PERSONAL

PERSONAL IDENTITY

Edited by

**Ellen Frankel Paul, Fred D. Miller, Jr.,
and Jeffrey Paul**

PUBLISHED BY THE PRESS SYNDICATE OF THE UNIVERSITY OF CAMBRIDGE
The Pitt Building, Trumpington Street, Cambridge, United Kingdom

CAMBRIDGE UNIVERSITY PRESS
The Edinburgh Building, Cambridge CB2 2RU, UK
40 West 20th Street, New York, NY 10011-4211, USA
477 Williamstown Road, Port Melbourne, VIC 3207, Australia
Ruiz de Alarcón 13, 28014 Madrid, Spain
Dock House, The Waterfront, Cape Town 8001, South Africa

http://www.cambridge.org

First published 2005

Printed in the United States of America

Typeface Palacio 10/12 pt.

A catalog record for this book is available from the British Library

Library of Congress Cataloging-in-Publication Data
Personal Identity / edited by Ellen Frankel Paul,
Fred D. Miller, Jr., and Jeffrey Paul.   p.   cm.
Includes bibliographical references and index.
ISBN 0-521-61767-7
1. Self (Philosophy)   2. Identity (Psychology)
I. Paul, Ellen Frankel.   II. Miller, Fred Dycus, 1944   III. Paul, Jeffrey.
BD438.5.P48   2005
126–dc22   2005045784

The essays in this book have also been published,
without introduction and index, in the semiannual journal
Social Philosophy & Policy, Volume 22, Number 2,
which is available by subscription.

CONTENTS

INTRODUCTION

What is a person? What makes me the same person today that I was yesterday or will be tomorrow? These are questions that philosophers have long pondered, and the history of this topic, as in other areas of philosophy, is a series of footnotes to Plato. In Plato's *Symposium,* Socrates recalls the argument he heard from Diotima that nature is governed by the principle of love, which manifests itself in the desire of mortal nature to live forever and to be immortal so far as possible. Living organisms manage to achieve some measure of immortality through sexual reproduction. On Diotima's view, however, something like this also happens within the lifetime of each organism:

> Even while each living thing is said to be alive and to be the same—as a person is said to be the same from childhood till he turns into an old man—even then he never consists of the same things, though he is called the same, but he is always being renewed and in other respects passing away, in his hair and flesh and bones and blood and his entire body. And it's not just in his body, but in his soul too, for none of his manners, customs, opinions, desires, pleasures, pains, or fears ever remains the same, but some are coming to be in him while others are passing away.... And in that way everything mortal is preserved, not, like the divine, by always being the same in every way, but because what is departing and aging leaves behind something new, something such as it had been.[1]

This argument implies that what we think of as our continuing personal identity is really an illusion. The people we are today are not, strictly speaking, the same as the people we were yesterday. Our bodies are not the same as the bodies that existed then, and our actions and thoughts are also different. We are "the same people" now as we were yesterday only in the sense that the people we are now are successors of, and are similar to, the people we were before. The argument in Plato's *Symposium* thus poses a problem about personal identity: on what basis can any of us reasonably claim that he or she is really the same person over time?

Aristotle proposed a solution to this problem: when a substance undergoes a change, there is something about it that remains the same, which Aristotle called the "substratum." Although a thing changes in many

---

[1] Plato, *Symposium*, trans. Alexander Nehamas and Paul Woodruff (Indianapolis: Hackett Publishing Company, 1989), 207d–208b.

ways over time, it retains the same substratum over time, because it has the same essence. This solution leads to other questions: Do things have essential properties? If so, what are they? And even if the people we were yesterday had the same essential properties as the people we are now, does this suffice to make them the "same" people?

In the modern era, John Locke criticized Aristotle's subtle metaphysical distinctions as obscure and unsupportable through empirical observation. He dismissed the Aristotelian substratum as a "something-I-know-not-what." Locke reformulated the problem of personal identity in his own way: Is a person a physical organism that persists through time, or is a person identified by the persistence of psychological states, by memory? Locke was also concerned about the implications of personal identity for moral responsibility. We might ask, for example, whether rationality requires us to exhibit equal concern for our earlier selves and our later selves.

The essays in this volume address these perennial and thorny issues, as well as the implications of various solutions for morality and public policy. Some of the essays defend general theories of identity—theories based on constitution, or on dualism, or on some form of bodily or psychological continuity. Some examine the work of Derek Parfit and other influential theorists. Other essays discuss how the conception of the person influences developments in various disciplines, including law, economics, and even literature. Still others relate personal identity to specific policy issues, asking how our concept of identity bears on the morality of cloning, genetic engineering, abortion, or private property rights.

The collection opens with a group of essays that examine various general theories of personal identity. In "Experience, Agency, and Personal Identity," Marya Schechtman explores the development of accounts of identity based on psychological continuity. The key challenge for such an account is to make sense of a person's survival (as the same person) over time, and one way to do so is to emphasize subjectivity—to adopt a view of the person as a subject of conscious experience. As Schechtman notes, however, Derek Parfit has argued that such a view is seriously flawed. If the view of a person as a subject of experience is to justify the importance we attach to identity, it will need to provide a deep unity of consciousness throughout the life of a person, and Parfit argues that no such unity is possible. In response, many philosophers have switched to a view of persons as essentially agents, claiming that the importance of identity depends on unity of agency rather than unity of consciousness. Schechtman acknowledges that this shift contributes significantly to the debate over identity, but she maintains that it does not offer a fully satisfying alternative. Unity of consciousness still seems to be required if identity is to be as important as we think it is. Drawing on discussions of identity as it relates to practical philosophy—and especially on the work of Christine Korsgaard and Harry Frankfurt—Schechtman sketches a new understanding of the unity of consciousness that attempts to answer Parfit's critique. She proposes an integrated view of identity that sees persons as both subjects and agents.

While Schechtman focuses on the role of psychological continuity in identity, other theorists have endeavored to ground human identity in our physical, biological nature. Lynne Rudder Baker adopts a version of this approach in her essay "When Does a Person Begin?" According to Baker's "constitution view" of persons, a human person is wholly constituted by (but not identical to) a human organism. Such a view, she believes, does justice both to our similarities to other animals and to our uniqueness. What distinguishes us from other animals is that each human person possesses a robust first-person perspective: the ability to have thoughts about oneself and to recognize oneself as the subject of those thoughts. In setting out her position, Baker defends the thesis that the coming-into-existence of a human person is not simply a matter of the coming-into-existence of an organism, even if that organism ultimately comes to constitute a person. She marshals support from developmental psychology in order to formulate a broadly materialistic account of the coming-into-existence of a human person. In the course of her essay, she distinguishes the constitution view from various alternatives, including substance dualism, biological animalism, and Thomistic animalism, arguing that these alternatives fail to capture what is essential about human nature. She concludes with a discussion of how the constitution view can be used to address questions about the morality of abortion.

In "Persons, Social Agency, and Constitution," Robert A. Wilson seeks to extend Baker's constitution view of persons, applying it to the realm of social agency. The key theoretical move Wilson makes is to conceive of constitution as a pluralistic relation, so that a single entity might constitute more than one thing; for example, a human body might constitute a person, but also a living thing, a member of a species, a moral agent, etc. Persons, in turn, may be seen as constituting many different types of rational and moral agents: police officers, businessmen, parents, policymakers, and so on. Wilson takes this analysis one step further, arguing that we can use the constitution relation to make sense of collective social agents such as organizations, corporations, and governments. These larger entities, he maintains, bear a special relationship to the collections of persons who make them up and through whom they act. This relationship, which Wilson calls "agency coincidence," is analogous to the relationship of "spatial coincidence" that exists between bodies and the persons they constitute. Understanding this relationship, he argues, can help us understand the nature of collective action in the social realm.

The relationship of body and mind (or soul) has been a central issue in the theory of personal identity, and one approach to addressing this issue—dualism—has been largely neglected in contemporary discussions. David S. Oderberg sets out to remedy this neglect in his contribution to this volume, "Hylemorphic Dualism." The version of dualism most commonly discussed, and rejected, by contemporary theorists is Cartesian dualism, the view that the mind is a separate and immaterial substance, bearing only a contingent relationship to the body it inhabits. But Oderberg contends that a more promising version of the theory is hylemorphic dualism, the version defended by Aristotelian and Thomist philosophers. On this view, all substances are said to be compounds of matter and form, and the form is said to actualize the matter, giving the substance its identity. The form of a human person is his or her rational nature. In his essay, Oderberg lays out the main lines of the hylemorphic dualist position, with particular reference to personal identity. He argues that overemphasis of the problem of consciousness has had an unhealthy effect on recent debate, and seeks to show why we should instead emphasize the concept of form. He offers an account of the concept of identity in terms of the notion of substantial form, and goes on to analyze the relation between form and matter. In the remainder of the essay, he argues for the immateriality of the substantial form of the human person (the soul) and for the soul's essential independence of matter. He concludes that although the soul is the immaterial bearer of personal identity, that identity is still the identity of an essentially embodied being.

The hylemorphic theory of identity also figures prominently in Edward Feser's essay "Personal Identity and Self-Ownership." Feser is a defender of the classical-liberal thesis of self-ownership, the view that each individual is the owner of his or her body, talents, labor, and so forth. Those who defend this thesis, Feser notes, generally focus on the "ownership" aspect and say little about the metaphysics of the self that is said to be self-owned. It makes sense, then, to ask which accounts of the self are consistent with robust self-ownership. Feser examines a range of theories—Cartesian dualism, bodily continuity, psychological continuity, and the identity theories of Robert Nozick and Derek Parfit—and finds that none of them are suitable for grounding a metaphysics of the self that is consistent with self-ownership. Having rejected these theories, Feser argues that the hylemorphic theory of Aristotle and Aquinas provides an account of the self that advocates of self-ownership can embrace. He acknowledges, however, that adopting this theory may lead us to a conception of self-ownership that differs from the standard libertarian or classical-liberal conception. On the hylemorphic view that Feser defends, individuals have a right to an environment in which they can develop moral virtues and exercise their self-owned capacities and powers. Governments may have an obligation to foster such an environment by placing some limits on how individuals may use their property and by regulating certain sorts of public activities.

Derek Parfit's theory of identity—a subject touched upon in Feser's essay—is the focus of Marvin Belzer's "Self-Conception and Personal Identity: Revisiting Parfit and Lewis with an Eye on the Grip of the Unity

Reaction." Belzer begins by sketching Parfit's reductionist account, according to which a person's identity over time is constituted by a series of interrelated mental states and events that are directly connected to one another through a continuity of memory, intention, belief, and desire. A crucial element of Parfit's theory is a thought experiment involving fission— the idea that a single person could divide into two separate persons, as amoebas and other simple organisms do. In a case such as this, Parfit argues, one would not survive the fission, but one would have "what matters in survival," since one's memories, desires, etc. would survive into the future. As Belzer observes, Parfit's analysis of the fission thought experiment involves the rejection of a common-sense intuition known as the "unity reaction": the intuition that self-unity is an essential characteristic of persons. Other theorists, such as David Lewis, have denied Parfit's claim that reductionism contravenes common sense. Belzer revisits the debate between Parfit and Lewis, arguing that Parfit wins it. He also examines another version of the reductionist theory, put forward by David Velleman, according to which fission does not conflict with the unity reaction. The key to making sense of cases of fission, Belzer contends, lies in taking up the perspective of a person who anticipates undergoing fission and forms intentions about his future, post-fission actions. After drawing out the implications of this approach, Belzer concludes that Velleman's theory fails to eliminate fission-based conflict with the unity reaction.

The next two essays deal with the relationship between identity and rationality. In "The Normativity of Self-Grounded Reason," David Copp proposes a standard of practical rationality and seeks to ground this standard in the idea of autonomous agency. He defines rationality as the efficient pursuit of one's values, where those values are aspects of one's identity. The concept of identity at work here is psychological rather than metaphysical. Specifically, Copp ties a person's values to his "self-esteem identity," defined as the set of propositions about his life that he believes and that ground emotions of esteem, such as pride and shame. According to this approach, it is plausible to view action governed by one's values as *self*-governed (autonomous) action. Agents are rational, Copp argues, when they comply with a standard that requires them to serve their values, and to seek what they need in order to continue to be able to serve their values. Copp offers examples of the values he has in mind (e.g., honesty and friendship) and describes them in terms of policies or intentions to act in a certain way under given circumstances. He goes on to defend the important role that autonomy plays in grounding his standard of rationality, addressing a number of objections. He concludes by noting the limits of his view: an agent may be rational according to the standard Copp has set out, yet may still lack moral values and moral reasons for action.

The link between rationality and repentance is the subject of Jennifer Roback Morse's contribution to this volume, "Rationality Means Being

Willing to Say You're Sorry." Morse begins with a pair of related questions: What does a person really want when he asks for an apology? And why do people so often find it difficult to give an apology? Repentance is relevant to personal identity, Morse contends, because the unrepentant soul has his own theory of identity. The unrepentant person believes that *he is his preference*, and that he is entitled to the behavior that flows from his preferences. Morse characterizes the unrepentant person in economic terms, drawing on the concept of *Homo economicus* (economic man). According to a simplified version of rational choice theory, *Homo economicus* analyzes the costs and benefits of various courses of action, using the information available to him, and decides which course of action maximizes his utility (understood in terms of his ordered preferences). This account of human action, Morse argues, can help us understand such phenomena as why people are so often reluctant to admit wrongdoing and why people place so much importance on receiving an apology. The actions of the unrepentant person are guided by something akin to this naive economic theory of human behavior. Such a person, Morse concludes, can never truly be sorry for anything, and as a result, will be almost impossible to live with. A person who identifies himself too closely with his preferences will bring misery to himself and to those around him.

In "Personal Identity and Postmortem Survival," Stephen E. Braude begins with the observation that the problem of personal identity can be viewed as either a metaphysical or an epistemological issue. Metaphysicians want to know *what it is* for one individual to be the same person as another. Epistemologists want to know how to *decide* if an individual is the same person as someone else. These two problems converge when we consider the subject of personal survival after death. In his essay, Braude discusses apparent examples of mediumship (communication with the dead) and putative reincarnation cases—phenomena that suggest personal survival after bodily death and dissolution. These cases make us wonder how it might be possible for a person to survive death and either temporarily or permanently animate another body. They also lead us to wonder how we could decide if such postmortem survival has actually occurred. In discussing these intriguing issues, Braude argues that metaphysical worries about postmortem survival are less important than many have thought. He then considers why cases suggesting postmortem survival can be so compelling, and he surveys our principal options for explaining these cases. Critics of the idea of postmortem survival point to a growing body of scientific evidence for the existence of an intimate link between brain states and mental states—evidence that would seem to rule out the survival of a person's consciousness after the destruction of his body. Braude maintains, however, that this evidence is not as convincing as some would suppose, and that the "container metaphor" (the idea that mental states are *in* the brain) is problematic. The conclusion Braude reaches is provocative: it may be that making judgments about whether someone has survived bodily death is not radically different from determining a person's identity in less exotic circumstances, such as when (for example) one re-encounters a former acquaintance.

John Finnis takes a novel approach to the topic of identity in his essay "'The Thing I Am': Personal Identity in Aquinas and Shakespeare." The identity of the human person, Finnis says, can be understood in terms of four elements, based upon the four kinds of order identified by Thomas Aquinas at the beginning of his commentary on Aristotle's *Nicomachean Ethics*. First, we can be understood as part of the natural order, as animals with certain natural capacities. Second, we are part of an "order of thought": we are conscious of ourselves and of others; we are capable of reason, judgment, and memory. Third, we are capable of deliberation and choice, and our choices serve to shape our character. Fourth, we are capable of mastering various skills and crafts, including the craft of self-expression. This fourth element includes our ability to adopt "personas" to convey to others some impression (whether true or false) about ourselves. Taking these four elements as a starting point, Finnis goes on to examine Shakespeare's dramatic works in order to discern his understanding of human identity. Finnis shows how Shakespeare conceives of identity as both (1) one's lasting presence to oneself as one and the same bodily and mental self, and (2) one's self-shaping by one's free choices, especially one's commitment choices. Finnis discusses several of Shakespeare's plays, especially *All's Well That Ends Well*, and seeks to demonstrate how Shakespeare explores these aspects of identity, quite deliberately, through cases of mistaken identity and the humiliation that his characters suffer when the personas they have constructed for themselves are exposed.

The final two essays relate to technological innovations and the impact they may have on personal identity. F. M. Kamm seeks to discover whether the prospect of human cloning represents a threat to the nonsubstitutability of persons—the moral principle that separate persons are not substitutable for one another when we perform a calculation of the harms and benefits of some proposed course of action. In "Moral Status and Personal Identity: Clones, Embryos, and Future Generations," Kamm divides entities into three rough categories: those that count morally in their own right in the sense that they give us reasons to constrain our behavior toward them (e.g., trees or works of art); those that have moral status (e.g., some nonhuman animals); and those that can have moral claims against us (e.g., persons). She argues that entities falling into the first categories enjoy only a weak form of nonsubstitutability (if any): such entities may give us reasons not to destroy them (and even reasons to help them), yet their good can sometimes be substituted by the good of other entities. In contrast, entities that can have moral claims (and can be owed duties) have a much stronger form of nonsubstitutability. Kamm goes on to apply her analysis to the issue of reproductive cloning. Critics of cloning argue that it would violate the dignity of persons, since we might be tempted to regard persons produced by cloning as something less than fully human. We can even imagine scenarios in which clones are produced in order to serve as mere means to the good of others (for example, by having their organs harvested for transplants). Kamm examines the objections raised against cloning and finds them unpersuasive: persons produced by cloning, she argues, would have the same dignity and status as those produced through sexual reproduction. She concludes by drawing out the implications of her analysis for cases involving the rights of future generations and the genetic enhancement of human embryos.

The collection's final essay takes a detailed look at the issue of genetic engineering and its potential impact on human identity. In "The Identity of Identity: Moral and Legal Aspects of Technological Self-Transformation," Michael H. Shapiro discusses various technologies that are being developed for significantly altering the traits of existing persons (or fetuses or embryos) via germ-line modification, and considers whether the concept of personal identity requires revision in the face of such technologies. He observes that our existing notions of personal identity (and related ideas such as personhood and autonomy) may seem unable to comfortably accommodate the possibilities of technologically directed trait formation and development. This is a matter of moral and legal importance because the assumed continuation of personal identity over time underlies interpersonal relationships, the assignment of rewards and punishments, and the very idea of what constitutes an autonomous person. Shapiro contends that efforts to enhance human traits, including merit attributes and other resource-attractive characteristics (e.g., intellectual and athletic abilities), may generate serious legal problems, and thus that some speculation is warranted on how trait change generally will be managed within our legal and socioeconomic systems. In particular, we need to consider the question of access to trait-altering technologies and how these technologies may have the effect of magnifying socioeconomic inequalities. In the end, however, Shapiro suggests that existing and projected technologies do not impel the abandonment or remodeling of the idea of personal identity. Nevertheless, we may have to reconsider some uses of this concept in different settings, rethink our understandings of ideas of merit and desert, and deal with issues of resource distribution that may lead to larger and more entrenched "distances" between social and economic groups.

The theory of personal identity has ancient roots in the history of philosophy, and questions about identity still hold a central place in contemporary philosophical discussions. These twelve essays offer valuable insights into the nature of human identity and its implications for morality and social policy.

ACKNOWLEDGMENTS

The editors wish to acknowledge several individuals at the Social Philosophy and Policy Center, Bowling Green State University, who provided invaluable assistance in the production of this volume. They include former Assistant Director Travis Cook, Mary Dilsaver, and Terrie Weaver.

The editors extend special thanks to Assistant Managing Editor Tamara Sharp for attending to the innumerable day-to-day details of the book's preparation, and to Managing Editor Harry Dolan for providing dedicated assistance throughout the editorial and production process.

CONTRIBUTORS

Marya Schechtman is Associate Professor of Philosophy at the University of Illinois at Chicago and a member of its Laboratory of Integrated Neuroscience. She received her Ph.D. from Harvard in 1988. Her main areas of interest are personal identity, practical reason, and the philosophy of mind. She is the author of *The Constitution of Selves* (1996) and numerous articles on personal identity and the philosophy of mind, which have appeared in such journals as *American Philosophical Quarterly*, *The Journal of Philosophy*, *Philosophical Psychology*, and *Philosophical Explorations*.

Lynne Rudder Baker is Professor of Philosophy at the University of Massachusetts, Amherst. She is the author of *Saving Belief: A Critique of Physicalism* (1987), *Explaining Attitudes: A Practical Approach to the Mind* (1995), and *Persons and Bodies: A Constitution View* (2000). She has published numerous articles in the philosophy of mind, metaphysics, and philosophical theology in such journals as *The Journal of Philosophy*, *Philosophical Review*, *Philosophy and Phenomenological Research*, *American Philosophical Quarterly*, *Philosophical Studies*, *Noûs*, *Mind and Language*, *Synthese*, and *Philosophical Explorations*.

Robert A. Wilson is Professor of Philosophy at the University of Alberta, having taught previously at Queen's University and the University of Illinois, Urbana-Champaign. He works chiefly in the philosophy of mind, cognitive science, and the philosophy of biology, and has recently published papers on the concept of realization, pluralism about the levels of selection, Locke's view of primary qualities, and the relationship between intentionality and phenomenology. His most recent books are *Boundaries of the Mind* and *Genes and the Agents of Life*, both published by Cambridge University Press in 2004.

David S. Oderberg is Professor of Philosophy at the University of Reading, England. He is the author of *The Metaphysics of Identity over Time* (1993), *Moral Theory* (2000), and *Applied Ethics* (2000). He is the editor of *Form and Matter: Themes in Contemporary Metaphysics* (1999) and of *The Old New Logic: Essays on the Philosophy of Fred Sommers* (2005), and the coeditor of *Human Lives: Critical Essays on Consequentialist Bioethics* (1997) and *Human Values: New Essays on Ethics and Natural Law* (2005). He has published many articles on metaphysics, philosophical logic, ethics, philosophy of religion, and other subjects, and is currently writing a book on essentialism. In 2003, he was a Visiting Scholar at the Social Philosophy and Policy Center.

Edward Feser is Visiting Assistant Professor of Philosophy at Loyola Marymount University in Los Angeles. He is the author of *On Nozick* (2003) and *Philosophy of Mind: An Introduction* (forthcoming), and of many articles in political philosophy, philosophy of mind, and philosophy of religion. During the summer of 2002, he was a Visiting Scholar at the Social Philosophy and Policy Center.

Marvin Belzer is Associate Professor of Philosophy at Bowling Green State University. He has published articles on personal identity as well as on deontic logic, including a series of articles on defeasible normative reasoning based on the deontic logic "3-D," which he developed in collaboration with Barry Loewer. His website, http://personal.bgsu.edu/~mbelzer, contains numerous works of philosophical fiction, including *The Z-files* and *Dialogues on Personal Identity and Morality*.

David Copp is Professor of Philosophy at the University of Florida. He is the author of *Morality, Normativity, and Society* (1995) and the editor of *The Oxford Handbook of Ethical Theory* (2005). He has published many articles in moral and political philosophy, and is an associate editor of *Ethics*.

Jennifer Roback Morse joined Stanford University's Hoover Institution as a Research Fellow in 1997. She received her Ph.D. in economics from the University of Rochester in 1980, and taught economics at Yale University and George Mason University for fifteen years. Her current book, *Love and Economics: Why the Laissez-Faire Family Doesn't Work* (2001), shows why the family is the necessary building block for a free society and why so many modern attempted substitutes for the family do not work. She was a founding member of the academic advisory boards of the Acton Institute for the Study of Religion and Liberty, the Institute for Justice, and the Women's Freedom Network. She currently lives in Vista, California, where she pursues her primary vocation as wife and mother, combined with an avocation of writing and lecturing.

Stephen E. Braude is Professor of Philosophy and Chairman of the Philosophy Department at the University of Maryland, Baltimore County, and past President of the Parapsychological Association. He has a long-standing interest in the philosophy of science and the philosophy of mind, and has most recently focused on problems in philosophical psychopathology. He has written extensively on the connections between dissociation and classic philosophical problems, as well as on central issues in parapsychology, and has published more than fifty philosophical essays in such journals as *Noûs*, *Philosophical Review*, *Philosophical Studies*, *Analysis*, *Inquiry*, *Philosophia*, *Philosophy, Psychiatry and Psychology*, the *Journal of Scientific Exploration*, and the *Journal of Trauma and Dissociation*. He is the author of *ESP and Psychokinesis: A Philosophical Examination*

(1979, 2002), *The Limits of Influence: Psychokinesis and the Philosophy of Science* (1986, 1991), *First Person Plural: Multiple Personality and the Philosophy of Mind* (1991, 1995), and *Immortal Remains: The Evidence for Life after Death* (2003).

John Finnis is Professor of Law and Legal Philosophy in the University of Oxford, a Fellow of University College, Oxford, and Biolchini Family Professor of Law at Notre Dame Law School, Notre Dame, Indiana. His books include *Natural Law and Natural Rights* (1980, fifteenth reprint 2003), *Fundamentals of Ethics* (1983), *Moral Absolutes* (1991), and *Aquinas: Moral, Political, and Legal Theory* (1998). He is writing and publishing with Patrick H. Martin of Louisiana State University on a hitherto unexplored contemporary of Shakespeare.

F. M. Kamm is Littauer Professor of Philosophy and Public Policy at the Kennedy School of Government and Professor of Philosophy at Harvard University. She is the author of *Creation and Abortion* (1992), *Morality, Mortality*, volumes 1 and 2 (1993, 1996), and numerous articles on normative ethical theory and practical ethics.

Michael H. Shapiro is Dorothy W. Nelson Professor of Law at the University of Southern California. He received his M.A. in philosophy from the University of California, Los Angeles, and his J.D. from the University of Chicago Law School. After practicing law for several years, he joined the University of Southern California Law faculty, where he has taught substantive criminal law, constitutional law, and bioethics and law. His main focus is the intersection of bioethics and constitutional law. He is the author of various law journal articles, including "The Technology of Perfection: Performance Enhancement and the Control of Attributes" (1991); "Who Merits Merit? Problems in Distributive Justice and Utility Posed by the New Biology" (1974); and "Constitutional Adjudication and Standards of Review Under Pressure from Biological Technologies" (2001). He is the editor (with Spece, Dresser, and Clayton) of the law school text *Bioethics and Law: Cases, Materials, and Problems*, second edition (2003).

EXPERIENCE, AGENCY, AND PERSONAL IDENTITY*

By Marya Schechtman

I. Introduction

Questions of personal identity are raised in many different philosophical contexts. In metaphysics the question at issue is that of personal identity over time, or of what relation a person at one time must bear to a person at another time in order for them to be, literally, the same person. There are two standard responses to this question in the current literature. One considers a person as essentially a biological entity and defines the identity of the person over time in terms of the continued existence of a single organism. The other follows John Locke in accepting a distinction between persons and human beings and defines the identity of a person in terms of the continued flow of psychological life.[1] This second response—the "psychological continuity theory"—has a great deal of appeal and enjoys a great many supporters. Both positions are still very much alive in the current discussion, suggesting that at the very least each response expresses some important aspect of our thought about what we are and how we continue. In what follows I will leave aside the dispute *between* these two accounts of identity and will focus only on the psychological side. Understanding what fuels the idea that personal identity should be defined in psychological terms, and what a viable psychological account of identity would look like, is an important goal in its own right and will put us in a better position to understand the relation between psychological and biological accounts of identity.

A central element in the motivation and defense of the psychological continuity theory of personal identity comes from the intimate connection between the concepts of identity and survival. One obvious way of understanding what it means for a person to survive is for there to be someone in the future who is she. Since surviving is, to put it mildly, a matter of the utmost practical importance, it seems that whatever relation defines personal identity over time should also bear the importance we attach to

---

* I am indebted to many friends and colleagues for their input in the course of writing this essay. I would like especially to thank David DeGrazia, Anthony Laden, Ray Martin, Marc Slors, and the editors of *Social Philosophy and Policy*.

[1] There are, of course, other positions that are and have been defended. Historically it has been popular to define personal identity in terms of the persistence of an immaterial soul, and this view still has its defenders. Others see identity as irreducible and unanalyzable. Continuity of organism and continuity of psychological life are, however, generally acknowledged as the basic candidates for an account of personal identity in the current discussion, and the vast majority of authors in the area defend one or the other of them.

survival. Psychological continuity theorists argue that when we ask our-selves which kind of continuation—physical or psychological—seems to bear this importance, the latter emerges as the better candidate. This view trades on the intuition that a situation where a person's body continues to function but his psychological life comes to an end (as in, e.g., a case of irreversible coma or total possession) seems like a failure to survive, while a situation in which psychological life continues despite the death of a person's body (as in, e.g., some of the traditional religious depictions of an afterlife) seems like a case of personal continuation.

It remains, however, for psychological continuity theorists to describe in more detail the kind of psychological continuation that constitutes survival. The initial and most natural idea is that persons should be construed as experiencing subjects, and that personal identity should be defined in terms of a deep unity of consciousness throughout an entire life, but this unity turns out to be difficult to define coherently. For this and other reasons, some identity theorists who support a psychologically based view have shifted from a picture of the person as a subject to a picture of the person as an agent, and from a definition of personal identity in terms of a deep phenomenological unity to a definition in terms of the unity of agency. This shift leaves us with the question of whether unity of agency is a strong enough relation to provide an account of what it is for a person, literally, to survive.

Some resources for answering this question can be found in other areas of philosophy—in particular, in discussions of free will, practical reason, and the theory of action, which I will refer to collectively with the term "practical philosophy." A prominent strand of thought there suggests that having deeply held projects and commitments is essential to being a person, and describes how a person can literally disintegrate from a lack of such projects and commitments. While this discussion does make a strong case that unity of agency must be part of any acceptable psycho-logical account of the persistence of the person, the original intuition that some sort of deep unity of consciousness is required for personal survival runs deep, and a view couched entirely in terms of unity of agency is unlikely to be fully satisfying. Fortunately, the insights gleaned by fol-lowing out the shift toward a view of the person as agent can help point to a way that something like phenomenological unity of consciousness might be introduced without so much difficult metaphysical baggage.

My main goal here is to follow out the way in which a picture of persons as essentially agents has found its way into the metaphysical discussion of personal identity, and to assess where this leaves us in our attempts to understand the conditions of personal persistence. I begin by showing how the internal pressures of the metaphysical discussion lead to the introduction of an understanding of persons as agents, and how work in practical philosophy can help support the plausibility of this understanding as a response to the metaphysical question of personal persistence. After this I discuss why a response to this question wholly in terms of agency is likely to remain unsatisfying, and I point very briefly to a possible strategy for reintroducing an understanding of the person as subject as part of a more integrated account.

II. What Matters in Survival and Peter Unger's Distinction

As I have already mentioned, the central considerations supporting the psychological continuity theory are based on the idea that it is psychological rather than physical continuation that captures what matters to us in survival. As discussion of this view has unfolded, many psychological continuity theorists have found reason to put aside the question of personal identity per se and ask directly about the conditions of survival and what we find important in it. The main impetus for this switch is a difficulty with using psychological continuity as a criterion of personal identity. Psychological continuity—at least as usually defined by these theories—does not have the logical form of an identity relation. The continuity relation, unlike identity itself, can be one-many, intransitive, and a matter of degree. Derek Parfit famously argues that this does not undermine the psychological continuity theory but rather reveals that what really underlies our interest in the question of personal identity over time is the issue of survival.[2] In ordinary circumstances, survival will involve identity; the person as whom one survives will be oneself. However, in certain imaginable science fiction scenarios, Parfit argues, it may be possible to survive as someone else. This might happen, for instance, if a person could split amoeba-like into two qualitatively identical people. Such a division hardly seems like death, he argues, yet the two resulting people, since they are clearly not identical with one another, cannot both be identical to the original person on pain of intransitivity. This "fission" scenario is thus a case in which a person enjoys what we take to be significant in survival despite the fact that there is no one in the future to whom she is identical.[3]

Parfit holds that our interest in questions of identity is an artifact of the fact that in ordinary circumstances survival requires identity with some future person. Once we see that we can have what matters in survival without identity, we can see that our main interest is with survival rather than identity itself. The question of whether or not we are going to sur-

---

[2] In fact, Parfit shifts his use of the term "survival" over the course of his work. In Derek Parfit, "Personal Identity," *Philosophical Review* 80 (1971): 3–27, he suggests that survival can come apart from identity, and suggests that we are interested in questions of survival. In his book *Reasons and Persons* (Oxford: Clarendon Press, 1984), Parfit seems to imply that, strictly speaking, survival requires identity, and that we are interested in "what matters in survival." I will be using the terminology in the former sense. For a full discussion of the evolution in Parfit's use of this term, see Marvin Belzer, "Self-Conception and Personal Identity," elsewhere in this volume, Section IIC.

[3] Parfit, *Reasons and Persons*, chap. 12.

vive undoubtedly bears a special significance for us. As John Perry puts it: "You learn that someone will be run over by a truck tomorrow; you are saddened, feel pity, and think reflectively about the frailty of life; one bit of information is added, that someone is you, and a whole different set of emotions rise in your breast."[4] What we are after with questions of diachronic personal identity (that is, questions about the conditions for the persistence of a single person over time), says Parfit, is the question of what relation to the future carries this importance—"what matters" in survival. Many theorists of personal identity who would define it in psychological terms have thus shifted their emphasis from identity to what matters in survival.

It might seem as if the shift of focus to "what matters" automatically turns the discussion to a more metaphorical or psychological notion than that with which we started, since we are now asking what makes our continuation a good rather than what makes us, literally, still alive. Most psychological continuity theorists would deny this, however. The survival they are trying to define is, they insist, quite literal, and the sense of "what matters" at issue should be read that way. This point is made most explicitly by Peter Unger, who says that there are different things we could mean by "what matters in survival," and that it is important for us to keep clear on which of them is under consideration. He distinguishes between three different uses of this term. One, to which I will return later, concerns the question of which features of survival *constitute* it as survival. For present purposes, the most important distinction is between the other two senses, which he calls the "desirability" and the "prudential" senses of "what matters." According to the desirability sense,

> 'what matters in survival' will mean much the same as this: what it is that one gets out of survival that makes continued survival a desirable thing for one, a better thing, at least, than is utter cessation. On this desirability use, if one has what matters in survival, then, from a self-interested perspective, one has reason to continue rather than opt for sudden painless termination.[5]

This is contrasted with the prudential use, which determines,

> from the perspective of a person's concern for herself, or from a slight rational extension of that perspective, what future being there is or, possibly, which future beings there are, for whom the person rationally should be "intrinsically" concerned. Saying that this rational concern is "intrinsic" means, roughly, that, even apart from questions

---

[4] John Perry, "The Importance of Being Identical," in Amélie Oksenberg Rorty, ed., *The Identities of Persons* (Berkeley: University of California Press, 1976), 67.

[5] Peter Unger, *Identity, Consciousness, and Value* (New York: Oxford University Press, 1990), 93.

of whether or not he might advance the present person's projects, there is this rational concern for the welfare of the future being.[6]

Unger suggests that there is a question of whether a future will be mine to experience—whether I will undergo what happens in it—which at least seems quite independent of my values, goals, ideals, or character traits.

If we are looking to answer literal, metaphysical questions about our survival, Unger argues, we should be looking for the relation that underlies the more fundamental, prudential connection between different moments of a person's life. The desirability sense of what matters may be an important thing to define in its own right, but it is not, he says, "highly relevant to questions of our survival."[7] To test for the prudential sense of what matters, Unger suggests that we use the "avoidance of future pain test." We are to imagine ourselves connected to a future person in some way, and then imagine that person being subjected to horrible torture or excruciating pain. The question we are to ask is whether our horror of the future pain is sympathetic in nature or rather the sort of concern we would feel if we were anticipating our own future pain. The latter response suggests that we have what matters in survival in the fundamental sense at issue in metaphysical discussions of personal survival.

Unger himself believes that attention to this question will lead us to a more biologically based account of personal survival, albeit one that requires the continuity of minimal psychological capacities (what he calls "core" psychology). Traditional psychological continuity theorists have rejected Unger's solution, but they seem to accept his basic insight. They suggest that the avoidance of future pain test reveals that what matters fundamentally in survival is the legitimate *anticipation* of future experiences. To survive we must bear a connection to the future that makes it rational for us to expect to have experiences then. These theorists do not accept Unger's solution because they deny, for reasons given by Locke, that the continuity of the body can itself be what legitimates anticipation of future experiences. (Locke famously argues through the use of hypothetical cases that continuity of body—or soul—with no continuity of consciousness cannot provide what we seek in survival.) For such anticipation we need a deep phenomenological connection to the future—a unity of consciousness over time. Continuity of the body might turn out to be one source of such a phenomenological connection; it might even turn out to be the only source. This would, however, be a contingent fact, and even if it were true it would not be the continuity of the body per se, but rather the unity of consciousness it produced, that would make our intrinsic concern for some future person rational. On this view, then, a *person* is most fundamentally an experiencing subject, and survival must

---

[6] Ibid., 94.
[7] Ibid., 93.

involve the unity of an experiencing subject over time. This is, in many ways, a very natural and appealing picture of what is involved in our survival as persons, but it is difficult to develop a coherent theory based on this picture, as the next section will explain.

III. Derek Parfit's Argument against the Person as Experiencing Subject

A compelling initial picture of what constitutes literal survival for those who take a psychological approach to this question is, as we have seen, a unity of consciousness over time.[8] Derek Parfit has argued quite forcefully, however, that this natural first idea of what defines survival cannot be defended—or even defined—in the end. He provides several arguments explicitly directed at the idea that personal identity cannot be defensibly defined in terms of the unity of a subject of experiences, but most of the fundamental insights behind these arguments can be found in the Teletransportation and Branch-Line cases with which he opens his discussion of personal identity in *Reasons and Persons*.[9] This pair of cases uncovers both the hold this conception of personal continuation has on us, and its problematic nature. In Teletransportation, a subject enters a booth where his body is scanned and dematerialized. A molecule-for-molecule duplicate of the original body is built on the destination planet, a duplicate who by hypothesis replicates the intrinsic character of the original person's psychological states exactly. The question is whether this is an efficient means of travel to distant planets, or death and replacement by an imposter. Parfit acknowledges that we are quite likely to think of it as the latter. Despite the exact similarity of the newly formed individual to the original person, we may well fear that the replica will lack a deep attachment to that person present in ordinary survival. We fear that while in ordinary survival one will *feel* one's future experiences, in Teletransportation one will feel nothing in the future—one's point of view, which would continue in the ordinary case, is snuffed out.

The presupposition underlying this fear is that there is a deep unity of consciousness within a given life that may be absent in our connection to a replica. It is not immediately obvious exactly what this deep unity of consciousness is, but the basic idea can be understood on the model of co-consciousness at a time. At a given time there is a brute difference between a set of experiences being present in a single consciousness and their being parts of distinct consciousnesses. This is why, for example, a decision about whether to tolerate a small pain in my shoulder now to avoid an excruciating pain in my foot now is different in kind from a

---

[8] As mentioned in note 2, for terminological simplicity in what follows I will refer to having what matters in this fundamental sense simply as "survival," meaning that in my use survival does not automatically imply identity.

[9] Parfit, *Reasons and Persons*, 199–201.

decision about whether to tolerate a small pain in my shoulder now to avoid *your* experiencing an excruciating pain in *your* foot now. The fear of Teletransportation reveals the supposition that we have a relation to our future experiences which is relevantly like the relation we have to our own present ones. This is why the decision about whether to suffer a small pain now to avoid an excruciating pain *later* is also different from the decision about whether to suffer a small pain now to keep someone else from suffering an excruciating pain later.[10] This difference is, of course, what the avoidance of future pain test proposed by Unger is testing for. When we fear that we will not survive Teletransportation, we are expressing the possibility that this connection to the future may not hold in cases of replication. In more concrete terms, we suspect that my attitude toward the replica's potential pains should be more like my attitude toward the potential pains of others than toward my own.

Since a teletransported replica is, by stipulation, completely identical to the original person in terms of the *contents* of her consciousness, whatever difference there is between ordinary survival and having a replica cannot be defined in terms of these contents. The previous discussion makes it clear, however, that it is supposed to be a difference in the *quality of experience*. To make the case that there could be such a difference, we thus need to be able to understand a phenomenological distinction between really continuing and being replaced by a replica which is not defined in terms of the contents of consciousness. Parfit's claim is that there is no defensible way to define such a distinction. The difference we are seeking cannot be explained by the fact that in one case we retain our original body, since the psychological account is based on the intuition that we could in theory have what counts as survival without continuation of the body. If the sameness of body plays a crucial role, it will have to be because continuing in a single body is experientially different from being replaced by a replica, and we still need to say something about the nature of this phenomenological difference.[11] Parfit thinks that we might have been able to make sense of this mysterious unity of consciousness over time if we accepted the view that we are simple, immaterial souls (although the Lockean arguments make this questionable in any event), but argues that there is no reason to believe such a thing, and many reasons not to.[12]

[10] Of course, in either case we may decide that suffering the small pain is the better thing to do. We can care as much or more about the pains of others as we do about our own. The point is just that the considerations that go into the decision making are different in each case.

[11] Of course, at this point we might revert to a biological criterion, saying that our special concern about our own futures is not based on a deep unity of consciousness, but only on the fact that the organism currently having experience will be present, sentient, and in pain in the future. There are many considerations in favor of this position, and Parfit also offers many arguments against it. For the present, I am only interested in following out the intuitions behind psychological accounts of identity. I will, therefore, only consider what would be required to make this approach work, and see where this leads us.

[12] Parfit, *Reasons and Persons*, 227–28.

Of course, the inability to define the deep unity of consciousness that we assume in our own lives—and fear might be absent in replication—may not be enough to convince us that it does not exist. It seems as if we actively experience this continuity and connection in our own lives. Moreover, it seems all too possible to imagine the flow of our own psychological life terminated or diverted despite the existence of a replica with qualitatively identical contents of consciousness. Kathleen Wilkes makes this point quite effectively in a footnote in *Real People: Personal Identity without Thought Experiments*. Discussing the transporter depicted on the science fiction series *Star Trek*, she says:

> Captain Kirk, so the story goes, disintegrates at place p and reassembles at place p*. But perhaps, instead, he dies at p and a doppelganger emerges at p*. What is the difference? One way of illustrating the difference is to suppose there is an afterlife: a heaven, or hell, increasingly supplemented by yet more Captain Kirks all cursing the day they ever stepped into the molecular disintegrator.[13]

Once the viewpoint of the original Captain Kirk is reintroduced, it seems natural to assume there is a unified flow of consciousness between the original Kirk and the disembodied Kirk—a flow of consciousness that does not exist between the original Kirk and his doppelganger. If we now simply take out the assumption of an afterlife, we can see that the connection between the original and doppelganger remains phenomenologically deficient.

Parfit himself is very sensitive to the pull of this idea, and this is why he introduces the variation on his Teletransportation case that he calls the "Branch-Line case." In the Branch-Line case, the traveler is scanned and a blueprint made, but the original body is not dematerialized. Instead, it is damaged in such a way that it can live only a few more days. At the same time, a healthy replica is built on the distant planet (here Mars) as in simple Teletransportation. There are now two people who are psychologically continuous (in Parfit's sense) with the original person: the replica on Mars and the person with the original body on Earth. It seems clear, Parfit acknowledges, that the connection between the person on Earth (now traveling on a branch line of psychological continuation) and the replica does not contain what matters most fundamentally in survival. Parfit imagines himself on the branch line talking to his replica on Mars:

> Since my Replica knows that I am about to die, he tries to console me with the same thoughts with which I recently tried to console a dying friend. It is sad to learn, on the receiving end, how unconsoling these

---

[13] Kathleen Wilkes, *Real People: Personal Identity without Thought Experiments* (Oxford: Clarendon Press, 1994), 46n.

thoughts are. My Replica then assures me that he will take up my life where I leave off. He loves my wife, and together they will care for my children. And he will finish the book that I am writing. . . . All these facts console me a little. Dying when I know that I shall have a Replica is not quite as bad as, simply, dying. Even so, I shall soon lose consciousness, forever.[14]

The replica is as like the branch-line person in terms of contents of consciousness as a person is like herself in the near future, but there is all the difference in the world for this person between her psychological life continuing several more decades and its being terminated while the replica continues for those decades—or so it seems. This is why, Parfit acknowledges, "it is natural to assume that my prospect, on the Branch Line, is almost as bad as ordinary death." Nonetheless, he goes on to say, "[a]s I shall argue later, I ought to regard having a Replica as being about as good as ordinary survival."[15]

He offers a variety of considerations in favor of this claim. These include a collection of arguments for a reductionist view of persons, arguments against the possibility of directly experiencing a deep unity of consciousness over time in our own lives, and thought experiments aimed at making it more plausible that the person on the branch line could survive as the replica. The case most directly addressing this issue is, importantly, not a science fiction case, but one that is part of a real life. Parfit describes a sleeping pill he has taken that takes a short time to work. After taking the pill, the person remains fully conscious for a while, but when he awakens he has no memory of the time between taking the pill and falling asleep. Parfit reports that having once taken such a pill, he apparently solved a practical problem before falling asleep, for he found a note the next morning under his razor advising him of the solution, despite having no memory of solving the problem or writing the note. He argues that the person who has taken such a pill can know, like the person on the branch line, that his stream of consciousness will end before morning, but he is unlikely to face this prospect as if he is facing death. Yet, Parfit argues, in terms of intrinsic relations of consciousness or phenomenology the relation of the person who takes this sleeping pill to the person in the morning is no different from the relation of the branch-line person to his replica on Mars. There are, indeed, a host of differences between the two cases, but they do not seem to be *intrinsic* differences, and so if we want to say that these make the difference between surviving and not surviving we will have given up on the idea that the importance of survival is linked to a deep diachronic unity of consciousness.

---

[14] Parfit, *Reasons and Persons,* 201.
[15] Ibid.

While there is much to understand—and to take exception to—in Parfit's arguments, the underlying theme is, I think, fairly simple and quite persuasive. What his arguments do at their most effective is direct us to commonplace examples of survival and undermine our conviction that there is any deep unity of consciousness there. The sleeping-pill case, for instance, tells us less about a heart-damaged person with a replica on Mars than about what happens to us all the time. We do not need to take sleeping pills to have gaps in our consciousness, or to know sometimes that what we are thinking and experiencing in the present will be entirely lost to future consciousness—this is why people make lists and keep journals. This challenge is reinforced by the sort of empirical work used by Daniel Dennett and Andy Clark, among others, to reveal that our unity of consciousness—even at a time—is not all that casual introspection might lead us to believe.[16]

Whatever the upshot of detailed engagement with Parfit's many arguments, he raises a powerful and serious challenge to one deep-seated understanding of what is involved in our survival, and its importance. A tempting and natural way to think about our continuation is in terms of a flow of consciousness that connects current experience to future experience in something like the way our current experiences are connected to one another. It is this flow of consciousness that seems to allow us to really have experiences in the future—to *be* there in the sense that is most important. Parfit's repeated challenge to this picture, emblemized in the Teletransportation and Branch-Line cases, is essentially David Hume's— that if we take the time to really look, we can find no such unity in our own lives. This is why Parfit finally says of Teletransportation: "I want the person on Mars to be me in a specially intimate way in which no future person will ever be me. My continued existence never involves this deep further fact. What I fear will be missing is *always* missing." [17] He thus draws the following conclusion: it is not, as he claimed earlier, that Teletransportation is about as good as ordinary survival, but rather that "ordinary survival is *about as bad as,* or little better than, Teletransportation. *Ordinary survival is about as bad as being destroyed and having a Replica.*" [18]

If Parfit succeeds in his challenge—which many think he does—the only psychological connection between one's present and one's future is a relation of similarity or association between the contents of consciousness at different times. Since our sense of the importance of survival seems to be based—at least largely—on the assumption of a deep, phenomenological connection to the future, that importance needs to be reassessed in light of Parfit's challenge. The most extreme possibility is that the psychological relations we really do bear to the future have no intrin-

---

[16] See, for instance, Andy Clark, *Being There* (Cambridge, MA: MIT Press, 1998); and Daniel Dennett, *Consciousness Explained* (Boston: Little, Brown, and Co., 1991).
[17] Parfit, *Reasons and Persons,* 208.
[18] Ibid.

sic importance, and hence that survival itself is not actually very important. As counterintuitive as this conclusion is, Parfit suggests that it is defensible, and in some ways liberating.[19]

This conclusion is not forced on us, however. To avoid it, one need only show that some relation that we really do bear to the future justifies, at least partially, the importance we attribute to survival. This might be done by revisiting the original arguments that favor a psychological account of identity and turning instead toward a biologically based view—a view that places the significance of survival in biological connections.[20] But the importance of survival might also be salvaged within the framework of a psychologically based view if it could be shown that the psychological relation that we do have to our futures can still bear the importance we attribute to survival despite the fact that it is not the deep phenomenological connection we thought we had. This strategy has been fairly popular, and it is here that we see a turn to a view of persons as agents in the metaphysical literature on personal identity.

IV. The Turn toward Agency

A. John Perry's distinction between the importance and constitution of identity

One good example of the switch to an agency-based approach to survival can be found in John Perry's work. Like Unger, Perry distinguishes between different senses of "what matters in survival." His distinction, however, is not quite the same as Unger's. He says that the phrase "what matters in survival" can mean either *"what is of importance"* in survival or "what makes a case of survival a case of survival."[21] Unger's prudential and desirability senses would thus both fall under Perry's category of importance. Although Perry is a psychological continuity theorist, he holds a version of this view in which identity-constituting psychological continuity is intimately interlinked with continuity of body. He therefore claims that not only is a person's replica not *identical* to her, but, strictly speaking, she does not *survive* as her replica either (he thus uses "survival" in a different sense than I have been using it). The puzzles which Parfit and others find concerning identity and survival, Perry argues, frequently involve a conflation of the two senses of "what matters" as he has defined them. The confusion stems from the expectation that the relation that defines survival will be intrinsically important, and when it

---

[19] Ibid., 281–82.
[20] This approach has become increasingly popular lately. A prominent example is Eric Olson's book *The Human Animal: Personal Identity without Psychology* (New York: Oxford University Press, 1997).
[21] Perry, "The Importance of Being Identical," 85–86.

is found not to be, this is taken as a challenge to the psychological continuity theory. What we need to understand, says Perry, is that the importance of survival—in both Unger's prudential sense and his desirability sense—is derivative rather than immediate.

To make this point, and to show from what the importance of survival derives, Perry uses a variant on Unger's avoidance of future pain test. He imagines a scenario in which a person, by pushing a button, can prevent someone from experiencing terrible pain the next day, and asks whether a person has different sorts of reasons to press the button if the pain she prevents will be her own—reasons that go beyond the simple fact that anyone's pain is bad and should, all things equal, be prevented. Perry argues that a person does, at least usually, have special reasons to push the button to prevent her own pain, but also that they are not the sorts of reasons we typically take her to have. On Perry's view, the legitimacy of our concerns about our future pains is not based on a deep phenomenological connection to the future, but instead derives from our concern for our projects. Each of us has many projects, and we have reasons to see those projects carried out. If we are in excruciating pain, we are less likely to be able to see our projects through, and so we have reasons to avoid excruciating pain. Given that we are the people most likely to carry out our own projects, we thus have special reasons to avoid our own pains. Perry is aware, of course, that in some instances there may be others who can carry out our projects better than we can. He adds, however, that it is extremely improbable that there is anyone else who could and would carry out *all* of our projects better than we would, and therefore our concern for our projects gives us reason to be specially concerned for ourselves.

Perry also acknowledges that the asymmetry between the likelihood that a person will carry out her projects and the likelihood that someone else will is a contingent rather than a logically necessary one. In the types of thought experiments used in the personal identity literature, this truism may not hold. Teletransportation, for instance, replicates a person's entire psychological life. In Perry's terminology, the people in these cases will not "survive" as their replicas, but the replicas will, by definition, be just as likely to carry out their projects as they would, and in just the same way. What is important in survival in the most fundamental sense will thus be captured in these cases, even though the original person does not, in Perry's sense, survive.[22] Perry agrees with Parfit that the importance of identity and survival is derivative and does not depend upon a deep, phenomenological connection between the different temporal parts of a person's life. It depends instead, he says, on our interest in carrying out our projects—that is, our interests as agents.

---

[22] That is, the person does not survive as Perry uses the term—as I am using the term "survival," however, the person does survive.

B. Carol Rovane and the reconnection of constitution and importance

The shift to a view of the person as agent is also made by Carol Rovane in *The Bounds of Agency: An Essay in Revisionary Metaphysics*. Rovane does not enter the debate in direct response to the challenge of explaining the importance of survival or capturing phenomenological unity, and so she does not explicitly address these issues. She does, however, undertake to offer a psychological account of personal identity that will capture its practical importance (and, although she does not herself use the distinction between identity and survival, the practical importance of survival as well). More specifically, Rovane sets herself the goal of providing an account of identity that explains the normative injunction that rational unity should be achieved within the point of view of a single person, but not beyond.[23] To achieve her goal Rovane offers a normative analysis of personal identity. "According to the normative analysis, the condition of personal identity is the condition that gives rise to a certain normative commitment, namely, the commitment to achieve overall rational unity."[24] Although her view is quite complex, the features relevant for our purposes are well-articulated in an analysis she offers of where her view stands relative to Locke's. She agrees with Locke, she says, that personal identity should be defined in terms of the unity of a first-person point of view, but adds that her "analysis will reject Locke's specific account of what a first person point of view is. He construed it as the phenomenological point of view of a unified consciousness. In contrast, the normative analysis takes it to be the rational point of view of an agent."[25] Central to Rovane's view is the claim that a rational and phenomenological point of view need not—indeed, likely will not—coincide.

Rovane thus argues that the view that personal survival should be defined in terms of a phenomenological unity does not explain the normative injunction to take into account all of one's own states, but not any one else's, in deliberations about what to do. Instead she offers a view in which identity is defined in terms of unity of agency. This unity requires as a background condition many of the types of psychological connections that are present in the psychological continuity theory, but "in addition, the set must include certain substantive practical commitments that serve as *unifying projects*."[26] There is, of course, a great deal more to her view than I have described here, but it is the fundamental insight that is

---

[23] This normative injunction says that "when I deliberate I ought to resolve all of the contradictions and conflicts within my own point of view, but I need not resolve all of my disagreements with you. Likewise, I ought to rank all of my preferences, but this ranking need not reflect your preferences. And more generally, when I arrive at all-things-considered judgments I should take into account all of my beliefs, desires, and so forth, but not yours." Carol Rovane, *The Bounds of Agency* (Princeton, NJ: Princeton University Press, 1998), 24.

[24] Ibid., 23.

[25] Ibid., 19.

[26] Ibid., 31.

important for our purposes. Translated into the terminology we have been using, Rovane says that the bounds of self-interested concern will be set not by phenomenological unity, but by agential unity, and thus that both what constitutes survival and what matters in it will be our continuation as rational agents, not as experiencing subjects.

C. Resources in practical philosophy—Christine Korsgaard and Harry Frankfurt

The idea that persons should be viewed primarily as agents, and the unity of persons as the unity of agency, is not, of course, limited to discussions in the metaphysics of personal identity. It is a standard position in practical philosophy as well. For the most part, the discussions of identity in metaphysics and practical philosophy have proceeded independently. This is unfortunate, as insights found in practical philosophy provide useful resources for those interested in developing an agent-based view of personal identity. However, one important point of contact between these two discussions can be found in Christine Korsgaard's essay "Personal Identity and the Unity of Agency: A Kantian Response to Parfit."[27] Here Korsgaard explicitly takes on Parfit's arguments against a deep unity in the life of a person. She urges the Kantian position that "subject" and "agent" represent two perspectives we can take on persons, but says that if we wish to find what unifies a person, we must understand persons under the latter description rather than the former. The unity of a person's life, she says, is a unity of agency, not of experience.

Korsgaard accepts Parfit's argument that there is no unity of consciousness of the sort we tend to assume. She very elegantly describes the naive view of phenomenological unity as follows:

> The sphere of consciousness presents itself as something like a room, a place, a lit-up area, within which we do our thinking, imagining, remembering and planning, and from which we observe the world, the passing scene. It is envisioned as a tunnel or a stream, because we think that one moment of consciousness is somehow directly continuous with others, even when interrupted by deep sleep or anesthesia. We are inclined to think that memory is a deeper thing than it is, that it is *direct* access to an earlier stage of a continuing self, and not merely one way of knowing what happened. And so we may think of amnesia, not merely as the loss of knowledge, but as a door that blocks an existing place.[28]

---

[27] Christine Korsgaard, "Personal Identity and the Unity of Agency: A Kantian Response to Parfit," *Philosophy and Public Affairs* 18 (Spring 1989).
[28] Ibid., 116.

Like Parfit, Korsgaard denies the accuracy of this picture of consciousness and acknowledges that if we are looking for a significant unity within the life of a person we will not find it by looking for a unified subject of experiences. If we think about persons as agents, however, a meaningful, nonarbitrary unity is easy to find. Korsgaard writes: "[S]uppose Parfit has established that there is no deep sense in which I am identical to the subject of experiences who will occupy my body in the future. . . . I will argue that I nevertheless have reasons for regarding myself as the same rational agent as the one who will occupy my body in the future." She goes on to clarify that "these reasons are not metaphysical, but practical."[29]

When we start out thinking of persons as agents, we will immediately come upon the obvious fact that as agents, we must act, and that means we must decide what to do—or not do, as the case may be. Once we concentrate on this aspect of human existence, Korsgaard says, it will be easy to see that in order to act we must conceive of ourselves as unified agents. To show this, she begins by asking us to consider what underlies our sense that we are unified *at* a time, and says that there are two elements of this unity. First, the need for unity is forced upon us by the fact that, at least in our world, we control one and only one body. If we are divided about what to do, we need to overcome our division to be able to act coherently and effectively. "You are a unified person at any given time because you must act, and you have only one body with which to act."[30] The second element is the "unity implicit in the *standpoint* from which you deliberate and choose." She says that "it may be that what actually happens when you make a choice is that the strongest of your conflicting desires wins, but that is not the way you think of it when you deliberate. When you deliberate, it is as if there were something over and above all your desires, something that is *you* and *chooses* which one to act on."[31] According to Korsgaard, this sense of ourselves as choosing necessitates that we have *reasons* for choosing one course of action over the others, and "it is these reasons, rather than the desires themselves, which are expressive of your will."[32] You must have a sense of yourself as a unified chooser with reasons in order to act.

Korsgaard goes on to argue that *this* unity, unlike unity of consciousness, can easily be seen as stretching over time as well as holding at a time. A person needs to coordinate action and motives over time as well as at a time, since almost anything we want to do will take at least a bit of time to unfold. Imagine, she says, that my body really is occupied by a series of subjects, changing from moment to moment. It is clear that they had better learn to cooperate "if together we are going to have any kind

[29] Ibid., 109.
[30] Ibid., 111.
[31] Ibid.
[32] Ibid., 113.

of a *life*."[33] But more than this, the need to think of oneself as a unified agent acting from reasons means that we must identify ourselves with those reasons, and those reasons may, and probably will, "automatically carry us into the future."[34] If you understand yourself as an agent "implementing something like a particular plan of life, you need to identify with your future in order to be *what you are even now*."[35] The basis for our unity over time is thus the necessity of acting once we are thrust on the scene, and not some metaphysical fact. As Korsgaard sums it up: "You normally think you lead one continuing life because you are one person, but according to this argument the truth is the reverse. You are one continuing person because you have one life to lead."[36]

Korsgaard realizes that to many it will seem that she has ignored the central issue. There may be some good practical reasons to act *as if* we will persist into the future, and to view ourselves as unified, but this does not really unify us. She rejects this description of the situation, however, for two reasons. First, she agrees with Parfit that our naive conception of the unity of a person rests on the assumption of a deep unity of consciousness over time, and that there is no such unity to be found in our actual lives, let alone in bizarre science fiction cases. Second, and most important, while our sense of our unity as agents may rest on practical rather than metaphysical facts, these facts are by no means trivial or arbitrary. It is not just an accident or convention that we take the body as the most relevant unit of agency; things would go badly for us if we didn't—indeed, after a while there might well not be any "us" for whom things would go badly. She allows, as does Rovane, that there can be units of agency bigger (and presumably also smaller) than the body—families, tribes, bowling leagues, or our teenaged selves might qualify. There is no denying, however, the necessity of viewing ourselves as unified agents (whatever the size of the unit), nor of taking a human life as a particularly basic such unit. Such unification is necessary, even if the necessity is not metaphysical.

The basic picture behind this view is developed further in recent work in practical reasoning that starts from the picture of the person as an agent and stresses the fundamental importance of our unity as agents, suggesting that our very survival depends upon it. Much of this work is Korsgaard's own. This picture is laid out in great detail in her book *The Sources of Normativity* and in her *Locke Lectures*. In the latter she tells us:

---

[33] Korsgaard therefore holds that personal identity will, in our world, be tied to the identity of the human being. She stresses that this is a contingent fact, however, in the sense that in a world where people had their bodies replaced with replicas on a regular basis, and these replicas continued their lives in something like the ordinary way, the unity of the agent could involve more than one body. See ibid., 113.

[34] Ibid.

[35] Ibid., 113–14.

[36] Ibid., 113.

Because human beings are self-conscious, we are conscious of threats to our psychic unity or integrity. Sometimes these threats spring from our own desires and impulses. The element of truth in the image of the miserable sinner who must repress his unruly desires in order to be good rests in the fact that we deliberate in the face of threats to our integrity, and act against them. What is false about the picture is the idea that we must repress these threats *in order to be good*. Rather, we must repress them in order to be one, to be unified, to be whole. We must repress them in order to maintain our personal or practical identity.[37]

If we do not unify ourselves as agents, we are in danger of real disintegration.

This general picture is shared by Harry Frankfurt. Although his view of personal identity differs from Korsgaard's in many important respects, he shares with her the idea that we must maintain unity of will to have any sort of life at all. Frankfurt tells us: "[T]here is, I believe, a quite primitive human need to establish and to maintain volitional unity. Any threat to that unity—that is, any threat to the cohesion of the self—tends to alarm a person, and to mobilize him for an attempt at 'self-preservation.' "[38] Although the term appears in scare quotes, elsewhere Frankfurt links these issues to "self-preservation" "only in an unfamiliarly literal sense—in the sense of sustaining not the *life* of the organism but the *persistence of the self*."[39] By giving us a way to think about unity of agency as central to our real persistence as persons, the work of Korsgaard and Frankfurt in practical philosophy adds a great deal to the plausibility of the approach suggested by Perry and Rovane. It provides a deep, nonarbitrary unity over the course of our lives that is not a unity of consciousness.

V. Unity of Consciousness Again

The switch to an agency-based view of persons and personal identity, especially supplemented by work in practical philosophy, represents an important development in our thought about these issues. There is a compelling case for the view that unity of agency is a real and important feature of personal identity. The question that remains, however, is whether this sort of unity is really strong enough to bear the kind of importance we attribute to survival. It may be that there is no unity of consciousness of the sort we typically assume there to be throughout the life of a person,

---

[37] Christine Korsgaard, *Locke Lectures*, Lecture I, 18. Available online at http://www.people.fas.harvard.edu/~korsgaar/Korsgaard.LL1.pdf.

[38] Harry Frankfurt, "Autonomy, Necessity, and Love," in Frankfurt, *Necessity, Volition, and Love* (Cambridge: Cambridge University Press, 1999), 139.

[39] Harry Frankfurt, "On the Usefulness of Final Ends," in Frankfurt, *Necessity, Volition, and Love*, 89.

and also that unity of agency is a more important unity than we generally take it to be, but that does not mean that it has the kind of visceral significance our naive-but-problematic notion of unity of consciousness did. To use Parfit's idiom, it is not clear whether an agency-based approach to personal identity is an alternative above and beyond those he conceived, or whether it is a version of the "moderate claim," giving survival some importance, but not as much as we originally believed.

When we look at a view like Perry's or Rovane's, it certainly seems the latter. Of course we care about our projects, but if *all* there is to survival is the continuity of projects, the difference between surviving and being survived by like-minded folk does seem trivial. Korsgaard and Frankfurt offer resources for seeing an agency-based view as more of a real alternative to the Parfitian approach. The brute importance of unity of agency, not as a nicety or refinement of our lives, but as a condition of them, suggests that this sort of unity may well be considered the condition of survival as we ordinarily conceive it. On this view, unity of agency is not a consolation for not having unity of consciousness, but the unity that carries the significance we usually attribute to survival. This perspective, however, works better when we look at the short term, and it becomes more problematic when we look on the time scale of a human life. Korsgaard makes an excellent case for the need for unity of agency in the short term as a precondition for taking any action, and thus as a precondition for anything we might recognize as a person. The need for unity of agency over the long term, however, is a more tenuous thing. I do need a unified will at a time to eat, drink, or get out of bed, but I don't necessarily need a unified will over time to do those things.

Korsgaard, of course, argues that in a real sense I do need a unified will over time to take even minimal actions now. The move here depends rather heavily on the need to have *reasons* for action. To unify my will now, on her view, I need to see myself as having reasons for my choices, and it is these reasons that carry me into the future by taking the form of general laws. This is why the necessity of unification of agency over time is based on the view of oneself as "implementing a life plan" or having "any kind of a life." So here the necessity of unification looks less like it comes from the desire to have *a* life and more like it comes from the desire to have a *meaningful* life. Frankfurt's position is similar in this respect. Although he does not think we need reasons to act, he does think we need to have fairly stable commitments to what we care about. His rationale for this claim is the same as Korsgaard's; such stability is necessary to have a meaningful life. In their later work, both philosophers thus stress the connection between unity of agency and a life that is "worth living." Korsgaard does this, for instance, in her discussion of our identification with a variety of "practical identities"—identities as mother, friend, patriot, union member, etc.—which provide us with reasons for action. She defines these practical identities as "a description under which you value yourself, a description under which you find your life to be worth living and your actions to be worth undertaking." [40] And Frankfurt describes a life of ambivalence as follows: "For someone who is unlikely to have any stable preferences or goals," he says,

> the benefits of freedom are, at the very least, severely diminished. The opportunity to act in accordance with his own inclinations is a doubtful asset for an individual whose will is so divided that he is moved both to decide for a certain alternative and to decide against it. Neither of the alternatives can satisfy him, since each entails the frustration of the other. The fact that he is free to choose between them is likely only to make his anguish more poignant and more intense. [41]

This provides us with a powerful motivation for seeking volitional unity over time, to be sure, but it does not make an overwhelming case for the fact that such unity is what defines our persistence. The distinction between a life integrated enough to be *a* life and one integrated enough to be a *meaningful* life thus becomes blurred.

This is problematic for agency-based accounts of personal identity because it seems all too possible for a person to live a life that has no meaning or direction, or to lose meaning only to find it again, and then perhaps lose it again. These are all crises *within* the life of a person and not crises that signify the end of a life. This idea is well-expressed in the opening question of Camus's *Myth of Sisyphus*—"why not suicide?" Camus denies the existence of a transcendent meaning that could unify a life, and asks whether and why we should go to the trouble of living if life has no meaning. While I do not mean to imply that Camus has a completely convincing conception of the nature of human existence, I do think he represents well one strain of thought that persists in our thinking about ourselves and our lives. The relation of this strain of thought to a position like Korsgaard's is complex, and worth investigating.

To begin, it might seem as if the very coherence of Camus's question challenges Korsgaard's position as I have interpreted it. If we are worried about having to live in the future despite the fact that life has no over-arching significance, it would seem that no such significance is required to continue living a life. But this is too quick. Even if we accept (as I do) that Camus is talking about suicide not only as the act of killing an organism, but as the act of killing a psychological self, his question in many ways supports Korsgaard's position far more than it challenges it. Camus is saying that without meaning we wonder whether it is worth the

---

[40] Christine Korsgaard, *The Sources of Normativity* (Cambridge: Cambridge University Press, 1996), 101.
[41] Harry Frankfurt, "The Faintest Passion," in Frankfurt, *Necessity, Volition, and Love*, 102.

effort of living. This means we do feel as if we have to decide what to do about the future—whether to perpetuate ourselves into it in a way that guarantees that we will have to keep acting and so take on the responsibility of deciding what to do, or whether to spare ourselves that effort. Considering such a drastic step, and for this reason, certainly suggests that we are identifying ourselves as the very agents who will be called upon to act in the future. This is why we need to make decisions now about what to do then. Suicide is a decision about what to do in one's future; it is the decision to do nothing.

The challenge to Korsgaard raised by Camus, such as it is, comes rather in the way that he argues that suicide is not an appropriate or rational reaction to the recognition that life has no meaning. Life can be lived all the better, he says, because it has no meaning. We can find a reason to live in the perpetual, self-expressive struggle against the arationality of the world. It is important to note that in some respects Camus and Korsgaard offer the same solution to the problem of meaninglessness. Neither relies on a transcendent purpose, outside of our natures, that provides our reason to live. Reasons for living and value must be provided by us, and are provided by us via our expression of ourselves as value-conferring or reason-giving beings. In fact, toward the end of *The Sources of Normativity*, Korsgaard gives an analysis of what is wrong with suicide that is in many ways very like Camus's.[42] There is, however, an important difference. Korsgaard's picture involves our taking the reasons we give ourselves seriously, which means recognizing that they give meaning to our lives insofar as we are true to them, and threaten to make our lives disintegrate into meaninglessness if we are not. Camus, on the other hand, suggests that we can only have a life worth living if we refuse to take these human meanings seriously, if we reject stability and find our value instead in the raw fact of our consciousness. Now, sometimes by "consciousness" he means consciousness *of* our condition—the continued awareness that we assert ourselves by struggling hopelessly against the absurd. But he also often means just the capacity to have experience—any experience. He tells us that "what counts is not the best living but the most living,"[43] that "no depth, no emotion, no passion, and no sacrifice could render equal in the eyes of the absurd man (even if he wished it so) a conscious life of forty years and a lucidity spread over sixty years,"[44] and that "the present and the succession of presents before a constantly conscious soul is the ideal of the absurd man."[45]

I do not mean to urge Camus's view as more accurate than Korsgaard's, but in its extremity it points to an important element that is not given suf-

---

[42] Korsgaard, *The Sources of Normativity*, 160–64.
[43] Albert Camus, *The Myth of Sisyphus and Other Essays*, trans. Justin O'Brien (New York: Vintage International, 1991), 63.
[44] Ibid.
[45] Ibid., 63–64.

ficient emphasis in her account—the value that we put on the sheer fact of being conscious, independent of any practical implications. Of course, Korsgaard does not deny that we care about consciousness, but I think Camus's picture shows more than just that; it shows how much we care about being perpetuated into the future as the same experiencing subject. The subject who is conscious now wants to act, and wants meaning, but she also just plain wants to *be there* in the future, with or without purpose. Two more months, even if there are no loose ends to tie up or projects to complete, are two more months. This does not mean that pain and depression cannot make the negative value of continuation so great that it is no longer deemed worthwhile—this is when we see suicide as an understandable response. But the significance of being there, just to be there, just to keep having experiences, just to have *a* life and not necessarily a *meaningful* life is, I think, an important part of "what matters in survival."

So, we seem to be back to the idea that the agency-based account of personal identity is some form of Parfit's moderate claim. The kind of survival that seems so important to us—the survival that psychological accounts of identity are trying to capture—requires a deep unity of consciousness over time, something that we now have reason to believe we do not, and cannot, have. This would mean that Parfit was right in claiming we are merely under an *illusion* that this unity exists, and therefore take identity and survival to have an importance that they do not actually have. But this is too quick. Our discussion of agency-based accounts of identity has hinted that they may be able to give us something more like our naive conception of psychological continuation than we might have thought. These hints are the suggestions that our conception of ourselves as unified agents can have a profound impact on the quality of our conscious experience, and on our experience of ourselves as persisting *subjects* as well as agents. Korsgaard talks about the way in which our reasons for action "carry us into the future" as agents, but they may also do so as subjects. In conceiving of ourselves as continuing as agents, we project ourselves into the future as subjects as well—imagining what will bring us satisfaction, when we will be filled with regret, what is likely to tempt us away from our purpose, and so on. To experience ourselves as unified agents, we may well also have to experience ourselves as unified subjects, and vice versa.

Another aspect of this connection is mentioned by Frankfurt in his discussion of why we need final ends. He has told us already that we need to have stable commitments that constrain our will (with our approval) because otherwise life will be meaningless, but he puts a particularly interesting gloss on this claim when he tells us that if we fail to find something we care about in this way we will get bored, and, he says,

> the avoidance of boredom is a profound human need. Our aversion to being bored is not a matter simply of distaste for a rather unpleas-

ant state of consciousness. The aversion expresses our sensitivity
to a much more basic threat. It is of the essence of boredom that
we don't care about what is going on. We therefore experience an
attenuation of psychic vitality or liveliness. In its most familiar
manifestations, being bored involves a reduction in the sharpness
and focus of attention. The general level of mental energy dimin-
ishes. Our responsiveness to conscious stimuli flattens out and
shrinks. Distinctions are not noticed and not made, so that our
conscious field becomes increasingly homogeneous. As boredom
progresses, it entails an increasing diminution of significant differentiation within consciousness.[46]

He goes on to explain:

At the limit, when consciousness is totally undifferentiated, this
homogenization is tantamount to the cessation of conscious experience altogether. When we are bored, in other words, we tend to fall
asleep. Any substantial increase in the extent to which we are bored
undermines, then, the very continuation of conscious mental life.
That is, it threatens the extinction of the active self. What is expressed
by our interest in avoiding boredom is therefore not simply a resistance to discomfort, but a quite primitive urge for psychic survival.[47]

It is not just activity that is threatened if we do not have long-term
commitments; it is our very consciousness. The danger, of course, is not
just literally falling asleep, but rather failing to project one's consciousness into the future in the ways we usually do.

Interestingly enough, Camus makes just the opposite claim. He says
that we need to reject long-term commitments and the meaning derived
from them if we are to retain our consciousness. Commitment breeds
complacency, and a rote, mechanistic implementation of a life-plan dulls
our consciousness. If we are to be really alive, and remain really conscious, he says, we must think of ourselves as faced with the world afresh
at each moment. Undoubtedly there is some truth to both of these perspectives. A failure to have passions may well dull consciousness, and so
may falling into a routine. Moreover, there is probably less of a distinction
between Frankfurt and Korsgaard on the one hand and Camus on the
other than it at first appears. While Frankfurt and Korsgaard do require
stability, they also emphasize that as agents we are forced to keep our
commitments in place, essentially by perpetually rechoosing them. These
issues are too complex to sort out here. For the present, I am interested
only in making the more general point that the quality of our conscious-

---

[46] Frankfurt, "On the Usefulness of Final Ends," 89.
[47] Ibid.

ness is going to be affected in a variety of ways by our recognition that we are agents and by our conception of ourselves as unified agents. The agency view thus need not be seen simply as a *substitution* of a picture of persons as agents for a picture of persons as subjects, but rather as a new way of thinking about persons as subjects, and the way in which subjects might be unified over time.

This discussion suggests that while we do, indeed, feel that a continuation of consciousness is a crucial part of the survival of the person, it is not the bare continuation of sentience isolated by Unger's prudential sense of what matters, nor the formal connections of similarity and association between the contents of consciousness offered by psychological continuity theorists. It is, rather, a continuing sense of ourselves as subjects moving through the world and experiencing it. This experience of ourselves as unified subjects may well require at some point the structure and organization that comes from conceiving of ourselves as unified agents, and may arise only under the practical exigencies of living in the world. This does not mean that this experience is not of independent value, nor that it cannot outlast the sorts of identifications and reasons that unify an agent over the long term. There may thus be a meaningful and significant question of whether I can anticipate having experience in the future that cannot simply be answered by looking at how I unify myself as an agent, even if the answer is not totally independent of that fact. The relations to which I am pointing are, admittedly, very vague at this point. If, however, there is reason to believe that they really exist, there is reason to think that we can come up with a more satisfying account of personal identity by uncovering and understanding them.

VI. CONCLUSION

The psychological approach to problems of personal identity seems to capture one very important aspect of our conception of what we are and the conditions of our persistence. It is not easy, however, to articulate the insight it provides. Originally it seems that the insight is that we are fundamentally subjects of experience, and that our survival requires a persistence of experiencing subjects. The naive understanding of this persistence is in terms of a deep, metaphysical unity of consciousness over time. Parfit and others have argued effectively that it is hard even to make this naive understanding coherent, let alone give reasons for believing that we have it in ordinary survival. This argument seems to imply that ordinary survival cannot have the importance we usually attribute to it, perhaps having no importance at all.

An alternative approach has developed suggesting that persons should be conceived as most fundamentally agents rather than subjects of experience, and thus that the unity of a person over time should be defined in terms of unity of agency rather than unity of subject. This approach is seen in both metaphysics and practical philosophy. Perry and Rovane offer their alternatives within the context of the metaphysical debate, while Korsgaard and Frankfurt develop theirs mostly within the context of discussions of practical reason. I have suggested that as revealing as these views are, they still seem to leave out the importance our conception of ourselves as experiencing subjects has for us, an importance that is described in Camus's *Myth of Sisyphus*. Using hints found in the development of agency-based views of personal identity, however, I have pointed to a possible reintroduction of the picture of the person as subject into the agency-based views we have considered.

   Coming from a Kantian perspective, Korsgaard says that persons are both subjects and agents, and we can take one perspective or the other depending on our purposes. I have suggested that for these purposes we must think of subjectivity and agency as inherently intertwined, and thus of unity of agency and unity of consciousness as separate but interdependent unities. In this way we can hope to regain a meaningful unity of consciousness as part of personal survival. Like the unity of agency described by Korsgaard, it will not have a metaphysical basis, but it will be nonarbitrary and deeply important nonetheless.

Philosophy, University of Illinois at Chicago

WHEN DOES A PERSON BEGIN?*

By Lynne Rudder Baker

I. Introduction

The answer to the question "When does a person begin?" depends on what a person is: If an entity is a person, what kind of being, most fundamentally, is she? Since the persons we are familiar with are human persons—persons with human bodies—one may simply assume that what we human persons are most fundamentally are animals.[1] I agree that it is often useful to think of us as animals—as long as we are thinking biologically, rather than ontologically. However, on my view, our animal nature, which we share with other higher primates, does not expose what we most fundamentally are. Ontology is not a branch of biology.

Nevertheless, my account of human persons roots us firmly in the natural world. Biologically, we are akin to other primates; but ontologically, we are unique. However, we are still material beings. I believe that we are fundamentally persons who are constituted by human organisms. Since constitution is not identity, human persons may come into existence at a different time from the organisms that constitute them. So I shall argue.

Unfortunately, this area of inquiry is clouded with terminological difficulties. The term "human being" (as well as "human individual") is used ambiguously. Some philosophers take "human being" to be a purely biological term that refers to human organisms.[2] Others take "human being" to name a psychological kind, not a biological kind.[3] And still other philosophers seem to trade on the ambiguity when they argue that human persons are human beings and human beings are human organisms; so human persons come into existence when human organisms come into existence. This is a non sequitur: Human organisms are a biological kind; human persons cannot pretheoretically be assumed to be a biological kind. The term "human being" may be used either for human organisms or for human persons, but—in a pretheoretical context—it is tendentious to use "human being" (or "human individual") for both.

* Thanks to Gareth Matthews and Catherine E. Rudder for comments. I am also grateful to other contributors to this volume, especially Robert A. Wilson, Marya Schechtman, David Oderberg, Stephen Braude, and John Finnis.
[1] Throughout this essay, I mean "we" to apply to the community of readers.
[2] For example, see John Perry, "The Importance of Being Identical," in Amélie Oksenberg Rorty, ed., *The Identities of Persons* (Berkeley: University of California Press, 1976), 70.
[3] For example, see Mark Johnston, "Human Beings," *Journal of Philosophy* 84 (1987): 64.

The term "human nature" inherits the ambiguity of "human being" and "human individual." "Human nature" may refer to biological character-istics (say, length of gestation period or brain size) that distinguish human organisms from nonhuman organisms. Or it may refer to rational and moral characteristics that distinguish human persons from nonpersons.[4]

Although I would prefer to use the term "human being" to refer to human persons, and "human nature" to refer to the nature of human persons (rather than of human organisms), I shall avoid these terms in order to steer clear of ambiguity. I take the term "human organism" to be interchangeable with "human animal," and I take the nature of a human organism to be whatever biologists tell us it is. I am a Darwinian about human animals. That is, I believe that there is important continuity between the most primitive organisms and us, and that we human persons have an animal nature. But I do not believe that our animal nature exhausts our nature all things considered. I shall use a biological theory of human organisms on which to build an ontological theory of human persons. Before turning to my view of persons, let us consider when a human *organism* comes into existence.

II. WHEN DOES A HUMAN ORGANISM BEGIN?

I take the question "When does a human organism begin?" to be a biological question. This empirical question stands in contrast to the phil-osophical question "When does a human person begin?" (Empirical data are relevant to philosophical questions, without being conclusive.) One frequently heard answer to the biological question is that a human organ-ism comes into existence at the time of fertilization of a human egg by a sperm. (But beware: There is not an exact moment of fertilization. Fertil-ization itself is a process that lasts twenty-plus hours.)[5] However, the view that a human organism comes into existence at—or at the end of—fertilization is logically untenable, because a fertilized egg may split and produce twins. If it is even physically possible for a fertilized egg to produce twins (whether it actually does so or not), a fertilized egg cannot be *identical* to an organism. As long as it is possible to twin, a zygote is not *a* human anything, but a cell cluster.[6] In the case of twinning, as philos-opher G. E. M. Anscombe explains: "Neither of the two humans that

---

[4] See Norman M. Ford, *The Prenatal Person: Ethics from Conception to Birth* (Malden, MA: Blackwell Publishing, 2002), 9, 15.

[5] Ibid., 55. Moreover, everything in the natural world comes into existence gradually: solar systems, cherry blossoms, jellyfish, tractors and other artifacts. Thus, every natural entity has vague temporal boundaries, and hence is subject to vague existence; but it does not follow that there is any vague identity. If $a = b$ and a is vague, then b is vague in exactly the same respects. I discuss this further in my essay "Everyday Concepts as a Guide to Reality," *The Monist* (2006).

[6] G. E. M. Anscombe, "Were You a Zygote?" in A. Phillips Griffiths, ed., *Philosophy and Practice* (Cambridge: Cambridge University Press, 1985), 111.

eventually develop can be identified as the same human as the zygote, because they can't *both* be so, as they are different humans from one another."[7] It is logically impossible for one organism to be identical to two organisms. And, of course, anything that is logically impossible is biologically impossible. In twinning, two (or more) twins come from a single fertilized egg. But neither of the twins is identical to that fertilized egg, on pain of contradiction. To see this, suppose that a zygote (a cell cluster) divides and twins result. Call the zygote "*A*," and one of the twins "*B*" and the other twin "*C*." If *A* were identical to both *B* and *C*, then—by the transitivity of identity—*B* and *C* would be identical to each other. But *B* is clearly not identical to *C*. Therefore, *A* (the zygote) cannot be identical to *B* and *C*. A human organism cannot come into existence until there is no further possibility of "twinning"—about two weeks after fertilization.

Thus, there is no new human organism until after the end of the process of implantation of a blastocyst in the wall of the womb (about fourteen days after fertilization). Even at implantation, an organism does not come into existence instantaneously. There is no sharp line demarcating the coming into existence of a new human individual organism. There is only a gradual process. But we can say this much: Soon after implantation (the primitive streak stage), the embryo is an individual, as opposed to a mass of cells.[8] At this point, there is an individual human organism that persists through fetal development, birth, maturation, adulthood, until death. There are differing views about whether the human organism ends at the time of death, but in no case does the human organism persist through the disintegration of the human body.[9]

This answers the biological question about human embryos. But there remains the ontological question—a further question that is not automatically answered by biology: Granting that a human embryo after implantation is an individual human organism, what is the relation between a human embryo and a human person? On my view, the relation is constitution: A human person is wholly constituted by a human organism, without being identical to the constituting organism. So the coming into existence of a human organism is not *ipso facto* the coming into existence of a human person. As we shall see, on my view—the constitution view—a human person is not temporally coextensive with a human organism, but

---

[7] Ibid., 112.

[8] This is a point that has been made by Roman Catholic writers. See, e.g., Norman M. Ford, *When Did I Begin? Conception of the Human Individual in History, Philosophy, and Science* (Cambridge: Cambridge University Press, 1988), 174–78. See also Anscombe, "Were You a Zygote?"

[9] Many philosophers identify human organisms with human bodies. For example, Fred Feldman holds that human persons are (identical to) human organisms and that human organisms persist after death as corpses. See Fred Feldman, *Confrontations with the Reaper* (New York: Oxford University Press, 1992), 104–5. Although I do not identify persons and organisms, I do identify organisms and bodies.

is nevertheless a material being, ultimately constituted by subatomic particles. Human persons have no immaterial parts.[10]

III. What a Person Is

So, what is a person? *Person*—like *statue*—is a primary kind, one of many irreducible ontological kinds. Everything that exists is of some primary kind—the kind that determines what the thing is most fundamentally. Things have their primary-kind properties essentially. Members of the kind *organism* are organisms essentially; members of the kind *person* are persons essentially. (If *x* has *F* essentially, then there is no possible world or time at which *x* exists and lacks *F*.) Thus, when a person comes into being, a new object comes into being—an object that is a person essentially.

What distinguishes *person* from other primary kinds (like *planet* or *organism*) is that persons have first-person perspectives. Just as a statue is not a piece of clay, say, plus some other part, so too a human person is not a human organism plus some other part. The defining characteristic of a person is a first-person perspective. Human persons are beings that have first-person perspectives essentially and are constituted by human organisms (or bodies). Martian persons, if there were any, are beings that have first-person perspectives essentially and are constituted by Martian bodies. Although *person* is a psychological kind, human persons are in the domains, not only of psychology, but also of biology, on the one hand, and of the social sciences, on the other.[11] A human person, like a bronze statue, is a unified thing—but the statue is not identical to the piece of bronze that constitutes it, nor is the person identical to the body that constitutes her. Your body is a person derivatively, in virtue of constituting you, who are a person nonderivatively. You are a human organism derivatively, in virtue of being constituted by your body that is a human organism nonderivatively.

In order to understand what a person is, the property to focus on is the first-person perspective. In mature persons, to have a first-person perspective is to be able to think of oneself without the use of any name, description, or demonstrative; it is the ability to conceive of oneself as oneself, from the inside, as it were.[12]

---

[10] Constitution is not a relation between parts and wholes. If *x* constitutes *y* at *t*, the difference between *x* and *y* is that *x* and *y* have different properties essentially and different persistence conditions. It is not a matter of *y*'s having a part that *x* lacks, or vice versa.

[11] By "social sciences" I mean the disciplines of sociology, political science, history, and other disciplines that have groups of people in their domain. The domain of psychology includes conscious beings with beliefs, desires, and intentions. In the absence of anything immaterial, where is the domain of psychology located? The domain of psychology is located where the conscious beings with beliefs, desires, and intentions are located. Not every phenomenon in a material world has a definite spatial location—e.g., where was Smith's purchase of Shell Oil stock located?

[12] I have discussed this at length in *Persons and Bodies: A Constitution View* (Cambridge: Cambridge University Press, 2000). See ch. 3.

Linguistic evidence of a first-person perspective comes from use of first-person pronouns embedded in sentences with linguistic or psychological verbs—e.g., "I wonder how I will die," or "I promise that I will stick with you."[13] The content of a thought so expressed includes ineliminable first-person reference. Call the thought expressed using "I" embedded in a sentence following a psychological or linguistic verb (e.g., "I am thinking that I am hungry now") an "I* thought."[14] What distinguishes an I* thought from a simple first-person sentence (e.g., "I am hungry now") is that in the I* thought the first-person reference is part of the content of the thought, whereas in the simple first-person sentence, the "I" could drop out: one's thought could be expressed by "hungry now." If I am wondering how I will die, then I am entertaining an I* thought; I am thinking of myself as myself, so to speak. I am not thinking of myself in any third-person way (e.g., not as Lynne Baker, nor as the person who is thinking, nor as that woman, nor as the only person in the room) at all. I could wonder how I am going to die even if I had total amnesia. I* thoughts are not expressible by any non-first-person sentences. Anything that can entertain such irreducibly first-person thoughts is a person. A being with a first-person perspective not only can have thoughts about herself, but she can also conceive of herself as the subject of such thoughts. I not only wonder how I'll die, but I realize that the bearer of that thought is myself.

A being may be conscious without having a first-person perspective. Nonhuman primates and other mammals are conscious. They have psychological states like believing, fearing, and desiring, but they do not realize that they have beliefs and desires. They have points of view (e.g., "danger in that direction"), but they cannot conceive of themselves as the subjects of such thoughts. They cannot *conceive of* themselves from the first-person. (We have every reason to think that they do not wonder how they will die.) Thus, having psychological states like beliefs and desires, and having a point of view, are necessary but not sufficient conditions for being a person. A sufficient condition for being a person—whether human, divine, ape, or silicon-based—is having a first-person perspective.[15] So, what makes something a person is not the "stuff" it is made of. It does not matter whether something is made of organic material or silicon or, in the

---

[13] Hector-Neri Castañeda developed this idea in several papers. See Castañeda, "He: A Study in the Logic of Self-Consciousness," *Ratio* 8 (1966): 130–57; and Castañeda, "Indicators and Quasi-Indicators," *American Philosophical Quarterly* 4 (1967): 85–100.

[14] The term comes from Gareth B. Matthews, *Thought's Ego in Augustine and Descartes* (Ithaca, NY: Cornell University Press, 1992).

[15] Gordon Gallup's experiments with chimpanzees suggest the possibility of a kind of intermediate stage between dogs (which have intentional states but no first-person perspectives) and human persons (who have first-person perspectives). In my opinion, Gallup's chimpanzees fall short of full-blown first-person perspectives (for details, see Baker, *Persons and Bodies*, 62–64). See Gordon Gallup, Jr., "Self-Recognition in Primates: A Comparative Approach to Bidirectional Properties of Consciousness," *American Psychologist* 32 (1977): 329–38.

case of God, no material "stuff" at all. If a being has a first-person perspective, it is a person.

A first-person perspective is the basis of all forms of self-consciousness. It makes possible an inner life, a life of thoughts that one realizes are her own. Although I cannot discuss it here, I believe that a first-person perspective is closely related to the acquisition of language. A first-person perspective makes possible moral agency and rational agency. We not only act on our desires (as, presumably, dogs do); we can evaluate our desires. It makes possible many new sorts of phenomena: memoirs, confessions, self-deception. It gives us the ability to assess our goals—even biologically endowed goals like survival and reproduction. And on and on.

The appearance of first-person perspectives in a world makes an ontological difference in that world: A world with beings that have inner lives is ontologically richer than a world without beings that have inner lives. But what is ontologically distinctive about being a person—namely, the capacity for a first-person perspective—does not have to be secured by an immaterial substance like a soul.[16]

IV. THE IDEA OF A RUDIMENTARY FIRST-PERSON PERSPECTIVE

What I have just described is what I shall call a *robust* first-person perspective. Now I shall distinguish a robust first-person perspective from a rudimentary first-person perspective, and then apply this distinction to the question of when a person comes into being.[17]

Since our stereotypes of persons are of human persons, my notion of a first-person perspective is tailored to fit specifically human persons. If there are nonhuman persons, they, too, will have robust first-person perspectives, but they may not have acquired them as a development of rudimentary first-person perspectives. But human persons begin by having rudimentary first-person perspectives:

> *Rudimentary FPP.* A being has a rudimentary first-person perspective if and only if (i) it is conscious, a sentient being; (ii) it has a capacity to imitate; and (iii) its behavior is explainable only by attribution of beliefs, desires, and intentions.

---

[16] The constitution view is an argument for this claim. The first-person perspective, along with the capacity to acquire a language, may be products of natural selection or may be specially endowed by God. But for whatever reason (either God's will or natural selection sans God), nonhuman primates have not developed robust first-person perspectives of the kind that we have.

[17] I was motivated to distinguish between a robust and a rudimentary first-person perspective by my many critics, including Marc Slors, Anthonie Meijers, Monica Meijsing, Herman de Regt, and Ton Derksen.

The requirement of consciousness or sentience for a rudimentary first-person perspective rules out security cameras as conscious, even though they may be said to have a perspective on, say, a parking lot. The capacity to imitate involves differentiation of self and other. The capacity to imitate has been linked by developmental psychologists to "some form of self-recognition" that does not require a self-concept.[18] Finally, a being whose behavior is not explainable except by attribution of beliefs and desires has a perspective and can respond appropriately to changing situations. For one's behavior to be explainable only by attribution of beliefs, desires, and intentions is to be a (minimal) intentional agent. Thus, a being with a rudimentary first-person perspective is a sentient being, an imitator, and an intentional agent.[19]

Human infants have rudimentary first-person perspectives. There is empirical evidence that human infants have the three properties required for a rudimentary first-person perspective. Human infants are clearly sentient. There is abundant research to show that they are imitators from birth. For example, two well-known psychologists, Alison Gopnik and Andrew Meltzoff, tested forty newborns as young as forty-two minutes old (the average age was thirty-two hours) in 1983.[20] They wrote of the newborns' gestures of mouth opening and tongue protrusion: "These data directly demonstrate that a primitive capacity to imitate is part of the normal child's biological endowment."[21] Imitation is grounded in bodies: a newborn imitator must connect the internal feeling of his own body (kinesthesia) with the external things that he sees (and later hears).[22] (Aristotle went so far as to say, in his *Poetics*, that imitation was a distinguishing mark of human beings.) And finally, according to Ulric Neisser, "Babies are intentional agents almost from birth."[23] So human infants meet the conditions for having rudimentary first-person perspectives. Indeed, developmental psychologists agree that from birth, a first-person perspective is underway.[24]

---

[18] Michael Lewis, "Myself and Me," in Sue Taylor Parker, Robert W. Mitchell, and Maria L. Boccia, eds., *Self-Awareness in Animals and Humans* (Cambridge: Cambridge University Press, 1994), 22.

[19] So, rudimentary first-person perspectives have what Robert A. Wilson calls "action-traction." See Section V of his essay "Persons, Social Agency, and Constitution," elsewhere in this volume.

[20] Gopnik is Professor of Psychology at the University of California at Berkeley, and Meltzoff is Codirector of the Institute for Learning and Brain Sciences at the University of Washington, where he is also Professor of Psychology.

[21] Alison Gopnik and Andrew N. Meltzoff, "Minds, Bodies, and Persons: Young Children's Understanding of the Self and Others as Reflected in Imitation and Theory-of-Mind Research," in Parker, Mitchell, and Boccia, eds., *Self-Awareness in Animals and Humans*, 171.

[22] Alison Gopnik, Andrew Meltzoff, and Patricia Kuhl, eds., *How Babies Think: The Science of Childhood* (London: Weidenfeld, and Nicholson, 1999), 30.

[23] See Ulric Neisser, "Criteria for an Ecological Self," in Philippe Rochat, ed., *The Self in Infancy: Theory and Research* (Amsterdam: North-Holland, Elsevier, 1995), 23. Neisser is a well-known cognitive psychologist at Cornell University.

[24] See, for example, Jerome Kagan, *Unstable Ideas* (Cambridge, MA: Harvard University Press, 1989). Kagan is the Starch Professor of Psychology at Harvard.

Higher nonhuman mammals seem to meet the conditions as well. Observation of household pets like dogs and cats suggests that they have rudimentary first-person perspectives. They are sentient—they feel pain, for example. (Their brains, as well as their behavior when injured, are similar enough to ours for this to be a secure judgment.) They are imitators; even ducks, who imprint on their mothers, engage in imitative behavior. Although there is some controversy regarding the research on animal intentionality,[25] higher nonhuman mammals appear to be intentional agents. Although we have apparently successful intentional explanations of animal behavior—e.g., "Fido is digging over there because he saw you bury the bone there and he wants it"—there are no adequate nonintentional accounts of Fido's behavior. Chimpanzees that pass psychologist Gordon Gallup's famous mirror tests even more obviously have rudimentary first-person perspectives.[26]

The conclusion I draw from the work of developmental psychologists is that human infants and higher nonhuman mammals have rudimentary first-person perspectives.[27] Moreover, rudimentary first-person perspectives exhaust the first-personal resources of human infants and higher nonhuman mammals; human infants and higher nonhuman mammals exhibit no more sophisticated first-personal phenomena than what rudimentary first-person perspectives account for. Although infants differentiate themselves from others from birth, they do not pass the mirror test until they are about eighteen months old. (And chimpanzees and orangutans "show every bit as compelling evidence of self-recognition as 18- to 24-month-old human infants.")[28] According to Jerome Kagan, it is "not at all certain that [human] 12-month-olds, who experience sensations, possess any concepts about their person, and it is dubious that they are consciously aware of their intentions, feelings, appearance or actions."[29] Daniel J. Povinelli and Christopher G. Prince report that "there is little evidence that chimpanzees understand anything at all about mental states."[30] Although more evidence is needed about the cognitive devel-

[25] See, for example, Cecilia Heyes and Anthony Dickinson, "The Intentionality of Animal Action," in Martin Davies and Glyn W. Humphreys, eds., *Consciousness: Psychological and Philosophical Essays* (Oxford: Blackwell, 1993), 105–20. Heyes is in the Department of Psychology at University College, London, and Dickinson is in the Department of Experimental Psychology at Cambridge University.

[26] See Gallup, "Self-Recognition in Primates." Discussion of the mirror tests has become so widespread that the phenomenon of recognizing oneself in a mirror is routinely referred to simply by the initials MSR (mirror self-recognition) in psychological literature.

[27] I do not expect the developmental psychologists to share my metaphysical view of constitution; I look to their work only to show at what stages during development certain features appear.

[28] Daniel J. Povinelli, "The Unduplicated Self," in Rochat, ed., *The Self in Infancy*, 185. Povinelli is in the Cognitive Evolution Group at the University of Louisiana at Lafayette.

[29] Jerome Kagan, "Is There a Self in Infancy?" in Michel Ferrari and Robert J. Sternberg, eds., *Self-Awareness: Its Nature and Development* (New York: The Guilford Press, 1998), 138.

[30] Daniel J. Povinelli and Christopher G. Prince, "When Self Met Other," in Ferrari and Sternberg, eds., *Self-Awareness*, 88.

opment of chimpanzees, there is no clear evidence that chimpanzees have the capacity to construct higher-order representations that would allow conceptions of themselves as having pasts and futures.[31]

Another similarity between human infants and higher nonhuman mammals is that they are social creatures. There seems to be general agreement among psychologists that developmentally there is a symmetry of self and other, that humans (as well as other higher nonhuman mammals) are social creatures. Ulric Neisser puts the "interpersonal self" in which the "individual engaged in social interaction with another person" at eight weeks.[32] Philippe Rochat flatly asserts that the developmental origins of self-awareness are primarily social.[33] The idea of a first-person perspective is not Cartesian or Leibnizian: we are not monads that unfold according to an internal plan unaffected by our surroundings.

Thus, human infants and higher nonhuman mammals all have rudimentary first-person perspectives, but I hold that human infants are persons and higher nonhuman mammals are not persons (or probably not). If having a first-person perspective is what distinguishes a person from everything else, and if a human infant and a chimpanzee both have rudimentary first-person perspectives, how can a human infant be a person if a chimpanzee fails to be? What distinguishes the human infant from the chimpanzee is that the human infant's rudimentary first-person perspective is a developmental preliminary to having a robust first-person perspective, but a chimpanzee's rudimentary first-person perspective is not preliminary to anything.

By saying that a rudimentary first-person perspective is "a preliminary to a robust first-person perspective," I mean to pick out those rudimentary first-person perspectives that developmentally ground or underpin robust first-person perspectives. Unlike chimpanzees, human animals are of a kind that normally develops robust first-person perspectives. This is what makes human animals special: their rudimentary first-person perspectives are a developmental preliminary to robust first-person perspectives. A being with a rudimentary first-person perspective is a person *only if it is of a kind that normally develops robust first-person perspectives.* This is not to say that a person will develop a robust first-person perspective: perhaps severely autistic individuals, or severely retarded individuals, have only rudimentary first-person perspectives. However, they are still persons, albeit very impaired, because they have rudimentary first-person perspectives and are of a kind—human animal—that develops a robust first-person perspective. We can capture this idea by the following thesis:

---

[31] Povinelli, "The Unduplicated Self," 186. So it looks as if the scope of the self-concept that Gallup postulated to explain mirror behavior is really quite limited, contrary to Gallup's speculation.

[32] Ulric Neisser, "Criteria for an Ecological Self," in Rochat, ed., *The Self in Infancy,* 18.

[33] Philippe Rochat, "Early Objectification of the Self," in Rochat, ed., *The Self in Infancy,* 54. Rochat is in the Emory University department of psychology.

(HP) x constitutes a human person at t if and only if x is a human organism at t and x has a rudimentary or robust first-person perspective at t,

where we take "x constitutes a human person at t" as shorthand for "x constitutes a person at t, and x is a (nonderivative) human organism." [34] Thesis (HP) gives only a necessary and sufficient condition for there being a *human* person. There may be other kinds of persons: silicon persons (constituted by aggregates of silicon compounds) and God (not constituted by anything). (HP) is silent about other kinds of persons.

In *Persons and Bodies*, I wrote that a person comes into being when a human organism develops a robust first-person perspective or the structural capacity for one. The effect of (HP) is to push back the onset of personhood to human animals with rudimentary first-person perspectives.

In the face of (HP), someone might mount a "slippery slope" argument against it. [35] The argument would be this: "Once we introduce the notion of a preliminary, we have no reason to stop with rudimentary first-person perspectives. If we consider a being with a rudimentary first-person perspective that is preliminary to a robust first-person perspective to be a person, why not also consider a being at a prior stage that is preliminary to a rudimentary first-person perspective to be a person, and so on?" Suppose that, in place of (HP), someone proposed (HP*):

(HP*) x constitutes a human person at t if and only if x is a human organism at t and either x has a robust first-person perspective or x has capacities that, in the normal course, produce a being with a robust first-person perspective. [36]

I reject (HP*), and with it the regress argument, [37] for the following reasons. In the first place, note that a robust first-person perspective is itself a capacity—but a capacity of a special sort. A first-person perspective (robust or rudimentary) awaits nothing for its exercise other than a subject's thinking a certain kind of thought. It is an in-hand capacity that can be exercised at will. Let us distinguish between a remote capacity and an in-hand capacity. A hammer has an in-hand capacity at t for driving nails whether or not it is actually driving nails; you have an in-hand capacity at t for digesting food whether or not you are actually digesting food. Unassembled hammer parts (a wooden handle and a metal head)

---

[34] This latter detail is a needed technicality since, on the constitution view, *person* is a primary kind, and there may be nonhuman persons. "Human person" refers to a person constituted by a human organism.

[35] Gareth Matthews suggested this argument.

[36] Robert A. Wilson suggested (HP*).

[37] "Regress argument" is a common philosophical term for the kind of argument sketched in the preceding paragraph.

have only a remote capacity at t for driving nails; an embryo has only a remote capacity at t for digesting food.[38] A remote capacity may be thought of as a second-order capacity: a capacity to develop a capacity. An in-hand capacity is a first-order capacity.

According to the constitution view—as revised to include (HP)—a first-person perspective (rudimentary as well as robust) is an in-hand capacity, not a capacity to develop a capacity. According to (HP*), a being with no in-hand capacities at all, but only with a capacity to develop a capacity, is a person. I do not believe that remote capacities suffice for making *any-thing* the kind of thing that it is. (HP) makes being a person depend on the more constrained notion of an in-hand capacity of a (rudimentary or robust) first-person perspective.

The second reason that I reject (HP*) is this: The properties in terms of which rudimentary first-person perspectives are specified are ones we recognize as personal: sentience, capacity to imitate, intentionality. Inso-far as we think of nonhuman animals as person-like, it is precisely because they have these properties. The properties that an early-term human fetus has—say, having a heart—are not particularly associated with persons, or even with human animals. Even invertebrates have hearts. So, not just every property that is a developmental preliminary to a robust first-person perspective in humans contributes to being a person. There is a difference between those properties in virtue of which beings are person-like (the properties of rudimentary first-person perspectives) and the broader class of biological properties shared by members of many taxa. The properties in virtue of which something is a person are themselves specifically personal properties.

Given (HP), then, human infants are persons: when a human organism develops a rudimentary first-person perspective, it comes to constitute a human person. Acquisition of the properties that comprise a rudimentary first-person perspective has different ontological significance for human organisms than for nonhuman primates. Acquisition of those properties by a human organism marks the beginning of a new person. Acquisition of those properties by a nonhuman organism, however, does not mark the beginning of a new person. The rudimentary first-person perspectives of higher nonhuman mammals are not developmentally preliminary to any-thing further. (If nonhuman primates did develop robust first-person perspectives, then they, too, would come to constitute persons.)

According to the modern synthesis in biology, we are biological beings, continuous with the rest of the animal kingdom. The constitution view recognizes that we have animal natures. The constitution view shows how to put together Darwinian biology with a traditional concern of

---

[38] I borrowed the example of the hammer from Robert Pasnau's excellent discussion of "has a capacity." See Robert Pasnau, *Thomas Aquinas on Human Nature: A Philosophical Study of Summa Theologiae 1a 75–89* (Cambridge: Cambridge University Press, 2002), 115.

philosophers—our inwardness, our ability to see ourselves and each other as subjects, our ability to have rich inner lives. This first-personal aspect of us—the essential aspect, in my opinion—is of no interest to biologists. The first-person perspective may well have evolved by natural selection, but it does not stand out, biologically speaking.

On the constitution view, when a human organism acquires a rudimentary first-person perspective, a new being—a person—comes into existence. When a quantity of bronze is cast into a likeness of a man, a new thing—a statue—comes into existence. Nonderivative persons are essentially persons—just as nonderivative statues are essentially statues. (Bodies that constitute persons are persons derivatively—just as pieces of marble that constitute statues are statues derivatively.) The relation between a human person and a human animal is the same as the relation between a bronze statue and a piece of bronze: constitution. The statue is not identical to the piece of bronze, nor is the person identical to the animal. Thus, the argument for the ontological uniqueness of persons does not require any special pleading. On this view, a human person comes into existence near birth: what is born is a person constituted by an organism.

On the constitution view, as we have seen, a human person comes into existence when a human organism acquires a rudimentary first-person perspective. There is not an exact moment when this happens—just as there is not an exact moment when a human organism comes into existence. But nothing that we know of in the natural world comes into existence instantaneously.[39] When a human organism acquires a rudimentary first-person perspective, it comes to constitute a new entity: a human person. In the next two sections, I shall examine some positions that contrast with the constitution view.

V. SUBSTANCE DUALISM

The constitution view is materialistic: All substances in the natural world are ultimately constituted by physical particles. There are no immaterial substances in the natural world. However, the constitution view has been accused (by philosopher Dean Zimmerman) of being a terminological variant of substance dualism. The charge takes the form of a dilemma:[40] When a person thinks, "I hope that I'll be happy," there is either one thinker of the thought or two. If there are two, then there are too many thinkers. But if there is only one real bearer of the thought, the critic claims, the constitution view is indistinguishable from substance dualism

---

[39] There is (ontological) indeterminacy at the beginning of everything that comes into existence by means of a process. See my essay "Everyday Concepts as a Guide to Reality," *The Monist* (2006).

[40] This is my interpretation of Dean Zimmerman's "The Constitution of Persons by Bodies: A Critique of Lynne Rudder Baker's Theory of Material Constitution," *Philosophical Topics* 30 (2002): 295–338.

of the sort that holds that immaterial souls are located in bodies that have mental states in virtue of their relations to souls. If there is only one thinker of the thought, then there are two substances (person and animal), distinguished by the fact that one of them is the thinker and the other one is not.

On the constitution view, "one thinker" would refer to the person-constituted-by-the-animal, and "two thinkers" would refer to the person (a member of one primary kind) and the constituting animal (a member of a distinct primary kind). When a person thinks, "I hope that I'll be happy," there is only one thinker that has the thought nonderivatively, the person-constituted-by-the-animal.

Thus, I take the first horn of the dilemma, but deny that it is substance dualism.[41] Zimmerman is right to say that to have a property derivatively is to be constitutionally related to something that has it nonderivatively, but he is mistaken to think that to have it derivatively is to not have it at all. I have argued at length that the constitution-relation is a relation of *unity*. If you take the constitution-relation seriously as a unity-relation, then "derivatively" is not "by courtesy." I suspect that Zimmerman's belief that to have a property derivatively is not to have it at all stems from what I take to be a metaphysical prejudice: the only properties that something *really* has are intrinsic to it. On this assumption, if x has a property in virtue of its relation to y, where y is nonidentical to x—even if the relation is as close as constitution—x does not *really* have the property. Since I have argued that many things have relational properties essentially, I consider it question-begging to criticize the view by assuming that to have a property in virtue of constitution-relations is not really to have it. The unity is a matter of constitution.

As I said, biologically, I'm a Darwinian: I believe that there is important continuity between the most primitive organisms and us, and that we have animal natures. But there is more to us than our animal natures. I do not believe that biological knowledge suffices for understanding our nature, all things considered. Like the substance dualist, I think that we are ontologically special: the worth or value of a person is not measured in terms of surviving offspring. But emphatically unlike the substance dual-

---

[41] Zimmerman asks how I differ from an emergent dualist (like William Hasker), who holds that a soul—a distinct substance, made of a unique kind of immaterial stuff—emerges from a body. Despite some affinities between my view and Hasker's, I think that it is implausible to suppose that there are immaterial substances in the natural world. Moreover: (1) On my view, the relation between a person and her body (as well as the relation between a person and the micro-elements that make her up) is an instance of a very general relation common to *all* macro-objects; whereas, according to Hasker, the relation between a person and her body is that a body is one part of a person, who also has a special immaterial part. (2) On my view, what emerges from material elements is never anything immaterial; on Hasker's view, the emergent self is an immaterial object. (3) I think that all the causal powers of a human person are constituted by causal powers at lower levels; whereas Hasker holds that the self has libertarian free will and can modify and direct the brain. See William Hasker, *The Emergent Self* (Ithaca, NY: Cornell University Press, 1999), 195.

ist, I do not account for what makes us special in terms of having an immaterial part.

Here are some fundamental ways that the constitution view differs from substance dualism. On the constitution view: (1) There are not just two kinds of substances—mental and physical—but indefinitely many kinds of substances. Each primary kind is ontologically special. (This is important because there is not just one big divide in nature between two disparate realms—mental and physical.) (2) The constitution relation itself is comprehensive, and is exemplified independently of any mental properties. Thus, in contrast to substance dualism, there is no special pleading for persons. (3) The derivative/nonderivative distinction is likewise comprehensive, and is exemplified independently of any mental properties.[42] So, I think that I escape the dilemma of either having to countenance too many thinkers or too many mental states or of falling into substance dualism.

According to substance dualism, there is a bifurcation within the natural world itself—not just, as traditional theists hold, a bifurcation of Creator and creation. Substance dualists take human persons to have two substantially different parts: one material (the body) and one immaterial (the mind or soul). (Whereas a substance dualist might say that we have one foot in heaven, I don't think that we have any feet in heaven.) A person comes into being, according to substance dualism, only when both the material and immaterial parts are present. Different versions of substance dualism locate the coming into being of a person at different times.

I do not believe that substance dualism is a plausible account of the natural world as we know it today. Although I reject scientism root and branch, empirical investigation of the natural world has produced an amazing body of knowledge with no end in sight.[43] Postulation of immaterial substances in the natural world should be a last resort. Since I think that we can do without postulating immaterial substances in the natural world, I think that we ought to do without them. According to the constitution view, nature itself is a unified whole with its own integrity, and human persons are a part of nature.[44] With the exception of one version (which I shall discuss in part B of Section VI), I shall put aside substance dualism.

---

[42] Substance dualists countenance only one-way borrowing: the body borrows mental properties from the soul. Zimmerman supposes that the "emergent dualist will surely regard [my two-way borrowing] as simply a question of semantics" (Zimmerman, "The Constitution of Persons by Bodies," 316). He does not say why the substance dualist's one-way borrowing of mental properties from the soul by the body should be considered a matter of metaphysics, but borrowing in the other direction only a matter of semantics.

[43] By "scientism" I mean the view that *all* correct explanations are scientific explanations. We must distinguish between scientific claims—claims made from *within* science—and claims made *about* science. One important claim about science (one that I reject) is that science is the arbiter of all knowable truth, that there is nothing to be known beyond what science delivers.

[44] This is so, I believe, whether there is a Creator or not.

Now let's consider two alternatives to the constitution view. Both these alternatives—which I reject—take persons to be ontologically in the same category as animals. I shall call these the "biological-animalist view" and the "Thomistic-animalist view," respectively. What I am calling the "biological-animalist view" is called simply the "animalist view" in the mainstream literature on personal identity. I am using the more awkward term, "biological animalism," in order to distinguish this view from a very different view that also takes human persons to be animals, but takes human animals to have immaterial souls. I am calling this latter view "Thomistic animalism."

VI. Persons as Animals

A. Biological animalism

On the biological-animalist view, what we are most fundamentally are human animals, and human animals are construed as biologists construe them. The animal kingdom is a seamless whole. According to the biological-animalist view, human animals (= human persons) are just another primate species—along with chimpanzees, orangutans, monkeys, and gorillas. The fact that human persons alone have inner lives (or any other psychological or moral properties) is not a particularly important fact about human persons. Proponents of the biological-animalist view have nothing to say about what distinguishes us from nonhuman primates. This is so, I suspect, because what distinguishes us from nonhuman primates is not biologically important.

On the biological-animalist view, what makes us the kind of beings that we are are our biological properties (like metabolism), and our continued existence depends only on the continued functioning of biological processes.[45] It is exclusively up to biologists to tell us what our natures are. A noted biological animalist, Eric Olson, says pointedly: "What it takes for us to persist through time is what I have called *biological continuity*: one survives just in case one's purely animal functions—metabolism, the capacity to breathe and circulate one's blood, and the like—continue."[46] Psychology is, as Olson says, "completely irrelevant to personal identity."[47]

Being a person and having the properties that are associated with being a person, on the biological-animalist view, are irrelevant to the kind of entity you fundamentally are. Person-making properties are temporary and contingent properties of human animals. Olson offhandedly refers to the properties in virtue of which a human animal is a person as "rationality, a capacity for self-consciousness, or what have you"; in Olson's

---

[45] Eric T. Olson, *The Human Animal: Personal Identity without Psychology* (Oxford: Oxford University Press, 1997), 30.
[46] Ibid., 16.
[47] Eric T. Olson, "Was I Ever a Fetus?" *Philosophy and Phenomenological Research* 57 (1997): 97.

view these are rather like properties of "being a philosopher, or a student, or a fancier of fast cars"—properties that are not part of one's nature.[48] According to biological animalism, what makes you you concerns the biological functions controlled by your lower brain stem.

If biological animalism is correct, then being a person is just an ontologically insignificant property of certain organisms. In that case, the question "When does a person begin?" would be ambiguous. Either it would mean: When does an organism—an entity that will acquire the property of being a person—begin? Or it could mean: When does an organism acquire the property of being a person? These questions have different answers: the time that a new organism begins is much earlier than the time that it acquires the property of being a person. But we need not decide which way a biological animalist ought to construe the question "When does a person begin?," because there are reasons to reject the biological-animalist view independently of how it answers this question.

The main reason to reject the biological-animalist view is that it renders invisible our most important characteristics. The abilities of self-conscious, brooding, and introspective beings—from Augustine in the *Confessions* to analysands in psychoanalysis to former U.S. presidents writing their memoirs—are of a different order from those of tool-using, mate-seeking, dominance-establishing nonhuman primates—even though our use of tools, seeking of mates, and establishing dominance have their origins in our nonhuman ancestors. With respect to *the range of what we can do* (from planning our futures to wondering how we got ourselves into such a mess), and with respect to *the moral significance of what we can do* (from assessing our goals to confessing our sins), self-conscious beings are obviously unique—significantly different from non-self-conscious beings.

I agree with the biological animalists about our biological nature—as I said, I am a Darwinian—I just think that our biological nature does not exhaust our nature all things considered. For example, if Darwin is right, there are only two ultimate goals for human animals: survival and reproduction. But people have ultimate goals that cannot be assimilated to survival and reproduction. (Think of people willing to die in the service of an abstract idea like freedom.) Thus, I think that biological animalism does not do justice to the reality of human persons. So, let's turn to Thomistic animalism.

B. Thomistic animalism

I use the term "Thomistic animalism" to describe a view that regards us as fundamentally animals, but does not construe human animals as biologists construe them. According to Thomistic animalism, any member of the biological species *Homo sapiens* is a person. But being a member of the

[48] Olson, *The Human Animal*, 17.

Homo sapiens species is not like being a member of other species. According to Thomistic animalism, all and only members of the *Homo sapiens* species have immaterial spiritual souls that are not recognized by biologists.[49] Thus, according to Thomistic animalism, human persons are animals, but there are two kinds of animals: nonrational animals that do not have immaterial souls and rational animals that do have immaterial souls.

Norman M. Ford, author of two informative and provocative books on the beginning of persons,[50] is a major proponent of the view that I am calling "Thomistic animalism." Ford is concerned with what he usually calls "the human individual." As he put it, "I shall use all three ways of referring to the members of our biological species *Homo sapiens* as interchangeable and with the same meaning—human individual, human being and person."[51] This may sound like biological animalism, but it is crucially different. Unlike biological animalism, Thomistic animalism does not take biology to be the arbiter of the nature of animals, at least of human animals. Ford does not believe that "the human person can be satisfactorily explained in purely empirical terms." A human animal is not "just a living body that has the capacity to engage in rational self-conscious acts."[52] On the Thomistic-animalist view, a human animal is animated by an immaterial spiritual soul or a "human life-principle," which, after death, "is no longer present in the corpse."[53] Ford sees a "fundamental psychosomatic unity of soul and matter within the ontological unity of the human individual."[54] (Thus, I take Ford's view to be a form of substance dualism.)[55]

Although, on Ford's view, "person" officially is just another name for members of the *Homo sapiens* species, the "core of our personhood" is not a matter of biology: "Rape and perjury are immoral everywhere. This is

---

[49] See Ford, *When Did I Begin?*; and Ford, *The Prenatal Person.*

[50] The thesis that Ford elaborates and supports is (what is commonly taken to be) the official view of the Roman Catholic Church after the First Vatican Council, 1869–70. However, it is not the view of Thomas Aquinas, nor is it just an updated version of Aquinas's view. Aquinas, following Aristotle, thought that until the presence of a rational soul—about twelve weeks into gestation—there was no human individual of any sort. See Robert Pasnau, *Thomas Aquinas on Human Nature*, 100–142. (An updated version of Aquinas's view, I believe, would place the beginning of a human person at the development of a brain that could support rational thought.) The Roman Catholic Church's official position is that human life must be protected from the time of conception. John Finnis pointed out to me that the doctrine is not that a fetus *is* a person, but that a fetus *must be treated as* a person. See, for example, Congregation for the Doctrine of the Faith, "Instruction on Respect for Human Life in Its Origin and on the Dignity of Procreation: Replies to Certain Questions of the Day," http://www.vatican.va/roman_curia/congregations/cfaith/documents/rc_con_cfaith_doc_19870222_respect-for-human-life_en.html (accessed April 4, 2004).

[51] Ford, *When Did I Begin?* 67.

[52] Ibid., 74.

[53] Ibid., 16; and Ford, *The Prenatal Person*, 13–16.

[54] Ford, *When Did I Begin?* 74.

[55] Although Thomistic animalists are substance dualists, I consider their view as a variety of animalism because they take their view from Thomas Aquinas, who followed Aristotle in holding that men (as he would say) are essentially animals.

so because morality is essentially related to the core of our personhood where human dignity and solidarity originate."[56] Thomistic animalism, then, takes us human persons to be fundamentally animals with important nonbiological properties that are unique to human persons. Moreover, Ford sometimes calls a spiritual soul "an immaterial life-principle."[57] If we need an immaterial life-principle to explain our being "living human individuals," why don't chimpanzees also need an immaterial life-principle to explain their being living nonhuman primates?

In any case, I think that Thomistic animalism is ultimately unsatisfactory for two principal reasons. First, Thomistic animalism tears apart the animal kingdom. Contrary to contemporary biological thought, Thomistic animalism makes membership in the species *Homo sapiens* very different from membership in any other species. It asserts that biology does not have the last word on *Homo sapiens*. Second, Thomistic animalism conceives of us human persons as having two parts: an immaterial soul and a material body. The constitution view offers an alternative that avoids both these difficulties while retaining moral and theological benefits of Thomistic animalism.[58]

On the constitution view, biology does have the last word on *Homo sapiens*; but biology does not have the last word on us human persons, all things considered. If we are constituted by human animals, but not identical to the human animals that constitute us, then we can give biology its full due—and with biologists, see the animal kingdom as a seamless whole—and still emphasize the very properties that Thomistic animalists insist on.

For example, unlike biologists, Ford locates the evolutionary difference between "a form of animal life" and human beings in a spiritual soul, evidence for which is that human beings have reflective self-awareness.[59] According to the constitution view, we can side with the biologists on the matter of the difference between human and nonhuman animals, and yet agree with Ford that reflective self-awareness does make us human persons unique. We just need to distinguish between human persons and human animals and refrain from using "human beings" or "human individuals" equivocally. We do not have to abandon standard biology in order to secure our uniqueness. Nor do we have to suppose that we have immaterial spiritual souls—or that any animal would need or have such a thing—in order to secure our uniqueness.

By conceiving of human persons as members of the species *Homo sapiens*, but essentially having nonbiological properties (immaterial souls),

[56] Ford, *The Prenatal Person*, 17.
[57] Ibid., 91.
[58] See my "Material Persons and the Doctrine of Resurrection," *Faith and Philosophy* 18 (2001): 151–67; and my "Death and the Afterlife," in *The Oxford Handbook of Philosophy of Religion*, ed. William J. Wainwright (Oxford: Oxford University Press, 2004), 366–91.
[59] Ford, *When Did I Begin?* 1. Moreover, Ford sometimes slips up and *contrasts* human persons and animals. See ibid., 75.

Thomistic animalism cannot make good sense of the respects in which we are like the rest of the animal kingdom and the respects in which we are not. By contrast, the constitution view clearly holds that we are part of the animal kingdom with respect to what constitutes us, but that our being essentially persons makes us unique in just the ways that Ford would like.

One consideration that is *not* among my reasons to reject Thomistic animalism is that it is presented as a Christian view.[60] Indeed, I think that theists who believe in (or even who want to leave open the possibility of) life after death have still another reason to reject Thomistic animalism: Animals essentially are organic; organic material essentially decays (it is corruptible). I do not see how an animal could possibly survive death. Ah, but the Thomistic animalist says, we are very special animals; we are animals-with-immaterial-souls, and an immaterial soul does not decay! In that case, if we are to survive death, we should be identified with the immaterial soul, not with animals at all. The constitution view, as I have argued elsewhere, is a better way to leave room for life after death than postulation of an immaterial soul.[61]

Thus, I believe that the constitution view is superior to both biological animalism and Thomistic animalism (as well as to substance dualism). Biological animalism does not recognize the ontological importance of the unique properties of human persons. Thomistic animalism, while recognizing the ontological importance of human persons, attributes the ontologically important properties to (putatively) immaterial features of members of the animal kingdom. By contrast, the constitution view both recognizes the ontological importance of the unique properties of human persons, and regards human persons as natural, material beings—without contravening any tenets of traditional theism or even of Christian doctrine. Now let's return to the matter of the coming into existence of a human person and its implications for thinking about abortion.

VII. THINKING ABOUT ABORTION

This is an essay in metaphysics—specifically in the metaphysics of personal identity. It is not an essay on public policy, nor is it an essay on the legal issues concerning abortion in the United States. These matters, though important, are logically subsequent to the ones at issue here.[62]

---

[60] For what it's worth, I am a practicing Episcopalian, who accepts the Nicene Creed.

[61] See my "Death and the Afterlife," in Wainwright, ed., *The Oxford Handbook of Philosophy of Religion.* I also believe that the constitution view can make better sense of the "two-natures" doctrine of Christ than can substance dualism. See my essay "Christians Should Reject Mind-Body Dualism," in Michael L. Peterson and Raymond J. VanArragon, eds., *Contemporary Debates in the Philosophy of Religion* (Malden, MA: Blackwell Publishers, 2004), 327–37.

[62] If I had written a different essay, U.S. Supreme Court cases—such as *Roe v. Wade* (1973) and *Casey v. Planned Parenthood* (1993)—would have been germane; but they are not ger-

Nevertheless, the constitution view has one logical implication that is relevant to thinking about abortion. Thus, I want to add a coda to discuss this implication and reasons why it is useful in thinking about abortion.

According to the constitution view, as we have seen, a human organism exists before a human person comes into being: a human person comes into being when a human organism develops a rudimentary first-person perspective—at birth, or shortly before.[63] The obvious consequence of the constitution view for the issue of abortion is this: Any premise that implies that abortion before development of a rudimentary first-person perspective is the killing of an innocent person is false. If the constitution view is correct, then no sound anti-abortion argument can be based on such a premise.[64] This is all that follows from the constitution view. But it answers—in the negative—an important question: Does every human organism have the same ontological and moral status as you and me? This question is an important philosophical one for everyone—legislators, judges, as well as private individuals who have no official social roles—who thinks seriously about abortion.

Using "fetus" as short for "fetus before development of a rudimentary first-person perspective," the metaphysical implication of the constitution view is the following thesis—call it "(O)":

(O) A human fetus is an organism that does not constitute a person.

Thesis (O) has no direct implications for condoning or not condoning abortion. It certainly does not justify abortion. Indeed, one may endorse (O) and be just as opposed to procured abortions of any sort as someone who holds that every human embryo is a person. Thesis (O) is, however, significant for thinking about abortion, because it removes a whole category of arguments that short-circuit careful moral thought. The thesis that every fetus is a person implies that abortion is the killing of an innocent person. If the fetus is a person, abortion is morally impermissible regardless of the circumstances of the pregnant girl or woman. Morally speaking, the thesis that the fetus is a person renders the pregnant female invisible: it simply forecloses any consideration of the woman or

---

mane to this metaphysical essay. Such legal considerations are at the wrong level of discourse for this essay.

[63] In "Was I Ever a Fetus?" Eric T. Olson argued that on views like mine, I was never an early-term fetus. Distinguo! There is no x such that x was a fetus at t and I am identical to x. However, there is an x such that x was a fetus at t and I am now constituted by x. For my full reply to Olson's article, see my "What Am I?" *Philosophy and Phenomenological Research* 59 (1999): 151–59.

[64] Moral theories like utilitarianism or Kantianism are of limited use in debates about abortion for two reasons: (1) The question of what beings qualify as being subject to moral theories is not answered by the theories themselves; and (2) in applying a moral theory to an actual case, all the "moral work" goes into describing the particulars of the case. In actual decisions about abortion, the particulars of the case carry the day.

girl per se who (for whatever reason) has an unwanted pregnancy. By contrast, (O) allows respect for pregnant females per se and not just as incubators. In thinking about abortion, it is morally important not to leave out respect for the pregnant girl or woman in her own right.[65] Thesis (O) opens up the field of discussion to include pregnant girls and women in their own right. There are three further reasons that (O) is helpful in thinking about abortion.

The first reason is that, by removing the premise that a fetus is a person, (O) clears the field of misleading arguments about, e.g., a "right to life." There can be no "right to life" until there is a person to be a subject of that right. It makes no sense to suppose that a nonexisting person has a right to be brought into existence. Moreover, "life" is used to refer both to biological life (taking in nutrition, locomotion, growing—biological characteristics that we share with other species) and to personal life (joys, hopes, plans for the future—nonbiological characteristics that appear in a biography). Human biological life derives value from making possible personal life. But to take human biological life—shorn of context and of considerations of quality—to be an absolute value in itself verges on idolatry. It puts allegiance to an abstract metaphysical view above the concrete needs of the actual people involved: it gives precedence to an abstraction—*life*—over the real lives of real people.

The second reason that (O) is helpful in thinking about abortion is this: Rejection of the thesis that the fetus is a person shifts the issue from a question about the morality of killing a person to a question about the morality of bringing into existence a person in various circumstances. The question of whether a person should be brought into existence is very different from the question of duties toward a person already in existence. This shift of questions—to whether a person should be brought into existence in various given circumstances—makes room for careful reflection that takes into account relevant considerations such as the health of the fetus, the health of the mother, the capacity of the mother (or others), financially and emotionally, to take on the responsibility of caring for an infant and bringing up a child, the quality of life that a child would likely have, the impact of a new child on the family, and the consequences for society of bringing a child into the world in the given circumstances. Discussions that assume that fetuses are persons simplemindedly screen off such morally relevant considerations from view.

Anyone who is considering an abortion is in a terrible situation. Everyone can agree that it would have been much better not to have become pregnant. But when the options are to have an abortion or to have a baby,

---

[65] Note that I am not using the fact that (O) allows respect for pregnant females per se, and not just as human incubators, as reason to accept (O), but rather as reason to welcome (O) as a consequence of the constitution view. The reason to *accept* (O) is that it follows from the constitution view, which is a comprehensive view defended on grounds having nothing to do with fetuses.

there are circumstances in which the choice to have an abortion is the morally better choice. One such circumstance is a situation in which the fetus is anencephalic. Anencephaly is a fatal condition in which brain formation begins but goes awry, leaving a defective brain stem and malformed hemispheres. Anencephalic fetuses are never capable of long-term survival. Delivery of such a baby carries a high risk of hemorrhage and extreme trauma for the mother. Bringing such a baby into the world is not a wise use of health-care resources.

In such cases, I believe that abortion would be morally the right course of action. The anencephalic human organism will never have a rudimentary first-person perspective and will never come to constitute a person. Even Ford, who still counsels against abortion, agrees that such a fetus "will never be able to express rational activities." But Ford holds that a fetus with "anencephaly is a human individual with a rational nature on account of a divinely created immaterial soul or life-principle and who, due to a malformed cortex and brain damage, will never be able to express rational activities." [66]

The point is this: If (O) were false [67] —if abortion were morally impermissible on the grounds that a fetus is a person—then morally speaking, there could be no exceptions to the prohibition of abortion in the case of anencephaly, or in the case of rape or incest, or in the case of saving the pregnant woman's life. None of these considerations would be relevant to allowing abortion. (That most abortions have nothing to do with these extreme circumstances is irrelevant to the logical point.) Thus, another reason to welcome (O) is that (O)—unlike its denial—allows consideration of morally relevant circumstances in deciding about an abortion.

The third reason that (O) is helpful in thinking about abortion is that abortion is a complex issue, and (O), unlike the denial of (O), allows the complexity to be recognized. For example, who should make decisions about abortion? If (O) is denied, there is no moral room for decisions about abortion to be made by anyone. Given (O), the following line of thought is available (though not forced upon one):

It is reasonable that, in *any* decision, whoever will bear the burden for the effects of the decision should have control over making it. The ultimate bearer of responsibility for having a baby is primarily the pregnant girl or woman, and to a lesser extent her sexual partner, her doctor, and other caregivers whom she may call upon for help.[68] A new person does not come into existence until the fetus develops a rudimentary first-

---

[66] Ford, *The Prenatal Person*, 95–96.

[67] Thesis (O) is false if and only if either a fetus is not an organism, or a fetus is a person. I shall assume that those who deny (O) do not deny that a fetus is an organism, but rather hold that a fetus is a person.

[68] Those who urge ill-prepared pregnant girls not to have abortions seem to melt away when the baby actually arrives; their concern for human life, as many have pointed out, seems to stop at birth.

person perspective, perhaps at birth, perhaps shortly before birth at the earliest.[69] Since fetal development is a gradual process, the closer the fetus comes to developing a rudimentary first-person perspective, the more cautious someone considering abortion should be. So, as long as we can be sure that there is no rudimentary first-person perspective—up through, say, the second trimester of pregnancy—the decision to abort should be in the hands of the pregnant girl or woman and her allies.[70]

This line of thought leads to individual choice about matters of great personal importance and intimacy, but not to moral relativism. There is an analogy here with religion. We may tolerate individual religious choice, while not advocating religious relativism. One can be convinced that someone else is wrong on a vitally important matter, without feeling justified in interfering with her decision. Thesis (O)—the thesis that a fetus is not a person—allows (but does not require) individual moral judgment and tolerance for others' moral judgments about their own lives.

Thus, there are three important differences between the thesis that a fetus is not a person—(O)—and the denial of (O). First, (O) allows but does not require giving precedence to the concrete and particular (actual pregnant girls and women) over the abstract and general (the idea of life considered in isolation from anyone's actual experience of life). The thesis that a fetus is a person does the reverse. Second, (O) allows but does not require attending to the moral significance of the circumstances of a pregnancy. The thesis that a fetus is a person renders those circumstances morally irrelevant. Third, (O) allows but does not require individual moral judgment and tolerance for others' moral judgments about the most intimate details of their own lives.

To sum up this section: The constitution view, which is supported by arguments that have nothing to do with abortion,[71] implies that a fetus before development of a rudimentary first-person perspective is not a person. This section gives reasons to welcome this consequence. The overall reason to welcome it is that it opens the door to discussion of

---

[69] Although a fetus may be sentient early on, it seems unlikely that it has a capacity to imitate or that it behaves in ways explainable only by attribution of beliefs, desires, and intentions until birth or shortly before birth. Thus, even in the absence of empirical research, I think it is safe to suppose that the requirements of a rudimentary first-person perspective are not met until birth or shortly before birth. I am not arguing from any attitude toward abortion of nearly full-term fetuses to a conclusion about the ontological status of the fetus. The thesis about the ontological status of the fetus—that a fetus before development of a rudimentary first-person perspective is not a person—follows from the constitution view, which was developed quite independently of these issues.

[70] The reason that one may want to leave the state out of these decisions until there is a rudimentary first-person perspective is that laws limiting abortion are made by legislatures and upheld at times by courts filled with people who sincerely believe that women find fulfillment in being subordinate to men. A compassionate public policy would not leave the fate of women and girls who get pregnant in the hands of such people.

[71] See my *Persons and Bodies*.

the considerations that I mentioned. If abortion were the killing of an innocent person, then none of the considerations that I mentioned— anencephaly, rape, incest, the pregnant person's suitability for parenthood, or the others—would even be relevant to the morality of abortion. There would be nothing to argue about. Putting aside the view that the fetus is a person is a necessary condition for discussion of the morality of abortion in various circumstances.

VIII. Conclusion

The constitution view of human persons is part of a comprehensive picture of the material world. It holds that human persons are constituted by bodies (i.e., organisms) without being identical to the constituting organisms. Such an account does justice both to our similarities to other animals and to our uniqueness. Moreover, I have argued that the constitution view is superior to biological animalism, Thomistic animalism, and other forms of substance dualism. According to the constitution view, a human person comes into existence when a human organism acquires a rudimentary first-person perspective. The onset of a first-person perspective marks the entry of a new entity in the world.

The constitution view has one important consequence for thinking about abortion. The consequence is that, for principled reasons that have nothing specifically to do with abortion, a fetus is not a person.[72] Just as a hunk of marble is in an ontologically distinct category from a statue, so is a fetus in an ontologically distinct category from a person. Thus, the constitution view gives one an *ontological* reason to deny that the fetus is a person. Anyone who takes it to be morally abhorrent to force a rape victim to bear the rapist's child has in addition a good *moral* reason to deny that the fetus is a person. Anyone who believes that there is even a possibility of morally relevant differences among pregnancies should welcome the thesis that follows from the constitution view: A fetus is not a person.

Philosophy, University of Massachusetts, Amherst

---

[72] Nor, of course, is an embryo a person. Thus, any argument against embryonic stem cell research that presupposes that an embryo is a person is also unsound.

PERSONS, SOCIAL AGENCY, AND CONSTITUTION*

By Robert A. Wilson

I. Introduction

In her recent book *Persons and Bodies* (hereafter *PB*),[1] Lynne Rudder Baker has defended what she calls the *constitution view* of persons. On this view, persons are constituted by their bodies, where "constitution" is a ubiquitous, general metaphysical relation distinct from more familiar relations, such as identity and part-whole composition.

The constitution view answers the question "What are we?" in that it identifies something fundamental about the kind of creature we are. For Baker, we are fundamentally persons. Persons are not capable simply of having mental states, nor merely of having a first-person perspective, a subjective point of view. Rather, persons are creatures that can conceive of themselves as having (or, presumably, lacking) a perspective: they have an awareness of themselves as beings with a first-person perspective. This is what, extending Baker's terminology, we might call having a *strong* first-person perspective, and it is this capacity that demarcates persons from other kinds of things in the world (*PB*, 64). Persons thus stand in contrast with most if not all nonhuman animals, and our status as persons entails that we are not merely animals. Thus, the constitution view contrasts both with more standard psychological views of what is special about human beings (views that have their historical home in Cartesian dualism and in John Locke's discussion of personal identity in *An Essay Concerning Human Understanding*), as well as with animalist views, which hold that we are, fundamentally, animals.

All of these views have implications for how we should think of diachronic identity—what it is that makes me today the same individual as I was yesterday or will be tomorrow. But Baker is concerned chiefly to defend the constitution view as an answer to the question "What am I most fundamentally?" I am a person; a person essentially has a (strong) first-person perspective and is related to her body constitutively. Thus, in contrast with classic dualism, the constitution view purports to be mate-

* A version of this paper was given in February 2004 to the philosophy colloquium at the University of Alberta; I thank my commentator, Bernard Linsky, and members of the audience for helpful feedback. I would also like to thank Lynne Rudder Baker and Gary Wedeking for their reactions to an earlier version of the paper, and the other contributors to this volume for their comments.
[1] See Lynne Rudder Baker, *Persons and Bodies: A Constitution View* (New York: Cambridge University Press, 2000).

rialist. Yet in contrast with both "psychological" and "bodily" forms of materialism, the constitution view claims that we are neither simply psychological creatures, nor creatures identical with our bodies. Rather, we are a certain kind of psychological creature, one that is also embodied in (but not identical to) the material stuff of the body.

II. CONSTITUTION: AN INTRODUCTION

Baker gives a precise characterization of constitution (more of which in a moment), but in general terms it is a ubiquitous, nonreducible "relation of unity that is intermediate between identity and separate existence" (*PB*, 27).[2] It applies to things, and is the relation that holds between a particular statue (David) and the piece of marble that it is made of (Piece), an example to which Baker returns throughout her articulation and defense of the constitution view. Baker says:

> Constitution is everywhere: Pieces of paper constitute dollar bills; pieces of cloth constitute flags; pieces of bronze constitute statues. And constitution applies not only to artifacts and symbols, but to natural objects as well: strands of DNA constitute genes. (Some philosophers hold that particular brain states constitute beliefs. Although I do not endorse this claim, the idea of constitution is poised to make sense of it.) (*PB*, 21, footnote omitted)

The examples should provide at least an intuitive feel for why constitution is not identity.

Consider, first, David and Piece. There are circumstances in which Piece could exist although David does not (imagine that Piece is formed by a lightning strike, rather than by a sculptor); in fact, some of these are circumstances in which Piece exists but there are *no* statues (imagine that there is no art world at all). If that is true, then David and Piece cannot be identical, since they are not coexistent across all possible circumstances, or, if we allow that existence is a property, it is not a property that they share across all possible circumstances. If identity is necessary, or if, in accord with Leibniz's Law, identical entities must have the same properties, then David and Piece are not identical.

---

[2] Apart from Baker's *Persons and Bodies* itself, other good sources for an introduction to the constitution view she defends include several recent book symposia, particularly that in *Philosophy and Phenomenological Research* 64 (2002): 592–635, with discussion by Dean Zimmerman, Michael Rea, and Derk Pereboom (together with a précis and reply from Baker); see also the symposium in the online journal *A Field Guide to the Philosophy of Mind*, 2001, featuring discussion by Brian Garrett, Harold Noonan, and Eric Olson; and Gary Wedeking, "Critical Notice of Lynne Rudder Baker, *Persons and Bodies*," *Canadian Journal of Philosophy* 32 (2002): 267–90.

The same general point holds for Baker's other examples: there are circumstances in which the very piece of cloth that constitutes my Canadian flag at home exists but there are no Canadian flags (no Canada); those in which the very piece of paper that actually constitutes a dollar bill exists but there are no dollar bills (no treasury); and those in which a given strand of DNA no longer constitutes genes (no downstream decoding machinery). This is because each of the entities constituted by some particular material entity is individuated, in part, by relational properties that the constituent entities themselves need not possess. That is, statues, flags, dollar bills, and genes all have at least some of their relational properties *essentially*, while the material entities that constitute them have those relational properties only contingently. So in circumstances in which those individuative relational properties are absent, only the constituent entities exist. Thus, these material entities cannot be identical to what they constitute.

Yet it would also be a mistake to think that David and Piece, or any of these other entity pairs, are simply separate entities, and so to count them distinctly or overlook the special relationship between them. For a start, in the actual world, David and Piece are spatially coincident. And many of the properties that we naturally attribute to David—its elegance, its emotional expressiveness—depend in some way on properties that we naturally attribute to Piece—the curve to the marble, its color. The relationship between David and Piece, as between all of our other pairs of entities, is intimate, but not so intimate that they are one and the same entity.

If this understanding of constitution is correct, then note two things about the generality of the constitution view. First, while many examples (and all but one that Baker appeals to) involve relations that are conventional or intentional, there will be a wide range of examples of entities that are individuated by *functional* relations. As Baker's sole "natural" example—that of genes—suggests, many of these will be biological: from cells and cellular machinery (genes, ribosomes, telomeres), to bodily organs and systems (hearts, livers, digestive systems), to kinds of organisms (predators, tree-dwellers, species).

Second, constituent entities themselves may be relationally individuated, provided that their essential relational properties are different from those individuating the entities they constitute, and do not entail the presence of those properties, in and of themselves. Corkscrews are functionally individuated, but so too are the bottle-openers that they constitute. (Corkscrews themselves are often constituted by a small number of parts, parts that are also functionally individuated.)

There is much that seems to me right about the constitution view, even if I think that Baker's defense of it is, in places, mistaken or misleading. What I am chiefly interested in here is the *scope* of the view. In particular, I should like to explore its aptness for thinking not simply about our paradigmatic persons—individual agents like you and me—but for conceptualizing such persons and what they in turn constitute. The issue I shall explore is how well the constitution view is placed to make sense of various forms of *social agency*.

To answer this question, I shall have to say a little more about the constitution view (Section III) and at least begin to explain its relationship to pluralistic views of ontology (Section IV).

III. THE CONSTITUTION VIEW: SOME ELABORATION

Although Baker provides an explicit and elaborate definition of constitution three times in her book (*PB*, 43, 95, 168), rather than recount that here I want to summarize it and convey its flavor.[3] Some object, x, constitutes some object, y, at a given time, t, just if four conditions hold: (i) x and y are spatially coincident at t; (ii) x exists in conditions necessary for things of y's kind to exist; (iii) if something, z, of x's kind, exists together with the circumstances required for something of y's kind to exist, then an instance of y's kind exists that is spatially coincident with z; (iv) it is possible for x to exist without there being anything of y's kind that is spatially coincident with x. Conditions (i) and (iii) identify why x and y are not simply separate entities, while (iv) specifies why they cannot be identified.

To make this a little more concrete, consider David and Piece at a given time. (Suppose David is on display at the Metropolitan Museum of Art in New York.) David is a statue. Piece is a piece of marble with a particular size, shape, color, and composition. David and Piece occupy precisely the same space at that time—so (i) is satisfied. However, neither statues nor pieces of marble are ubiquitous. Among the conditions necessary for statues to exist are certain kinds of human practices, institutions, and intentions. For example, practices of sculpting, institutions of artisan craftsmanship, and the intentions to produce particular, meaningful works of art are all conditions necessary for the production of statues in the past and present. Of course, as cultures shift, these conditions may change, and we might think that none of them is strictly necessary for statues to exist, as evidenced by the production of statues by machines and with the intention to make as much money as possible (artistic intention be damned). But the general point is that some such conditions must hold if there are to be statues, rather than merely pieces of marble, and in general these

---

[3] There are several reasons for this. The first is that Baker's own definition is cast in terms of the notion of a *primary kind*, a notion that itself requires some elaboration and that raises its own set of complications; I shall have some things to say about this notion in the following sections. The second is that the definition that Baker herself provides in *Persons and Bodies* has been modified in several ways as the constitution view has been elaborated and critiqued; see, for example, her replies in the *Philosophy and Phenomenological Research* book symposium cited in note 2 above.

conditions concern the nature of the world beyond the physical boundaries that David and Piece share.

So suppose that Piece is in these circumstances—so that (ii) is satisfied.
Given these circumstances, to say that David is constituted by Piece is to
say that any time you have a piece of marble with the properties that
Piece has—its shape, size, color, composition—then you also have a statue
that is spatially coincident with that piece of marble—so that (iii) is satisfied. Yet precisely because these conditions are contingent and distinctively necessary for statues, it is possible simply for a piece of marble to
exist, as alike to Piece qua piece of marble as you like, without there being
a statue at all, let alone David—thus, (iv) is satisfied.

To summarize: Constitution exists just when there is (complete) spatial coincidence between two entities, together with a set of distinctively contingent conditions that are metaphysically sufficient for the
presence of the object constituted, given the presence of the constituent
object or something very much like it. The constitution view says that
just this relationship exists between persons and their bodies. They are
spatially coincident, and the conditions that, in some sense, need to be
"added" to a mere physical body to create a person—those needed to
create a strong first-person perspective—are both distinctively contingent and metaphysically sufficient for there being persons, given the
existence of bodies.

IV. CONSTITUTION AND PLURALISM

In contrasting constitution with other metaphysical relations, particularly with mereological relationships that hold between a thing and its
parts, Baker says, "constitution is construed unambiguously as a vertical
relation" (PB, 182). By this, and in light of the examples she provides and
concentrates on, I take this metaphor to tie with another, one especially
common in the philosophy of mind: that of higher and lower levels.
Constitution is an asymmetrical relation, one that relates objects described
at one level to those described at another. Since the existence of a constituted entity requires that there be some set of conditions in addition to
those necessary for the existence of a constituent entity, it is natural to
think of the former as an instance of a higher-level kind, and the latter as
an instance of a lower-level kind.

There is nothing in the constitution view, or in the full and explicit
characterization of constitution, to rule out one entity's being constituted
by many different entities, or one entity's constituting many different
entities. In fact, it is important to my extension of the constitution view—
and, I think, to its broader applicability—that constitution relations be
many-many. To put this together with the appeal to constitution as a
vertical relation and the talk of levels that it relies on, this is to say that

there can be many lower-level constituents for any higher-level entity that has a constituent, and many higher-level entities that any lower-level entity constitutes.[4]

For example, a person is constituted by her body, but also by an aggregate of body parts (e.g., heart, lungs, stomach), a causal network of bodily systems (the circulatory, respiratory, and digestive systems), and a particular arrangement of elementary particles. Conversely, a given body can constitute not just a person, but also a living thing, a member of a particular species or genus, and a moral or rational agent. If these are real kinds of things, then a many-many constitution relation is poised to make sense of them.

Something similar is true of David and Piece. Piece constitutes David, but also constitutes a piece of art, a valuable artifact, and a work by Michelangelo. The conditions for the existence of each of these kinds of things are different from one another. Pieces of art need not be valuable artifacts, and although works by Michelangelo are both in the actual world, this need not have been the case—not least of all because Michelangelo might have died as a baby and never produced any art. More to the point for the constitution view, the spatial coincidence at a time of Piece and any one of these things is contingent, and the existence of a piece of marble like Piece in conditions sufficient for the existence of each of these kinds metaphysically suffices for the spatial coincidence of that piece of marble and the resultant piece of art, valuable artifact, or work by Michelangelo.

Conversely, David is constituted by Piece, but David is also constituted by an aggregate of the elementary particles on or inside Piece, and by the sum of the marble on the surface of Piece and all the marble inside the surface of Piece. Neither of these entities is strictly identical with Piece, for they exist embedded within the larger piece of marble from which Piece was sculpted, a condition in which Piece itself does not exist.

Baker herself would, I think, deny these particular claims about persons and bodies, and about David and Piece, for a reason that we will shortly see. But broader features of her view suggest ambivalence about

---

[4] The idea of constitution as a many-many relation may trouble materialists, particularly those who characterize materialism in terms of the notion of supervenience. For while materialists have traditionally had few qualms about the "one-many" relation of multiple realization (perhaps too few), they have usually balked at its converse, "emergent realization." Provided that constitution (as a relation between things) can be mapped onto notions like supervenience and realization (usually construed as relations between properties, or sets of properties), a many-many view of constitution countenances both. This topic deserves further discussion than I can give it here (and than Baker gives it in *Persons and Bodies* on pp. 186–87); thanks to Alex Rueger for reminding me of it. On multiple realization, see William Bechtel and Jennifer Mundale, "Multiple Realizability Revisited: Linking Cognitive and Neural States," *Philosophy of Science* 66 (1999): 175–207; Jaegwon Kim, *Supervenience and Mind* (New York: Cambridge University Press, 1993); Lawrence Shapiro "Multiple Realizations," *Journal of Philosophy* 97 (2000): 635–54; and Lawrence Shapiro *The Mind Incarnate* (Cambridge, MA: MIT Press, 2004).

the more general issue of whether the constitution view should countenance a many-many constitution relation.

On the one hand, Baker champions a form of ontological pluralism, according to which there are myriad kinds of things in the world. In addition to the examples we have already seen, there are many kinds of things that feature in Baker's own elaboration of the constitution view and the broader ontological view of which it is a central part. There are lumps of clay and aggregates of material particles (*PB*, 25), landscape paintings and carburetors (*PB*, 38), airliners, personal computers, anvils, and doorstops (*PB*, 41), deans (*PB*, 47), and coaches (*PB*, 51). On Baker's view, all of these things exist, and presumably each is a material object, and thus at least a candidate for subsumption under the constitution view. This ontological pluralism takes as its point of departure the "pragmatic realism" that has guided much of Baker's previous work, a realism that attempts to understand the everyday, lived world of objects, their properties, and their relations (*PB*, 22–24). If there are deans, persons, bodies, and aggregates of material particles in your ontology, and you are tempted by the thought that none of these entities is strictly identical to any other, then you might well turn to a many-many constitution relation to make sense of the relations between them. This would be one way to deflate the ontological extravagance of your pluralism (cf. persons and bodies).

On the other hand, Baker is clear that she thinks that there is a limit to just how ontologically extravagant the commitments of pragmatic realism are. This is manifest in her explication of a notion central to her explicit definition of constitution, that of a *primary kind*. She says:

> Each concrete individual is fundamentally a member of exactly one kind—call it its 'primary kind'. To answer the question 'What most fundamentally is x?' we cite x's primary kind by using a substance noun: for example, 'a horse' or 'a bowl'. x's primary kind is a kind of thing, not just stuff: Piece's primary kind is not just marble, but a piece of marble; the Nile's primary kind is not just water, but a river (of water). (*PB*, 39–40)

Although Baker, along with everyone else, lacks a theory of primary kinds, she points to clear cases that help to mark the distinction between a change that creates a new primary kind and one that merely results in things of the same primary kind acquiring or losing properties. Being a husband, she claims, is not a primary-kind property, for a "world like ours except that it lacked the institution of marriage (and hence had no husbands) would not thereby have fewer individuals in it than our world" (*PB*, 40). An anvil can be used as a doorstop, but this is a case of one thing, an anvil, coming to acquire a property—rather than a new primary kind, doorstops, coming into existence (*PB*, 40–41).

Baker's general idea for distinguishing the two sorts of case is that it is only when we have the creation of "whole classes of causal properties" that we have a distinct primary kind. Thus, a person is constituted by her body, but a doorstop is not constituted by the anvil, because only in the former case do we have entities that belong to distinct primary kinds; only in the former case is there a whole class of causal properties that mark the existence of a distinct primary kind. Likewise, I suspect that Baker would see only the causal differences between persons and bodies — and not those either between persons, deans, and moral and rational agents, or between bodies, aggregates of particles, animals, and causal networks of bodily systems — as marking a boundary significant enough to call for distinct primary kinds.

While I share Baker's intuition that there is a distinction to be drawn between mere property change and entity creation, a proper understanding of the basis for that distinction seems to me unlikely to eliminate the need for a many-many constitution relation, either in general or in the case of persons and bodies (or, for that matter, in the case of David and Piece). We can (perhaps should) think of primary kinds as things bearing distinct causal clusters of properties and powers. But it is a central part of pragmatic realism not to privilege *intrinsic* properties and powers over relational properties, as Baker herself makes clear (*PB*, 24). So those clusters of powers can exist in part because of features of the circumstances that entities find themselves in. Statues, rivers, deans, coaches, landscape paintings, carburetors, doorstops, and anvils all possess distinctive causal powers, given not just possible circumstances but the world as it actually is. Thus, it is difficult to see a motivated way to rule them out, a priori as it were, from the set of primary kinds. Moreover, once you embrace the idea that there are many, many kinds of things, there seems little reason to insist that the special relation of constitution holds only between pairs of them. If one accepts the ontological pluralism implied by pragmatic realism, together with a generalized version of the constitution view, then one should view constitution as a many-many relation.

The existence of many-many constitution relations radicalizes the constitution view. For not only are there two things, person and body, related by constitution, where we might have thought there was one, but there are many things — person, rational agent, moral agent, bearer of mental properties, body, aggregate of body parts, living thing, causal network of bodily systems — that stand in a more complicated set of constitutive relationships to one another. Prima facie, at least any of the first four — person, rational agent, moral agent, bearer of mental properties — is constituted by at least any of the final four — body, aggregate of body parts, living thing, causal network of bodily systems. But this does not, obviously, exhaust the ontological relationships between instances of these kinds, which themselves are just examples of the myriad kinds of things that exist in a case like this. Call this the *many-many problem* for the constitution view.

Even if what we are, essentially, are persons, the relationship between persons and their bodies is no longer special in virtue of being unique. This is a welcome aspect of the constitution view, I want to suggest, since it further serves to defuse the binary opposition between entities that are mind-like (persons) and entities that are matter-like (bodies). But then we need some account of whether there is any reason to focus on the person-body relation, rather than any of the other constitutive relations that typically exist when we have a person. Two different (but not incompatible) responses to the many-many problem are suggested by my comments above.

The first tack, which I tend to favor, would be to embrace ontological pluralism wholeheartedly and supplement it with some kind of subjectivist or relativist account of why the categories of person and body might be thought to be special and deserving of distinct treatment. However wholehearted one's endorsement of pluralism here, clearly it needs to be tempered by a recognition of the distinction between entity creation and mere property change. Baker's own approach to marking this distinction, cast in terms of distinct causal clusters of powers, may be on the right track, but it seems to me unlikely to be sufficient in itself to complete the task. (For one, I suspect that an ineliminable reference to the duration of the cluster's existence will be necessary.)

A second response, which I suspect Baker would find more conducive, would be to attempt to limit even the appearance of ontological extravagance here by arguing that some of these entities—body, animal, and organism, for example, to take a trio that Baker herself equates—are not the names of distinct objects, while others—aggregate of body parts seems like a plausible candidate—are not governed by the constitution view because they are not themselves things or objects. The essential challenge that this sort of response must meet is to show that an ontologically less extravagant (but still robust) application of the constitution view to the kinds of things that exist in the world beyond Baker's stock examples (of persons and bodies, David and Piece) does not compromise the constitution view's position on such examples.

Both strategies of response to the many-many problem are likely to prove problematic in their own way, but here is not the place to articulate or defend that claim.[5] Instead, I want to consider how we might frame-shift the constitution view from persons and their constituents to what entities persons themselves might be thought to constitute.

---

[5] My own hunch is that the first response is likely to run into problems concerning the objectivity of the distinction between entity creation and property change and thus the objectivity of the kinds of things there are; the second response and the challenges it faces are further complicated by taking seriously my claim that constitution is a many-many relation. These are matters that I begin to explore in a paper in progress, "Non-Mereological Constitution and Metaphysics."

V. Agency, the Mind, and Social Action

What seems to me clearly right about the constitution view, regardless of what one says about the many-many problem that I have touched on in the previous section, is that the category of person is important for thinking about the question "What am I?" Moreover, something like having a strong first-person perspective seems necessary to articulate that concept in a way that implies that human persons are special not just in being constituted by a human body, but in the sort of agency that persons, including human persons, manifest.

I should say something about how I think about agency.[6] I take agents to be individual entities that are capable of acting in the world and that typically do so act. They are differential loci of actions. I am happy to be quite pluralistic about the kinds of agents there are in the world. There are *physical* agents, including elementary particles and atomic elements, every-day physical objects (such as tables and rocks), and larger and more distant objects (such as stars and tectonic plates). There are *biological* agents, such as proteins, genes, cells, organisms, demes, species, and clades. And there are *social* agents, including not only individual people, but also groups and collections of people, institutions, and perhaps even whole communities and nations. Agents are causes, but not mere causes, for they are individuals with some kind of physical boundary—or at least they are in nearly all of the examples I have cited above. (The exceptions here concern kinds of collective agents; I will have more to say about these in the next section.)

Even though human beings are paradigmatic agents in many respects, it is also true that the kind of agency they manifest is special in that it is either unique or shared with only a small minority of the agents that there are in the physical world. There are different ways to articulate what is special here. But all the ways that I know of presuppose that human agency goes hand-in-hand with a relatively rich mental life, whether it be acting on the basis of reasons (rather than mere causes), engaging in particular forms of reasoning (means-ends, deliberative, evaluative, infer-ential), or having a qualitatively distinct phenomenal life that makes a causal difference to how we react to and interact in the world. And although this may be slightly more controversial, I take it to be very plausible to think that however this idea of a rich mental life is spelled out, it consists in more than merely having mental episodes of some kind or other, or being causally governed by distinctively mental, internal states.

Given that, I do not intend to challenge the constitution view's characterization of a person as an entity that has, or has a capacity for, a strong

---

[6] For more elaboration on this view of agency, see my *Genes and the Agents of Life* (New York: Cambridge University Press, 2004), chapters 1–3.

first-person perspective. However, I do want to suggest that this capacity is insufficient for any kind of agency, including distinctively human agency. For this view is what we might call an *input-based* or *internally-based* view of persons in that it identifies persons independent of their reactions to or interactions with the world beyond their own boundary. It is not acting as an embodied agent with a (strong) first-person perspective that is crucial to being a person, according to Baker, but simply having (or even possessing the capacity for having) a first-person perspective. On this view, someone who could only register thoughts such as "I am here," "I believe I am late," or "I want to know more" would count as a person, provided that she could wonder about those thoughts, entertain their falsity, and attempt to explore their implications.

In his book *Mental Reality*,[7] Galen Strawson defended the idea that a race of sentient, intelligent creatures, the Weather Watchers, who were individuals rooted in the ground and with a range of mental states, were possible, even though they lacked even the physiology necessary for action. This is mentation as pure registration, as reflection on internal states that are either simply registered or reflections on that registration, and part of Strawson's point in introducing the Weather Watchers was to argue that behavior had no conceptual connection to the concept of the mental. Despite Baker's own externalist sympathies in the philosophy of mind, her emphasis on the first-person *perspective* in her account of persons places her views here closer to Strawson's than one might have expected.[8]

Suppose that we were to concede a conception of the mind that is internalist in the way that Strawson's is, and even concede that such bearers of mental states are persons. My point here is that such individuals would not be agents. Unless they can at least see themselves as capable of acting in the world, of either adjusting their position with respect to it or modifying the world itself in some way, it is difficult to credit them with the sort of agency that creatures with our sort of rich mental life take for granted. If we wish to adapt the constitution view to apply to anything like the full range of human agency, then we need to go beyond the input- or internally-based conception of persons that it employs. This is just to recognize that despite the centrality of the concept of a

---

[7] Galen Strawson, *Mental Reality* (Cambridge, MA: MIT Press, 1994).

[8] Baker has articulated her externalism about the mind in two previous books, and it surfaces in several places in *Persons and Bodies*. She relies on it, for example, in arguing (pp. 72–76) that any being with a (strong) first-person perspective must have concepts of other things, and to have those it must interact with other (those other?) things. Since both premises in this argument seem to me false (even despite Baker's discussion of them), I don't see this as a promising path linking the first-person perspective to externalism. For Baker's previous work on the mind, see her *Saving Belief: A Critique of Physicalism* (Princeton, NJ: Princeton University Press, 1987), and *Explaining Attitudes: A Practical Approach to the Mind* (New York: Cambridge University Press, 1995).

person (so understood) to agency, there is more to human agency than being a person.

There are several ways in which one might read this very point into the constitution view itself. For example, human persons, perhaps unlike other persons (such as angels or God), are *embodied*, and bodies are just what provide for the possibility of human action in the world—action-traction, as we might call it. And we can see human agency as going beyond mere personhood in Baker's discussion of "the importance of being a person." For part of its importance is that it allows one to be both a rational and a moral agent (*PB*, chap. 6), where at least the latter of these involves being subject to certain kinds of norms, some of which are presumably made possible only when a person has action-traction. Personhood, as characterized by the constitution view, is necessary for the sort of agency that humans possess, but it does not seem sufficient, because it is input- or internally-based.[9]

Being a person seems crucial not just to rational agency, but to the possibility of a fully-fledged social life. More specifically, being a person creates the possibility of such a social life, one that involves what we commonly call *interpersonal* relations. These social relations include those of care and friendship, of love and hate, of rivalry and jealousy, of compassion and empathy, of malice and spite, of forgiveness and kindness, of respect and admiration, of revenge and defiance. Or, to express this in a way that more accurately depicts what I consider the likely developmental and evolutionary story here, persons (on an input- or internally-based conception) and social agents coexist as nonidentical but mutually reinforcing kinds of being.

I implied earlier in this section that social agency should not be conceptualized simply in terms of the actions of individual agents but also in terms of what institutional and collective agents do. Banks can foreclose on your mortgage, city councils can raise your property taxes, and Her Majesty's government can request the pleasure of your company. As economic, political, and legal entities, each of these agents can bring about effects, sometimes effects that matter a great deal to us. They act through the agency of individual persons, to be sure, but it is only as a representative of a bank, a council, or Her Majesty's government that the acts of particular persons count as foreclosing our mortgage, raising our property taxes, or imprisoning us. I shall argue in what follows that the constitution view can be readily and fruitfully adapted to shed some light on social agency, including the collective forms that it takes, and its relationship to persons.

---

[9] Baker herself argues in chapter 6 of *Persons and Bodies* that being a person is necessary *and sufficient* for being both a rational and a moral agent, and thus does not herself seem to allow for the sort of gap that I am positing between human persons (embodied and all) and human agents. As I hope my argument in the text below makes clear, I view this as a mistake.

VI. The Constitution View and the Social Domain

Recall the many-many problem facing the constitution view of the relation between persons and bodies. If bodies constitute persons, then so too do many other things, such as aggregates of body parts, causal networks of bodily systems, and living things. And persons are not the only kind of thing that bodies constitute, for they also constitute (among other things) rational and moral agents, and individual social agents—bankers, tax assessors, and policemen, for example. The many-many problem suggests that the ontological pluralism entailed by the constitution view is extravagant, and the problem is to decide whether to embrace this extravagance or to find ways to deny that it is an implication of the view. Although the many-many problem is quite general in that it applies not just to the case of persons and their bodies but in principle to any case where a pair of things stand in a relationship of constitution, there are reasons to think that the problem will be acute when persons are one of the relata in the constitution relation.

This is especially the case where a person is not the constituted entity (as in the person-body relation) but the *constituent* entity. Thus far, I have not explicitly considered in detail any examples in which this is so, but I hope it does not come as a complete surprise to learn that I think that social agents and persons can be viewed as standing in a relation of constitution, much as persons and bodies can.

Consider, first and perhaps most contentiously, rational agents and persons. Essential to being a rational agent is not simply having means-ends reasoning, where ends are goals typically manifest as desires, but having the ability to evaluate both that reasoning and the behavior that it results in. Rational agents are *deliberative*. We might require more of rational agents—perhaps they need at least some emotional life, or to have a grasp of certain basic rules of inference, or to have some minimally coherent belief-desire set. But it is hard to see how we could require less, at least if we take ourselves as paradigms of such agents.

Suppose that we consider Kim, who is both a rational agent and a person. Intuitively, rational agency, at whose heart lies the notion of deliberation, is something distinct from, and more than simply having, a strong first-person perspective. Both rational agents and persons are reflective or contemplative, but rational agents have, in addition, some kind of action-traction that is an optional extra for persons, even embodied persons. Moreover, it is plausible to think that if there is this sort of difference between rational agents and persons, then there will be a large cluster of powers that rational agents have that mere persons lack, namely, all of those powers that concern how one can and does act in the world. Just as having a strong first-person perspective creates significant powers above those that merely mental creatures (those with a weak first-person perspective) have, so too with being a rational agent and being a person.

Rational agent is a primary kind, and it is a different primary kind from person.

Here is another way to come at the difference between persons and rational agents. A person has a strong first-person perspective (by stipulation), but that perspective could be directed entirely at the "input" side of her mental life: at her perceptions, her beliefs, the grounds she has for these, the connections between them. A rational agent, by contrast, in addition to all of this higher-order mental life has an action-oriented, motivational dimension to what it is like to be that agent. She not only has goals and desires, but evaluates them and strives to achieve them, or engages with the world to increase the goodness of fit between actual states and goal states. Call this *practical rational agency*, if you like; my point is that it is something more than merely being a person.

To see that it is something more, consider several ways in which having a first-person perspective and being a rational agent can come apart in the actual world. Individuals who feel powerless to act can withdraw from the world, and can come to see themselves as incapable of exercising effective control over their own body. In extreme cases, they dissociate themselves from all action, a dissociation that is accompanied by depression, fear, and anxiety. Cases of dementia, of extreme memory loss, or other forms of what we call "mental breakdown" can also compromise rational agency short of compromising action itself. But part of what is so disturbing about both kinds of cases is that there remains a being with a first-person perspective, a person who has become unhinged from herself as a rational agent. In general, if we think that people can fail to be rational in ways extreme enough to justify viewing them as different kinds of beings—irrational or arational agents— but remain nonetheless persons, then rational agency is something distinct from mere personhood.

We can turn to the characterization of constitution recounted in Section III to make the point here in terms of one relationship that holds between persons and rational agents. Suppose that Person Kim exists in the circumstances favorable for the existence of rational agents: Person Kim has deliberative capacities, a motivational set of mental states that engage her with action, and a perspective on herself as an agent. Simplifying a little further than we have already, a relation of constitution exists between Rational Agent Kim and Person Kim just if (a) Person Kim and Rational Agent Kim are spatially coincident in some circumstances; (b) these circumstances suffice for any person to be spatially coincident with a rational agent; and (c) these conditions are distinctively contingent, such that Person Kim could exist even if Rational Agent Kim does not.[10] Con-

---

[10] In effect, I have compressed conditions (ii) and (iii) in the articulation of the constitution view given at the beginning of Section III into (b) above in order to facilitate the application of the view to this example and others.

dition (a) should simply be granted. But the set of conditions that make for rational agency, above and beyond those that make for a strong first-person perspective, are deliberative and action-oriented, and involve both specific cognitive and motivational capacities and action-traction with the world. These conditions, and thus rational agency, could fail to exist even when there are creatures with a strong first-person perspective—and so (c) is satisfied. But given that they do exist, anything that is a person is also a rational agent—and so (b) is satisfied. Thus, rational agents are constituted by persons.

One response that would seem in keeping with Baker's own discussion in *Persons and Bodies* (especially chapter 3) would be to maintain that person and rational agent are not *distinct* primary kinds, or that any conditions sufficient for one are also sufficient for the other. The idea here is that although our concepts of person and rational agent are distinct, they travel hand-in-glove, such that there are no circumstances in which persons exist but rational agents do not. Thus, persons and rational agents do not satisfy condition (iv) in my earlier characterization of constitution, and so condition (c) above.

While there are certainly ways of conceiving of the two for which this would be true, this response is an option for Baker only if she is prepared to make one of two moves: either build more action-traction into the conception of a person than does the first-person perspective view, or adopt a view of rational agency that has looser ties to action than I have suggested it has. My hunch is that either move (but particularly the former) will reduce the extension of "person," such that both very young and very old human beings will typically fail to be persons, as will others who suffer long-term or irreparable diminishment of motivational and action-oriented aspects to their mental lives.

The relationship between moral agents and persons seems to me less controversially constitutive. I take moral agency essentially to involve interpersonal phenomena. Certainly many of the beliefs, desires, emotions, and judgments that we make in the moral domain are other-regarding, and moral agents typically operate within a series of increasingly encompassing moral communities: family, kin, local communities, cities, and so on. Moral agency lies not just in having certain internal mental states but also in acting in ways that are subject to certain kinds of normative evaluations. Plausibly, the conditions necessary for moral agency include facts about groups and communities of people.

Consider Tim, both a moral agent and a person. Moral Agent Tim and Person Tim are spatially coincident at some time—thus, (a) is satisfied. But the conditions that make for the possibility of moral agency—the existence of other people, some sense of them as people or as agents, perhaps certain social conditions—are distinct from those for the existence of persons—thus, (c) is satisfied. And these conditions, when present, metaphysically suffice for anything that is a person, including Person

Tim, to be a moral agent, including Moral Agent Tim—thus, (b) is satisfied. Thus, Moral Agent Tim is constituted by Person Tim.

Least controversial with respect to satisfying the "distinct existences" clause of the definition of constitution, are cases that involve social agents whose agency lies in the roles they play in certain institutional frameworks: the bankers, the tax assessors, and the policemen I have previously mentioned. Suppose that Diane is a banker. Are there two entities, Banker Diane and the person Diane, that stand in a relation of constitution? Provided that banker is, in Baker's terminology, a primary kind, it would seem so. For suppose that the person Diane exists in the circumstances necessary for a person to be a banker: there is the institution of banking, she is employed by a bank, she is paid for her services, etc. If Banker Diane exists, then surely she is spatially coincident with the person Diane—so (a) is satisfied. Now, if there is anything that is a person that exists in just those circumstances that Diane exists in, then that thing will also be spatially coincident with a banker—so (b) is satisfied. And the distinctive contingency of those conditions makes it possible for there to be persons but no bankers (as history shows)—so (c) is satisfied. Thus, Banker Diane is constituted by the person Diane, just as that person is constituted by (among other things) Diane's body.

The point here is quite general. It applies to agents defined in terms of their employment (bankers, presidents, miners), their family roles (father, sister, cousin), their living and social conditions (neighbor, volunteer, coach), and the economic and legal institutions they are subject to (debtor, criminal, citizen). The crucial issue, in each case, is whether each of these socially defined roles carries with it a distinctive cluster of causal properties and powers sufficient to warrant considering it a distinct primary kind. In keeping with my earlier remarks about ontological extravagance at the end of Section IV, I have no doubt that this is *not* always true. But the real issue seems to be whether it is *ever* true; for if it is, then it seems that at least certain kinds of individual social agents are constituted by persons. Certainly there are circumstances where occupying some of these social roles makes a massive difference to one's place in the causal net. Presidents of powerful countries can bring about massive changes in the world; being a father at least sometimes makes a large difference to what one cares about, how one spends one's time and money, and one's broader moral perspective; and there is a battery of statistics about criminals qua criminals, tracking causal regularities about limitations to their employment prospects, their likelihood of being imprisoned, and their longevity.

Thus, while I share the intuition that such forms of social agency need not be causally impactful enough to create entities of a new primary kind, there also seem to be cases where it is hard to deny that they meet this criterion. In each case, the constituent entity is a person or, recognizing constitution as a many-many relation, a person is one of the entities that constitute any individual social agent. Persons are important because lots of the kinds of things we are, the kinds of things in virtue of which we make a differential causal impact on the world, are constituted by persons in the very same sense articulated by the constitution view of persons.

One response we saw to the claim that persons constitute rational agents claimed that persons and rational agents were not distinct primary kinds. A second response, one that would allow one to address the many-many problem more generally and the ontological extravagance that it seems to pose, would be to adopt a modified view of constitution as holding not only when two things are of distinct primary kinds but when they occur *at distinct ontological levels.* This would allow one to rest less heavily on the notion of a primary kind, or on particular construals of concepts such as person and rational agent, but would place a corresponding burden on the metaphor of levels. Either of these responses could be used to buttress the intuition that while persons may be distinctly existing entities, social agents are simply determinate forms that such entities may take, what philosophers and linguists might call phase-sortals of the category "person," much as "teenager" and "child" are.

Applied to persons, this further modification of the constitution view could grant that while person, rational agent, moral agent, and bearer of mental properties are distinct primary kinds, these occur "at the same level," and thus there can be no constitution relations between them. (The same could be said of body, aggregate of body parts, living thing, and causal network of bodily systems.) Constitution would remain a many-many relation that applies to the social domain, but social agents (including rational and moral agents) would be kinds of person, not kinds constituted by persons. This would preserve the intuition, which I think Baker herself shares, that there is something fundamental about the division between persons and bodies that is not shared by any of the other distinctions that can be drawn "within a level."

There are three reasons for caution here. The first is the burden that this view places on talk of levels, talk that despite (or is it because of?) its ubiquity is seldom recognized as metaphorical, or cast in more precise terms. (The burden here may be greater for Baker herself than for others, since she is resistant to incorporating part-whole notions into the constitution view; mereology, the study of such relations, has provided the resources for most of the literal accounts of levels-speak.)[11] The second reason for caution is the generality (and conversely, the *ad hocness*) of this modification. It would have to apply to David (as a statue, a work by Michelangelo, a piece of art, a valuable artifact) and Piece, as well as the other examples of constitution that Baker mentions (e.g., dollars and pieces of paper; genes and strands of DNA), and would have to provide

---

[11] My own doubts here are fairly general and arise from a decade of work in both the philosophy of mind and the philosophy of biology, where levels-speak is near ubiquitous. For some doubts in the context of debate over the "levels of selection," see Robert A. Wilson, "Pluralism, Entwinement, and the Levels of Selection," *Philosophy of Science* 70 (2003): 531–52.

a principled account of the relationships between entities at any given level. Finally, this kind of restriction on the application of the constitution view runs the danger of undermining the view's application to its paradigm case, that of persons and bodies. For if persons and social agents are better thought of as standing in the relation of determinable to determinate, or primary kind to phase-sortal of that kind, rather than in a relation of constitution, then the very same might be argued to be true of body and person.

VII. Collective Social Agents and the Constitution View

Individual social agents are persons. Indeed, if what I have suggested up until the final two paragraphs in the previous section is on track, then persons stand in the particularly intimate relation of constitution to at least some social agents. In the final substantive section of this essay, I want to consider collective and institutional agents—banks, city councils, and Her Majesty's government—and the issue of whether the constitution view might be used to shed some light on both their actions and their place in the causal order of things.

Collective and institutional agents are something other than simply aggregates of individual social agents. Like all agents, they are knots in the causal net, loci of action, and there is some intuitive sense in which they are "higher-level" entities than individual persons. But they are not themselves persons (the phrase "corporate person" notwithstanding). Persons are, however, important to understanding collective and institutional social agency in a number of ways. Consider just two.

First, and perhaps most obviously, such social agency presupposes the existence of persons in order to act at all, not just as role-fillers but as cognitive agents who are able to plan, to make decisions, to inquire, to communicate, to judge, to set goals, to evaluate outcomes, to make estimates, to readjust schedules, to comfort and console. It is not simply bodies that fill these roles, but creatures with a first-person perspective, for many of the skills that these roles require are those of persons.

Second, and less obviously, we often use a kind of cognitive metaphor in describing the activities of collective social agents, in effect treating them as cognitive agents in their own right.[12] Corporations reach decisions, governments distrust one another, and the school band refuses your generous offer to play the harmonica with them. If we build enough into the idea of having a strong first-person perspective, such that an entity must have second-order states directed at a *phenomenal* life, then

---

[12] The idea of a group mind is experiencing something of a revival of late. See, for example, Philip Pettit, "Groups with Minds of Their Own," in Frederick F. Schmitt, ed., *Socializing Metaphysics* (Lanham, MD: Rowman and Littlefield, 2003); and Robert A. Wilson, *Boundaries of the Mind: The Individual in the Fragile Sciences: Cognition* (New York: Cambridge University Press, 2004), part IV.

organizations, institutions, and even whole cultures are seldom, if ever, treated as persons, even if they are treated as if they were cognitive agents of some kind. The cognitive metaphor, at least as it is applied in the social sciences, is never complete, and tends to focus on intuitively more cognitive and behaviorally grounded psychological states and traits. Yet what happens in such cases is that collective social agents are *personified*, at least in part, just as are many biological agents—selfish genes, cell recognition, immune defense as self-defense—when the cognitive metaphor is used in the biological sciences.[13]

One reason that collective social agents do not seem like apt relata for the relation of constitution, however, is that they are not physically bounded entities. As such, they seem unlikely candidates for satisfying the first condition of constitution: spatial coincidence. Boards of directors, trade unions, philosophy classes, families, and the welders in a factory are or can be agents of some kind, but they are not continuous, spatially bounded, physical agents, and thus cannot be spatially coincident with entities that have these features.

What I want to suggest instead is that such social agents are what I shall call *agency coincident* with the collections of persons that belong to them, whose members are (typically but not exclusively) the means through which they act. If this is correct, then I think we can defend an analogue of the constitution view relating collective social agents and such persons.

Two objects are spatially coincident at *t* just if they occupy precisely the same parts of space at *t*. Two agents are agency coincident at *t* just if they undertake precisely the same actions at *t*. To be agency coincident *simpliciter* is to be agency coincident at all times (cf. spatial coincidence). Collective social agents can act, of course, through the agency of just one or more individual agents, as when a president acts on behalf of a nation to declare war on another country (or even on a phenomenon, such as "terror"); those agents need not even be part of the collective social agent, as when a lawyer acts on behalf of shareholders to remove a wayward director. Yet this is compatible with (say) the shareholders and the collection of individual shareholders being agency coincident, so long as the action of the lawyer is that of the shareholders just if it is also that of the collection of individual shareholders. (And the action of the president is an action of the nation just if it is an action of the collection of individuals that belong to the nation.) Since there are many social mechanisms, institutions, and practices that authorize individuals and small groups of individuals to act on behalf of many individuals considered as members of a collective social agent, it would be a mistake to focus exclusively on

---

[13] I discuss biological and social uses of the cognitive metaphor both in *Boundaries of the Mind*, part IV, where I focus on some recent discussions of the idea of a group mind in the biological and social sciences, and in *Genes and the Agents of Life*, parts II and III, where my focus is on organisms, genetics, and developmental biology.

unanimity, consensus, or even majority decision as our model for how collective social agents act.

To make the case that collective social agents are agency coincident with the collections of individuals that belong to them and that they represent is a large task that I do not propose to undertake here. But I would not raise it as a possibility if I thought that it had no prima facie plausibility. What I do want to argue for, though, is the claim that if agency coincidence were established, then by showing how collective social agents and individuals (for short) or persons satisfied the metaphysical sufficiency and contingency conditions of the constitution view, we would have shown how to adapt the constitution view of persons to make sense not only of individual agency but of collective social agency.

It is relatively easy to show that collective social agents and persons do satisfy these conditions. Consider the collection or group of persons who belong to or are represented by a given collective social agent at a given time. Clearly, that group of persons could exist without that social agent existing. Each member of the board of directors could exist without the social institutions presupposed by the existence of the board itself, or the mechanisms making just those individuals members of the board. But if we have a group of persons, and those conditions are in place—the corporation exists, those persons have been appointed to the board, etc.— then we must also have the corresponding collective social agent, in this case, a board of directors. As in the standard cases of constitution, this is guaranteed by the nature of these conditions; thus, taking an agent that is a kind of constituent—a group of people—and adding these conditions is metaphysically sufficient to create a collective social agent.

VIII. CONCLUSION

The constitution view of persons deserves (and is receiving) much consideration in its own right. My aim here has been to take what seems central to the view and right about it in order to explore a domain for which the view was not really designed, the domain of the social. We could, as one might expect, come full circle and use the perhaps strained applications and adaptations of the constitution view that I have suggested to probe further into the constitution view proper, though by now it will surprise no one to learn that I am happy to leave that as a (further) exercise for the reader. (For those willing to undertake the exercise, note that the ease with which one can generate distinct higher-level agents, including social agents, with the machinery of the constitution view will provide some with reason to think that view too unconstrained. The many-many problem looms large here.)

I have argued that the constitution view applies directly to the relationship between individual social agents and individual persons. In addition, the constitution view can be tweaked to express the relationship that exists between collective social agents and collections of persons. These are independent proposals concerning how one might understand the metaphysics of the social domain by drawing on a notion of constitution, and the plausibility of each will turn on broader ontological commitments.[14] One virtue of these suggestions, if they (particularly the latter) can be defended in full generality, is that they provide a way of walking that thin line between holistic, nonreductionist views of social ontology and explanation and their individualistic, reductionist counterparts. We can do justice to the former views by recognizing the distinctive status of both individual and collective social agents, while acknowledging that the latter views are correct in insisting that collectivities are, in some sense, nothing more than the individuals that comprise them. Since this is also a chief virtue of and motivation for the original constitution view—persons are neither strictly identical to nor entirely separate from their bodies—it must be time to bring this essay to a close.

Philosophy, University of Alberta

---

[14] For discussion of some of these commitments, see the essays in Schmitt, ed., *Socializing Metaphysics.*

HYLEMORPHIC DUALISM*

By David S. Oderberg

I. Introduction

Despite the fact that it continues to have followers, and that it can be said to have enjoyed something of a micro-revival in recent years, dualism either in the philosophy of mind or in the theory of personal identity persists in being more the object of ridicule than of serious rational engagement. It is held by the vast majority of philosophers to be anything from (and not mutually exclusively) false, mysterious, and bizarre, to obscurantist, unintelligible, and/or dangerous to morals. Its adherents are assumed to be biased, scientifically ill-informed, motivated by prior theological dogma, cursed by metaphysical anachronism, and/or to have taken leave of their senses. Dualists who otherwise appear relatively sane in their philosophical writings are often treated with a certain benign, quasi-parental indulgence.[1]

* I am grateful to Stephen Braude, John Cottingham, John Haldane, David Jehle, Joel Katzav, Eduardo Ortiz, and Fred Sommers for helpful comments and discussion of a draft of this essay. I would also like to thank Ellen Paul, whose suggestions have helped greatly to improve the essay's style and content.
[1] Here, in no special order, are some typical examples illustrating the claims of this paragraph, nearly all in the context of discussions of Cartesian dualism or property dualism (see the text below). (1) For David Braddon-Mitchell and Frank Jackson, dualism is akin to explaining lightning in terms of Thor's anger, and hence is fundamentally primitive and prescientific. See Braddon-Mitchell and Jackson, *Philosophy of Mind and Cognition* (Oxford: Blackwell, 1996), 8. (2) For Colin McGinn, to believe in dualism is ipso facto to believe in "supernatural entities or divine interventions," the attribution being clearly pejorative. See McGinn, "Can We Solve the Mind-Body Problem?" reprinted in Richard Warner and Tadeusz Szubka, eds., *The Mind-Body Problem: A Guide to the Current Debate* (Oxford: Blackwell, 1994), 100. (3) For Patricia Churchland, "the concept of a non-physical soul looks increasingly like an outdated theoretical curiosity." See Churchland, *Brain-wise: Studies in Neurophilosophy* (Cambridge, MA: MIT Press, 2002), 173. (4) Robert Cummins gives a one-page caricature, and a highly inaccurate and misleading one at that, of the sort of position defended in this essay, which involves putting the word "form" in upper-case letters rather than seeking to explain just what form is supposed to be: "Mind-stuff inFORMed," etc. See Cummins, *Meaning and Mental Representation* (Cambridge, MA: MIT Press, 1989), 2. (5) Needless to say, Gilbert Ryle's vivid metaphor of the "ghost in the machine" has helped to stifle serious debate for decades. See Ryle, *The Concept of Mind* (Chicago: University of Chicago Press, 1949). (6) Daniel Dennett, for instance, refers approvingly to Ryle's having "danced quite a jig on the corpse of Cartesian dualism." See Dennett, *The Intentional Stance* (Cambridge, MA: MIT Press, 1987), 214. (7) David Armstrong describes Cartesian dualism as "curiously formal and empty." See Armstrong, *A Materialist Theory of the Mind* (London: Routledge and Kegan Paul, 1968), 23. These and countless other examples are not meant to imply that the critics do not always offer arguments, of varying degrees of insight, against dualism in its several forms; but in general the opposition tends toward the curt, the dismissive, and the incredulous.

The "dualism problem," as one might call it—the problem of the odd place of dualism as no more than an intellectual curiosity in current debate, its adherents characterized as "swimming against the tide"[2]—is complicated by the fact that when it comes to attempts to describe and then, predictably, refute dualism, it is almost without exception the Cartesian form that takes center stage. There is, true to say, a respectable place for property dualism,[3] the theory that although the mind is material, mental *properties* such as consciousness are not reducible to material properties such as states of the brain; and event dualism has begun to attract attention,[4] this being the view that the correct distinction is between mental and physical *events*, such as thoughts on the one hand, which are irreducible to brain processes on the other. Still, Cartesian dualism has clear and unassailable pride of place as the whipping post on which dualists are ritualistically flailed. The idea that the mind is a separate, immaterial substance in its own right, with only a contingent relation to the body it inhabits, is said to raise a host of problems. How could such an entity interact causally with a physical body? Exactly what sort of relationship does this spiritual substance have to a body? What are the identity conditions for such a substance, and how in the end can such an obscure kind of thing explain anything about human mental life?

My aim in this essay is not to defend Cartesian dualism. Rather, it is to set out the groundwork for the sort of dualism that gets little attention and that, if any form of dualism is defensible, is by far the best candidate. It is called "hylemorphic dualism," and is the dualism of Aristotle and the Aristotelians, most notably St. Thomas Aquinas and his followers. It has lagged behind the other dualisms as far as the number and prominence of its contemporary defenders are concerned, though there are signs of renewed interest and serious intellectual attention.[5] Until it acquires more supporters, it will continue to be conspicuous by its absence from stan-

---

[2] To use Keith Campbell's term in his discussion of John Foster's book *The Immaterial Self: A Defence of the Cartesian Dualist Conception of Mind* (London: Routledge, 1991): see Campbell, "Swimming against the Tide," *Inquiry* 36 (1993): 161–77.

[3] This is mainly associated with Thomas Nagel: see Nagel, "What Is It Like to Be a Bat?" *Philosophical Review* 83 (1974): 435–50, and reprinted in many places; see also Frank Jackson, "Epiphenomenal Qualia," *Philosophical Quarterly* 32 (1982): 127–36, and Jackson, "What Mary Didn't Know," *Journal of Philosophy* 83 (1986): 291–95. David Chalmers's so-called naturalistic dualism looks also like a kind of property dualism, identifying mental properties with irreducibly nonphysical properties, but these are wholly material in the broad sense and governed by unknown laws of natural science: see Chalmers, *The Conscious Mind* (Oxford: Oxford University Press, 1996).

[4] See, e.g., Paul Pietroski, *Causing Actions* (Oxford: Oxford University Press, 2000).

[5] Defenders of hylemorphic dualism include John Haldane, "A Return to Form in the Philosophy of Mind," in David S. Oderberg, ed., *Form and Matter: Themes in Contemporary Metaphysics* (Oxford: Blackwell, 1999), 40–64; Haldane, "Analytical Philosophy and the Nature of Mind: Time for Another Rebirth?" in Richard Warner and Tadeusz Szubka, eds., *The Mind-Body Problem: A Guide to the Current Debate* (Oxford: Blackwell, 1994), 195–203; and J. P. Moreland and Scott B. Rae, *Body and Soul: Human Nature and the Crisis in Ethics* (Downers Grove, IL: InterVarsity Press, 2000). See also Edward Feser's contribution to this collection.

dard accounts of personal identity and expositions of the philosophy of mind.

Dualism is a thesis in both of these fields. The account that follows will concentrate on dualism as a position in the theory of personal identity, though the material will inevitably overlap with issues in the philosophy of mind per se. I will set out and defend the primary theses of hylemorphic dualism, with the aim not of a comprehensive account that defends against all reasonable objections and explains every unclarity, but of showing that the theses taken together present a coherent, distinctive, and compelling picture of the nature and identity of the person.

Briefly, the central theses to be defended are as follows. (1) All substances, in other words all self-subsisting entities that are the bearers of properties and attributes but are not themselves properties or attributes of anything, are compounds of matter (*hylē*) and form (*morphē*). (2) The form is *substantial* since it actualizes matter and gives the substance its very essence and identity. (3) The human person, being a substance, is also a compound of matter and substantial form. (4) Since a person is defined as an individual substance of a rational nature, the substantial form of the person is the rational nature of the person. (5) The exercise of rationality, however, is an essentially immaterial operation. (6) Hence, human nature itself is essentially immaterial. (7) But since it is immaterial, it does not depend for its existence on being united to matter. (8) So a person is capable of existing, by means of his rational nature, which is traditionally called the soul, independently of the existence of his body. (9) Hence, human beings are immortal; but their identity and individuality does require that they be united to a body at some time in their existence.

II. Identity, Consciousness, and Psychology

The questions of personal identity and of the nature of mind have, I would argue, been skewed in recent years by the thought that *if* there is a residual puzzle that has not yet been solved by the twentieth-century's onslaught of materialism, naturalism, and physicalism, it must be the problem of *consciousness*. Hence the attention that David Chalmers attracted when he published *The Conscious Mind*,[6] a book that for many people summed up what has come to be known as the "hard problem." If there really is something that materialists cannot successfully grapple with, it is the phenomenology of conscious experience, the felt quality of our interaction with the world. Everything else about the mind, according to Chalmers, can be captured within a physicalistic functionalist model. To be sure, there is still the problem of explaining how to *identify* the correct functional analysis of human psychological operation; but that there is one,

---

[6] See note 3 above.

and that it is at least in principle realizable in inorganic systems such as computer models, is something already taught to us by cognitive science.

This bifurcation of the question of the nature of the mind—into a question about human cognition on the one hand, and a separate question about the special "problem of consciousness" on the other—and then the subsequent focus on the "problem of consciousness" as *the* outstanding conceptual issue in the quest for a total naturalistic theory, is, in my view, the biggest wrong turn in the recent history of the subject. First, however, I should explain what I am *not* claiming. I do not deny that there is indeed a "problem of consciousness," and that many of the central claims of the nonreductionists, including so-called "naturalistic dualists" like Chalmers, are correct: principally, that there is no explanation of the subjective nature of conscious experience in physicalistic terms. What I do deny, however, is that this is not a problem affecting the psychological in general. For it is at least plausible to claim that there is also a *phenomenology of psychology* as much as of conscious experience, and the typical responses to such a claim look, as they do in respect of conscious experience, to be question-begging.

By a phenomenology of psychology I mean simply the "what it is like" of ordinary psychological operations such as judging, reasoning, and calculating. There is, I claim, even "something that it is like" to calculate that two plus two equals four. It may not be qualitatively identical for all people, but then neither is the taste of strawberry ice cream exactly the same for all people, one might suppose, while at the same time noting that our similar physiological structures imply that the individual experiences for each kind of act should be highly similar. Indeed, one might assert that these experiences contain a certain phenomenological core, and that the class of such experiences is such that its members are all more similar to each other, all things being equal, than they are to any experience of a different mental act, state, or process.

It might be objected that the phenomenology of calculating that two and two make four, if there were such a thing, would hardly be different from that attending the calculation that four and four make eight, thus reducing the idea to absurdity—a distinction without a difference. Yet this would be as misplaced as denying the distinct phenomenologies of seeing reddish yellow and yellowish red because they are so similar. That there are such phenomenological differences in calculation is not something for which there is nonintrospective proof any more than there is for the standard kinds of qualia to which nonreductionists (such as Chalmers and Frank Jackson) draw attention.[7] Yet introspection does, I believe, make apparent the qualitative character of calculation, a character easily heightened by comparing, say, the experience of doing algebra with that

---

[7] For a useful and detailed list, see Chalmers, *The Conscious Mind*, 6–11. For Jackson's work, see notes 1 and 3 above.

of doing calculus. Again, there is a conscious experience of performing a piece of deductive reasoning that differs from that attending the judgment of a single proposition. I cannot offer here a taxonomy of such experiences, nor anything like a catalogue of dimensions of similarity such as can be done, to some degree, for the usual perceptual experiences on which the debate always settles. All I propose for consideration is that there is a phenomenology of psychology, whatever the details.

It will not do to respond (as would most defenders of the idea that artificial intelligence captures the essence of human cognition) that since computers can do arithmetic, and by their very nature have no conscious experience, it must be the case that what I claim to exist for people is an illusion. For the response assumes that what we do and what computers do when they calculate that two and two make four is the same in the first place. As a matter of scientific sociology, for what it is worth, no one has the faintest idea of what *humans* do when they do arithmetic, specifically, what goes on in the brain when even the simplest of calculations is carried out. Ipso facto there is no agreement on what physical system best models what we do.[8] But the logical point is that one may not assume that what humans and computers do is fundamentally the same; rather, this is a proposition that has to be proven. Moreover, the phenomenological evidence in the human case is so strong that we have a priori reason for thinking that *whatever* physical model is proposed, it will not capture what we do. One could, of course, seek to show that some physical model captures what we do *if* one took there to be no problem concerning the reduction of conscious experience in the first place. However, this is a claim that dualists of all stripes deny, so minimizing the problem will gain no traction. Nor, again, is it of any force to claim that since humans can perform unconscious calculation, such an activity can have no phenomenology. For the question is not about what we can do unconsciously. Similarly, if unconscious perception were a genuine phenomenon (a matter of dispute),[9] this would not disprove the existence of subjective experience during conscious perception. Thus, one cannot neutralize the claim that there is a phenomenology of psychological activity by appealing to unconscious kinds of the same or similar activity.

It might seem to be a somewhat exotic if not irrelevant claim to assert that there is a problem of consciousness for psychology as much as for sensory experience. Yet it is important for our purposes, since it highlights the error for the theory of personal identity of corralling consciousness into a corner of the mind, particularly that corner associated with the

---

[8] For an idea of the vast difference between kinds of physical models of cognition that currently have supporters, see Timothy van Gelder, "What Might Cognition Be, If Not Computation?" *Journal of Philosophy* 92 (1995): 345–81.

[9] See, for example, Philip M. Merikle, and Eyal M. Reingold, "On Demonstrating Unconscious Perception: Comment on Draine and Greenwald," *Journal of Experimental Psychology: General* 127 (1998): 304–10.

mind's lowest function, namely perception. It is no more than a perpetuation of the Cartesian error of identifying the soul with awareness. It positively invites a dichotomizing of the human being into a conscious self plus the physical add-ons, which for the Cartesian dualist means identifying the person with the soul, and, for the reductionist reacting in a perfectly understandable way to the ontological split, means doing away with the Cartesian soul as a piece of obscure metaphysical baggage and reducing the person to some collection or other of physical states of whatever complexity.[10] Dualists must resist both errors, and they can only do so by insisting on the essential unity of the person. To point to the fact that human psychology is shot through with phenomenology is but one way of emphasizing that unity; and it is that unity which is at the heart of the kind of dualism I will set out and defend.

That the problem of personal identity is not primarily a problem about consciousness—at least in the narrow sense that dominates current debate—is also shown by the fact that consciousness does not *constitute* personhood; rather, it *presupposes and reveals* it. The point is well known from the classic objections of Thomas Reid and Joseph Butler to the Lockean theory of personal identity:[11] there is a vicious circularity in trying to analyze personal identity, as Locke does, in terms of memory or of consciousness in general, since these phenomena presuppose identity (i.e., that it is the *same* person who remembers or is conscious). Yet it is a point that cannot be repeated often enough. A person is not merely aware—he is aware *of something*, and that something is, fundamentally, himself. There has, of course, been an attempt to get around the problem by invoking non-identity-presupposing relations such as "quasi-memory," but such notions are of doubtful coherence at best.[12] Any attempt to synthesize personal identity out of a manifold of conscious states will founder on the task of specifying just what the content of those states is supposed to be,

---

[10] In speaking of the Cartesian position in this essay, I recognize that Descartes does not always appear to adhere to the position traditionally attributed to him. In the *Treatise on Man* (1664), he speaks of the person as "composed of soul and body," while at the same time attempting what looks like a purely mechanistic explanation of human action; see Descartes, *Treatise on Man*, in *The Philosophical Writings of Descartes*, trans. J. Cottingham, R. Stoothoff, and D. Murdoch (Cambridge: Cambridge University Press, 1985), vol. 1: 99ff. (See also Descartes, *The Principles of Philosophy*, no. 189, ibid., 279–80.) When I speak of the Cartesian view, then, I am referring to the view traditionally ascribed to him, which is also the position that most clearly emerges from the central works published during his life.

[11] See Joseph Butler, *The Analogy of Religion*, first appendix, 1736, reprinted in John Perry, ed., *Personal Identity* (Berkeley: University of California Press, 1975), 99–112; and Thomas Reid, "Of Mr. Locke's Account of Our Personal Identity," chapter 6 of "Of Memory," in his *Essays on the Intellectual Powers of Man*, 1785, reprinted in Perry, ed., *Personal Identity*, 113–18. Locke's theory is in his *Essay Concerning Human Understanding*, II.27, ed. P. H. Nidditch (Oxford: Clarendon Press, 1975), 328–48.

[12] See Sydney Shoemaker, "Persons and Their Pasts," *American Philosophical Quarterly* 7 (1970): 269–85; and Derek Parfit, *Reasons and Persons* (Oxford: Oxford University Press, 1984), 220ff. I criticize the notion in David S. Oderberg, *The Metaphysics of Identity over Time* (New York: St Martin's Press, 1993), 180–85.

and I take this to be a point extendable beyond persons to the identity of any conscious being, such as an animal. More generally, the circularity objection is a special case of the general one against all attempts to give a non-identity-presupposing, and hence noncircular, theory of diachronic identity (identity over time) for any kind of object—about which I will soon have more to say.

It would be specious to deny that either phenomenology or consciousness in general were relevant to the problem of personal identity: any plausible theory must, for example, account for a person's sense of self as an enduring entity, capacity for higher-order conscious states, and awareness of itself as a being endowed with freedom and responsibility. What I am denying, however, is that the problem of person identity is primarily one about phenomenology or consciousness. Rather, it is about psychology in general, taken in the broad, traditional sense: the problem concerns the specific mental operation of the human being in particular, and of any person at all, whether there be angels, animals that are persons, or other disembodied minds. To broach the problem, we must begin with the concept of *form,* since this will take us directly to the concept of identity by focusing consideration on the nature, function, and operation of substances.

III. Form and Identity

Here is a standard definition of form: "The intrinsic incomplete constituent principle in a substance which actualizes the potencies of matter and together with the matter composes a definite material substance or natural body."[13] It is "intrinsic" because it is a constituent of the substance and solely of the substance. It is a "constituent" in the sense of being a real part or element of it, though not on the same level as the substance's natural parts, for example, the branch of a tree or the leg of a dog; rather, it is a radical or fundamental part of the substance in the sense of constituting it as the kind of substance it is. It is a "principle" in the sense of being that from which the identity of the substance is derived— that *in virtue of which* the substance is what it is. It is "incomplete" in the sense that it does not and cannot exist apart from its instantiation by a particular individual, contra Platonism. (This does not, however, contradict the possibility of a certain kind of form's existing independently of *present instantiation in matter,* as we shall see.) It "actualizes the potencies of matter" in the sense of being the principle that unites with matter to produce a finite individual with limited powers and an existence circumscribed by space and time. Together with matter, it composes the distinct individual substance.

[13] Bernard Wuellner, S.J., *Dictionary of Scholastic Philosophy* (Milwaukee: Bruce Pub. Co., 1956), 48.

These ideas will be expanded as we proceed. For the moment, it is the question of identity itself that needs clarification. The problem of personal identity is a problem about identity over time. Since there is no non-identity-presupposing analysis of diachronic identity in general, there is no non-identity-presupposing analysis of personal identity.[14] The most popular current proposal for analyzing identity over time is the four-dimensionalist account, according to which every persisting object is taken to be a four-dimensional "space-time worm." Inspired (if not necessarily justified) by contemporary relativistic physics and the supposed amalgamation of the three spatial dimensions and that of time into a "four-dimensional manifold," this theory has it that persisting objects are really complexes of "temporal parts," more or less momentary "slices" or "stages" of matter across space-time. What we think of as three-dimensional objects persisting through time are, on this view, four-dimensional objects "smeared out" across the space-time manifold.[15] Yet four-dimensionalism, whatever its version, suffers from many flaws,[16] one of the fundamental ones being that there is no way of analyzing temporal parts that does not either invoke the very phenomenon of identity that is supposed to be analyzed, or else reduce to absurdity by the invocation of literally instantaneous object-stages that cannot give rise to any temporally extended object.

One way out that has gained a little in popularity is to take identity to be primitive.[17] Yet there is a right way and a wrong way of interpreting this. The right way is to take the phenomenon of identity per se to be primitive. In other words, there is no way of defining identity across time in other terms: it is a basic, unanalyzable phenomenon. The wrong way is to take it as meaning that the identity of specific material substances themselves is primitive: in other words, it would be incorrect to claim that when it comes to identity, *nothing further can be said* about why it is that an object of a certain kind, existing at a given time, is numerically identical to an object of a certain kind identified at a later time; or why an object at one time is identical to *this* object rather than *that* object at a later time. It would, to elaborate a little, be wrong to claim that when it comes to *kinds* of things,

---

[14] I argue for the general claim in *The Metaphysics of Identity over Time*, with brief reference to personal identity at 59–62 and 185–95. Other authors to cast doubt in one way or another on the idea of finding a non-identity-presupposing criterion of identity include Michael Jubien, "The Myth of Identity Conditions," in James E. Tomberlin, ed., *Philosophical Perspectives 10: Metaphysics* (Oxford: Blackwell, 1996), 343–56; Trenton Merricks, "There Are No Criteria of Identity over Time," *Noûs* 32 (1998): 106–24; and Michael Rea, "Temporal Parts Unmotivated," *Philosophical Review* 107 (1998): 225–60.

[15] For some standard expositions, see Eli Hirsch, *The Concept of Identity* (Oxford: Oxford University Press, 1982); Mark Heller, *The Ontology of Physical Objects* (Cambridge: Cambridge University Press, 1990); and Theodore Sider, *Four-Dimensionalism* (Oxford: Clarendon Press, 2001).

[16] See, e.g., my *The Metaphysics of Identity over Time*; see also my "Temporal Parts and the Possibility of Change," *Philosophy and Phenomenological Research* 69 (2004): 686–708; Rea, "Temporal Parts Unmotivated"; and Roderick Chisholm, *Person and Object* (La Salle, IL: Open Court, 1976), appendix A.

[17] See the authors in note 14, including myself.

the criterion of identity for a given kind is primitive, that nothing further can be said about why, say, objects of kind K continue to exist in certain conditions but cease to exist in others—other than that's just how things are for things of kind K. But even if a sympathizer with nominalism were to say that there *are* no real *kinds* of objects, that every object is purely an individual, it would still be wrong to assert that nothing further can be said about why individuals persist in these circumstances rather than those.

The reason the wrong way is wrong is that it simply ignores self-evident truths of identity. We can explain why it is, for instance, that Bessie the cow seen at t_1 is not identical to Rover the dog observed at t_2, and why Rover at t_2 is not the same as Fido at t_3—and why, say, a Lego house at t_3 is distinct from the pile of Lego bricks at t_4 that constituted it at t_3. In all such cases, we do not rest content with saying that Bessie is Bessie and Rover is Rover, that Fido and Rover are just not the same, and that a Lego house is something different from its Lego bricks. Even if the criteria of identity invoked are quite simple, they are informative: a cow and a dog are different kinds of animals; this cow and this dog have different properties; the two dogs are of different breeds, or else differ otherwise in their properties; a pile of Lego bricks does not make a house; and so on. The notion of primitive substance identity does not explain what we *do* when we account for the identity of substances.

Clearly what we do is more than simply make assertions about what is identical with what. And what emerges is that the criteria we invoke all, whether directly or indirectly, refer back to the forms of things, and, *pace* the nominalist, to those forms considered as universal entities instantiated in particular cases. The identity of the substance is primitive in this sense—that it cannot be decomposed into elements that do not themselves presuppose either the identity that is the subject of analysis in the first place or the identity of other things on which the identity in question is dependent. So the identity of Rover, for instance, is *evidenced* by those features we typically point to as features of Rover—Rover's bark, Rover's bite, Rover's characteristic way of chasing postmen. But it would be patently circular to claim that Rover's identity *consisted* in these things. Or, in the case of a bare natural formation, say, such as a river, the identity is evidenced by typical features of that thing—its characteristic shape or flow. Aggregates such as a pile of bricks have an identity wholly dependent on the identity of their constituents, which need not commit us to mereological essentialism—the idea that even the slightest addition to or replacement of parts destroys a thing—even though it is notoriously difficult to say just how many bricks need to stay the same for the pile to be the same pile. We refer to evidence, and evidence is all we have to go on. Even the much-vaunted phenomenon of spatiotemporal continuity only gives us evidence rather than an analysis.[18]

---

[18] See my *The Metaphysics of Identity over Time*, esp. chap. 2.

The sorts of features to which we point, however, when we try—impossibly—to analyze identity (as distinct from the actual practice of reidentification, which we do successfully all the time) are notable for having this in common: they are all features referable back to, and deriving from, the form of the object in question. In general, what matters are the congeries of powers, operations, activities, organization, structure, and function of the object, whether it be something as bare as shape in the case of the diachronic identity of a circle drawn on a piece of paper, or something as complex as character in the case of the identity of a relatively higher animal such as a dog. Hence, it is Rover's special way of barking at dinner time that is of more relevance than his color—after all, he could have been swapped for a twin from the litter—and it is his mournful mien when refused a walk in the park that is of more relevance than his enthusiasm for chasing postmen. There seems to be a hierarchy of attributes to which we attach relative importance in grasping a thing's identity; it is better, perhaps, to think of it as a series of concentric circles, moving from the periphery where certain attributes—perhaps (but not necessarily) color, shape, posture, having been at a certain place at a certain time—have a fairly transitory importance, toward the center where, in the case of, say, a higher animal, features such as manner of behavior and characteristic function assume dominance. The closer we get to the center, the nearer we approach what we think of as the *essence* of the thing.

Why can we not simply refer identity criteria back to spatiotemporal characteristics? Apart from the impossibility of an analysis in terms of spatiotemporal continuity, and apart also from the well-known Max Black–style counterexamples to the Identity of Indiscernibles,[19] the possibility of exact spatiotemporal coincidence of objects precludes any analysis in terms solely of such characteristics. I have argued elsewhere that coincidence is impossible for substances of the same kind because of the problem of individuation, and that for non-substances (at least of certain kinds) it is possible since individuation is effected by appeal to the identity of the coincident objects' ontological sources, since non-substances are ontologically dependent entities. For instance, coinciding objects such as two shadows or two beams of light, one on top of the other, are individuated by their sources (the distinct occluding objects and the dis-

---

[19] Black invites us to consider two qualitatively identical spheres existing in a homogeneous space devoid of any other entity. Since, according to the Identity of Indiscernibles, objects that have all their features in common must really be one and the same thing numerically, these distinct spheres must be discernible in respect of their qualities. Yet, argues Black, what quality distinguishes them? They are intrinsically the same; further, all their relational properties and spatiotemporal properties are the same, since they are the only two things in an otherwise void, homogeneous space. Thus, he concludes, the Identity of Indiscernibles must be false. The alleged counterexample and his interpretation of it are, to say the least, controversial. See Max Black, "The Identity of Indiscernibles," *Mind* 61 (1952): 153–64.

tinct light sources, respectively).[20] Again, for substances of different kinds, if coincidence is possible it will be referred back to distinct identity criteria for those substances, and this may include modal features, that is, features concerning how things *might* have been with respect to one or both objects (these being genuine features of objects as much as their nonmodal features such as shape or size). For instance, if a statue is a substance then it is distinct from the lump of marble constituting it because of the different identity criteria for statues and lumps of marble; one *could* have existed without the other, say, if the lump had been rearranged into a differently shaped object.[21] In all cases where coincidence is possible, reference to distinct identity criteria entails reference to the distinct forms possessed by the entities in question, substances or not. (In the case of non-substances of the same kind, such as property instances, or such entities as shadows and beams of light, reference is to the identity criteria for the substances on which they are ontologically dependent.)

The moral of the story is that form is the root cause of identity: another way of putting it is that identity has a *formal cause*. Since, however, substances are individuals and form is not of itself individual, we have to posit a *material* cause of identity as well: in other words, the identity of a substance is given by the form as instantiated in matter. That the matter is not the root cause of identity is shown by the fact that most macroscopic objects can and often do change all their matter without ceasing to persist.[22] No substance can change its form—that is, its *substantial* form— and continue to exist. Another way of expressing the proposition that

---

[20] See David S. Oderberg, "Coincidence under a Sortal," *Philosophical Review* 105 (1996): 145–71, sec. 5; I call examples such as shadows and beams of light "Leibnizian cases." For the concept of ontological dependence, see E. J. Lowe, "Ontological Dependency," *Philosophical Papers* 23 (1994): 31–48, substantially reprinted in chapter 6 of his *The Possibility of Metaphysics* (Oxford: Clarendon Press, 1998); see also Roderick Chisholm, "Ontologically Dependent Entities," *Philosophy and Phenomenological Research* 54 (1994): 499–507.

[21] See note 20, and also E. J. Lowe, "Coinciding Objects: In Defence of the 'Standard Account'," *Analysis* 55 (1995): 171–78, replying to Michael B. Burke, "Copper Statues and Pieces of Copper," *Analysis* 52 (1992): 12–17.

[22] Despite what is often proposed to philosophy undergraduates, however, human beings do not turn over all of their cells during their adult life. Most neurons and muscle cells are not replaced. A girl is born with all the egg cells she will ever have, all in an arrested stage of cell division. Then, after puberty, ordinarily just one cell each month finishes its process of cell division to produce the released egg. Some organisms have fixed numbers of cells: the lobster has exactly nine nerve cells in its cardiac ganglion that are fixed for life; the adult roundworm *Caenorhabditis elegans* has exactly 959 somatic cells (not counting sperm and eggs) which are never replaced. Much of the physical material forming our cells is replaced, though. Even the mineral in our bones is constantly being turned over. The DNA is a prominent exception. Although there are some attempts to correct errors in the sequence that may accumulate with time, once a DNA molecule is produced, it stays unchanged until the cell divides or dies. When the cell divides, one of the old strands ends up in each new cell unchanged. That one strand may go unchanged through many cell divisions until the cell it happens to reside in dies. Another structure not replaced is the lens of the eye. Damage to these cells or to the proteins in them tends to accumulate so that our vision is constantly deteriorating. (Thanks to Richard Norman, Associate Professor of Biology at the University of Michigan, Dearborn, for this information.)

identity has a formal cause is to say that form is the *bearer* of identity. For a substance to persist is for it to possess *this* substantial form: not merely *a* substantial form, but a form instantiated by *this* matter—where *this* matter is not identified by there necessarily being a single parcel of atoms or other stuff, since as noted this may itself change over time. The matter is simply the matter of the persisting substance. Only if this were offered as an analysis of identity would there be a problem of circularity; rather, what is offered is an analysis of the causes of identity, and seen as such there is no circularity: a substance persists because it consists of a form instantiated in matter, the form being the actualizing principle in virtue of which the substance is what it is, and the matter being the limiting principle of that form in virtue of which the substance is individual.[23]

Since a person is, following the classic definition of Boethius (480–524 A.D.), an individual substance of a rational nature,[24] it follows that a person persists in virtue of its form. The form just is the person's rational nature; it is also called the person's *soul.* Anyone who objects to the term "soul" as metaphysically or theologically loaded can simply use the term "rational nature" wherever "soul" appears in what follows. It is now necessary to understand exactly *of what* the soul is the form.

IV. BODY, UNICITY OF FORM, AND PRIMORDIAL MATTER

We can only grasp what the soul is the form of, however, via a defense of two central doctrines of hylemorphism, namely, those of the unicity of substantial form and of the existence of primordial (or prime) matter. Unicity of form means that for any substance, there is one and only one substantial form that it possesses. This is because a substance is one kind of thing, and substantial form determines the kind of thing it is. Hence, when a substance comes into being, it does so in virtue of acquiring a single substantial form, and when it loses that form it ceases to exist altogether as that kind of thing, even if something else is left over that is not that kind of thing. Thus, when a lump of clay is smashed to pieces it ceases to exist altogether even though other, numerically distinct lumps of clay may come into existence in virtue of the persistence of clay material that is not itself a lump of any kind but rather the referent of the mass term "clay." Suppose, on the contrary, that the lump of clay possessed two substantial forms, that of *lump* and that of *clay.* Then we would have to say that if the lump form were removed, say by smashing, the clay form would remain and the lump of clay, not having been completely destroyed, would continue to exist. But how could it exist? One might think it exists

---

[23] On matter as the principle of individuation, see David S. Oderberg, "Hylomorphism and Individuation," in John Haldane, ed., *Mind, Metaphysics, and Value in the Thomistic and Analytical Traditions* (South Bend, IN: University of Notre Dame Press, 2002), 125–42.

[24] Boethius, *Liber de persona et duabus naturis contra Eutychen et Nestorium,* c. ii.

as the clay itself. But this is absurd: in what sense has the *lump of clay* persisted—as clay? But a lump of clay is not mere clay. Or suppose it exists as in some respect "partially identical" to the clay. Yet this is unintelligible, whatever the proponents of "degrees of identity" or peddlers of the idea of "survival" (a kind of persistence short of full identity) may think. Further, it would then seem impossible even to *destroy* a lump of clay without removing the clay form as well, which would require disintegrating it into its atomic or subatomic parts—but surely destroying a lump of clay cannot be *that* difficult.

Whatever one might say about the substantiality of such objects as lumps of clay—and some recent writers have cast doubt on it[25]—the unicity doctrine is even more apparent in the case of objects over whose substantiality there is no dispute, such as living things. Let us go back to Fido. If substantial forms were multiple in Fido, the multiplicity theorist would have to say either that one substance, Fido, instantiated two substantial forms, or that there were actually two substances where it looked as if there were only one. Take the first alternative. Suppose we say that Fido, being both a living thing and a dog, falls under the two substantial kinds *living thing* and *dog*. These being distinct forms, why could they not come apart, with Fido instantiating one but not the other? One scenario is that Fido goes the way of all doggy flesh, leaving behind a canine corpse. It might be said, pointing at the corpse, "There is Fido," meaning that Fido is still a dog, albeit a dead one. But a dead dog is not a kind of dog any more than the proverbial rubber duck is a kind of duck, or, to change the analogy, than a dead parrot is anything other than an ex-parrot. A substantial form, as defined earlier, supplies the proper functions and operations of its instances. Since no such functions and operations take place in a dead dog[26]—indeed, the processes undergone by and taking place in a corpse are in general the very *reverse* of those undergone by and taking place in a functioning dog—clearly a dead dog does not fall under the substantial kind *dog*.

Another scenario is that Fido acquires the powers of Proteus and morphs into various other kinds of substance, while retaining the form of *living creature*. Does this indicate that Fido would have ceased to fall under the substantial form *dog* while continuing to instantiate the separate form of a living creature? No, because in the case of Protean change the transient forms are not substantial but accidental: they do not determine the kind of thing Protean Fido is in his *essence* or *nature*, but merely the diversity of forms which that essence or nature allows him to take on. Observing

[25] The writers are not themselves (at least overt) hylemorphists, it should be noted. See, e.g., Joshua Hoffman and Gary Rosenkrantz, *Substance: Its Nature and Existence* (London: Routledge, 1997); Trenton Merricks, *Objects and Persons* (Oxford: Oxford University Press, 2001); Peter van Inwagen, *Material Beings* (Ithaca, NY: Cornell University Press, 1990).

[26] We can safely leave aside such transient phenomena as the continued growing of hair and nails postmortem.

Protean Fido in his canine form, we do not behold a substance that is essentially a dog and a Protean living thing, but an essentially Protean living thing that has taken on the form of a dog. Therefore, neither of the scenarios just described gives us a way of positing distinct substantial forms possessed by a single substance.

Might there, taking the other alternative, be two substances where there only appeared to be one? We can easily dispense with this thought in respect of Protean Fido, because we cannot plausibly say, observing the living creature in its canine form, that here there are *two* things, namely, a dog *and* a Protean organism: rather, there is one thing, a Protean organism appearing *as* a dog. For the organism, the sortal "dog" is as much a phase sortal[27] as the sortal "teenager" is for a thirteen-year-old person, in which latter case there do not exist two things, a human being *and* a teenager. More plausibly, however, it might be argued in the case of normal Fido that there are two substantial forms, namely, those of *dog* and of *body*, and that either there are two substances (for example, a certain body constituting a dog) or there is one substance instantiating the forms of both body and dog. The basic confusion at the root of both proposals is that they misunderstand the concept of substantial form. Substantial forms do not make up a hierarchy within a substance—the canine form is not an add-on to the inferior corporeal form, for example. For how would one specify exactly what kind of body the canine form was superadded to? We can eliminate the idea that the canine form is the form of a certain kind of corpse. It is tempting to think that a living dog just is a dead dog plus something extra, and one might imagine dead Fido's being miraculously brought back to life and call that the re-addition of canine form to canine matter. But dead flesh is not a formally impoverished kind of living flesh: in dead flesh, from the moment death occurs, not only is the substantial organic canine form absent but it is replaced by the very form of a dead thing, in which new functions of decay and disintegration immediately begin to occur. The reanimation of dead Fido by means of the re-addition of the organic canine form would involve not merely the super-addition of something to a corpse, but the actual *reversal* of disintegrative processes already commenced. In other words, Fido's form qua living dog is the form of living flesh; that is, the living flesh has a formal cause in Fido's substantial form. There simply is no metaphysical space for another kind of flesh to which the organic canine form is added to produce a living, breathing dog.

Another way of putting the point is to say that substantial form *permeates* the entirety of the substance that possesses it, not merely *horizon-*

---

[27] A sortal term, here "dog," tells us what sort of thing—in the most liberal sense—an object is. A phase sortal is a sortal term applying to a thing that goes through a temporary stage or phase denoted by the term; e.g., "teenager" is a phase sortal under which human beings fall. A *substance* sortal, in contrast, is such that an object that falls under it *must* fall under it or else cease to exist altogether, e.g., "human" for human beings.

tally in its parts—there is as much dogginess in Fido's nose and tail as in Fido as a whole[28]—but also *vertically*, down to the very chemical elements that constitute Fido's living flesh. To use the traditional scholastic terminology, the chemical elements exist *virtually* in Fido, not as compounds in their own right but as elements fully harnessed to the operations of the organism in which they exist, via the compounds they constitute, and the further compounds the latter constitute, through levels of compounds, proteins, the DNA the latter code for, the organelles that make up the cells, the organs made up of the cells, and so on.[29] Supposing there to be elementary particles (a proposal I deny),[30] and supposing these to be quarks, it does not follow from the fact that every material substance is *made* of quarks that every substantial form is the *form* of a bundle of quarks, because in the existing substance the quarks *have* no substantial identity of their own, their behavior having been fully yoked to the function and operations of the substance in which they exist. The substantial forms of the particles exist *virtually* in the substances they constitute. In other words, the quark is ontologically dependent on the whole of which

[28] Note that this does *not* imply, absurdly, that Fido's nose is a dog, only that Fido's nose is nothing other than a canine one. The canine form is not partially present in the nose: it is wholly present but it informs the nose and every other part according to its own exigencies qua canine form. The way a substantial form informs the parts of, say, a dog is thus not essentially different from the way an accidental form such as whiteness informs the parts of a white object: a white object has white parts, a canine substance has canine parts. The difference lies in the relative heterogeneity of the parts, which depends on the forms themselves. Organisms generally have sharply differentiated parts, whereas color is relatively homogeneous. See also St. Thomas Aquinas, *Summa contra Gentiles*, II.72, trans. James F. Anderson (Garden City, NY: Image Books, 1956), 213–15.

[29] The same point applies to such phenomena as the transplantation of foreign DNA or cells into another species. Fido may have had mouse cells inserted into him by an experimenter, but if those cells really do enter into the dog's very makeup, taking their operative place within the genome, then they have no substantial identity of their own any more than they did in the body of the mouse from which they were taken. Outside any creature—sitting, say, on a petri dish—the cells are substances in their own right, but when yoked to the nature of the creature into which they are inserted, their existence is virtual, not substantial. Contrast the case of parasitism, where the parasite inside the organism retains its substantial identity because, however closely it may interact with and depend upon the functioning of its host, it does not enter into the very nature of that host, it does not become part of what *informs* that host or determines its specific identity.

[30] To be clear on what my denial amounts to: I recognize that physicists currently believe there to be "elementary particles," i.e., particles with no structure and no parts, in particular, leptons and quarks. But I regard it as a metaphysical, rather than a physical, truth that no spatially extended object can be essentially elementary and hence indivisible. Thus, I take it that strict metaphysical atomism is false a priori. Leaving aside the raised eyebrows such a philosophical claim might cause given the supposed empirical evidence to the contrary, note that what physicists *actually* hold is that if quarks (for instance) have a structure, it must be smaller than 10^{-16} cm, but measurements cannot yet reach that far. Further, if it turned out that quarks *did* have a structure, they would, as physicists quite rightly admit, no longer merit the name elementary. What this shows is (a) that there is at least no law of nature, as currently understood, that prevents quarks from having structure and hence parts, and (b) that merely calling a particle "elementary" does not mean that it really is so. It is, then, unjustified to claim that my denial of the existence of elementary particles has simply been proven false by physics.

it is a part, but its causal powers persist, albeit in a way radically limited by the whole. The substantial form is what determines the permissible and impermissible behavior of the quarks in the body, which is why some chemical reactions typically occur, others rarely, and others not at all. Nor is there any particular bundle of quarks of which the form could even be the form, given the familiar fact that every body loses and gains quarks all the time. Again, it is the form that determines the when, how, and how much of the loss and gain that may occur, with external circumstances merely operating upon predetermined possibilities.[31]

According to the hylemorphic theory, the unique substantial form of any material substance must be united to something to produce that substance, since in itself it is only an actualizing principle. What does it actualize? It does not actualize anything whose actuality already presupposes the existence of the substantial form. Here it is useful to distinguish between two senses of "of" in the expression "x is the form of y." In one sense, the substituend for "y" is simply that whose identity depends on the substituend for "x," as when we say that a father is the father of his son ("He is his father's son"). In the other sense, the substituend for "y" is the object whose identity does not so depend, the object with its own real existence apart from that to which it is functionally related, as when we say that a father is the father of a person. In the first sense, then, we can say with Aristotle, when speaking about life, that the soul, understood as the organic principle, is the first actuality of a natural body with organs.[32] In other words, the soul is the form of an organism, that which makes the organism an organism; we could also say that the soul is the form of a body that has *these* kinds of properties. In terms of the real unity relation, however, the soul is the form of something else, something not itself shot through by the very soul to which it is united—and this is what the hylemorphist calls primordial matter. There is no space here to enter into a detailed explanation and defense of primordial matter: for our purposes, it is enough to know that although I have called it a something, it is, in the well-worn phrase, not a something but not a nothing either. It is the closest there is in the universe to nothingness without being nothingness, since it has no features of its own but for the potential to receive substantial forms. There has to be something to which form unites, and primordial matter is the only thing that can fill that role.

---

[31] Joel Katzav has drawn my attention to the similar position adopted by A. N. Whitehead: see Whitehead, *Science and the Modern World* (Cambridge: Cambridge University Press, 1926), 98–99 and the pages leading up to these. At p. 99, he says: "Thus an electron within a living body is different [substantially?] from an electron outside it, by reason of the plan of the body. . . . But the principle of modification is perfectly general throughout nature, and represents no property peculiar to living bodies." This appears to be wholly in accord with the scholastic doctrine, at least if "different" is taken to mean "substantially different."

[32] Aristotle, *De Anima*, II.1, 412b4.

To return now to our main concern, which is persons, the situation is this. A person, like any other substance, is actualized by a substantial form. For human beings, the kind of person that is our focus, the substantial form is that principle in virtue of which the person is a person, and that means the principle of life, of consciousness, and of rationality. These are all one principle since the doctrine of unicity applies as much to persons as to any other substance. The fact that persons are also sentient and alive does not mean that there are three forms, the form of life, the form of sentience, and the form of rationality, for what could this mean? There are not three distinct substances—the organism, the animal, and the rational creature. There is one substance, a person, who is both living, and sentient, and rational. There is not one substance instantiating three distinct substantial forms—life, sentience, and rationality—because they are all constituents of one set of powers. What gives the *person* life is precisely what makes the *person* sentient, and what makes him sentient is just what makes him rational, even though canine sentience, by contrast, does not give rise to canine rationality. The reverse also holds: for instance, what makes the *person* rational is also what makes him organic, since the sort of rationality persons have essentially involves the use of sensation, and sensation requires life. There may be—indeed are—kinds of rationality that do not require sensation, but they are irrelevant to consideration of the human person.

The person, then, like any substantial kind of thing, is an essential unity manifesting a multiplicity of operations: one nature, many manifestations of that nature. The nature is called by hylemorphists the soul, the term having been traditionally used for all living things, even plants, but now restricted to human beings. In what sense, then, is hylemorphism a kind of dualism?

V. Soul and Knowledge

The hylemorphic theory is dualistic with respect to the analysis of *all* material substances without exception, since it holds that they are all composites of primordial matter and substantial form. When it comes to persons, however, the theory has a special account. The soul of Fido, for instance, is wholly material—all of Fido's organic and mental operations are material, inasmuch as they have an analysis in wholly material terms. The soul of a person, on the other hand, is wholly immaterial, the argument for this being that a person has at least some mental operations that are not wholly explicable in material terms—and we can deduce what a thing's nature is from the way it necessarily acts or behaves. If, however, some such operations are not wholly materially explicable, the soul itself cannot be anything other than wholly immaterial because there is no sense in postulating a soul that is a mixture of the material and the immaterial.[33]

To take the last point first, if the soul were a mixture of the material and immaterial it would be subject to contrary properties: qua material it would have spatiotemporal characteristics, qua immaterial it would not; qua material it would have parts, qua immaterial it would not; qua material it would be divisible, qua immaterial it would not.[34] Although very much imperfect, the analogy with abstract objects is useful: the color red, for instance, though wholly dependent on material tokenings for its existence, is in its own nature an immaterial, abstract object, not a mixture of the material and the immaterial. Its very immateriality is what allows it to be wholly instantiated in more than one place at one time, which is not possible for material objects. But if it is true of immaterial objects wholly dependent on material instantiation that they are not a mixture of the material and the immaterial, how much more will it be true of immaterial objects that are not wholly materially dependent? (We will see this lack of dependence later.) Note also that this point does not exclude the following. (i) The *person*, being a *compound* of matter and form, is a compound of the material and the immaterial. In this sense one can speak loosely of the person's being a "mixture" of the material and the immaterial. The

---

[33] A word of explanation is in order. Lest it be thought that hylemorphic dualism commits itself to an absurd position concerning the immortality of purely material objects such as tables and chairs, or dogs and cats, it must be emphasized that the theory is not one about universals but about particulars. As abstract objects, universals such as *chairness* and *felinity*, and even *humanity*, are immaterial. Nevertheless, just what that means for a universal is a difficult and complex issue that cannot be explored here. If, as it seems, it is correct to say that universals are wholly present wherever and whenever they are instantiated, we are compelled to assign to universals a kind of spatiotemporal location that must still be compatible with their essential immateriality. But their immateriality does not entail that they can exist without their instances: on the Aristotelian view of universals, the ceasing to exist of, say, all the green things means the ceasing to exist of the universal *greenness*, even though *greenness*, qua abstract object, is immaterial. Of course, *greenness* continues to exist even if this particular tree is destroyed, as long as there are other green things; but the total absence of green things entails the absence of *greenness*. Hence, we cannot deduce from the facts that a universal F is an immaterial entity and that F is instantiated in some particular object, that F can survive the destruction of that object (for it might be the only instance of F). Even more importantly for present purposes, however, is the point that every particular instance of a universal is distinct from the universal itself: the hunger of Felix, for example, is a *property instance* ("trope," as it is now called; "mode," as it is traditionally called), to be distinguished from the universal *hunger*. Property instances are *concrete* entities, not abstract ones, and as such are not essentially immaterial. Thus, one cannot read off from hylemorphic dualism the view that an individual instance of some universal is immaterial because the universal is immaterial, and hence the absurd conclusion that every substance is immortal simply because—to revert to the Aristotelian terminology—it possesses a substantial form. As possessed by a substance, the substantial form is *particular*, not universal, and *concrete*, not abstract. If it is immaterial, it will not be because it instantiates an immaterial universal, e.g., *human nature* or *felinity*, but rather because there is something *about* the instances of the relevant universal such that they themselves are properly to be regarded as immaterial. In the human case, this is the idea that the human intellect is immaterial in its essential operations.

[34] Aristotle, *De Anima*, III.4, 429a25.

soul, however, does not have parts and thus is not itself a compound object (this I assume rather than argue for in the present essay): so it would really possess contradictory properties were it to be both material and immaterial. (ii) The soul, although immaterial in itself, can be described as having a certain essential relation to matter, in that its complete operation requires embodiment. Again, however, this does not mean that the soul has contradictory properties.

Now, if the soul is immaterial, it follows that human nature is immaterial, since the soul of a person just is that person's nature. We can see this by understanding the concept of a hierarchy of capacities. Although some may balk at the idea of such a hierarchy, in fact the idea is easily explained by saying that F-type capacities are superior to G-type capacities just in case the former entail the latter but not vice versa. It follows that sentience is superior to nutrition because sentient operations require nutritive ones but not vice versa—we have abundant examples of such. Hence, the nature of an object that has sentience and nutrition as capacities is sentient, and by implication nutritive, but not merely nutritive. In other words, the nature of a thing is defined in terms of its highest capacities. Human rationality is superior to both human sentience and human nutrition according to the definition given, so human nature is defined in terms of the rational capacity. If the rational capacity is immaterial, however, it follows that human nature, that is, the substantial form of the human person, is immaterial. (This does not imply that nutrition, say, is an immaterial process, only that human nature, being essentially immaterial, contains a *power* of nutrition that can exist apart from any embodiment. But in the absence of the requisite material conditions—embodiment and objects upon which to act—that power cannot be exercised.)

There are various ways of establishing the immateriality of human reason, or the human intellect, and one of these does indeed appeal to consciousness. But as I have claimed, an excessive focus on consciousness is deleterious both to the debate about personal identity (and the mind-body problem) and to our very conception of human nature. Instead, hylemorphists take their primary cue from Aristotle, who asserts that the intellect has no bodily organ.[35] In other words, intellectual activity—the forming of ideas or concepts, the making of judgments, and logical reasoning—is an essentially immaterial process, a process that is intrinsically independent of matter, however much it may be *extrinsically* dependent on matter for its normal operations in the human being.[36] Aristotle's

---

[35] Aristotle, *De Generatione Animalium*, II, 736b28: "for bodily activity has no share in the activity of reason [*nous*]"; see also note 34 above, and *De Anima*, II.1, 413a6.

[36] Extrinsic dependence is a kind of nonessential dependence. For example, certain kinds of plants depend extrinsically, hence nonessentially, on the presence of soil for their nutrition, since they can be grown hydroponically; but they depend intrinsically, hence essentially, on the presence of certain nutrients that they normally receive from soil but can receive via other routes.

position, it must be emphasized, is not that hylemorphism *of itself* entails the immateriality of the intellect, but that within the hylemorphic conception, considering the *specific function* of the human person, the intellect must be immaterial. The central theses of hylemorphism in general then tell us in what manner and to what extent the human person is immaterial, as will be explained in due course.

The reason for the proposition that the intellect is immaterial is that there is an essential ontological mismatch between the proper objects of intellectual activity just mentioned and any kind of potential physical embodiment of them: we might call this the *embodiment problem,* but looked at in a slightly narrower way, in cognitive-scientific terms, it might be called the location or storage problem. Concepts, propositions, and arguments are abstract; potential material loci for these items are concrete.[37] The former are unextended; the latter are extended.[38] The former are universals; the latter are particular. Nothing that is abstract, unextended, and universal—and it is perhaps hard to see how anything abstract could be other than unextended and universal—could be embodied, located, or stored in anything concrete, extended, and particular. Therefore, the proper objects of intellectual activity can have no material embodiment or locus.

To complicate the problem even more for the materialist, consider those concepts that are not only universal, unextended, and abstract, but also semantically simple. Suppose, *per impossibile,* that the materialist could overcome the problem of the first three features of concepts, adding that those that are semantically complex, such as the concept of a black dog, had their locus in the brain spatially distributed in a way that mirrored their complexity: thus, the concept black had location A, the concept dog had location B, and some kind of structural relation between A and B constituted the relation between these concepts as elements of the unified concept of a black dog. (Whether it is even right to analyze complex concepts in this way is another matter that cannot be discussed here.) Now what about simple concepts such as the concept of unity, or of being, or of identity? Such concepts do not admit of analysis into semantic parts, though it is possible to explicate the notions contextually, illustrate them, and so on. They are, nevertheless, semantically simple. So there is not

[37] The point here is not one about *instantiation,* since the instantiation of the abstract by the concrete is a commonplace (which is not to say that it is easily understood) that reveals nothing special about the human mind. Human beings and human minds do not instantiate concepts, they possess and store them. The ontological problem, then, is how an abstract object such as a concept, with all its sui generis properties, could ever be stored in or possessed by a concrete object such as a brain.

[38] The thought here is that concepts are not even *categorially capable* of embodiment due to a lack of extension, the lack being not merely a privation, such as when a concept happens not to have a possessor, but an intrinsic incapability of possession, as in the case of a number's not being red. Looked at this way, it is arguably straight nonsense to claim that a concept is either extended or unextended; but this supports my point equally well, since it does make sense (and is true) to say that a brain is extended, and so the ontological mismatch is preserved. (Thanks to Fred Sommers for emphasizing this point to me.)

even a prospect of finding a material locus for such concepts, assuming all the other difficulties could be overcome, unless the putative locus were materially simple, in the sense of being material and yet metaphysically indivisible. But the very idea of a material simple makes no sense. If a material object were simple it would be unextended—but then in what sense would it be material? An extensionless point is not a something but a nothing, and thus cannot be a locus for concepts, which are something. Further, extensionless points cannot have any constitutive relation to the extended, which is why Aristotle was adamant that the infinite divisibility of space is only potential, not actual. Suppose, however, we could make sense of the idea of a material simple—could it be the candidate locus for simple concepts? Well, are we to postulate a simple located in the brain? If so, is it the same simple that embodies all simple concepts? It would have to be if we were to postulate a single mind having those concepts. But it is hard to make sense of the idea of multiple simple concepts in one materially simple location—about as hard as making sense of many dimensionless points located at one dimensionless point. Yet if we proposed multiple material loci, we would have to account for the mental unity by which one mind has many concepts. All of this without yet having accounted for the possibility of complex concepts, like that of a black dog, in a material simple—how could that be? Yet if there were a non-simple location for these, how again could we account for mental unity given that the simple concepts had simple locations? All in all, the existence of simple concepts merely aggravates the already immense difficulty of smoothing over the fundamental mismatch between concepts and their putative material embodiment.

Needless to say, one of the fundamental problems of cognitive science, in its ubiquitously materialistic contemporary guise, has been to explain the storage of concepts. And needless to say, again, most of the research is either beside the point insofar as it attempts to solve the embodiment problem, or else yields precious little knowledge. For example, one recent paper notes: "A common feature of all concrete objects is their physical form [note the use of the term 'form', which in the context of the paper means something more than shape]. Evidence is accumulating that suggests that all object categories elicit distinct patterns of neural activity in regions that mediate perception of object form (the ventral occipitotemporal cortex)." [39] The authors go on to describe how functional brain-imaging techniques show that representations of different object categories are located in discrete cortical regions that are "distributed and overlapping," embedded in a "lumpy feature-space." To be sure, functional imaging may well reveal *correlations* between certain intellectual activities and certain cortical activities: for the hylemorphic dualist, such correlations are only to be expected,

---

[39] Alex Martin and Linda L. Chao, "Semantic Memory and the Brain: Structure and Processes," *Current Opinion in Neurobiology* 11 (2001): 194–201, at 195.

since persons as embodied beings require corporeal activity in order to interact with the world. Persons are not pure spirits capable of immediate intellectual apprehension or action upon the environment (assuming such things
to exist for the purpose of contrast). Nevertheless, the substantial form is
what directs and controls corporeal activity, whether by acting upon physical inputs or producing physical outputs.

The authors of the paper go on, prudently, to say: "Clearly, it would be
difficult, as well as unwise, to argue that there is a 'chair area' in the brain.
There are simply too many categories, and too little neural space to accommodate discrete, category-specific modules for every category. In fact,
there is no limit on the number of object categories."[40] Indeed, this latter
observation points again to the ontological mismatch between concepts
and their putative material embodiment. The intellect is capable of grasping a potential infinity of concepts, but no corporeal organ can harbor a
potential infinity of anything.[41] In particular, the intellect is distinguished
by this feature: that it can grasp a potentially infinite number of *categories*
of concepts, and within each category a potentially infinite number of exem-
plars. In other words, there is no limit to the number of kinds of things the
intellect can recognize, and no limit to the number of examples of each kind
that it can grasp. By contrast, the eye or ear, for instance, can only receive
colors and sounds, respectively; and within each kind of sense datum, they
can only receive a limited number of examples—hence, we cannot naturally see certain colors or hear certain sounds. The very physical finiteness
of the organs of sight and hearing means they are bounded with respect to
what kinds of information they can take in. This is patently not so for the
intellect—and it does *not* exclude the fact that the intellect, being finite in
its own way, cannot discover certain things. There is a difference between
the intellect's not being able to reach certain truths by its own operation,
and its suffering an intrinsic *material* limitation on the kind of information
it can take in. The absence of such a material limitation, again, is consistent
with its being *extrinsically* limited in respect of the physical information it
can take in: for example, not having the concept of a color that is beyond
the visual spectrum available to the eye. But if the sort of limitation I have
been talking about applies to the eye and the ear, it must apply to *any* proposed organ for embodying concepts. The features of the eye and ear that
make them singularly unsuitable for intellectual operation apply equally
to the brain, the nervous system, or any other proposed material locus. It
is the very materiality of such a locus that prevents it from embodying the
proper objects of intellectual activity.

[40] Ibid., 196.
[41] One does not need to resort to exotic arguments to prove that the mind can grasp a
potential infinity of concepts: one need only refer to the possibility of iteration or of grasping, say, a potentially infinite conjunction. Noam Chomsky's emphasis on "linguistic creativity" is relevant here. See, e.g., Chomsky, *Aspects of the Theory of Syntax* (Cambridge, MA:
MIT Press, 1965), chap. 1, sec. 1.

If researchers into functional imaging have shown anything, then, it is merely that category-specific object recognition is correlated with activity in certain distinct, if highly diffuse and non-discrete, regions in the brain. But this sort of research, as interesting and as potentially useful for brain-damaged patients as it might be, goes no way to even beginning to provide a theoretical or empirical foundation for the idea that concepts, judgments, and inferences themselves have a physical location.

There are, of course, many kinds of challenges that might be leveled against the defense of the immateriality of the intellect I have given. One might level a Rylean-style charge of illegitimate reification against the very idea of concepts as things.[42] One might object that an appeal to immateriality to solve the embodiment problem is a classic case of *obscurum per obscurius*. One might deny that there are concepts in any meaningful sense at all, and claim that there are only distinct, particular acts of representation. There is no space here to canvass these and other objections. But as a general reply we should emphasize that a refusal to reify concepts means an inability to explain fundamental semantic and logical phenomena: not merely the fact that the concept of a black dog is a function of the concept of black and the concept of dog, but that the *concept-possessor* understands this, which is more than saying he can *recognize* a black dog only if he can recognize black things and dogs. Rather, it means that if he has those concepts, he can *see* how one is derived from the others. Mutatis mutandis for judgments and for inferences. And if a person *grasps* a certain concept, and if that concept is an object (*pace* Gottlob Frege's worries about the concept horse),[43] then the person grasps an object. Since this is a mental act, his mind must take hold of something, and if it takes hold of a thing then that thing must make a kind of contact with it—which means, since there is no other plausible way of understanding it, that the concept must somehow be in its possessor's mind. But if the concept is not the sort of thing that can be physically inside the possessor's brain, his mind cannot be his brain, and moreover must be immaterial since only an immaterial thing can be suited to laying hold of the concept.

---

[42] See Gilbert Ryle, *The Concept of Mind* (London: Hutchinson, 1949), for a sustained attack on what he saw as the illegitimate practice of taking the mind to be an entity or substance of some kind, rather than as a concept denoting various kinds of behavior. In attacking the supposed conceptual mistake of making a thing out of what is not a thing, Ryle was, of course, heavily influenced by Ludwig Wittgenstein.

[43] Due to the distinctive features of Frege's semantic and syntactic theory, an expression such as "the concept horse" ought to refer to an object—namely, the concept of a horse. But since he radically distinguishes between concept and object (objects, such as the horse Dobbin, *satisfy* concepts, such as the concept ". . . is fast"), how could one and the same thing be both a concept and an object? See G. Frege, "On Concept and Object," in P. Geach and M. Black, eds., *Translations from the Philosophical Writings of Gottlob Frege* (Oxford: Blackwell, 1952). I suspect that this paradox in Frege is genuine, and I take it to count against his rigid distinction between concept and object.

VI. Soul, Identity, and Material Dependence

What, then, of the complex relationship between the soul, the person, and the matter the soul informs to produce the person? The first thing to note is that the soul is not the person.[44] The person is the human being, the substantial compound of matter and form. A person is an individual substance of a rational nature, but the soul is not such a substance—for it *is* the rational nature, not a substance *with* a rational nature. Hence, the fundamental flaw in the Cartesian conception of the person is the illegitimate identification of the person with the soul, taking them to be one and the same substance. It might with good reason be said that Descartes, having given up on the notion of substantial form,[45] yet eager to preserve personal immortality, had nowhere else to go. Yet the mistake is basic, and leads to so many of the problems that have dogged Cartesian dualism ever since.

Next, given the unicity of substantial form, one cannot take there to be separate, lower orders of soul or nature in the human person. Growth,

---

[44] St. Thomas Aquinas, *Summa Theologiae* (hereafter *ST*), I, q. 75, a. 5, trans. Fathers of the English Dominican Province, 2d ed. (London: Burnes Oates and Washbourne, 1922), vol. 4: 13–16. For a contrary view, though not couched in terms of souls, see E. J. Lowe, "Form without Matter," in Oderberg, ed., *Form and Matter*, 1–21, at 8–9, where Lowe identifies the individual concrete substance with its own substantial form, suggesting later that perhaps persons are examples of matterless substances, i.e., forms without matter (21). But it is not clear from his discussion why the two must be identified. For if, using his example, the form of a statue is the property (although it is dangerous to use this term for reasons apparent from the above discussion) of its particular *being a statue of such-and-such a shape,* and if the individual statue itself is an instance of the substantial kind *statue of such-and-such a shape,* then the form as property and the statue as concrete substance are not one and the same. The statue is a compound of matter and form (however one wishes to construe matter, and it should be noted that Lowe eschews prime matter in favor of proximate matter such as *lump of bronze*), and it is this that is the instance of the kind. The form remains only a part of that compound, its very individuality being given by the matter with which it is united (though again, Lowe rejects the idea of matter as the principle of individuation).

[45] Descartes says this about substantial forms:

> For they were not introduced by philosophers for any other reason than that by them an explanation might be given for the proper actions of natural things, of which the form is to be the principle and root, as was said in an earlier thesis. But clearly no explanation can be given by these substantial forms for any natural action, since their defenders admit that they are occult and that they do not understand them themselves. For if they say that some action proceeds from a substantial form, it is as if they said that it proceeds from something they do not understand; which explains nothing.

He also says that "the prophets and apostles, and others who composed the sacred scriptures at the dictation of the Holy Ghost, never considered these philosophical entities, clearly unknown outside the Schools," and that substantial forms are "nowhere, we think, clearly mentioned in Holy Scripture. . . ." Descartes's letter to Regius, January 1642, in Charles Adam and Paul Tannery, eds., *Oeuvres de Descartes III: Correspondance* (Paris: Cerf, 1899), 502, 506. Although Descartes is here responding directly to the charge by the Calvinist theologian Voetius that the former's denial of substantial forms is inconsistent with Scripture, the context suggests that he is more than happy to sound triumphant about there being no clear biblical mention of them, as though this lent positive support to his denial. Contrary to popular parody, however, scholastic method hardly takes reference in Holy Writ to be a criterion for the acceptability of a philosophical concept.

nutrition, reproduction, sentience, perception—all of the operations of the organism belong to the unique human nature of the person. A human being is an essential unity, not a plurality. Some of those operations, however, depend essentially on matter—such as reproduction and sensation—and others, such as the operations of the intellect, as we have seen, do not. But if the person is not to be broken down into a plurality, how do we reconcile the partial dependence and partial independence of matter that we find in human nature? We have to say something like the following. The person, being essentially embodied, depends for its existence and identity on embodiment, as also for some of its operations. Whether it exists at all depends upon its having a human nature individualized in matter; and *which* person it is depends on which material individualization it is. Again, this is not proposed as an analysis of identity in other terms, but rather as an account of the *causes* of that identity.

To say, however, that the person is existence- and identity-dependent on its embodiment does not entail that all of its parts depend for their existence on being united in the embodied person. As an imperfect analogy, we observe that a broom cannot exist without a brush but the brush can exist without the broom to which it belonged. That is, it is not a universal truth that if an F cannot exist without a certain part P, then P cannot exist without F: it depends on the kind of thing one is talking about. In the case of nonrational animals, we can say that the animal cannot exist without its soul, but neither can the soul exist without embodiment in the animal since all of the animal soul's operations are wholly material, not rising beyond sensation and perception of the concrete particular. On the other hand, since some of the operations of the intellectual soul are not material, it can exist without its embodiment in matter. The principle at work here is the following: x can exist without y if and only if x can operate without y. The first half is that if x can exist without y then x can operate without y: if x exists without y, then x's nature is actualized without y; but if x's nature is actualized, then x possesses the very operations given to it by its nature, and thus can operate according to that nature without y. It might be the case that x operates in an imperfect way because of the lack of y, but its essential nature and the functions proper to that essential nature will not in themselves be destroyed. Fido can exist without his tail, so he can function without his tail even though the lack of a tail impairs that function. He cannot exist without a head, however, and so cannot function without a head.

The second half of the biconditional says that if x can operate without y, then x can exist without y. If x can operate without y, albeit perhaps imperfectly, then x must have a nature that can be actual without y's being actual. But for x to be actual is for x to exist, and for y not to be actual is for y not to exist. So x can exist without y. I can function without ten fingers; so I can exist without ten fingers. I might not be able to hold a baseball bat without ten fingers, but holding a baseball bat—indeed, being able to hold anything—is not essential to my functioning as a human being. By contrast, I cannot function without a heart, or without something that fulfills the role of a heart; hence, I cannot exist without a heart. Whether or not the biconditional is true for any x and y or only for material substances, the hylemorphist only needs it to be true for living things in order to make his point about human souls as opposed to other souls. Since the human soul can operate without matter, it can exist without matter. It might exist in an imperfect state, since it cannot, for instance, perform acts of sensation that require material stimuli and the formation of mental images, but it can still exist apart from matter.[46]

Although the soul of the person is not existence-dependent upon matter, in the way I have claimed (it does not require material embodiment to exist), it is not plausible to deny that its existence depends upon matter in the following sense: that it must be embodied at *some* time during its existence. This is a weaker form of existence-dependence, and it follows from the fact that the human soul just *is* the rational nature of an individual substance belonging to a certain *kind*. Human persons just are embodied creatures, and thus not only must their souls be attached to their bodies—at least at *some* time in their history—for them to exist, but also their souls, in order to be *souls of persons*, that is, in order to be what they are, must be at some time the forms of bodies. This means that the idea of a human person disembodied throughout its history is incoherent. Such a being might be a disembodied person, but it would not be a disembodied *human* person because human persons are just not that kind of thing. In which case, if the human soul has a disembodied existence, that existence can only be made possible by its once having been the form of a body.[47] Further, it is also *identity-dependent* on its once having been the form of a body.[48] In other words, to be the particular soul that it is, it must once have been the form of a particular body making a particular individual substance of a rational nature; just as, in its embodied state, the soul's identity depends on

---

[46] The idea that form can exist without matter might seem repugnant to the very Aristotelian conception of substance that I have been concerned to defend. But it is not, and is not to be confused with Platonism about universals, which is of course repugnant to Aristotelianism. For an interesting recent defense of form without matter that seeks to stay faithful to both the *Categories* and the *Metaphysics*, see Lowe, "Form without Matter."

[47] What about the possibility of a soul's having begun to exist in a disembodied state, with its existence and identity being dependent not on its having once been the form of a body, but on its becoming *at a future date* the form of a body? This depends on whether one can make sense of the idea of backwards material causation—the idea that x exists at t_i because of the matter to which x will be united at t_j ($t_i < t_j$). There are of course epistemological problems with the idea of identifying something on the basis of its future matter, but perhaps there is no straightforward metaphysical problem if the future is at least knowable in principle, say to an omniscient mind.

[48] For more on the concepts of identity-dependence and existence-dependence, see Lowe, "Ontological Dependency."

whose, that is, which person's, soul it is.[49] In short, the principle of
individuation for persons must be *cross-temporal*.[50]

As I claimed earlier, the form is the bearer of the identity of a substance,
in the sense that it is the primary part of the substance responsible for the
substance's being the substance it is over time. The soul, as form of the
body, is therefore also the bearer of personal identity. From the subjective
point of view, when I reflect upon my own identity as a person it is my
soul that exercises that intellectual operation, recognizing itself as the
bearer of my identity as a person. This does not mean that the first-person
pronoun is ambiguous, only that it refers to me as a person by means of
referring to that person's chief part, which is the soul, just as, when I say
"I am in pain" after I stub my toe, "I" refers to me as a person by means
of one of my parts, in this case my toe: I am in pain because my toe is in
pain. I take the primary reference of the first-person pronoun, as used by
me, to be myself as a person; but I propose tentatively that the reference
to my soul (in the case of thought) or my toe (when I stub it) is a kind of
secondary or *instrumental* reference.

In the disembodied state, I continue to exist—that is, the person that is
me persists despite my physical *death*, which is the separation of my form
from my matter—even though one of my constituents, namely my body,
does not. What this means, then, is that my death results in the person
that I am *continuing to exist as my chief part*, namely the part in virtue of
which I am specifically different, or different in kind, from any other kind
of animal. When the body my soul informs ceases to exist, as surely it
does at some time, then the person I am dies but does not thereby cease
to exist; hence, death and cessation of existence, for entities like us, are not
the same event.[51] I persist both *as a person* and as the form that once was
the form of the body that was a part of that person. My soul is the bearer
of my identity as a person, but I am not, and was never, strictly numer-

---

[49] Howard Robinson sums up this position succinctly, in answer to the Aristotelian question of "why and how a soul should be—in this life at least—tied to a particular body as a
substantial unity": "the soul is the form of the body, for the individualized identity of a form
depends necessarily on the matter in which it is individualized, so there can be no worry
about how it comes to belong to this body." See Howard Robinson, "Form and the Immateriality of the Intellect from Aristotle to Aquinas," in Henry Blumenthal and Howard
Robinson, eds., *Aristotle and the Later Tradition* (*Oxford Studies in Ancient Philosophy*), ed. Julia
Annas (Oxford: Clarendon Press, 1991), 207–26, at 225–26.

[50] Hence, it should be clear that although human nature per se is universal, a human
person, being an individualized human nature, is particular.

[51] Just as the soul, having intrinsic existence independent of matter, does not cease to exist
via separation from matter, so by parity of reasoning it would seem that the soul cannot
come into existence by the very fact of the coming into existence of the person as compound
of soul and body. In other words, neither the soul's generation nor its corruption depend on
matter. As Aristotle puts it in *On the Generation of Animals* 736b21–28, the rational soul is
unique in having to come "from outside." It requires further argument, be it philosophical
or theological, to determine whether "from outside" entails pre-existence (Plato) or immediate creation (Christianity).

ically identical with my soul.[52] Another imperfect analogy helps to make the point. Suppose it were technically possible to reduce my organic existence to that of a head.[53] Then I would exist *as* a head, but I would not be numerically identical *with* a head any more than I would have been numerically identical with my whole body—there being no reason to affirm one and deny the other, transitivity of identity would be violated. And yet in *some* sense I am a head: perhaps, to use a much-discussed concept, we can say that I am *constituted* by a head, as I was once constituted by a whole body (let us leave aside the soul for the moment—the point should be graspable by materialists as well). Although the concept of constitution is not well understood, I think that the best way of interpreting it in this context is to say that my existing as a head just means my being reduced to one of my parts, my existing in a radically mutilated state.

Finally, the consequences for personal responsibility must be something like the following. If persons die when their souls leave their bodies—which is no more than a special case of the general truth that substances cease to exist when their form and matter are no longer united—then can any sense be made of a soul's bearing any responsibility for the acts of the whole person of which it once was a constituent? To pursue the gory analogy of the bodiless head, there does not appear to be anything repugnant to reason in the idea that a person existing solely as a head should be punished for crimes committed while the head was connected to a body. Yet perhaps intuitions differ strongly on this question. I think we can accommodate any divergence by considering generally whether sense can be made of the idea that a part of an F can be held responsible for the

[52] Although the overwhelming textual evidence from Aquinas is that this is exactly what he believes, there is also a particularly tricky sentence from his *Commentary on 1 Corinthians*, referred to by John Finnis in "'The Thing I Am': Personal Identity in Aquinas and Shakespeare" (elsewhere in this volume), to which attention should be drawn. In his commentary at 15.2 on chapter 15, verses 13ff. ("If there be no resurrection of the dead, then Christ is not risen again. . . . [I]f the dead rise not again, your faith is in vain," etc.), Aquinas says: "My soul is not me [anima mea non est ego]; and so even if my soul should attain salvation in another life, still neither I nor any man would have attained it." This looks as though he is denying that the person survives death and asserting that only the soul does so. Read in context, however—both the context at hand and that of all his other remarks on the subject (including those referred to in this essay)—I do not think that this is what he has in mind. Immediately prior to the quoted assertion, he points out that the soul is a part of the man, and not the whole man (totus homo). So by going on to say that the man does not achieve salvation after death, he implicitly means this of the *whole* man, and this is correct, since the person after death is deprived of his body. Moreover, since he is commenting on St. Paul's claim that without the resurrection of the dead, faith is in vain, and since he explains that man has a natural desire for his salvation (naturaliter desiderat salutem sui ipsius), he must be taken to be pointing out that what a person desires is the salvation of his whole self, body and soul—not of himself in some reduced or impoverished way, as a mere part, namely, the soul. Hence, the sort of salvation ultimately desired, which prevents faith from being in vain, is that represented by Christ's resurrection, to wit that of the entire person, body and soul, in his fullness.

[53] Gruesome as it may sound, patents have already been taken out on just such a procedure (see U.S. Patent no. 4666425).

acts of a whole F. To see that such an idea is not only coherent but has real-world application, consider the case of a corporation (a legal and moral person) whose chief executive is held responsible for that corporation's illegal actions. Considering the corporation as a kind of aggregate or collectivity, and its directors as constituent parts of that collectivity, we can see that the chief executive as a part of the corporation can be held responsible for the latter's transactions, as can the directors in general.[54] It is true but irrelevant that the courts have traditionally been reluctant to impute such responsibility in a blanket fashion, their reluctance being motivated not by metaphysics but by a recognition of the disincentive such blanket responsibility would be to anyone thinking of becoming a director, let alone CEO, of a corporation. All we need to see is that it is coherent to suggest that a part might be held responsible for the actions of the whole—moreover, that not any part will do, but only that part (or those parts) which are, as it were, in the driver's seat. The soul, if it is part of the person at all, certainly is in the driver's seat, so if any part of the person can be held responsible, it must be the soul. But since, as I have argued, the person I am continues to exist *as* a soul (even though I am not numerically identical *with* a soul), it must be me who is responsible precisely for what I did when my soul informed a certain body.[55] But doesn't this imply a twofold responsibility, and hence a twofold punishment or reward (if there be such after death)? No, because the soul is held responsible solely in virtue of its being the chief part whereby *I*, the person, did whatever I did that incurred responsibility. As Aquinas puts it, I am rewarded or punished "in the soul" for what I did when my soul informed my body. To return to the example of my being reduced to a bodiless head, if it is true to say that the head suffers a punishment, it does not do so *qua head*, but qua the part that now constitutes *me*: if there is to be any punishment at all of bodiless me, the only way it can be carried out is *by* punishing my head.

VII. Conclusion

My aim in this essay has been to set out the main lines of the much-neglected hylemorphic theory of the person, and of the dualism that is at its heart. It has not been possible to canvass the many questions and objec-

---

[54] In *ST,* I, q. 75, a. 4 (1922 ed., vol. 4, p. 12), ad 1, St. Thomas himself uses the analogy of governor and state to support the idea that what the person does can be imputed to the soul. The soul then, according to him, can after a fashion be called the man (= the person), though it is not strictly identical with the man. This is compatible with the proposition that the man (= person) continues to exist *as* a soul, i.e., in a radically mutilated form.

[55] Having said that each man is an individual person (*ST,* III [Supp.], q. 88, a. 1 [1922 ed., vol. 21, p. 12], ad 1), Aquinas goes on to explain that the "particular judgment" due to him "is that to which he will be subjected after death, when he will receive according as he hath done in the body (2 Corinthians 5:10), not indeed entirely but only in part since he will receive not in the body but only in the soul."

tions that may be raised. If the essay shows nothing more than that the theory is worthy of far more serious attention than it has commonly been given, that will be enough. I do, however, want to conclude with a general observation. The theory that I am not strictly identical with my soul, hence that soul and person are distinct, the person having an essential connection to its body as well as its soul, seems more strange to dualist ears than it should. The "problem of personal identity," as it has come to be known, has a relatively recent currency (due to Locke) and is more fitted to a metaphysical viewpoint that at the very least takes the ideas of disembodied existence and of the immateriality of the soul to be at best highly problematic, at worst not even worth a place in the conceptual landscape on which the problem is grappled with. More strongly, I would venture to say that the problem of personal identity is a problem made for materialists—at least those materialists who take seriously the peculiar ontological status of the mental, the existence of free will and rational agency, and perhaps even the possibility of a future life. The contemporary dualist reaction to materialism, however, has tended to be one of recoiling from the idea of any essential connection between body and soul, and hence between person and both. This has led, in turn, to making the apparently "obvious" move (for the dualist) of identifying person with soul, or at least of regarding person and soul as having an exclusive essential relationship.

For the hylemorphic dualist, on the other hand, the acceptance of a genuinely immaterial element in human nature means a greater flexibility in trying to comprehend just how human persons persist. The concept of form can be pushed heavily into service, as can the idea of the person as a compound substance, in this respect just like a material substance—namely, a substance composed of matter and form. Nevertheless, the hylemorphic dualist must avoid the disastrous fall into Cartesianism or Platonism, both of which diminish the role of the body in personhood. Once the soul is united to a body, it is the form of that body for all time, even after that body has ceased to exist. Its identity after death—and hence the identity of the person that is reduced to it—depends on its having once informed certain matter. The soul must always have a retrospective character, one that looks back on what choices it made when it actualized that matter, and hence on what the person did of which it was once the chief part. (Again, think of the chief executive who, long after his corporation's demise, is forever tarred with the brush of responsibility for those decisions *he* made—and hence his corporation made—when he was its chief constituent.) The soul has, as it were, the indelible stamp of personhood, and due to its very nature as an actualizing principle of matter it has an essential tendency or direction toward the full flowering of its capacities in matter. Whether it may also look forward to a reuniting of itself with matter is, however, beyond the scope of philosophy to answer.

Philosophy, University of Reading, England

PERSONAL IDENTITY AND SELF-OWNERSHIP*

By Edward Feser

I. Introduction

The thesis of self-ownership is the principle on which many classical liberal and libertarian theorists, from John Locke to Robert Nozick, have founded their political philosophy. The "ownership" part of the thesis, touching as it does on the concepts of property and rights with their obvious political relevance, has understandably been the focus of debate over the principle. Still, it is curious that the other component of the thesis—the "self" that is said to be self-owned—has received so little attention from either the advocates of the thesis or its detractors. Could it be that this neglect is justified? Could it be that questions about the nature of the *self* are simply tangential to the question of self-*ownership* per se, and can safely be bracketed off by political theory and left to the metaphysicians? I want to suggest that they cannot be. The thesis of self-ownership, I want to argue, is simply not compatible with just every philosophical conception of the self on offer—and not compatible even with certain conceptions some advocates of the thesis are likely at least implicitly to be committed to when their attention is not on matters of political philosophy. Indeed, as I will try to show, the thesis may in fact be compatible with only *one* general approach to the metaphysics of the self. Since I am an advocate both of that metaphysical approach and of the thesis of self-ownership itself, as well as of many of the consequences the thesis is generally taken to have, the fact that there is at least this one viable conception comes as a relief, personally speaking. But it might not come as a relief to all advocates of self-ownership. For a correct understanding of the self may, as we shall see, imply a correction to certain construals of self-ownership and its implications proffered by many of the thesis's advocates.

Justifying these claims will require a consideration of the thesis of self-ownership in light of the major theories of the self put forward by metaphysicians and philosophers of mind, theories largely coextensive with the major theories of personal identity. The focus of my investigation will accordingly be the relationship between personal identity and self-ownership. The first order of business is to get clear on the nature of the

* For comments on earlier versions of this essay, I thank Christopher Kaczor, Ellen Frankel Paul, the participants at an Institute for Humane Studies current research workshop in January 2004, and the other contributors to this volume.

thesis of self-ownership itself. Then I shall consider its compatibility or lack thereof with each of the major theories of personal identity.

II. Self-Ownership

The thesis of self-ownership, as generally understood, holds that each individual has complete ownership of or property rights in himself—in his body and its parts, his talents and abilities, his labor and energies, and so forth. Among the less controversial consequences of the thesis is that no innocent person can legitimately be made a slave, for to take a person as a slave would be to steal him from himself;[1] among the more controversial is that, in the words of Nozick, the most influential advocate of the thesis in twentieth-century philosophy, "taxation of earnings from labor is on a par with forced labor," a subtle kind of slavery.[2] The claim is not necessarily that *all* taxation amounts to forced labor—the taxation that goes to fund the libertarian minimal or "nightwatchman" state is consistent with self-ownership, in Nozick's view, for reasons too complicated to enter into here.[3] But redistributive taxation, for the purposes of realizing some pattern of distribution (egalitarian, say) or providing others with certain benefits (social insurance, socialized medicine, or pretty much "social" or "socialized" anything), gives others—the state, or the recipients of the state's largesse—an "enforceable claim" on your labor and its fruits; it "makes them a *part-owner* of you; it gives them a property right in you," which violates your self-ownership.[4] The consequences for political philosophy are, in turn, that the only morally legitimate sort of polity is one that is characterized by a very limited central government and one that at least allows for, though it does not strictly require, a free market or capitalist economic system; egalitarian liberalism and socialism, faceless welfare bureaucracies no less than gulags, are absolutely ruled out as merely different gradations on a spectrum of state-sponsored slave labor.

---

[1] I use the qualifier "innocent" because an advocate of the thesis of self-ownership could at least argue that a person who has seriously violated the rights of another might thereby have forfeited his own rights to such an extent that he could legitimately be taken into slavery. One of the traditional justifications of (some forms of) slavery, for example, held that enemy combatants captured in a just war could, since they had by participation in an unjust cause forfeited their rights to their very lives, have no legitimate objection to suffering the lesser penalty of lifelong servitude to their conquerors. Some advocates of self-ownership would also argue that a person could, as a self-owner, voluntarily sell himself into slavery, though perhaps the semantics of the term "slavery," seeming as it does to include involuntariness as an essential component, would rule out the possibility of *voluntary* slavery by definition. In any case, taking *innocent* persons as slaves *without* their consent—as was the case, for example, in the African slave trade—would unambiguously be ruled out by the thesis of self-ownership.

[2] Robert Nozick, *Anarchy, State, and Utopia* (New York: Basic Books, 1974), 169.

[3] See part I of Nozick, *Anarchy, State, and Utopia*. For a defense of Nozick's defense of the minimal state and of his moral critique of most taxation, see Edward Feser, *On Nozick* (Belmont, CA: Wadsworth, 2003).

[4] Nozick, *Anarchy, State, and Utopia*, 172.

These qualifications—"very limited *central* government" and "at least allows for, though it does not strictly require"—are important, both intrinsically and for the position I will ultimately be advocating in this essay, though they are almost never noticed by Nozick's critics or emphasized enough by Nozick himself. It is almost universally held by those critics that Nozick's position would entail in practice that the poor would be abandoned to sleeping on grates and starving en masse, that there would be widespread environmental devastation, etc. But this is hysterics rather than serious analysis. I say this not only because of the enormous body of serious scholarly work that has been done comparing the results of government action in matters of welfare, conservation, education, and so forth versus action in the "private sector," mostly to the detriment of the former.[5] I say it primarily because the critics ignore the details of Nozick's overall position in political philosophy, which does not at all fit the standard caricature of classical liberal or libertarian thinking as conceiving of individuals as isolated atoms struggling for survival within the forbidding context of ruthless competition between mammoth corporations lightly governed by a distant and uncaring minimal state.[6]

As is made evident especially by the much-neglected third part of Nozick's *Anarchy, State, and Utopia*, what Nozick favored was the sort of organic social order that develops "from below," on a small scale and in a localized fashion, through voluntary interaction among people of shared values (and we might add in a conservative vein, though this is not stressed by the individualistically-inclined Nozick himself, shared traditions and shared histories), rather than an artificial and regimented regime imposed "from above," via regulation, indoctrination, and the threat of litigation or prosecution, by the regulatory, educational, and legal bureaucracies of a massive centralized state. Such localized organic communities may well require, even by ordinance, any degree of public-spiritedness and self-sacrifice of their members; but they would operate within the overarching context of a central government—the minimal state—which itself requires only that those within its jurisdiction contribute to the common defense and a common juridical system. And such communities would also respect the right of exit of those who may decide to abandon their communities (communities which may, again, nevertheless retain any level of control over those who agree to remain within them); and this right of exit would be enforced by the minimal state. The social picture that results, however reflective of a commitment to the dignity of the individual and the importance of consent, is nevertheless not that of "atomistic individualism," but something closer to the emphasis put by

---

[5] The literature is vast, but Feser, *On Nozick*, contains an overview of some of the major themes (in chapter 2) and a useful bibliography.

[6] In fact, *no* prominent classical liberal or libertarian theorist's vision of social life fits this silly caricature—certainly not Adam Smith's or F. A. Hayek's, and not even Herbert Spencer's—but that is another matter.

Burkean conservatives on the need for a healthy society to be based on strong "intermediate institutions"—intermediate, that is, between the individual and the state—or the notion of subsidiarity in Catholic social doctrine.[7] Those who assume that to strip the centralized modern state of its Leviathan-like powers *must* be to leave the individual helpless reveal merely the limits of their own imaginations, not any flaws in Nozick's political philosophy, or in self-ownership inspired political thinking generally.

There is another reason for the inadequacy of the caricature, however, one stemming from the very nature of self-ownership, and made evident in the work of philosopher Eric Mack. It is not enough to respect an individual's self-ownership merely to refrain from killing, injuring, or enslaving him, or in other ways to avoid interfering with what happens within, we might say, the boundary formed by his skin. One must also recognize and respect the implications of the fact that the capacities and powers that the individual owns in owning himself are inherently *world-interactive*. A self, we might say, is by its nature directed at the world and to functioning within the world. It follows that fully to respect another's self-ownership, one must not use one's own property—one's own justly and exclusively held pieces of the world—in a way that undermines the capacity of the other person to interact with the world. To squeeze someone's windpipe until he suffocates would obviously be to violate his self-ownership; but so too would it violate his self-ownership to leave his body untouched but remove all the air surrounding it. To force an innocent person into a cage by manhandling him, thereby imprisoning him, would violate his self-ownership; but so too would refraining to touch him at all while nevertheless building a cage around him while he sleeps peacefully in a field. If one acquires some air or a cage as one's private property, one may have all the rights over those things that are normally associated with private property, but one must nevertheless not use one's air or one's cage in a way that completely undermines another's capacity to interact with the world. This constitutes what Mack calls a "self-ownership proviso" on the use of one's private property: one may use that property however one sees fit, so long as such use does not nullify

---

[7] The classic formulation of the notion of subsidiarity is Pope Pius XI's statement in *Quadragesimo Anno:* "It is an injustice and at the same time a great evil and disturbance of right order to assign to a greater and higher association what lesser and subordinate organizations can do" (sec. 79). In this connection, one might note that whereas localized and noncoercive socialist communities, though allowed for by Nozick's position, would nevertheless not be likely to flourish given their evident economic inefficiency and incompatibility with human nature (note the decline of the kibbutz in Israel), the sort of agrarian and even quasi-anarchical but private property respecting communities envisioned by critics of industrial society like *Catholic Worker* editor Dorothy Day would be realistic options. That Day was closer in spirit to the libertarian right than to the socialist left is a proposition defended by Bill Kauffman in "The Way of Love: Dorothy Day and the American Right," reprinted in Christopher Hitchens and Christopher Caldwell, eds., *Left Hooks, Right Crosses: A Decade of Political Writing* (New York: Thunder's Mouth Press, 2002).

another's ability to use his self-owned world-interactive powers and capacities. This proviso follows, in Mack's view, as a corollary of, indeed an implicit part of, the thesis of self-ownership itself.[8]

It is important to note that the self-ownership proviso is *not* a constraint on the acquisition of property. Even to acquire, by legal and voluntary transactions, all the water in the world and sell it to individuals at the price they would have had to pay anyway to get it themselves would not violate the proviso. To refuse to sell it to them, however, or to charge them prices the paying of which would reduce them to bare subsistence, *would* violate it, for it would effectively undermine their capacity to use their self-owned powers. The proviso must therefore be distinguished from the Lockean proviso associated with John Locke's theory of property, on which one must, in acquiring any kind of property, leave "enough and as good" for others to acquire.[9] The self-ownership proviso is, again, a proviso on the *use* of one's justly held property: one could in principle come to own all the water in the world, but could nevertheless not use that water in a way that nullifies others' self-owned capacities, including by denying them access to it.[10]

The thesis of self-ownership, and the sort of political philosophy generally understood to flow from it, accordingly do not have the consequence that, in Herbert Spencer's words, "save by the permission of the lords of the soil, [those without property] can have no room for the soles of their feet."[11] To be sure, the implications of the proviso governing self-ownership are in no way egalitarian: inequalities of wealth of vast scale are compatible with it. But then, egalitarianism per se is simply not the same thing as concern for the plight of the poor and propertyless,

---

[8] See Eric Mack, "The Self-Ownership Proviso: A New and Improved Lockean Proviso," *Social Philosophy and Policy* 12, no. 1 (1995): 186–218; Eric Mack, "Self-Ownership, Marxism, and Egalitarianism, Part I: Challenges to Historical Entitlement," *Politics, Philosophy, and Economics* 1, no. 1 (February 2002): 75–108; and Eric Mack, "Self-Ownership, Marxism, and Egalitarianism, Part II: Challenges to the Self-Ownership Thesis," *Politics, Philosophy, and Economics* 1, no. 2 (June 2002).

[9] John Locke, *Two Treatises of Government*, ed. P. Laslett (Cambridge: Cambridge University Press, 1967), *Second Treatise*, section 26. Nozick endorsed a modified, and less egalitarian-sounding, version of the Lockean proviso, but most commentators, whether critics or sympathizers, have not been satisfied with his account of it. Mack's development of the self-ownership proviso is intended in part to salvage what is plausible in the idea of a Lockean proviso while avoiding the philosophical difficulties and apparent back door to egalitarianism that seem to come with it.

[10] There is a parallel here (one relevant to the position I shall be defending) to the distinction drawn in Thomistic natural law thinking between the right to *own* private property, which is absolute, and the right to *use* one's private property, which is not absolute. (See St. Thomas Aquinas, *Summa Theologiae* II-II, question 66.)

[11] Herbert Spencer, *Social Statics* (New York: Robert Schalkenbach Foundation, 1995), 104. It must be noted that Spencer did not *approve* of such a dire consequence; indeed, in the original edition of *Social Statics* he devoted a chapter to "The Right to the Use of the Earth" (from which the quote above is taken) precisely in order to avoid it, though this chapter, deemed threatening because it seemed too egalitarian a position to sit comfortably with the rest of Spencer's philosophy, was omitted from later editions.

however often egalitarians blur the distinction. A society with great inequalities in wealth may nevertheless be a society in which everyone is able adequately to provide for himself and his family. The self-ownership proviso requires at most that society be set up so that the latter is possible; it does not require strict equality, or even anything close to equality. Indeed, it is doubtful that the proviso could justify very much state intervention at all in the context of a modern capitalist society, where almost all people are almost always capable of bringing their self-owned powers to bear on the world via some form of employment or other, however menial (and almost never as menial as the sort of hard labor required for bare subsistence in circumstances where stable private property does not exist).[12] In requiring what it does require, however, the proviso does entail—and this is a point that will be relevant to what follows—that one's use of the resources that one acquires as one's private property can at least *in principle* be regulated, where that use threatens to nullify others' exercise of their self-owned powers. One's self, being self-owned, is utterly inviolable. But what one acquires out of what is *external* to oneself—private property in portions of the natural world—is, though one can form very strong property rights to it, nevertheless subject in some (narrowly confined) circumstances to interference by others, including potentially the state, when one's use of it threatens to violate the self-ownership proviso.[13]

All this raises many questions, of course, but they are not questions that can be or need to be addressed here.[14] The foregoing will suffice for our purposes, namely, providing a working conception of self-ownership and its implications. We need now to proceed to the question of primary interest: Which conceptions of personal identity, if any, are compatible with self-ownership?

---

[12] See David Schmidtz, "The Institution of Property," *Social Philosophy and Policy* 11, no. 2 (1994): 42–62, for an excellent discussion of how people are in general vastly better off under a regime of private property rights than they are when resources are held in common.

[13] It is important to emphasize that it is at most interference with *external* resources that is in question here. Some readers of earlier versions of this essay raised the objection that a right to the use of another's body for sexual purposes would seem, absurdly, to be entailed by the proviso, given the unique manner in which our sexual organs and drives are inherently world-interactive (i.e., they require use of *another's* sexual organs). But this will follow, if at all, only if one's sexual organs are external to one's *self*; and as I will argue in Section VIII below, one's body and its parts are *not* external to one's self. Might this objection be a problem for theories on which the body *is* external to the self, such as the theories I shall be examining in Sections IV through VII? Not necessarily, if, as I would argue, it is a necessary (though not sufficient) condition of the proper use of one's sexual faculties (in the natural law theory sense of "proper use") that the one with whom one engages in sexual activity be a willing participant. But defending this claim would require an excursus into issues of sexual morality that is beyond the scope of this essay.

[14] I have addressed some of them elsewhere, defending the thesis of self-ownership in chapter 3 of *On Nozick* and defending the self-ownership proviso, and criticizing the Lockean proviso that the self-ownership proviso is intended to replace, in Edward Feser, "There Is No Such Thing as an Unjust Initial Acquisition," *Social Philosophy and Policy* 22, no. 1 (2005).

III. Personal Identity and the Self

Theories of personal identity and theories of the self are not, to be sure, always exactly the same thing. They are, however, intimately related. Theories of personal identity are, among other things, theories about what it is to be a *person*; for to give the identity conditions of a thing is in part to give an account of what sort of thing that thing is. And the concept of a person is clearly tied to the concept of selfhood. As a rough characterization of the relationship, one might say that "person" and "self" are two descriptions of one and the same kind of entity, the first from the "outside," the second from the "inside." To conceive of something as a person is to conceive of it as a self, and as something that at least normally has a sense of being a self; and to conceive of one's self is to conceive of being a particular person. To present a theory of personal identity is thus implicitly to give an account of the self that the thesis of self-ownership claims the self owns.

It is also arguably to give a more *useful* theory of the self for our purposes than an outright theory of the self per se would be. There is a sense in which the thesis of self-ownership can seem just obviously true, a semantic consequence (though not necessarily a trivial one) of the very *concept* of "self." To say, for example, "This is my hand, but I don't own it" appears outright contradictory—at least when the speaker has not detached and sold his hand, say, making it no longer *his*, strictly speaking. As political theorist Michael Zuckert has put the point in the context of characterizing Locke's understanding of self-ownership: "The self in its very nature is posited as self-owning, a fact witnessed in our most elementary locutions—I, me, mine, to quote an old Beatles' song." [15] *Any* theory of the self per se would thus count as a theory on which the self owns itself, by definition.

Of course, some would deny that this apparent *conceptual* fact about self-ownership implies any *moral* consequences concerning rights over or property in one's self. My own suspicion is that, on the contrary, the intrinsic connection between the notions of *self* and *ownership* implies precisely that we cannot coherently take something to be a self without taking it also to be the bearer of the rights implied by ownership. The notion of "self," that is to say, is an *inherently moralized* one. But that is the problem. So closely does the concept of the self seem to be tied to irreducibly moral concepts that it is difficult to focus on its purely metaphysical aspects. We are, as it were, too close to the self per se to get an objective fix on it. What we need is an account of the self from a broader point of view—from the outside, as it were, where we can see it not as an "I" aware of what is "mine," but rather from a more neutral third-person

---

[15] Michael P. Zuckert, *Launching Liberalism: On Lockean Political Philosophy* (Lawrence: University Press of Kansas, 2002), 195.

perspective. We need the concept of a person, and thus an account of personal identity.

IV. CARTESIAN DUALISM

An obvious candidate for a conception of persons that would be congenial to self-ownership is René Descartes's dualistic conception of human nature, which goes directly from the first-person point of view of the self to an objective account of persons as immaterial substances conjoined to material bodies. I know with certainty that I exist by virtue of the very fact that I am thinking about the matter, Descartes argued, but I do not thereby know that my *body* exists, for it is at least possible that I could be hallucinating it (say, under the influence of an evil spirit). The self and the body could conceivably come apart, then, in which case they cannot be the same thing. What *I* am, metaphysically speaking, therefore, is not a body, but something incorporeal or nonphysical, a soul outside space and merely causally connected with, but not identical to, my body. Moreover, I am, being immaterial, also a *simple* substance in Descartes's view, one without parts. Thus, there can be no aspect of *me* which is not in the strictest sense *mine*. I simply *am*—my self *is*—identical to all of its concrete features. The gap between the self and what the self purportedly owns is accordingly in this case much narrower than that which exists in generally uncontroversial cases of ownership—ownership of a pen, say, or even of one's body parts, which could conceivably be removed—for *there just is no gap at all.* There is no part of me, on a Cartesian view, which can be removed without removing me along with it. If I could conceivably own anything at all, then, I must surely own at least myself. We might say that if a *Cartesian* self does not own itself, *nobody* owns *anything*.

There are, however, in fact serious problems in reconciling Cartesian dualism and self-ownership, at least if Cartesian dualism is construed in the way it usually is and if self-ownership entails what I have characterized it as entailing. My reasons for saying this are not the predictable ones, to the effect that Cartesian dualism is philosophically indefensible, unscientific, etc., and thus unfit for adoption by advocates of self-ownership or any other serious theorist. On the contrary, *something like* Cartesian dualism is in my view *true*—at least the "dualism" part of it is, and even to some extent the "Cartesian" part, when this is properly understood. For Descartes did not, as is commonly thought (and as my potted characterization above implies), take a person to be identical with an immaterial substance all by itself, with the body being inessential. Though he did regard mind and body as distinct substances capable of existing apart from one another, he also took their combination to constitute a third kind of (compound) substance, and to constitute also a *person,* who when existing disembodied must be considered incomplete. Much of this seems to me to be correct—not for reasons that can fully be explored here, though for reasons that will become at least partially evident by the end of this essay.[16]

On the usual construal of Cartesian dualism, however—which for the time being I shall go along with—a person *is*, again, identical to an immaterial substance, full stop, and the body is inessential to the person qua person. It is this construal that I take to be problematic for self-ownership. For on this interpretation, the body turns out to be a resource *external to the self* in a manner analogous to the way other resources—land, water, food, etc.—are external to the self. In that case, however, the self-ownership proviso will apply at least in principle to the use of one's own body just as it does to one's use of any other external resource one owns. Recall that on that proviso, if I acquire all the water in the world, or for that matter any significant monopoly on an external resource that is irreplaceable and necessary to people's use of their world-interactive self-owned powers, then there are moral grounds for others, including the state, to intervene in and regulate my use of such resources if I use them in a way that prevents others from using said powers. But what if an irreplaceable resource exists in my body itself? As seems plausible even on a dualistic view, certain skills are at least partially realized in bodily features and processes: neural wiring, a certain configuration and development of the muscles, optimal functioning of the eyeballs, and the like. Surgical skills would be a good example. Suppose that such skills become scarce, while the need for them remains as it is or even grows—after a natural disaster, perhaps. Wouldn't we have grounds, given the self-ownership proviso, for intervening in the lives of surgeons, demanding that they use the scarce resources, external to their selves, which they have taken as their property—their skill-realizing bodies—to provide surgical services to others? True, we would not be justified in *directly* forcing them to perform surgery, exactly; that would infringe on their right to use their self-owned immaterial substances, which must volitionally move their bodies if they are to do anything competently surgical at all. We could intervene *indirectly*, however, by interfering with force whenever the surgeons insisted on using their bodies to do something which, because it effectively squandered the skills realized in those monopolized bodies, violated the self-ownership proviso. If a small group who owned all the water in the world and refused to allow everyone access to it would thereby violate the proviso, surely a small group of surgeons who owned all the surgical-skill-realizing bodies in the world—resources as external to the surgeons themselves (who are nothing more than immaterial substances) as water

---

[16] They are explored more fully in Edward Feser, *Philosophy of Mind: A Short Introduction* (Oxford: Oneworld Publications, 2005). The proper interpretation of Descartes's dualism is the subject of a number of volumes, including two with virtually the same title: Gordon Baker and Katherine J. Morris, *Descartes' Dualism* (London: Routledge, 1996); and Marleen Rozemond, *Descartes's Dualism* (Cambridge, MA: Harvard University Press, 1998).

is—and refused to allow everyone else access to them would also be violating it.

Someone might object that the skills inherent in the surgeons' bodies are only there in the first place as a result of the influence of the distinctly mental capacities inherent in the surgeons' immaterial substances: since the skills would not have been in the bodies if the surgeons' immaterial substances had not interacted with them, those embodied skills cannot be treated as external resources. But such an objection would fail to get to the nub of the matter; after all, getting at water (and, sometimes, making it potable) also requires at least some undeniably self-owned powers, but that does not keep the self-ownership proviso from governing the use of water. Surgical skills, however dependent in part on the self-owned attributes of the immaterial substance that constitutes the surgeon, are also and obviously at least partly the result of having certain inherently bodily capacities: you cannot have surgical skills without *some* body or other, after all; and if you end up having a particular aptitude for surgery, that is no doubt at least partly the result of genetically influenced bodily endowments.

Furthermore, we can imagine that given belief in (the standard interpretation of) Cartesian dualism, people might start to acquire what would otherwise be the bodies of other people, at conception. As Fred is conceived, say, and before his immaterial substance begins to interact with his body (whenever that is), others—Fred's parents, say, or scientists to whom his parents have given the right to his body—"mix their labor," Lockean-style, with Fred's body (perhaps during the course of an in vitro fertilization) and thereby come to acquire it as their property. So as to respect the self-ownership proviso as it applies to Fred, they are always careful ever after to allow Fred to use his body in such a way that he is able to bring his self-owned mental capacities to bear on the world. They nevertheless attach certain conditions to that use, so that the proviso is also respected in application to everyone else. In particular, they require that should Fred decide to develop surgical skills—skills *he* will be the one putting into the body, to be sure, but nevertheless into a body he would not be able so to develop at all unless others who already owned it allowed him the use of it—he will have to agree to use them in the service of whomever the owners of his body decide should be benefited by them. The idea here is that just as people come to be born into an external world the portions of which (raw materials, land, houses, water, food, etc.) are already owned by others, so that such portions can only be accessed when one is freely given them, sold them, or allowed to labor for or with them, so too might bodies come to be pre-owned before one has a chance to access them, if Cartesian dualism, as usually characterized, is correct. A body might fail to have any interesting capacities until an immaterial substance interacts with it, but so too are external natural resources pretty useless until someone does something with them. So if the latter are governed by the self-ownership proviso, why not the former?[17]

There are other, perhaps more disturbing, cases where (the standard caricature of) Cartesian dualism coupled with the self-ownership proviso leads to consequences like those just described. Consider the well-worn example of terrorists threatening to kill a number of innocent people unless a certain other innocent person is turned over to be murdered by them. The advocate of the thesis of self-ownership would seem at first glance to be committed to refusing the terrorists' demands no matter what the consequences, for to turn over the innocent person would seem clearly to violate his absolute rights over himself. If we take a Cartesian dualist view, however, a person's body is not really essential to him in the first place—*he* will not die even if his body does. So why not turn him over? You may be interfering with his use of his body, but on this interpretation that would be like interfering with his use of his water or land: ordinarily impermissible, but in certain emergency circumstances allowable, at least given the self-ownership proviso.

One might object that those threatened by the terrorists with death if the innocent person is not turned over would also be losing merely their bodies, not their selves, so that their self-ownership rights per se would not be violated if we refused to turn over the innocent person—thus undermining the case for turning him over. But this would still involve balancing the prospect of *many* bodies lost against the loss of only *one* body, in which case the violation of one person's property rights in his body would seem less objectionable than the violation of many persons' property rights in *their* bodies. Furthermore, the example can be altered slightly so that it *does* involve violations of self-ownership. Suppose that the terrorists plan in effect to *torture* many innocent people by releasing a deadly nerve agent—thereby violating their self-ownership by causing severe pain, a mental state realized in their self-owned immaterial substances and thus in their *selves*—while planning only painlessly to kill the innocent person's body, thus destroying his external property (his body, analogous to destroying his water or land) but leaving the innocent person's self per se untouched. Surely in this case, avoidance of the violation of the self-ownership rights of many people would trump avoidance of the violation of the external property rights of one person.

Still, it might be replied that even if the body is an external resource, and thus in principle subject in its use to interference from others so as to

---

[17] Cartesian dualism arguably has troubling consequences not only for what happens to the body before birth, but also for what happens to it after death: if the body is completely distinct from the self, an external resource like any other, why would it not be legitimate, in principle, for government to require mandatory postmortem organ harvesting for the sake of those urgently needing transplants (assuming one has not already bequeathed one's organs to some other specific person)? Wouldn't someone who refuses to become an organ donor be like the water monopolist who refuses access to a natural resource necessary to others' survival?

fulfill the self-ownership proviso, actually to *destroy* that body by turning it over to the terrorists would violate the self-ownership proviso with respect to the innocent person himself, who now has had *his* self-owned world-interactive properties nullified by being deprived of a body with which to interact with the world. Again, however, the example can easily be modified to meet the objection, in this case by supposing instead that the terrorists do not want to *kill* the innocent person's body, but only seriously to modify it (by tattooing it, say, or surgically adding a third arm just for laughs—and while he is under anesthesia so that the procedure is painless) and not in a way that will nullify his ability to use his body to interact with the world. The basic point remains: if (the usual caricature of) Cartesian dualism is true, then given the self-ownership proviso, there will be grounds in principle in at least some cases for others seriously to interfere with a person's use of his body.

Now such a consequence is not, strictly speaking, incompatible with the thesis of self-ownership. If a self *really is* just a Cartesian immaterial substance, with the body being an external resource, then nothing I have described is really a violation of *self-ownership* per se, but merely an extension, surprising but justifiable, of the application of the self-ownership proviso to the body, now understood as one external resource among others. Still, such a result would seem to be at least in tension with the *spirit* of the thesis of self-ownership. If self-ownership cannot guarantee even the inviolability of one's own body, it is much less attractive a principle than it at first appeared, and the concrete political and moral implications it seemed to have seem less secure.

V. Bodily-Continuity and Psychological-Continuity Theories

If Cartesian dualism—again, as typically construed, anyway—leaves something to be desired where robust self-ownership is concerned, then bodily-continuity theories, which in effect identify a person with his body, might seem a great improvement. After all, the problem with dualism was that it divorced the body from the self, was it not? So how could a bodily-continuity theory fail to be superior? Quite easily, actually. There is in fact an obvious respect in which bodily-continuity theories must be, from the point of view of the self-ownership advocate, just as bad as Cartesian ones; and there is another, less obvious but still hard to deny respect in which they are *worse*.

Let us take first the respect in which bodily-continuity theories must be "just as bad" as Cartesian ones. Like all theories of personal identity, the bodily-continuity theory is concerned in part with what makes for identity of persons *over time*: what makes it the case, for example, that you at five years old and you at thirty-five years old are the same person, despite the great physical and psychological changes that occur during the course of a lifetime. Cartesian dualism holds that what makes for sameness of person throughout such changes is that the same immaterial substance is present. Bodily-continuity theories hold that it is the presence of the same *material* substance—the body, say—that is crucial. But such theories typically qualify this claim significantly. First of all, *exact* sameness of body is not necessary, for not only does a human body obviously change considerably as a person grows from infancy through adolescence to adulthood and senescence, but a person might make other radical changes to his body—organ transplants and the like—and yet remain the same person. What is important, then, is that there is a traceable *continuity* from one stage of the body to the next, that the changes to the body, however significant, are gradual rather than sudden. Even continuity of the body per se seems inessential, however, since we can imagine cases where a person's brain is transplanted from one body to another and his old body destroyed, but where it would be plausible to say that he has survived as the same person in this new body. So it is, strictly speaking, continuity of a particular *part* of the body—the brain, the physical seat of one's personality and psychological traits in general—that is crucial to personal identity on a bodily-continuity theory.

Perhaps the problem is now obvious. If the *brain* is what is essential to personal identity on a bodily-continuity theory, then the *rest* of the body becomes as much a resource *external* to the self on such a theory as it did on the Cartesian dualist theory.[18] The self-ownership proviso will once again apply to the use of the body as much as to the use of any other external resource, and the untoward consequences described above (apart from those involving the brain, which now becomes essential to the self) more or less follow for the bodily-continuity theory as for the Cartesian theory.

Thus, the bodily-continuity theory is at least just as bad as the Cartesian dualist theory where advocacy of an attractive and robust notion of self-ownership is concerned. Why might it even be worse? Consider one of the bizarre science-fiction scenarios often used by philosophers to illustrate the conceptual puzzles posed by personal identity—the "fission" scenario. We can imagine that the two halves of a person's brain are divided and placed into two different bodies cloned from the person's original body. It is at least possible (so those who make use of the scenario assure us, anyway) that the psychological characteristics associated with the person's original, united brain could carry over unaltered into each of

[18] But isn't the brain, unlike a Cartesian immaterial substance, dependent on the body for its very survival? And if so, wouldn't the body be essential to it (and thus part of the self)? The answer to both questions is no: the brain could at least in principle survive without its body (e.g., in a vat of nutrients); and even if it couldn't, this wouldn't make the body any less external to the brain (and thus, on the proposal in question, the self) than is any other resource one depends on for survival (e.g., food and water).

the halves (since we know from neuroscience that the functions associated with a part of the brain that becomes damaged or even destroyed can often be taken over by other parts of the brain). The result would be two persons, each of whom thinks of himself as the original person and each of whom is continuous brain-wise with the original person.

Such a scenario poses obvious difficulties for any possibility of robust self-ownership. For example, the original person no doubt acquired a certain amount of wealth with his self-owned labor—wealth that, in general (and other than the part of it that he ought to pay to help fund the minimal state, etc.), he was entitled to on the view of the self-ownership advocate. But which of the two persons resulting from the fission is now entitled to that wealth? Given that they are both physically continuous with the original, the bodily-continuity theorist would presumably have to say that they are both entitled to it. But they cannot both keep all the wealth. And if one of them takes it all, the other can legitimately claim that his self-ownership rights have been violated; after all, he is equally continuous with, and thus also the same person as, the person whose self-owned powers originally acquired the wealth. However, if instead the wealth is divided between them, they both now have cause to complain, for neither gets the full amount to which he is entitled.[19] The bodily-continuity theory, then, even more than Cartesian dualism, seems to have untoward consequences for self-ownership.

These considerations bring to mind another sort of personal identity theory, namely psychological-continuity theories—and also indicate that these theories too will suffer from the same problems as bodily-continuity theories do where self-ownership is concerned. Psychological-continuity theories—sometimes called psychological continuity and connectedness (or psychological C & C) theories—hold that it is not continuity of the body or brain per se that is crucial to personal identity, but rather continuity of psychological characteristics, such as personality traits, behavioral patterns, and memories. (This sort of theory descends from Locke's memory theory of personal identity, which is really just a special case of a psychological C & C theory.) If a later person has psychological characteristics that are continuous with those of an earlier person, and the continuity of those characteristics is due to the right sort of causal connection between the earlier and later persons, then the later person is identical to the earlier one. (The inclusion of the idea of "the right sort of causal connection" in the theory is intended to allow it to avoid counterexamples where, say, some delusional person alive today has Napoleonic

---

[19] This scenario also implies that even "the brain," full stop, cannot be essential to a person, and thus untouched by the self-ownership proviso. All that can really be so untouched is *however much of the brain is necessary to preserve continuity of the self.* If that turns out to be 50 percent of the brain, say, then the other 50 percent becomes as much a resource external to the self as the rest of the body is, and can in principle be interfered with if the self-ownership proviso requires it.

personality traits and vivid pseudo-memories of fighting at Waterloo, but nevertheless is obviously not Napoleon.)

Psychological C & C theorists typically hold the "right" sort of causal connection to involve continuity of brain processes—for example, the later person must have not only the memories, say, of the earlier one, but those memories must be linked to a brain that is continuous with that of the earlier person—so that the brain becomes as central to the psychological-continuity theory as it is to the bodily-continuity theory. But then the problems resulting from the possibility of fission and the like plague the former theory as much as they do the latter. Psychological C & C theories also face unique bizarre and problem-generating scenarios of their own, such as the "teletransportation" scenario, wherein a person steps into a teleportation machine on Earth, all the information about his brain and body is scanned by a supercomputer and beamed to Mars, and his body is then destroyed as an exact copy of it appears in a similar machine on the red planet.[20] The person who walks out of the machine on Mars could have all the psychological characteristics of the person who stepped into the machine on Earth, and given that he is thus psychologically continuous, we can conclude that he is the same person as the latter. We can also imagine, however, that the copy walks out of the machine on Mars while the body on Earth is *not* destroyed, or that due to some programming glitch or a prankster operating the machine on Mars, *two* copies rather than one walk out of the machine. Here we have a scenario analogous to the fission scenario, and with the same problematic consequences for a robust and attractive conception of self-ownership.[21]

VI. Nozick's "Closest Continuer" Theory

Of course, given that it seems impossible that *both* persons resulting from the fission or teletransportation glitch could be identical to the original person, since they are clearly not identical to *each other*, many philosophers would argue that in such cases the original person in effect *ceases to exist* when the split occurs, to be replaced by two new and distinct persons. They would suggest that the continuity emphasized by the theories we have been discussing must be *unique* or "non-branching" if personal identity is to be preserved. But this does not sit well with the intuition that continuity of the brain and/or of psychological traits is the key to continuity of the person. For there *is* such continuity in these cases:

[20] See Derek Parfit, *Reasons and Persons* (Oxford: Clarendon Press, 1984), 199–200.

[21] An additional problem with psychological C & C theories is that insofar as they imply that personhood exists only when certain psychological characteristics do, they thereby imply (as I earlier suggested the Cartesian view does) that the body of an infant, or at least a fetus, which has not yet developed these characteristics can be regarded as a raw natural resource which may in principle be acquired by others as their property (since there is no person associated with it who can be said to own it).

how can it fail to guarantee that the person survives the fission or the teletransportation glitch? Suppose that after the halves of the brain had been divided and one of them placed in a cloned body, the other half had been completely destroyed, or that the teletransportation had gone exactly according to plan, so that there was in either case only one person continuous with the original. In these cases it would seem plausible that the original person has survived. How, then, can the existence of a *second* person continuous with the original make any difference?

Nozick himself put forward a theory of personal identity intended to deal with this question.[22] In his view, it is not strictly speaking just *any* later person who is continuous with, or who "continues," the earlier person, who is identical to him; it is, rather, the later person who *most closely* continues the earlier one, who is identical. If we imagine that in the fission case the person's brain is divided not in half exactly, but rather that 51 percent of it goes into one body and 49 percent into the other, we can say that the person who wakes up in the first body, having more of the original person's brain, more closely continues the original, and is thus identical with the original. The second person, having less of the brain—and thus, though continuous with the original person, not the *closest* continuer—is not identical to the original person, but is rather a new person. In the variation on the teletransportation case where the original body is not destroyed, it is the person in that original body who most closely continues the original person and is thus identical with the original, with the person appearing on Mars being a new person. In cases where there is no single closest continuer, though—such as in the original 50-50 fission scenario or the "prankster" variation on the teletransportation case in which the original body is destroyed and *two* copies appear on Mars—there is no survival of the original person. That original person has, in effect, died and been replaced by mere duplicates.

An interesting—and bizarre—feature of this theory (and of "non-branching" continuity theories too) is that it makes the identity and survival of a person dependent on factors completely external to him. Consider again the post-fission person with 49 percent of the original's brain. Had the other 51 percent not been transplanted but instead completely destroyed, then the person with the 49 percent of the brain *would* have been the closest continuer of the original and thus *would* have been identical with him. Indeed, if the person with the 51 percent of the original brain were to die only a few moments after he and the person with the 49 percent both awoke from the transplant surgery, it would seem to follow that the latter would suddenly *become* identical with the original person after a few moments of *not* being identical, having suddenly become the closest continuer to the original! Consider again also the "prankster"

---

[22] Robert Nozick, *Philosophical Explanations* (Cambridge, MA: Belknap Press, 1981), chapter 1.

variation on the teletransportation case. When the two copies walk out of the machine on Mars, Nozick's theory says that neither is identical to the original—who has, in effect, died—because neither is the *closest* continuer. But suppose the prankster, having quickly grown bored with his joke, pulls out a ray gun a few seconds after the teletransportation and disintegrates one of the copies. Does the remaining copy now suddenly become identical to the original person, since he is now the single closest continuer? Has the original, who had "died" a few seconds before, now suddenly been "resurrected"—by virtue of some other, duplicate body having been destroyed?!

As these strange possibilities indicate, Nozick's theory takes personal identity to be an *extrinsic* relation, determined at least in part by factors outside of the person himself. One and the same individual—a post-fission recipient of 49 percent of someone's brain—may or may not be identical to an earlier person depending on factors completely unrelated to anything going on in that individual. If someone else gets the remaining 51 percent percent, the recipient of the 49 percent is *not* identical; if that 51 percent is instead destroyed, he *is* identical. Either way, what happens in the body, brain, and mental life of the recipient of the 49 percent is insufficient for identity. Similarly, whether an individual who steps out of the machine on Mars is identical to the original depends, ultimately, not on whether his psychological traits are continuous with the original's, but on whether a second individual steps out of the machine. The prankster's whim (whether or not he decides to fiddle with the wiring of a machine, say), and not what is going on in the body or mind of the person who walks out of the machine, determines whether that person is identical to the original, and thus whether the original has survived.

This has, understandably, seemed to many philosophers to be counterintuitive, even absurd. More relevant to our interests, though, is that it makes the closest continuer theory (and indeed, any "extrinsic" theory of personal identity) incompatible with a robust and attractive notion of self-ownership (ironically enough, given that Nozick, perhaps the foremost champion of self-ownership in contemporary philosophy, originated the theory). For example, it can hardly be said that one's self-ownership-generated rights to the fruits of one's labor are secure when the metaphysics of the self makes its survival hinge on the proper functioning of a machine thousands of miles away or the presence or absence of a few neurons. A person waking up from a fission operation must worry about whether he will be entitled to the wealth he remembers working many long years to accrue or whether he will be left penniless: his fate will be determined, not by whether his physical and psychological characteristics are continuous with the person he seems to remember being (for they are so continuous), but rather by whether the neurosurgeon has, through malice, whim, or error, placed one or two neurons in this body or that, or instead just thrown them into the trash. A person stepping out of the teletransporter must have similar worries, since *his* fate may be determined by something as trivial as a power surge or a machine operator's morbid sense of humor.

There is also the fact that the closest continuer theory is in essence merely a modification of a bodily continuity or psychological C & C theory. Such theories, as we have seen, have a tendency to isolate the locus of selfhood at whatever part of the brain is responsible for maintaining continuity of psychological characteristics. Like these other theories, then, the closest continuer theory must make the body something largely external to the self, and thus eligible for interference by others, given the self-ownership proviso. Indeed, a similar problem will afflict every theory—whether Cartesian or materialist—that "externalizes" the body, making it less than essential to the self.[23]

VII. PARFIT'S THEORY

The non-Cartesian theories we have been considering may be even worse, where compatibility with self-ownership is concerned, than has been suggested already. The bodily-continuity, psychological C & C, and closest continuer theories are, unlike the Cartesian view, all *reductionist* accounts of the self. They all hold that the self is not the simple, unified, and irreducible entity Descartes took it to be, but ought instead to be analyzed as being really "nothing but" something else—a continuous chain of bodily stages or psychological characteristics, say. Derek Parfit has argued that if we endorse such theories, we ought to go on to conclude that personal identity per se does not matter.[24] The objective facts about personal identity turn out, on these theories, to consist of nothing more than facts about the continuity of certain bodily and/or psychological characteristics. Such continuity, then, is all that really matters, and identity as such drops out as irrelevant, and even misleading. We ought not to be puzzled or concerned over whether a person would survive a fission operation or teletransportation glitch, because the facts about the continuities involved are all the facts there are in the first place. To assert or deny that any person who wakes up after the operation or steps out of the machine is or is not identical to the original is, in Parfit's view, not to assert or deny anything factual or objectively true or false. All that can be said of a factual nature is that there are certain degrees of continuity. Anything more than this—in particular, any talk about whether the self or

---

[23] This will include, e.g., functionalist theories that make the self out to be a kind of computer program, only contingently connected to the "hardware" of the body it is "implemented" in.

[24] See Parfit, *Reasons and Persons;* and Derek Parfit, "The Unimportance of Identity," in Raymond Martin and John Barresi, eds., *Personal Identity* (Oxford: Blackwell, 2003).

person does or does not continue to exist—is a matter of mere linguistic convention, a decision about how to use the *words* "self" and "person."

Parfit's view has its own dire consequences for self-ownership. Consider an example of Parfit's involving his brain being removed from his paralyzed body and being put into the healthy body of a hypothetical twin brother, whose own diseased brain has ceased to function.[25] Who will be the person who wakes up after the transplant operation? On some versions of the bodily-continuity theory, it would be Parfit's brother who wakes up, for the body of the person who wakes up will be mostly continuous with that of the brother. On other versions, such as the ones we have been considering, and on the psychological C & C theory, it will be Parfit himself who wakes up. Parfit's own view is that the question simply does not matter. There will be certain continuities between, on the one hand, the post-surgery person who wakes up, and on the other hand, the pre-surgery Parfit and his twin brother; and there also will be certain discontinuities. And that is all that can be said. There is no fact of the matter beyond the various continuities and discontinuities about which person has survived or even if either of them has survived.

But let us alter the example slightly by imagining that Parfit's hypothetical twin brother had a mental life qualitatively identical to Parfit's own—because they were both controlled by the same mad scientist or Cartesian demon, or whatever. Now suppose that Parfit *murders* the twin brother to get the body, and his own brain is transplanted into it. Who wakes up after the operation? Advocates of the theories we have been considering could make equally good cases for any possible answer; and Parfit himself would again answer that there is no fact of the matter. But then it seems that there just is no one who has been harmed by, and thus no one who has any reason for complaint about, the murder that Parfit would have committed in order to make the operation possible. Indeed, there would not truly have *been* a murder in the first place, since there was no one alive before the "murder" who can plausibly be said, on Parfit's view, not to exist now. But not only is this counterintuitive, it is clearly inconsistent with any robust and interesting concept of self-ownership: surely self-ownership becomes meaningless when a murder does not count as a murder.

That his theory of personal identity is incompatible with self-ownership is not likely to trouble Parfit, however, for by his own reckoning that theory is really incompatible with any robust notion of the *self* in the first place. Parfit takes his view—and indeed, any reductionist theory—to be committed to a "bundle" conception of the self of the sort associated with David Hume and some varieties of Buddhism.[26] On such a view the self

[25] Parfit, "The Unimportance of Identity," 308–9.
[26] See David Hume, *A Treatise of Human Nature* (Oxford: Clarendon Press, 1978), book I, part IV, section VI; and, for quotes from some relevant Buddhist texts, Parfit, *Reasons and Persons*, 502–3.

is nothing more than a collection of qualities or characteristics, such as a continuous chain of certain bodily and/or psychological traits; or rather, strictly speaking, such traits are all that exist, and there *is no* self per se at all. Surely the apparent consequences for self-ownership could not be more drastic: if there is, strictly speaking, no self, then there is also, strictly speaking, nothing there either to own or to be owned.[27]

Parfit would no doubt be untroubled by this result; indeed, he finds the abandonment of the notion of the self "liberating, and consoling," and suggests that such abandonment is bound to make one less selfish and "more concerned about the lives of others."[28] Indeed, he takes views like his to herald a bold and hopeful new beginning in human history, and the possibility of a distinctly "non-religious ethics" the "free development" of which will not be "prevented [by] . . . belief in God."[29] One might reasonably doubt the wisdom of such sanguinity, however, unless one thinks it an accident that the political freedoms, economic prosperity, and consequent material and social well-being that the modern world has brought us developed in the very civilization that has made the inviolability of the individual its central social value: the Judeo-Christian West. There can be no meaningful notion of rights, in either the political or the economic sphere, without a concrete individual self to bear those rights; nor can there be any genuine respect for persons, in the Kantian sense of refusing to treat them as mere means, if there are no persons in the first place. Accordingly, it seems hardly surprising that it is precisely in the West, the cultural story of which has largely been one of an increasing emphasis on the dignity of the person—made in the image of a God who is Himself essentially personal, who became incarnate in a particular individual human being, and who created the world precisely for human habitation—that the concepts of natural rights and a Kantian respect for persons, with all the beneficial sociopolitical implications that these have had, first appeared. Nor is it surprising that they did *not* appear in the East, with its tendencies toward impersonal and abstract conceptions of deity, and toward seeing the self as an illusion and human history as an insignificant eddy in an endless, pointless river of time. Metaphysical *avant-gardists* of the Parfitian stripe ought to think twice before abandoning concepts so central to the heritage of the West and so foundational to its moral and social achievements, achievements most of them would profess to value.

---

[27] Something similar can be said for any other view that is less than realist about the self. Instrumentalist views of intentionality, for instance, on which the mind (and thus the self) is but a convenient fiction—a useful concept to apply when predicting human behavior, but one which fails to refer to any objective reality—would seem obviously deficient as a basis for a robust conception of self-ownership. Eliminativist views about the mind, which regard it as a fiction full stop, are even more blatantly incompatible with robust self-ownership.

[28] Parfit, *Reasons and Persons*, 281.

[29] Ibid., 454.

VIII. Hylemorphism

In any event, the question that now arises is whether there is any notion of personal identity left that can ground self-ownership. Such a conception would, if Parfit is right, have to construe the self as irreducible, as Descartes held it to be, and thus not subject to the bizarre consequences plaguing the various reductionist views we have looked at; but it would also have to avoid the Cartesian tendency to externalize the body. Is there such a conception? There is: the hylemorphic conception of human nature associated with the Aristotelian and (especially) Thomistic traditions.[30] The term "hylemorphism" derives from the Greek words *hyle* (or "matter") and *morphe* (or "form"), and the view holds that the relationship between the body and the soul—the seat of rationality and personality—is an instance of the relationship between matter and form generally. The soul, that is to say, is the substantial form of the body—that which makes it the distinct kind of thing it is. The human *person*, on this conception, is thus a composite of form and matter, soul and body: neither the soul alone nor the body alone counts as a complete person, any more than a chunk of matter counts as a desk apart from its having the form of a desk, or than the form of a desk counts as a desk without having matter to instantiate it.[31] Of course, especially on the view of Thomas Aquinas, the soul is uniquely associated with mental life, and, being immaterial, can continue to exist beyond the body's death (making the view in question a kind of dualism); but it does *not* continue to exist *as a complete person*— hence the need in Aquinas's view, if personal immortality is fully to be secured, for a resurrection of the body and its reunion with the soul. In this regard, the hylemorphic view is like the Cartesian view as I said earlier it *ought* to be understood, as opposed to the standard caricature of the Cartesian view. It is also like the Cartesian view in taking the soul to be simple and irreducible. But since it conceives of the soul as a *form*, and

---

[30] See Aristotle's *De Anima* and Aquinas's *Summa Theologiae* I, questions 75–89, for the classic statements of the view, and David Oderberg's essay in this volume for a more detailed exposition and defense than I have space to give here.

[31] This distinguishes hylemorphism from a view that might appear similar to it, namely, the variation on the bodily-continuity theory that takes a human being to be identical to a kind of *animal*. See, e.g., Eric T. Olson, *The Human Animal: Personal Identity without Psychology* (New York: Oxford University Press, 1997). For that view seems to entail that our psychological traits are not essential to us: were your cerebrum to be removed and put into another body, the rest of your body would, if it survived, still be the same animal (now just missing an organ) and thus the same human being. It, and it alone, would be *you*—even though some other body (the one that received your cerebrum) would now have (what used to be) your thoughts, memories, etc. On the hylemorphic view, though, you are essentially an *embodied soul*: both the bodily and the psychological (and thus distinctly personal) aspects are essential. Note also that insofar as the "animal" view seems to externalize one's distinctly psychological traits, it may entail that they are as subject to outside interference as I have argued bodily traits are on the Cartesian and bodily- and psychological-continuity theories, so that the "animal" view is equally incompatible with robust self-ownership.

in particular the form *of the body,* it does not have the Cartesian difficulty of leaving it mysterious how the body could be part of the self.[32]

Of course, this view like any other requires defense. My purpose here, however, is to determine whether it is compatible with self-ownership; and I would argue that it is. Given that, on the hylemorphic view, the body is as essential to a person qua person as the soul is, there is no danger of the body's being "externalized" or alienated from the self, and thus made subject in principle to interference by others on the basis of the self-ownership proviso.

But what of the bizarre and problematic scenarios we have considered, which like the standard interpretation of the Cartesian view seem in principle to undermine the possibility of a robust and attractive concept of self-ownership? Aren't these as possible on the hylemorphic conception as on the various reductionist accounts? In fact, they are not. The reason is the same as the reason they must be counted impossible on a Cartesian account. If the self is, as Cartesianism holds, a simple immaterial substance, then no amount of surgery or teletransportation, involving as they do the manipulation of purely *material* substances, can do anything more than duplicate mere bodies; they cannot, that is, create duplicate *persons.* These scenarios can be ruled out a priori, then. Similarly, since the soul, being a form, is on the hylemorphic view something simple and immaterial, there can be no question of duplicating it via fission or teletransportation. These scenarios are thus as a priori impossible on hylemorphism as on Cartesianism. This claim might seem implausible, but only if one assumes that there is no strong case to be made for Cartesianism or hylemorphism. If there *is* a strong case, though, then that case will ipso facto be a case for ruling out fission and the like a priori.[33]

---

[32] Strictly speaking, then, the Cartesian view *rightly understood,* as opposed to the stock caricature of the Cartesian view, is as compatible with self-ownership as I hold the Thomistic view to be. But the Thomistic view is, I think, metaphysically superior, partly for the reasons hinted at in the text.

[33] I try to make such a case—for Thomistic hylemorphism in particular, but also for the cogency of Cartesian arguments against materialism—in Feser, *Philosophy of Mind: A Short Introduction.* I would also tentatively suggest, as a way of mitigating the apparent implausibility of ruling out the fission and teletransportation cases a priori, that these scenarios be interpreted as follows: In the teletransportation case, if two people really *do* step out of the machine, then this is due to the creation by God of a new soul (and thus a totally new person) to go along with the new body, leaving us with psychologically identical twins; one of the two is the original and the other the duplicate, though only God, Who created the new soul, will know who is who. (Of course, this presupposes theism, but theism is something the Thomist is going to argue for independently in any case—and theism is hardly more eccentric than the teletransportation scenario itself!) In the fission case, what we have is neither the death of the original person, nor the creation of two new persons, but rather the continuation of the original person in a highly eccentric form. The organs of his body—of which his (necessarily still fully intact) soul, with its psychological characteristics, is the form—have been spatially separated, but are still organs of the same one person. And if the placement of the two brain halves in different bodies now results in two streams of experience, this is merely an extreme case of the dissociation and incoherence that can result from any kind of brain damage: the one person now gets sensory input via two bodies and his

If I am right, then, a commitment to self-ownership must entail a commitment to an Aristotelian-Thomistic hylemorphic conception of persons. But one might wonder whether advocates of hylemorphism, and in particular Aristotelians and Thomists, could *welcome* the addition to their ranks of self-ownership theorists. For isn't self-ownership simply too modern and too individualistic an idea to sit comfortably with the sort of political and moral philosophy usually associated with Aristotle and Aquinas?

This is a large topic, to say the least. Suffice it for now to make the following observations. It is true that the classical political philosophy associated with Aristotelianism and Thomism take man to be a social animal, and a political animal. To be a social animal, however, is not the same as to be a *socialist* animal; and to be a political animal is not the same as to take all matters of social concern rightly to be settled by litigation and the setting up of a vast central government. It cannot be emphasized too strongly that the modern representatives of classical Aristotelian, and especially of Thomistic, political thinking, including (what must be a significant fact for Thomists) the modern popes from Leo XIII to John Paul II, have often been as strident in criticizing socialism, and sometimes also the bureaucratic welfare state, as have the most ardent defenders of capitalism. Moreover, the *reasons* for the criticism have overlapped to a very great extent: a respect for the right of a man to the fruits of his labor and for private property in general, and an emphasis on subsidiarity as essential to a just and humane social order, leading the popes no less than modern libertarians to prefer, as far as possible, that social problems be dealt with by the intermediate institutions of civil society, and without resorting to state intervention. Of course, to claim that an explicit commitment to the thesis of self-ownership is common to both sets of reasons would be to go too far; but it would also go too far to deny that there may be important implicit conceptual connections between these sets of reasons. Again, the writings of the popes are instructive here. It has often been remarked how *Lockean* are some of the arguments in Leo XIII's encyclical *Rerum Novarum*.[34] And a quasi-Kantian respect for persons permeates the Thomistic personalism of John Paul II, echoing the Kantian

---

cognitive processes are thereby massively disrupted, but he remains the same one person nonetheless. These suggestions would, of course, require further development and defense to be fully convincing.

[34] Leo XIII, *Rerum Novarum*, reprinted in *Catholic Social Thought: The Documentary Heritage*, ed. David J. O'Brien and Thomas A. Shannon (Maryknoll, NY: Orbis Books, 1992). See especially the discussion of private property in sections 4–8, where among other things Leo says (in section 7, echoing Locke's "labor-mixing" theory of the initial acquisition of property): "Now, when man thus spends the industry of his mind and the strength of his body in procuring the fruits of nature by that act he makes his own that portion of nature's field which he cultivates—that portion on which he leaves, as it were, the impress of his own personality, and it cannot but be just that he should possess that portion as his own, and should have a right to keep it without molestation." The similarity to Locke is discussed in Robert A. Sirico, CSP, "Catholicism's Developing Social Teaching," *The Freeman* 41, no. 12 (December 1991).

prohibition of using people as means that Nozick takes to go hand in hand with self-ownership.[35]

It is true that one finds no full-throated endorsement of capitalism in the writings of the popes, and indeed often finds criticism of conditions extant in capitalist societies (especially in Pius XI's encyclical *Quadragesimo Anno*). But one also never finds an outright *rejection* of capitalism as such, as one finds a decisive rejection of socialism; indeed, one even finds (especially in John Paul II's *Centesimus Annus*) a qualified acceptance of capitalism as compatible in principle with a broadly Thomistic social philosophy, and as unavoidable in practice. And the notions of *ownership* and *property*, so central to the arguments of defenders of capitalism in general and self-ownership advocates in particular, are arguably also central to the social thought of writers in the Thomistic natural law tradition, with all the "individualism" that that implies. As G. K. Chesterton noted, the broader Christian tradition of which the natural law tradition is a part holds to an ethic, not of "sharing," but of *giving* and of *sacrifice*.[36] One "shares" what one holds in common with others. But one can only give and sacrifice what is one's to give or sacrifice in the first place—that is, what one *owns*. This can hardly fail to be as true of one's self—and one is called within Christianity to give of oneself and to sacrifice oneself—as it is of any external piece of property.

Given these considerations, and also the too often ignored subtleties in the Nozickian position in political philosophy elaborated earlier, the gap some might see between the thesis of self-ownership and the kind of moral theory usually associated with defenders of hylemorphism may be more apparent than real. Moreover, it is surely significant that many advocates of the thesis of self-ownership, and/or of the social and political consequences it is normally thought to have, take their inspiration from Aristotle and the Thomistic natural law tradition.[37] This is not to deny that spelling out the precise relationship between a broadly Aristotelian or Thomistic metaphysics and ethics (on the one hand) and the ideas of self-ownership and capitalism (on the other) is a matter of great complexity; the point is rather that there is no good reason to dismiss the possibility of harmony between them as a priori implausible. Nor is it to

---

[35] For accessible introductions to the philosophy of John Paul II (a.k.a. Karol Wojtyla), see Peter Simpson, *On Karol Wojtyla* (Belmont, CA: Wadsworth, 2001); and Rocco Buttiglione, *Karol Wojtyla: The Thought of the Man Who Became Pope John Paul II* (Grand Rapids, MI: William B. Eerdmans, 1997).

[36] G. K. Chesterton, "Why I Am Not a Socialist," reprinted in *The Chesterton Review* 7 (August 1981): 189–95.

[37] For writers influenced by the Aristotelian tradition, see, e.g., Fred D. Miller, Jr., *Nature, Justice, and Rights in Aristotle's "Politics"* (Oxford: Clarendon Press, 1995); and Douglas B. Rasmussen and Douglas J. Den Uyl, *Liberty and Nature: An Aristotelian Defense of Liberal Order* (La Salle, IL: Open Court, 1991). For writers influenced by natural law, see, e.g., Alejandro A. Chafuen, *Faith and Liberty: The Economic Thought of the Late Scholastics* (New York: Lexington Books, 2003); and Murray N. Rothbard, *The Ethics of Liberty* (New York: New York University Press, 1998).

deny that an Aristotelian and/or Thomistically inspired account of self-ownership is bound in many ways to differ in substance from the understanding of self-ownership sometimes operative in popular libertarianism: even if the former account should allow for a significant degree of liberty in the economic and political spheres, it will surely *not* allow for libertinism. To claim to own oneself need not be to avow moral subjectivism. The notion of self-ownership might instead be better understood as just the application of the seventh commandment to persons: one has, in general, no more right to take from a man without his consent his labor and its fruits than one has the right to steal his property.

There may even be implications for the extent to which the state may intervene to shore up traditional morality, as understood from a natural law perspective. Given the self-ownership proviso, the state has, at least in principle and in some circumstances, the right to keep one from using one's property in a way that nullifies another's self-owned capacities and powers. Among those capacities and powers, however, are distinctly *moral* capacities; and on an Aristotelian and Thomistic conception of morality, such capacities can only be developed through training and practice of the virtues, and in the context of an environment conducive to such practice. An environment resolutely hostile to such practice can severely impede the possibility of developing moral virtue, and even, in children at least, nearly nullify it altogether. There would seem in principle to be grounds, then, for government to ensure, to some extent, that individuals do not use their property in such a way that they practically nullify the capacity for persons, especially children, properly to develop their self-owned moral powers: for government to fail to do so would be for it to violate the rights of its citizens, who have a natural right, given the self-ownership proviso, to an environment in which the practice of the virtues is possible. Such considerations would not justify the law in interfering with what goes on between consenting adults behind closed doors, and of course, the general libertarian concerns about placing too much authority in the hands of central government still hold. But these considerations may in principle allow at least local governments to regulate *public* activities that have a dramatic effect on the moral climate of a community. Advocacy of self-ownership, when informed by the Thomism that I have argued is its only secure metaphysical foundation, may have conservative implications as well as libertarian ones.[38]

IX. Conclusion

I suggested earlier that the concept of the self is an inherently moralized one, making it difficult to get an objective fix on the concept. It

---

[38] I develop and defend these suggestions at greater length in "Self-Ownership, Abortion, and the Rights of Children: Toward a More Conservative Libertarianism," *Journal of Libertarian Studies* 18, no. 3 (2004).

should not be thought, however, that such objectivity is exclusively, or even primarily, a difficulty for the partisans of self-ownership, as opposed to their critics. For it may be that the ownership arguably entailed by selfhood is precisely part of what moves certain critics of self-ownership, and of allied moral notions like those of rights and property, to adopt certain theories of personal identity—theories on which the self effectively disappears, and with it the offending moral notions. Indeed, there do seem to be connections, both conceptual and sociological, between (on the one hand) a robust conception of the self and an ethic of strong private property rights, and (on the other hand) a weak conception of the self and hostility toward private property. The mainstream tradition of the West confirms the former correlation. The recent history of the Western intelligentsia, with its attachment to socialism and to skeptical and reductionist metaphysical conceptions, and its hostility toward monotheism and fascination with non-Western, depersonalized conceptions of deity and of reality in general, confirms the latter. So too does the Marxist tendency to combine a program of abolition of private property with a crudely materialistic conception of human beings as mere cogs in a vast social-historical machine, and the Rawlsian tendency, criticized by Nozick, to treat every concrete attribute of persons, including their talents, labor, and the products of these, as "arbitrary from a moral point of view" and subject to the redistributive machinations of the state.[39]

Metaphysics and morality cannot be divorced. The Thomistically-inspired metaphysics of the person that I would endorse is not something I have tried to defend here, nor have I tried to refute rival views.[40] I have, however, tried to show what moral and social implications those rival views might have, implications that include a denial of any robust conception of self-ownership. Insofar as the history of the twentieth century gives considerable reason to believe that the abandonment of the notion of a self-owning bearer of inviolable rights cannot fail to have unhappy practical consequences, that history also gives considerable reason to take a hard look at those rivals before one endorses them—and to take a second look at the Thomistic alternative.

Philosophy, Loyola Marymount University

[39] John Rawls, *A Theory of Justice* (Cambridge, MA: Harvard University Press, 1971), 72.
[40] But see Feser, *Philosophy of Mind*, for such defense and criticism.

SELF-CONCEPTION AND PERSONAL IDENTITY: REVISITING PARFIT AND LEWIS WITH AN EYE ON THE GRIP OF THE UNITY REACTION*

By Marvin Belzer

I. Introduction

Derek Parfit says in *Reasons and Persons* that he decided to study philosophy "almost entirely because [he] was enthralled" by the possibility of personal fission, that is, a person dividing in the manner of an amoeba.[1] In 1971 he published an article, "Personal Identity" (hereafter '71),[2] in which he sketched the themes that he later developed (with a few revisions) in Part III of *Reasons and Persons* (hereafter *R&P*). One of his themes is the so-called *reductionist* thesis that

> personal identity through time is constituted by ("reduced to") relations between mental and physical states and events in the absence of anything like a necessarily determinate and indivisible soul.

A second general theme is that some of our commonsensical beliefs about rationality and morality need to be revised given the reductionist thesis (especially its rejection of a necessarily determinate entity at the center of our existence as persons). The possibility of fission plays a central role in Parfit's arguments for the practical ramifications of the reductionist thesis. For example, he argues that identity is not "what matters," and his argument is based on his analysis of fission—in such a case, he argues, one would not survive the fission but nonetheless one would have *what matters* in survival (that is, one would have what one should care about insofar as one wishes to survive into the future).

* Earlier versions of this paper were presented at the philosophy departments at Rutgers University and Bowling Green State University. I am indebted to many members of these audiences, and to the other contributors to this volume, for their comments—especially Frank Arntzenius, Michael Bradie, David Copp, John Finnis, Jerry Fodor, Brian Loar, Barry Loewer, Colin McGinn, Fred Miller, Mark Moyer, David Oderberg, Marya Schechtman, David Schmidtz, David Sobel, and Sara Worley. Special thanks to David Sanford. I am also grateful to graduate students in my seminar at Bowling Green during the spring of 2003, for urging me to take seriously the grip of the unity reaction; I am especially grateful for the comments of Nico Maloberti, Jonathan Miller, John Milliken, Robyn Peabody, Jennifer Sproul, Jessica Teaman, and Sherisse Webb.

[1] Derek Parfit, *Reasons and Persons* (Oxford: Clarendon Press, 1984), 518. For Parfit's description of fission, see in ibid., 254–55.

[2] Derek Parfit, "Personal Identity," *Philosophical Review* 80 (1971): 3–27. Reprinted in John Perry, ed., *Personal Identity* (Berkeley: University of California Press, 1975).

This startling conclusion conflicts with our common-sense self-conceptions insofar as we would tend to assume that we can imagine having *what matters in survival* only by *continuing to exist,* no matter how far-fetched the situation may be. Roderick Chisholm said it was "clear and distinct" to him that in fission either he determinately would survive as one or the other of the post-fission people (and would have what matters in survival by virtue of being identical with one or the other), or he determinately would not survive at all (and determinately would *not* have what matters in survival). Chisholm simply sets aside the idea that as persons we are subject to the vagaries, including puzzles about fission, to which ordinary physical objects like ships and tables are subject.[3] The intuition of essential self-unity to which Chisholm appeals is indeed "very strong in us."[4] Simon Blackburn holds that a "unity reaction" to the fission thought experiment has an "absolute grip" on our understanding of our roles as agents who deliberate and act on the basis of practical reasoning; the presupposition of essential unity is ineliminably at the core of our self-conceptions as agents. The "unity reaction" might be expressed as follows:

> As persons we are essentially unified, indivisible, even in the absence of anything like a necessarily determinate and indivisible soul.

The central issue arising out of reflection on fission—"the only specific problem in the area," as Blackburn says—is "that of understanding and giving due weight to the unity reaction."[5]

Parfit's own formulation (and rejection) of the unity reaction is found in his argument that "identity is not what matters" as well as in his later "Extreme claim" arguments that, given the reductionist thesis, personal existence through time does not underwrite justifiable anticipation, punishment, commitment, or intrapersonal compensation.[6] In response to Parfit's '71, however, David Lewis downplayed the conflict between reductionism and common sense, arguing that there is no real conflict between common-sense self-conceptions and a reductionist interpretation of fis-

---

[3] Roderick M. Chisholm, "Reply to Strawson's Comments," in H. E. Kiefer and Milton K. Munitz, eds., *Language, Belief, and Metaphysics* (Albany, NY: SUNY Press, 1970).

[4] As Judith Jarvis Thomson puts it. Even though she is inclined to resist the intuition of essential unity, Thomson suggests that "it has not been taken seriously enough in the contemporary literature on personal identity: people do not ask exactly why it has such a grip on us." Judith Jarvis Thomson, "People and Their Bodies," in Jonathan Dancy, ed., *Reading Parfit* (Oxford: Blackwell, 1997): 225.

[5] Simon Blackburn, "Has Kant Refuted Parfit?" in Dancy, ed., *Reading Parfit,* 181.

[6] Derek Parfit, "Comments," *Ethics* 96, no. 4 (1986): 832–72. In *Reasons and Persons,* Parfit had mentioned such claims but had not tried to defend them. "Intrapersonal compensation" means benefiting a person at one time for sacrifices made by that person at a different time (as, for example, in disciplining a child for the sake of the future adult he or she will become).

sion.[7] Lewis claims on behalf of common sense that the reductionist need not posit a revisionist logical wedge between personal identity and what matters in survival.

If Lewis is right, there is no serious conflict between the reductionist thesis and the unity reaction. The debate between Parfit and Lewis on this point is worth revisiting because an examination of some details of their dispute will help clarify the relationship between the unity reaction and the reductionist thesis. There are five basic points (with the final two points to be stated shortly). I will explain (1) why Parfit wins the point with Lewis about the question of whether their shared metaphysical views entail conflict with common sense, since Lewis simply assumes that identity (that is, commonsensical self-unity) does not matter. I also will explain (2) why Parfit's own reply to Lewis fell short. Moreover, (3) if one accepts Lewis's presupposition that his own unity relation (the I-relation) need not be an equivalence relation, an alternative account that treats Lewis's I-relation as not symmetrical provides a superior treatment of fission. Yet this superior treatment just *is* Parfit's '71 account, and thus, bracketing a few differences, we can speak simply of *the* '71/Lewis account.

The '71/Lewis account has virtues that are lacking in the slightly revised version that Parfit himself offered later, in 1984, in *Reasons and Persons*, and upon which he bases the arguments in his "Comments" in *Ethics*, in 1986, for the Extreme claims. In '71, Parfit had suggested a revisionist conception of *survival* according to which one could *survive* fission (albeit without *being numerically the same person*), and Lewis developed this idea. The '71/Lewis account does not support Parfit's Extreme arguments in the *Ethics* discussion; at the same time, it need not be used in a superficial reconciliation of the reductionist thesis with the unity reaction (as in Lewis), since the revision in the concept of *survival* can be made perfectly explicit. It says, in a precise and coherent way, *that one could survive fission but without self-unity.*

Although the '71/Lewis position may sharpen the central issue pertaining to conflict between the reductionist thesis and the unity reaction, it does not settle anything. Indeed, the defender of the unity reaction has a pretty quick reply—simply setting aside the revised use of *survival* as glib wordplay. Thus, I believe it is important to see that we can develop forms of psychological reductionism that frame the central issue in other ways, and some of them do not conflict with the unity reaction. Thus, I will show how David Velleman's conception of reductionism can be used to give a precise account of the unity reaction. Then, however, I will argue (4) that this view by itself does not in fact show that we *should* think of psychological continuity in such a way as to eliminate fission-based con-

---

[7] David Lewis, "Survival and Identity," in Amélie Oksenberg Rorty, ed., *The Identities of Persons* (Berkeley: University of California Press, 1976), 17–40.

flict with the unity reaction. A pay-off of reflection on these matters is (5) a distinction that may help us understand the conflict itself.

II. Parfit's Psychological Criteria of Personal Identity and What Matters in Survival

Even though there is general agreement in the metaphysical accounts of persons presupposed by Lewis and Parfit, there also are some formal differences. To begin, I will try to reconstruct their accounts in an accurate way so as to be able to focus on some formal differences that turn out to be significant.

Parfit's version of the Psychological Account of personal identity through time does not change much from '71 to *R&P*, the main difference pertaining to the use of "survival," as I will note. A person's identity through time consists in the occurrence of a series of interrelated mental states and events, where such states and events can be "directly connected" with each other. Relevant direct connections include memory, intention, and continuity of belief and desire.[8] Assume that *person stages* are collections of such states and events.[9] The relations of *psychological connectedness* and *psychological continuity* between stages provide a basis for the Psychological Account of personal identity through time. These relations can be understood generally and schematically in the following ways.

(1) *Psychological connectedness* is characterized as follows, for person stages x and y:

x is *psychologically connected* with y just in case there is some event e in x and some event f in y such that e is directly connected with f.

---

[8] They also include "quasi-" forms of these states. See Parfit, *Reasons and Persons,* 220; and Sydney Shoemaker, "Persons and Their Pasts," *American Philosophical Quarterly* 7 (1970): 269–85.

[9] See Lewis, "Survival and Identity," 20; and "Postscript" in David Lewis, *Philosophical Papers,* vol. 1 (Oxford: Oxford University Press, 1983), 76–77. Parfit does not use the term "person stage," but his account can be reconstructed accurately enough for present purposes by borrowing it from Lewis. Grice used the term "total temporary state" for all the experiences any one person is having at any given time; see H. P. Grice, "Personal Identity," in John Perry, ed., *Personal Identity* (Berkeley: University of California Press, 1975), 86. Parfit says little about the synchronic unity of a person, but he suggests it is due to "states of awareness" (*Reasons and Persons,* 250). Parfit's suggestion is supported by Galen Strawson's discussion of the awareness-based and short-lived "self." Galen Strawson, "The Self," in Shaun Gallagher and Jonathan Shear, eds., *Models of the Self* (Thorverton, UK: Imprint Academic, 1999), 1–24. In contrast, Shoemaker's functionalist psychological approach provides him with an account of synchronic unity of the mental states of a person that is different from Parfit's. Since the relevant states are ontologically dependent upon the existence of a person, including the various relations in which the states stand to each other over time, synchronic unity (unity at a time) is derivative from diachronic unity (unity through time). See Sydney Shoemaker, "Personal Identity: A Materialist's Account," in Sydney Shoemaker and Richard Swinburne, *Personal Identity* (Oxford: Blackwell, 1984).

(Notice that mental events are "directly connected" whereas stages are here said to be "psychologically connected." Parfit also speaks of persons at times being connected; we will get to that in a moment.)

Let us abbreviate *x is psychologically connected with y* as Ψxy. Relation Ψ (psychological connectedness) is not transitive, Parfit says, since the mental relations that constitute connectedness are not transitive.[10] Let us leave open for the moment whether or not Ψ is symmetrical. It may seem arbitrary, but this will turn out to be an important question.[11] Ψ is scalar (comes in degrees); and the degree of connectedness between two person stages x and y depends on the number and significance of the direct psychological connections between x and y.[12]

(2) The idea of *strong psychological connectedness* between person stages is central to Parfit's account.[13] For stages x and y, I will let Ψ*xy abbreviate *x is strongly psychologically connected with y:*

Ψ*xy if and only if x is psychologically connected with y and the degree of connectedness of x with y exceeds a certain threshold.

That is, Ψ*xy just in case there are *enough* direct psychological connections between the events in x and y. Any specific formula for the threshold — for what is *"enough"* — is going to be somewhat arbitrary, so there will be borderline cases.[14] This means that no matter how the threshold is characterized, there are going to be conceivable cases in which there are stages

---

[10] Parfit, "Personal Identity," 214.

[11] A relation Q is transitive just in case for all x,y,z, if Qxy and Qyz then Qxz. Q is symmetrical just in case for all x,y if Qxy then Qyx. Q is reflexive just in case Qxx for all x. A relation Q is an equivalence relation just in case Q is transitive, symmetrical, and reflexive.

[12] Parfit seems to treat connectedness as a quantitative notion, but probably it is qualitative as well, with some connections counting for more than others in determining the degree of connectedness between stages, which might be understood on analogy with the varying "weight" of norms within a normative system.

[13] As developed in Parfit, *Reasons and Persons*. (In "Personal Identity," Parfit does not distinguish connectedness from strong connectedness.)

[14] About the relevant threshold, Parfit says there is *enough* connectedness for strong connectedness if there are *at least half* of the mental connections that occur in one day for a normal adult. It is difficult to believe, however, that he would have intended this formula to be taken seriously, since it is so clearly arbitrary to treat the connections over one *day* as the relevant standard. Why is one day the right interval to use? Why not use two-day intervals as the right period of time? Or one hour? Or five-second intervals? As with degree of connectedness, it is difficult to think of strong connectedness as a purely quantitative notion. Could one count the connections? And aren't some more important than others? Robert Nozick argues, for example, that degree of connectedness (or "closeness") should be determined relative to a person's values (for example, what the person values *in survival*). See Robert Nozick, *Philosophical Explanations* (Cambridge, MA: Harvard University Press, 1981), 62–71. Similarly, Korsgaard emphasizes types of connections involved in practical reasoning and agency. See Christine Korsgaard, "Personal Identity and the Unity of Agency: A Kantian Response to Parfit," *Philosophy and Public Affairs* 18 (1989): 101–32. No matter what the specific formula might be, however, because "connectedness is a matter of degree, we cannot define precisely what counts as enough" (Parfit, *Reasons and Persons*, 206).

for which it will not be determinate whether or not there is strong connectedness between those stages.[15]

As for the formal properties, Ψ^* is symmetrical if Ψ is; but clearly Ψ^*
is not transitive since obviously there can be cases in which there is
enough connectedness for Ψ^* between x and y, and enough between y
and z, but not enough between x and z, as is represented in Figure 1.

$$\Psi^* \quad \Psi^*$$

$$\circ\,-\,-\,-\,\circ\,-\,-\,-\,\circ$$

$$x \qquad y \qquad z$$

FIGURE 1. Strong psychological connectedness

(3) Finally we come to *psychological continuity*, which can be defined as
the ancestral of Ψ^*. That is, letting Rxy abbreviate *there is continuity from
x to y*:[16]

Rxy if and only if there are stages i, i+1, . . . , i+n such that $\Psi^*(x,i)$ and
$\Psi^*(i,i+1)$ and . . . $\Psi^*(i+n,y)$.

That is, R holds between two stages just when there is a *chain* of strong
psychological connectedness linking them. This, I think, is what Parfit has
in mind when he says there is continuity when there are "overlapping
chains of strong connectedness"—although in this explication one chain
will do (there may not be overlapping *chains*, but they are possible).

[15] The claim that it can be indeterminate whether or not there is strong connectedness
between stages is not the claim that Ψ^* is scalar (comes in degrees). To see this, suppose it
is determinate that there is enough connectedness for strong connectedness between stages
x and y as well as between x^* and y^* in another case. But suppose as well that there is more
connectedness in the first case, between x and y, than there is in the second, between x^* and
y^*. It is important to note that this is not to say that the first case has "more" *strong*
connectedness than the second. The two cases are equal with respect to strong connectedness insofar as the threshold is exceeded in both cases. So Ψ^* is not scalar.

[16] The abbreviation "R" should be used with some caution, since Parfit and Lewis together
use "R" in four distinct ways: (1) In *Reasons and Persons*, Parfit explicitly defines the R-relation
as continuity and/or connectedness (215, 262, and elsewhere), which means there is R if
there is Ψ (that is, connectedness, where only one connection is sufficient for connectedness).
This explicit definition is a relatively harmless mistake, since Parfit never uses "R" in a
context in which it makes sense to interpret it as referring to connectedness. (2) "R" means
continuity when Parfit says the Psychological Criterion treats personal identity as "non-
branching R" (*ibid.*, 216, 267). (3) "R" means continuity plus some connectedness when
Parfit claims that it is R that matters (*ibid.*, 287). I am using "R" here in conformity with
Parfit's use (2), and will use "R_Ψ" for (3). Additionally, (4) Lewis uses "R" for yet a fourth
notion, as we will see, which can be expressed as $R_\Psi xy$ or $R_\Psi yx$. I will use "R_L" for Lewis's
relation. See my "Notes on Relation R," *Analysis* 56, no. 1 (1996): 56–62.

There can be continuity between two stages even if they are not strongly connected or perhaps even if there are not any direct connections at all between them. For example, consider Figure 1, presented above to illustrate that Ψ^* is not transitive. In that case we supposed we do not have Ψ^*xz, but we do have Rxz—by virtue of Rxy and Ryz.

R is transitive by definition. As for symmetry, R is symmetrical if Ψ^* is.[17] We earlier left open the question of whether or not Ψ^* is symmetrical. A reason for treating R as *not* symmetrical goes back to the directed nature of direct connections due, in some cases, to the causal nature of these relations, with later person stages arising out of earlier ones but normally not conversely. In any case, Parfit consistently assumes that R is *not* symmetrical in order to avoid R-relatedness of post-fission stages in the fission thought-experiment. In the fission example as diagramed below, both y and z arise out of x; but x arises out of neither y nor z. We have stages x, y, and z such that Rxy and Rxz:

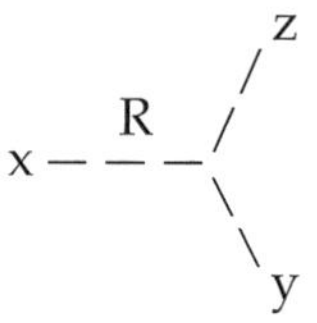

FIGURE 2. Fission

Given symmetry of R, we would have Ryx, and given transitivity, we would have Ryz (from Ryx and Rxz). Now I do not see that saying Ryz is incoherent,[18] but in any case it is contrary to what is intended by Parfit.[19]

---

[17] To see this, suppose Ψ^* is symmetrical. Suppose there are stages x and y such that Rxy, which means there is some Ψ^* chain between x and y. Since we are supposing Ψ^* is symmetrical, there is a similar chain from y to x, which means Ryx. Thus, R is symmetrical if Ψ^* is.

[18] John Perry reconstructs H. P. Grice's account so that it has this consequence. See Perry, "The Problem of Personal Identity," in John Perry, ed., *Personal Identity* (Berkeley: University of California Press, 1975), 3–30.

[19] That R is nonsymmetrical is what Parfit means when he says that "the chain of continuity must run in one direction of time" ("Personal Identity," 23 n. 29); and in *Reasons and Persons* when he says that continuity is transitive, but we would not treat it as transitive "if we allow it to take both directions in a single argument" (302). Because Parfit's phrasing is awkward, one can understand why critics have been confused. E.g., Anthony Brueckner argues that Parfit would be committed to R holding between stages y and z in fission (as diagramed in Figure 2). See Anthony Brueckner, "Parfit on What Matters in Survival," *Philosophical Studies* 70 (1993): 1–22. In his reply to Brueckner, Parfit says "psychological continuity is only transitive when considered in one direction in time"; see Parfit, "The Indeterminacy of Identity: A Reply to Brueckner," *Philosophical Studies* 70 (1993): 24. What Parfit means here, more simply put, is that continuity is not symmetrical, and since R is nonsymmetrical we cannot use the transitivity of R together with Rxy and Rxz to infer Ryz. If R were symmetrical, we could reason like this: Rxy, so by symmetry, Ryx. And given transitivity, Ryx and Rxz entail Ryz. (Notice, by the way, that nonsymmetry is not asymmetry. Asymmetry means Rxy entails ~Ryx, whereas nonsymmetry means only that Rxy

Given that Parfit's R definitely should not hold between z and y, and since his R equally definitely is transitive, we have a reason for treating R as not symmetrical (and so also, then, given earlier results, for going back down the line and also treating both Ψ^* and Ψ as not symmetrical).

In both '71 and *R&P*, Parfit can be understood as treating *copersonality*, or (let us say) *self-unity*, as R-relatedness among stages in the absence of "branching":

> x is *self-unified* with y (Pxy) just in case Rxy or Ryx and there is no-branching on the R-path between x and y.[20]

Parfit does not use the terms "copersonal" or "self-unity," but the notion defined here is useful in the discussion of his account. P is the "unity relation" for persons—"the relation that holds between different experiences, person stages, etc., just in case they belong to one and the same person."[21] Self-unity as thus conceived is an equivalence relation (reflexive, symmetrical, and transitive), assuming individual experiences, stages, etc. are not shared by two or more people. (I will return to this point later in my discussion of Lewis, since Lewis's unity relation is not an equivalence relation.)

Finally, "what matters," Parfit argues in *R&P*, is continuity plus connectedness, which I will abbreviate as R_Ψ. $R_\Psi$xy says "Rxy *and* Ψxy." R_Ψ is neither symmetrical nor transitive: it is not symmetrical because R is not symmetrical, and R_Ψ is not transitive because of the role of Ψ (and degrees of Ψ) in R_Ψ.[22] Parfit's argument that identity does not matter is grounded in the fact that P (self-unity) is an equivalence relation whereas R_Ψ is neither symmetrical nor transitive, as I discuss further below.

A. Continuity and identity of persons

The relations Ψ (psychological connectedness), Ψ^* (strong psychological connectedness), R (psychological continuity), and R_Ψ (psychological continuity-and-connectedness) have sets of person stages as their domains

---

does not entail Ryx. I will assume that Parfit treats R as nonsymmetrical but not as asymmetrical—this leaves open the possibility that there could be cases in which Rxy and Ryx due, for example, to there being a causal loop. Conceivable even if outlandish, it requires not merely temporally backward causation, but such causation where, for example, an experience at t2 causes a memory at t3 which then backward-causes, say, an intention at t1 which is a cause of the experience at t2 [where t1 < t2 < t3].)

[20] See Parfit, "Personal Identity," 208, and *Reasons and Persons*, 207. The details about what "no-branching" means are not very easy to spell out, a task made even more difficult in explication of Parfit since he wants to admit, along with Nozick, that some branching is consistent with self-unity.

[21] Sydney Shoemaker, "Parfit on Identity," in Dancy, ed., *Reading Parfit*, 139.

[22] For Parfit's argument that what matters includes Ψ as well as R, see *Reasons and Persons*, 301–2.

and ranges. Parfit often speaks, however, as if persons also are in the domains and ranges of these relations. Indeed, his Psychological Criterion, for example, speaks this way when it speaks of a person X being *continuous* with Y.[23] Even though a person's existence at a time just consists in the occurrence of the events in a certain stage (so to speak), Parfit envisions a form of psychological reductionism that would not simply identify the person with the series of interrelated stages in which his or her existence consists;[24] rather, his or her existence is *constituted by* the series of interrelated stages.[25] We formally can accommodate the sort of reductionism that Parfit envisions by supposing that there is a function F that maps any person A and time t on the person stage in which A's existence at t consists.[26]

A is *constituted by* x at t if and only if $F(A,t)=x$.

Various statements about persons can be constructed out of the descriptions of stages and their relations.[27] If $F(A,t)=x$ and $F(B,t^*)=y$:

A at time t is *connected to* B at t^* if and only if Ψxy.
A at t is *strongly connected with* B at t^* if and only if $\Psi^* xy$.
A at t is *continuous with* B at t^* if and only if Rxy.

Moreover, we also may want to talk about continuity of persons (without any mention of times):

A is *continuous* with B if and only if there are times t and t^* such that A at t is continuous with B at t^*.

The Psychological Criterion of personal identity through time[28] can be expressed as follows in terms of "self-unity" (P) as defined above (recall that P is non-branching R). If $F(A,t)=x$ and $F(B,t^*)=y$, then

---

[23] Ibid., 207.

[24] Ibid., 211.

[25] Parfit, "The Unimportance of Identity," in Henry Harris, ed., *Identity: Essays Based on Herbert Spencer Lectures Given in the University of Oxford* (Oxford: Clarendon Press, 1995), 13–45. On the constitution of facts about personal identity, see Mark Johnston, "Human Concerns without Superlative Selves," in Dancy, ed., *Reading Parfit*, 154.

[26] This works only as a first approximation. I should say "stage *or stages*," assuming the coherence of temporally overlapping (concurrent) copersonal stages (given, for example, the coherence of time travel, as is discussed later in this essay). Thus, F should pick out a set of stages, and the following uses of F should be modified accordingly. In the text, however, I assume the simpler function, since ordinarily, in the absence of temporal overlapping, $F(A,t)$ will be a unit set.

[27] Alternatively, the domain and range of R could be extended in an obvious way as follows (similarly for "connected" and R^*):

$R(\langle A,t \rangle, \langle B,t^* \rangle)$ if and only if there are x,y such that $F(A,t)=x$ and $F(B,t^*)=y$ and Rxy.
$R(A,B)$ if and only if there are t and t^* such that $R(\langle A,t \rangle, \langle B,t^* \rangle)$.

[28] Parfit, *Reasons and Persons*, 207.

A at t is the *same person* as B at t* if and only if Pxy.

Finally, Parfit says in *Reasons and Persons* that his most important claim is that "personal identity is not what matters,"[29] and that it is continuity plus connectedness that matters in survival. This can be reconstructed as follows, given $F(A,t)=x$ and $F(B,t^*)=y$:

A at t has in B at t* *what matters in survival* if and only if $R_\Psi xy$.

B. Parfit's argument that identity does not matter

The main argument that Parfit gives for the claim that identity does not matter depends on the possibility that R (and R_Ψ) branch in the fission cases.[30] The argument is as follows: In fission, one would have what matters in survival (at least twice); but one would be identical with no one living afterward—in anticipating a fission, one's current stage will not be self-unified with any post-fission stages. Therefore, identity (self-unity) is not what matters in survival. In fission, Frost has in ZFrost what matters in survival since $R_\Psi xz$ is true (if "Frost" refers to the person constituted by x in Figure 3, and "ZFrost" refers to the person constituted by z). But Frost is not the same person as ZFrost, since Pxz is not true—for there is not *non-branching* R between x and z; and we have to deny both Pxz and Pxy since otherwise the transitivity and symmetry of P will guarantee the result that Pzy—a result that Parfit regards as counterintuitive.[31] Therefore, personal identity is not what matters in Frost's survival. Speaking of stages, we equally can say that self-unity is not what matters in survival (since the branch between x and z undermines Pxz even though $R_\Psi xy$ holds).

FIGURE 3. Frost fission

[29] Ibid., 241.
[30] Ibid., 261ff.
[31] While some do not accept this analysis of fission, the poet Frost appears to accept it: *Two roads diverged in a narrow wood / And sorry I could not travel both / And be one traveler / Long I stood....* From "The Road Not Taken," in Robert Frost, *Mountain Interval* (New York: Henry Holt, 1916), 9.

C. Survival

The argument that identity does not matter can be found in both '71 and *R&P*, but there is a shift in Parfit's assumption about the relation between survival and identity, which is the only important difference between Parfit's views in '71 and in *R&P*. The '71 position would define survival simply as R_ψ, so that, letting $F(A,t)=x$ and $F(B,t^*)=y$:

A at t *survives as* B at t^* just in case $R_\psi xy$.

Both continuity and connectedness are necessary for survival, and it is the inclusion of connectedness that makes survival a "matter of degree."[32] Parfit in '71 also introduced the notion of a "future self," and this idea can be linked to survival. Given $F(A,t)=x$ and $F(B,t^*)=y$:

B at t^* is a *future self* of A at t if and only if $R_\psi xy$.[33]

On this reconstruction, "survival as" and "future selfhood" are necessarily coextensive with each other, as well as with "what matters in survival":

A at t *survives as* B at t^* if and only if B at t^* is a *future self* of A at t,

and

B at t^* is a *future self* of A at t if and only if A at t *has* in B at t^* *what matters* in survival.

Neither survival nor "future selfhold" entails either personal identity or self-unity; thus, as in fission, y can be a future self of x ($R_\psi xy$) even though x is not self-unified with y ($\sim Pxy$).

Parfit suggests in '71 that the concept of "survival" should be pried apart from "identity," so that "I will survive" does not entail "there will be someone alive who is the same person as me." This would be a revision in our normal concept of "survival as" — since "survival as," as normally used, entails identity. On the revisionist interpretation, one could *survive* fission even though afterward there would be no one alive with whom one is identical.[34]

---

[32] Parfit, "Personal Identity," 211.

[33] In which case, A at t is a *past self* of B at t^*. Parfit also introduces the distinct notions of ancestral (descendant) selves: these notions can be reconstructed as follows directly in terms of R. Given $F(A,t)=x$ and $F(B,t^*)=y$:

A at t is an ancestral self of B at t^* if and only if Rxy.
A at t is a descendant self of B at t^* if and only if Ryx.

[34] Georges Rey says Parfit's '71 wedge involves a "travesty of ordinary talk" since "a person, on this account, may *survive* yet not continue to *exist*, since she may survive as [each of] two different persons." Georges Rey, "Survival," in Amélie Oksenberg Rorty, ed., *The*

Parfit did not develop this idea in *R&P*, where he does not say much about survival. When he does talk about survival, however, he does so in such a way that it entails personal identity.[35] As Sydney Shoemaker does in his essay "Personal Identity,"[36] Parfit in *R&P* argues *not* that survival should be pried apart from identity, but that *what matters in survival* should be pried apart from both survival *and* identity. One can have what matters in survival, and one would have it in a fission case, even though one would not survive.

Although Parfit shifted his position about whether we should pry survival apart from identity, in both cases Parfit argues that we can have *what matters in survival* without personal identity. In both cases, that is, he holds that the best interpretation of fission will establish what Penelope Maddy called a "logical wedge" between what matters in survival and personal identity.[37] The difference between the '71 and *R&P* positions has to do with where the wedge is placed. In the '71 article, the wedge is placed between survival and identity (and Parfit does not envision a wedge between survival and what matters in survival), whereas in *R&P* the wedge is placed between survival and what matters in survival (and he does not discuss the earlier wedge between survival and identity). In the following diagram, let $\Rightarrow$ represent entailment and let $\Downarrow$ indicate where Parfit places the logical wedge in each case:

$$
\begin{array}{cc}
R\&P & \text{'71} \\
\Downarrow & \Downarrow
\end{array}
$$
(1) what matters $\Rightarrow$ (2) survival $\Rightarrow$ (3) personal identity

The *R&P* wedge denies that

(1) A has in B what matters in survival

entails

(2) A survives as B

whereas the '71 wedge denies that (2) entails

(3) A is the same person as B.

Identities of Persons (Berkeley: University of California Press, 1976), 42. Despite "the obvious awkwardness of this manner of speaking," Rey nonetheless goes on to argue that given the alternatives, we should accept the wedge between survival and identity: "Identity, I submit, should never have been the primary source of our concern with survival; it is, rather, survival, and our belief that our survival depended upon our continuing identity, which was the significant source of our concern with that identity" (ibid., 43).

[35] See, for example, Parfit, *Reasons and Persons*, 261.

[36] Shoemaker, "Personal Identity: A Materialist's Account" (see note 9 above).

[37] Penelope Maddy, "Is the Importance of Identity Derivative?" *Philosophical Studies* 35 (1979): 151–70.

Given the reconstruction so far, we have the logical wedges in the right place for Parfit given the two divergent conceptions of survival.[38]

Although the two treatments are significant for framing the conflict between the reductionist thesis and the unity reaction, as I will argue later, the differences between '71 and *R&P* are irrelevant to Parfit's general argument that identity does not matter, at least as he presents the argument. For in both cases, Parfit places a logical wedge between (1) what matters (R_Ψ) and (3) personal identity (self-unity, that is, relation P), and it is this feature that grounds his argument that identity does not matter. No matter what your form of reductionism, he holds, you should conclude that identity does not matter. Insofar as Parfit wanted his argument to convince any reductionist that identity does not matter, the argument is challenged by theories like Lewis's that claim to drive no logical wedges at all between what matters in survival and identity.

III. Lewis's Reply: The Nontransitive I-Relation

Lewis claims that the metaphysical picture of persons that he shares with Parfit is consistent with the commonsensical assumption that there is no Parfitian wedge between what matters and identity:

> [T]he opposition between what matters and identity is false. We can agree with Parfit (and I think we should) that what matters in questions of personal identity is mental continuity and connectedness, and that this might be one-many or many-one, and admits of degree. At the same time we can consistently agree with common sense (and I think we should) that what matters in questions of personal identity— even in the problem cases—is identity.[39]

---

[38] "Survival as" is transitive in *R&P* but not in '71, and is symmetrical in neither. There are two basic differences between the '71 and *R&P* treatments of survival. The first is that *R&P* requires self-unity for survival whereas '71 does not. The second difference is that *R&P* does not require any degree of Ψ for survival (since P does not require any degree of Ψ): the bottom-line difference in the two treatments of survival, then, is that '71 links survival with continuity and connectedness (R_Ψ) whereas *R&P* links survival with self-unity (P). If we bracket the second difference (requiring some degree of connectedness in both cases), we can spell out the first difference as follows. For '71, the relation between stages that constitutes survival ("Sxy") is simply R_Ψ (which means

$$S_{'71}: \quad S = R + \Psi$$

since $R_\Psi = R + \Psi$). For *R&P*, on the other hand, Sxy is $R_\Psi xy$ plus Pxy (which means

$$S_{R\&P}: \quad S = P + \Psi$$

since $R_\Psi = R + \Psi$ and P entails R). Since P is just non-branching R, the difference between the two conceptions boils down to whether *no-branching* on R is required for survival (*R&P* saying *yes*; '71 saying *no*)—which of course corresponds to the question of whether or not one "survives" in a fission case.

[39] Lewis, "Survival and Identity," 19.

The appearance of conflict is due to the fact that "we make an unequal and inept comparison"[40] between (a) *what matters* conceived as a relation between stages and (b) *identity* conceived as a relation between continuant persons. Lewis notes that it is "pointless" to compare these relations as such[41] since the *relata* of the two relations are different: in the one case stages, in the other continuant persons. To mark the distinction Lewis has in mind, let us distinguish *stage-level* statements such as those about the relations between person stages (Ψxy, Rxy, $R_\Psi xy$, Pxy, and so forth) from the *person-level* statements about relations between continuant persons (A at t is continuous with B at t*; A is continuous with B; A at t is the same person as B at t*; A at t survives as B at t*; and so forth—where it is important to remember that, on this analysis, "A at t" refers to a continuant person, not a person stage).

The distinction is important, but there can be relationships between the two levels insofar as persons are constituted by stages and the relations between stages. And, of course, Lewis does not deny that relations between the two levels can be described. For example, he freely combines them in his key expression of the commonsensical position that what matters in survival is identity: "*you* have what matters in survival if and only if *your present stage* is I-related to future stages."[42]

Lewis agrees with Parfit that what matters, expressed in person-stage level terms, is "mental continuity and connectedness." There is, however, a formal difference with Parfit about this relation, and since Lewis's "continuity and connectedness" does not correspond exactly to Parfit's R_Ψ, let us introduce "R_L" for Lewis's version of "continuity and connectedness," which is developed as follows.

Lewis seeks an account in which "continuity and connectedness" will be necessarily coextensive with his unity relation, which he calls the *I-relation*—the relation "that holds between the several stages of a single continuant person."[43] Now since Lewis assumes that the I-relation must be symmetrical,[44] he also seeks to define R_L so that it turns out to be symmetrical. He does so by abstracting away from the "direction" of continuity and connectedness, even while acknowledging that it "has a direction." In the following passage, Lewis uses simply "R" wherever "R_Ψ" or "R_L" appears; I make the replacements for coherence with the discussion here so far:

> If a stage S2 is mentally connected to a previous stage S1, S1 is available in memory to S2 and S2 is under the intentional control of S1 to some extent—not the other way around. We can say that S1 is

---

[40] Mark Johnston, "Fission and the Facts," *Philosophical Perspectives* 3 (1989): 385.
[41] Lewis, "Survival and Identity," 21.
[42] Ibid., 22, emphasis added. I discuss the I-relation in the text below.
[43] Ibid., 21.
[44] Ibid., 23.

R_Ψ-related *forward* to S2, whereas S2 is R_Ψ-related *backward* to S1. The forward and backward R_Ψ-relations are converses of one another. . . . But although we can distinguish the forward and backward R_Ψ-relations, we can also merge them into a symmetrical relation. That is the R_L-relation I have in mind: S1 and S2 are R_L-related *simpliciter* if and only if S1 is R_Ψ-related either forward or backward to S2.[45]

Formulated in the terms I used earlier to explicate Parfit, the forward relation is simply R_Ψ and the backward relation is R_Ψ^{-1}, the inverse of R_Ψ. Lewis is saying that he will guarantee that his version of "mental continuity and connectedness" is a symmetrical relation by defining it so that $R_L = R_\Psi \cup R_\Psi^{-1}$ (the union of R_Ψ and R_Ψ^{-1}), which means

$R_L xy$ if and only if $R_\Psi xy$ *or* $R_\Psi yx$,

that is,

$R_L xy$ if and only if $(Rxy$ & $\Psi xy)$ or $(Ryx$ & $\Psi yx)$.

R_L is symmetrical by definition, but R_L is not transitive due to the role of Ψ in R_L: as I noted earlier, there can be stages x, y, z such that Ψxy (there are connections from x to y) and Ψyz (connections from y to z) but not Ψxz (no connections from x to z). With R_L defined in this way, and since Lewis posits the necessary coextension of R_L and I, it turns out that the I-relation is symmetrical but not transitive.

The nontransitivity of I=R_L plays a crucial role in Lewis's interpretation of fission. Something is a continuant person if and only if it is a maximal I-interrelated aggregate of person stages:[46] Lewis identifies the person with the entire series of interconnected stages, whereas Parfit resisted this identification. In fission with two post-fission descendants, there are for Lewis two continuant persons. In fission, Lewis grants $R_L xz$ and $R_L xy$ (which entails $R_L zx$ and $R_L yx$, given symmetry of R_L). But neither $R_L zy$ nor $R_L yz$ can be derived because R_L is not transitive.

FIGURE 4. Fission in Lewis

[45] Ibid.
[46] Ibid., 22.

In particular, we cannot reason: "$R_L xz$, so $R_L zx$ by symmetry [for Lewis, that step is okay]. And [here is the mistake] $R_L zx$ and $R_L xy$ together entail $R_L zy$." This *is* a mistake because it assumes that R_L is transitive. Lewis is committed to neither $R_L zy$ nor $R_L yz$ (which means neither Izy nor Iyz, since R_L and the I-relation are necessarily coextensive, so there is no continuant person of whom z and y are stages). And Lewis consistently can hold that the I-relation is the relation between stages that matters in survival, assuming, of course, that two distinct continuant persons share the pre-fission stage x.

On this account, there is indeed no "wedge" between what matters (R_L) and the I-relation, since they are defined to be necessarily coextensive. But this is not a successful reconciliation of the reductionist metaphysics with common sense, because the I-relation, not being transitive, is not an equivalence relation, whereas common sense surely presupposes that self-unity is an equivalence relation just like identity itself (both relations being reflexive, symmetrical, and transitive). One aspect of self-unity is *distinctness from others*, including not sharing stages. That self-unity is an equivalence relation (as we assumed earlier in defining P) is simply the stage-level correlate to the person-level assumption that personal identity is an equivalence relation.

Lewis pointed out rightly that what matters, as a relation between stages, should not be compared directly with identity as a relation between continuant persons. All the same, what matters, as a relation between stages, coherently can be compared with relation P, self-unity, since it also is a relation between stages. Parfit's revisionist claim that fission shows that identity does not matter can be expressed equally well by saying that fission shows that relation P, *self-unity*, does not matter. Stages x and y are not related by P in fission, but since $R_\psi xy$, the relation between x and y has what matters. Self-unity, P, is one-one, but R_ψ is not one-one; therefore, P is not what matters.

Put this way, it becomes stunningly clear that rather than opposing Parfit's revisionist position, Lewis simply *assumes* it! That is, Lewis presupposes a logical wedge between his I-relation (= R_L) and self-unity, P:

Lewis
$$\Downarrow$$
$$I \Rightarrow P$$

Since the I-relation is necessarily coextensive with what matters in survival on his view, Lewis presupposes a logical wedge between what matters and self-unity just as surely as did Parfit. Insofar as he uses the term "survival" so as to entail I-relatedness but not P-relatedness, the wedge that Lewis presupposes is simply Parfit's '71 wedge between survival and self-unity. The relation between stages by virtue of which there is "survival" for Lewis (the I-relation) can hold even when P fails to hold. Lewis says, for instance:

If you wonder whether you will survive the coming battle or what-not, you are wondering whether any of the stages that will exist afterward is R_L-related to you-now, the stage that is doing the wondering.[47]

Since $R_L=I$, the account of survival presupposed in this statement is as follows, assuming $F(A,t)=x$ and $F(B,t^*)=y$:

A at t *survives as* B at t^* if and only if Ixy and t^* is later than t.[48]

And since the right side here does not entail Pxy, for Lewis survival does not entail self-unity.

The *commonsensical* platitude that what matters in survival is identity is *not* in fact expressed by Lewis's claim that you have what matters in survival if and only if your present stage is *I-related* to future stages.[49] This will sound good to common sense only on the assumption that the I-relation is P. But relation I is not relation P, and the platitude, properly expressed, is that you have what matters in survival just in case your present stage is *P-related* to future stages.

A. Why Parfit failed to explain what was wrong with Lewis's reply

Lewis's wedge between what matters and self-unity does not reveal itself in person-level statements about fission, for the following reason. If we use terms like "Frost" or "Frost at t" intending to refer to the pre-fission person constituted by stage x, we make ambiguous reference. Two continuant persons share stage x, so there is no unique continuant person constituted by x. Thus, even though Ixy and ~Pxy in the fission case, Lewis's theory never generates *person-level* conflict between competing statements like the Ixy-based "Frost is the same person as ZFrost" (where "ZFrost" refers to the person constituted by z) and the ~Pxy-based "Frost is not the same person as ZFrost." Why not? Because "Frost" is an improper description in this case. The name "Frost" is used ambiguously, since more than one continuant person shares the stage x. It must be granted that Lewis drives no wedge between what matters and *identity*—but this is only because all the relevant person-level identity statements that cor-respond to I-relation statements are ill-formed whenever there is failure of transitivity of I, for those are just the cases when continuant persons overlap (share stages).

---

[47] Ibid., 20, with "R_L" replacing "R."

[48] But see below for a refinement in terms of the distinction between external and per-sonal time.

[49] Ibid., 22.

It is for these reasons that Parfit failed to explain Lewis's magic. In his reply to Lewis, Parfit imagines his own forthcoming fission, and asserts the following:

> The claim that the R_ψ-relation is what matters in survival must involve the claim that what matters in *my* survival is that future stages be R_ψ-related to *my* present stage. Only if these future stages are stages of *me* . . . can we also claim that it is identity which is what matters.[50]

The problem with this objection to Lewis is that even first-personal reflexive thoughts and statements about "me" will, for Lewis, be subject to ambiguity if I, the thinker of those thoughts, am about to undergo fission. Parfit's objection sounds plausible, but pre-fission thoughts like "I am about to undergo fission" or "Sorry I could not travel both" do not succeed in referring to a unique continuant person according to Lewis's theory, since two continuant persons share "my" current stage when I think "I am about to undergo fission."[51]

I do not believe that *person-level* objections to Lewis's account of fission, such as Parfit's, can succeed, since Lewis suggests plausible ways to talk coherently about pre-fission stage-sharing without positing a wedge between what matters and identity. Nonetheless, as I have shown, Lewis has to posit a logical wedge at the *stage*-level between what matters and self-unity.[52]

It is widely accepted that (if one is willing to go along with pre-fission stage-sharing) Lewis succeeded in sketching a theory in which identity

---

[50] Derek Parfit, "Lewis, Perry, and What Matters," in Rorty, ed., *The Identities of Persons*, 95, with "R_ψ" replacing "R."

[51] See Lewis, "Postscript," in *Philosophical Papers*, 75: a pre-fission desire expressed by "let me survive" cannot be satisfied, since "it rests on the false presupposition that they [the two people sharing the stage] are a single person." Of course, this "Postscript" analysis undercuts the following claim in Lewis's original article:

> What matters in survival is survival. If I wonder whether I will survive, what I mostly care about is quite simple. When it's all over, will I myself—the very same person now thinking these thoughts and writing these words—still exist? Will any one of those who do exist afterward be me? ("Survival and Identity," 18)

Since these questions rest upon the false presupposition that "I" and "me" refer to a single person (when used by the pre-fission person), Lewis is committed to saying either that the questions are meaningless or that they should be answered *no* (depending on how he treats questions that make false presuppositions), but either interpretation is inconsistent with the claim that because of R_L-relatedness "I will survive." Given his "Postscript" comments, Lewis would have to withdraw the comments just quoted from his original article.

[52] Are there any cases in which Lewis's logical wedge between I and P could manifest at the person level, as a wedge between personal identity and identity *simpliciter*? I believe the answer is no, which can be seen as follows. If there were a case in which A is the same person as B, B is the same person as C, but A is not the same person as C (where the nontransitivity of I results in a failure of transitivity at the person level), it would be due to the failure of transitivity of I=R_L. Suppose A is constituted by x at t1, B by y at t2, and C by z at t3. And suppose Ixy, Iyz, but ~Ixz (as Lewis suggests might hold with long-lived people like Methuselah).

and what matters in survival do not come apart in fission.[53] While this widely held consensus is partly right, it is mostly wrong. It is partly right because, indeed, person-level judgments about what matters and identity do not diverge for Lewis, for the reasons just explained. But for Lewis what matters can diverge from commonsensical self-unity, explicated as P. The odd thing about the debate, then, is that Lewis already was a giant step ahead of the revisionist Parfit—already working, that is, within a framework that assumes that commonsensical self-unity, P, does not matter, even while misleadingly presenting himself as the commonsensical conservative in the debate![54] The virtues of Parfit's original '71 account emerge more fully in the next subsection, where I will explain (1) why Lewis does not offer a satisfactory treatment of fission cases in terms of his symmetrical nontransitive R_L-relation, and (2) why the formal revisions he should make will turn his account into the one presupposed originally by Parfit in '71.

B. Why Lewis's account of fission is unsatisfactory on its own terms

The nontransitivity of $R_L=I$ is essential for the use to which Lewis puts it in replying to Parfit about fission, as I have explained. R_L fails to be a transitive relation for the same reason that R_Ψ is not transitive: because *connectedness* (Ψ) is a component of those relations. Even though Lewis for consistency must deny that $R_L yz$ holds in the fission as diagrammed

$$R_L \qquad R_L$$
$$x - - - y - - - z$$
$$A \qquad\quad B \qquad\quad C$$
$$t1 \qquad\quad t2 \qquad\quad t3$$

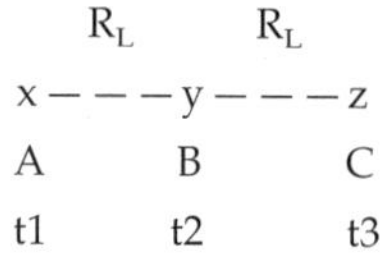

FIGURE 5. Methuselah

If the failure of transitivity of R_L appears at the person level, it would turn out that A is the same person as B, B is the same person as C, but A is not the same person as C, where each of the terms A, B, and C are well-formed. Now since A is the same as B, A is constituted by y at t2; and since B is the same as C, C also is constituted by y at t2. But this means that "B" was not in fact well-formed—"B" is used ambiguously to refer to two distinct persons, since its reference is fixed by saying that B is constituted by y at t2 and two (or more) distinct people share stage y.

[53] Ray Martin classes Lewis with the "neoconservatives" who hold that "identity really is what matters primarily in survival." Ray Martin, *Self-Concern* (Cambridge: Cambridge University Press, 1998), 56. See also Carol Rovane, *The Bounds of Agency* (Princeton, NJ: Princeton University Press, 1998), 55.

[54] Lewis was carried so far by his own rhetoric as to claim that were he to have to choose between the platitude of common sense and his philosophy, he would have to go with common sense because otherwise "it would be difficult to believe one's own philosophy" ("Survival and Identity," 18). By the way, I am not claiming that it is incoherent to define copersonality so that it is not an equivalence relation, as Lewis does; rather, my point is that in doing so Lewis already has departed from the platitude of common sense. I am grateful to Mark Moyer for discussion of this point.

above (in Figure 4), he lacks an explanation why R_L *must fail* to hold between any post-fission stages y and z. To see this, notice that we coherently can imagine a fission case in which there is some degree of connectedness between y and z, due perhaps to an implanted memory:[55]

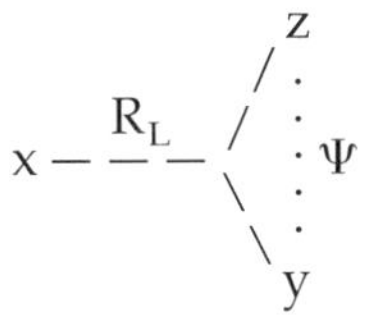

FIGURE 6. Fission in Lewis with some Ψ from z to y

Given the symmetry of R_L, Lewis has no reason to deny $R_L$zy in this case. After all, we have $R_L$xz (hence by symmetry $R_L$zx) and we have $R_L$xy. Now we cannot simply infer $R_L$zy, since the R_L-relation generally can fail to be transitive, as noted, because of the failure of connectedness. In this imagined case, however, we do have Ψzy. So Lewis cannot appeal to the role of Ψ to explain why $R_L$zy fails to hold in this case. In fact, in his account, there is no reason why $R_L$zy should fail to hold here. But certainly one random implanted memory connection should not (or need not) make a difference in the analysis of this type of case, and I do not believe that Lewis would have wanted to admit that given the random connection, it turns out after all that z and y would be R_L- and I-related (stages of one continuant person).

Before pressing my argument, let me consider a possible response. Even though Lewis cannot appeal to the lack of connectedness to explain why $R_L$zy fails to hold, he might reply that $R_L$zy fails to hold, even given the connectedness between z and y, because $\sim R_\Psi$zy (there isn't "forward" continuity and connectedness between z and y); and if $\sim R_\Psi$zy (and $\sim R_\Psi$yz) then $\sim R_L$zy. He can say this because continuity (R) itself is not symmetrical (talking now about R, not R_Ψ): from Rxz we cannot infer Rzx, so we cannot get Rzy in this case. So Lewis can say $\sim R_L$zy because $\sim$Rzy even though Ψzy.

I agree that this is a coherent reply for Lewis, but it would be odd for him to appeal to the nonsymmetry of R (continuity) in this case after scrambling to guarantee that his R_L (continuity and connectedness) *would be* symmetrical. Recall that in introducing these notions to reconstruct Parfit's views, it appeared more or less arbitrary what we said about *symmetry* on the relations of R continuity, R^* strong connectedness, and Ψ connectedness; and yet having defined R so that it is transitive, Parfit had a conclusive reason for treating R as not symmetrical in order to avoid

[55] See Parfit's "Venetian Memories," in *Reasons and Persons,* 220.

R-relatedness of the post-fission stages. And Parfit consistently denies symmetry on R (and consequently on R_Ψ) in order to prevent Rzy (and $R_\Psi$zy) in the fission cases. Of course, the nonsymmetry of continuity can be motivated independently in terms of the nonsymmetry of the causal and intentional processes by virtue of which later person stages arise out of earlier ones but normally not conversely (since there normally are not causal loops involving backwards causation). In the fission example, both y and z arise out of x; but x does not arise out of either y or z. My point is that it is the nonsymmetry of R_Ψ, not its nontransitivity, that is relevant to the failure of Pzy (and for Lewis, Izy) in fission: just as x does not arise out of z, neither does y. Even given some degree of connectedness between z and y, and even given $R_\Psi$xy and $R_\Psi$xz, we need not posit $R_\Psi$zy because there is not the right sort of causal or intentional relatedness between z and y.

Lewis's up-front motivation for ensuring the symmetry of R_L was to have a relation that corresponded with the symmetrical I-relation, and yet he grants that

> we can imagine the immediate postfission stages to be pretty much alike, wherefore they can all be strongly R_L-related to the immediate prefission stages.[56]

If what matters really *is* symmetrical, then y has it relative to x just as surely as x does to y (referring to Figure 6 again); and since x has it to z as well, it follows that z has it to y unless an inference based on *transitivity* can be blocked. While it is true that generally inferences based on the transitivity of R_L are not valid (since the relation is not transitive), the failure of transitivity of R_L, when it fails, is due to the failure of Ψ (connectedness). Therefore, in a case where there is connectedness between z and y, as in the implanted memories case discussed above, the claim that inference based on transitivity should be blocked rings false. It is more plausible to suppose that $R_L$zy fails in fission because the relevant relations are *not symmetrical*[57]—and nontransitivity becomes relevant to the denial of R_L over long spans of

---

[56] Lewis, "Survival and Identity," 40 n. 8, with "R" replaced by "R_L."

[57] The problem for Lewis here is made vivid by recalling H. P. Grice's worry, which (translated into the terms I am using in this essay) is that one might have experiences in stages that later were not connected to any future stages (such as in repressed memory or Alzheimer's cases). See Grice, "Personal Identity," 87–88. Grice *posits* the symmetry of his version of the R-relation precisely *in order to be able* to make those stages copersonal *despite* the branching. For my informal discussion Grice's views, see http://personal.bgsu.edu/~mbelzer/mulderscullyrepsychtheory.html. Of course, Lewis ignored this sort of problem and imposed symmetry on R_L in order to establish the desired necessary coextension of R_L with I; and, given symmetry, Lewis is committed to $R_L$yz in a fission case in which there also is *some degree* of connectedness between the post-fission stages y and z.

R-relatedness, because there is not any connectedness, as in the case of long-lived people like Methuselah.[58]

It seems to me, then, that Lewis should deny symmetry for R_L and the I-relation in order to handle fission cases properly; and if he denies it for both, then he can maintain their necessary coextension.

This conclusion is supported by the fact that Lewis faces an additional related problem due to the symmetry of his R_L. Lewis points out that

> you have what matters in survival if, and only if, your present stage is I-related to future stages.[59]

Call this "the future orientation of survival claim." Let us use "I^*" for the relation "being I-related to *future* stages" (where I^*xy if and only if Ixy and the time of y is later than the time of x).

The future orientation of survival claim says that what matters in survival is coextensive with I^*. But I^* is not R_L, for R_L was defined so that $R_L=I$, and $I^* \neq I$. Relation I is symmetrical for Lewis, whereas I^* (being I-related to *future* stages) is not a symmetrical relation: if Ixy and y is future relative to x, then it is not the case that x is future relative to y. And yet, of course, what Lewis says—the future orientation of survival claim—is correct: what matters in survival, as a relation between stages, is not symmetrical. The earlier stage has it relative to the later, but not conversely. The point is that having what matters in survival is coextensive only with the forward-looking I^*-relation.

This raises a problem for Lewis because "future," as it is used in his phrase "your present stage is I-related to *future* stages," needs to be interpreted relative to *personal* time (not external time). The orientation to the future in survival is one's "personal" future. As Lewis himself made clear in his essay on time travel, we coherently can imagine time travel scenarios in which personal time diverges from the "external" future.[60] One might *survive*, for example, by virtue of stages occurring *earlier than the present* in external time; and equally one might not survive until t even though one has stages at t. But his symmetrical $I=R_L$ offers Lewis no conception of personal time. To see this, suppose there is a stage y that is future, externally, to the one that constitutes me now—that is, it is future in *external* time (now it is 2004, but the stage is in, say, 2020). And suppose additionally that the stage is prior to my present stage in *personal* time (I have time-"traveled" backwards, from after 2020 until prior to now), and suppose that after a couple of moments (in external time) there will be no

---

[58] Lewis, "Survival and Identity," 29–31. See the discussion of Methuselah above in note 52.

[59] Ibid., 22.

[60] David Lewis, "Paradoxes of Time Travel," in Fred D. Miller, Jr., and Nicholas D. Smith, eds., *Thought Probes: Philosophy through Science Fiction* (Englewood Cliffs, NJ: Prentice-Hall, 1981).

stages future to me now in personal time. In other words, after a few moments in external time, there will be no stages that are R_Ψ-related to the one that constitutes me now. In the following diagram, z is my current stage and y is a stage of mine in 2020, and we suppose that $R_L yz$:

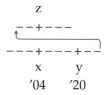

FIGURE 7. Time travel

Can I now say, from within stage z, that I will have what matters in survival when 2020 arrives? No. My current stage z is not properly related to any stages in 2020. I in 2020 may be said to survive (now) by virtue of my current stage z in 2004; but I now will not survive by virtue of that relation since I now (speaking from within z) have only the *backwards*-R_Ψ relation to those stages: I now have already been there.[61] My present stage z will not be forward-R_Ψ-related to any stages in 2020. It might be interesting to be able to *remember* what *will happen* then, but that, obviously, is different from surviving.

The problem for Lewis is that he is committed to telling me (as constituted by z): *yes, you will survive;* for on his account, there is a "future"

---

[61] Of course, in external time there is (as diagrammed in Figure 7) a distinct stage x of me, concurrent with z, from within which I can correctly anticipate surviving by virtue of the 2020 stage. Stages x and z overlap (that is, are concurrent in external time) but nonetheless are ordered in personal time by continuity and connectedness—they are self-unified. The possibility of concurrent self-unified stages by virtue of time travel is coherent for the reductionist, and it can generate conflict with the unity reaction in a way that is different from fission. In such cases (e.g., think of the concurrent distinct stages of Marty McFly near the end of the movie *Back to the Future*) there is a linear order of stages according to R_Ψ, hence no branching, hence relation P. For the reductionist, it seems to me, there should be no deep puzzles at all about personal identity and self-unity in such cases (whereas fission is more puzzling since there is no linear ordering of stages in fission). Time-travel overlap does not undermine relation P, diachronic self-unity, yet there could be times when there are two or more centers of consciousness for a single person, as in McFly's situation. Thus, time travel can undermine *synchronic* self-unity. For this reason, time-travel overlap may be better than fission in exploration of Blackburn's "unity reaction," as I discuss later in this essay. By the way, the possibility of time-travel overlap also defeats the reason Parfit gives in *R&P* for "no survival" being the best interpretation of fission, when he refers to the oddness of one's playing tennis with oneself, given a dual-survival interpretation of fission (*R&P*, 256–57). This admittedly would be pretty weird, but it is conceivable—at least for a reductionist. See Barry Dainton, "Time and Division," *Ratio* 5, no. 2 (1992): 102–28.

I-related (that is, R_L-related) stage y that is future to z in external time. The symmetrical R_L as such does not order stages so as to generate personal time, and my point is that Lewis himself needs a nonsymmetrical I-relation to make the relevant distinction between personal and external time (if the I-relation is going to be necessarily coextensive with what matters in survival).

We defined the needed I-type relation I* so that

I*xy if and only if Ixy and the time of y is later than the time of x.

I have just argued that "time" here should be understood in terms of personal time, not external time, so it turns out that I* just is the *forward-looking* subset of R_L, that is, R_Ψ; so

$$I^* = R_\Psi$$

This means, however, that the requisite I*-relation is necessarily coextensive with Parfit's '71 conceptions of survival and "future selfhood" as these notions were explicated earlier when expressed as relations between stages. Recall that each of these relations in '71 were treated as necessarily coextensive and as distinct from P (self-unity) insofar as the '71 wedge is placed between survival and self-unity.

Earlier I argued that Lewis simply presupposed Parfit's '71 logical wedge between survival and commonsensical self-unity. Now I have argued that, in order to handle fission properly and to be able to account for the future orientation of survival, Lewis should adjust his account of the I-relation to I*, which turns out to correspond *exactly* with the "future self" (survival) relation R_Ψ in Parfit's '71 article. In other words, Lewis needs to fall back on *exactly* that allegedly counter-commonsensical account to which he was *attempting to reply on behalf of common sense!*

IV. The Reductionist Thesis and the Unity Reaction

As for the general question about what matters in survival—the question about which Parfit and Lewis argued—there is no foreseeable consensus on the relationship between identity and what matters to us in survival. Some not-unreasonable reductionist interpretations of fission will even refuse to place a logical wedge anywhere in this chain:

what matters in survival → survival → personal identity → identity *simpliciter*

For example, some say one would have *none* of these in fission (Ernest Sosa, Mark Johnston),[62] and others say one would have *all* of them (unlike Lewis, John Perry's reconstruction of H. P. Grice's account results in a theory in which there is presupposed no relevant logical wedge).[63] Such views are coherent and will reject at least one of the two premises in Parfit's fission-based argument that identity does not matter: that you would have what matters; or that you would not be identical with any post-fission person. This means, I believe, that Parfit's general argument is bound to fail (even though Lewis's argument does not show it). Similarly bound to fail are Parfit's other fission-based arguments for practical ramifications of reductionism, as presented in *Reasons and Persons* and in his 1986 *Ethics* piece.[64]

Parfitians probably should just forget about trying to formulate fission-based person-level arguments. It seems to me, however, that reflection on fission still may be useful in exploring the more fine-grained central issue pertaining to the relation between the reductionist thesis and the unity reaction. (Recall that the unity reaction maintains that as persons we are essentially unified even given the absence of anything like an indivisible soul.) For it is plausible that reductionism might motivate changes in self-conception if both (a) the unity reaction is at the core of our self-conceptions, and (b) the reductionist thesis conflicts with the unity reaction. The '71/Lewis account countenances *survival* in fission, by virtue of relation R_Ψ, and since this use of "survival" is a conceptual revision, the departure from ordinary self-conceptions is made explicit (but without leaping to anything close to eliminativism as Parfit did with the Extreme claims). And of course, the reductionist should expect some revisions in our self-conceptions, insofar as the reductionist thesis appears to generate the puzzles associated with fission and time travel, whereas the unity reaction at the core of our self-conceptions will simply tend to set such puzzles aside.

With the '71/Lewis account, the reductionist has a position that initially seems to conflict with the unity reaction: in fission there is survival without self-unity. Minimizing the significance of fission relative to prac-

---

[62] Ernest Sosa, "Surviving Matters," *Noûs* 24 (1990): 297–322; Mark Johnston, "Fission and the Facts," *Philosophical Perspectives* 3 (1989): 369–97.

[63] Perry, "The Problem of Personal Identity."

[64] Derek Parfit, "Comments," *Ethics* 96, no. 4 (1986): 832–72. See Johnston, "Fission and the Facts." For an informal dialogue on why the fission-based arguments are bound to fail, see my http://personal.bgsu.edu/~mbelzer/tent1B.html. Parfit has acknowledged the failure of his original argument for the claim that "identity does not matter" (see his "The Indeterminacy of Identity: A Reply to Brueckner"). But Parfit attempts to revive the argument by replacing the premise that one would not be identical with a post-fission person with the premise that it is *indeterminate* whether one would have identity in fission. See Parfit, "The Unimportance of Identity." This new argument will not work either, however, since it trades on the two types of indeterminacy that are exhibited respectively in Parfit's Combined Spectrum argument and in fission. See my "Why Fission Arguments Fail" (forthcoming).

tical reasoning and action, then, the reductionist minimizes the significance of self-unity. This gives Kantian philosophers, and others like Simon Blackburn, a precise target and a challenge—to explain exactly why deliberation and intentional action must be incoherent in such a case. Of course, it is a bit too easy to reply—they can simply point to, and reject or even ridicule, the revised use of the term "survival." The impasse suggests that it would be better to frame the issues in more precise terms.

Of course, '71/Lewis is not the only way to develop the reductionist thesis, which by itself does not require any person-level interpretations of fission at all (relative to concepts of survival, identity, and what matters in survival).[65] The claim that $R_\psi xy$ would hold across the branching point (that is, pre-fission stage x could be R_ψ-related to a post-fission stage y), together with the claim that R_ψ normally constitutes self-unity, is sufficient to generate the challenge to the unity reaction (without *any* accompanying person-level claims at all).

On the other hand, a reductionist can *deny* that R_ψ *could* hold across that branch point, as we will see in subsection A below. This means that the reductionist thesis does not necessarily conflict with the unity reaction. R_ψ can be formulated so that fission not only undercuts personal identity and self-unity, but also undercuts R_ψ as well. It is an open question, then, whether R_ψ could hold across the fission branch point, and thus, it seems to me, it is an open question whether the reductionist thesis conflicts with the unity reaction.

A. A reductionist defense of the unity reaction

I will now examine a reductionist thesis from David Velleman that can be used to attempt to explicate the unity reaction, although Velleman did not formulate the thesis for that purpose.[66] Velleman focuses on special types of direct connections between mental states and events that "function like memory in giving us first personal access to other points of view."[67] In memory there is a relation such that the memory has "first-personal access" to earlier states. First-personal access is explicated in

[65] There are sutras in the Pali canon in which the Buddha is depicted as refusing to engage in what I have called "person-level" speculation about personal identity. Asked directly whether the person who does an action is the same or different from the one who experiences the causal results of the action, he says that either answer is "extreme" and shifts attention to the specific processes (relations within what I have called R_ψ) that give rise to suffering and/or happiness. See *Samyutta Nikaya* XII.46, *Aññatra Sutta*, trans. Thanissaro Bhikku (Geoffrey DeGraf), available at http://www.accesstoinsight.org/canon/sutta/samyutta/sn12-046.html.

[66] David Velleman, "Self to Self," *Philosophical Review* 105 (1996): 39–75. While Velleman indicates (in a footnote) that he sees his work as related to Blackburn's, he does not explain the connection with Blackburn's "unity reaction." Velleman primarily seems to see his work as extending that of Parfit, both in refining the concept of psychological connectedness and also offering a new type of "identity does not matter" argument.

[67] Ibid., 42.

terms of "unselfconscious" (identity-free) reference that "does not rely on antecedent specification" of the target of the reference; such thoughts "require no other thought about whom they refer to."[68] This is precisely the type of first-personal consideration relative to agency that, according to Blackburn, grounds the unity reaction:

> If practical reasoning is essentially conducted from within a first-person perspective, imagining *my* doing something is a very different matter from imagining *someone else* doing something. The imagining is quite different, and ... this difference is absolute, and will not succumb to indeterminacies in constitutive questions of identity of anything through time.[69]

These comments by Blackburn are quite general. Velleman offers a precise explanation of why it should be so.

Working within the general parameters of Parfit's Psychological Criterion, Velleman restricts the relevant connections for relation Ψ to those with a certain *type* of "reflexive" content. For the simple causal view (associated with Parfit), a stage x is connected to y insofar as events in x cause events in y but not conversely, whereas on Velleman's "reflexive content" view of connectedness, a stage y is connected to x because events in y have genuine identity-free first-person access to events in x.[70] As for the fission puzzle, Velleman holds that in anticipating fission I could not think "first personally" about each of two (or more) later post-fission successors. Even though I could be "psychologically engaged" with each (and each later could have genuinely first-personal reflexive thoughts about me now), I cannot now have genuinely first-personal reflexive thoughts about either of them—which means generally that Velleman's version of relation R_Ψ could not hold across the fission branch point.

Velleman's view is based on the distinction between the *notional subject* of a thought and its *actual subject*. In imagining that I am Napoleon surveying a battle scene, I am the *actual* subject of the imagining, whereas

---

[68] Ibid., 60.

[69] Blackburn, "Has Kant Refuted Parfit?" 198.

[70] Parfit and Velleman can agree that psychological connectedness, Ψ, is not generally symmetrical. There is an important difference, however, in their reasons for the nonsymmetry of Ψ. Whereas Parfit's Ψ cannot be symmetrical if he is to make sure branching is possible, for Velleman Ψ is not symmetrical because of the direction of genuinely reflexive unselfconscious first-personal reference. Suppose stages x and y contain events e and f, respectively, where memory f makes genuine first-personal reference to the person constituted by x, by virtue of x's containing e (due to the notional subject of f and the relevant causal chain). Now it is not necessarily the case that e (or any other state in x) makes a similar genuine first-personal reference to the person constituted by y. So connectedness between stages is not necessarily symmetrical (just as "being connected" is not necessarily symmetrical between relevant states and events). So even though Parfit and Velleman agree that "connectedness" is not symmetrical, they can get different results in some cases, such as fission, as to the *direction* in which the relation may fail.

Napoleon is the *notional* subject. Intention and anticipation also have "a notional subject whom they present as 'me',"[71] where intentions "project" themselves into the future in two ways: they represent the world from a future point of view, and they are "sent" into the future, "by depositing them in memory for future retrieval"—but I do not have to specify "a person from whose point of view I am trying to frame my intention, because that point of view is fixed by the future causal history of the intention itself."[72] And the referent of "me" in the later context is "simply whoever fills the role of subject within that perspective" (that is, the perspective in the future at which the intention arrives to guide action). Under normal circumstances, my later self

> will turn out to occupy the position of notional subject in my inten-
> tion, and so he will turn out to be the person of whom I was thinking
> first-personally in the context. Being accessible to unselfconscious
> first-personal thought on my part, he qualifies as my real future
> self.[73]

To say that thoughts are "unselfconscious" about their reference is to say that they require "no other thought about whom they refer to":

> [G]enuinely reflexive thoughts don't rely on an antecedent specifi-
> cation of their target: they just point to the subject, at the center of
> thought.[74]

This is Velleman's way of expressing the "identity freedom" of thoughts that refer to a subject even without there being any activity of picking out the subject as the thing being referred to.

Using these concepts, Velleman develops, as follows, his argument that before undergoing fission I could not make either successor person "the notional subject of my anticipations unselfconsciously":

> Suppose that I try to think ahead into some future moment at which
> I shall have two psychological successors. If I try to picture the moment
> as it will appear in an experience specified merely as forthcoming, or
> to follow, I won't succeed in picking out the perspective from which
> I'm trying to picture it, since my picture may be followed, in the
> relevant sense, by two different experiences of the moment in ques-
> tion, and I cannot be trying to draw it from both perspectives at once.
> Similarly, my anticipation may be remembered in two different per-

---

[71] Velleman, "Self to Self," 70.
[72] Ibid.
[73] Ibid., 72.
[74] Ibid., 60.

spectives, and so I cannot frame it from a perspective specified merely as that in which it will be remembered. In order to specify the perspective from which I'm trying to picture the future, I'll have to identify it with one of my psychological successors or the other. That is, I'll have to pick out the person whose perspective is the intended target and destination of my projective thoughts—whereupon I'll be doing exactly what I do when imagining that I am Napoleon. My anticipation of the future will be nothing more than an act of imagination. By depriving me of *unique future perspectives,* fission would deprive me of *real future selves.*[75]

If this argument is successful, it would show that a reductionist thesis does not necessarily conflict with the unity reaction, since Velleman gives a reductionist account that supports the unity reaction to fission—indeed, his account is a more fine-grained explanation of the general points adduced by Blackburn. There is not self-unity in fission (in Velleman's terminology, the "self"-relation must fail) because relation Ψ (understood now in terms of reflexive content) cannot hold across the fission branch point.

B. Why Velleman's argument is not successful

Under ordinary circumstances we do *not* have "unique future perspectives," and thus the fact that there would not be unique future perspectives after fission cannot be what results in there not being real future selves in such a case. Under ordinary circumstances, I am confronted with distinct future perspectives insofar as I now can anticipate and prepare for each of several different future circumstances (for example, being in San Francisco tomorrow, and in New York next week).

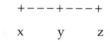

If at x I try to picture my perspective at y "specified *merely* as forthcoming" (what Velleman says I cannot do with respect to my fission successors), then it is relevant to point out that if this were an objection against being self-related to the fissionees, it also would be an objection against being Ψ-related to myself at several different points in the future. Likewise, about my anticipation of y at x in fission, Velleman says, "I cannot frame it from a perspective specified merely as that in which it will

[75] Ibid., 74–75, emphasis added.

be remembered"; but again, if this is an objection against Ψ-relatedness in fission, it also appears to defeat Ψ-relatedness in ordinary circumstances as well, since of course (in either case) the anticipation of y at x might be remembered at z as well. Right now I do not have a *unique* future successor in the sense that there is one unique momentary perspective awaiting me (at least, so I hope)—normally there will be many such perspectives in many different places and times, including places like nice beaches in the Caribbean. My first point, then, is that indeed we do plan for and anticipate divergent future perspectives.

Naturally, Velleman does not wish to deny that. More to Velleman's point, of course, would be the case in which the two unique future perspectives are perspectives on *the same spatiotemporal situation*. He says, "I cannot be trying to draw it from both perspectives at once."[76] But is it inconceivable to do this? Velleman's objection to the coherence of first-personal attitudes to each of the two fissionees turns out to be an objection much like Parfit's objection to the dual survival of fission view—that, for instance, one could end up playing tennis with oneself[77]—but for the reductionist this sort of thing is indeed easily conceivable.

To make it vivid, consider time travel once again—for example, the situation in which Michael J. Fox's character, Marty McFly, is observing himself in the parking lot at the end of the movie *Back to the Future* (see Figure 8).

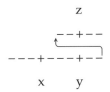

FIGURE 8. Time-travel overlap

Even though stages y and z overlap in a single spatiotemporal situation, I do not see why there could not be genuinely reflexive thoughts in x that are inherited by both y and z. Suppose I am a basketball player, preparing at t for an upcoming game at t*. Anticipating the time-travel scenario and knowing the person constituted by y and the one constituted by z (me in each case) will be on different teams, and indeed will guard each other, I now practice both defense and offense. I form strategies for both offense and defense, where "strategies" make explicit the highly conditional fea-

[76] Ibid., 75.
[77] Parfit, *Reasons and Persons*, 256–57.

ture of normal intentions insofar as strategies spell out what to do under
various circumstances.

Now suppose I play in a basketball game and then time travel and play
in it again (so to speak). In each case, I can be acting on the strategies I
developed in practice. ("When the opponent fakes a shot, don't stupidly
just jump"; "when planning to make a shot, give a head fake first"; and
so forth.) The relevant question here is whether in practice I could make
strategies that in the game are implemented by both *me*'s in the game—
and it is coherent to say so. This is not to say, of course, that I can practice
both roles at the same moment. With respect to each role, however, I can
practice it now just as easily as I can first go over what I need to do
tomorrow when I get to San Francisco, and then next week when I get to
New York (even though it would be difficult to go over both plans in my
mind at once). Adding the time-travel twist introduces an unusual element: that there will be (or could be) situations in which I am implementing my strategies in two different ways in a single situation.

Imagining what I will do in such a situation, given the time-travel twist,
does not require new conceptual resources. I rely on my ability to strategize
(to formulate conditional plans and intentions) and on the fact that I
expect to have future selves in diverse situations. The fact that, given the
time-travel twist, my future selves might interact by playing basketball
against each other does not necessarily undermine my ability to do anything that I normally can do. Velleman talks about a "future moment
when I have two successors," and he talks about trying to picture that
moment as it will appear in an experience specified "merely as forthcoming." The point of the time-travel discussion here is that because (a) in
ordinary circumstances we do confront a whole series of divergent future
perspectives and can and do routinely plan for them, and because (b) it is
coherent to suppose that stages could overlap temporally, given the coherence of time travel, it follows that it is coherent to suppose that in a single
situation my current strategies could be implemented simultaneously in
divergent ways within two or more distinct stages. Just as I can now
envision what I will be doing in San Francisco tomorrow and then in New
York next week, so also I can envision interaction of my two future stages
on the same basketball or tennis court.

I return now to the case of fission. When Velleman says "my anticipation may be remembered in two different perspectives, and so I cannot
frame it from a perspective specified merely as that in which it will be
remembered,"[78] we cannot read this uncharitably so that it would defeat
ordinary planning when I am coordinating what I will do in San Francisco tomorrow and then in New York next week. My planning for each
of the two successors (one in San Francisco and one later in New York) is,
in each case, conditional on expected perceptions and memories that each

[78] Velleman, "Self to Self," 75.

will have at the time when action will be appropriate, first in San Francisco, then in New York. As for fission, then, why couldn't planning for each of two *simultaneous* successors work in just the same way? Why can't conditionalization of plans and so forth work there just as it must be brought in to make sense of how we coordinate more than one future self? About fission, Velleman says:

> In order to specify the perspective from which I'm trying to picture the future, I'll have to identify it with one of my psychological successors or the other. That is, I'll have to pick out the person whose perspective is the intended target and destination of my projective thoughts. . . . My anticipation of the future will be nothing more than an act of imagination.[79]

Reflection on the time-travel case shows, it seems to me, that one *could* plan for two simultaneous successors in just the way that one can plan for two successive successors under ordinary circumstances. The simultaneity of successors in itself does not introduce complications with which we are not already familiar because of the fact that we can plan for diverse nonsimultaneous future perspectives. So it cannot be the fact that, in fission, my successors may overlap in time that defeats my ability to anticipate and plan for each in a genuinely first-personal way.[80]

It seems to me that Velleman has not shown that the fission case differs in relevant ways from ordinary planning when we know that we will have more than one future perspective later. True, my planning for fission would have to distinguish successors in the sense that the plans I make are conditional upon my being in one place rather than the other: when I picture seeing the Empire State Building, this picturing will be associated with other plans and expectations, so that it is correct to say that I identify this image with only one of my successors, namely, me in New York. But this surely does not mean that I "have to pick out the person" who is the intended target, since as Velleman has argued, ordinary intentions do not require that the person be picked out as such.

---

[79] Ibid.

[80] Moreover, because fission does not require temporal overlap, we can imagine stories in which there are no times at which stages from the two branches will overlap in external time (as with Parfit's philosopher and psychologist who do not overlap in external time; see *Reasons and Persons*, 264). In such a case, my plans for my fission successors could be much like my plans for myself at later times under ordinary circumstances—intending for each of them is much like intending for different parts of my normal future when I will be in San Francisco tomorrow and in New York next week. Of course, in such a case, I will not be able to assume that the later later-self will probably know things just because the earlier later-self learns them. In planning now for the later later-me, however, I can assume that the later later-me knows pretty much what I know now—discounting for forgetting, as we normally do, and so writing things down, and of course the earlier later-me can also write notes for the later later-me (like the thirty-minute branch in Parfit's "sleeping pill" case does; see ibid., 287). In any case, where is the conceptual difficulty here?

In ordinary deliberation I may formulate several different courses of action, dependent upon what happens. In so doing, I may think at a certain time t* that if p then I will do A at t; but if ~p, then I will do B at t, where p or ~p is something that will be settled at some time just before t. Before the time when p or ~p gets settled, I have no unconditional plan concerning A or B. At t* I do not know whether I will do A at t or B at t, but nonetheless I can anticipate doing one or the other, and moreover I can envision doing each of them. Whether I do A at t or B at t, in either case I regard the agent of the envisioned action "unselfconsciously as me" and identical with the notional subject of the thoughts at t* by virtue of which I envision each of the possible act types. If it turns out that p becomes settled as the case, and I do A at t, then in doing A I make it turn out that I am the actual subject referred to in the thought "I will do A at t, if p" when at t* I was making my plans.

I assume that these points about deliberation are not controversial. When I realize that p has been settled, and then do A at t, as a result of my earlier intending to do A at t, given p, then the agent who does A at t is (or will be) me, since I will turn out to "occupy the position of notional subject in my intention," and I will "turn out to be the person of whom I was thinking first-personally"[81] when I formed the conditional intentions. Of course, what is true of the agent who does A at t, would also have been true of the agent who would have done B at t, had ~p rather than p been settled prior to t. On some occasions, I may even rehearse (so as to be ready) what I will do, given p—as well as what I will do, given ~p.

Now in a fission case, let us suppose, there are circumstances that can be known beforehand concerning the diverse situations of each of the two successors later, and thus I now form intentions that are conditional upon those differences. For example, I believe that one of me will be in New York and the other will be in San Francisco. Let p be "I am in New York at t." I now intend conditionally to do A at t, given p, where p or ~p will be settled at some time shortly before t. I also conditionally intend to do B at t, given ~p. Just as I can form the conditional intentions in a case in which I assume that I will perform A or B at t, but not both, I also can form the conditional intentions in a situation in which I believe that I will both perform A at t and perform B at t. Suppose, relative to Figure 8, that incident y contains the performance of A at t, and suppose z contains the performance of B at t, while the earlier x includes the conditional intentions. We are examining the idea that x cannot be Ψ-related to y. Again, however, it seems to me that if in ordinary deliberation of the sort described above, x can be Ψ-related to y because of the action in y based on the conditional planning in x, then x can be Ψ-related to y in this case as well.

In saying that I believe I will perform A at t and that I will perform B at t, I do not wish to imply that I believe that I will perform A&B at t.

---

[81] Velleman, "Self to Self," 72.

Normally, of course, if I intend to A at t and B at t, then by some principle of "composition" there is some sense in which I intend to A&B at t. The details about this composition principle are not relevant here, since I mention it only to point out that, whatever the details, there is no such intention in this case (although there is a sense in which it would be true according to interpretations of fission where I survive as each of the successors). No principle of composition like that should be pre-supposed in characterizing a logic of intention that will be useful in planning for fission (or time-traveling) successors—and it does not need to be presupposed.[82]

Generally, then, I deny that we have "unique future perspectives" in ordinary experience that differ in any fundamental way from the "unique future perspectives" that we would have in future time travels or fissions. There are differences, of course, but can the differences be shown to be relevant to the question of Ψ-relatedness?

It is not difficult, of course, to imagine fission situations in which before-hand I would be overwhelmed by the number of anticipated fissionees or the complexity of coordination so as to be unable to do it very well, if at all.[83] The questions of complexity and conceivability should be kept dis-tinct, however. Even with one thousand fissionees, it as at least coherent that I intend (for example) to go to a certain football stadium and find a seat in the stands, and that each of the fissionees inherits this intention and acts on it in such a way that I become the actual subject of his mental states and actions as he makes his way to the stadium. I suppose numbers could be distributed at the stadium, or the seats numbered, etc., as part of some plan I might make up so as to coordinate further in this macabre scenario. If I knew now that it was going to happen, I might get really serious about doing it, using committees. And even though I probably could predict the outcomes of the committees, Peter Unger surely is right that I could not really anticipate very much about each of the future experiences of any of the fissionees insofar as I stayed focused on a complex plan that really would guide each of them.

My primary interest here is conceivability, not dealing in any detail with the relative complexities of two- or seven- or 1,000-person fissions. Yet it seems to me that Velleman's reflexive Ψ-relatedness is conceivable even with many fission descendants. There could be genuinely reflexive

---

[82] For logics that are applicable to intentions and that do not validate the principle of composition, see Marvin Belzer and Barry Loewer, "Deontic Logics of Defeasibility," in Donald Nute, ed., *Defeasible Deontic Logic* (Dordrecht: Kluwer Academic Publishers, 1997), 45–57.

[83] See Unger about 1,000 fissionees and the difficulty of identifying with each: Peter Unger, *Identity, Consciousness, and Value* (Oxford: Oxford University Press, 1990), 269–75. Similarly, Ray Martin points out that "a person may be able to anticipate the experiences of two fission descendants more fully than she can anticipate the experiences of any of a thousand fission descendants." Ray Martin, "Self-Interest and Survival," *American Philosophical Quarterly* 29 (1992): 319–30, p. 324.

first-personal thought between me now and each of many future fission successors. The main point here has been to reply to the idea that Ψ-relatedness in fission is undermined because of the impossibility of first-person anticipation and intentions across the fission branch point. I have tried to argue that the fact that we can form first-person conditional intentions for diverse future circumstances (in San Francisco tomorrow, in New York next week) allows us to see how it is possible to have genuinely first-person intentions for each post-fission successor.

It might be claimed that, even if I am right, we could not form unconditional intentions, or have unconditional anticipatory thoughts, by virtue of which we are Ψ-related to any post-fission successor. But I do not see why even this more modest point should be accepted generally. Suppose I now look forward to playing basketball, without anticipation of fission. I plan unconditionally to play and I am looking forward to it. My anticipation is in terms of a *type* of action, not some token action. There are infinitely many token events that later may realize my unconditional intention to play. If I also now anticipate fission, but know both fission successors will be playing in the game, it seems to me that my anticipatory thought, occurring before the fission, is such that each of the successors can become the actual subject of the thought in just the normal way. The fact that two or more of them are doing it is irrelevant. Just as Velleman grants that each can be Ψ-related back to me now, so also I now can be Ψ-related to each of them.

One might believe that unconditional intention involves straightforwardly intending individual actions. But this claim depends upon an assumption about intending and planning that is false. David Makinson has argued that individual actions are seldom obligatory, since there will be infinitely many ways to perform any obligatory act (type).[84] For instance, regarding obligations, suppose that I am obligated to give you a dollar; there is no individual action that my obligation requires. It requires me to do some individual action or other that is of the type "giving you a dollar." The individual act itself can be performed in infinitely many ways (handing you a dollar with my right hand, with my left hand, leaving it on the table, and so forth).

Likewise we seldom if ever intend individual acts. Rather, we intend act types. The individual action as performed is not intended as such in all its details, but it is intended as a type of action. Since plans and intentions typically involve planned or intended types of actions, not the token actions themselves by virtue of which our plans and intentions are realized, our planning and intending is highly conditional in nature (even when implicitly so). I intend to walk across the street. This means implicitly, if there is a truck coming, to wait, then look again. Since intentions are

---

[84] David Makinson, "Individual Actions Are Seldom Obligatory," *Journal of Non-Classical Logic* 2 (1983), 7–13.

highly conditional in this respect, it is not at all difficult to extend our normal planning to imagine a single situation in which I am at once drawing from two distinct sets of experiences of that situation as the situation unfolds. So suppose, prior to fission, I intend simply to go to the living room after the fission—this looks like an unconditional intention (or at least it can be interpreted that way if any intention can be). Each of my fissionees inherits the intention, so each thinks when he wakes up, "Oh, I should go to the living room now"—and each of me gets up and goes to the living room (except for maybe two or three of me who are struck by weakness of will and fall back asleep). Each performs an individual act due to the intention to do the act type "going to the living room." I do not see why each of the fissionees in thinking what he thinks, as he acts so as to realize the intention, cannot thereby become an actual subject of the pre-fission thought by virtue of which I intend to go to the living room after fissioning.

Of course, there could be thoughts now that could logically have only one successor subject, such as "Tomorrow I will play basketball with only one self in the game" (what I might be thinking when I decide *not* to fission). If I think that way, but undergo fission anyway (due to my fission addiction) so that two of me later show up to play, then admittedly neither successfully can do what I intended to do so as to become the actual subject of *that* intention. But so what? Obviously fission would change many things; this particular intention could not be satisfied, but even in that case there still could be enough reflexive connectedness for Ψ-relatedness with each of the two later selves.

I conclude that it would at least be coherent, then, for one to adopt Velleman's account of Ψ and nonetheless hold that one *can* be Ψ-related across the fission branch point. Thus, his explication of the reductionist thesis fails to reconcile it with the unity reaction; more importantly, it fails to give us a fine-grained version of the types of considerations to which Blackburn appeals in saying that the unity reaction has an "absolute grip" on us. Even if we give a central place to a reflexive-content based conception of Ψ, it is still plausible to suppose that there can be Ψ-relatedness without diachronic self-unity. The openness of the future that is assumed in ordinary deliberation corresponds formally to what one would encounter were one to be in a situation in which one were anticipating fission. The conditional and unconditional intentions that we form in the face of an uncertain future can be employed to provide for action on each of the different strands in the fission case. The complexities of such a case would not necessarily undermine agency even across a fission process.

I conclude that Velleman's "reflexivist" account does not support Blackburn's claim that the unity reaction has an "absolute grip" on our reflections about fission. Nonetheless, the initial plausibility of Velleman's account can help us to understand why the intuition of essential self-unity is "very strong in us."

C. The relation between the failure of the reflexivist explication of the unity reaction and Parfit's failure to explain why Lewis's account did not work

Blackburn has written that "[i]f practical reasoning is essentially conducted from within a first-person perspective, imagining *my* doing something is a very different matter from imagining *someone else* doing something."[85] But practical reasoning from within the first-person perspective does not necessarily involve my explicitly imagining "*my* doing something." Practical reasoning can be conducted without my explicitly making any judgments at all about *me* as such; that is, I do not need to make any person-level judgments from within the first-person perspective required for practical reasoning. Indeed, as Velleman points out, in intending to act I *do not have to specify* "a person from whose point of view I am trying to frame my intention." So even though it is true that imagining *my* doing something is different from imagining *someone else* doing it (as Blackburn says), this does not show that the unity reaction has an absolute grip on practical reasoning itself. In planning for tomorrow, my thoughts do not have to specify anything about *me*—my plans can be more like a list of action types ("put the garbage out; stop at the store"). And, as I have argued, because we use conditional intentions ("buy bananas if they are on sale") we *could* plan for diverse actions of disunified successors without having to introduce person-level thoughts that explicitly identify one or another successor as being the one from whose perspective X should be done. Of course, I do not at all wish to say that such person-level thoughts are always absent or that they would or should be absent in the bizarre cases.

We should distinguish, then, between (a) person-level descriptions of the first-person attitudes involved in agency, and (b) the first-person perspective that is itself involved in agency. Instead of supporting the grip of the unity reaction, Velleman's fine-grained analysis can help us see why the unity reaction does *not* have an absolute grip on our self-conceptions as agents. *In practical reasoning from within the first-person perspective, no person-level assumptions at all about identity or unity need to be made.* But of course these assumptions naturally are made when we *describe* first-person practical reasoning and agency—as in Blackburn's statement that imagining *my* doing something is different from imagining *someone else* doing it.

The same distinction was relevant to Parfit's failure to diagnose what was wrong with Lewis's response to the '71 account. Parfit relied on *person*-level statements to express his objections, but Lewis's response was immune to such objections. Nonetheless, looking into the stage-level details of Lewis's account, it became clear that he had failed to reconcile psychological reductionism with commonsensical assumptions about self-

---

[85] Blackburn, "Has Kant Refuted Parfit?" 198.

unity. Similarly, the '71/Lewis account, with its revised person-level use of "survival," did not help us much in sharpening the central issue about the relationship between the unity reaction and reductionism.

In each case, we find that what I have called *person-level* judgments are misleading or superfluous, given the reductionist framework. The '71/Lewis account makes for a simple impasse with the unity reaction. Objections against Lewis formulated in terms of *person*-level judgments (like those of Parfit) are going to fail to explain why he does not reconcile psychological reductionism about personal identity with commonsensical assumptions about self-unity. Likewise, Blackburn's general comments about the absolute grip are plausible, but they stay at the person level; and when we look more closely into the details, we do not find that anything at all about first-person practical reasoning supports the absolute grip of the unity reaction. One could make plans and form intentions to guide the actions of post-fission successors, and one could do so from within the normal first-person perspective, but person-level descriptions like Blackburn's obscure this fact.

V. Conclusion

In a recent paper, Sydney Shoemaker attempts to explain how an R_Ψ-based form of reductionism about personal identity is compatible with the idea that the self is a substance.[86] That the self is substantial is a traditional way of expressing the unity reaction. But since Shoemaker's account *is* R_Ψ-based, persons are (like tables and ships) subject to the vagaries of fission and other conceivable puzzles. Shoemaker attempts to articulate a reconciliation, but admits that he does not know how to do it:

> [T]here are conflicting tendencies in our thinking. There are tendencies that might be summed up in the slogan that the self is a substance. . . . And there are tendencies that emerge when we think about certain possible situations . . . and put ourselves in the place of those in those situations.[87]

Shoemaker concludes his paper by saying, "[T]here is a conflict here I do not know how to resolve."

A first step toward understanding the conflicting tendencies in our thinking is to see the distinction between person-level descriptions of

---

[86] Sydney Shoemaker, "Self and Substance," in James Tomberlin, ed., *Philosophical Perspectives 11: Mind, Causation, and World* (Oxford: Blackwell, 1997), 283–304.

[87] Shoemaker also discusses and sets aside the idea that we should not expect our concept of a person to be applicable in merely imaginary situations. See ibid., 301.

first-person states and the first-person perspective itself. The view of self as substance—and the grip of the unity reaction—arise out of forms of normal reflection upon, and *person-level descriptions* of, our first-person states. From *within* the experience of the first-person perspective itself, however, we quite naturally are free of the grip.

Philosophy, Bowling Green State University

THE NORMATIVITY OF SELF-GROUNDED REASON*

By David Copp

I. Introduction

In this essay I propose, and then attempt to ground, a standard of practical rationality. According to this standard, to a first approximation, rationality consists in the efficient pursuit of what one values.[1] This standard differs from the familiar principle of instrumental reason, which requires us to take the most efficient means to our ends, for it gives special emphasis to those of our ends that qualify as our values. It also differs from the principle of self-interest, which requires us to pursue our own good, both because we might value the good of others as much as our own good, and because, if we are unwise, we might value things that are bad for ourselves. I speak of the conception of rationality I develop as "self-grounded" because it requires the pursuit of a person's *own* values, and also because, as I shall argue, a person's values are grounded in her *identity*, on one useful conception of the identity of persons.

The idea of *grounding* a standard of rationality will require some discussion. The term comes from Immanuel Kant, as does my strategy, broadly understood, for I aim to ground the standard of self-grounded reason in the idea of autonomous agency, which of course is a strategy inspired by Kant's work in the *Groundwork of the Metaphysics of Morals*.[2] The account

* I am grateful to many people for helpful comments and discussion over the many years in which I have been developing the ideas in this essay. With apologies to those whose help escapes my memory, I would like to thank Nomy Arpaly, Sam Black, Michael Bratman, Justin D'Arms, Dan Farrell, Pat Greenspan, Don Hubin, Dan Jacobson, Marina Oshana, Michael Ridge, Michael Robins, David Sobel, Pekka Väyrynen, and David Velleman. I presented early versions of some of the ideas in this essay to audiences in the departments of philosophy at the University of Alberta, the University of Maryland at College Park, l'Université de Montréal, the University of Southern California, and the University of Florida, to the 1999 Conference on Moral Theory and Its Applications, Le Lavandou, France, and to the 2001 Conference on Reason and Deliberation, Bowling Green State University. I am grateful for the helpful comments of those who participated in the discussions on all of these occasions and especially to the other contributors to this volume, and its editors. I owe special thanks to Ellen Paul for encouraging me to integrate my thinking on identity with my thinking on rationality and for her useful comments.

[1] This formulation ignores a qualification I have discussed elsewhere. See David Copp, *Morality, Normativity, and Society* (New York: Oxford University Press, 1995), chap. 9; and David Copp, "Rationality, Autonomy, and Basic Needs," in Neil Roughley, ed., *Being Humans* (Berlin: de Gruyter, 2001), 334–55.

[2] Immanuel Kant, *Groundwork of the Metaphysics of Morals*, trans. James W. Ellington (Indianapolis: Hackett, 1981). See p. 50 (Ak 448). In references to the *Groundwork*, I refer first to the pagination of the Ellington translation and then to the pagination of the Prussian Academy Edition (Berlin: de Gruyter, 1902–).

I shall give of autonomous agency is very different from Kant's, however, and my conception of rationality is modest by comparison with a Kantian conception.[3] Most importantly, it does not guarantee a strong Kantian link between rationality and morality, for a person can exhibit a rational efficiency in the pursuit of what she values even if her values are morally abhorrent. Moreover, the grounding that I shall propose is compatible with naturalism; it does not rest on claims that purport to be synthetic a priori, nor does it depend on a nonnaturalistic metaphysics.

The basic idea is this: To be autonomous is to be *self*-governing. To be rational is at least in part to be self-*governing;* it is to do well, by a standard that we need to specify, in *governing oneself.* I argue that a person's values are aspects of her *identity* in a way that most of her ends are not, and that it therefore is plausible to view action governed by one's values as *self*-governed. This is also plausible on independent grounds. Given this, I say, rational agents comply with a standard—the "values standard"—that requires them to serve their values, and to seek what they need in order to continue to be able to serve their values.[4] I argue, then, that there is *reason* for an agent to serve her values and to seek what she needs in order to continue to be able to serve her values. An agent's values are a source of reasons—reasons of a kind that any rational person would take into account in deliberation, if she were aware of them, just in virtue of being rational. I call such reasons "self-grounded reasons," or "reasons of autonomy." I sometimes call the conception of self-grounded rationality the "autonomy conception."

The autonomy conception combines an account of the *content* of the standard of rationality with an account of its *grounding.* I begin, in Section II, by outlining some of the advantages of the conception. In Sections III and IV, I explain the conception of autonomous agency, and I briefly discuss Michael Bratman's model of such agency. In Section V, I develop an account of the identity of persons, and in Section VI, I propose a conception of an agent's values and link it to my account of identity and through it to the conception of autonomous agency. I then turn to the content of the standard of rationality. In Section VII, I outline the values standard, and, in Section VIII, I address an important objection, the objection from ungrounded ends. In Sections IX and X, I explain the idea of

---

[3] Christine Korsgaard has recently suggested that "the normativity" of the principle of instrumental rationality "must be traced to the agent's self-government, specifically to his capacity to be motivated to shape his character in accordance with an ideal of virtue." See Christine Korsgaard, "The Normativity of Instrumental Reason," in Garrett Cullity and Berys Gaut, eds., *Ethics and Practical Reason* (Oxford: Clarendon Press, 1997), 220 n. 13. My account does not invoke a moralized conception of autonomy.

[4] In speaking of "serving" a value, I mean to cover both cases of taking means that are instrumental to fulfilling or realizing something one values and cases of doing what is constitutive of fulfilling or realizing a value. For this usage, see Gavin Lawrence, "The Rationality of Morality," in Rosalind Hursthouse, Gavin Lawrence, and Warren Quinn, eds., *Virtues and Reasons* (Oxford: Clarendon Press, 2002), 90.

grounding a standard and argue that the values standard can be grounded in the conception of autonomous agency. Finally, in Section XI, I explain the way in which, on the autonomy conception, rationality has priority for practical deliberation.

II. Why Take This Road?

I believe that the autonomy conception has both intuitive and theoretical advantages over the familiar alternatives. One advantage is that it is compatible with a pluralistic view of reasons and normativity, a view that could be called "reasons pluralism." I do not aim to defend reasons pluralism in this essay, and an advocate of the autonomy conception could consistently deny it. Nevertheless, I think reasons pluralism is plausible. To focus the discussion, I offer an example.[5]

Imagine a group of mountain climbers who, after weeks of struggle, are within a day's climb of the summit of Everest. They will have to turn back tomorrow. Just after they begin their final push for the summit, they come across a small party of climbers who are huddled together, clearly in terrible need of help. These people, "the victims," are in their predicament as a result of an extraordinary combination of circumstances, including unusually extreme weather. They need to be helped down to a lower elevation, and their needs are immediate and life-threatening. The first group might realize that, morally, they ought to help. Yet they are indifferent to moral considerations; they do not care whether they are doing what they morally ought to do. They hurry on to the summit. In doing so, they are being extremely selfish and callous, but, intuitively, this is compatible with their being entirely *rational.*

This example brings out several intuitive points about our ideas of rationality and reasons for action, points that are accommodated by the autonomy conception.

First, the example suggests that a person can be rational in knowingly doing something morally wrong. Kant would disagree, I take it, but I shall not argue against the Kantian view in this essay.[6] My focus will be on developing the autonomy conception rather than on arguing against alternatives or exploring the relation between rationality and morality.

One might think that if the climbers believe they ought morally to help the victims, then they have moral values, and thus, on the autonomy conception, they have a self-grounded reason to help. I will argue, however, that an agent's values (in the relevant sense) are not beliefs. Despite their beliefs, the climbers may lack moral values, and thus, on the autonomy conception, they may be rational to ignore any temptation to help

---

[5] The example is based on an event described in Jon Krakauer, *Into Thin Air: A Personal Account of the Mount Everest Disaster* (New York: Anchor, 1998).
[6] Kant, *Groundwork*, 50–51 (Ak 447–49).

the victims. Rationality does not ensure moral virtue. A rational person may have moral values, but she need not.

Second, I think the example supports the intuitive plausibility of reasons pluralism—the view that there are different kinds of reasons, including moral reasons, self-grounded reasons, reasons of etiquette, and so on. And the example suggests, third, that if rationality is a matter of responsiveness to reasons, it is a responsiveness to reasons of a certain kind. Even if there are reasons of etiquette, for example, a rational person might decide not to give them any weight, just as, in the Everest example, the climbers decide to set aside moral considerations. On the autonomy conception, the reasons that a rational agent takes into account in deciding what to do, if she is aware of them, simply in virtue of being rational, are self-grounded reasons—these are (roughly) facts about the impact the agent's alternatives would have on what she values.[7]

Fourth, in the example it seems intuitively plausible both that the climbers rationally ought to continue the climb and that they morally ought to help the victims. Intuitively, just as there are different kinds of reasons, there are different kinds of "ought." This raises the question of what the climbers ought to do *simpliciter*. I have argued elsewhere that there is not a highest-order normative standard or kind of reason relative to which there is in general something that ought to be done *simpliciter*.[8] If I am correct, there is no answer to the question of what the climbers ought to do *simpliciter*, but I will not be arguing for this position here. The autonomy conception is compatible with the thesis that the rational action is required *simpliciter*, but does not entail it.[9]

One might object that when we are making a decision, we want to know what to do *period*, not merely what to do *rationally*. My account speaks to this concern, but not by assigning a special *metaphysical* status to self-grounded rationality. Rather, as I shall explain, it assigns a *deliberative* priority to self-grounded rationality. Self-grounded reasons play a central role in rational deliberation that is not played by other kinds of reasons, such as moral reasons—unless the agent has the relevant values. One might insist in light of this that, on my account, self-grounded rea-

---

[7] Philippa Foot rejects reasons pluralism in "Morality as a System of Hypothetical Imperatives," in Philippa Foot, *Virtues and Vices* (Berkeley: University of California Press, 1978), 161 and 168 n. 8. Yet she appears to agree with me that moral considerations are not a source of reasons of a kind that any rational person would take into account in deliberation, if she were aware of them, just in virtue of being rational.

[8] David Copp, "The Ring of Gyges: Overridingness and the Unity of Reason," *Social Philosophy and Policy* 14, no. 1 (1997): 86–106.

[9] There is risk of terminological confusion. Some writers think that the English expression "ought" refers, when unqualified, to what I would say "ought rationally" to be done. For example, where Gavin Lawrence speaks of "what the agent ought unsubscribed (that is *qua* rational) to do," I speak of what an agent "ought rationally" to do. See Lawrence, "The Rationality of Morality," 120. I think there is no answer to the question of what the climbers ought to do *simpliciter*, but I do think that, in the example as I understand it, they ought *rationally* to continue the climb.

sons are the only *genuine* or genuinely *normative* reasons. But there are moral considerations that count for and against our decisions, and it would obscure this fact if we denied that moral reasons are "genuine" or "normative." But this is a side issue. It concerns how best to formulate reasons pluralism, not how best to formulate the autonomy conception.

The autonomy conception has certain theoretical advantages in addition to its intuitive advantages. First, it seeks to *ground* the values standard. Donald Hubin has proposed that rationality consists in conformity to something like the values standard, but he sees no need to ground the standard.[10] Admittedly, it will not be clear why it is an advantage to provide a grounding until I have explained what this involves, but the objective is to explain the normativity of the values standard.[11] It is to explain why so-called self-grounded reasons deserve the label "reasons." I agree, then, with Christine Korsgaard that a principle of practical reason "needs a normative foundation."[12] Second, my account offers a kind of realism about rational requirements that is compatible with metaphysical naturalism. On my account, thoughts about rational action and choice are beliefs with naturalistic truth conditions.

In short, I think that the autonomy conception is at the core of an intuitively plausible view about reasons and rationality, which can be integrated into a plausible overall view of deliberation and choice. In the Everest example, if we think the climbers were acting rationally in pressing on to the summit, it is because we understand them as efficiently pursuing their underlying values. Of course, our concern with our *own* rationality is not due, at least not primarily, to a concern to *understand* what we are doing. It is due to a concern, inter alia, to do well in governing our lives.[13] The autonomy conception can explain this. It conceives of rationality as consisting in a kind of success in serving one's values, and as I conceive of valuing, it is partly constitutive of having values (in the relevant sense) that a person have certain policies for her own behavior. On this picture, as I will explain, rational behavior instantiates a kind of self-government.

III. AUTONOMOUS AGENCY

The literature on autonomous agency is primarily concerned to explain how we can be self-governing despite the variety of causal influences

---

[10] See Donald C. Hubin, "The Groundless Normativity of Instrumental Rationality," *Journal of Philosophy* 98 (2001): 445–68.

[11] There are different conceptions of normativity. I discuss some of the varieties in David Copp, "Moral Naturalism and Three Grades of Normativity," in Peter Schaber, ed., *Normativity and Naturalism* (Frankfurt: Ontos-Verlag, 2004), 7–45.

[12] Korsgaard, "The Normativity of Instrumental Reason," 218, 249.

[13] David Velleman proposes that "self-understanding" is the "constitutive aim" of action—in something like the way in which "truth" is the "constitutive aim" of belief. David Velleman, *The Possibility of Practical Reason* (Oxford: Oxford University Press, 2000), 16–24, see 22. My account does not require postulating a "constitutive aim" of action. A thorough discussion of Velleman's proposal is beyond the scope of this essay.

on our actions and despite the possibility of causal determinism. The explanandum in this literature is free intentional action. My project is a different one. I shall set aside the worry about determinism. Moreover, the explanandum in my project is, crudely, intentional action that is *governed* by the agent in a way that she "identifies" with. It is action that is autonomous in a different, "thicker" sense. Cases of *akrasia* or weakness of will count as autonomous action in the thinner sense, if any actions do, but in general they do not count as autonomous in the thicker sense that concerns me, for an *akratic* agent normally does not identify with her action in the relevant way. I shall focus on the thicker notion.

Autonomy is a matter of being "self-governing." Consider the idea of a self-governing country or state. States are affected in many ways by the actions of other states and by the environment in which they operate, but excessive outside interferences of certain kinds are incompatible with self-government. In a self-governing state, law and public policy originate in decisions of the government, and the government is able to implement its decisions without being subject to certain kinds of interference. By analogy, an autonomous person is someone capable of deciding for herself what to do, and capable of executing these decisions without interference of certain kinds. To be autonomous, one must meet conditions of two kinds. There are "internal" conditions, including the requirements of being able to make decisions, to form intentions, and to act on one's intentions, and there are "external" conditions, including the requirement of being free of certain kinds of interference, including coercion and manipulation.

The external requirements of autonomy do not play a role in my account of rationality, for one can deal rationally with external interferences, such as coercion and manipulation. The autonomy conception explains rationality in terms of the internal requirements of self-government; thus, for my purposes here, we can set aside the idea that there are also external requirements.[14]

The internal requirements of autonomy are psychological and physical properties and capabilities. First, one must have a will. That is, one must have a structure of beliefs, values, and desires, and the ability to decide how to act and to form intentions to act on the basis of these beliefs, values, and desires. Second, one must have the ability to make one's will effective in leading one to act. That is, one must have the ability to act on one's decisions, to act intentionally. One must have the power to perform bodily movements that, if one is successful, will constitute doing what

---

[14] Our values are shaped by the values of our family and culture, but such influences do not undermine our autonomy. Were it not for such influences, we might not be capable of the kind of planning required for autonomy. See Will Kymlicka, *Multicultural Citizenship* (Oxford: Oxford University Press, 1995), chap. 5, esp. 82–84. See also Marina Oshana, "Personal Autonomy and Society," *Journal of Social Philosophy* 29 (1998).

one has decided to do. The notion of intentional action needs to be explicated, but I believe it is clear enough for my purposes. Autonomous behavior is intentional, in that the agent could in principle give her reason for acting as she does, where her reason is a function of her intention in acting. Of course, intentional action can be irrational, so it is not necessary that the agent's reason for acting be a good reason.

There are important distinctions to be drawn among conative states. Most important for my purposes is the distinction between ordinary desires and intentions. I might desire to eat some ice cream, even though I intend not to do so, and I might intend to do something, such as to adhere to rigid guidelines about grading, even though, in the ordinary sense of the term, I have no desire to do so. Michael Bratman has proposed that intentions are "planful states" in a way that desires are not.[15] The key point, however, is that there is a distinction.[16]

There is also an important distinction between "intentions in action" and "prior intentions."[17] A prior intention can be a specific intention—an intention to do some relatively specific kind of thing at a specific future time. But some intentions govern a kind of action in kinds of situations that I might find myself in on many occasions. An example is my intention to wear a seatbelt when driving. Bratman suggests that we think of general intentions of this kind as "policies." The idea can be usefully extended to intentions that can be achieved only if a plan is implemented over time, where this involves acting on various more specific intentions that are components of the plan. Policies are intentions that are functionally general in that they guide the formation of various specific intentions over time.[18]

To understand the thicker notion of self-governing agency, we need to focus on the idea of *governing* something, understood as a matter of regulating the thing, or exercising systematic control. Autonomous agency is agency that is controlled or regulated by the agent.[19] The ability to have policies or plans is necessary to self-governing agency, so understood; and to the extent that we are self-governing, we shape our lives in accord

---

[15] Michael Bratman, *Intentions, Plans, and Practical Reason* (Cambridge, MA: Harvard University Press, 1987).

[16] Korsgaard has suggested that "willing an end just is *committing* yourself to realizing the end" (Korsgaard, "The Normativity of Instrumental Reason," 245). She understands such commitment normatively, as analogous to "making a promise" (ibid., 245 n. 60). In my view, to will an end is to form a kind of intention, which is not essentially a normative matter. Korsgaard's view is disputed in R. Jay Wallace, "Normativity, Commitment, and Instrumental Reason," *Philosophers' Imprint* 1 (2001): 3–10. http://www.philosophersimprint.org/001003/.

[17] John Searle, *Intentionality: An Essay in the Philosophy of Mind* (Cambridge: Cambridge University Press, 1983), 84–85.

[18] Gideon Yaffe pressed me to explain the sense in which policies are general.

[19] For a valuable discussion of the agential control of action, see John Martin Fischer and Mark Ravizza, S.J., *Responsibility and Control: A Theory of Moral Responsibility* (Cambridge: Cambridge University Press, 1998).

with our policies or plans. At a minimum, we are not simply driven by our strongest desires, but we select which desires to satisfy and which to treat as ends. There is, for example, the experience, when standing on a tall observation platform, of feeling drawn to jump. To the extent that we are autonomous, we can ignore such desires; we can refrain from treating their objects as goals to achieve. This ability to decide which of our desires to act on is part of what is involved in the ability to plan.[20] Beyond this, in planning, we decide among alternative future courses of behavior, settle on priorities and strategies for achieving our priorities, and of course, if we are self-governing, we act on the basis of such strategies and plans. A person may have various plans or policies, and qualify as acting autonomously in the thin sense, even if she fails in various ways to control or regulate her action systematically on the basis of her plans or policies. She might follow her plans only in a haphazard manner; her decisions might not tend to serve her plans well, or they might not reflect the priorities she has settled on in her planning, and so on. Hence, an agent can be autonomous in the thinner sense without being self-governing in the thicker sense that interests me.

In this thicker sense, I shall argue, a self-*governing* person regulates or controls her actions on the basis of intentions and plans that serve her values, or are at least constrained by her values, such that serving those intentions and plans does not conflict with serving her values. I shall argue that our values are a central subset of our policies, but this is a different point. Here the point is that the values of an autonomous agent constrain the rest of her policies and goals—the ones that do not qualify as values. Hence, the policies and goals that shape her decisions have been shaped by her values. Of course, autonomous agents can act on urges and desires, but they indulge such things within boundaries set by their values. In what follows, when I speak of autonomous agency, I shall intend self-governing agency in this thick sense.

IV. MICHAEL BRATMAN ON AUTONOMOUS AGENCY

In introducing the thick notion of autonomous agency, I described it as agency that is controlled and regulated by the agent herself in a way she "identifies" with. I have not yet explained in what sense an autonomous agent identifies with the way she controls actions that are governed by her values. Before proceeding to explain this, it will be useful to consider a different model of self-governing agency, the model that has been pro-

---

[20] Michael Bratman stresses the ability we have to decide whether to take the object of a desire to be an end. See his "Identification, Decision, and Treating as a Reason," *Philosophical Topics* 24 (1996): 1–18. Bratman cites Rachel Cohon, "Internalism about Reasons for Action," *Pacific Philosophical Quarterly* 74 (1993): 265–88.

posed by Michael Bratman.[21] His model is similar to mine, and my proposal builds on his work in the theory of action. The main difference between our views is that Bratman invokes a metaphysical conception of the identity of persons in order to explain the sense in which self-governing behavior issues from the self. I invoke, instead, a nonmetaphysical idea, the idea that an agent can "identify" with a way of controlling action.

Bratman aims to provide a model of the "core elements of autonomy" in at least a significant family of cases of autonomous agency, which he calls cases of "hierarchical self-governance."[22] His model agrees with mine in seeing autonomous action as regulated by a subset of the agent's policies. But whereas I think the relevant policies are our *values*, in Bratman's model they are "self-governing policies."[23] These are second-order policies concerned with the functioning of desires and other conative states in practical reasoning. An example would be my policy of giving weight in deliberation to my desire for safety. Such policies function to guide deliberation. Moreover, because they typically are stable across time, and because guidance by them involves reference to plans and desires the agent has at other times, they play a role in organizing the agent's life across time. They play this role by means of "continuities and connections" of the kind that, as Bratman reminds us, are central to Lockean accounts of personal identity.[24]

I need to explain this. At any time that a person is conscious, she is having various experiences, thoughts, feelings, emotions, and so on. As time passes, the person has new experiences, remembers past experiences, anticipates the future, regrets the past, forms plans, adopts goals, learns new things, and so on. These events in the psychological life of a person are related to one another in a variety of ways that go beyond their mere ordering in time. We are not dealing with a kaleidoscopic flux of unrelated events. For instance, there are memories of previous experiences and anticipations of future experiences; there are plans that are formulated at one time and carried out in specific intentions at a later time. A person might have forgotten many childhood experiences by the time she is in middle age, but as a teenager she likely still remembered many of them, and in middle age she might remember much of what occurred to her as a teenager. In this way, events in childhood might be linked to the memories of middle age by an overlapping chain of memories. Given all of this, the Lockean idea is that a person *is* essentially a

---

[21] Bratman presents his account in a series of papers. A useful overview is in Michael Bratman, "Planning Agency, Autonomous Agency," in James Stacey Taylor, ed., *Personal Autonomy* (Cambridge: Cambridge University Press, 2004), 33–57.

[22] Ibid., 35–36.

[23] Ibid., 43.

[24] Ibid., 41–42. Bratman refers to Derek Parfit, *Reasons and Persons* (Oxford: Clarendon Press, 1984), 206–8, for a contemporary discussion of a Lockean view of personal identity.

stream of psychological events and states that is unified by the fact that the events and states in the stream are linked together in a chain by the kinds of psychological continuities and connections to which I have been referring.

We can now return to Bratman's view. His idea is that self-governing policies function to guide deliberation in a way that involves reference to plans and desires the agent has at other times, including especially future times. These policies therefore organize the agent's life across time by means of continuities and connections of the kind that, in Lockean accounts of personal identity, organize what would otherwise be merely a kaleidoscopic sequence of psychological events into a unified life of a single person. Because of this, Bratman argues, self-governing policies are fitted to constitute "the agent's practical standpoint."[25] They are fitted to do this provided the agent is "satisfied" with them. Bratman explains the latter idea negatively: to be satisfied with a self-governing policy P is for P *not* to be in conflict with one's other self-governing policies (and quasi-policies) in a way that tends to undermine the role of P in supporting Lockean continuities and connections.[26] Finally, Bratman points out, the policies that figure in his model will be self-referential because they will speak to their own functioning.[27] In sum, Bratman holds that, "in a basic case," self-governing agency consists in "the known guidance of practical thought and action by [reflexive] self-governing policies with which the agent is satisfied."[28]

This is an important and elegant model of self-governing agency, and it deserves a sustained discussion beyond what I can give it here. But I have two worries.

First, I believe it is a mistake to think that autonomous action is typically guided by self-governing policies. I think that what is crucial to self-government is that one's life be governed by one's *values*. In order to make it fully clear why I say this, I need to develop my accounts of values and identity, which I will do in the next two sections of the essay. But the basic point is simple. I value my safety, for instance, and values of this kind are not self-governing policies because they are "first-order." In valuing my safety, I am concerned directly with my safety, not with my conative states or with my practical deliberation. It seems to me, however, that actions that are controlled or governed by first-order values of this kind have at least as good a claim to qualify as autonomous as do actions that are controlled or governed by Bratman's self-governing policies. Most

---

[25] Bratman, "Planning Agency, Autonomous Agency," 42.

[26] For Bratman, a "quasi-policy" is a "higher-order, policy-like" concern that is not, strictly speaking, a self-governing policy. Michael Bratman, "Reflection, Planning, and Temporally Extended Agency," *Philosophical Review* 109 (2000): 57–60 and 49–50. See also Bratman, "Planning Agency, Autonomous Agency," 44, 38–39.

[27] Bratman, "Planning Agency, Autonomous Agency," 44.

[28] Ibid.

of the values of a typical person are not self-governing policies, since they are first-order. It seems to me that self-governance by such values is typical of autonomous agency.

In response, Bratman could point out that seeming first-order values often consist in clusters of policies that include self-governing policies.[29] For example, valuing my safety might involve a policy of not permitting my love of adventure to outweigh safety in my deliberation. Still, presumably I would have this policy because I value safety. In general, it seems plausible that self-governing policies are adopted to serve our values. So I see no reason to privilege self-governance by self-governing policies by comparison with first-order policies, such as the simple policy of seeing to my safety. Hence, I think Bratman's model describes a special case of autonomy rather than the typical case.

Second, I think we need a richer account of the agent's endorsement of, or identification with, the elements of her practical standpoint. "Satisfaction" with reflexive self-governing policies is inadequate. To see this, imagine an obsessive person who is obsessed with giving no weight in practical deliberation to her obsessions (including this one). This obsession appears to qualify as a self-referential self-governing policy, and the person may count as "satisfied" with it since its Lockean role may be unimpeded by conflict with any other self-governing policies (or quasi-policies).[30] If so, then it may qualify as part of the person's practical standpoint. This seems to be a mistake, because the person neither endorses this obsession nor endorses its having a role in her deliberation. If it has such a role, she might be ashamed that it does. After all, she is obsessed with giving it *no weight*. So I think we should exclude it from her "practical standpoint."

It seems to me, then, that there are two main problems with Bratman's account. In my view, autonomous action is, roughly, action guided by a person's values, where, as I will explain, a person's values figure in her "identity" in a sense that ensures that she endorses their governing her action. A person's values can be first-order, so my view avoids the first problem with Bratman's account. Moreover, as I will explain, the fact that a person's values figure in her identity ensures that they are relevantly endorsed, so my view also avoids the second problem.

---

[29] Bratman urged this point in a helpful correspondence about my criticisms of his view. See also Michael Bratman, "Autonomy and Hierarchy," *Social Philosophy and Policy* 20, no. 2 (2003): 160–63.

[30] Her other obsessions may conflict with it, but they typically would not be self-governing policies (or quasi-policies). An obsession with her hair, for example, would be first-order, so it would not be a self-governing policy or quasi-policy, and it might not affect her deliberation, for her obsession not to give weight in deliberation to her obsessions stands in its way. If so, it would not impede the Lockean role of the latter. On Bratman's account, she counts as satisfied with the latter provided that no self-governing policy or quasi-policy undermines its Lockean role. See note 26 above.

V. Autonomy and the Identity of Persons

The life of an autonomous agent is governed in some important sense by the agent *herself*. This may suggest that an adequate account of autonomy needs to invoke a metaphysical conception of what agents *are*—a metaphysical conception of the *identity* of persons. As we saw, Bratman invokes a Lockean conception of the person. I think, however, that an account of autonomy should be neutral among various metaphysical accounts of the person. What we need, to use Bratman's term, is a viable conception of the agent's "practical standpoint," which can be understood, roughly, as the set of psychological states of the person that, when they control her behavior, qualify that behavior as *self-governed action*. The idea of a practical standpoint presupposes that we can identify a person in order to draw a distinction within the person's psychology between different ways that action is controlled, so it assumes that the metaphysics of persons is not at issue. The issue we face is psychological, not metaphysical.

In this section, I shall propose an idea of the psychological identity of persons, and use it to develop a conception of the agent's practical standpoint. The basic idea is that certain of a person's beliefs about her life constitute a whole that we can call her "identity" because of the way that these beliefs ground emotions of esteem, such as pride and shame. Such emotions are related to a person's conception of herself because she "identifies" in a relevant way with their objects. Philippa Foot has written: "The characteristic object of pride is something seen . . . as in some way a man's own." [31] I think that a corresponding point could be made about shame and other emotions of esteem. I propose, then, to take a person's identity—her "self-esteem identity"—to be constituted by (roughly) the set of propositions about her life that she believes and that ground emotions of esteem. [32] A person's practical standpoint can be seen as that part of her identity that is concerned, inter alia, with plans for her life—plans which are such that her beliefs about her success or failure in accomplishing them ground emotions of esteem.

The use of the term "identity" to express a psychological notion of the sort I have in mind is fairly recent. [33] Korsgaard has proposed that a

---

[31] Philippa Foot, "Moral Beliefs," in Foot, *Virtues and Vices*, 113–14. Foot's dictum would need to be reformulated to deal with cases in which pride takes a propositional object, for a proposition is not viewed as "a man's own." A person may be proud of a painting, or proud *that* he made the painting. Following Foot, we could perhaps say, in cases of the latter kind, that the object of a man's pride is a proposition about an actual or possible state of affairs involving the man—where, she would add, the obtaining of that state of affairs is viewed as some sort of achievement or advantage.

[32] I develop this suggestion in detail in David Copp, "Social Unity and the Identity of Persons," *Journal of Political Philosophy* 10 (2002): 365–91.

[33] The 1933 edition of *The Oxford English Dictionary* (Oxford: Clarendon Press, 1933) does not give an entry for "identity" with anything like the relevant meaning. In the 1976 *Supplement* to the O.E.D., however, the term "identity crisis" is given, with the first cited usage being 1954. Perhaps, then, we should speak of the "baby boomer conception of identity."

person's identity is a system of characteristics that the person has and values having.[34] But I want to allow for cases in which a person disvalues an aspect of her identity. During apartheid in South Africa, blacks were abused and humiliated on account of being black, and it is likely that many of them disvalued being black. Yet being black is a property that I would want to treat as part of their identity. K. Anthony Appiah has suggested that the identity of a person is a set of "properties important for social life," which might "matter to their bearers in very different ways." [35] But a person might be tormented by an apparently trivial event that she takes to be quite central to her life even though, and perhaps because, it was not important socially. I would want to treat this as an aspect of her identity.

We should evaluate accounts of identity on the basis of their explanatory usefulness. Different accounts might have different explanatory merits. I initially developed the idea of self-esteem identity in order to cast light on some issues in political philosophy, especially the power and importance of nationalism and patriotism. In this essay, I will use the idea to illuminate the difference between self-governed action and action that is intentional but that conflicts with our values or is governed only by relatively shallow and perhaps transient goals or desires.

I have suggested that the life of an autonomous agent is governed by her own policies and plans, and, more specifically, by her *values*, which are a subset of her policies and plans. The connection with the idea of identity is, I shall argue, that a person's values qualify as aspects of her identity. This remains to be explained, but if we assume it to be correct, then we can see a connection between governing one's life on the basis of one's values and governing one's life *oneself*. I have introduced the idea that an agent who regulates her life on the basis of her values qualifies as self-*governing*. I am now suggesting that she also qualifies as *self*-governing, for her values figure in her identity and constitute her practical standpoint. They ground emotions of esteem that reveal the shape of her self-conception. Moreover, I want to argue, *any* self-governing agent governs her life on the basis of her values. For otherwise, given that her values are aspects of her self-esteem identity (as I will explain), she would be ashamed or disappointed in herself on account of her actions, which would indicate a failure in self-government as she herself sees things. I want to say, then, that an agent is self-governing just in case she governs her life on the basis of her values. Self-governed behavior is not merely intentional and uncoerced. It is regulated by our values, and given that our values are deep psychological features of ourselves that affect our fundamental atti-

---

[34] See Christine Korsgaard, *The Sources of Normativity*, ed. Onora O'Neill (Cambridge: Cambridge University Press, 1996), 101. Korsgaard speaks of our "practical identity."

[35] K. Anthony Appiah, "Identity, Authenticity, Survival: Multicultural Societies and Social Reproduction," in Charles Taylor et al., *Multiculturalism: Examining the Politics of Recognition*, ed. Amy Gutmann (Princeton, NJ: Princeton University Press, 1994), 150–51.

tudes toward ourselves, and thereby figure in our identity, self-governed behavior also in this way *expresses* the agent's *identity*. The argument turns on the idea of self-esteem identity, which I shall now proceed to explain.

I need to begin with a brief discussion of the concept of self-esteem.[36] Self-esteem is a matter of the degree to which one feels satisfied with oneself on balance, and this is a matter of the degree to which one has a sense of *worth*. A sense of worth should not be identified with a set of beliefs about one's value. A person might believe herself to be valuable, or even to be superior to others, but have low self-esteem, feeling unworthy and insecure. Another person might believe herself to be mediocre, but, despite this, have a solid sense of self-esteem. Self-esteem involves an emotional assessment of oneself, or an emotional stance toward oneself.

A range of emotions is involved. Call them "emotions of esteem."[37] On the positive side, a person can feel good about herself, satisfied or comfortable with herself, or have a sense of worth or security or confidence in herself. A person can take pride in various things to which she takes herself to be related in a relevant way. A person can feel enhanced by something. On the negative side, a person might feel worthless or dissatisfied or uncomfortable with herself, or have a sense of insecurity, or lack confidence. She can feel shame, humiliation, or embarrassment. She can feel diminished by something. All of these emotions can bear on a person's self-esteem.

A person's emotions of esteem are grounded in her beliefs, often in a cluster of beliefs, in one of two ways. First, an emotion of esteem might take as its object a proposition that the person believes. For example, a person might be ashamed that she stole a radio. Second, the person might have a belief she would cite, or the propositional object of which she would cite, to explain her feeling. For example, a person might explain being ashamed that she stole the radio by remarking that she knew at the time she was doing something wrong.

Emotions of esteem can be fleeting. It might be a temporary and short-lived fact about me that I feel ashamed of myself for leaving a miserly tip for a waiter. But even if the shame I feel about the tip is short-lived, it might be a relatively enduring fact about me that I feel ashamed when I recall gaffes I have committed, such as leaving a small tip. We are inter-

---

[36] In this and the following six paragraphs, I follow the argument in David Copp, "Social Unity and the Identity of Persons."

[37] Gabriele Taylor speaks of "emotions of self-assessment" in her essay "Shame, Integrity, and Self-Respect," in Robin S. Dillon, ed., *Dignity, Character, and Self-Respect* (New York: Routledge, 1995), 168. Taylor holds that self-esteem is primarily to be understood in terms of pride and humiliation (p. 173). See also John Deigh, "Shame and Self-Esteem," in Dillon, ed., *Dignity, Character, and Self-Respect.* Deigh relates self-esteem to a range of emotions of the kind I mention (pp. 135–39). He links the idea of having disgraced oneself and the idea of shame with the idea of who one is, and he links the ideas of disgrace and shame to self-esteem.

ested in stable and enduring facts of this kind about a person's emotions of esteem and their grounds.

Consider, then, the set of propositions about a person that are believed by the person and that ground emotions of esteem in her in one of the two ways given above, in a stable or relatively enduring way. Let us provisionally define a person's self-esteem identity as consisting in this set of propositions. Suppose, for example, that you are proud that you have Greek ancestry, ashamed that you cannot speak Greek, embarrassed that you have a tendency to leave miserly tips, and mortified that you stole a radio. In this case, your belief in certain propositions explains these emotions (or the propositions are the objects of the emotions). These propositions are included in your identity.

We need to amend this account, for there are cases in which people would feel emotions of esteem in various hypothetical circumstances that seem diagnostic of their identity. Imagine a man who is not proud of his Greek ancestry, but who would feel diminished if he somehow came to believe that he did *not* have Greek ancestry. If this is true of him, his having Greek ancestry ought to be counted as part of his identity. There are also cases in which a person's emotions of esteem would be affected if, counterfactually, she believed certain things about other people, or about a group or an entity, to which she takes herself to be relevantly related.[38] For example, the man might feel pride if someone else whom he believes also to be Greek won the Nobel Peace Prize. In this case too, having Greek ancestry ought to be counted as part of the man's identity.[39]

Here, then, is the proposal.[40] The self-esteem identity of a person at a particular stage in her life is the set of propositions about herself, each of which she believes, where her belief grounds an emotion of esteem. In some cases, her belief "actively" grounds such an emotion. In other cases, her belief grounds such an emotion "potentially" in one of two ways. Either it *would* ground an emotion of esteem if she had certain relevant beliefs about other people or about a group or entity to which she takes herself to be relevantly related, or, if she came to believe its negation, this new belief would ground an emotion of esteem. More formally:

The proposition that she has property F or that she is R-related to an entity E is an element of S's identity during a stage *s* of her life just in case S believes the proposition during *s* and *either*

(a) this belief grounds an emotion of esteem in a stable and relatively enduring way during *s*, or

---

[38] For this purpose, we consider the closest possible world in which the person has the beliefs in question. I am assuming the account of counterfactuals in David Lewis, *Counterfactuals* (Oxford: Blackwell, 1973).

[39] Nomy Arpaly helped me with this kind of example.

[40] This paragraph is taken with some modifications from my "Social Unity and the Identity of Persons."

(b) it would do so, if S had certain beliefs about E or about other
people whom she believes to be F, or to be R-related to E, or
(c) if S were to come to believe during s that she is not F, or that she
is not R-related to E, then, other things being equal, this belief
would ground an emotion of esteem in a stable and relatively
enduring way during s.

For present purposes, the important point is the connection between
self-esteem identity and self-government. Suppose that you have planned
your life around various projects, such as raising a family, excelling in
your career, being fair in your dealings with others, and so on. The degree
to which you are content with yourself will be grounded, among other
things, in the degree to which you believe you are finding success in these
projects. Since self-contentment is an emotion of esteem, this means that
the fact that these are your projects and that you are succeeding in them
is an aspect of your identity. Moral commitment and moral character are
also entangled with your identity. If a person subscribes to a moral principle, attitudes of shame, guilt, or contentment would be grounded in her
record of compliance with the principle. Indeed, the fact that she subscribes to the principle likely would be an aspect of her identity, for she
likely would feel ashamed if she came to believe that she does not actually subscribe to the principle. And the things a virtuous person believes
about her moral character also normally ground emotions of esteem such
as pride or shame, either actually or potentially. A virtuous person would
see herself as honest, as not manipulative, and so on, and she would feel
ashamed or diminished if she came to see herself as dishonest or as
manipulative. Hence, her identity would normally include propositions
such as that she is honest and nonmanipulative.

Similar considerations show that a person's *values* are aspects of her
self-esteem identity. If a person values honesty, she would tend to feel
ashamed of herself if she were to realize she had acted dishonestly, for
instance, and she would also feel ashamed of herself if she came to believe
that she is not an honest person. Hence, the fact that she values honesty
will be an aspect of her self-esteem identity. Nor is this merely likely to be
the case. It seems to me that a person who values honesty must have a
tendency to feel ashamed if she thinks she has acted dishonestly or if she
comes to believe she actually is not honest. This is why the presence or
absence of such emotions is evidence of a person's values.[41] In general,
then, on my account of valuing, and on my account of identity, a person's
values are aspects of her identity.

There is a technical difficulty that needs to be addressed. A person's
identity is a set of propositions she believes. The difficulty is that, on my

---

[41] Aristotle suggests that our character is revealed in our feelings. See Aristotle, *Nicomachean
Ethics*, book 2, chapter 3, 1104b3ff. I owe this reference to Elaine Sternberg.

view, as I will explain more fully in the next section, a person's values are policies or general intentions rather than beliefs. Moreover, such a policy can be merely implicit in the sense that one might not be able to formulate it and one might not follow it self-consciously.[42] Hence, if I want to maintain that a person's values are "aspects" of her identity, it appears I need to say what proposition a person believes when she values V such that (a) it qualifies as an element of her identity on my account of self-esteem identity, and (b) it concerns V in a relevant way or is appropriately related to V. Suppose, then, that you value honesty. In this case, I think you would believe that you have a policy of being honest. This belief might be merely implicit, in that you might not have it consciously in mind; and it might be rather inarticulate, in that, for example, you might not think of yourself as having a "policy" rather than simply a desire to be honest.[43] Nevertheless I think some such belief would be present. Jay Wallace has argued that our intentions are ordinarily "fairly accessible to consciousness," given the role they play in shaping our deliberation. He argues, in fact, that someone who does not believe that she intends to do x "cannot really be described as having the intention to do x."[44] The point, of course, is that policies are general intentions. My proposal, then, is that if a person values V, the proposition that she has a policy of pursuing V is an element of her identity. Indeed, a cluster of beliefs regarding V will normally be included in her identity, including especially beliefs about her success or failure in serving V. For example, if she believes she missed an opportunity to serve V, she will tend to be disappointed in herself. A person's values are revealed by the emotions of esteem that she feels or tends to feel, and these values are embedded in her psychology in virtue of their connection with such emotions. Given all of this, I think it is appropriate to speak of a person's values as being "aspects" of her identity.

A person *endorses* the role of her values in governing her actions in that she is content with herself when she deliberates and acts in accord with them, is ashamed to fail to do so, and so on. To see the importance of this, notice that a person with an obsession might be ashamed of her obsession and ashamed to indulge it. In such a case, the fact that she has the obsession would be an aspect of her identity, but we would not want to count indulging it as an instance of self-government. This is for two reasons. First, the obsession is not an aspect of the person's identity in the

---

[42] We presumably have a policy of speaking grammatically, but we might not be able to formulate the rules of grammar and might not follow the policy self-consciously. The policy is "implicit" in this sense. Frank Jackson describes grammar as an "implicitly understood theory." See Frank Jackson, "Cognitivism, A Priori Deduction, and Moore," *Ethics* 113 (2003): 569.

[43] Jay Wallace speaks of beliefs that are not "explicitly and articulately present to the consciousness of the agent" but that "are implicit in the agent's understanding of their situation." Wallace, "Normativity, Commitment, and Instrumental Reason," 21 n. 52.

[44] Ibid., 22.

right way. Control of one's deliberation and actions by one's values is control by an aspect of one's identity that is endorsed in one's identity, where such control is also endorsed in one's identity. Obsessions are not normally endorsed in this way, nor is their role in one's life. Second, an obsession is not normally a policy, and the compulsive nature of an obsession subverts the control of one's actions by policies. In discussing Bratman's view (in Section IV), I gave an example of an obsessive policy, but the policy in that example was in part a policy of giving itself no weight in deliberation, so the agent did not endorse its playing a role in her deliberation.

Let me then return to the argument that began this section. If an agent regulates her life on the basis of her values, she qualifies as *self*-governing, for her values figure in her identity. Her actions express her self-conception. And she qualifies as self-*governing*, for she endorses control of her actions by her values and endorses her values. Moreover, if an agent is self-governing, she governs her life on the basis of her values, for otherwise she would be ashamed or disappointed in herself on account of her actions, which would indicate a failure in self-government as she herself sees things. Hence, as I claimed, an agent is (thickly) self-governing just in case she governs her life on the basis of her values. Her values constitute her practical standpoint.

VI. Values as Policies for Action

I have argued that (thickly) autonomous agency is agency that is regulated by the agent's values. And I have suggested that our values are a kind of policy, where a policy is a kind of general intention. I now need to defend this suggestion. I suggested that our values figure in our *identity* in a way that ordinary policies and plans need not. I want to argue that, because of this, and because we endorse control of our actions by our values, to the extent that we are *self*-governed, our actions are shaped and constrained by our values. To make the argument go through, however, I need to show that values can be understood as things that *can* regulate behavior, and to achieve this, I want to argue that values are a kind of policy for action. I also need to argue that our values are basic or fundamental policies that, to the extent we are self-governed, constrain the more occasional and instrumental plans and ends that shape action. The fact that our values are *intrinsic* policies helps to support this view, as I shall explain, as does the fact that our values figure in our *identity* in a way that ordinary policies and plans do not. The latter fact means that there are emotions of esteem to back up the controlling and regulating function of our values. It means that the engine of self-esteem helps to regulate the actions of a self-governing agent.

Let me begin to explain why I hold that our values—or our values "for action"—are a kind of policy. We need to distinguish, of course, between the things that a person values and her state of valuing those things. Consider, for example, what would be involved in valuing honesty, friendship, and so on. I think it is plausible that a person who values honesty must have a policy of being honest. She might sometimes fail to be honest, of course, but honesty must be her policy. It is not enough, for example, that she be honest merely as a result of finding honesty in her best interest from time to time. T. M. Scanlon suggests that to value friendship is among other things to have a policy of being a "good friend," of being loyal to friends, of being concerned with their interests, of spending time with them, and so on. It is also to have a policy of seeking to have friends, to keep the friends one has, and to want those we care about to have friends of their own.[45] Thus, I think that to value honesty and friendship would be, inter alia, to have a set of rough-and-ready policies regarding truth-telling, spending time with friends, and so on. In general, I think, to value something "for action" is, inter alia, to have a kind of policy with respect to it.

More is involved in valuing than having policies. The policies in question must be relatively stable. Our values do not switch on and off like lightbulbs. They are policies of and for temporally extended beings. Normally, moreover, a person who values something is satisfied with the relevant policy and does not regret it or desire to lose it.[46] Of course, we can imagine circumstances in which a person who values honesty would regret her honesty. Perhaps honesty has cost her a friend, for example. A person can have a kind of alienation from her values, perhaps viewing herself as naive for valuing honesty the way she does.[47] Nevertheless, such regret or alienation cannot go too far. For if a person values honesty, she would tend to feel shame or guilt or disappointment in herself, or regret, if she failed to be honest on a given occasion. Some of our policies are not like this. For example, even if I have a policy of reading the newspaper every morning, I would not feel disappointed in myself if, on some occasion, I listened to the news on the radio instead. This shows, I think, that I do not *value* reading the newspaper as such. Perhaps I value getting the news, but if so, then I would feel disappointed in myself if I failed to do anything at all to get the news. Our values for action, therefore, are part of our self-esteem identity, as I have already explained.

I now want to add that I have in mind things that we value *intrinsically*. Our values are "intrinsic policies." This idea is easiest to characterize negatively, as follows. If a policy is intrinsic, we do not have it merely because we think that carrying it out will be or may be instrumental to carrying out other policies that we have or achieving other things that we

---

[45] T. M. Scanlon, *What We Owe to Each Other* (Cambridge, MA: Harvard University Press, 1988), 88.

[46] Here I am influenced by Bratman's views about self-governing policies, in his "Planning Agency, Autonomous Agency," 41–45.

[47] Kadri Vihvelin suggested that a person can be alienated from her own values.

want.[48] Instrumental plans and ends rest on other ends, but intrinsic policies do not. For example, my policy of wearing a seatbelt is not intrinsic, since I have that policy only because complying with it contributes to my safety. But my policy of seeing to my safety is intrinsic. I do not have it merely for instrumental reasons. Thus, given that our values are intrinsic policies, they are more basic in the government of our lives than our more occasional and instrumental plans and ends.

I propose, then, that for a person to value something "for action" is at least in part for her to have an intrinsic policy of choosing or acting in relevant ways, a policy that is relatively stable, that on the whole she is content to have, a policy compliance with which affects her emotions of self-esteem and which is therefore partly constitutive of her identity, and a policy whose role in governing her actions she endorses.[49] This account could be taken as a stipulative, but I think it meshes with an ordinary understanding of what is involved in valuing.

One might object that there are cases in which valuing does *not* seem to involve having policies for action, at least not centrally. These are cases in which we value things we believe we cannot affect in any significant way. For example, I might value the accomplishments of Aristotle.[50] I realize I can do nothing to affect the accomplishments of Aristotle, so my valuing them would seem not to involve my having any policies.

In response, I propose that, even in cases of this kind, a person must have relevant *dispositions*. Suppose, for example, that a person values the pristine environment of Ellesmere Island. If she came to know that the island is threatened by pollution, she surely would have a tendency to support calls for conservation and the like. Having such dispositions is the kind of thing involved, inter alia, in having a policy of the relevant kind. Moreover, the problem cases seem to be ones in which a person values an instance of a kind that she values, where valuing the *kind* involves having a relevant policy. For example, a person who values Aristotle's accomplishments may value them as an example of philosophical accomplishment, and if so, she would have corresponding policies, such as a policy of encouraging, supporting, and applauding such accomplishments. But the important point is that there is such a thing as having a policy, and valuing something "for action" does involve having relevant policies.

My proposal, after all, is to explain rationality and self-grounded reasons in terms of the values standard, and the values standard is to be

---

[48] Compare Scanlon, *What We Owe to Each Other*, 79.

[49] In *Morality, Normativity, and Society*, I explained valuing in a slightly different way, in terms of subscribing to a standard, but there is a close connection between subscribing to a standard and having a policy. See 177–78, 84, 87–88. I proposed a different kind of account in "Reason and Needs," in R. G. Frey and Christopher Morris, eds., *Value, Welfare, and Morality* (Cambridge: Cambridge University Press, 1993), 112–37. It was criticized in Gilbert Harman, "Desired Desires," ibid., 138–57.

[50] Various people pressed me to discuss examples of this kind.

understood as concerned with our values for action, values the having of which involves, inter alia, having relevant policies. Our "values for action" are a subclass of our values. (If this is doubted, as I said, we could take my usage to be stipulative. The values standard would then be concerned with policies of the relevant kind.)

Various other proposals have been made about what is involved in valuing something. Scanlon holds that to value something is to take oneself to have *reasons* for holding positive attitudes toward it and for acting in certain ways in regard to it.[51] There are several problems with this proposal. First, it makes valuing something more of an intellectual matter than seems plausible, since it seems to imply that one must have the concept of a reason in order to value anything. Second, it seems that a person's values might run contrary to her beliefs about reasons. A person might take herself to have (aesthetic) reasons to hold positive attitudes toward listening to classical music, but she might not value listening to it. She might not enjoy it, and she might have a policy of avoiding it.[52] If she enjoyed jazz and listened to jazz on a regular basis, then it would be more revealing, I think, to describe her as valuing jazz rather than classical music, regardless of whether she would agree that she has (aesthetic) reasons to listen to jazz. Finally, and most important, Scanlon's proposal is not open to me. He aims to explain valuing in terms of taking oneself to have a reason, but one thing I am trying to explain is what a person would be thinking, in thinking she had a reason. I need an account of valuing that does not use the notion of a reason because my goal is to explain self-grounded reasons in terms of the attitude of valuing.

One might suggest that to value something is to *believe* it is valuable. It seems to me, however, that this proposal also makes valuing more of an intellectual matter than is plausible. A person might have no *beliefs* about the value of listening to music yet still *value* listening to jazz. The proposal also runs into difficulty with pluralism about the bases of value. A person might believe that listening to classical music is aesthetically valuable yet think that listening to jazz is valuable as a source of pleasure. Her values might track the latter beliefs rather than the former. Finally, a person's values might run contrary to her beliefs about what is valuable. She might believe that listening to classical music is valuable, yet she might strongly dislike it and have a policy of seeking out jazz. We *could* say that she "values" listening to classical music, simply to report her belief, but in most contexts, I think it would be misleading to say this.

It is plausible, nevertheless, that valuing something (in my sense) typically goes hand in hand with believing the thing is valuable or good, in at least some respect. Such belief is not necessary, however. In many cases, valuing something (in my sense) *precedes* believing that the thing is valu-

[51] Scanlon, *What We Owe to Each Other*, 95; see also 87–100.
[52] This example was suggested to me by Richard Schubert.

able. For example, in most cases, I believe, people come to value having a family without first having beliefs about the value of a family. There is perhaps a biological basis to our valuing having a family, which would help to explain this. For my purposes the important point is that, as the example suggests, a *belief* in the value of something is not invariably prior in the order of explanation to *valuing* the thing (in my sense). Moreover, the example shows that it need not be *irrational* for a person to value something in a case in which the fact that she values it (in my sense) is not explained by a belief that the thing is valuable. And it shows as well that it need not be irrational to value something (in my sense) *without* believing it is valuable. We are not irrational to value having a family in the years before maturity brings an understanding of why having a family is valuable.

One might object, however, that it *would* be irrational to value something (in my sense) while believing that the thing has *no* value *at all* or that it is not good in *any* respect. It might seem that there would be a kind of incoherence in this combination of valuing and belief. A person is content with herself when she acts in accord with her values, but it might seem that it would be incoherent to be content with oneself for acting in accord with a policy if one believes that it, or its object, has no value at all. In response, I concede that emotions of esteem depend on one's beliefs in subtle ways.[53] Yet, despite this, a person can value something that she believes not to be good in any respect, and can do so, I think, without irrationality. Someone might value listening to jazz even if she believes there is nothing good at all about listening to jazz. When asked why she spends so much time listening to jazz, she might reply that she loves it even though she can't explain why. I am not convinced that there would be an incoherence in her state of mind or an irrationality in her behavior.[54]

My proposal, then, is that to value something is, inter alia, to have a policy. Bratman has suggested that to have a policy is to have a general intention governing kinds of action in kinds of situations.[55] If this is correct, it is no surprise that deliberation that begins with our values can lead to action. If I have a policy of seeing to my safety, and if this involves having a general intention, then we can see why I form an intention to wear a seatbelt on getting into a car since I believe that wearing a seatbelt serves my safety. If to value something is to have a general intention, then in reasoning about how to achieve what we value, we will form more

---

[53] This idea has been addressed by many writers on the emotions. See Foot's brief groundbreaking discussion in her essay "Moral Beliefs," 113–14.

[54] This point needs more discussion. Steven Wall helped me to see the need to mention it.

[55] Having such a policy could be understood as a matter, inter alia, of intending to comply with certain relevant standards or norms. This suggestion brings my discussion of valuing into contact with Allan Gibbard's moral psychology, which postulates the state of norm acceptance, and the psychology I have proposed, which postulates the similar state of subscription to a standard. See Allan Gibbard, *Wise Choices, Apt Feelings* (Cambridge, MA: Harvard University Press, 1990); and Copp, *Morality, Normativity, and Society.*

specific intentions and, when appropriate, form the intention to act, other things being equal. In this way, the account of valuing that I recommend makes transparent the relation between valuing, deliberation, and action. This is a theoretical advantage of the account.

In this section, I have been defending my view that our values are central to the autonomous regulation of behavior. First, I explained that our values are a kind of policy. Second, I argued that because they are intrinsic policies, to the extent that we are self-governed they govern our formation of specific instrumental plans that then constrain and guide our actions. Moreover, given this, and because of the way our values are components of our identity, cases in which we govern our actions by our values qualify as cases of self-government.

VII. RATIONALITY AND VALUES

According to the autonomy conception, the concept of rationality is closely related to the concept of autonomy. Rationality is a matter of doing well at self-government (understood in the thick sense) and at securing the requirements of self-government. Controversy would center on what governing oneself well consists in. I have been arguing that governing oneself (understood in the thick sense) is basically a matter of living in accord with one's values. If so, governing oneself well must consist basically in doing well at living in accord with one's values (and securing the requirements of doing so). This then is what I propose rationality to consist in. Ignoring certain qualifications, I propose the following standard, which I call the "values standard":

> A person is to serve her values as well as she can, overall and in aggregate, and in situations where more than one alternative would maximally contribute to serving her values, she is to serve her (other) intrinsic goals as well as she can, overall and in aggregate.[56]

To a first approximation, I hold that this is the standard that agents comply with insofar as they are rational—assuming that they have approximately accurate beliefs about what they value and about how to achieve what they value. It suggests the following principle:

---

[56] A person's goal is intrinsic if the person does not have it merely because she thinks that achieving it will be or may be instrumental to achieving other things that she wants. The formulation in the text ignores some of the caveats I mention in what follows. I need to leave the notion of "serving" one's values unexplicated. But see note 4 above. Important complexities lurk under the surface here. Philip Pettit has proposed that "serving" something one values might consist in "promoting" it or in "honoring" or "expressing" it. In some cases, it may seem more appropriate to "honor" something we value than to "promote" it. See Philip Pettit, "Consequentialism," in Peter Singer, ed., *A Companion to Ethics* (Oxford: Blackwell, 1991), 230–40.

> Agent S is rationally required to do A in circumstances C just in case either (a) doing A in C is the action that would best serve S's values, overall and in aggregate, or (b) doing A is one of a group G of actions open to S in C, each of which would serve her values, overall and in aggregate, better than anything else she could do, and, of all the actions in G, doing A in C would contribute most to serving her (other) intrinsic goals, overall and in aggregate.

One might have various objections to this proposal, including the objection that a person's values can be pernicious. I will not be able to address every objection, but I will discuss those that seem most important. Before doing so, however, I need to mention four caveats.

First, there are constraints on the overall structure of a person's values, goals, and beliefs. To the extent that a person is rational, her values and beliefs are coherent with one another, and her (other) intrinsic goals are coherent with her values and constrained by them and by her beliefs, as well as coherent among themselves. Whether an agent is rationally required to attempt to achieve coherence in a given case depends on the costs and benefits of doing so, given the time and effort that would be required and given the agent's values and situation.[57] Second, a rational person serves her values as well as she can in light of the information available to her. She can be led by misinformation to believe that some action will serve her values when it will not, or to think that something will not serve her values when it will. Yet when her beliefs are reasonable, she may be acting rationally in acting on those beliefs.[58] To be sure, a rational person seeks information that is relevant to her capacity to serve her values and goals. She seeks such information to the extent that she is reasonable to believe that she should, given her values, her epistemic standards, and her epistemic situation.[59] And she assesses what to believe in a given epistemic situation in light of her epistemic standards or values.[60] Third, a rational

---

[57] There are complexities here that I must pass over. Compare John Rawls, *A Theory of Justice* (Cambridge, MA: Harvard University Press, 1971), 143. See Scanlon, *What We Owe to Each Other*, 121–22.

[58] Hence, the autonomy conception makes room for both kinds of error that Gavin Lawrence thinks any "proper theory" would accommodate. See Lawrence, "The Rationality of Morality," 121.

[59] A person's "epistemic standards" are norms she accepts that pertain to the rational formation of belief. An example is the rule to believe something only if the evidence or supporting reasons on balance make its truth significantly more likely than its falsity. By a person's "epistemic situation"—with respect to a given proposition—I mean her situation as it bears on the reasonableness of believing the proposition, given her epistemic standards.

[60] I pass over the problem of grounding epistemic standards. It is plausible that epistemic standards are appropriately grounded when, roughly, conformity with them would serve us well, in the typical circumstances in which we human beings actually find ourselves, in attaining true beliefs and avoiding false beliefs. On the account of practical rationality I am proposing, it is possible, even if unlikely, that a person who qualifies as practically rational might have epistemic standards that are not grounded in this way. For her epistemic standards may be such that conformity with them serves *her* well in pursuing what she values

person assesses her values and goals in light of new information when she believes she has reason to reconsider them in light of the new information. Fourth, where a person's serving her values (or goals) would put at risk her ability to sustain herself as an autonomous agent, rationality permits her to choose to sustain herself as an autonomous agent, by seeing to it that she is able to meet her basic needs.[61]

Even if we set aside these caveats, however, there is more to rational agency than merely acting *in accord with* the values standard, since this could happen by chance. Rationality is a matter of *governing* oneself well, and how well a person is doing at governing herself depends on the way in which she makes her decisions and not merely on what she decides to do. Setting aside various complexities, the basic idea is that rational behavior is *guided* by one's *values*. Such guidance seems to require a person to have at least approximately accurate beliefs about the content of her values, and to act in the belief that her action "makes at least as much sense," given her values, as would anything else.[62] In some cases, an agent is guided by her values in an explicit way. She deliberates about what to do, beginning with her values, considering how best to effect them, and finally reaching a decision about what to do. In many cases, however, an agent acts without consciously going through any reasoning. If she is guided by her values, there is something she values such that she does what she does *because* she thinks that her action *makes sense* in light of that thing. But she normally would not think that the key property of the thing she values is just that she values it.[63] She need not be guided by the values standard as such.[64] Thus, ignoring certain complexities:

---

even though it is not the case that conformity with them would serve human beings well, in typical circumstances, in attaining truth and avoiding falsehood. See Philip Kitcher, "The Naturalists Return," *Philosophical Review* 101 (1992): 53–114; e.g., 63. Compare Rawls, *A Theory of Justice*, 397.

[61] Meeting one's needs is a precondition for an autonomous life, so this qualification fits within the autonomy conception of rationality. I am not certain how the qualification should be worded. It should perhaps be restricted to emergency situations. The idea would be that rationality permits securing one's needs in emergency situations, even if doing so is contrary to serving one's values. For example, even if a rescue worker values his work, he may be rational to balk at going into a burning building when the risk to his life is excessive. By an emergency situation, I mean a situation with two key characteristics. First, it is reasonable for the agent to believe that serving her values would undermine or put seriously at risk her ability to sustain her status as an autonomous agent, not in a merely temporary or minor way, such that she could later compensate for neglecting her needs, but in a permanent and decisive way. And second, it is reasonable for her to believe that sustaining her status as autonomous would permit her to carry on in the future to serve at least some of her values. A version of the values standard that is qualified in the relevant way could be called the "needs and values standard."

[62] The locution "makes sense" is used in Gibbard, *Wise Choices, Apt Feelings*.

[63] For a related point, see Philip Pettit and Michael Smith, "Backgrounding Desire," *Philosophical Review* 99 (1990): 565–92.

[64] That is, a rational agent need not use the values standard as a decision procedure.

In a circumstance where agent S is rationally required to do A, and where S has approximately accurate beliefs about what she values, and about how to serve or achieve what she values, S is fully rational in acting only if (1) S does A intentionally, and (2), where V is something S values, S does A for the reason that, among other things, S judges that doing A will best serve V, and (3), where V, $V_1, \ldots V_n$, is the set of things S values, S judges that doing A makes the most sense given V, $V_1, \ldots V_n$.[65]

The reasons *for which* she acts should correspond to the self-grounded reasons that there are.

This suggests the following picture: A rational person—a person who complies with the values standard—governs herself on the basis of her values, making decisions that serve her values well given the priority she assigns to different values, and given the information she has. In situations in which all of her options would do equally well at serving her values, her values give her discretion, and she can do what will best satisfy her other intrinsic goals. She seeks information she needs in order to govern herself well, and she assesses the information and decides what to believe in light of her epistemic standards. She also seeks to sustain her ability to govern herself in this manner, at least insofar as doing so is compatible with her values, given her information. Rationality permits her to reconsider what to value, even if it calls for doing this in light of other things that she values. If a person values a life spent in the great outdoors, say, then, other things being equal, she lives this way despite the temptations of the city. But if she has values that would better be served by an urban life than by life in the woods, she might face difficult decisions. She might decide that her other values argue against the outdoors life, and she might give it up. Eventually she might cease to value it. This kind of change of values, in the interest of furthering one's ability to serve one's values, can be entirely rational.[66]

---

[65] I ignore the possibility of situations in which the agent judges that several actions would serve her values equally well. Where agent S is rationally required to do A because doing so will best serve her values, our assessment of the rationality of S's performance should be sensitive to, among other things, (1) whether S does A intentionally, (2) whether S does A for the reason that it will best serve her values, and (3) whether S believes that doing A makes the most sense given her values. In ordinary *akrasia*, the agent satisfies (3) but fails to do A. She may succeed, however, in serving something else that she values or takes as an end. Some cases of this kind will qualify as cases of "cleverness," as Wallace uses the term in "Normativity, Commitment, and Instrumental Reason," 1. In inverse *akrasia*, the agent succeeds on count (1), and perhaps also on (2), but believes that something other than A makes the most sense. In another kind of case, the agent succeeds on counts (1) and (3) but acts for the wrong reason. See Nomy Arpaly, "On Acting Rationally against One's Best Judgment," *Ethics* 110 (2000): 488–513.

[66] A similar point is made by Hubin, "The Groundless Normativity of Instrumental Rationality." David Schmidtz points out that having certain "final ends" can be a means to satisfying certain ends regarding our ends. See David Schmidtz, *Rational Choice and Moral Agency* (Princeton, NJ: Princeton University Press, 1995), 61, 77.

VIII. The Objection from Ungrounded Ends

One might object to the values standard on the ground that a require-ment to serve one's values can be plausible only for values that are themselves supported by reasons. People can have irrational and immoral values. Stephen Darwall writes: "If one had no reason to adopt A (or worse, reason not to do so), then maybe [instead of *serving* A], one should give up A." He writes: "From the facts that one has adopted A as an end and that B is a necessary means to A, it does not follow that one ought or has reason to B." It follows at most that one is required *either* to take the necessary means to A *or* to give up A.[67] Call this the "objection from ungrounded ends." In effect, the objection is that because people can have irrational and immoral values, compliance with the values standard can-not be a requirement of rationality.

I agree, of course, that the values standard needs to be grounded, and I shall propose a strategy for grounding it. This proposal will be the heart of my reply to the objection. There are, however, some preliminary responses to consider, the most important of which turns on a distinction between rationality and what I will call "wisdom."

It will be useful to begin by considering a related objection, the objec-tion that the values standard needs to be amended to take account of *irrational* values. I agree that a *set* of values can be irrational—the values of a rational person must be coherent with one another. But I deny that a value can be irrational, just as such, merely in light of its content.[68] One might object that since I hold that the values standard is grounded in autonomy (in a way I shall explain), I ought to admit that counter-autonomous values—values that are not compatible with one's autonomy—are irrational. Perhaps it is irrational to have a policy of always deferring to one's parents.[69]

I do not want to accept this proposal. A person who has a policy of always deferring to her parents may be doing well at governing herself in light of this policy. I do not want to say that such a person is automatically irrational. For I want to distinguish objections to her values from criti-cisms of her success in governing her life in accord with her values. I say that objections to a person's values do not speak against her rationality. I do not want to view people from cultures that do not value autonomy as

[67] Stephen Darwall, *Welfare and Rational Care* (Princeton, NJ: Princeton University Press, 2002), 7. See also John Broome, "Normative Requirements," *Ratio* [new series] 12 (1999): 398–419; Patricia Greenspan, "Conditional Obligations and Hypothetical Imperatives," *Jour-nal of Philosophy* 72 (1975): 259–76; and Korsgaard, "The Normativity of Instrumental Rea-son," 252. Korsgaard writes: "Hypothetical imperatives cannot exist without categorical ones, or anyway without principles which direct us to the pursuit of certain ends, or anyway without *something* which gives normative status to our ends" (ibid., 250).

[68] I ignore values that are logically impossible to satisfy. For useful discussion, see Donald C. Hubin, "Irrational Desires," *Philosophical Studies* 62 (1991): 23–44, esp. 24–26.

[69] I owe this objection to Steven Davis and Melinda Ammann.

irrational simply on the ground that they have counter-autonomous values. To do so would blur the important distinction between rationality,
understood as a matter of how one governs oneself, and "wisdom," understood as a matter of having values that are morally and otherwise acceptable. The objection from ungrounded ends also blurs this distinction,
since it denies the rationality of serving values that are not based in
reasons.

The intuitive basis of the distinction between rationality and wisdom is
suggested by the Everest example. The climbers were not *wise* to give
such importance to climbing Everest, but, despite this, we see them as
having been rational in their pursuit of their goal. The values of a rational
person may be subject to a variety of criticisms; they may be immoral or
impolitic or self-aggrandizing or foolish. A good navigator may not be
navigating toward a good destination. Of course, nothing turns on my
choice of words to mark the distinction. It would not be a misuse of
English to call the climbers irrational for giving such importance to climbing Everest, or to say it would be irrational to have a policy of deferring
to one's parents. The important point is that there is a distinction between
evaluating how well a person does at governing herself, given her values,
and evaluating a person's values. I am concerned with evaluations of the
former kind.[70]

Let me return, then, to the objection from ungrounded ends. I agree
with Darwall that the fact that one has adopted an end does not entail
that one has a reason to serve it, and I agree with Wallace that there is "no
genuine requirement to take the means that are necessary for realizing
ends that one merely happens to desire."[71] First, the values principle is
concerned with serving values, not ends. A value is not an end that one
merely happens to desire. A person might be rationally required *not* to
pursue an end, if doing so would conflict with serving her values. Thus,
the fact that I have a given *end* does not mean that I have any reason to
serve it. Second, I can agree that it does not *follow* from the fact that I value
something that I have reason to serve it. The values principle is a substantive principle that needs to be grounded.

---

[70] Gavin Lawrence discusses a view he calls the "end-relative account," which is similar
to the conception of self-grounded reason that I am defending. He says that on this account
"there is simply no question of whether an end is good or worth pursuing." See Lawrence,
"The Rationality of Morality," 115, 128. I am claiming that it *is* possible to evaluate a person's
values but that this is a different matter from evaluating the rationality of her actions.
Korsgaard says that "the instrumental principle," which is similar to the values standard,
cannot stand without "*something* which gives normative status to our ends." Yet she concedes that this status may be very thin. She allows that a "heroic existentialist" might
endorse his ends for no "further reason," without thinking his ends are good. See Korsgaard,
"The Normativity of Instrumental Reason," 251 n. 74, and 252. I have said that an agent
"endorses" her values and the role of her values in governing her actions. This is not to say,
however, that an evaluation of the rationality of an agent's actions in terms of the values
standard requires or involves an evaluation of the agent's values.

[71] Wallace, "Normativity, Commitment, and Instrumental Reason," 1.

To be on target, then, the objection needs to be reformulated. The objection is that I have not explained why or how it can be that "ungrounded" *values* are a source of reasons. Michael Bratman has pointed out that this objection may be especially difficult for me, given my view that values are general intentions or policies.[72] *Specific* intentions do not seem to be a source of *basic* or *underived* reasons.[73] If I form the intention to go to the gym, this gives me reason to take my gym clothes with me, but it does not give me a new reason to go to the gym. General intentions may seem to be similar: we adopt general intentions on the basis of reasons, but perhaps they are not sources of new reasons. The objection is that if values are just a kind of general intention, I need to explain why or how they can be a source of basic reasons when other intentions are not.

A fundamental response to these objections will have to wait until I discuss the grounding of the values standard. But I want here to bring out the plausibility of the idea that values can be a source of basic reasons—even if values are not themselves grounded in reasons, even if they are simply a kind of intention, and even if specific intentions are not a source of basic reasons.

Nevertheless, I think that a specific intention *can* be a source of a basic reason. If, on a whim, I form the intention to smell a nearby rose, this ordinarily would give me a reason to smell it, assuming that doing so would not conflict with my values. This reason would be basic, in that it would not be derived from any other reason.[74] But suppose I form an intention to act in a way that, I realize, conflicts with doing what would best serve my values. Suppose, for example, that I decide on a whim not to wear my seatbelt. Since I value my safety, I have reason *to* wear the seatbelt, and—in the given example—*no* reason *not* to wear it. Intuitively, even if I have no *reason* to value my safety, my value gives me a reason to wear the seatbelt, but my whim gives me *no* reason *not* to wear the seatbelt. A decision or intention motivated by a whim does not give a person a reason to act contrary to her values. Two factors seem crucial to explaining this.

---

[72] Bratman pressed this objection in personal correspondence.

[73] Scanlon, *What We Owe to Each Other*, 70. Bratman stresses that once one has formed an intention to A, one is under certain rational constraints with respect to this intention, such as the constraint not to change the intention without reason. But this is not to say that one acquires a new reason to A merely in virtue of forming the intention. See Bratman, *Intentions, Plans, and Practical Reason*.

[74] But would the reason be derived from a reason given to me by the whim or urge to smell the rose? There is a temptation to say so. However, an urge or whim can instead be viewed as an occurrence that is not in itself reason-giving. A person can decide whether to indulge it or not, and either way, arguably, she makes no mistake, other things being equal. If she forms the intention to indulge it, then, arguably, she thereby acquires a reason to do so. On this view, a person who stops to smell a rose on a whim may be no more responsive to reasons than would have been the case had she not stopped. Yet, of course, in the latter case, we might doubt her wisdom in eschewing an innocent opportunity for enjoyment.

First, values are intrinsic. Ordinary policies and intentions typically are formed because we see acting in accord with them as means to serving our values. This is why action in accord with our values is fundamental to governing ourselves in a way that action in accord with ordinary policies (and whims) is not. Second, and more important, our values are aspects of our identities in a way that our ordinary intentions, policies, ends, and whims are not. Failing to live in accord with our values negatively affects our self-esteem. In this sense, a person's values are linked to her sense of self. The self-esteem of a person who sees herself as having failed to comply with her own values is shaken to some degree by a sense of failure and disappointment in herself or a sense of shame or regret. A knowing failure to serve one's values is a kind of self-betrayal.[75]

Let me return, then, to the original objection, reformulated as the objection from ungrounded values. The objection is that a person who values A without having any reason to value A is rationally required, at most, *either* to serve A *or* to give it up; she is not rationally required to serve A. But consider the alternatives. A person does not have the *option* of giving up a value in the way that she has the option of giving up an ordinary goal, such as to smell a rose. We cannot change our identities at will, and our values are embedded in our identities. Of course, our values can *change*—even as a result of decisions we make. A person might rationally try to change her values in light of other things that she values. But we cannot *decide* to give up a value, or even an ordinary end, in the way we can decide what to do. At the point of action, our values are set. Hence, if a person with a value is rationally required either to give up the value or to serve it, then since she lacks the option of giving it up, it is plausible that she is required to serve it. It is plausible that to the extent that she is rational, she will govern her action in accord with it.

The point here is not simply that we cannot change our values at will. The reason we cannot change our values at will is, in part, that they are embedded in our identities: they are grounds of our self-esteem and aspects of our self-conception. Otherwise they would not function as they do, as compasses in our lives.[76]

IX. Grounding a Conception of Rationality

A theory of rationality can be viewed as proposing a standard or a norm, such as the values standard. The theory then claims that its pro-

---

[75] Similar suggestions have been made before. Donald Hubin has suggested an account of reasons for action based on what a person "intrinsically values," and he suggests that our values are "expressions of our selves." See Donald C. Hubin, "Hypothetical Motivation," *Noûs* 30 (1996): 47. Korsgaard has said that an adequate account of normativity "must appeal, in a deep way, to our sense of who we are, to our sense of identity." Korsgaard, *The Sources of Normativity*, 17–18. For Korsgaard, your identity is "a description under which you value yourself." See ibid., 101.

[76] See the discussion of giving up an ideal in Sarah Buss, "The Irrationality of Unhappiness and the Paradox of Despair," *Journal of Philosophy* 101 (2004): 186–87.

posed standard *is* the standard of rationality—the standard that rational agents would comply with to the extent that they can, given their knowledge, just in virtue of being rational. This claim needs to be substantiated by providing the standard with an appropriate grounding. Let me explain what would be involved in doing this.

We can formulate any number of purely arbitrary standards. There is, for example, a standard calling on everyone to do a pirouette every night at midnight. We do not think that this standard corresponds to a normative requirement or that it has any bearing on how we are to act. To ground the values standard, I need to show that it is not similarly arbitrary. I need to show that it has a status in virtue of which it is relevantly "authoritative" or "normative."

To show this, I need to show, at least, that the values standard has a status such that those who fail to comply with it have thereby failed in a significant way. There is a problem specifying the *kind* of significance this failure would have. There are irrational people, so we cannot insist that it must be a kind of failure that *anyone* would be motivated to avoid. If the values standard is the standard of rationality, then a knowing failure to serve one's values would be *irrational*, but to say this would be question-begging and unhelpful. Given the content of the values standard, those who fail to comply with it face a loss, and perhaps a significant loss, since they fail to serve their values as well as they could. This is a kind of loss virtually anyone would be motivated to avoid, but would they be motivated in the way, or for the reason, we are motivated to avoid irrationality?

Donald Hubin suggests that a norm calling on us to pursue our values stands in no need of grounding.[77] He compares his view of the status of this norm to H. L. A. Hart's view of the status of the fundamental "rule of recognition" in a legal system. He seems to think that just as, for Hart, it is enough that the rule of recognition be treated a certain way by officials in the legal system, so it is enough that the norm calling on us to pursue our values be treated a certain way by us. At root there are simply certain brute facts, such as that we pursue what we value, and we at least sometimes assess our actions in terms of our values. And Hubin writes: "[T]he property of being rationally advisable just is the property of being properly related to these brute facts."[78] However, if the pursuit of what one values is "rationally advisable," then if a person fails to pursue what she values, this is not simply a departure from a brute psychological regularity. It is a failure in some interesting normative sense. The challenge is to explain this.

There is an analogous issue about politeness. Consider a rule that calls on us not to wear hats indoors. We might think that this rule is pointless

[77] Hubin, "The Groundless Normativity of Instrumental Rationality."
[78] Ibid., 467; see 463–68. See H. L. A. Hart, *The Concept of Law* (New York: Oxford University Press, 1961).

and deny that it has any bearing on how to act, even if we understand that compliance with this rule is locally taken to be a matter of politeness. Nevertheless, in a culture where there are rules that are taken to define politeness, there will be a widely accepted second-order standard, which we could call the "standard of politeness," that calls on people to comply with the local standards of conventionally acceptable behavior, such as the rule about hats. We cannot suppose that the standard of politeness has a bearing on how we are to act if we think that it is just as arbitrary and pointless as the rule about midnight pirouettes. Those of us who think that politeness has a bearing on how to act—that it is a significant failure of some kind to be impolite—must therefore think that the standard of politeness has some relevant authority or status.

There is an obvious way to think about this. The point of etiquette is to contribute to comfortable and pleasing social interaction. The standard of politeness is relevantly authoritative in virtue of the fact that compliance with it helps to make for comfortable and pleasing social interaction. It plainly is not the case that everyone values comfortable and pleasing social interaction, but the proposal is not that the standard of politeness is authoritative in virtue of the fact that we *value* comfortable and pleasing social interaction. The proposal is instead that there is reason to comply with the standard of politeness in virtue of its status as facilitating social interaction. Call this the "social interaction theory" of politeness.

A complete theory of rationality must be supplemented by a theory that has a similar form and a similar purpose to the social interaction theory of politeness. On anyone's view, rationality requires acting in certain ways, ways that could be expressed in a standard calling for us to do such and such in such and such circumstances. Any proposal about the content of the standard of rationality is incomplete unless it is accompanied by some account of the basis or authority of the standard.[79] This, then, is the grounding problem. To solve it, I think we need to understand the *point* of evaluating people and their actions as rational or irrational.

It might seem that if we can provide an analysis of the *concept* of rationality, and show that a given standard best captures our concept, we have done all that can be done to ground it. I hope that we can do something different from this. Suppose that the concept of rationality is the concept of the kind of virtuosity in the pursuit of what one values specified by the values standard. If so, then we rightly call people who comply with the standard "rational." But this does not yet give us any reason to view the standard as authoritative. Even if we rightly consider

---

[79] Elsewhere, I have proposed a schema according to which a basic normative proposition of kind K is true only if a corresponding K standard or norm has a relevant kind of status or justification. See Copp, *Morality, Normativity, and Society,* chap. 2. An account of the grounding of the standard of rationality could be plugged into this schema to yield an account of the truth conditions of claims about rationality. For further discussion of this idea, see Copp, "Moral Naturalism and Three Grades of Normativity."

ourselves "rational" insofar as we conform to the standard, we might wonder whether the standard has any status in virtue of which it actually imposes a requirement on us. Perhaps it will be replied that our concept of rationality is the concept of an *authoritative* standard—so that if the values standard *is* the standard of rationality, it *follows* that it is authoritative. But if this is correct, then if we are in doubt as to whether the values standard is authoritative, we are committed to being equally in doubt as to whether it is the standard of rationality.[80]

The issue is one that Kant apparently had in mind in the *Groundwork of the Metaphysics of Morals*, where he discussed the "possibility" of an "imperative." In my terms, a Kantian imperative is an "authoritative" standard, one that sets out an actual requirement. The possibility problem for Kant is to explain how to conceive of "the necessitation of the will expressed by an imperative in setting a task" and to show that there is such necessitation.[81] In my terms, that is, regarding a proposed standard of rationality, the problem is to explain how such a standard can be "authoritative" or "normative," such that it actually imposes a requirement.

X. Grounding the Values Standard in Autonomy

I have been arguing that the concept of rationality is closely related to the concept of autonomy. To be autonomous is to be *self*-governing, and to be rational is to do *well* in *governing* oneself. From one side, this suggests that the *content* of the standard of rationality should be determined by investigating what is involved in governing oneself. From the other side, it suggests a strategy for explaining the *grounding* of the standard of rationality.

The idea in outline is that rationality serves self-government— understood in the thick sense in which self-government involves regulating our actions by our values. The point of assessing the rationality of a person's actions is to appraise her success in manifesting or securing her self-government. That is, if the values standard is the standard of rationality, its grounding or warrant is that to comply with it furthers or instantiates one's self-government. Irrationality is a failure of self-government, a departure from governing oneself well. (Of course, irratio-

---

[80] Kant writes: "Whoever wills the end, wills (so far as reason has decisive influence on his actions) also the means that are indispensably necessary to his [ends] and that lie in his power. This proposition, as far as willing is concerned, is analytic." Kant, *Groundwork of the Metaphysics of Morals*, 27 (Ak 417). However, unless there is a requirement of some sort that we be fully rational, then even if it is analytic that fully rational agents do intend the means to their ends, it does not follow that there is a requirement to intend the means to our ends. Hence, in Kant's terms, it does not follow that the standard calling on us to intend the means to our ends is an *imperative*.

[81] Kant, *Groundwork of the Metaphysics of Morals*, 27 (Ak 417). I discuss some of Kant's arguments in David Copp, "The 'Possibility' of a Categorical Imperative: Kant's Groundwork, Part III," *Philosophical Perspectives* 6 (1992): 261–84.

nal people may be autonomous in the thinner sense; they do poorly at governing themselves in the thicker sense.) The proposal is not that we are rational to manifest and secure our autonomy because we value autonomy. It is that we are rational to manifest and secure our autonomy, even if we do not value autonomy, because manifesting and securing one's autonomy is what rationality consists in.

Call the condition that a standard meets when complying with it furthers or instantiates one's self-government, the "autonomy condition." If what I have argued is correct, it should be plain that the values standard meets this condition. It calls on us to govern ourselves on the basis of our values, or, where our values do not dictate what to do, on the basis of our other intrinsic goals. To act in a way that would not serve our values as well as something else we could do would be to fail to control our actions on the basis of our values. But our values are policies we have that are central to our identity and that are intrinsic in that they are not grounded in any other policies or intentions. They are aspects of our self-conception. Thus, to fail to govern our actions on the basis of our values would be to fail in *self*-government. And in a case where more than one thing we could do would serve our values equally well, to fail to serve our other intrinsic ends as well as we could, while serving our values as well as we can, would be to fail to follow our own policies, despite being able to. This too would be to fail in self-government. Hence, it is plausible that compliance with the values standard furthers or instantiates *governing* oneself.

The autonomy condition is meant to play the same kind of role in grounding the values standard as the condition of furthering pleasing and comfortable social interaction played in grounding the standard of politeness. One might object that to establish genuine normativity, something much more ambitious than this must be done in order to ground the values standard. For if the grounding of the values standard is analogous to the grounding I proposed for the standard of politeness, then rationality is not a practical virtue that is superior to politeness. There are several things to say in reply to this objection, but I limit myself to two. First, recall that I am working here on the assumption that reasons pluralism is true. I think that there are reasons of etiquette just as there are self-grounded reasons. For this reason, I think it is an advantage that my grounding of the values standard is analogous to the grounding of the standard of politeness. Second, although I accept reasons pluralism, I agree that rationality is a special kind of practical virtue. It is special, not *metaphysically*, but because of its role in *deliberation*, as I will explain.

One might object that since many people and many cultures do not value autonomy, the autonomy condition cannot do the work I want it to do in explaining the authority of the standard of reason. For, one might think, a plausible account of rationality must be culturally neutral and neutral among our substantive values. Moreover, if some of us do not value autonomy, then the fact that compliance with my proposed standard of rationality would serve our self-government would not show that every person has reason to care about being rational.

In response, I want to say, first, that my account does not imply that it is irrational to fail to value autonomy. In fact, it implies (although with a qualification I am ignoring) that it is irrational to fail to promote satisfaction of one's values, *whatever* they are, even if one values a non-autonomous way of life.[82] According to the values standard, no one is ever rationally required to promote her autonomy unless her own values require her to do so. Second, no plausible theory of rationality can avoid implying that a person might be rationally required to conform with a standard she does not accept. For *any* theory needs to leave room for irrational persons. Finally, virtually anyone *would* want to do what she is required to do, according to the values standard. For the standard merely calls on us to serve our values. When we value something, we naturally are motivated to act appropriately, barring fatigue or depression or the like.[83] Motivation by our values is psychologically deep, for we tend to feel shame or guilt or disappointment in ourselves if we fail to act according to our values. Thus, to understand how we can be motivated to act in accord with the values standard, it is not necessary to suppose that we value promoting our own autonomy in addition to valuing such things as friendship. If irrationality is the failure of self-government, we can see why people typically care to avoid irrationality.

The objection seems to assume that the autonomy condition seeks to justify rationality as instrumental to autonomy. But this is a mistake. The view is, rather, that in being rational we *instantiate* our autonomy. The view is not that self-grounded reasons bind us only insofar as we *desire* to be autonomous, or only insofar as we *value* autonomy.[84] Many of us do not value being autonomous and have no desire to be autonomous.[85] Nor does my view depend on the idea that autonomy is *valuable*—though I do not deny that it is. To a first approximation, rationality requires us to serve our *values* because serving our values instantiates being autonomous, and because rationality consists in instantiating autonomy. This is

---

[82] I refer to the qualification about meeting one's needs. See note 61 above.

[83] Valuing something involves having a policy, or a general intention. One who has such an intention has at least a background standing disposition to act appropriately.

[84] If this were my view, then the argument would show, at best, that the requirement to comply with the values standard is hypothetical, or conditional on our valuing autonomy. This is not so, however. When we are rationally required to do something A, in most cases the requirement is conditional on, roughly, our having values such that doing A best serves those values in the circumstances. But the requirement to comply with the values standard itself is not conditional on our having any values in particular. Whatever our values, in complying with the values standard, we best serve those values.

[85] David Velleman argues to the contrary that agency has a "constitutive goal" such that any agent must aim to be in conscious control of her behavior—which he says amounts to the aim to be autonomous. It is in virtue of this fact that agents are subject to reasons. See J. David Velleman, "The Possibility of Practical Reason," *Ethics* 106 (1996): 719. See note 14 above. My account does not require postulating a "constitutive aim" of agency.

why, *whatever* a person values, she is rationally required to serve her values. My claim is not about what rationality requires her to value. It is about what rationality requires her to do *given* what she values.

XI. DELIBERATIVE PRIORITY

My account assigns priority to rationality by comparison with other practical virtues, but not by assigning it a special *metaphysical* status. Instead, it assigns rationality a priority in *deliberation*. When agents with the necessary self-understanding and necessary information deliberate about what to do, the "default" is that their decision is in accord with the values standard.[86] Of course, in my view an agent who decides otherwise is to that extent less than fully rational. But the priority-in-deliberation thesis is that it is a law-like truth that, given the nature of practical deliberation, when agents who have approximately accurate beliefs about what they value, and about how to achieve what they value, deliberate about what to do and reach a decision based on their deliberation, other things being equal, they decide to do what they are required to do according to the values standard.[87] This is the default case.

This thesis is supported by claims I have made about what is involved in valuing something, given that the values standard calls on us to serve our actual values. First, values are policies or general intentions. We would not count you as valuing safety, for example, unless you had a tendency to act with caution when faced with known dangers. Second, your values are an aspect of your identity. This means that emotions of self-esteem are harnessed to your values and help to ensure that you have a tendency to pursue what you value. Moreover, the thesis is supported by a picture of the nature of practical deliberation—deliberation that leads to decisions about what to do. According to this picture, in central cases, practical reasoning involves reasoning from general intentions or policies to specific intentions in action. It is means-end reasoning in the sense that it concerns how to carry out general intentions. Given this picture, if a person is rationally required to A according to the values standard, then, other things being

[86] Korsgaard holds the stronger view that compliance with the "instrumental principle" is *constitutive of deliberate action*. She writes: "[I]f you don't put one foot in front of the other you will not be walking and you will get nowhere. . . . The instrumental principle is, in this way, a constitutive norm of willing, of deliberate action. If you are going to act at all, then you must conform to it" (Korsgaard, "The Normativity of Instrumental Reason," 249). But Korsgaard insists that failures to conform to the instrumental principle must be possible if the principle is normative (ibid., 247–48, 228). Surely, however, a person who fails to conform to the instrumental principle may have acted. Agents sometimes perform *akratic* actions. If the climbers had failed to serve their values in the Everest example, but had instead stopped to help the victims, their helping would have been an action. It therefore seems implausible that conformity with the instrumental principle is constitutive of "deliberate action."

[87] The idea of a defeasible law-like generalization is discussed in Mark Lance and Margaret Little, "Defeasibility and the Normative Grasp of Content," *Erkenntnis* (forthcoming).

equal, she would form the intention to A if she were to deliberate cogently about what to do in light of her values.

There can be exceptions. The person might be depressed or exhausted and might for this reason fail to form any intention to act. Or she might fail to reach any conclusion about how best to serve her values. She might be unable to see how to resolve conflicts among her values. She might not understand what she values, or she might lack relevant information about how to serve her values. Deliberation might lead her to become perplexed about what she values. She might lack the fortitude to resist an impulse to act contrary to her values. She might be *akratic*. Or, perhaps paradoxically, she might *have* the strength to resist the impulse to act in *accord* with her values. In a moment of clarity, she might see that her values are morally unacceptable and decide to do the right thing. The climbers in the Everest example might decide to abort the climb and to help the victims, thereby acting out-of-character and irrationally, but doing the right thing.

With these caveats understood, we can see that the account of rational agency I have proposed explains how reasoning about what to do can lead to a decision, and thus to the forming of an intention. And we can see how rational decision-making can be the default case, assuming approximately true relevant beliefs. Our values are partly constituted by general intentions or policies, and the default is to be guided by them to form specific intentions that will implement or further or express our values. Suppose you are trying to decide whether to watch a tennis match or to read a novel. Your decision likely will turn on such considerations as how much you are enjoying the novel, how often you find time to watch tennis or to read, who is playing in the match, and so on. Let us suppose that you value the simple pleasures of life, which, for you, include reading novels and following tennis. If you realize that this is the only thing you value that will be affected by your choice, you will pay attention to which of the activities in question promises more enjoyment. Once you have reached a conclusion about this, if all goes well, your value—which is, inter alia, a general intention—will lead you to form a specific intention either to read or to watch tennis. In the default case, if you have been reasoning with accurate information, your intention will be to do what the values standard implies that you rationally ought to do.

The important point here is that self-grounded reasons—facts about the impact the agent's alternatives would have on the things she values— have a role in deliberation that other kinds of reasons do not generally have. When agents who have the necessary self-understanding and the necessary information decide to act, the default is that their decision is in accord with the values standard. The corresponding thing cannot be said of morality or etiquette, for example. It is not the case that when a person with the necessary self-understanding and information decides what to do, the default is that she decides to act morally or politely. This is true only of people with the corresponding values.

One might object that a person who is deliberating about what to do is trying to decide what to do *period,* not merely to decide what *rationally* to do. To see this, consider again the Everest example. Given the values of the climbers, suppose that the values standard would require them to press on to the summit. This would mean that carrying on is what the climbers ought *rationally* to do. But I have been supposing that they ought morally to stop and help the victims. One might object that a reflective climber would want to decide what to do *period,* not merely what she ought rationally to do. On my own view, it might seem, the values standard cannot tell the climbers what they ought to do *period.* For as I said earlier, I hold that there is no answer to the question of what the climbers ought *simpliciter* to do in the imagined situation. That is, I am assuming that there *is* an answer to the question of what they ought rationally to do, and that there *is* an answer to the question of what they ought morally to do, but I hold that there is no overarching normative standard that determines what they ought to do *simpliciter.* Now it is not part of my goal in this essay to defend my view about "ought *simpliciter,*" so I could avoid the objection by giving up my view. I do not need to do this, however; for the objection is based on a misunderstanding.

The upshot of practical deliberation is not a belief about what one ought to do; it is a decision or an intention. On my view, the values standard cannot tell the climbers what they ought to do *simpliciter,* but only what they ought *rationally* to do. But the climbers are trying to decide what to do. They are not trying to decide what to believe to be the rational thing to do. And a climber's decision about what to do would be a flat-out decision, a decision either to help the victims or to carry on with the climb. I agree that a reflective climber would want to decide what to do *period,* but on my account she would do so. That is the nature of decisions.

It is true that if someone decides to do something, and if her deliberation is relevantly informed and fully rational, then she ought *rationally* to do it. This does not entail, however, that she ought *simpliciter* to do it. For deliberation is carried out from one's own practical standpoint, not from the standpoint of a metaphysically overarching standard that determines what one ought to do *simpliciter.* I have argued, in effect, although with caveats, that one's practical standpoint is constituted by one's values. If a climber decides to carry on with the climb, she would be confused if, after the climb, she claimed to have made the mistake of failing to decide what to do *period.* Her decision may have been morally indefensible, but it was a flat-out decision. Her mistake was a moral mistake, not the mistake of failing to make a flat-out decision.

XII. Conclusion

I have distinguished two issues that a theory of rationality must address. First, it must specify the content of the standard of rationality. Second, it must ground the standard in order to support its claim that the standard is the standard of rationality. I have proposed the values standard, and I have claimed to ground the values standard in the autonomy condition. *Rationality* is in the service of self-*government*, I have argued.

In closing, I would like to emphasize the modesty of the view. According to the autonomy conception, rational agents are necessarily disposed to comply with self-grounded reasons, just in virtue of being rational. But rational agents are not necessarily disposed to comply with moral reasons, even if they recognize that there are moral reasons that bear on their actions. A rational person *could* have moral values, so moral reasons *could* be reasons for which she acts. A morally virtuous agent has exactly the moral values it is morally best to have, and thus, for such a person, moral reasons are also self-grounded reasons. It is not necessarily true, however, that rational agents have moral values, so it is not necessarily true that they are rationally required to do what they believe they have moral reason to do. A person who ignores reasons of this kind is not necessarily failing to govern herself in light of her values.

Philosophy, University of Florida

RATIONALITY MEANS BEING WILLING TO SAY
YOU'RE SORRY

By Jennifer Roback Morse

I. Introduction

This essay examines the problem of repentance and apology. What is so powerful about the three-word utterance, "I am sorry?" People who feel offended spend time and energy demanding an apology from the offender. People who have given offense often seem to have difficulty giving an apology. I want to ask two basic questions. What does a person really want when he asks for an apology? Why do people so often find it difficult to give an apology?

These questions may not seem to have anything to do with the issue of personal identity. But personal identity is relevant to repentance because one common difficulty with apologizing is that the person is reluctant to admit wrongdoing. The offender is willing to disrupt a relationship, bear costs himself and impose costs on others, rather than admit he did something wrong. Likewise, the victim is infuriated by the offender's failure to say, "I am sorry," with sufficient sincerity. These are very curious behaviors. I believe that one explanation for these curious behaviors lies in a particular kind of self-understanding: the person identifies himself with his preferences and the behaviors that flow from them. In other words, the unrepentant soul has his own theory of personal identity, quite apart from anything any philosopher might have to say about it. The unrepentant person believes *he is his preferences,* and that he is entitled to the behavior that flows from those preferences.

This person uses something akin to a naive economic theory of human behavior. Economists have a specific view of personal identity: a person is defined by a set of stable preferences. I am going to use *Homo economicus,* or economic man, as a foil for analyzing repentance, apology, and forgiveness. The naive version of *Homo economicus* can never truly be sorry for anything, and as a result, will be almost impossible to live with.

This essay takes the form of an "if-then" statement: If one interprets and applies the economic paradigm in this particular way, then deleterious consequences will result, both for economic analysis and for individuals themselves. I do not claim that every economist takes the position I criticize: I know for a fact that they do not. Nor do I claim that this position is necessary for doing economics: the problem I identify can be solved within rational choice theory suitably amended. But my purpose is neither to defend economic theory from misinterpretation, nor to rescue it by amending it, even though I think both tasks could be accomplished. I simply want to show that a person who identifies himself too closely with his preferences will bring misery to himself and those around him. And an unrepentant individual is surely unjustified in invoking economic analysis to justify his behavior. Starting with economics helps the analysis, however, because it helps to clarify the issues at stake, including the mistakes that the unrepentant person is making.

To convince the reader that repentance matters, I begin with examples of public situations. The criminal justice system certainly seems to care whether a person is repentant or not. I then go on to look at the very private behavior that is the main focus of this essay. I depict an obnoxious encounter with an unpleasant, unrepentant person, who views himself as economic man.

II. Why Repentance Matters

Suppose a person commits a crime. He is caught, arrested, tried, and convicted. Let us suppose this criminal regrets being caught, but is not sorry for what he did. He shows no remorse. The judge and jury are more likely to be sympathetic with a truly repentant criminal than with one who merely regrets being caught.

Veronica Gonzales and her husband are on California's death row for the brutal torture and murder of their four-year-old niece. The evidence indicated that while both were active participants in the child's death, the husband was more culpable. Veronica tried to argue that since she, too, had been victimized by her husband's violence, she should not be held responsible. Dan Goldstein, the deputy district attorney who prosecuted their case, offered this opinion as to why the jury had voted for the death penalty for Veronica:

> To this day, I think if Veronica had been a little more honest, she could have helped herself out. Instead, she got up and hid behind the battered-woman-syndrome defense. I talked to a couple of the jurors after the case. Several of them said that when Veronica was testifying, their impression was she was lying. And in their minds they kept thinking, "Don't lie to me. If you lie to me, I am going to have to vote death."[1]

The news recently reported the release of Lionel Tate, a sixteen-year-old Florida boy who had killed a six-year-old child, when he was himself a mere twelve years old. He had kicked, stomped, and beaten a little girl

[1] Leslie Ryland, "What Made Them Kill," *San Diego Weekly Reader* 32, no. 8 (February 20, 2003), 43.

who weighed forty-eight pounds. He said he was imitating what he saw on TV, on World Wide Wrestling.[2]

The mother of his victim, who stated that she had forgiven him for killing her daughter, nonetheless added that she hoped he would stop saying it was an accident. "We wanted Lionel to step up and say, 'Look, I have done something wrong here. I'm guilty of this. I'm sorry about this.' " Florida governor Jeb Bush didn't mention forgiveness, but made a similar point about repentance: "I do hope that Lionel will express remorse, at a minimum, for what occurred."

Why did the jury care whether Veronica was lying or not? They were probably using truthfulness as a proxy for repentance. If she thought she was entitled to lie, she was unlikely to be genuinely sorry for what she did. This raises the next question: Why did the jury care whether Veronica was sorry? Why did anyone care whether Lionel was repentant or not?

If a person is not repentant, then we suspect that he is either justifying his offense, or indifferent to it. If a boy can justify killing a six-year-old, he is more likely to commit a similar crime. Indifference is not much better. To kill a child in the brutal way that he did, required him to ignore her cries of pain. It is difficult to imagine the callousness of continuing to kick and stomp a small child until she finally died. Anybody, of any age or intelligence level, who could do that once, could probably do it again. Even if his cause-and-effect thinking was so distorted that he didn't understand that the other child would die, this doesn't much matter. He is highly likely to be a problem to other people. In contrast, if he genuinely understands that what he did was wrong, he will be more likely to restrain himself and less likely to give way to his passions, whatever they might be, that would urge him to stomp another child to death.

With this in the background, let us examine the unrepentant person who uses a variant of economic reasoning to justify himself. I will ultimately show that the rational choice economic paradigm can be amended to account for a rational choice both to ask for and to give apologies. First, however, I want to ask whether the naive version of *Homo economicus,* or economic man, can ever truly be sorry or repentant for anything. I am not going to examine him in the process of committing spectacular crimes like these. Instead, I am going to follow *Homo economicus* around the house and watch him try to interact with his family. First, let me outline the key assumptions of the economists' approach to human behavior.

III. The Economists' View of the Person

Economists have a very specific view of personal identity: a person is a utility function. A utility function describes a person's preference ordering of every possible set of goods and services. If we want to know how

---

[2] "Teen Who Killed Playmate, 6, Is Freed," *San Diego Union-Tribune,* January 27, 2004.

an individual ranks various bundles of apples and oranges, holding all other things equal, the utility function tells us. These preference orderings are assumed to be stable, at least in comparison with the constraints the person faces when making choices. The major constraints economists analyze are prices and income, broadly defined. Any changed behavior we observe is, in general, not the result of changes in preferences, but of changes in these factors that are external to the person.

Even Gary Becker's pioneering work on preferences assumes a stable "extended preference" function.[3] Becker places some structure on this utility function, and asks about its relationship to ordinary utility functions that depend directly on observable goods and services. Becker argues that ordinary utility functions appear to be unstable, but that the underlying extended preference function remains constant. In this way, he addresses questions such as habit formation and addiction as a variant of capital theory. A person accumulates "consumption capital," which changes his future evaluation of goods in systematic and predictable ways. When making a current consumption decision, the person takes into account its impact on his future enjoyment of goods. The initial utility function, upon which all future preferences hinge, is the individual's most fundamental decision-making parameter. In this sense, this initial utility function still defines the individual.

Just as personal identity has a particular interpretation within economics, rational choice also means something specific in economics. *Homo economicus* or economic man uses all available information about the costs and benefits of various courses of action, calculates which course of action maximizes his utility, and carries out that course of action. The exceptions to this general approach have to do with economizing on the use of information. For instance, economists hypothesize that people might devise some cost-effective strategy for sifting through mountains of data, rather than be stymied and overwhelmed by trying to process every available fact. I will have more to say below about these economizing strategies for using new information. With these words of explanation behind us, let us address the main question.

IV. Can *Homo Economicus* Be Sorry?

He cannot. A rational economic man, who always maximizes his own personal happiness, taking into account all the relevant costs and benefits of his actions, and using fully all the available information, cannot repent of anything. If an individual chooses to live his life using these textbook assumptions behind *Homo economicus*, he cannot be sorry, and thus will be almost impossible to live with.

---

[3] Gary S. Becker, *Accounting for Tastes* (Cambridge, MA: Harvard University Press, 1996), 4–12.

To see how this is the case, make a distinction between regret and remorse (as the jury in the Veronica Gonzales case seemed to do). A person feels regret for two principal reasons. A person might feel regret upon discovering information that he did not have in the first place. He had originally taken a course of action, using all available information, but he was not in possession of some crucial fact that only became available as his actions unfolded. If he had known this information initially, he would have decided and acted differently from the way he did.

A person also might feel regret because some probabilistic event did not turn out as he had hoped. We can easily imagine *Homo economicus* feeling regret because he bought stock knowing that, as the prospectus states, "the stock market is inherently risky and not suitable for all investors." He regrets that he didn't sell all his shares of JDS Uniphase in 2000 when it was selling for $150, instead of holding onto it until now when it is trading at $3 per share. But he isn't irrational because things might have turned out otherwise. He isn't and shouldn't be repentant because he didn't do anything morally blameworthy. He just made a mistake.[4]

Feeling remorse means something different. Remorse is the feeling associated with an admission of wrongdoing. The person was not just poorly informed, not just mistaken, but wrong, and he admits it. He has some feelings, both about the wrongdoing itself and about admitting it. A working synonym for "remorse" would be "shame." Being sorry or repentant means admitting I was wrong. This admission is what someone is looking for when they ask for an apology.

What are the possible responses of the rational person to a request for an apology? The other person says something along the lines of: "I don't like what you did. You hurt me. I want you to apologize." Here are three general categories of responses:

1. I didn't know I hurt you. I didn't know (in advance) that what I was about to do would be hurtful to you. I regret hurting you.

This is, in effect, a plea of imperfect information. I only have regrets that things did not turn out as I had expected and hoped. I am not truly sorry, because I was only ignorant, not actually wrong or guilty of anything. Regret, rather than contrition, is appropriate, assuming I am telling the truth and not rationalizing. If the other person believed that I was acting out of ignorance, he or she might be inclined to forgive me.

---

[4] There are other situations in which people's decisions do not turn out as they expected. For instance, a phenomenon called "projection bias" involves people systematically underestimating costs or benefits associated with consuming certain goods, such as addictive substances, visits to the health club, or snack foods at the grocery store. People's preferences are not exactly what they expect them to be, and therefore planned consumption and actual consumption diverge. But even these cases do not involve anything recognizable as repentance. The person regrets how things turn out. See George Lowenstein, Ted O'Donoghue, and Matthew Rabin, "Projection Bias in Predicting Future Utility," *Quarterly Journal of Economics* 118 (November 2003).

2. I wanted to hurt you. I knew it would hurt you. I am entitled to hurt you if I feel sufficiently aggrieved with you, or with life in general. I am allowed to come home from a crummy job and kick the cat, yell at the kids, and snarl at you. I did what I wanted to do. I didn't expect you to like it. I knew you would probably yell at me. But I was then, and am now, willing to pay the price of your displeasure.

This is *Homo economicus* all right, rational and calculating. But you would not want to be married to him. I doubt very seriously that his friend or spouse would say compliantly, "Oh well, maximizing your utility involved hurting me. Gee, I understand. That makes everything okay." The friend is likely to either exit the relationship or punch him in the nose. Nobody wants to be held in so little regard as this "rational" person seems to do in this case.

3. I didn't particularly want to hurt you. I hurt you as a by-product of something else I wanted to do. I do not plead ignorance, or imperfect information. Nor can I honestly say that I wanted to hurt you and felt entitled to do so. In this intermediate case, I simply state that what I wanted to do was more important to me than your feelings about it.

Notice that in none of these cases does the person offer a genuine apology. The unrepentant person is, in each case, using a variant of economic man to get himself off the hook for the need to apologize. In the first case, the rational person might be willing to offer a statement of regret; but contrition is not really appropriate, since he was just ignorant, not malicious. In the latter two cases, the rational person knew there was some probability that his actions would displease the other person, so he cannot plead ignorance. *Homo economicus* believes he is entitled to do what he wants, even if it hurts the other person. In case 2, the extreme case, he not only believes himself entitled to inflict harm, he actively wants to hurt the other person.

Now a reader might object that no one really behaves like this. No one really uses an economic rationale to relieve himself of the obligation to apologize for bad behavior. I reply that I have known quite a few people like this, and most of them are not economists. These are people whose need to justify themselves and unwillingness to apologize borders on the irrational. And oddly enough, their justification for their behavior is that they are acting in their own interest. They might borrow the title of the best-selling book and say they are "looking out for number 1."[5] Disagreements with these people, or requests for an apology from these people, often seem to end with, "I don't have to and you can't make me."

I want to do two things in what follows. I want to show that economic analysis, properly understood or suitably amended, really cannot be used to justify a flat-out refusal to apologize. I also want to use a variant of

---

[5] Robert Ringer, *Looking Out for #1* (New York: Random House, 1978).

economic analysis to show why the whole topic of repentance presents so many difficulties.

To do this, I am going to focus for a moment on the intermediate case, in which one person hurts the other as a by-product of something else he wants to do. This case is most interesting, because it is sometimes understandable. It is easy to imagine situations in which we would feel it was acceptable or even appropriate to hurt someone as a by-product of something else we wanted to do. We can imagine situations in which we would feel fairly treated if someone did this to us. Context is everything. This intermediate case also helps us understand why citing rationality as an excuse for not apologizing is more a rationalization than genuinely rational behavior.

V. A Conflict between *Homo Economicus* and His Spouse

Suppose a husband refused to accompany his wife to a dinner that was important to her. He knows she wants it, and that she will feel bad if he doesn't go. He chooses to do something else instead. He claims he is making a rational choice, by doing his most preferred activity, all things considered. We, as impartial spectators,[6] cannot judge this situation in the absence of further information.

Suppose the dinner is an event honoring the wife for winning the Nobel Prize in economics. *Homo Economicus* (or HE for short) refuses to go because he does not want to miss his card club, which will be meeting during the trip. His plea of rationality would probably not gain much sympathy, either from us, the impartial spectators, or from his wife. We would probably conclude that there was something skewed about his preferences.

Suppose instead that the dinner is at her mother's house. Her mother is a shrew who can't shut up and continually criticizes everyone in sight, including and especially her son-in-law, whom her daughter never should have married in the first place. The husband says he would prefer to do just about anything rather than go to this dinner and endure his mother-in-law's criticism. His wife is *Sly Homo Economica* (SHE for short). SHE proclaims that she is hurt, demands that he always act to avoid hurting her, and pronounces him an inconsiderate lout.

This set of facts makes the case seem quite different. As impartial spectators, it is difficult to sympathize with the wife. We might even conclude that SHE is using her pain to manipulate her husband.

---

[6] Adam Smith used the term "impartial spectator" as a key part of his moral discourse in his analysis of sympathy. Would an "impartial spectator" approve of a course of conduct? Smith recommends this question as a guideline for moral action. See Adam Smith, *The Theory of Moral Sentiments* (1759), ed. D. D. Raphael and A. L. Macfie (Indianapolis: Liberty Press, 1984).

But one thing is for sure about both of these cases: "rational choice" is not a stand-alone justification for the behavior. No one is obligated to accept the husband's calculation that his card club is more important than honoring his wife's accomplishments. Likewise, her claim to be hurt is not an open-and-shut argument that her husband must instantly comply with her wishes. In each case, the offender (or purported offender) needs to supplement the cost-benefit calculus with a justification for the preferences themselves. The wife in the first case does not think that traveling to Sweden should count as a cost. The husband in the second case does not think that visiting his mother-in-law should count as a benefit. The argument is over these issues, not over whether anybody calculated accurately. In fact, pleading rationality sounds a lot like changing the subject.

In personal situations like these, the rationality argument is a distraction from the main issues of the worthiness of my preferences, and my willingness to accommodate you in the grand scheme of my preferences. The argument is over whether HE is entitled to place such a high weight on the card club, or whether SHE is entitled to place such a great weight on visiting her mother. The hurt that each one feels comes from knowing that he or she is not really very important to the other person.

Here is another sure thing: A person who habitually pleaded the rationality argument, in the absence of these other contextual considerations, would be extremely difficult to live with. In fact, it would be difficult to commit to a relationship with such a person. You could never know in advance how highly your feelings would count in the person's calculus. You would always be wondering whether HE really wanted that card game, or whether HE just did not want to be inconvenienced. You would wonder whether SHE really was hurt, or whether SHE was manipulating you. Because you could not predict all these preferences and choices in advance, you would almost certainly feel aggrieved some of the time.

The person claiming that this is rational behavior could stand to read a few articles on rational altruism or economic theories of social interaction.[7] These theories hypothesize that people gain utility from the happiness of others or from the esteem of others. But even these theories might provide solace to the hardened soul, determined to be unrepentant. For these theories assume that the individual has a stable overarching set of preferences that incorporate both the utility of other people and the potential change in one's own preferences over time. Thinking in terms of maximizing one's own utility might very well lead a person to conclude that the significant work of choosing has already been done in the initial period of choice. Once I have made my initial consumption choices, upon which all future choices depend, I need not be reflective any longer. All I need do is to calculate the costs and benefits, based on how things seem

[7] See, for instance, Gary S. Becker, "A Theory of Social Interactions," *Journal of Political Economy* 82, no. 6 (1974): 1063–93.

to feel at the moment. I am still not required to apologize or offer an account of myself.

VI. The Rational Choice among Mates

As an example of such thinking, one might argue that in choosing to enter a serious relationship with a person, a rational person would consider all of the other person's preferences as part of the decision-making process. If you cannot live with the other person's preferences, you shouldn't get involved and you certainly should not get married. It is plausible to argue that a person could and should screen out completely unsuitable people in this way. One can easily conclude that members of a street gang have preferences so different from one's own that there would be no point in pursuing their friendship.

If we are imagining the choice of whom to marry, however, it is not credible to suppose that one could accurately predict the details of every ranking one's potential spouse might ever make among all possible goods, services, activities, and moral values over the course of an entire lifetime. This approach would press the rationality assumption to an absurd extreme. *Homo economicus* would not only need to know his own preferences; he would also need to be perfectly informed about the preferences of his spouse and friends. More than that, he would need to be this thoroughly informed about each potential spouse, otherwise, we could not say that he made a rational choice among them.

In effect, this argument for the rational choice among potential spouses takes the economist's view of personal identity to an extreme in the following way. The person is a utility function: he can be perfectly described by all of his preference rankings among every possible combination of goods, services, and moral values. When he goes looking for a spouse, he is shopping among other individuals, who also can be perfectly described by a set of preference orderings. He is shopping among utility functions, with which he can interact. To make a rational choice among spouses, he must be perfectly informed about each potential spouse's utility function.

Friedrich A. Hayek's argument about the limits of knowledge would certainly apply to this situation.[8] It is one thing for economists to make an analytical assumption that a person can be defined and described by his preferences. It is quite another to claim that any individual can actually articulate those preferences for himself or accurately reveal them to another person. Hayek made an impressive argument that individuals are unable to articulate a huge percentage of the knowledge that they routinely and accurately use. He called this "tacit knowledge" and argued that the

---

[8] Friedrich A. Hayek, "The Use of Knowledge in Society," *American Economic Review* 35, no. 4 (1945): 519–30; and Hayek, *Law, Legislation, and Liberty, Vol. 1, Rules and Order* (Chicago: University of Chicago Press, 1973).

inability to articulate or reveal all this information completely would flummox any attempt to centrally plan an economy. Likewise, the claim that making a rational choice among spouses implies a commitment to be content with whatever choices they might make over the course of a lifetime assumes far too much knowledge of oneself and the other person.

In point of fact, one of the charming facets of lifelong friendship is the element of surprise and serendipity. A friend can bring ideas and activities into my life that I would never have even considered. I cannot possibly have a preference ordering among goods I have never thought of. Since he might bring completely new things to my attention, I cannot very well argue that the decision to be friends with this particular person entailed a tacit decision to honor all of his possible choices equally. I will be delighted by some of the things my friend or spouse brings into my life, disgusted by others, and utterly indifferent to still others.

This is why it is not plausible to claim that a rational choice among spouses makes a person who habitually pleads the rationality argument any easier to live with. To be specific, there is no way that I can make a "rational choice" among spouses that would completely obviate any need to consider the impact my behavior has on my spouse, or that his behavior has on me. I am not necessarily entitled to insist that he always act in a way that pleases me, just because he made a "rational choice" to marry me, and he knew perfectly well what this would mean. Nor can I claim that I am entitled to do whatever I want, without regard to his feelings about it, since he knew what sort of person I was when he married me. I cannot reasonably claim that he has no cause for legitimate complaint because he knew, or should have known, that I was the sort of person to do that sort of thing.

Even if both people accepted the basic premise of the rational choice of spouses, that still would not get them very far. Neither could trust the other to truthfully reveal their preferences if it inconvenienced them to do so. The rationality argument—"I did it because I wanted to, all things considered"—does not help much if you are trying to be in a relationship, trying to understand the other person, trying to have genuine intimacy with the other person. Hovering around the rationality argument is an implied clause: "when I considered all things, you and your feelings didn't get a very high ranking."

An economist might attempt to bring *Homo economicus* out of his isolation and into a more social mode of being, by explicitly including friendships and other relationships among the things that give a person happiness. One way to do this would be to enter my friend's well-being or happiness into my utility function. His happiness makes me happy. Alternatively, we might try to capture the friendship's impact on my happiness by saying that spending time together, doing anything or nothing in particular, is a good in itself. Being together gets a weight of its own in my decision making, independently of whatever it is that we are doing.

Either of those alternatives allows another person to matter enough to the rational person that he takes the other's responses into account in deciding what to do. Both friends say that they no longer get to do anything they want without considering other people.

Neither of these reformulations of utility completely prevents the genuinely unrepentant person from looking for a rationalization to refrain from apologizing. They just push the problem back a step. "I did what I wanted, all things considered. And by the way, my dear, you know perfectly well that you and your feelings were among the things I considered." The "by the way" clause is certainly a major improvement over "I did what I wanted and you don't matter." But I still might owe you an apology on occasion, and I still might want to ask for one from you. If I really do consider your feelings about my actions and take them into account in my calculations about what to do, that does not necessarily imply that you will never be aggrieved with me or disappointed in me.

In a way, the argument that I have already taken you into account makes the problem deeper, because it becomes harder to understand how and why you could ever get mad at me. How could you justifiably be angry, when I have already taken you and your feelings into account? Do I owe you an apology, just because you are mad at me, and have asked for an apology? What exactly would an apology mean in this context?

We are right back to the three choices with which we began: I didn't know it would hurt you. I knew and I wanted to hurt you. I knew and I didn't care.

VII. Is the Demand for Repentance Rational?

Let us turn this question around for a moment to shed some different light on it. Instead of asking whether a rational person could ever be sorry, let us ask ourselves whether a rational person could ever ask for an apology. What might the request, or demand, for an apology mean? Suppose I want you to apologize for something. What is it that I want you to say or admit? And is my desire reasonable?

One possibility is that I want you to admit that you were irrational. You didn't really mean it when you assigned an inappropriately low weight to me and my feelings. Or you didn't really know the impact your actions would have on me. This interpretation of an apology corresponds to the argument from ignorance. If I accept an apology based on ignorance, I am in effect letting the person off the hook.

Another, deeper possibility is that I want you to change. You admit knowing what you were doing; and I agree with that, but it doesn't make me feel any better. It actually makes me feel worse. My problem with you is that I don't like what you wanted. I want you to apologize, because that would tell me you agree that there is something wrong with you and your preferences. Either you assigned too low a weight to my feelings, or your values are so different from mine that I cannot accept or respect yours. The wife in our example might say, "Thinking your card club is more important than my Nobel Prize is beyond the pale." Or the husband might say, "Telling me that I don't love you unless I put up with your mother's nagging is telling me that your mother is more important to you than I am."

Each spouse can say to the other, with some justification, "I cannot accept your preferences. I don't have to change my preferences in this particular matter, and you can't make me. I think I am right, and I am not going to be bullied out of my position by your claim to autonomy, or your claim to be hurt, or your right to choose, or anything else."

The request for an apology might have a third possible meaning: Work with me. Help me understand. I want to understand. Offer an account of yourself, beyond "I did it because I wanted to." Give me an explanation of your preferences, your values. I would really like to be on good terms with you, and not be mad at you. But if you can't offer me an explanation that satisfies me in some form or fashion, I give myself permission to be mad at you.

This third case illustrates that justification is really the heart of the issue. If I ask you for an apology, I am asking you to justify yourself. If you can't, then I am justified in being angry at you because you did something I didn't like.

Whether the person offers an explanation of his behavior, or something closer to a genuine apology, the demand for an apology has placed some costs on him. This helps explain why the victim would go to the trouble of asking for an apology. The hard work of apologizing functions a bit like posting a performance bond for good behavior. The offender bears some cost of apologizing. By bearing this cost, the offender signals that he is willing to take responsibility for his behavior and the impact it has on others. He is not going to keep trying to see if he can wear the victim down, and eventually get away with it. Nor is he counting on the victim to continually monitor and correct him. An apology, particularly a costly apology, helps the victim feel that the offender is really serious about improving his behavior.

So we can understand why someone might ask a normal person for an apology. Does it make sense, however, to ask *Homo economicus* for one? Rational economic man has his justification prepared: he has already optimized. He has considered all costs and benefits, including the impact of his actions on other people. He cannot really be sorry for anything. He has already done the best he can do. A lame sort of "I am sorry you were hurt" is as close to an apology as we're going to get from him.

So asking *Homo economicus* for an apology is not rational, since we know in advance what he is going to say. The rational choice is to save our breath and not bother. We are forced to conclude that the naive version of rational economic man can neither give nor request an apology. We need some explanation for the fact that people do request and receive apologies.

The philosophers and theologians who are skeptical of the rational choice model altogether are perhaps chuckling at this point. They might think the obvious solution is to throw the whole rational choice apparatus overboard, along with *Homo economicus* and all his relatives. But this economist is not quite ready to admit defeat. There may be a way to account for this apparently irrational behavior.

VIII. Willful Blindness

We can get some insight by turning the question of repentance around once again: Why should repentance be so difficult? My spouse didn't like what I did. I didn't know he would be so upset about it. If I had really known all about the impact my actions would have on me and others, I would have chosen otherwise. When he asks for an apology, why do I resist? Why not just say, "Gee, I didn't realize this would bother you so much. I am sorry."

And of course, in many cases, this is exactly what we do. Oftentimes, the issue at hand is not a big enough deal that the offender has any problem offering an apology. In some situations, it really is a matter of new information: I honestly didn't know this was going to upset you.

But these "no big deal" cases do not exhaust the full set of situations in which people either ask for or give an apology. When a person has resisted giving an apology, and finally pleads ignorance, her partner might still be dissatisfied. He might very well respond, "What do you mean you didn't know how much it would bother me? How could you have not known? I don't believe you didn't know." The truth may very well be that the other person did not want to know.

This is the real source of the problem, both for our hypothetical married couple and for rational choice theory. My spouse has a different, and perhaps more realistic, picture of my behavior than I do. He wants me to change because I am giving him trouble in some way and he wants to be more comfortable. If I saw myself the way he saw me, I might agree that it is somehow in my interest to change. But I resist knowing this, especially if my husband is in my face about it. Whether his assessment of the situation is correct or not has little bearing on how easy it is to listen to.

This refusal to see is quite often at the source of the demand for an apology. One person feels wronged and the other sees no need for repentance. The demand for an admission of guilt can be a demand that the other person stop his willful blindness and see, really see, the impact that his actions have had on the person who has been wronged.

This phenomenon of self-deception also helps us to see why the plea of ignorance can be so infuriating to the person who feels wronged. If somebody is clueless about his own behavior, the claim of ignorance is not really satisfying. "I didn't know this bothered you" is an explanation that can easily be worn out by overuse. After hearing this a few times, the other person doesn't care whether you didn't know. Not knowing is what they want you to get over.

An example of this phenomenon took place during the 2004 Super Bowl, the major championship game in American professional football. During the halftime show, broadcast on the CBS network, singers Janet Jackson and Justin Timberlake "accidently" had a "wardrobe malfunction" that resulted in Jackson's breast being exposed on nationwide television. Brent Bozell, president of the Parents Television Council, made precisely this point that a plea of ignorance is no substitute for an apology: "We do not accept the apology of CBS, nor do we accept the statements of regret by MTV [which produced the halftime show]. It is absolutely reckless for CBS to claim that it had no prior knowledge that such activity was likely to take place. MTV is known for exactly this type of conduct. MTV and CBS are both owned by Viacom. Whether or not CBS executives did or did not know in advance is irrelevant; Viacom executives had the duty to know."[9]

Willful blindness presents a problem for rational choice theory as well. Rational choice theory would have us believe that I would always welcome accurate information about myself. But I think every adult knows what I am talking about when I say that I sometimes resist knowing the truth about myself. If my husband is in my face about an irritating habit, knowing he is right does not make me feel any better. In fact, I would rather he bugged me about something that wasn't true, so I could dismiss him as an idiot. (How a Rational Economic Woman chooses to marry an idiot, or convinces herself that she has chosen to marry an idiot, is an interesting problem I shall not pursue.)

I somehow doubt that this refusal to see the truth about oneself is unique to the Morse household. Nor is it confined to married couples. I imagine that every reader can picture someone who matches one of these descriptions of the willfully blind. The drunk in denial refuses to see the harm he does to himself, as well as to others. An abusive person thinks the other person has it coming, or that she or he really doesn't mind. The neglectful parents believe their child is really okay, even though he is alone watching TV in his room all the time. The self-important snob talks constantly about himself without noticing that no one is listening and everyone is avoiding him. The indulgent parents do not see that the complaints of their child's teacher are valid. Instead, they stick up for their precious little darling who has never done anything wrong in his whole life. The control freak can never manage to see that other people

---

[9] Statement by Brent Bozell, president of the Parents Television Council, in response to the Super Bowl halftime show display by Janet Jackson and Justin Timberlake. Press release, February 2, 2004; available online at http://www.parentstv.org/PTC/publications/release/2004/0202.asp (accessed October 16, 2004).

might possibly have something to contribute, and cannot understand why no one feels like cooperating with her.

The phenomenon of self-deception, then, is not an obscure or insignificant one. People are capable of bearing substantial costs rather than embracing certain kinds of information about themselves. The challenge for rational choice theory is to offer an account of why rational people would resist absorbing accurate information, freely offered. This is a particular challenge when the information is about something as intrinsically important as how we affect the people closest to us.

IX. THE WISH TO THINK WELL OF ONESELF

Putting this phenomenon of self-deception into a rational choice framework requires specific assumptions about the content of people's preferences. We can account for the refusal to see the negative impact we have on others by hypothesizing the existence of a particular good: the wish to think well of oneself. Virtually everyone has this good in his or her utility function to some extent. Positing the existence of a preference for something like this good helps account for our resistance to updating our beliefs about ourselves. For convenience, I suggest a shorter, more compact term for this thing we seem to value so much: *pride.*

We can see how pride plays a part in generating willful blindness by looking back to my short list of deluded individuals in the previous section. The alcoholic does not want to surrender his image of himself as a sober, upstanding citizen who can hold his liquor as well as anyone else. The abusive person does not want to surrender either the power he has over his victim, or his fantasy that his violence is somehow the other person's fault. The neglectful parents, who are perhaps absorbed in themselves, do not want to see that their child needs something from them. Nor do they want to surrender their view of themselves as good parents because they are good providers. The snob especially enjoys his good opinion of himself. He is totally deluded about the fact that other people lost interest in him long ago. The indulgent parents view their child as an extension of themselves. When the child causes problems at school, these parents prefer to blame the school rather than correct the child. Not only is blaming the school easier than correcting a difficult child, but this helps them preserve their image of themselves as good parents. All of the control freak's self-esteem depends upon being in control of every detail of every situation. Giving way to another person, or even giving credit to another person, feels like an intolerable loss of status.

In all of these cases, the cost of accepting negative information about the self is that we must forgo some part of our good opinion of ourselves. We must bear this cost in addition to any intrinsic difficulties of changing our behavior. This is a rational choice approach to accounting for the self-deception we see all around us. The cost of embracing accurate, but negative, information about ourselves is that we must surrender our pride.

The rational choice approach would say that a person will only embrace negative information about himself when the cost of remaining ignorant exceeds the benefits of clinging to his good opinion of himself. This would account for the common perception that an alcoholic has to "hit bottom" before he will be willing to sober up. The alcoholic must overcome more than the physical costs of going through withdrawal. If the physical costs were the only issue, alcoholics would talk about their situation quite differently from the way they typically do. They would say something along the lines of: "I recognize that I am addicted to alcohol. I choose not to give up drinking because quitting is too hard." The addict more often claims he is not addicted, that he can quit anytime he wants to, that other people are exaggerating the problems, and so forth. We surmise that the greater cost to the typical alcoholic is the cost of admitting that he is not the upstanding citizen he imagines himself to be. It is a testimony to the power of pride that the costs of continuing to drink have to be enormous before the alcoholic will make a serious effort to change.

The economists' way of looking at things also helps us see why the sin of pride has always been considered a deadly sin. The wish to think well of oneself is not wrong in itself. If that wish induces a person to ignore or resist accurate information, however, then it has morphed out of something legitimate and understandable and into something more serious, and even sinister. It is always irrational to refuse to use accurate information, when that information is presented to us without search costs or processing costs. Therefore, an economist would conclude that pride at the cost of self-deception is not rational. And that is really saying something, since "irrational" is the only word economists have that means "bad."

We might rescue this individual from the charge of irrationality by invoking the concept of satisficing, rather than maximizing. This hypothesis about information management suggests that people are not in a continual frenzy of gathering more and better information. Rather, people make a rational choice about how much information will suffice for the purpose at hand. In the present example, the individual does not continually update his beliefs about himself and his own preferences as a result of the input from other people. Instead, he waits until he has accumulated a critical mass of vital information to make an adjustment. He is willing to absorb some costs associated with bothering other people and losing their esteem in the meantime.[10]

This argument does not entirely rescue our self-deceiving friend. It only moves the behavior from the category of irrational and into the category of rational satisficing. But satisficing is a rational strategy only if there are

---

[10] Herbert A. Simon won the Nobel Prize for the idea of satisficing. His classic work is *Administrative Behavior*, 4th ed. (New York: Free Press, 1997).

substantial costs of gathering and processing information. In these cases of self-deception, gathering the information is not the problem. Mrs. *Homo Economicus* is literally right in her husband's face with more information than he wants to hear. It is the cost of processing the information that the person does not want to bear. His self-deceptive behavior is incomprehensible without seeing that forgoing pride counts as a substantial cost. Plainly, the individual would be better off with a lower cost of processing negative information about himself.

X. The Costs and Benefits of Apologies

So this is, in the end, what is so difficult about apologizing. Apologizing requires us to admit that we were wrong. The cost of that admission is surrendering some of our good feelings about ourselves. We give up some of our pride. Seeing this helps us to see what a person is looking for when he asks for an apology.

When someone asks for an apology, he is asking the other person to concede that there was something wrong about the other's preferences. If I ask you for an apology, I want you to admit that you were wrong in what you wanted, in the weights you assigned to different things, and in particular, in the weight you assigned to me and my feelings. This is exactly why giving an apology is so difficult. We have to admit we were wrong in what we wanted, as well as in how well we pursued our own interests.

The economists' perspective actually helps us to see just how acute this difficulty is. Economists define the person by his preferences as a matter of analytical convenience. This is not the same thing as hypothesizing that individuals literally identify themselves with their preferences. But if people choose to identify themselves in this way, they are less likely to surrender their preferences. Admitting to some wrong in the preferences is admitting to some substantial disorder in the soul. If you tell me there is something wrong with what I want, we are not just having a minor difference of opinion. You are telling me there is something intrinsically wrong with me. In other words, an attack on a person's preferences amounts to an attack on the person's identity. It is a lot more problematic than somebody saying they don't like my hairstyle. I can change my hairdo more easily than I can change my preferences.

To get a better idea of the point, think about someone for whom hair is identity. Many teenage girls have their identity all wrapped up in their appearance. If somebody tells her she has bad hair, a teenage girl becomes hysterical. The same comment to a more mature woman, or to a man of any age, is likely to be a big yawn. The teenage girl says to herself, "I am my appearance." The extreme version of economic man says, "I am my preferences."

Some features of the problem of repentance suggest that this view of the self has some plausibility. For instance, this helps account for the intense conflicts that sometimes arise over what ought to be simply matters of taste. We might think that arguments over preferences would be fairly tame. You want what you want; I want what I want. Live and let live.

But this turns out to be not quite true for the person who identifies himself with his wants. A complaint about tastes is more like a personal attack than a simple difference of opinion. If you make such a complaint, I have to put a stop to this assault on the interior of my soul. I can either sever my relationship with you, so I don't have to listen to you and your nonsense about my preferences being bad, or I can argue with you about your views, and hope that I can bludgeon you into submission. In neither case is the "live and let live" position quite stable.

Taking the economists' approach seriously, then, helps us to zero in on a couple of features about repentance we might not otherwise have noticed. The more reluctant a person is to receive negative information about himself, the less likely he will be to be repentant or to apologize. Self-deception is almost synonymous with a reluctance to absorb negative information about the self. A person's level of self-deception is related to two other factors: his level of pride and the extent to which he identifies himself with his preferences. In particular:

1. The greater the person's pride, the less open he will be to negative information about himself. Therefore, increases in pride will be correlated with increases in self-deception and other forms of irrational behavior. Increases in pride will also be correlated with a greater reluctance to apologize.

2. The more closely the person identifies himself with his preferences, the less open the person will be to negative information about those preferences. He will therefore be less willing to apologize. The more someone identifies himself with his preferences, the more defensive he will be about any confrontation regarding the content of his preferences.

Changes in preferences really are the heart of repentance. When we ask someone to apologize, we want him to do more than say he made a mistake. We want him to have new preferences so that he will be less likely to want to do the things that were hurtful to us. We want him to monitor himself, so we don't have to confront him every time. And if we do have to confront him, it will be a lot easier if he already understands that he needs to change. If he adopts new preferences, we don't have to convince him each and every time that there was something twisted about his original preferences.

We can put this into economic terms by observing that both excessive pride and excessive attachment to one's preferences operate as increases in the costs of processing new and accurate information about oneself. Higher processing costs make a person worse off than lower processing costs, precisely because these costs act as a barrier to using accurate information.

This is why it is a mistake for our unrepentant friend to claim he is using rational choice theory to justify his refusal to apologize. He is unwilling to say that his pride is more important than the relationship, that his good opinion of himself is more important than his spouse's feelings about him. He is unwilling to update his preferences to include significant information about the impact his behavior has on other people. He is unwilling to offer an account of his preferences. He expects the people in his life to "take his preferences as given," the way an elementary economics textbook might do. Hiding behind rational choice theory is a rationalization, not a reason.

XI. PUT ON THE NEW MAN

The issue of repentance raises the question of whether it is safe to assume that preferences remain unchanged. Some cases of remorse and apology are straightforward; others are life-changing. The repentant person is a new person.[11] He has renounced his old preferences and committed himself to live according to new ones.

Recall Lionel Tate, the Florida teenager who killed a six-year-old girl. Part of Lionel's process of repentance will have to include a changed understanding of himself. If his wish to think well of himself requires him to justify his every act, no matter the consequences to others, his behavior is unlikely to change. However, he may be able to change his behavior, if he is able to say, "I killed someone. I was wrong to do it. My reasons were not good enough. My reasons were excuses." He will, at least temporarily, think badly of himself and what he did. He has to find a different way of thinking well of himself. If he is really going to change, he has to both see what he did and develop a desire to behave differently.

The unrepentant soul claims that he is entitled to have preferences that are completely self-contained and self-referential. The problem of self-deception gives a hint that there is something mistaken about this. If a person places too great a weight on pride, and if he is too strongly attached to his preferences, he will behave in an utterly irrational manner, in exactly the economists' sense: he will ignore accurate information. That accurate information concerns the impact he has on other people. Our subjective feelings may well be facts, but they are not primal, nonnegotiable facts. There comes a point at which our feelings are just not the most important fact about a situation.

A person who is truly committed to rational behavior will be willing to accept all accurate information, even if that information implicates his preferences in some way. This person is more rational, but less apt to identify himself closely with any one set of preferences. This person, if he

---

[11] "Put on the new man" was St. Paul's advice to the Ephesians, 4:24 (1953 New Catholic edition of the Bible, a revision of the Challoner-Rheims version).

thinks in terms of preferences at all, will be more likely to be looking outside himself for guidance about how to behave. He may very well end up with a higher level of utility than would be possible with any one set of closely held preferences. In plain English, he is more likely to be happier more of the time, if he is less attached to the details of his preference ordering and more attentive to the information he can obtain from outside himself.

Once the person has made this kind of commitment, it seems that he can reasonably say, "I like my new preferences better." The vantage point from which one can say, "I like my new preferences better," has to include a substantial component of input from the world outside the individual himself. We need somehow to make that statement from a position outside, or above, both our current and our previous preferences. In other words, we need a God's eye view.[12]

Now, one need not claim to have a personal telephone line to God Himself in order to make the claim that the God's eye view would be superior to a purely subjective view of our preferences. Indeed, we need not even believe that such a God exists, in order to understand the idea that if He did exist, His perspective would be superior. God knows more than I do. God has a longer time horizon than I do. He can see how my actions will unfold over the long term, for a larger number of people, far better than I can. Finally, the God's eye perspective takes the good of more people truly into account. Since I am a social being, I actually do care about others. Since I am limited and finite, I am unable to fully comprehend or apprehend the impact I have on others. Therefore, God's way will be superior.

We could intelligibly argue that the more closely I align my preferences with the preferences God has for me, the happier I will be. I can meaningfully say, "I like these better." Under this approach, rationality means something quite different from successfully maximizing utility, using a completely subjective, self-derived set of preferences. A person is more rational, the more closely he conforms himself to the standard that exists outside himself.

Even without a specific religious tradition, we might still be able to discover something about the God's eye view, or at least, a view broader than our own preferences. Repentance is a key part of this process. For the

---

[12] The God's eye view has both similarities to and differences from the view of the "impartial spectator" cited above (in Section V). We might say that the impartial spectator was Adam Smith's attempt to "despiritualize" the conscience. Instead of using God's will as the standard for moral behavior, Smith and others in the Scottish Enlightenment suggested using the standard of the impartial spectator. What would a reasonable and decent person, detached from the situation, think was good conduct? Smith and his fellows assumed (and probably safely) that the ordinary person of their time had a robust, well-formed conscience. For instance, Smith seemed to assume that the ordinary Scotsman would eschew as bad manners excessive gloating over an unexpected turn of good fortune. See Smith, *The Theory of Moral Sentiments*, I.ii.5.2.

process of repentance compels a person to recognize that he is not God. Part of being repentant is admitting that I don't know everything, that I am not always right, and that I do not always care as much about others as I would like to think. It is in my interest to listen to what other people have to say.

That willingness to take in new information is part of what allows a person to detach from a particular set of preferences, and change. Being detached from particular preferences makes a person more rational, in exactly the economists' sense of using more information at lower cost. Being detached from our high opinion of ourselves also reduces the costs of processing negative information about ourselves. This openness to new information is also part of what allows people to be in genuine relationship with others. We can be less self-referential and more able to actually grow. One need not believe in an omniscient God to see that having some detachment from the self and openness to others is superior to trying to maximize utility based on a completely self-contained, self-defined set of preferences.

In fact, any moral code based upon a "living exemplar" (a virtuous person used as a model) offers a way out of the closed loop of personal preferences. Aristotle enjoins us that the way to become virtuous is to practice virtuous acts, under the tutelage of a virtuous person.[13] This process of following the virtuous person directs our gaze outward— rather than exclusively inward, on ourselves and our own feelings.

Of course, we must make a decision about whom to follow; and of course, we might pick out a knave or worse. There is no escaping the possibility of self-deception in the service of self-gratification. But if we choose to focus entirely on the self, we excuse ourselves from even trying to choose a guide to follow. The choice of an exemplar forces some process of self-examination and self-reflection that pulls people out of their natural preoccupation with themselves.

XII. CONCLUSION

The problems of apology and repentance offer a few surprising twists on the understanding of personal identity. Far from concluding that all preferences are equal and deserving of equal respect from the analyst, we can see that some behaviors are irrational in exactly the economists' sense. A person who cites self-interest as an excuse for not apologizing is a person who is very likely behaving in an irrational manner.

The greater the person's pride, the less open he will be to negative information about himself. Increases in pride will be correlated with increases in self-deception and other forms of irrational behavior. Increases

---

[13] Aristotle, *Nicomachean Ethics*, trans. David Ross, revised by J. L. Ackrill and J. O. Urmson (Oxford: Oxford University Press, 1984), book II, chapters 1–3, pp. 28–33.

in pride will also be correlated with a greater reluctance to apologize. The more closely the person identifies himself with his preferences, the less open the person will be to negative information about those preferences. He will therefore be less willing to apologize. The more someone identifies himself with his preferences, the more defensive he will be about any confrontation regarding the content of his preferences.

A more practical alternative is to see that I am better off if I allow my preferences to adapt to the information I get from the complaints of those around me. I can increase my utility by swallowing my pride, listening to what others have to say, and allowing myself to be changed. And as we economists watch people growing in happiness in this way, we may be motivated to take a fresh look at rationality. To be rational is not simply to maximize the pleasure I derive from a completely self-referential set of preferences. To be rational is to be successful at conforming myself, including my preferences, to what is.

Economics, Hoover Institution, Stanford University

PERSONAL IDENTITY AND POSTMORTEM SURVIVAL

By Stephen E. Braude

I. Introduction

As many have noted, what is often called the "problem" of personal identity can be understood either as a metaphysical issue or as an epistemological (and somewhat more practical) issue. Metaphysicians typically want to know *what it is* for one individual to be the same person as another. People undergo many changes over time, and some people resemble others quite closely. The metaphysician wants to know, for example, what makes me—the chronologically challenged, mostly bald philosopher Stephen Braude—the same unique individual as the infant who appeared on the scene many years earlier, despite the considerable evolution in my appearance and in my psychology during the interim. However, epistemologists are concerned (at least sometimes) with a different problem: how to *decide* if an individual is the same person as someone else. For example, are these decisions rooted in judgments about physical continuity, psychological continuity, or both? In virtue of what, for example, do we identify a person as me, despite (so I'm told) my remarkable resemblance to other chronologically and follically challenged individuals? Granted, in real life this potential problem seldom stops us in our tracks. Although some have trouble distinguishing identical twins, and although we sometimes mistake a person for someone else, those problems are uncommon, and usually they are quickly resolved. In fact, that is about as difficult as it gets for everyday identifications. Fortunately, we seldom deal with drastic or sudden changes in a person; physical or psychological changes in those we know are usually subtle or at least gradual. And few of us are forced to deal with really rare or exotic puzzles over a person's identity. For example, we needn't worry about whether our acquaintances are being skillfully impersonated; we seldom receive phone calls or other communiqués from people we thought had died; and most of us never contend with identity puzzles generated by cases of DID (dissociative identity disorder—formerly, multiple personality disorder).

However, there are some severe and real cases, suggesting the survival of bodily death and dissolution, which are not all that uncommon, and which many people have pondered even if they have not dealt with them personally. And here, the metaphysical and epistemological problems of personal identity seem to converge. That is because our interest in postmortem survival concerns something more interesting and personal than the scenario envisioned by some Eastern religions and New Age pundits: a kind of merging with the infinite, or being-in-general (a grand soup of consciousness). Although that might count as a form of *life after death*, it is certainly not the *survival of death* that people have anticipated, feared, or desired for centuries. Merging with the infinite would be a condition that obliterates whatever is distinctive about us, including our merely numerical individuality. But people who wonder about personal postmortem survival wonder about such things as whether *they* will be able to meet up with their deceased relatives, communicate with the still-living members of their families, reincarnate, or enjoy a postmortem existence in which they simply get their hair back. In general, they wonder whether *they* will continue to exist in some form or another after bodily death. And they wonder whether that future individual bears something like the same relationship to their present self that their present self bears to their physically and psychologically remote infant self. As a result, these cases present the epistemological challenge of deciding whether they provide evidence for postmortem persistence of a specific individual. And they present the metaphysical challenge of explaining how such persistence is possible.

Thus, when mediums appear to channel information from, or dramatically impersonate, our deceased friends or relatives, or when children seem to display the memories, traits, and abilities of deceased strangers in cases of ostensible reincarnation, we have good reason to be puzzled, whether we are metaphysicians or folk who are less relentlessly abstract. Metaphysicians often wonder whether we can use the concepts *identity* or *person* intelligibly when we talk about postmortem survival. For example, if we believe (as many do) that our personhood and personal identity are intimately and essentially tied to our physical embodiment, then we might wonder whether *anything deserving to be called "Stephen Braude"* could survive my bodily death. And for those not troubled by this metaphysical problem, there remains a difficult practical problem. If the deceased's body no longer exists, "it is hard to see what . . . could possibly count as distinguishing between Jones having survived the death of his body (though we don't understand how) and its being now and again transiently *as if* he had survived it (though again we can't make sense of it)." [1]

In the next section, I shall argue that metaphysical worries about postmortem survival are less important than many have supposed. In Section III, I shall consider briefly why cases suggesting postmortem survival can be so intriguing and compelling, and I shall survey our principal explanatory options and challenges. In Section IV, I shall consider why we need to be circumspect in our appraisal of evidence for mind-body correlations. And in the final section, I shall try to draw a few tentative and provocative conclusions.

---

[1] Alan Gauld, "Philosophy and Survival: An Essay Review of R. W. K. Paterson's *Philosophy and the Belief in a Life after Death*," *Journal of the Society for Psychical Research* 62 (1998): 453–462, p. 458.

II. The Primacy of the Practical

Initially, it might seem that we need to solve the metaphysical problem of identity before we can decide what to say when confronted with a good case of ostensible mediumship or reincarnation. That is, if we cannot even begin to explain how survival *could* occur following bodily death and dissolution, and especially when we have philosophical concerns about whether disembodied survival is even possible, then how could we decide if postmortem survival has occurred in fact? But that position is questionable for a number of reasons.

First, it is clear that most of us satisfactorily make decisions about *pre*mortem identity without having anything of interest or substance to say either about the nature of personal identity or about the empirical basis for our successful everyday judgments about identity. Obviously, we do not need a theoretical grasp of the metaphysics of identity simply to make correct identifications. Most people know nothing about the metaphysics of identity, and those who do don't come close to a consensus on the issues. In fact, probably any of several different metaphysical theories will be compatible with our everyday, preanalytic judgments of personal identity. If a metaphysical theory plays any *useful* role at all, it might merely be to show how we could theoretically ground our successful practice of identifying persons. Moreover, most people are largely ignorant of the received medical, biological, or psychological basis for determining bodily or psychological continuity. Nevertheless, our strategies for identifying others are generally workable, and probably they have remained stable for millennia. At the same time, however, our prevailing philosophies and scientific background theories have changed profoundly. Apparently, then, we have not been prevented, either by our ignorance, theoretical naiveté, or shifting conceptual trends, from making successful judgments about identity.

The philosopher R. W. K. Paterson, in a generally sensible and well-informed book on postmortem survival, makes a related observation about our ability to identify persons successfully without the aid (or hindrance) of a well-developed underlying metaphysics.[2] After commenting on the intractability of familiar philosophical puzzles about identity, he writes:

> From our failure to discover the *fons et origo* [source and origin] of the continuing and unique identity we ascribe to living persons it follows that we have no special, imperative, inescapable intellectual obligation to discover it and set it forth in the case of deceased persons.[3]

---

[2] R. W. K. Paterson, *Philosophy and the Belief in a Life after Death* (New York: St. Martin's Press, 1995).
[3] Ibid., 23.

More contentiously, however, Paterson argues further that we can dispense with the usual metaphysical puzzles, because personal (or at least numerical) identity is one of a large number of unanalyzable facts that we unhesitatingly accept as facts. Now I would agree that some facts are unanalyzable,[4] but it is not clear that Paterson and I are making the same claim here. In fact, it is not clear what sort of impossibility Paterson has in mind when he claims that some concepts cannot be analyzed. In any case, I want to focus on another feature of his view. To illustrate what he has in mind, Paterson argues that "although we all understand what time is, we cannot give a clear explication of what it is; we cannot say what we mean when we speak of a 'past' event . . . and yet we and our hearers know perfectly well what we mean."[5] Similarly, "even if we are unable to give a full and correct analysis of the claim that some disembodied person is numerically absolutely identical with the ante-mortem Winston Churchill, we understand *what* is being claimed and are entitled to weigh up such evidence as is available on behalf of this claim."[6]

That does not seem quite right, however. First, whether we are making claims about time or about identity, it is somewhat misleading, or at least unclear, to say that we understand (or "know perfectly well") what we are saying. In fact, I would argue that not even metaphysicians are as clear about their claims as they sometimes like to believe, and the rest of us needn't have even a shared idea of what we are saying—much less a metaphysical view of *what it is* for an event to be past or of *what it is* for a postmortem individual to be the same person as a premortem individual.

One problem here concerns fundamental issues in the philosophy of language, and for reasons of space, I must wax dogmatic for a moment. Some would contend—I believe, correctly—that neither meanings nor concepts are determinate or clear things at all, and in fact that the meaning of a sentence is no more determinate or specifiable than the humor or compassion of a sentence. If that is true, however, then to think that we know or can specify what exactly we are saying when we make these judgments presupposes an untenable view of language and meaning. It presupposes not simply that meanings can be determinate but that some expressions must be intrinsically unambiguous—that is, the ones we reach when disambiguation comes to an end.[7] As far as identity judgments are concerned, at best we know—only roughly—what sorts of considerations would lead us to *decide* that two individuals are the same. Whatever personal identity amounts to, whatever we mean when we talk about

[4] Stephen E. Braude, *The Limits of Influence: Psychokinesis and the Philosophy of Science*, rev. ed. (Lanham, MD: University Press of America, 1997).

[5] Paterson, *Philosophy and the Belief in a Life after Death*, 44.

[6] Ibid., 45, italics in original.

[7] I use the term "disambiguation" here to refer to the general process of clarifying the meaning of our utterances, which involves rendering them both less ambiguous and less vague.

identity, or whatever justifies or undergirds our decision that two things are (or are not) identical, is then something we can try to determine or (more likely) dispute indefinitely.

Every sentence we utter rests on numerous tacit background assumptions, which ordinarily need not be considered, evaluated, or even understood by the speaker in order to determine what the sentence means or whether the sentence is true. For example, when I say, "The table is brown," I make numerous assumptions about the nature of observation and the stability of physical objects and their properties over time. It is only when we are engaged in philosophical analysis, or when actual problems emerge in communicating with others, that we are likely to recognize some of those assumptions and appreciate the role they play in determining what our utterances mean. Perhaps more importantly, it is only in these problematical contexts that we are likely to realize how vague and ambiguous our statements are.

Admittedly, analyzing our utterances and arguments is often a fairly straightforward matter. But that is seldom (if ever) because our statements on those occasions are inherently clearer or more precise than on other occasions. Rather, it is usually because the prevailing context of inquiry is relatively undemanding. Understanding or clarifying what we mean is challenging only in relatively arcane contexts, or when the need for clarification is unusually urgent or the requirements particularly exacting. In most cases, however, we tolerate a great deal of ambiguity and vagueness, and we seldom need or demand further clarification. But that is not because our utterances in those cases are inherently clear, or significantly clearer than in contexts where disambiguation is more difficult or pressing. It merely reflects the pervasiveness of shared background assumptions underlying our linguistic practices generally and the specific topic of conversation in particular. That is why we might take a sentence to be deeply obscure in certain contexts but not in others (e.g., where there is no need to question or examine our background assumptions).

For example, the sentence "We create our own reality" might seem perfectly intelligible and acceptable at a conference celebrating so-called New Age thinking, whereas in many academic contexts it would be considered mysterious at best or blatantly false at worst. Similarly, "Good neighbors come in all colors" might seem both clear and true at a town meeting on racial integration, but in other contexts (e.g., a logic or art class) the sentence would be considered false, because no humans are (say) forest green, aquamarine, or vermilion.

If these observations are correct, then it is not the case that either ordinary or philosophical talk about persons or identity is especially or helpfully clear and precise. Nevertheless, it is significant (as Paterson recognizes) that when we make identity judgments we are able in most cases to get along quite nicely, despite our apparently inevitable conceptual fuzziness. To the extent we even have *a* concept of personhood or personal identity, it is as loose and elastic as most of our concepts. And ordinarily it serves us quite well; we have little if any trouble deciding who's who. Moreover, when we identify persons, we rely generally on both physical and psychological continuity, and under optimal conditions we can identify people with respect to continuity of both sorts. In many cases, however, our empirical resources are less robust. We might interact verbally with someone via telephone or email but not see the person's body. We might see a person but observe no psychologically significant behavior. And even if we believe all along that a person's psychological properties supervene on the bodily, in making identity judgments we weight psychological and physical continuity differently in different cases, relying sometimes on only one of them.

Of course, philosophers like to concoct various science-fiction or theological scenarios to challenge our general strategies for judging identity and (allegedly) thereby sharpen our thinking about identity. But real-life cases do this as well—among them, cases of dissociative identity disorder (DID) and cases suggesting postmortem survival. I would say that none of these real or imagined cases threatens to undermine our ordinary concepts of a person or personal identity.[8] There is no reason to think that an adequate concept should handle all cases it might be thought to cover, no matter how exotic. Our ordinary concepts tend to be just fine for ordinary cases. The weird cases are ones we cannot resolve without an uncommonly reflective decision on the matter. Moreover, "some hypothetical cases may not be decidable by any means at all, let alone by some 'criterion'."[9] At any rate, the ostensible postmortem cases strike us as particularly vexing because they apparently undercut both our familiar reliance on bodily continuity as well as common assumptions about how psychological properties depend on physical states of affairs. However, some observations about this predicament are in order.

First, we need to keep in mind the cultural variability in the concept of a person, which might help combat our tendency to assume smugly that there is something privileged about our common presuppositions about personhood. For example, although for many of us the presumption of one person/one body is the default presumption in most instances, that is not the case in other cultures (e.g., the Ndembu, the Ashanti, and the Bushmen of the Kalahari) that have interesting approaches to what they perceive as the conceptually problematic birth of twins, triplets, etc.[10]

---

[8] For a fuller discussion, see Stephen E. Braude, *Immortal Remains: The Evidence for Life after Death* (Lanham, MD: Rowman and Littlefield, 2003).

[9] Bruce Aune, *Metaphysics: The Elements* (Minneapolis: University of Minnesota Press, 1995), 91.

[10] See Stephen E. Braude, *First Person Plural: Multiple Personality and the Philosophy of Mind*, rev. ed. (Lanham, MD: Rowman and Littlefield, 1995). Dan Gowler, "On the Concept of the Person: A Biosocial View," in Ralph Ruddock, ed., *Six Approaches to the Person* (London and Boston: Routledge and Kegan Paul, 1972), 37–69.

Moreover, in our culture, our rough-and-ready ordinary concept of a person is largely *normative* (what Locke termed a "forensic" concept). When we use the term "person" in everyday life we are not picking out a *natural kind*—that is, either some a priori specifiable piece of ontological furniture or at least something whose nature scientific inquiry will decide (for example, something that inevitably links persons to the biological species *Homo sapiens*).[11] Our ordinary concept of a person concerns things we value about ourselves and each other, and it rests on various presuppositions about the ways people should be treated. In our culture at least, we typically regard persons as (among other things) entities who have (or could have) an inner life relevantly similar to our own, who have various rights and perhaps obligations, and who deserve our respect, consideration, and so on. And we accept the normativity of this conception of personhood irrespective of our views (if any) about how persons might (or must) be configured biologically or otherwise—for example, whether fetuses, dolphins, computers, brains in a vat, alternate personalities, or disembodied spirits, could be persons. In fact, I would argue (along with philosopher Anthony Quinton)[12] that what we value most about persons are their psychological traits and that this is why we are often content to make identity judgments (even in exotic cases such as DID and apparent postmortem survival) solely on the basis of psychological continuity.

Some might protest that although the concept of a person is loose and variable, the concept of identity is not. Paterson, for example, claims it is a simple fact that something is strictly identical with another thing, or (even more clearly) that it is self-identical.[13] In the same spirit, philosopher Steve Matthews (in an exchange we had recently regarding DID) argues, "I agree . . . that the concept of personhood is elastic. But the concept of numerical identity of self over time is necessarily not elastic because the concept of numerical identity is not: everything is identical with itself and no other thing."[14] Arguably, a similar position on the concept of identity underwrites the recent revisionist view in philosophy that identity is not what matters in survival.[15]

---

[11] For a discussion of the slippery concept of a natural kind, see Barry Stroud, "The Charm of Naturalism," *Proceedings and Addresses of the American Philosophical Association* 70, no. 2 (1996): 43–55.

[12] Anthony Quinton, "The Soul," in John Perry, ed., *Personal Identity* (Berkeley: University of California Press, 1975), 53–72; originally published in *The Journal of Philosophy* 59, no. 15 (1962): 393–409.

[13] Paterson, *Philosophy and the Belief in a Life after Death*, 44–45.

[14] Steve Matthews, "Blaming Agents and Excusing Persons: The Case of DID," *Philosophy, Psychiatry, and Psychology* 10 (2003): 169–74, p. 169. See also Steve Matthews, "Establishing Personal Identity in Cases of DID," *Philosophy, Psychiatry, and Psychology* 10 (2003): 143–51; and Stephen E. Braude, "Counting Persons and Living with Alters: Comments on Matthews," *Philosophy, Psychiatry, and Psychology* 10 (2003): 153–56.

[15] Raymond Martin, *Self-Concern: An Experiential Approach to What Matters in Survival* (Cambridge: Cambridge University Press, 1998); Derek Parfit, *Reasons and Persons* (Oxford: Oxford University Press, 1984).

But the concept of numerical identity is not especially clear or simple. For one thing, there is no single preferred thing we mean when we say "everything is self-identical." And for another, concepts are not isolable or independent entities. In fact, the concept of numerical identity seems to be elastic and variable in a way similar to that in which the concept of a person is elastic and variable.

First, as I noted earlier, our talk about both persons and identity—in fact, our language generally—is fundamentally vague and ambiguous. Second, as I also mentioned above, whether we regard something as a person depends on various other beliefs we hold—for example, beliefs shaped by culture, religious upbringing, general education, or philosophical training. It also depends on the practical needs of situations we actually confront or at least might confront. For example, it depends on whether we are dealing with aliens, androids, or (more realistically) ordinary cases of recognizing people, or even with the urgent need to decide how our spouse's alternate personality—or a criminal defendant suffering from DID—should be treated.

Apparently, then, it is implausible to suppose that there is something that qualifies as *the* concept of a person, or that there is an inherently privileged analysis of what we mean by "person," or that this meaning can be specified with the kind of crispness or finality to which some philosophers aspire. But an analogous situation holds in connection with numerical identity. To see this, consider first the expression

$$(x)(x = x)$$

usually interpreted as "anything x is such that it is identical to itself," or more colloquially, "everything is self-identical." The acceptability of this alleged law of identity is not something we can decide by considering this law alone. Regarded merely as a theorem of a formal system, it has no meaning at all; it is nothing more than a sanctioned expression within a set of rules for manipulating symbols. As an interpreted bit of formalism, however, it is acceptable only with respect to situations in which we attempt to apply it. And perhaps more interesting, it is *intelligible* only as part of a larger network of commitments. That is, what we mean by "everything is self-identical" depends in part on how we integrate that sentence with other principles or inferences we accept or reject.

To see this, consider whether we would accept as true the statement

(1) Zeus = Zeus.

To many, no doubt, that sentence seems as unproblematical as the superficially similar

(2) Steve Braude = Steve Braude.

However, in many systems of deductive logic containing the rule of existential generalization (EG), from the symbolization of (1)—namely,

(1') $z = z$

we can infer

(3) $(\exists x)\; x = z$

or, in other words,

(4) Zeus exists,

and of course, many consider that result intolerable.

Not surprisingly, philosophers have entertained various ways of dealing with this situation. One would be to taxonomize different types of existence and interpret the rule of existential generalization as applying only to some of them. Another approach would be to get fussy about the concept of a *name*. We could decide that "Zeus" is not a genuine name and that genuine names (like "Steve Braude") pick out only real existent individuals—not mythical or fictional individuals, for example. Both these approaches concede certain (but different) sorts of limitations to standard predicate logic and the way or extent to which it connects with ordinary discourse. Others prefer to tweak the logic directly, either syntactically or semantically. For example, some simply reject the rule of existential generalization and endorse a so-called (existence) *free* logic. Alternatively, some retain EG but adopt a substitutional interpretation of the quantifiers "(x)" and "$(\exists x)$," so that instead of reading (3) as

(3') There is (or exists) some x such that x is identical with z (Zeus),

we read it as

(3") Some substitution instance of "$x = z$" is true.

The latter, they would say, is acceptable and carries no existential commitments.

The reader needn't understand all these options. The moral, however, should be clear enough. All these approaches raise concerns about what should be regarded as a *thing* in certain contexts. The statement "everything is self-identical" is not simply true *no matter what*. Its truth (and indeed, meaning) turn on a number of other decisions as to which other principles or inferences are acceptable, and that whole package of decisions can only be evaluated on pragmatic grounds. Moreover, it is perfectly respectable to decide that some solutions to this conundrum are appropriate for some situations and that other solutions are appropriate for others. We are never constrained to select one solution as privileged or fundamental.

III. Confronting the Evidence

As I noted earlier, we often make identity judgments satisfactorily on the basis of psychological continuity alone, even if we suspect or believe strongly that the psychological supervenes on the physical. Moreover, we typically make these judgments in the face of considerable philosophical ignorance or indecision about what constitutes identity, as well as scientific ignorance about the physical or biological basis for asserting bodily continuity. That is enough, I think, to undercut the claim that we cannot acceptably make identity judgments in cases of ostensible postmortem survival when we do not know how to explain survival in the apparent absence of bodily continuity. So let's consider briefly how, in a state of comparative metaphysical or scientific innocence, we would assess apparently good evidence for postmortem survival. Presumably (and as we will see), what we would want to say depends largely on the same thing that concerns us most deeply in everyday cases: *how we value persons.*

However, empirical considerations still matter, and the empirical landscape is strewn with obstacles. The issues here are numerous and complex, and I have discussed them at length elsewhere.[16] For present purposes, we need only note the following key points.

Generally speaking, a case suggests postmortem survival because (a) some living person demonstrates knowledge or abilities closely (if not uniquely) associated with a deceased person, and (b) we have good reason to believe that this knowledge was not obtained, or the abilities developed, through ordinary means. For example, suppose that a medium purports to channel information from my late Uncle Harry. And suppose that she provides information—for example, the location of a secret will—that no living person besides Harry ever knew (at least by normal means). And suppose that, although the medium never met my uncle, she takes on various of his characteristics, such as his quirky interests and perspective on politics, his distinctive laugh and caustic sense of humor, and his idiosyncratic syntax and inflection. And suppose the medium also demonstrates Uncle Harry's ability to speak Yiddish, even though she never studied (or better, was never exposed) to that language.

Before we can accept even an impressive case as indicating postmortem survival, however, we have to rule out a number of counter-hypotheses,

---

[16] Braude, *Immortal Remains.*

some more obvious and easier to eliminate than others. First, we need to consider what I call the Usual Suspects: fraud, the closely related misreporting and malobservation, and cryptomnesia or hidden memories (the ability to remember something without consciously realizing it). For some cases, these are clearly live options, but for others they are not. That is one reason the topic of postmortem survival is so interesting: the best cases easily deflect counter-explanation in terms of the Usual Suspects.

But the Usual Suspects are merely the first wave of skeptical counter-explanations, and they posit nothing more than relatively normal (or possibly abnormal) processes as alternatives to postmortem survival. However, a second wave of more exotic counter-explanations are more refractory, and these proposals fall into two classes. The first class posits clearly abnormal or rare processes, such as dissociative pathologies, rare mnemonic gifts, extreme or unprecedented forms of savantism, or equally rare latent creative capacities. For example, it is significant that prodigies and other gifted people manifest various abilities without having first to undergo a period of practice. And it is significant that savants display abilities that seem radically discontinuous with their usual, limited repertoire of capacities. Some calculating savants, for instance, can factor any number presented to them, even though they cannot add the change in their pockets. One famous musical savant was spastic until he sat down to play the piano. Clearly, these cases must be considered when evaluating a medium's suddenly manifesting an ability associated with an ostensibly deceased person.[17] I call these alternatives the Unusual Suspects, and although they seem to be ruled out in the very best cases, advocates of the survival hypothesis (hereafter *survivalists*) have, in general, done a poor job of countering them.

The second class of exotic counter-explanations posits something even more difficult to rule out—namely, *psychic functioning among the living*, presumably displayed in a way that simply gives the appearance of postmortem survival. This counter-hypothesis is actually difficult—perhaps impossible—to rule out in principle, since apparently any evidence suggesting postmortem survival can be explained solely in terms of (perhaps convoluted) psychic processes involving the living. For example, so long as obscure information provided by a medium can be verified, it can be explained by appeal to extrasensory perception (ESP). Intimate facts verified by consulting someone's memories can be explained by telepathy, and facts verified by consulting physical states of affairs (for example, the location of a hidden will) can be explained by clairvoyance. Advocates of postmortem survival cannot object to these counter-explanations as a matter of principle, because ironically they also must posit comparably impressive feats of ESP, simply to explain how mediums interact with

---

[17] For examples of how anti-survivalists would frame counter-explanations in terms of these abnormal or unusual capacities of the living, see Braude, *Immortal Remains*.

deceased communicators and how deceased communicators are aware of current physical states of affairs.

At any rate, these types of counter-explanation will not be entertained by anyone who refuses to accept the existence or possibility of ESP or psychokinesis (i.e., remote control by the deceased of the medium's body).[18] And clearly, this is not the place to review the evidence, either for relatively humdrum forms of psychic processes or for the more refined or extensive forms believed necessary to accommodate the evidence for survival—what is often called "super psi." I *will* lay my cards on the table and say that I believe the evidence for both ESP and psychokinesis has been satisfactorily demonstrated.[19] For now, however, we needn't worry about that. What matters here is what we would say if we were confronted with a slam-dunk, ideal case suggesting postmortem survival, and what impact such a case would have on our thinking about identity.

Presumably, an ideal survival case would be one for which appeals to the Usual and Unusual Suspects have no plausibility whatever. It would also be one that, while perhaps not conclusively ruling out appeals to psychic functioning among the living, nevertheless strains that hypothesis to the breaking point—that is, a case where even people sympathetic to such paranormal conjectures would be inclined to throw in the towel. In *Immortal Remains,* I offered a list of desirable features of a postmortem survival case, some of which are as follows.

(1) The case would be etiologically distinct from cases of DID or other psychological disorders. For example, in a reincarnation case the phenomena should not manifest after the subject experiences a traumatic childhood incident. (2) The manifestations of a previous personality (or discarnate communicator) should not serve any discernible psychological needs of the living. (3) Those manifestations should make most sense (or better, should only make sense) in terms of agendas or interests reasonably attributable to the previous personality. (4) The manifestations should begin, and should be documented, before the subject (or anyone in the subject's circle of acquaintances) has identified and researched the life of a corresponding previous personality. (5) The subject should supply verifiable, intimate facts about the previous personality's life. (6) The history and behavior of the previous personality (as revealed through the subject) should be recognizable, in intimate detail, to several individuals, preferably on separate occasions. (7) The subject should also display some of the previous personality's idiosyncratic skills or traits. (8) These skills or traits should be as foreign to the subject as possible—for example, from a

---

[18] Conceptually, the distinction between this form of psychokinesis and telepathic influence is very hazy. For a discussion of this and related terminological issues, see Stephen E. Braude, *ESP and Psychokinesis: A Philosophical Examination,* rev. ed. (Parkland, FL: Brown Walker Press, 2002).

[19] I have defended these conclusions at length in Braude, *The Limits of Influence* and *ESP and Psychokinesis.*

significantly different culture. (9) Skills associated with the previous personality should be of a kind or of a degree that generally require practice,
and that are seldom (if ever) found in prodigies or savants. (10) In order
for investigators to verify information communicated about the previous
personality's life, it should be necessary to access multiple, culturally and
geographically remote, and obscure sources.

It is one thing to consider the issues here purely in the abstract, and
another to imagine in more detail what an overwhelmingly impressive
case would look like. However, I think the latter is precisely what we
need to do, not simply to appreciate how the evidence might challenge us
conceptually, but to show how, in practice, concerns about bodily continuity may play no role whatever. Consider, then, what we would do if
confronted with the following case of ostensible mediumship.

Mrs. B is a gifted medium. As far as her education is concerned, she
never completed primary school, and as a result she has only an average
fourth-grader's level of literacy. Moreover, Mrs. B's exposure to the world
has been confined exclusively to her immediate small-town environment
in the American Midwest. She has never traveled beyond her hometown
or expressed any interest in books, magazines, or television shows about
other locales. Similarly, she has had no exposure to the world of ideas, to
literature (even in cinematic form), or to the arts. In fact, when she is not
channeling communications or caring for her home and family, she devotes
her time to prayer and developing her psychic sensitivity.

One day Mrs. B gives a sitting for Mr. X, who lives in Helsinki. The
sitting is what is known as a *proxy* sitting, because the person interacting
with the medium is substituting for someone who wants information
from the medium. In the most interesting cases, proxy sitters have little or
no information about the person they represent, and they know nothing
about the individual the medium is supposed to contact. Clearly, then,
good proxy cases help rule out some Usual Suspects, because we cannot
plausibly assert that the medium is simply extracting information from
the sitter by means of leading questions, subtle bodily cues, etc. In the
present case, Mr. X (using a pseudonym) sends a watch, once owned by
a dear friend, to the Parapsychology Foundation in New York, requesting
that someone there present it to Mrs. B on his behalf. So no one at the
Parapsychology Foundation knows (at least by normal means) the identity of either Mr. X or the original owner of the watch.

When Mrs. B handles the watch, she goes into trance and, speaking
English as if it were not her native tongue and with a clear Scandinavian
accent, purports to be the surviving personality of the Finnish composer
Joonas Kokkonen. She also speaks a language unknown to anyone at the
séance, which the sitters record and which experts later identify as fluent
Finnish. At subsequent sittings, native speakers of Finnish attend, along
with the proxy, and converse with Mrs. B in their language. All the while,
she continues to speak Finnish fluently, demonstrating an ability not only

to utter, but also to understand, sentences in Finnish. In both Finnish and accented English, Mrs. B provides detailed information about Kokkonen's life and his music, demonstrating in the process an intimate acquaintance with Finnish culture, a professional command of music generally, and a knowledge of Kokkonen's music in particular. For example, on one occasion she writes out the final bars to an uncompleted piano quintet and requests that they be given to Kokkonen's former colleague, Aulis Sallinen, who she claims has possession of the original score, so that the quintet can be assembled into a performing edition. In fact, Sallinen does have the original score, in the condition described by the Kokkonen communicator.

These sittings cause a minor sensation in Finland and elsewhere, and before long many of Kokkonen's friends travel to have anonymous sittings with Mrs. B. Because Kokkonen was a major international musical figure and had friends and colleagues throughout the world, many of those friends are not Scandinavian. So at least those sitters provide no immediate linguistic clue as to whom they wish to contact. In every case, however, Mrs. B's Kokkonen-persona recognizes the sitters and demonstrates an intimate knowledge of details specific to Kokkonen's friendship with them. When speaking to Kokkonen's musician friends, the Kokkonen-persona discusses particular compositions, performances, or matters of professional musical gossip. For example, with one sitter, the Kokkonen-persona discusses the relative merits of the Finlandia and BIS recordings of his cello concerto (neither of which the sitter has heard), and then complains about the recording quality of the old Fuga recording of his third string quartet. With another sitter, the Kokkonen-persona gossips enthusiastically and knowledgeably about a famous conductor's body odor. When speaking to nonmusician friends, the trance-persona speaks in similar detail about matters of personal interest to the sitter. Some of these later sittings are themselves proxy sittings. For example, the composer Pehr Nordgren arranges, anonymously, to be represented by a Midwestern wheat farmer, who takes with him to the séance a personal item of Nordgren's. Mrs. B goes into trance immediately, mentions a term of endearment by which Kokkonen used to address Nordgren, and begins relating a discussion the two composers once had about Nordgren's violin concerto. Communications of this quality continue, consistently, for more than a year.

I submit that if we actually encountered a case of this quality, we would have to agree with philosopher Robert Almeder that it would be irrational (in some sense) not to regard it as good (if not compelling) evidence of survival,[20] even if we did not know how to make sense of it theoretically, and (in the most extreme scenario) even if our underlying metaphysics

---

[20] Robert Almeder, *Death and Personal Survival* (Lanham, MD: Rowman and Littlefield, 1992).

was clearly uncongenial to the idea of postmortem survival. Moreover, if several cases of (or near) that quality appeared, they would have a cumulative force. They would obviously comprise precisely the kind of evidence that could lead us to revise, abandon, or at least seriously reconsider a conventionally materialist worldview. Philosophical intransigence in the face of such cases would not demonstrate admirable tough-mindedness. Instead, it would betray indefensible intellectual rigidity.

Unfortunately, we do not encounter cases of this quality; even the best of them disappoint in some respects. Nevertheless, the very best cases are rich enough to give us pause—at least if we do not have a metaphysical axe to grind. At any rate, one virtue of looking at hypothetically ideal cases is that they remind us it is not an idle enterprise to consider less-than-ideal cases, even if the evidence is consistently frustrating in one way or another. The quest is not futile; the evidence *can* point persuasively (if mysteriously) to postmortem survival, at least in principle.

Interestingly (as philosopher C. J. Ducasse noted),[21] the mediumistic scenario we have been envisioning is similar in critical respects to a more familiar situation, one in which identity judgments are—and more importantly—*need to be* made without relying on evidence of bodily continuity. Suppose I received a phone call over a noisy connection from an individual purporting to be my friend George, whom I thought had died in a plane crash. Although I cannot establish the speaker's identity by confirming his bodily continuity to the George I knew, and although the noisy phone line sometimes makes it difficult to hear what the speaker is saying, nevertheless my conversation can provide a solid practical basis for concluding that George is really speaking to me. The speaker could demonstrate that he had certain memories that no one but George should have, and he could exhibit characteristically George-ish personality traits, verbal mannerisms, as well as idiosyncratic motives and interests. Whether or not the persistence of these traits satisfies a metaphysician's criteria of identity, they will often suffice for real-life cases.

Similarly, if my phone conversation were with a person who claimed to be speaking to George and relaying his words to me (and vice versa), this situation would be analogous to cases where a medium conveys messages from communicator to sitters. Obviously, it is more difficult to discern the communicator's personality traits under these conditions, and that clearly deprives us of one type of evidence of survival. Nevertheless, if the content of the conveyed information is highly specific and intimate, it might justify concluding that George lives and is communicating directly to the person on the phone.

Apparently, then, we should be able to apply to postmortem cases the same psychological criteria of identity that we apply, usually unproblem-

---

[21] C. J. Ducasse, *A Critical Examination of the Belief in a Life after Death* (Springfield, IL: Charles C. Thomas, 1961).

atically, in everyday cases. Granted, we might still feel puzzled by the postmortem cases, and we may be unable to explain (or say anything interesting about) how survival could occur following bodily death. We may simply be at a loss philosophically and scientifically. As I noted earlier, however, that is hardly unique to postmortem cases. Besides, it is pretty much irrelevant—although it may still be annoying—that hypothetically ideal postmortem cases challenge us conceptually and even violate some people's physicalist assumptions. Although philosophers are often reluctant to admit this, practical considerations trump abstract philosophy every time, and if we really encountered a case as good as those we can construct, and especially if the case mattered to us personally, our reflective metaphysical scruples would count for nothing. We would not hedge our bets and say that it is not really survival, but only the persistence of what matters to us in survival. We would say that the deceased individual had actually (if mysteriously) survived bodily death.

To that extent I sympathize with the "Minimalism" advocated by Mark Johnston.[22] Johnston writes:

> The Minimalist has it that although ordinary practitioners may naturally be led to adopt metaphysical pictures as a result of their practices, and perhaps a little philosophical prompting, the practices are typically not dependent on the truth of the pictures. Practices that endure and spread are typically justifiable in nonmetaphysical terms. To this the Minimalist adds that we can do better in holding out against various sorts of skepticism and unwarranted revision when we correctly represent ordinary practice as having given no hostages to metaphysical fortune.
>
> In the particular case of personal identity, Minimalism will imply that any metaphysical view of persons that we might have is not indispensable to the justification of our practice of making judgments about personal identity and organizing our practical concerns around those judgments.[23]

IV. Dueling Metaphors and Hidden Assumptions

I realize that, for many, the foregoing considerations will not dispel the lingering lure of physicalism. One reason, no doubt, is the clear—and still growing—body of evidence indicating an intimate connection of some kind between brain states and mental states.[24] That body of evidence

---

[22] See, e.g., Mark Johnston, "Reasons and Reductionism," *The Philosophical Review* 101 (1992): 589–618.

[23] Ibid., 590.

[24] For both a detailed summary and philosophical criticism of the empirical literature, see M. R. Bennett and P. M. S. Hacker, *Philosophical Foundations of Neuroscience* (Oxford: Blackwell, 2003).

obviously cannot simply be ignored. But survivalists contend that our mental states—indeed, characteristic dispositions and large chunks of personal psychology—can persist after bodily dissolution. It seems fair, then, to ask them why our mental capacities and states at least *seem* to be so bodily dependent. Traditionally, survivalists deal with this question by claiming that the deceased's brain is merely one kind of *instrument* for expressing mental states. After death (they would say), either the deceased uses some other instrument (for example, the medium's brain or an astral or secondary body), or else the deceased uses no physical or quasi-physical instrument at all (for example, if communication is telepathic).

I am fully aware that many will be unmoved by this gambit, and this reaction is not difficult to understand. However, it may not be defensible, and to see why, consider the following.

The evidence suggesting postmortem survival is evidence counting prima facie against reductionistic physicalism and epiphenomenalism. Granted, some have tried to demonstrate the compatibility of physicalism and postmortem survival,[25] but their proposals cannot accommodate the more interesting case-types studied by psychical researchers.[26] At any rate, it is fair to say that the evidence suggesting survival (however mysterious it may be, at least right now) calls into question familiar forms of physicalism. In that case, however, it is unclear to what extent physicalists can cite neurophysiological data in support of their objections to postmortem survival. After all, the reason people seriously entertain the survival hypothesis is that some evidence seems at least prima facie to support it. But that suggests that our mental states may not be dependent on our brain states in the ways many suppose. But in that case, we should be prepared to entertain alternatives to the received interpretations of some neurophysiological data.

We need to remember (a) that scientific data do not come preinterpreted and (b) that there is no such thing as a purely empirical science. Every science rests on numerous abstract presuppositions, metaphysical and methodological, and all too often we lose sight of what those presuppositions are (especially as a science becomes more developed). Moreover, even though a background theory may be well entrenched, it is always subject to challenge, especially in the light of new data. In fact, apparently obvious interpretations of novel data may reveal more about our unexamined theoretical presuppositions (or lack of imagination) than they do about the phenomena in question. One of my favorite episodes from the history of psychology illustrates the point nicely.

---

[25] See, e.g., Kevin Corcoran, "Physical Persons and Postmortem Survival without Temporal Gaps," in Kevin Corcoran, ed., *Soul, Body, and Survival* (Ithaca, NY: Cornell University Press, 2001), 201–17. See also Trenton Merricks, "How to Live Forever without Saving Your Soul: Physicalism and Immortality," in Corcoran, ed., *Soul, Body, and Survival*, 183–200.

[26] For details, see Braude, *Immortal Remains*.

In the 1920s, Karl Lashley thought he could determine the location of a rat's memory in its brain. He trained rats to run a maze, and then he excised the portion of the brain where he believed the acquired memory to be. To his surprise, the rats continued to run the maze. So Lashley cut out even more of the brain, but the rats still navigated the maze (though with a bit less panache). This surprising result persisted as Lashley continued excising portions of the rats' brains. Only when a small fraction of the brain remained were the rats unable to run the maze. Unfortunately, at that point they also could do little else.[27] Later, others looked at these results and concluded that the rats' memories must have been located in the brain in the way information is distributed diffusely in a hologram. In fact, Karl Pribram has been heralded as a pundit for that questionable inference and his resulting holographic theory of memory traces.[28] In my view, however, Pribram's apparently easy recourse to a holographic model indicates that he was merely in the grip of a standard mechanistic and physicalistic picture. To those not antecedently committed to mechanistic analyses of the mental, Lashley's data take on a different kind of significance. In fact, they can easily be taken to support the view—held in some quarters— that the *container metaphor* (i.e., that mental states are *in* the brain) was wrong from the start and that memories are not localized *anywhere* or *in any form* in the brain. Moreover, that antimechanistic position can be supplemented by deep and apparently fatal objections to trace theories of memory generally. For example, some claim that trace theories must posit an infinite regress of homunculi (or additional rememberers) to explain how the appropriate trace is activated, or else that trace theories must rely on the unintelligible notions of *intrinsic similarity* (to explain how traces relate to things in the world) or *intrinsic meaning.*[29]

The evidence suggesting postmortem survival invites similar displays of metaphysical myopia. For example, in a recent interesting article on reincarnation,[30] physician and economist David Bishai challenges the famil-

[27] Karl S. Lashley, *Brain Mechanisms and Intelligence* (Chicago: University of Chicago Press, 1929), and Lashley, "In Search of the Engram," *Symposia of the Society for Experimental Biology* 4 (1950): 454–82. See also F. A. Beach et al., eds., *The Neuropsychology of Lashley: Selected Papers of K. S. Lashley* (New York: McGraw-Hill, 1960).

[28] Karl H. Pribram, *Languages of the Brain* (Englewood Cliffs, NJ: Prentice Hall, 1970); Pribram, "Holonomy and Structure in the Organization of Perception," in U. M. Nicholas, ed., *Images, Perception, and Knowledge* (Dordrecht: Reidel, 1977). See also Karl H. Pribram, M. Nuwer, and Robert J. Baron, "The Holographic Hypothesis of Memory Structure in Brain Function and Perception," in David H. Krantz, R. Duncan Luce, and Patrick Suppes, eds., *Contemporary Developments in Mathematical Psychology*, vol. 2 (San Francisco: Freeman, 1974).

[29] For detailed criticisms of trace theory, see Bennett and Hacker, *Philosophical Foundations of Neuroscience*; Howard A. Bursen, *Dismantling the Memory Machine* (Dordrecht: Reidel, 1978); John Heil, "Traces of Things Past," *Philosophy of Science* 45 (1978): 60–67; Norman Malcolm, *Memory and Mind* (Ithaca, NY: Cornell University Press, 1977); and Braude, *ESP and Psychokinesis.*

[30] David Bishai, "Can Population Growth Rule Out Reincarnation? A Model of Circular Migration," *Journal of Scientific Exploration* 14 (2000): 411–20.

iar anti-survivalist argument that, as philosopher Paul Edwards has put it, "reincarnation appears to be refuted by population statistics"[31] — namely, by the fact that the world's population continues to increase. Bishai shows how various assumptions about the "dwell time," or period between incarnations, yield different predictions about the rate of human population growth. Then he sketches a simple "circular migration model" that does, in fact, account for the data from a reincarnationist perspective. He also shows that the alleged incompatibility between the reincarnation hypothesis and the facts of population growth rests on a very controversial assumption: namely, that "the mean duration of stay in the afterlife has been constant throughout human history."[32] Apparently, Edwards did not realize that his condescending and allegedly hard-nosed attack on reincarnationists was as deeply (and inevitably) metaphysical as the view he opposed. And no doubt he would have been hard-pressed to defend his required assumption about dwell time against alternative reincarnationist assumptions. At any rate, the major lesson of Bishai's study is that metaphysical assumptions are unavoidable no matter where one stands on the issue of reincarnation and population growth.

One would think, then, that both in this case and in the case of apparent mind-brain correlations, we need to be circumspect in our assertions about what the data shows. Nevertheless, survivalists still need to address the more obvious cases suggesting at least the causal dependency of the mental on the physical. For example, it is undeniable that changes in or damage to the brain can affect (and sometimes seem to obliterate) memory. Even if we grant that the brain is an instrument that needs to be intact in order to respond properly, we might still be reluctant to assert further (as survivalists do) that memory and other cognitive functions do not require that instrument. As physiologist, parapsychologist, and Nobel laureate Charles Richet put it, "It is as if I were to say that in an electric lamp the passage of the current and the integrity of the mechanism of the lamp are not necessary for the production of its light."[33]

This analogy, and others like it, are initially seductive. Their appeal may, however, reflect little more than our familiarity with a certain conventional picture of how the world works generally and of what the mind is in particular. If we are really engaged in an open-minded appraisal of exotic and challenging bodies of evidence, then we must be ready to entertain alternative pictures and alternative analogies. And in fact, other analogies—much more congenial to the survivalist—are not that difficult to find, as philosopher J. M. E. McTaggart demonstrated some time ago.[34]

---

[31] Paul Edwards, *Reincarnation: A Critical Examination* (Amherst, NY: Prometheus Books, 1996), 227.

[32] Ibid., 419.

[33] Charles Richet, "The Difficulty of Survival from the Scientific Point of View," *Proceedings of the Society for Psychical Research* 34 (1924): 107–13, p. 109.

[34] J. M. E. McTaggart, *Some Dogmas of Religion* (Bristol: Thoemmes Press, 1930/1997).

Indeed, McTaggart's discussion is an exemplar of somewhat old-fashioned, but admirably cautious, metaphysics.

To appreciate McTaggart's contribution to this debate, we should note first that survivalists apparently must express their position in terms that many will find either simply unfamiliar, quaint, or downright peculiar. Because they reject physicalistic reductionism, survivalists claim that the self (whatever, exactly, it is) is not something identical with one's physical body or a part of the body (for example, the brain). And because they reject epiphenomenalism, they must claim that the self is also not merely a by-product of bodily activity, or something totally causally dependent (or supervening) on (part of) one's physical body. Survivalists must say that the self (whatever, exactly, it is), as we know it introspectively and through our earthly commerce with others, is something that *has* a body.

Of course, anti-survivalists might object that this language is question-begging, because it presupposes precisely what is at issue: namely, that the self might not be embodied. That is false, however. Granted, the language makes room for the claim that the self might be disembodied. But (as we will see below) it seems only to presuppose that the self might not have *its current body*. In any case, survivalists must be allowed to use the locution that the self has a body. *Pretheoretically*, it is no less legitimate than the competing, and equally theory-laden, terminology of physicalists (i.e., that the self is, or supervenes on, a body). Granted (as I have noted), physiological evidence apparently casts doubt on the survivalist position. It is precisely what draws many people to some form of the identity theory or epiphenomenalism. According to McTaggart, however, survivalists can concede that physiological discoveries pose at least an initial challenge to their position. That is why Richet's analogy seems compelling. But good survival evidence has a theoretical pull in the opposite direction and poses an apparently comparable prima facie challenge to the anti-survivalist. Moreover, as we will see below, McTaggart believed that survivalists can appeal to analogies of their own, and he believed that they are at least as weighty as analogies more congenial to physicalists.

McTaggart's discussion merits a close study, but for present purposes the following paraphrase will suffice. What McTaggart wanted to do was to expose several inferential leaps that we make all too unreflectively. We can grant that our sensations and our mental life *seem* invariably linked to bodily processes of some kind. No matter how intimate the mind-body connection seems to be, however, the data would show, at most, "that *some* body was necessary to my self, and not that its present body was necessary."[35] And even that may be going too far; strictly speaking, the data show us only what *is* the case, not what *must be* the case. If our evaluation of the evidence for postmortem survival is to be genuinely open-minded, then we need to suspend (if only temporarily) our familiar

[35] Ibid., 104, italics in original.

physicalist or reductionist assumptions or biases. But in that case it is clear that the data do not establish limits on the *possible* manifestations of selfhood. In particular, nothing in the data compels us to conclude that a self must be linked to a physical body. Thus, on a more circumspect or conservative appraisal of the data, we might conclude simply that "*while a self has a body*, that body is essentially connected with the self's mental life." [36] McTaggart argued:

> [I]t does not follow, because a self which has a body cannot get its data except in connexion with that body, that it would be impossible for a self without a body to get data in some other way. It may be just the existence of the body which makes these other ways impossible at present. If a man is shut up in a house, the transparency of the windows is an essential condition of his seeing the sky. But it would not be prudent to infer that, if he walked out of the house, he could not see the sky because there was no longer any glass through which he might see it. [37]

McTaggart made a similar point with regard to the more specific, and apparently intimate, relation between brain states and mental states:

> Even if the brain is essential to thought while we have bodies, it would not follow that when we ceased to have brains we could not think without them. . . . It might be that the present inability of the self to think except in connexion with the body was a limitation which was imposed by the presence of the body, and which vanished with it. [38]

McTaggart's view is important and insightful. Strictly speaking, the physiological evidence does not show that selfhood or consciousness is *exclusively* linked to bodily processes, much less the processes of any particular physical body. Probably, physicalistic interpretations of the data seem initially compelling because physicalistic presuppositions are widespread and deeply rooted. If so, it may be a useful intellectual exercise to try to divest ourselves of those presuppositions and then take a fresh look at the data. We might find, then, that McTaggart's (or the survivalist's) interpretation seems more immediately appealing.

V. CONCLUSION

I think it is clear, then, that we can have at least prima facie evidence for postmortem survival, however mysterious that evidence may be to us, both scientifically and philosophically. Hypothetically ideal cases illus-

---

[36] Ibid., 105, italics in original.
[37] Ibid., 105.
[38] Ibid., 106.

trate how compelling the evidence *could* be, and the best actual cases illustrate further that thinking about postmortem survival is not just idle speculation. And I think it is clear that, if the evidence is compelling enough, our ignorance about how such survival could occur is simply an annoyance we would have to accept but which we can hope to dispel.

But how compelling *is* the evidence? That is a very complex matter we cannot assess here, and I have examined it elsewhere in considerable detail.[39] Moreover, other philosophers have taken a close and critically open-minded look at the evidence.[40] Regrettably, others are apparently more hasty and too easily dismissive. For instance, Derek Parfit concedes that we could in principle have evidence strongly supporting the belief in reincarnation, but then he adds—without supporting argument or even references—that there is no such evidence.[41]

Moreover, we have not yet addressed psychologist Alan Gauld's concern (mentioned at the beginning of this essay): "it is hard to see what . . . could possibly count as distinguishing between Jones having survived the death of his body (though we don't understand how) and its being now and again transiently *as if* he had survived it (though again we can't make sense of it)."[42] We cannot now consider this in great detail, because if we opt for the "as if" interpretation of survival cases, in the best of them we have no choice but to adopt an interpretation positing impressive psychic functioning among the living. To answer Gauld's question, then, we must evaluate the relative merits of super-psi and survivalist interpretations of the evidence. And of course, how we decide between those two options—both of which many take to be unsavory—is a complex matter, and I can only refer readers to my book *Immortal Remains*.

However, a different sort of point can be made now, about what is at stake conceptually if we feel pulled in the direction of accepting postmortem survival. My view du jour is similar to that expressed by philosopher Terence Penelhum.[43] Penelhum has suggested that because bodily continuity would be broken in any genuine case of postmortem survival, it becomes "optional" whether we say that the premortem and postmortem individuals are identical. Prior to that decision, it is neither true nor false that those individuals are identical. And in that case, it is up to us to decide whether to identify them on the basis of some kind of psychological continuity.

---

[39] Braude, *Immortal Remains*.

[40] See, e.g., Almeder, *Death and Personal Survival*; C. D. Broad, *Lectures on Psychical Research* (London: Routledge and Kegan Paul, 1962); David Ray Griffin, *Parapsychology, Philosophy, and Spirituality: A Postmodern Exploration* (Albany: State University of New York Press, 1997); Raymond Martin, "Survival of Bodily Death: A Question of Values," in Daniel Kolak and Raymond Martin, eds., *Self, Cosmos, God* (New York: Harcourt Brace Jovanovich, 1993), 141–56; and Paterson, *Philosophy and the Belief in a Life after Death*.

[41] Parfit, *Reasons and Persons*, 227–28.

[42] Gauld, "Philosophy and Survival," 458.

[43] Terence Penelhum, *Survival and Disembodied Existence* (London: Routledge and Kegan Paul, 1970).

If I understand Penelhum, the principal difference between us on this matter connects with issues noted in my earlier discussion about the deep fuzziness and context- and assumption-relativity of language. In my view, it is *always* up to us to decide what counts when making identifications (i.e., even when there is bodily continuity), and every one of those decisions is appropriate only against a background of needs and interests. In some cases, it is correct to say that I am not the same person I was as an infant, or before my first divorce. In other (possibly more artificial, philosophical) contexts, it would be correct to say that I *am* the same person. Neither claim has a privileged status conceptually, and the phrase "same person" has no pre-ferred meaning. The fact that in some cases we decide very easily what to say indicates relatively little about the cases in question and more about us, our patterns of life, and various of our shared presuppositions.

And besides, as the literature on personal identity demonstrates all too clearly, it is difficult to figure out what to say even in a rigorously phil-osophical context. Depending on what philosophical enterprise we are engaged in, it is not a straightforward matter either to decide what a person is or to conclude that I am the same person now that I was as an infant. Like the principle of identity discussed earlier, these matters hinge on a variety of other philosophical decisions that are equally open to revision or rejection. For example, if we take persons to be real things, we might then consider whether they are the sorts of things that come into being and pass away. And then we might consider the consequences of taking those processes to be nongradual, unlike the process of becoming a human being.[44] A different set of issues hinges on how we handle Leibniz's Law: if two things are identical, then all properties of one are properties of the other, and vice versa. On certain interpretations of Leib-niz's Law (and also on a decision to consider person-stages as persons), we might want to say that I had no youth. Alternatively, we might want to distinguish different senses of "identity."[45] Or we might want to dis-tinguish different kinds of properties—for example, tensed and tenseless (i.e., time-variable and time-stable) properties—and consider different ways to reformulate Leibniz's Law with those distinctions in mind.[46] Or we might opt for something like the four-dimensionalism of David Lewis, according to which human persons are four-dimensional objects occupy-ing specific regions of space-time.[47] But of course, once we are in this

---

[44] Roderick. M. Chisholm, "Coming into Being and Passing Away: Can the Metaphysician Help?" in John Donnelly, ed., *Language, Metaphysics, and Death* (New York: Fordham University Press, 1978), 13–24.

[45] Roderick M. Chisholm, "The Loose and Popular and the Strict and Philosophical Senses of Identity," in Norman S. Care and Robert H. Grimm, eds., *Perception and Personal Identity* (Cleveland: Case Western Reserve University Press, 1969), 82–106.

[46] For an interesting discussion along those lines, see George I. Mavrodes, "The Life Everlasting and the Bodily Criterion of Identity," *Noûs* 11 (1977): 27–39.

[47] David Lewis, "Survival and Identity," in Lewis, *Philosophical Papers, Vol. 1* (New York: Oxford University Press, 1983), 55–77.

particular conceptual thicket, we have to contend with puzzles noted at least since the Middle Ages,[48] puzzles that reveal (once again) how philosophical problems cannot be solved—or even formulated—independently of a network of other complex philosophical decisions. And this is merely the tip of the iceberg. The literature on the nature of persons and identity is huge, and the range of approaches to the issues is daunting.

My suspicion, then, is that determining whether someone has survived bodily death is not radically different from determining identity in more familiar cases. Granted, due to the absence of (at least overt) bodily continuity,[49] there are empirical concerns in postmortem cases that typically do not arise in ordinary situations. And postmortem cases bump up against entrenched assumptions that more ordinary cases seldom threaten. In all cases, however, our decisions about identity turn on a variety of other assumptions, none of which are either privileged or immune from philosophical doubt. And even in ordinary cases where we rely on bodily continuity, we can raise interesting questions—not even touched on here—about what we mean by "same body" or similar locutions.[50]

If there is a big lesson to be learned from apparent postmortem cases about the so-called problem of identity, it applies both to the metaphysical problem of determining what personal identity consists in and to the epistemological problem of deciding whether two things are identical. In all cases, our judgments rest on a complex network of interrelated, often unexamined, and obviously controversial assumptions. Thus, it may be that the concepts of identity and personal identity are so deeply and inevitably flawed, system- or context-dependent, or arbitrary that we should simply abandon the quest for a generally satisfactory consensus on what the issues are—much less a one-size-fits-all solution to either our metaphysical or our epistemological concerns. Or, more likely, it may be that our varying everyday procedures for deciding identity are fine as they are and can (perhaps with occasional hesitancy) be extended to many (though not all) exotic cases. And that may allow us to end the interminable philosophical debates over identity and resolve them by the same means that work satisfactorily in life. In that case, there really is no *problem* of identity. There are only problem cases.

Philosophy, University of Maryland, Baltimore County

---

[48] See, e.g., John Buridan, *Sophisms on Meaning and Truth,* trans. Kermit Scott (New York: Appleton Century Crofts, 1966).

[49] By "at least overt" I intend to leave room for varieties of resurrectionist theories (see, e.g., Corcoran, "Physical Persons and Postmortem Survival"; and Merricks, "How to Live Forever without Saving Your Soul"), not to mention more exotic theories positing astral or secondary bodies (which, as C. D. Broad has argued reasonably, may not be as outlandish as many unreflectively suppose—see Broad, *Lectures on Psychical Research*).

[50] For a sample of the relevant issues, see, e.g., Harold W. Noonan, ed., *Identity* (Aldershot: Dartmouth, 1993); and David Wiggins, *Sameness and Substance* (Oxford: Blackwell, 1980).

"THE THING I AM": PERSONAL IDENTITY IN AQUINAS AND SHAKESPEARE

By John Finnis

I. Four Irreducibly Distinct Explanations of Personal Identity

Questions about identity are questions about what some object of attention and inquiry is and whether it is the same as, or different from, another object of attention and inquiry. So, for example, one might attend to the uttering of this paragraph, on some occasion, by a speaker. Considering the speaking source of the beginning of the utterance and the speaking source of the end of it, one might ask whether—and if so, how and why—one and the same object, this speaking person, was the source of the whole utterance. Explanatory affirmations or denials of identity will be as irreducibly various as the kinds of explanation that, in any field of inquiry whatever, are available for fruitfully answering pertinent questions.

At the beginning of his commentary on what in fact, though not in name, is Aristotle's main treatise on persons, the *Nicomachean Ethics*, Thomas Aquinas set out what he considered the four irreducibly distinct kinds of explanation (i.e., of *scientia*), corresponding to four irreducibly distinct aspects of reality or, more precisely, real kinds of order.[1] Followers of Aquinas have, to their cost, paid scant attention to this foundational analysis. More generally, many of the failures that mark the history of philosophy and learned discourse involve neglect of the fundamental complexity of reality and the corresponding necessity of diverse kinds of explanation. And as will be immediately obvious, the four kinds of order, understood in the four kinds of explanation, are instantiated paradigmatically in the human person, whose *what-it-is* includes being a *who-(s)he-is*—being an object that is also a subject.

The first kind of order is that of nature, of things that are what they are independently of our considering them and understanding them to be so—the kind of order that is the subject of all the natural sciences in the

---

[1] I have given an account of this part of the prologue to Aquinas's commentary in John Finnis, *Aquinas: Moral, Political, and Legal Theory* (Oxford and New York: Oxford University Press, 1998), 20-23; see also John Finnis, *Natural Law and Natural Rights* (Oxford and New York: Oxford University Press, 1980), 135-39.

broadest sense of that term (which will include a philosophical explanation of the kind being pursued here). Each of us, each human person, is by nature an animal with the naturally given capacity not only for all the kinds of activity found in other animals but also for the kinds of understanding, reflection, explanatory judgment, language, and community with other persons that open up to us in and by being understanding speakers (and readers) of the linguistically communicated—for example, of this sentence. In this order and its corresponding mode of explanation, one has one's identity, one's personal identity, as a given (independently of one's thinking about it, or about anything else), as one's subsisting and continuity as this animal.

The second kind of order is that of thought itself, of consciousness, observation, attention, consideration, inquiring, understanding, reasoning, and judging. In this order, one has one's identity, one's personal identity, in and by subsisting as knowing, as conscious of one's remembered childhood ignorance, one's present improved but incomplete understanding, and one's envisaged and intended future increase of knowledge. So the primary aspect of one's identity in this order is one's identity as the *subject* of knowing (and erring), who knows (and errs about) oneself along with other objects (as what Shakespeare, as we will see, regularly calls "the thing I am"). The secondary aspect, then, is precisely one's identity as *object* of one's knowing (and erring), as something of which one has reflexive knowledge both immediate and inferential, in and in respect of one's awareness (and inattention), observing (and oversight), knowing (and erring), choosing and character, self-expressive activity (and ineptitude), and one's whole makeup as someone whose given capacities and exercise of them in activities include all this, remembered, present in consciousness, and anticipated. In this order there can be self-awareness, self-deception, and more or less (un)perceptive self-consciousness. Grasp of oneself as object is difficult. Even great philosophers—but not Aquinas—have often failed to notice themselves adequately as objects within the subject-matter of their general propositions, and have thus fallen into the self-referential inconsistency that disqualifies so many philosophical theories. That is why one's identity as object of one's understanding is secondary to one's identity as the subject of coming to know whatever, in all orders of explanation, one knows and intends to come to know.

The third kind of order is that which is anticipated and shaped in deliberation, choice, intentional actions, and thus—because choices last in the chooser until negated by a contrary choice—is instantiated in one's subsisting character as self-centered or generous, constant or treacherous, converted or perverted, and so forth. In this order one has one's personal identity both as self-determining and as self-determined. The latter, the identity that has the content of one's unrepented choices, is the more important: what counts is what one becomes in choosing *what one chooses*.

Self-determination, the fact of autonomy and its exercise, is not itself, as such, a good, but rather is simply the fact that one can and does make oneself good or evil, and that this freedom is a necessary condition for the moral goodness which is the proper measure deployed (even if only implicitly) in fully adequate explanations and explanatory descriptions in this third order.

The fourth of the four irreducibly distinct kinds of order is that of culture, or mastery over materials (in the broadest sense of material)—every kind of *techne*. This order includes not only language but also all (or important elements in all) the crafts of self-expression—of rhetoric, poetry, drama, lectureship, essay writing—and not only these as crafts but also the adopting of a persona (or personas) whereby one communicates to others some truth or falsehood about oneself. Of course, the adoption of such a "personal identity" is a morally significant act in, and to be assessed by, the third order. (So too is a choice to attend to one's health, or to engage in intellectual activity, or to exercise self-discipline in one's choosing.) But the persona is an artifact, intelligible and assessable as a means of communication, and by all the criteria applicable to the arts.

In this essay, I shall elaborate and illustrate these four senses of personal identity by pointing out some of the consideration given to them by two great masters of reflective openness to and appropriation of the complexity and depths of human nature and existence. Most if not all the aspects of reality that are alluded to, since the late seventeenth century, with the phrase "personal identity" are central to Shakespeare's work. Very many of the thoughts his plays and poems are intended to convey, and/or do in fact suggest, are conveyed or suggested in the resonant opening words of *Hamlet*: "Who's there?"—when those words are heard or read in the context not only of the whole of that play but also of the entire Shakespearean corpus. Shakespeare is a writer who conveys his own understanding of human existence, nature, and personality not didactically like Aristotle, Aquinas, Locke, or Hume, or even dialogically like Plato, but for the most part dramatically. Characters in a play, such as those I shall recall and discuss a little in this essay, are not persons we could bump into and who could make free choices. Everything they are presented as doing is necessitated by their playmaster's choice to make them so. But when the playwright has made us appreciate something of the force and depth of his understanding of human persons, we can reasonably make his characters and their doings material for reflection comparable to the material we find in biographies and autobiographies, which also, after all, present us with a kind of drama in which the reality of the life stories narrated is more or less overlaid by masks, misunderstandings, fabrications, and various (other) principles of selection of parts from a whole known adequately, no doubt, to no one.

II. BODILINESS, CHOICE, AND IDENTITY IN AQUINAS AND SHAKESPEARE

In Aquinas's account, the foundation of one's[2] identity as an individual person is one's material, bodily reality as this body, something that is both distinct from other bodies (human or nonhuman, animal or inanimate) and a subsisting thing in virtue of its physical, chemical, and biological unity and continuity as an organism. Organic existence is life or living existence. The principle—*principium,* fundamental element and source—of this life, giving unity and continuity to the shifting material components of the organism, is the factor that Aquinas, like Aristotle, calls soul: the very *form* and lifelong *act(uality)* by which the matter of one's bodily makeup is constituted the unified and active subject/object, this organism, this human being, this person, from one's outset until one's death.[3]

In her vapid infatuation with Bottom, the weaver magically given an ass's head visible to all but himself, Titania, queen of the fairies in *A Midsummer Night's Dream,* promises him that she "will purge thy mortal grossness so, / That thou shalt like an airy spirit go" (3.1.153–54). But she doesn't, and even when imaging the fantasy of magical transformations, Shakespeare never loses hold of the personal identity that each of his characters has by being this living body rather than that. "What I am" is (includes) for each of us, even the most elevated in rank, the corporeal susceptibility to "the icy fang / And churlish chiding of the winter's wind, / Which . . . bites and blows upon my body / Even till I shrink

---

[2] The English semantics of "one"—taken always in the first-person singular—is highly convenient for expounding the philosophy of personal existence, of action, and of social reality as a function of the existence, activity, and dispositions to act, of individual human persons.

[3] Taking his natural science (biology, embryology, etc.) largely from Aristotle's empirical studies, Aquinas was unaware of the role of the male and female gametes in human generation. He envisaged it as resulting from the active, formative influence of male semen on essentially passive and inanimate (though not formless) female menstrual blood. He therefore supposed that it must naturally take some time (about forty to sixty days from the outset of conception) for the process of generation to yield a body sufficiently elaborated (*complexionatum*) and organized (*organizatum*) to receive and be organized anew by the rational, specifically human soul. See, e.g., Thomas Aquinas, *Summa contra Gentiles* (hereafter *ScG*) II c. 30 n. 12; c. 89 n. 6; IV c. 44 n. 5. It seems clear that, had he known of the extremely elaborate and specifically organized structure of the sperm and the ovum, their chromosomal complementarity, and the typical, wholly continuous self-directed growth and development of the embryo or embryos from the moment of insemination of the ovum, Aquinas would have concluded that the specifically human, rational (and sensitive and vegetative) animating form and act (soul)—and therefore personhood (*personalitas: ScG* IV c. 44 n. 3)—can be and doubtless is present from that moment. If in some cases a single embryo divides to become twins, he would equally have understood this as an unusual (though not in any other sense unnatural) form of generation, either of two new embryos from one now deceased or of one new one from the older one that began a few days earlier and now continues as the newer one's sibling-parent. (On nonsexual generation by division in some animals, see *ScG* II c. 86 n. 3.)

from cold. . . ." [4] Of course, Shakespeare has his characters enunciate the common Christian belief in souls surviving death in a life—perhaps heavenly, perhaps purgatorial, or even hellish—after death but prior to the miracle of bodily resurrection. So Lorenzo uses a Pauline-sounding image and conception of the relation between body and soul in his rhapsody for his young Jewish lover Jessica: "Such harmony is in immortal souls, / But whilst this muddy vesture of decay / Doth grossly close it in, we cannot hear it" (*The Merchant of Venice*, 5.1.63–65).[5] And in four of Shakespeare's plays there is a ghost or ghosts, a kind of reappearance of someone lately living but now dead.[6]

But the ghost in *Hamlet*, the only Shakespearean ghost visible to more than one character onstage, has no part in the play's resolution—and may even be a devil who has assumed the appearance of Hamlet's father, rather than a genuine remnant or reappearance, from Purgatory, of the father himself.[7] And all in all, there is little reason to think that Shakespeare would object to Aquinas's radical insistence on the unity of soul and body, and on one's body—with all its aspects and dynamisms—as the principle of one's soul's individuality. This insistence is very firm: Aquinas maintains that "[m]y soul is not me (*anima mea non est ego*); and so, even if [my] soul attained salvation in another life, still neither I nor anybody else would have attained it."[8] A human soul is not a human person. (Thus, between death and resurrection there can survive of me only a remnant, a remnant of a person.)[9] Or again: "Bodiliness [*corporeitas*], since it is the substantial form in a human being, cannot be other than the rational soul, which—since it is the act of some *body*—requires that its own matter have three dimensions" and have the makeup not merely of a substantial thing, and a living organism, and an animal, but

---

[4] *As You Like It*, 2.1.612–15. This famous speech by the exiled Duke goes on: "Even till I shrink from cold, I smile, and say / 'This is no flattery. These [icy winds] are counsellors / That feelingly persuade me *what I am.*' / Sweet are the uses of adversity. . . ." Note: all emphases in quotations have been added by the author of this paper. Act and scene divisions and line numbers are taken from the Folio text as presented by Internet Shakespeare Editions: http://ise.uvic.ca.

[5] Cf. 1 Corinthians 15:42, 53 (Geneva Bible) ("The body is sown in corruption and is raised in incorruption. . . . For this corruptible [body] must put on incorruption, and this mortal [body] must put on immortality." The Vulgate Latin for "put on" is *induere*, to clothe or vest oneself or another; *indumentum* means a garment = vesture.) Note that Aquinas sums up the body-soul dualism that (not unfairly: see *Alcibiades* 129d–130c) he ascribes to Plato (and rejects) in the metaphor of the soul using the body as one uses a garment (*homo utens indumento*): *ScG* II c. 57 n. 4.

[6] *Richard III, Julius Caesar, Hamlet*, and *Macbeth*.

[7] See, e.g., Harry Morris, *Last Things in Shakespeare* (Tallahassee: Florida State University Press, 1985), 19–33.

[8] Aquinas, *Commentary on I Corinthians*, 15.2 (on v. 19). See also Finnis, *Aquinas*, 318n, 179n.

[9] We should not expect to understand this remnant until we understand better than we do the interrelation between time and eternity. Cf. Peter Geach, *God and the Soul* (London: Routledge and Kegan Paul, 1969), 17–29, with Peter Geach, *The Virtues* (Cambridge: Cambridge University Press, 1977), 57–66.

of a particular thing of the human kind (nature and species).[10] In short, one's bodiliness is the foundation of one's personal identity, a subsisting identity that precedes consciousness and lasts through even protracted terminal unconsciousness until death.

Neither in Aquinas nor in Shakespeare does this stress on bodiliness blunt their acute, meditated, and appropriated awareness of one's capacity to be uniquely, particularly ("personally") present to oneself in one's perceiving other things, as also in one's reflecting, deliberating, choosing, and carrying out one's choices in acting. At the very outset of his work, in the first pages of his youthful *Commentary on the Sentences*, Aquinas articulates a datum of our conscious life: "in one and the same operation I understand something intelligible and understand that I understand."[11] This he calls one's presence (*praesentia*) to oneself,[12] and of course it is an experience,[13] and understanding,[14] not only of one's acts of understanding narrowly understood, but also of one's active existence as someone feeling,[15] perceiving with one's senses, inquiring, deliberating, judging, choosing, and physically carrying out one's choices.[16] One must be cautious about the word "experience" here, however, lest it be taken to connote that one's consciousness of, say, choosing (at the moment of choice) is passive, a matter of undergoing something like a dream or a feeling of dizziness; rather, it is an awareness (a comprehending awareness) of one's own doing something, of acting in the precise sense of making the choice one is making. The "mastery of [or over] one's own acts" that Aquinas makes so central to

[10] Aquinas, *ScG* IV c. 81 n. 7; see also Finnis, *Aquinas*, 178n. A spirit that is not the form and act of a body—an angel—cannot both share its nature with and yet be an individual distinct from other individuals of the same nature: so each angel is of a different species from every other angel: Thomas Aquinas, *Summa Theologiae* (hereafter *ST*) I q. 50 a. 4.

[11] Aquinas, I *Scriptum super Sententiis* (hereafter *Sent.*) d. 1 q. 2 a. 1 ad 2; see also Finnis, *Aquinas*, 177n.

[12] Aquinas, I *Sent.* d. 3 q. 4 aa. 4c and 5c; see also Finnis, *Aquinas*, 177–78.

[13] "Experitur enim unusquisque seipsum esse qui intelligit"—each of us experiences that [= is conscious that] it is he himself that understands: Aquinas, *ST* I q. 76 a. 1c.

[14] Thomas Wright, S.J.—who in or before 1597, while associated with the Earl of Essex, wrote an English treatise, *The Passions of the Mind*, clearly following Aquinas, and dedicated the book's second edition (1604) to the Earl of Southampton (close friend of the late Earl of Essex)—says at the end of chapter 1 that what the ancient injunction "Know thyself" tells us to seek is a knowledge that "principally consisteth of a perfect experience every man hath of himself in particular, and an universal knowledge of men's inclinations in common. The former is greatly helped by the latter, the which knowledge is delivered in this treatise." Aquinas treats what Wright calls "experience [of oneself]" as itself an understanding, albeit an understanding that can be enhanced by reflection and a philosophical anthropology based on information and reflection on human beings and their inclinations and actions in general.

[15] See Aquinas, *ST* I q. 76 a. 1c: "ipse idem homo est qui percipit se et intelligere et sentire"—one and the same human person [man] perceives himself both to understand and to have sensations/feelings.

[16] Thinking/contemplating, too, is a physical act, even if it is also much more than a physical act. So too is mental prayer, whether or not it is divided and distracted as when "my words fly up, my thoughts remain below" (*Hamlet*, 3.3.97).

his entire philosophy of human matters[17] is not to be understood as if some ghost or homunculus were controlling the parts of some body (and their movements) "from within," but is rather one's being in a position to adopt, and adopting, a proposal for action—one's own action—in preference to some alternative action(s) (of one's own) that one has envisaged and been interested in.

One has no direct, unmediated, noninferential knowledge of oneself (as distinct from knowledge of characteristics of human beings in general) other than of what one experiences as happening to one corporeally (which includes psychologically) and of what one is doing or actively inclined to do, whether spontaneously or compulsively, or by one's free choices.[18] This knowledge is of a being extended in time, who can decide to respond to a question with reflective search for an answer, discover what seems to be the answer, communicate it to the questioner, and when it has been communicated *know* that the question was given a relevant answer—that I who heard the question found and gave an answer, and that it is not the same answer as I gave or would have given when I first came across a question of that content in another country forty-eight years ago. *All's Well That Ends Well*, the Shakespeare play on which I shall be focusing, is saturated, from its title and its opening page all the way to its last, with reference, explicit and implicit, to time and the passing of human existence in time, that necessary condition for all my opportunities of commitment and achievement, and all the perils of deflating failure, discredit, and humiliation. The experience of all this is made possible only by memory, prime witness and testimony to one's personal identity. But from Aquinas's striking readiness to appeal to personal consciousness, his, yours, and mine, as the very pivot of his argument[19] for the radical unity of the animal human person as *corpore et anima unus*,[20] and from his readiness to affirm the consequences of this unity (*anima mea non est ego*) notwithstanding the obvious difficulties this sets up for talking of immortality, we can infer that he would not have been impressed by the thought experiments which tempted Locke and his followers to take memory, "consciousness of the past," to be not merely a witness and testimony to one's subsisting personal identity but its very reality, that in which that identity consists.[21]

---

[17] Aquinas, *ST* I-II prol. and q. 1 a. 1.

[18] That thesis is an implication of Aquinas's pervasive thesis that one understands (comes to know) the nature of something only by understanding its capacities, and understands its capacities only by understanding its act(ivitie)s: see Finnis, *Aquinas*, 29–33.

[19] Aquinas, *ST* I q. 76, a. 1c.

[20] Meaning: "by/in body and soul one [human being/human person]." The phrase does not occur in Aquinas but is used by the Second Vatican Council, Pastoral Constitution *Gaudium et Spes* (1965), sec. 14, as a compressed formulation rightly judged to convey the essence of Aquinas's position (a position rejected by virtually all theologians when first articulated by Aquinas).

[21] John Locke, *An Essay Concerning Human Understanding*, II, xxvii.

Especially when taken as an account of one's subsisting identity as one and the same human being, rather than, as Locke often claims,[22] an account only of one's "forensic" responsibility, Locke's position defies our most elementary knowledge of ourselves and others as beings who subsist and can and must acknowledge our authorship of our own acts notwithstanding decay or destruction of memories.[23] Locke's radical evasiveness about whether his accounts of *personal identity* are metaphysical (ontological) or merely forensic (moral) lends plausibility to the thought that *personal identity* is perhaps a pseudo-concept.[24] Whatever should be said about the character of residual existence as an intelligence separated from the body of which it was the very form and act(uality), or about a cobbler equipped by a philosophical magus with the memories of a prince,[25] must remain a speculation incapable of undermining one's primary experience and understanding of one's identity as someone who was born on a day one knows only by testimony, verifiably did things both forgotten and remembered, began this inseparably past and present, conscious, intelligent, and physical act of reading, listening to, or writing this sentence, and should regard oneself as responsible (in due measure)[26] for everything one has ever chosen to do.

[22] See, e.g., ibid., II, xxvii: "21 . . . whatsoever to some men makes a man, and consequently the same individual man, wherein perhaps few are agreed, personal identity can by us be placed in nothing but consciousness (which is that alone which makes what we call self). . . . 26. Person, as I take it, is the name for this self. Wherever a man finds what he calls himself, there I think another may say is the same person. It is a forensick term appropriating actions and their merit; and so belongs only to intelligent agents capable of a law, and happiness and misery. This personality extends itself beyond present existence to what is past, only by consciousness, whereby it becomes concerned and accountable, owns and imputes to itself past actions, just upon the same ground, and for the same reason that it does the present. All which is founded in a concern for happiness, the unavoidable concomitant of consciousness; that which is conscious of pleasure and pain, desiring that that self that is conscious should be happy. And therefore whatever past actions it cannot reconcile or appropriate to that present self by consciousness, it can be no more concerned in, than if they had never been done."

[23] The classic critiques of Locke on personal identity: George Berkeley, *Alciphron* (1732), VII. viii; Joseph Butler, Dissertation I, "Of Personal Identity," appended to *The Analogy of Religion, Natural and Revealed, to the Constitution and Course of Nature*, 2d ed. (London, 1736); Thomas Reid, *Essays on the Intellectual Powers of Man* (Edinburgh, 1785), 319–20, from essay III, chap. 4, "Of Identity." A recent restatement of them: David Wiggins, *Sameness and Substance Renewed* (Cambridge: Cambridge University Press, 2001).

[24] That it is a pseudo-concept is argued, without explicit reference to Locke, but drawing on Aquinas and Geach (who however does use the phrase) by Christopher F. J. Martin, "Thomas de Aquino y la Identidad Personal," *Anuario Filosófico* 26 (1993): 249–60. Cf. also Robert Sokolowski, "Language, the Human Person, and Christian Faith," *Proceedings of the American Catholic Philosophical Association* 76 (2003): 27–38, taking up the thought that "person" is not a sortal noun.

[25] Locke, *Essay Concerning Human Understanding*, II, xxvii, 15: "[S]hould the soul of a prince, carrying with it the consciousness of the prince's past life, enter and inform the body of a cobbler, as soon as deserted by his own soul, every one sees he would be the same person with the prince, accountable only for the prince's actions: But who would say it was the same man?"

[26] Being responsible is one thing; being held responsible is another, even when everyone concerned knows all the facts of the case and is currently acting reasonably.

III. Nature, Inclinations, Character, and Honor in *All's Well That Ends Well*

At the most obvious level, mistaken identity is the hinge of plots, subplots, and countless scenes in most of Shakespeare's comedies and romances and many of his tragedies.[27] The ways in which particular characters respond to, and under, their own and others' mistakes of identity convey much of what the dramatist wishes to say about what is most personal to each of them.[28] Shakespeare does not use "identity" or "individual" or their cognates. The phrase quoted in the title of this essay, "the thing I am," is from *All's Well That Ends Well*. This remarkable comedy—one of the three known to twentieth-century critics as Shakespeare's "problem plays"—thematizes many aspects of personal identity, both structurally, through a highly patterned set of personal humiliations induced by or involving mistakes of identity,[29] and discursively, through the articulations of several philosophically and theologically lucid characters whose statements are richly supplemented by the author's own linguistic and imagistic patternings.

Like almost all of Shakespeare's drama, this comedy takes for its core a story well known to many in the sophisticated courtly audiences and well-educated readership for which the plays were obviously intended.

[27] As George T. Wright, *Hearing the Measures: Shakespearean and Other Inflections* (Madison: University of Wisconsin Press, 2001), 75, observes:

> Compared with earlier Elizabethan playwrights, Shakespeare complicates and multiplies the false supposes under which his gullible characters labor; like theatrical audiences—like *us*—they seem hungry for supposes. Throughout his work characters adopt disguises, change costumes, are misidentified, misread visual or political clues, make verbal mistakes, play-act, pretend to beliefs or affections they do not hold, or are miraculously transformed into other creatures or into people they never supposed they could become. Lies, deceptions, mistakes, and impersonations make his characters' dramatic lives treacherous for them and appealing or appalling to his audience. . . . Mistakes by the deceived and maskings by their deceivers mirror their counterparts in life and in the theater and are followed at some point in most of the plays by unmaskings, by moments in which the masking personages resume their original identities, disclose or discover their true ones, undeceive their victims, or adopt new masks.

[28] "Personal" is used by Shakespeare in a variety of relevant senses, e.g., "no mightier than thyself or me in personal action" (*Julius Caesar*, 1.3.77); "I know no personal cause to spurn at him" (ibid., 2.1.11). He does not use "character" in the modern sense of personal individuality.

[29] Joseph G. Price, *The Unfortunate Comedy: A Study of "All's Well That Ends Well" and Its Critics* (Liverpool and Toronto: Liverpool University Press and Toronto University Press, 1968) is a valuable account of the many misunderstandings of this play down to 1964, and a fine vindication (pp. 133–72) of its many excellences, showing how "the play is tightly knit through parallels, parodies, anticipations, and commentaries" and unified through its theme of honor, or rather, the "nobility of virtue" (p. 171). The introductory essay in the New Cambridge Shakespeare edition shows that this "is a great play whose time has come round": Russell Fraser, ed., *All's Well That Ends Well* (Cambridge and New York: Cambridge University Press, 1985), 8. Neither Price nor Fraser, however, understands Parolles as fully as may be desired.

Here the tale derives from Boccaccio's *Decameron* (1353), and Shakespeare copies enough of the story's main lines, and of its characters' names, to keep it in the reader's mind, thereby pointing up the substantial changes he makes to both plot and character, and the wholly new (and evidently original, unsourced) subplot he introduces; that subplot will be the focus of Section VI below. Boccaccio's tale is set in the part of the *Decameron* that tells of people who win what they want through their personal initiative and ingenuity. The daughter of a physician falls in love with a young man of much higher social status, a young count. Following him to the French court, she uses one of her late father's secret prescriptions to heal the king, who accordingly keeps his promise to bestow her in marriage to whomever she nominates. She nominates the young count, but he bitterly objects to being married to a woman of such inferior origin and, when the king insists on the marriage, refuses to consummate it. Instead, he goes away to the Italian wars, stating that he will never live with her until she possesses the ring on his finger and bears him a son—two "things impossible" because of his deliberate absence far away. But she follows him from France to Florence, where she finds him courting a poor but honest young Florentine woman. The abandoned wife reveals her identity to this young woman and her impoverished mother, and arranges with them to allow the count to have intercourse, in a dark room, with someone he supposes is the young woman he loves but in fact is his wife. And they make it a precondition of these liberties that he send ahead his ring as a token of his love. In this way, his wife both obtains his ring and conceives by him a son, indeed twin sons. Thus, when he has returned to his stately home in France, she is able, in due course, when he is holding a great feast, to confront him with the ring and his offspring. In admiration for her "good wit," he acknowledges her as his wife and they live happily ever after.

All's Well That Ends Well retains (while subtly changing) all these elements except the twin sons and the great feast at the end. That is replaced by an immensely more elaborate scene in which the young count, Bertram, is comprehensively humiliated in the presence of the king and court and his own mother. The young Florentine woman Diana, whom he thought he had brought to bed with insincere promises of marriage, confronts him at the French court with the ring he gave away as his love-game, or purchase price. As he had mistaken his wife Helena for Diana, in a dark room in Florence, so in the broad daylight of the crowded French court Bertram takes Diana to be the woman to whom he made love and gave his ring. He lies to the king repeatedly about both the woman and the ring, representing Diana as a mere camp follower who could be bought at market rate. His multiplying and excruciatingly public[30] lies are soon

---

[30] The play's audience knows what Bertram's courtly audience does not, that Diana was poor but honest and that Bertram's various stories about how he parted with the ring are false.

enough exposed by Helena's appearance on the scene, carrying her (one) child (of unknown sex) in her womb rather than, as in Boccaccio, her arms. Utterly discredited, the young count repents[31] and declares emphatically that when all has been explained to him, he will love her dearly, ever dearly.

All's Well's philosophically minded interest in the interrelation of nature and virtue (or vice) in personal identity is opened up early in its first scene. Helena's father's skill as a physician "was almost as great as his honesty," says the count's mother, using "honesty" in the sense in which it is still close to *honestus,* worthy, virtuous; if his skill had "stretched so far [as his moral worth, it] would have made nature immortal" (1.1.23–24). And this man's daughter Helena, says the old countess (her guardian), is having an education that

> promises her dispositions [that] she inherits, which [education] makes fair gifts fairer: for where an unclean mind carries virtuous qualities, there commendations go with pity; they are *virtues and traitors too*. In her they are the better for their simpleness. She derives her honesty and achieves her goodness.   (1.1.42–47)

Recent Oxford and Arden editors have thought that the "virtuous qualities" that can be carried by an unclean mind ("virtues and traitors too") are accomplishments of "learning without reference to morality," as contrasted with "the inborn bad disposition." But much more probably the playwright is resuming the classical and medieval problematic of the unity of the virtues (*connexio virtutum*): as Aquinas explains, virtues like courage, whether "in us by nature" or by usage (*sive a natura sive ex assuetudine*), are radically imperfect unless the individual person who has them has no vices but rather *all* the virtues, especially the unifying and directing virtue of practical reasonableness, *prudentia*.[32] In Helena, says the countess, all the virtues are to be found unmixed with vice, and thus "the better for their simpleness." This theme the countess interweaves with that of heredity and accomplishment: Helena "derives [from her father] her honesty and achieves [through her education, understood in the broadest sense of that word] her goodness," that is, her being an unqualifiedly good person (not merely someone good *at* . . . , or good

---

[31] Some deny this, and certainly everything essential in the play's last minutes is compressed to the barest minimum. But the reality of his repentance is made more plausible for the audience by the play's thesis that Helena's cure of the king's ailment was miraculous and the choice to wager herself on achieving it was divinely approved: Price, *The Unfortunate Comedy*, 152, 161. E. M. W. Tillyard, speaking as "a modern," reaches the same conclusion in his *Shakespeare's Problem Plays* (London: Chatto and Windus, 1961), 117: "[W]hen Bertram goes on to say that he will love Helena 'dearly, ever dearly', we should believe him implicitly. Helena has got her man; and he needs her moral support with such pathetic obviousness that she never need fear his escape."

[32] Aquinas, *ST* I-II q. 65 a. 1c.

as . . .).[33] Moments later, the countess applies the same analysis, optatively, to her son the young count: "Be thou bless'd, Bertram, and succeed thy father / In manner as in shape. Thy *blood and virtue* / Contend for empire, and thy *goodness* / *Share with thy birthright*" (1.1.63–66). This theme — inherited qualities must be appropriated and nurtured by personal choices ("adoption")[34] — is then taken up by the king, after his healing. Confronted by the young count's refusal to marry a "poor physician's daughter," the king judges that the young man is confusing names with realities. The social rank, standing, and repute ("title" and "honor") that Helena lacks can be bestowed upon her by the king, but what *merits* honor depends upon her own gifts of nature and then, decisively, upon her own acts:

> The property [= quality of character] by what it is should go,
> Not by the title. She is young, wise, fair;
> In these to nature she's immediate heir,
> And these breed honor. . . .
> . . . Honors thrive
> When *rather from our acts we them derive*
> *Than our foregoers.* . . .
> Virtue and she
> Is her own dower; honor and wealth from me.
>
> (2.3.1032–46)

As the play shows, the king's characterization of Helena as "young, *wise,* fair," like the old countess's assumption that Helena has complete *prudentia,* is simplistic. Nature, her own nature (personality) as a rational animal of strong appetite, makes her susceptible to the infatuation that

[33] The property of being "good alone" —that is, good *simpliciter,* i.e., without qualification—is taken up, again in relation to Helena, by the king in 2.3.1019–31, where he equates it with her being "all that is virtuous." A recent Cambridge editor, in a generally illuminating commentary, says, "[W]e are told how Helena inherits her 'dispositions', and also her 'honesty'. She achieves her goodness, though (1.1.30–35). Evidently, natural disposition makes an antithesis to goodness. The papist and the puritan come down hard on this antithesis, but their psychology is disabling, and they fail to grasp what it means. Goodness involves a return on the talents which a provident man puts out at interest . . ." (Fraser, ed., *All's Well That Ends Well,* 24). Whatever Fraser may mean by "come down hard on," it is clear that neither the play nor the central ("papist") tradition suggests an "antithesis" between natural disposition and the human goodness *simpliciter* of perfect virtue (being simply "a good person"). The gifts *dispose* one to virtue, but only by one's free choices and acts is one actually virtuous, straightforwardly good. The play emphasizes the priority of grace to freedom, and the gratuity and transcendence of grace and Providence: see Section IV below, though in this essay I largely abstract from this important dimension of the play.

[34] In relation to the adoption of children into a family, the countess declares (1.3.469–70): "Adoption strives with nature, and choice breeds / A native slip to us from foreign seeds." In the context of her moral-anthropological analyses, this remark casts the light of analogy onto the problematic of becoming a good person, even when one has admirably virtuous parentage and gifts and natural dispositions.

disables her judgment of the count, "a bright particular star . . . so above me in his bright radiance and collateral light . . . the lion . . . his arched brows, his hawking eye, his curls . . ." (1.1.90–98). Indeed, the play sets out, it seems, to show from many angles the commingling of good and bad dispositions in each of the persons in whose character it takes an interest. This commingling, and its universality, is articulated by two French noblemen, captains in the count's French regiment fighting in support of the Florentines, who reflect like a chorus on the count's seduction of—as he and the two commentators suppose—Diana, the young Florentine gentlewoman "of most chaste renown," in the "spoil of [whose] honor" he "fleshes his will":

> FIRST LORD: Now, God delay our rebellion! *As we are ourselves, what things are we!*

> SECOND LORD: Merely our own traitors. And, as in the common course of all treasons we still see them reveal themselves till they attain their abhorred ends, so *he* [the count] *that in this action contrives against his own nobility, in his proper stream o'erflows himself.*   (4.3.2125–31)

And then, more generally: "The web of our life is of a mingled yarn, good and ill together. Our virtues would be proud if our faults whipped them not, and our crimes would despair if they were not cherished by our virtues" (4.3.2177–80).

The play looks to ends, and tells us that Heaven, using weak human instruments, is capable of great works of healing and restoration and—why not?—conversion, especially when such results were least expected.[35] The ending well that the play projects (without guaranteeing) is the happy marriage that Helena's energetic and ingenious self-possession deserves, a marriage that truly remedies the urges of the flesh not by suppressing them nor by following them where they drive, but by taking them up into the integrity of love's person-to-person commitment—no longer a yearning love pouring like water through a sieve,[36] nor yet the lust that makes a person overflow his proper stream.

---

[35] See Helena's speeches to the king, 2.1.745–54, 757–61 (quoted in the text after footnote 46 below), ratified by the king (2.1.786–89), by events, and by Lafeu and Parolles (2.3.893–929).

[36] See 1.3.532–38:

> I know I love in vain, strive against hope;
> Yet *in this captious and inteemable sieve*
> *I still pour in the waters of my love*
> And lack not to lose still: thus, Indian-like,
> Religious in mine error, I adore
> The sun, that looks upon his worshipper,
> But knows of him no more.

IV. SELF-CONSCIOUSNESS AND COMMITMENT IN AQUINAS
AND SHAKESPEARE

When one tries to extend one's awareness of one's identity, beyond the awareness of one's psychosomatic unity and continuity of being, to an understanding and knowledge of one's own character as formed by one's commitments and other choices, the way to knowledge is beset by pitfalls at least as much as any other kind of search for knowledge. Shakespeare spends much of his play *Richard II* showing this. King Richard is strongly interested in himself, at once self-conscious and self-regarding in the idiomatic senses of those terms—indeed, self-centered. Yet he shows himself to be a man who never understands that he is being deposed in response to his own and his henchmen's crimes, negligences, and injustices—misconduct that he never admits to himself, nor even really denies. For all his regrets, he never approaches or even contemplates repentance. In *Richard III*, his successor, awakening from a dream of visitation by the ghosts or visible souls of associates and friends whom he has murdered, articulates with utter clarity the difficulties, indeed the incoherence, inherent in the self-determining[37] commitment he had made years before "to have his way,"[38] to make the Crown and winning it "my heaven."[39] The division within himself, in the end suppressed, is wonderfully articulated in his dialogical soliloquy:

O coward Conscience! how dost thou afflict me?
The Lights burn blue. It is no[w] dead midnight.
Cold fearful drops stand on my trembling flesh.
What? do I fear my Self? There's none else by;
Richard loves Richard, that is, I am I.
Is there a Murderer here? No; Yes, I am:
Then fly; What, from my Self? Great reason: why?
Lest I Revenge. What? my Self upon my Self?
Alack, I love my Self. Wherefore? For any good
That I my Self, have done unto my Self?
O no. Alas, I rather hate my Self,
For hateful Deeds committed by my Self.
I am a Villain: yet I Lie, I am not.
Fool, of thy Self speak well: Fool, do not flatter.
My Conscience hath a thousand several Tongues,
And every Tongue brings in a several Tale,
And every Tale condemns me for a Villain;

---

[37] *The Tragedy of Richard III*, 1.1.30–32: "and therefore, since I cannot prove a lover / To entertain these fair well-spoken days, / I am determined to prove a villain. . . ."
[38] *3 Henry VI*, 3.2.1663.
[39] Ibid., 3.2.1692.

Perjury, in the high'st Degree,
Murder, stern murder, in the dir'st degree,
All several sins, all us'd in each degree,
Throng all to'th' Bar, crying all, Guilty, Guilty.
I shall despair, there is no Creature loves me;
And if I die, no soul shall pity me.
Nay, wherefore should they? Since that I my Self,
Find in my Self, no pity to my Self.[40]

So Richard III, too, fails to repent, or even to consider repentance as a serious option. Indeed, it would be more accurate to say: he refuses to repent; he does not really try, and his nonrepentance is an(other) (guilty) exercise of his self-determination. But at least he understands himself rather well, if not fully.

In the soliloquy just quoted, the typographer of the First Folio (1623) has maximized the apparent reference to a "self," or even two "selves," within oneself. Latin syntax is less open to the illusions that English syntax and orthography may generate hereabouts. Take, for example, Aquinas's treatment of one's first free choice(s). Until one reaches a certain age, the "age of reason" as we say, one cannot make free choices. When one does reach it, one is immediately confronted, Aquinas says, with the rational necessity of deliberating *about oneself* (*de seipso*), and about the direction, the integrating point, of one's whole life (*salus sua*), so that in that choosing one (a) treats oneself like an end in oneself to which other things are related as quasi-means (*de seipso cogitet, ad quem alia ordinet sicut ad finem*), and (b) either does or fails to do "what is in oneself" (*quod in se est*).[41] This thesis has sometimes been understood as asserting that one's first choice is somehow uniquely dispositive or self-determining, and/or as asserting that there are choices whose precise object is to dispose of "one's whole self" in a "fundamental option," e.g., for or against God. Both those readings are mistaken, I believe. Aquinas, in these passages, is pointing to the self-determining character of any significant choice, at any stage of one's life; the precise object of such a choice can be quite ordinary.[42] Aquinas holds that every particular choice one makes, even a choice to do something morally neutral in *kind*, is either morally good or morally bad, because of the place or role it has in contributing to or detracting from one's orientation toward wider purposes (ends) that are not morally neutral.[43] Moreover, he understands the intransitivity of every chosen act, that is, the fact that it remains *in one*, as part of one's

[40] *Richard III*, 5.3.3641–65.

[41] Aquinas, *ST* I-II q. 89 a. 6c ad 3; II *Sent*. d. 42 q. 1 a. 5 ad 7; *De Veritate* q. 28 a. 3 ad 4; and see *De Malo* q. 7 a. 10 ad 8.

[42] John Finnis, "Law and What I Truly Should Decide," *American Journal of Jurisprudence* 48 (2003): 107–29 at 109–11, discusses one such kind of choice.

[43] Aquinas, *ST* I-II q. 18 a. 9 and parallel passages from *Sent*. (early) and *De Malo* (late).

character: this, after all, was the basic Aristotelian distinction between the ethical and the technical in one's doings.

Still, it may be that Aquinas exaggerated the extent to which acting persons integrate their choices around relatively or absolutely "ultimate" purposes (ends). He may have underestimated, or at least understated, the extent to which such integration does not take place without more or less explicit *commitment*—of a kind that not everyone makes, not even every healthy and active adult—to wide-ranging, open-ended ways of thinking and acting: ways of life like a religious faith, a marriage, a vowed religious (e.g., monastic) state, a profession embraced as a vocation. Such character-shaping commitments, by which one constitutes, we can say, a distinct personal identity, are made by choices, and such choices have in a straightforward way the characteristics that Aquinas spoke of in relation to the child's first choice. Such choices are *de seipso*, about oneself, and by them one does *quod in se est*, "what is in one."

This last phrase might, of course, be taken to allude to some idea of intrinsically good and virtuous authenticity by fidelity to a somehow given "real self," which it is one's business to discover and follow, as if it were some supra-moral standard of right judgment and action. But by "what is in one" Aquinas surely has in mind nothing other than the capacities, inclinations, and dispositions one has, in the first instance as givens of one's makeup, that is, "by nature," as "seeds of the virtues"— capacities, that is, to pursue and do *good* and avoid evil (which is never more than good's negation). Love of neighbor has as its standard and measure love of self, but this normativity of love of self would be unintelligible unless love of self means wanting for oneself what is truly good, the fullness of virtue(s) in action.[44] As Shakespeare's choric French captains put it, in response to their own question ("As we are ourselves, what things are we?"), we are "merely our own traitors," each in rebellion against himself, and "in his proper stream o'erflow[ing] himself," when he "contrives against his own *nobility*." Against one's faults and crimes, one's vices, one should indeed contrive. One's true self, if we wish to speak like that, one's proper self, is the changing self that it is appropriate for one to choose to be, in all the circumstances of one's existence. The *standard* of appropriateness in those circumstances is always the same: simply the moral law: love of neighbor *as* oneself—that is, by the same sense of worth, of intrinsic goods, as makes intelligible one's choices for oneself. Richard earl of Gloucester, later Richard III, tried to integrate himself around an end that, in the interests of his self-love, involved treating his "neighbors" as other than what they truly are: persons of intrinsically equal dignity with himself. The attempt was transitively effective enough, but resulted intransitively not in real integration of his own

---

[44] On the tightly inter-defined circle of practical reasonableness (*prudentia*), justice, flourishing (*beatitudo*), virtue, and love of self and neighbor, see Finnis, *Aquinas,* chap. 4.

character but in the incoherence of self-love and self-hate, a self-pitying awareness of a paralyzing inability—but (whatever he tells himself) this inability is not radical or ineluctable—to take pity on himself or others by repenting and renouncing the path of slaughterous injustice.

Aquinas is quite clear that one's individual nature may contain flaws, such as proneness to anger or lust or sloth, in a form or measure particular to oneself.[45] The fact that there are flaws such as these in my nature, present in my makeup as givens, not as the result of my own or even others' free choices, does not make them other than flaws to be overcome by the choice of (prospectively) self-discipline and (retrospectively) repentance, reform, conversion. Still less is it the case that such givens are to be taken to be a greater part of, or to have a greater influence in, my developed character than the vices or virtues—the settled and ready dispositions to make and carry out morally bad or good choices—by which, as master of my own acts and of my own willingness to act, I constitute myself the developed, decent or misshapen, thing I am.

Though he does not, I think, articulate it, Aquinas would not have dissented from the summary thesis that (to put it in slogan form) "faith is the fundamental option"—that the most fundamental and pervasively self-determining, identity-shaping option and commitment one can make is faith, understood not in the classic Protestant sense of an awareness of having been saved, but as the choice, lived out in action and constantly reaffirmed, to believe in God's self-disclosure and offer of adoption into the divine household, and to accept his love as object, and living in it as motive, of all one's most basic orientations to action in which one's neighbor is as valued as oneself.[46] In reaction against the misunderstandings encapsulated in the Reformers' *sola fide* (by faith alone), Catholic contemporaries of Shakespeare preferred to frame their practical theology in terms of love, and Shakespeare too makes no explicitly articulated theme of religious faith. But theme it is, for all that. Without the thematizing of belief in divine intervention through human agents by Helena and the count's mother (and by other characters we shall meet, Lafeu and Parolles), the moral conversion of the count, without which nothing can end well, would be too abrupt to carry the play's conclusion. With that thematizing, it does—which does not make the thematizing mere machinery:

---

[45] Aquinas, *ST* I-II q. 41 a. 3c; q. 78 a. 3c; q. 31 a. 7c; *De Malo* q. 16 a. 2c; Finnis, *Aquinas*, 93.

[46] See Aquinas's explanation of the virtue of faith (informed by *caritas*), and of its primacy, in *ST* II-II q. 4. That faith is the fundamental option is proposed, within a broadly Thomist tradition, by Germain Grisez, *Christian Moral Principles* (Chicago: Franciscan Herald Press, 1983), secs. 16-E, 16-G, 23-C, 25-A, 25-F, 26-B, 27-E, 32-D; John Paul II, Encyclical *Veritatis Splendor*, 6 August 1993, sec. 66; see also sec. 65: "[F]reedom is not only the choice for one or another particular action; it is also, within that choice, a *decision about oneself* [*de seipso*] and a setting of one's life for or against the Good, for or against the Truth, and ultimately for or against God."

HELENA: He that of greatest works is finisher
Oft does them by the weakest minister.
Holy writ in babes hath judgment shown,
When judges hath been babes. Great floods have flown
From simple sources, and great seas have dried
When miracles have by the great'st been denied. . . .

KING: I must not hear thee. . . .

HELENA: Inspired merit so by breath is barr'd.
It is not so with [H]im that all things knows
As 'tis with us that square our guess by shows;
But most it is presumption in us when
The help of heaven we count the act of men.
Dear sir, to my endeavours give consent;
Of heaven, not me, make an experiment. . . .

(2.1.745–63)

The king's "health shall live free, and sickness freely die" on the presupposition, Helena says, of "the greatest [G]race lending grace" (2.1.770). And grace was so lent, the play seems to say. But the heavenly promised reward, a husband of her choice, remained more nominal than real until she had demonstrated in action the partial truth of her earlier statement about the relation between human freedom and divine providence:

Our remedies oft in themselves do lie,
Which we ascribe to heaven; the fated sky
Gives us free scope; only backward pull
Our slow designs when we ourselves are dull.

(1.1.223–26)

None of Helena's formulations precisely articulates the subtle truth about the relation(s) between grace and freedom, but each attempt comes close, and together they approximate it well enough.

V. COMMITMENT AND IDENTITY IN MARRIAGE

Comparable to the identity-shaping commitment of religious faith is the commitment of marriage, a commitment to which, once made, Aquinas and the tradition for which he speaks give the same name, *fides*—understood not in the thin modern sense of avoiding "infidelity" but rather as the disposition of this man and this woman, the spouses, to be maritally united to each other and to no other creature in that unique *societas* and friendship, their marriage.[47] This uniquely personal kind of union of two

---

[47] Finnis, *Aquinas*, 143–54.

human persons—a union procreative in kind if not in the event—is cel-
ebrated by Shakespeare in most if not all of his comedies, plays whose concern to intimate serious truths, ethical, metaphysical, or theological, is clear
to careful readers. But the most remarkable of his reflections on the implications of true marriage for personal identity are in his untitled poem known
as *Phoenix and Turtle*. It has recently been shown, as I think, that this enig-
matic and unparalleled piece memorializes the marriage and death of a
young husband and his widow, shortly after her execution for religion, her
ever-devoted husband having earlier died in exile for religion.[48] But this
only confirms what should be clear from the poem, that it is a married
couple whose unity is affirmed,[49] not without hyperbole, but with high
seriousness:

> Love and Constancy is dead,
> Phoenix and the Turtle fled,
> In a mutual flame from hence.
>
> So they loved as love in twain,
> Had the essence but in one,
> Two distincts, Division none:
> Number there in love was slain.
>
> Hearts remote, yet not asunder;
> Distance, and no space was seen,[50]
> 'Twixt this Turtle and his Queen;
> But in them it were a wonder.
>
> So between them Love did shine,
> That the Turtle saw his right
> Flaming in the Phoenix sight;
> Either was the other's mine.
>
> Property[51] was thus appalled,
> That the self was not the same:

---

[48] John Finnis and Patrick Martin, "Shakespeare's Intercession for Love's Martyr," *Times Literary Supplement*, 18 May 2003, 12–14.

[49] The poem's final lament ("threne") says that they now rest to eternity "Leaving no posterity, / 'Twas not their infirmity, / It was married Chastity."

[50] Here, it seems, is the poem's disclosure, for some of its original readers, of the identity of the two "birds"; the Euclidean definition of a line—length and no breadth—points via "Distance and no space" to Roger and Anne Line, whose name is then echoed in the next stanza's "shine" and "mine." There are many other pointers to this young couple in the poem and the circumstances of its origin. Anne Line was executed in London in February 1601 for having a priest perform a religious ceremony in her house.

[51] That is, individuality (though the word is also punning, I believe, on the disinheritance—for his religion—of the husband allusively referred to throughout, Roger Line—and "appalled" alludes to the pall, the cloth that hides the chalice before and after the canon of the mass). In such a totally true marriage, the original individuality of husband and wife is so clothed and hidden "that the self [is] not the same" (a line that equally bears further meanings). In the background throughout is a metaphysical theology like the Friar's in *Romeo and Juliet* (2.6.1430): in sacramental marriage, "holy Church incorporate[s] two in one."

Single Nature's double name
Neither two nor one was called.

Reason in itself confounded,
Saw Division grow together,
To themselves yet either neither,
Simple were so well compounded

That it cried, how true a twain,
Seemeth this concordant one,
Love hath Reason, Reason none,
If what parts, can so remain.

Whereupon it made this Threne
To the Phoenix and the Dove,
Co-supremes and stars of Love. . . .

Abstractly (at least on the surface) but with an intensity that gives substance to its hyperbole, the poem articulates the philosophical and theological understanding of interpersonal love as a thoroughgoing unity (amounting even to a shared "single nature") without, however, any loss of personal identity—"neither two nor one," a twain, concordant, of *co*-supremes: a union initiated and maintained, until death, by free choice and the willed virtue of constancy, of being "true," in a measure which Reason itself affirms, "as Chorus," but which is far beyond reason in its attaching of this person to that, compounding this "simple" with that "simple." All this is the more remarkable if it affirms, as I think it does, that there can be, and concretely has been, such a unity of spouses even though they have chosen to renounce the sexual intercourse, open to procreation, which is the rationale for this *form* of union.

   At the end of *All's Well*, Diana brings to its close her extended tour de force of riddling allusion to the substitution of Bertram's supposedly dead wife Helena for Diana in the latter's supposedly "unchaste composition" with Bertram in Florence:

> So there's my riddle: one that's dead is quick,
> And now behold the meaning
>   *enter Widow, Helena*
> KING: Is there no exorcist
> Beguiles the truer office of mine eyes?
> Is't real [w]hat I see?
> HELENA: No, my good lord;
> 'Tis but the shadow of a wife you see;
> *The name and not the thing.*
> COUNT BERTRAM: Both, both, O pardon!
>
>   (5.3.3037–46)

"The greatest Grace lending grace," and human choices responding as they ought—not least with Bertram's "dearly, ever dearly"—this suffices to make the marital union of Helena and Bertram begin to be real and live, and, as Helena declares by indirection, makes fanciful any prospect that "deadly divorce" will "step between me and you." Her direct response to Bertram's plea for pardon is an allusion (her second) to what she discovered in what was, in fact, the consummation, highly anomalous but not incontestably unreal, of their marriage: "O my good lord, when I was like this maid / I found you wondrous kind." [52] Though the play's (happy) ending carefully disclaims the fixity of a Last Judgment, it affirms the prospect that, as Helena's love will no longer be poured away as in a sieve, so Bertram, in loving her ever dearly, will no longer o'erflow his stream. Rather—so we are encouraged at least to hope—he will have the quiet strength of a self-contained and virtuous identity, as a man and a husband.

VI. HUMILIATION AND IDENTITY IN ALL'S WELL THAT ENDS WELL

The humiliation of Count Bertram has, as I said, its artful parallel in a brilliantly comic subplot. The playwright has provided the count with a flamboyant and eloquent personal assistant, Parolles ("Words"). Upset at the loss of the regimental drum in the Sienna-Florence wars, Captain Parolles boastfully undertakes to recapture it by a lone mission behind the enemy lines. Other French officers in the count's regiment, anticipating that Parolles will lack what it takes to accomplish such a difficult mission, ambush him as he is excogitating some deceitful cover story to explain away his failure. They blindfold him, and then act—albeit farcically—as if they were a foreign military unit, perhaps Muscovites, and with threats of death and torture interrogate him about the dispositions of the French forces and the personal character of the very officers who, unrecognized by him, are interrogating him—and who now include the count, his master. Just as in a dark bedroom the count will mistake the identity of the woman he is lying with, so Parolles in the darkness of a blindfold mistakes the identity of his interrogators and, in love with his own life, acts the traitor—or at least, enacts the identity of a traitor. He betrays (so it seems) the dispositions of the forces and extravagantly defames his master and the other principal officers until, pretending to be

---

[52] *All's Well That Ends Well*, 5.3.3047–48. "Kind" means both affectionate/generous and nature/species, and both meanings are here in play. "Found/find" is one of the play's theme-words (used more than twice the average rate for Shakespeare's plays), and its primary reference is to discovering what or who someone *really* is, in their personal/individual nature. So Helena's words here directly echo the words of the chastened Parolles to his new master, Lord Lafeu: "O my good lord, you were the first that found me" (5.2.2683); Parolles' "every braggart shall be found an ass" (4.3.2434); and many other instances in the play.

about to execute him, they take off his blindfold and let him experience, not death but crushing humiliation. Mocking him with politesse and irony, they all depart, leaving him alone on stage:

Yet am I thankful: if my heart were great
'Twould burst at this: Captain *I'll be no more,*
But I will eat and drink and sleep as soft
As captain shall. *Simply the thing I am*
Shall make me live: who *knows himself* a braggart,
Let him fear this; for it will come to pass
That every braggart *shall be found* an ass.
Rust sword, cool blushes, and Parolles live
Safest in shame: being fooled, by foolery thrive;
There's place and means for every man alive.

(4.3.2428–37)

The scene immediately shifts back to the main plot; Helena, having accomplished her purpose in doing what was necessary to conceive by her husband (and obtain his ring), is conferring with Diana and her mother about the next phase in her "business." Many earlier plays in the European repertoire had involved the bed-trick, as does Shakespeare's *Measure for Measure* (probably written a couple of years before *All's Well*). The biblical prototypes of this substitution ruse were well known.[53] But *All's Well*, perhaps uniquely, seeks to give us a glimpse of the inwardness of it, of what it is like to go through with it. Shakespeare prepares for this, much earlier, when underlining the humiliation for Helena in her husband's rejection of her, and introducing—as an element unknown to Boccaccio—Helena's own sense that she ("poor thief") has stolen the position of wife, that her doing so is cause of the count's imperiling himself in the wars (3.2.1521–38), and that her "ambitious love hath so in me offended" that she must go on barefoot pilgrimage "my faults to have amended" (3.4.1561–63). The direct humiliation that was involved, along with much else, in the successful bed-trick is now conveyed with compression and delicacy in two sentences, prefaced by Helena's characteristic expression of faith in providential order; speaking to Diana's widowed mother, she says:

Doubt not but heaven
Hath brought me up to be your daughter's dower,
As it hath fated her to be my motive

---

[53] Leah and her father play the bed-trick on Jacob (Genesis 29:21–24). One of Leah's sons, Judah, has the bed-trick played on him by his widowed daughter-in-law Tamar (Genesis 38:14–26) in circumstances that include getting his ring as a precondition, and conception of twins from one act of intercourse.

And helper to a husband. But O, strange men,
That can such sweet use make of what they hate
When saucy trusting of the cozened thoughts
Defiles the pitchy night! So lust doth play
With what it loathes for that which is away.

                                                    (4.4.2460–67)

"Sweet use" alludes directly to the pleasure of what, for her, was (as well
as was not) a *usus matrimonii*, marital intercourse;[54] "defile," "saucy" (= in
Elizabethan, lascivious), and "lust doth play with what it loathes" allude
with equal directness to the painful indignity of her involvement, her
presence to the act as if by proxy, as someone as radically misidentified as
can be—subject of the deception in which her own husband in his very
thoughts (and acts!) is "cozened," that is, deceived and betrayed,[55] and

---

[54] Her prospective first *usus matrimonii* was floridly evoked by Parolles (2.4.1251–57) as
go-between excusing the count's purportedly initial and temporary refusal to participate
in it:

> The great prerogative and rite of love,
> Which, as your due, time claims, he does acknowledge;
> But puts it off to a compell'd restraint;
> Whose want, and whose delay, is strew'd with sweets,
> Which they distil now in the curbed time,
> To make the coming hour o'erflow with joy
> And pleasure drown the brim.

Notice also that Shakespeare takes great care to depart from Boccaccio by having Helena
arrange that Bertram receive letters informing him of her death—information which arrives
just before their tryst. Thus, though his intent in courting Diana was probably adulterous,
his eventual act of intercourse did not involve him willing to go through with adultery; it
was at least open to him to be willing the marriage he probably but not certainly insincerely
promised Diana in order to get her agreement (as he thought) to surrender to him her
virginity. Notice, thirdly, that Aquinas would doubtless point out the equivocation or error
in "*both* not sin" in Helena's on the whole remarkably clearheaded moral analysis of the
bed-trick as "wicked meaning [Bertram's] in a lawful deed, / And lawful meaning [hers] in
a lawful act, / Where both not sin, and yet a sinful fact [Bertram's probable intent to
fornicate]" (3.7.1906–8).

[55] The deception/betrayal is, on a first level, by the ruse of Diana and Helena, but on a
second level is by the count's own desire/lust/"will." This becomes clearer when one
notices the association of ideas and images—so characteristic of Shakespeare's works—
between this passage (taken with the parallel cozening of Parolles, the "hoodman" [4.3.2227]
deceived behind a blindfold) and the passage in *Hamlet* where Hamlet denounces, in a series
of hyperboles, the decision of his mother to go in marriage to the bed of Claudius. The
hyperboles are constructed for the relish of readers familiar with a philosophical vocabulary,
and conclude that in Gertrude "reason panders will." The thesis is that in preferring Claudius
to her true husband Gertrude has acted on "compulsive ardure" [ardor] and her "judgment"
or "sense" has been and is "apoplex'd, for madness would not err, / Nor sense to ecstasy
was ne'er so enthrall'd / But it reserv'd some quantity of choice / To serve in such a
difference. What devil was't / That thus hath *cozen'd you at hoodman-blind?*" (3.4.2454–56
[Folio and Second Quarto synthesized]). The "devil" or "hell" is not, however, anything
outside Gertrude, but is—this is Hamlet's argument—the lust that "mutine[s] in" her
"matron's bones" (2458), bringing her to "live / In the rank sweat of an enseamed bed, /
stew'd in corruption, honeying and making love . . ." (2468–70). (To note the parallel and its
sense is not to assume that Hamlet's accusation is sound in relation to Gertrude.)

thus reduced to object even as she is made (albeit by making herself) the object of his "use" in an act that should be but is not (even while, at the level of behavior, it is) the height of inter-*subject*ivity.

The wintriness of this personal experience beneath its sweetness is suggested two sentences later, in a passage like a patch of color in this most monochrome of Shakespeare's plays—a passage further emphasized by its explication of the play's own title, as Helena turns away from Italy toward her home country:

> But with the word the time will bring on summer,
> When briars shall have leaves as well as thorns,
> And be as sweet as sharp: we must away,
> Our wagon is prepared, and time revives us;
> All's well that ends well; still the fine's the crown;
> Whate'er the course, the end is the renown.[56]

$$(4.4.2475–80)$$

"As sweet as sharp": this is one of several metaphors for the play's motif (see Section IV above), the commingling of good and bad dispositions in a single character, the "web of our life" being "of a mingled yarn, good and ill together" (4.3.2177–78).

How does this evocation of mingled yarn apply to Parolles? There can be no other character in Shakespeare who is the object of more unbridled denigration—denigration first at the hands of every substantial character in the play, and thereafter by virtually every critic. As he enters for the first time, Act 1 scene 1, Helena says to herself and the audience, "I know him a notorious liar, / Think him a great way fool, solely a coward. . . ."[57] In Act 2, not very long after he has engaged in a remarkable dialogue with good old Lord Lafeu, an aria in duet that shows them as of one mind about the miraculous nature of Helena's cure of the king,[58] Parolles is rounded upon by Lafeu, who apparently all unprovoked unleashes a torrent of insults, writing Parolles off as "my good window of lattice. . . . Thy casement I need not open, for I *look through thee*" (2.3.1120–22). Indeed, everyone (except, for a time, his master the count) claims to be able to *see through* and *find out* Parolles, and loudly declaims against what they "find" and "see." The play's Clown writes Parolles off as a fool, and Lafeu returns to the charge: "there can be no kernel in this light nut. The soul of

---

[56] This triplet of substantially identical saws seems to echo the Latin triplet near the end of (pseudo-) Aquinas's commentary on (pseudo-) Boethius, *In Boethii De Scholarium Disciplina*: "*exitus acta probat* et item *finis coronat* et insuper *a fine omnia denominari.*" There were sixteenth-century editions of this commentary available in England.

[57] *All's Well That Ends Well*, 1.1.105–6. However, Helena is the only one of his denigrators who does not condemn the man wholesale, for she goes on (1.1.108–9): "Yet these fixed evils sit *so fit in him* / That *they take place when virtue's steely bones / Looks bleak i'th' cold wind.*"

[58] Ibid., 2.3.893–929. That the cure is miraculous is a considerable shift from Boccaccio.

the man is his clothes. Trust him not in matters of heavy consequence"
(2.5.1314–16). The count's distinguished mother's first words about Parolles
are: "A very tainted fellow, and full of wickedness. My son corrupts a well
derived nature / With his inducement" (3.2.1495–97). In Florence, a citizen onlooker denounces him as he approaches on horseback alongside
the count: "one Parolles: a filthy officer he is in those suggestions for the
young earl" (3.5.1626–28). Diana, the object of the count's desire, likewise
points to Parolles: " 'Yonds that same knave / That leads him [the count]
to these places. Were I his lady, / I would poison that vile rascal. . . . that
jackanapes with scarves" (3.5.1707–11). One of the French officer noblemen describes him to the count: "he's a most notable coward, an infinite
and endless liar, an hourly promise-breaker, the owner of no one good
quality worthy of your lordship's entertainment" (3.6.1741–44). The claims
to know *what Parolles is* continue uninterrupted to the end: "so bad an
instrument," says Diana; "I saw the man today, if man he be," says Lafeu;
and now the young count himself, self-servingly, joins the chorus: "What
of him? / He's quoted for a most perfidious slave / With all the spots
a'th'world taxed and debauched, / Whose nature sickens but to speak a
truth. Am I or that or this for what he'll utter, / That will speak anything?" (5.3.2928–35).

What the play *shows* about Parolles is rather different. True, he is shown
to be a braggart whose boasts trap him into attempting the impossible,
and who is (he says) prepared to lie on oath to save face. And his letter
to Diana, warning her against Bertram's unscrupulousness and immaturity, is indeed "tainted," addressing her as if she were willing to sell her
favors, if not hinting that he would be a better beneficiary of them than
his master. But the accusations that he leads Bertram into wickedness are
never verified: the playwright makes it clear that it was the count's own
decision to go to the Tuscan wars rather than attend to his wife, and the
count's decision to pursue Diana. So far as the play indicates, Parolles
does no more than second these decisions and act as an agent and
go-between (not wholly reliable) in carrying them out. When he is beg-
ging for his life, he pours out purported details of the French and other
pro-Florentine forces and of their officers' bad character. But nothing
shows that the details are really military secrets of use to the enemy, or at
all—his purported counting of the infantry asserts that numbers totaling
3,600 total 15,000—and the character sketches he offers are either fair
enough (as when he says the count his master is "a foolish idle boy but
for all that very ruttish"), or so laughably exaggerated that no real enemy
would give them a moment's notice. And whatever the truth about his
character before his humiliation and self-knowledge, he afterward acts as
a teller of the truth, who at appropriate royal command says what he
knows about Bertram's relationship with Diana, and does so without
dishonoring him (or her). As the play reaches its benign resolution, his
new master, wise old Lord Lafeu, weeping with joy, confers on Parolles a

subtly new status, raised from the depths, by asking for a handkerchief for his own use from "Good Tom Drum."

We must conclude that Parolles' carefully constructed persona, his sartorial and rhetorical flamboyance and his affectation of military zeal, was a failure of technique. As a means of getting and keeping influence with the immature, it was engaging and seductive, but as a means of gaining the confidence of the relatively mature, it was the failure that Lafeu encapsulates with his dismissive "no kernel in this light nut; the soul of this man is his clothes. Trust him not. . . ."

The phrase "the thing I am," in Parolles' meaning, signifies what was true about him all along (so to speak), underneath his bragging and overreaching of himself in foolhardy action and shamefaced deception. We, like so many of the play's leading characters, *suppose* we know the nasty truth about him, but perhaps, led on by all his critics, are mistaken about his real identity, that is, his true character. Certainly it seems that he does not confront or acknowledge the whole truth about himself, and his resolution to eat, drink, and sleep soft in a lower station—indeed, in "foolery"—is neither morally uplifting nor true to his own manifest talents.[59] Still, there is no reason to doubt what the play suggests, that the humiliation has induced in him a renunciation of his constructed social persona, and a kind of humbling that is an at least partial reshaping of his personal identity, under the description (we may suggest) of gaining or regaining *authenticity.* Two or three years earlier, in *As You Like It,* Shakespeare used the same phrase, "the thing I am," to mark a moral conversion—of the wicked eldest brother Oliver—a repentance that must, if that play is to make sense, be thoroughgoing. (The young count's conversion or repentance in the final moments of *All's Well* must equally be thoroughgoing, if that play is to end as its audience must unequivocally wish.) By recall-

---

[59] These talents are first shown in the brilliance of his bawdy, philosophical, but crisp exposition (1.1.140–54) of the case against virginity (and in favor of procreation rather than libertinism)—an exposition with echoes of Erasmus's colloquy on marriage and of William Gager's Latin Oxford play *Meleager*; see John Finnis and Patrick M. Martin, "An Oxford Play Festival in 1582," *Notes & Queries* 50 (2003): 391–94. The talents are soon shown again in his equally brilliant duet with Lafeu about the miraculous character of Helena's cure of the king, "the rarest argument of wonder that hath shot out in our latter times"—a duet that ends:

> PAROLLES: Nay, 'tis strange, 'tis very strange; that is the brief and tedious of it; and he's of a most facinerious [abominable] spirit that will not acknowledge it to be the—
> OLD LAFEU: Very hand of heaven.
> PAROLLES: Ay, so I say.
> OLD LAFEU: In a most weak—
> PAROLLES: And debile minister, great power, great transcendence, which should indeed give us a further use to be made than alone the recov'ry of the king, as to be—
> OLD LAFEU: Generally thankful.
>
> (2.3.899–929)

The play, moreover, seems to back this hypothesis against "our philosophical persons [who] make modern [= everyday] and familiar *things supernatural and causeless*" (2.3.894–95).

ing from its outset the parable of the prodigal son, *As You Like It* shaped itself toward the multiple conversions, moral and religious, with which it ended. And the murderously wicked elder brother revealed his own unanticipated moral transformation with the words:

> I do not shame
> To tell you *what I was,* since my conversion
> So sweetly tastes, *being the thing I am.*
>
> (4.3.135)

The thing I am thus stands over against *what I was;* more cautiously put, there has been a vital change—"my conversion"—in the one and the same *I.*

VII. Repentance and Identity

Thus, to the radical shaping of personal identity by religious faith and by commitment to one's spouse in marriage can be added its shaping in conversion or repentance. Parolles' change of heart is left ambiguous, like his future relationship with his new master, Lafeu. Most critics take it at its surface appearance, a future as the old lord's fool, but Lafeu's "I'll make sport with thee" may well envisage something much less unequal, such as riding together to the hunt. Be that as it may, Parolles' resounding "simply the thing I am shall make me live" echoes two of Shakespeare's earlier articulations of a convert's change of personal identity. Oliver's we have just seen articulated by one who was the vicious would-be murderer of his own brother, and who, finding himself the beneficiary of that brother's generosity of spirit in action, is transformed by repentance into someone fit to love and marry a woman of high character and charm. Perhaps more well known is the new King Henry V's repudiation of Sir John Falstaff, entertaining enough but fundamentally vile, come up to Westminster on stolen horses to claim high office in the court of the new monarch, his long-time companion in low life:

HENRY V:

> *Presume not that I am the thing I was;*
> For God doth know, so shall the world perceive,
> That *I have turn'd away my former self;*
> So will I those that kept me company.
> When thou dost hear I am as I have been,
> Approach me, and thou shalt be as thou wast,
> The tutor and the feeder of my riots:
> Till then, I banish thee, on pain of death,
> As I have done the rest of my misleaders. . . .[60]

---

[60] *The History of King Henry IV, Part Two,* 5.5.3268–76. Modern audiences, directors, and readers tend to side with Falstaff, but are deeply and to some extent willfully mistaken—seduced.

The new king does not deny that, as Falstaff's companion Prince Hal, he has been the kind of person that Falstaff happily assumed him to be—just the kind of person that the old king denounced him as being, an enemy of the kingdom's common good, a favorer of ruffians, wild dogs, scum. This "dear and deep rebuke" by the dying king elicited from the prince the same response as Bertram makes to his humiliation at the end of *All's Well*: "O pardon me. . . ." The articulation of the new king's new identity in repudiating Falstaff affirms in act the repentance and reform that he chose, it seems, when he was at the king's deathbed, his conscience scoured by that rebuke. To all this we must add, however, that when this play is taken with its companion play *Henry IV Part One*, the reality of this repentance, reform, and conversion remains in doubt, along with the reality of the depravity that the prince affected and appeared to share with Falstaff. For at the end of the first occasion when we are shown these two men together, the prince discloses to us in soliloquy that in consorting with Falstaff in crime, he'll "so offend to make offence a skill" so that in due course "when this loose behaviour I throw off . . . like bright metal on a sullen ground, / My reformation, glitt'ring o'er my fault, / Shall show more goodly and attract more eyes / Than that which hath no foil to set it off" (1.2.309–16). Yet the seriousness of Henry's reformation seems vouched for by much in the preceding scenes, including his testing by his dying father, and his own testing of and by the Chief Justice. The fact is that the playwright teases us, across three whole plays, with the possibility that Henry V was never really debauchee, never really convertite, and so, perhaps, never the authentic Christian king he ends up seeming. Dissipation and conversion, too, can be masks, personas in the word's oldest sense. The choice of masks both shapes and reveals the person who chooses them, but only to one who knows that the choice has been made and persisted in. The Shakespearean soliloquy puts an audience in such a Godlike position—or seems to.

VIII. MATURITY AND DECAY

Both *All's Well* and *As You Like It*, comedies of repentance or conversion, also make searching play of aging as maturation and decay. Early in *All's Well*, the king, who in his own long and apparently incurable illness has "persecuted time with hope" (a hope he has by now abandoned), reports and seconds the saying of Helena's late father, the great physician whose skill, had it stretched as far as his honesty, would have "made [his] nature immortal" (1.1.18, 24). Speaking to the young count Bertram, the king says:

> "Let me not live," quoth he,
> "After my flame lacks oil, to be the snuff
> Of younger spirits, whose apprehensive senses
> All but new things disdain; whose judgments are

Mere fathers of their garments; whose constancies
Expire before their fashions."[61] This he wish'd.
I, after him, do after him wish[62] too,
Since I nor wax nor honey can bring home,
I quickly were dissolved from my hive
To give some laborers room.

                                                        (1.2.305–14)

This contrast between younger and older is part of the play's strong surface structure, in which old king, old countess, old Lord Lafeu, and old Florentine widow are foils to the immaturities, ventures, achievements, follies, fecundity, and resource of Helena, Bertram, and Diana. And as the play's last act opens, the king is again speaking to Bertram, now returned from Florence and both prematurely and casually asking forgiveness (for having gone away to the wars against a royal prohibition):

KING: The time is fair again.
BERTRAM: My high-repented blames
            Dear sovereign, pardon to me.
KING: All is whole,
            Not one word more of the consumed time;
            Let's take the instant by the forward top;
            For we are old, and on our quick'st decrees
            Th'inaudible and noiseless foot of time
            Steals ere we can effect them.

                                                        (5.3.2740–48)

As You Like It gives to its maverick melancholic Jaques a bravura rendering of late-sixteenth-century reflections on the "seven ages of man," finishing up:

                                      Last scene of all,
            That ends this strange eventful history,
            Is *second childishness and mere oblivion,*
            Sans teeth, sans eyes, sans taste, sans everything.

                                                        (2.7.1142–45)

The stagey morbidity of Jaques's reflections is undercut by the immediate entrance of the hero's aged servant, the venerable Adam, a man of unalloyed goodness and constancy. Almost eighty, he has in an earlier

---

[61] Note the orderly philosophical sequence: "apprehensive senses," "judgment," "constancy [of will]."

[62] It now, regrettably, seems necessary to observe that this wish is not even conditionally an intent or willingness to commit suicide or accept euthanasia.

scene declared himself, somewhat optimistically, "strong and lusty": "my age is as a lusty winter, / Frosty but kindly. Let me go with you, / I'll do the service of a younger man / In all your business and necessities" (2.3.756–59). However, the hungry journey into exile does prove too much for him, physically. And in any case, Jaques's depiction of decrepitude does tell a truth.

Does it tell the whole truth about the personal identity of someone thoroughly disabled by age? The question is difficult, and not directly answered, I think, by either Shakespeare or Aquinas. But just as neither believes that the dissolution of the person in death leaves no surviving remnant awaiting resurrection in heaven, purgatory, or hell, so neither believes that descent into the darkness of senility or other like disorder of mind expunges the identity shaped by free choices—by a freedom now lost. The choice to repent can cancel vice, but decay cannot cancel virtue or merit, the personal identity known to him who is "the top of judgment." As the heroine of another of Shakespeare's three "problem plays" says:

ISABELLA: How would you be,
        If He, which is the top of judgment, should
        But judge you as you are? O, think on that;
        And mercy then will breathe within your lips,
        Like man new made.
                                (*Measure for Measure*, 2.2.827–31)

She is pleading for her brother's life with a man at the height of his powers, in the full pride of life, and of unshaken repute for his austerely virtuous character. She assumes that in the eye of God this man's character is nonetheless not free from vice—and so is in need of forgiving mercy—but she will be astounded and for a time incredulous when such vices, and very great ones, are disclosed to her later in their encounter. It is not too hazardous to think that Shakespeare and Aquinas, with the whole tradition in which they work, take for granted that what matters in divine judgment on human persons is not how weak they are through immaturity, illness, or senility at the time of their death, but *what they are* in the identity they have *made for themselves*. For they make this identity (if they do) by their free choices, during the time, short or long, that they can freely choose. And in the view of Aquinas, whereas God can remedy all deficiencies of nature such as immaturity or senility, giving to each the psychosomatic condition of a human being of the age Christ had at his death and resurrection,[63] even "the greatest [G]race lending grace" (and by divine mercy making one "new made") does not and cannot override

---

[63] Aquinas, *ST* Supp. q. 81 a. 1; *ScG* IV c. 88 n. 5 [4231]—"by reason of the perfection of nature which is found in that age alone."

the freedom by choice to make oneself what one's choices determine one to be, until (if ever) one chooses to repent or reverse them sometime later in this life.[64] Such seems to be Shakespeare's working assumption, too—not merely his character Isabella's.

IX. CONCLUSION

As Germain Grisez, who took up and developed incipient elements of Aquinas's philosophical understanding of the person, rightly says:

> A person is in all four of the orders, and he embraces all of them in himself. In the person the four orders are distinct, irreducible, yet normally inseparable. The unity of the person is unlike the unity of any entity which is enclosed within one of the four orders. The unity of the person is mysterious and must remain so. This unity is immediately given in human experience, and it cannot be explained discursively, since reason cannot synthesize the distinct orders in a higher positive intelligibility.[65] . . . The unity of the person is not an intelligible principle of a fifth order, distinct from the four, nor is it something like an entity belonging to one or another of the four orders hidden behind all of them. The four aspects of the person all involve and in a way include one another, as the four orders always do. . . . The person is the self who *unifies* these four distinct and irreducible but normally inseparable aspects. The self [which in the next paragraph Grisez speaks of, synonymously, as the soul] is a unifying principle. . . .[66]

Grisez's account seems intended to suggest that he does not accept Aquinas's account of the human soul as the substantial form of the human body, an account that looks as if the soul and thus too the human person as a whole is to be understood and explained as simply a reality in the first (natural) order. But in speaking of the soul as that which—we know not *how*—unifies all the irreducibly distinct but interpenetrated aspects of the person, including the bodily (that is, the psychophysical), Grisez retains the elements of Aquinas's account that I have emphasized, above all its insistence that when (for example) I deliver a lecture, that which is producing physical and psychophysical effects by audibly speaking, and being acted upon physically and psychophysically by hearing, is identical—

---

[64] Aquinas, *ST* I-II q. 113 aa. 3 and 4. So until death ends the personal narrative, we can say no more of someone than what the king says in the play's last lines: "All yet [so far] *seems* well. . . ."

[65] Germain Grisez, *Beyond the New Theism: A Philosophy of Religion* (Notre Dame and London: University of Notre Dame Press, 1975), 349. On the four orders, see Section I above.

[66] Ibid., 351.

qua human person, I myself—with that which is reasoning logically (or perhaps correcting or failing to correct logical invalidity), *and* carrying out a choice to devote precious time to this act of communication, *and* using internalized technical resources, especially the English language and the techniques of effective utterance.[67]

In short, there is the identity I have as the particular human being I have been since I was formed in my mother's womb with all the radical capacities, and thus the nature, of a human person. There is the identity I have as a person conscious of much that I have experienced and thought since first I began to be aware of myself (my toes and my fears . . .) in relation to other things including people, and began to inquire and assert and deny and argue. There is the identity I have as a person with the character I have made for myself by the choices I have made within the constraints, and between the opportunities, that have arisen from the nature of things, the choices of others, and the accidental conjunctions, by *all* of which factors, as Shakespeare and Aquinas each depict, divine providence "shapes our ends, / rough hew them how we will" (*Hamlet*, 5. 2.3509–10). And there is the identity I have as an object of cultural forms (a citizen of Australia) and a user of them (English-speaking, tie-wearing) and a projecter of new and partly new personas.

The literary critic Gary Taylor has recently suggested that Shakespeare errs in trying to "flatter the would-be transcendentalism of the ego":

> Maybe we should not believe Hamlet, or Shakespeare, when he tells us "I have that within which passeth show" [*Hamlet*, 1.2.266]. Middleton did not believe him. Middleton answered Shakespeare . . . "You're the deed's creature." What is within does not matter, if it does not come out; the secret subjectivity that you imagine for yourself is irrelevant, by comparison to the substantive social and material identity created by what you have actually done. You are created by, and a slave to, your actions, not your self-regarding fantasies.[68]

[67] On the philosophical significance of the distinction between *langue*, language as resource (found in dictionaries and in the competence of speakers), and *parole*, language as use of that resource in acts of communication (of inexhaustible variety and, often, novelty), see David Braine, *The Human Person: Animal and Spirit* (Notre Dame and London: University of Notre Dame Press, 1992), 353–63, 461–65, etc. Braine's entire book is of great value as a thorough-going rethinking and restoration of an Aristotelian-Thomistic understanding of the human person and personal identity, making rich use of natural science and of recent English-language "analytical" philosophy. Not unlike Grisez, he concludes that the soul is what gives nature, identity, unity, and operation to the human body and its parts and that "we can utilize the much more general Aristotelian conception of 'formal cause' and apply it to the soul, but it is . . . entirely optional whether we apply to the soul the separate (and in the development of Aristotle's thought, later) idea of 'form' as the correlate of 'matter'" (527).

[68] Gary Taylor, "The Cultural Politics of Maybe," in *Theatre and Religion: Lancastrian Shakespeare*, ed. Richard Dutton, Alison Findlay, and Richard Wilson (Manchester and New York: Manchester University Press, 2003), 242–58 at 256. The allusion is to Thomas Middleton (1570–1627), *The Changeling* (first performed 1624), 3.4.140.

Aquinas and Shakespeare, I have argued, would agree that we are each, in some respects, created by our actions, as well as by our experiences and skills, and scarcely by our self-regarding fantasies; and that as creatures of our actions we will be slaves to them unless we choose to reassert the mastery over them that we had when first we chose them. They would agree that "the secret subjectivity that you imagine for yourself" matters far less than "the substantive social and material identity created by what you have actually done." But they would add that what one has actually *done* was the carrying out of intentions—proposals shaped, however rapidly, in deliberation and adopted by choices—and that one's deliberative shapings of intention, extended (by those choices and their execution) into one's actions, are one's real subjectivity, at once secret and made known. And they would also add that one's "social identity" may be a mask of which one might, in principle, be stripped as of a blindfold, revealing even to oneself something partly the same but partly different.

Law and Philosophy, University of Oxford

MORAL STATUS AND PERSONAL IDENTITY: CLONES, EMBRYOS, AND FUTURE GENERATIONS

By F. M. Kamm

I. Introduction

The permissibility of our actions can sometimes depend on the identities of those who will be affected by them. Investigating this phenomenon has been a traditional focus of deontological ethics. Deontological ethics claims that what we ought to do is not always a function of what will produce the best outcome: we could be morally constrained from producing the best outcome because it would require harming someone who would not himself benefit from our action, though others would. John Rawls referred to this as the moral relevance of the separateness of persons.[1] One way of expressing this idea has been that persons are not, in general, substitutable for one another when we do a calculation of harms and benefits. More precisely, harm to person A may not be compensated for by benefit to B just because it would be compensated for by the same benefit to A himself. In Section II of this essay, I shall briefly canvass some ways in which the differing identities of those affected by our acts can bear on the permissibility of imposing harm on them without any accompanying benefit for them. I shall also consider what sorts of properties an entity must have in order to make it the case that harms imposed upon it are not compensated by benefits that flow to another.

In Section III, I shall examine the validity of concerns about reproductive cloning that focus on the fear that cloned people will become substitutable for each other. In Section IV, I shall consider whether substitutions of harms and benefits that would be impermissible interpersonally are permissible when we act on embryos, even when there will be continuity between any such embryo and the person that will arise from it—and thus, possibly, there is identity over time of a human being (if not a person). If such substitutions are permissible, this will serve as a criticism of those who would argue that the moral status of an embryo should be that of a person if it will definitely give rise to a person (as opposed to merely having the potential to give rise to a person). I shall also consider how this bears on what is called the Non-Identity Problem and the distinction between person-affecting and non-person-affecting moral principles.

---

[1] See John Rawls, *A Theory of Justice* (Cambridge, MA: Harvard University Press, 1971), p. 29.

II. Types of Entities and the Importance
of Personal Identity

A. *Ways of mattering morally*

When we say that something counts morally *in its own right*, we are often said to be thinking of its intrinsic worth or value rather than its instrumental value. If it were morally right to treat animals well only because this would promote kindness between persons, then animals would count morally only instrumentally. That is, they should be treated well not because of what they are in their own right, but only because of the effects on others of treating them well. Philosopher Christine Korsgaard has argued, however, that the true contrast to mere instrumental value is having value as an end, not having intrinsic value.[2] That is, if the animal counts morally in its own right, there is no further end that need be served by our treating the animal well in order for us to have a reason to treat it well. If something is an end (in this limited sense), this need not mean that it has value that can never be trumped, or that it can never be treated as a mere means. At minimum, it means only that its condition can provide a reason (even if an overrideable one) for attitudes or actions appropriate to its moral worth, independent of other considerations. Korsgaard argues that some things may be ends in virtue of their intrinsic properties, but others may be ends in virtue of their extrinsic properties. A thing's intrinsic properties are all its nonrelational properties.[3] Its extrinsic properties are properties it has in virtue of standing in relation to other things. For example, Ronald Dworkin claims to have a theory of the intrinsic value of even nonsentient, nonconscious life, such as is found in an early embryo. However, he also says this value comes from the history of the embryo, in particular the investment that nature or God has made in it. This is not a theory of the intrinsic value of a life but of its extrinsic value, since it derives the value of the embryo from its particular history rather than from properties it has independent of this history.[4] Further, an entity's ability to produce an effect is a relational property holding between it and the effect. It is possible, given what Korsgaard has said, that something could be worth treating as an end because it is capable of causing a certain effect, even if it never does.

A work of art or a tree may count morally in its own right in the sense that it gives us reason to constrain our behavior toward it (for example, not destroy it) just because that would preserve this entity. That is, independent of the pleasure or enlightenment that it does or will cause in

---

[2] See Christine Korsgaard, "Two Distinctions in Goodness," *The Philosophical Review* 2 (April 1983): 169–95.

[3] Note, however, that a thing's intrinsic properties might include relations between its parts.

[4] See Ronald Dworkin, *Life's Dominion: An Argument about Abortion, Euthanasia, and Individual Freedom* (New York: Knopf, 1993).

people, a thing of aesthetic value gives us reason not to destroy it. In that sense, it counts morally. Nevertheless, this is still to be distinguished from constraining ourselves *for the sake of* the work of art or the tree. I do not act for its sake when I save a work of art, because I do not think of its good and how its continuing existence would be good for it when I save it. (Nor do I think of its exercising its capacities or performing its duties. Acting for the sake of its exercising capacities or performing duties might also involve acting for the entity's sake, though it need not involve seeking what is good for it.) Rather, I think of the good of the work of art, its worth as an art object, when I save it for no other reason than that it will continue to exist. By contrast, when I save a bird, I can do it for the bird's sake, because it will get something out of continuing to exist and it could be a harm to it not to continue. It seems that something must already have or have had the capacity for sentience or consciousness in order for it to be harmed by not continuing on in existence. This is because an entity must be able to get something out of its continuing existence, and a capacity for sentience or consciousness seems to be necessary for this. (I do not think either capacity is a *necessary* condition for us to be able to act for the sake of the entity, since each without the other is sufficient. Having the capacity is not the same as actually being sentient. It is also not the same as merely having the potential to be sentient, where the latter implies that an entity merely has the potential to have the capacity.) I shall say that *an entity has (positive) moral status when in its own right, for its own sake, it gives us reason to help it and to refrain from destroying it.*

On this account, a nonsentient, nonconscious embryo lacks moral status but could count morally in itself (e.g., could give us reason in its own right not to destroy it) because of its intrinsic and extrinsic properties, such as what its potential is. This is different from its merely having instrumental value because it will in fact give rise to a person that has moral status. For even if the embryo is not instrumental to there being a person (because it is deprived of an environment in which to develop), I believe its having the potential could still give it greater value than an embryo that lacks the potential. (Similarly, a Chippendale dining table may have value in itself and may have more value if it can also turn into a magnificent writing desk, though it will not.) Notice, however, that the instrumental value of an embryo might be greater if it will generate Beethoven rather than an ordinary person, even if the moral status of these two persons does not differ. Similarly, an embryo can have greater value in its own right if it has the potential to become an extraordinary human being (e.g., Beethoven) rather than an ordinary human being, even if these persons have the same moral status, and the embryo will not, in fact, generate anyone.

All this does not mean, however, that an embryo's continued existence is good for it or that it is harmed by not continuing on. Similarly, an ordinary table might, by magic, be turned into a table that can develop into a person, and it may be good to be a person, but can a table be the sort of thing that is harmed by not getting the good of its transformation? It does not seem so. The person that would come from the embryo also cannot be harmed by never coming to exist. But we can act for the sake of a person who will develop from the embryo by doing things to the embryo not for its sake but for the sake of the person who will exist. (I shall return to this issue in Section IV below.) The fact that an embryo may have value in its own right in virtue of its extrinsic properties could account for why it might be wrong to use it for frivolous purposes. If so, the ground for objecting to such acts would be like the ground for objecting to making lampshades of the flesh of deceased human beings (who had died of natural causes). The flesh has no moral status (as I am using the term), but it has an extrinsic relation to once-living human persons who had moral status, and thus it may give us reason in its own right not to use it in certain ways. (The embryo's particular intrinsic and extrinsic properties, of course, differ from those of the dead flesh.)

Those things for whose sake we can act when we save their lives may or may not give us as much reason to save them as entities whose existence cannot be extended for their own sake. For example, if we had to choose whether to destroy the Grand Canyon or a bird (holding constant the number of people who would get pleasure or be enlightened by each), it could be morally wrong to choose the Grand Canyon. This illustrates how something like a bird can count morally because it can get something out of life, without its giving more reason to act, in the sense of how significant its continuing in existence would be, relative to other things. Sometimes the remarkableness of something (such as the Grand Canyon) or its uniqueness calls for more protection than something else's having moral status.

Not all things whose lives we could save (or not destroy) for their own sake are things it would be wrong not to save or to destroy (for example, dangerous dogs). But if we did have a duty sometimes to save or not to destroy such entities, this still does not imply that all the entities that have moral status are entities *to whom we owe it* to save or not destroy their lives. There is a difference between one's having a duty to do something and having a duty *to* a specific entity to do it. The latter is known as a directed duty, and typically it has a correlative that is a right or a claim possessed by the entity to whom the duty is owed against the person who owes it.[5] Correspondingly, there is a difference between doing the wrong thing (for example, not fulfilling a *non*directed duty) and *wronging* some entity by failing to perform the duty owed to her. The entity who is owed a duty is not necessarily the entity who is benefited or affected by the object of the duty. For example, if you owe it to me to take care of my

---

[5] An exception may exist if there are duties one has to oneself, for one cannot have rights against oneself.

mother, I am the right-holder, not my mother, even though the object of the duty is to benefit her, and you wrong me, not my mother, if you fail to help her. Arguably, the idea of respect for persons and the dignity of the person amounts to the idea that one *owes it to a person* to behave in certain ways, rather than simply that it would be wrong to treat her in certain ways because, for example, one owes it to God not to do so or because it would not maximize utility to do so and one has a general duty as a rational being (but not a duty owed to anyone) to maximize utility. Thus, just as only some entities that count in their own right are entities that have moral status (as I have defined it), so only some entities that have moral status have rights against us.

To what sort of entities is it possible to owe things or behaviors? Thomas Scanlon has argued that only entities capable of judgment-sensitive attitudes are entities to whom we can owe certain treatment.[6] (Scanlon does not speak of rights as the correlatives of directed duties, but I believe the addition of rights talk in his system would be appropriate.)[7] Entities capable of judgment-sensitive attitudes form attitudes or decide on actions on the basis of evaluating certain factors as reasons, that is, as considerations in favor of an attitude or action. For example, they do not just respond to aspects of their environment (as a cat would); they see these aspects as considerations in favor of or against action. Scanlon's view seems to be that if some entities can evaluate our conduct toward them (so that they can see a reason for us to act or not act in that way), then we may potentially owe it to them to act or not act in that way.[8] He also seems to think that a creature capable of judgment-sensitive attitudes governs itself in the light of reasons, and thus it is only to self-governing creatures that we can owe things. (It is possible, however, to imagine that the capacity for judgment-sensitive attitudes does not go so far as to involve self-governance in the light of reasons. For example, a creature might take certain factors in the environment as true reasons to pursue food but might not be self-conscious and thus not self-governing. I am not sure what Scanlon would say if these two conditions were pulled apart.)

Scanlon thinks animals count morally in their own right and give us reasons to act for their sake. Hence, our conduct toward them can be right or wrong, independent of further considerations, but it cannot be owed to them and they cannot be wronged when we behave wrongly. This is because (he assumes) they are not capable of judgment-sensitive attitudes. Furthermore, he thinks that while we have a reason to help an

---

[6] Thomas Scanlon, *What We Owe to Each Other* (Cambridge, MA: Harvard University Press, 1999).

[7] I suggest this addition in my discussion of Scanlon's book; see F. M. Kamm, "Owing, Justifying, and Rejecting," *Mind* 111, no. 442 (April 2002).

[8] I have criticized Scanlon's use of his account of "owing to others" as the basis of an account of what it is for something to be wrong. I suggest it may better be understood as what makes it possible to wrong someone. See my "Owing, Justifying, and Rejecting."

animal in need, we can have the same reason to help a rational being in need plus an additional reason absent in the case of the animal: that is, we can owe it to the rational being to help him. On this account, the "greater" moral importance or value of rational beings (persons) gets fleshed out (in part) as the additional factor present in our relations with them: that is, we owe things to them or, as I would say, they have rights against us.

B. The bearing of personal identity on our treatment of persons

Having considered some different types of entities, I now want to consider whether and how we may take account of or ignore the facts of personal identity when we are dealing with persons.

There may be conflicts between satisfying interests or respecting rights and maximizing satisfaction of interests intrapersonally and interpersonally. (I will refer to interpersonally maximizing interests satisfied as "producing the greater good.") Consider first the conflict between negative rights and great goods *not* protected by rights.[9]

It is often said that part of the reason why one person's right not to be paralyzed should take precedence over the greater good (when they conflict) is that others, not he, will receive the benefit of his sacrifice. Sometimes, however, it will be even worse to harm a person for his own greater benefit than it would be to harm him for the good of others. This is when we act against his will, for the charge of paternalism arises in the former case but not in the latter. In other cases, it seems that the reason for not imposing harm on one person is not that he will fail to be benefited, but rather that the greater good we produce is of the wrong sort. For example, it may consist in many small goods aggregated over many other persons, rather than a large benefit to any one other person. Consider a case in which someone has a negative right to not have his car damaged. I might nevertheless permissibly damage his car in the course of using it to rush someone else (who would otherwise die) to the hospital. If it were possible that, by damaging the car, I could produce a comparable number of additional years of life by giving an enormous number of people one minute each of additional life, would this be permissible too? It seems not. But is it really the separateness of the beneficiaries that stands in the way? Suppose that each of the beneficiaries of the small benefit faced as bad a prospect as the one person who would die (that is, suppose they were each on the point of death). Might not the small goods to many separate people then justify the imposition of harm on the one person?[10] If we still think that the large, concentrated benefit of the life saved, and not the small benefits to each soon-to-die person, justifies the imposition in these cases, it is nevertheless true that aggregating some small benefits

---

[9] Under "goods," I include both benefits and the avoidance of harm.
[10] Derek Parfit emphasizes this in his *Rediscovering Reasons* (unpublished).

to people (each of whom would be very badly off) might sometimes justify a larger imposition on a person who would not be as badly off.

In the case just discussed, we have compared individuals one person at a time to see who will wind up worse off and who will get what, if we act one way rather than another. This procedure is called "pairwise comparison." A proponent of pairwise comparison claims that the fact that potential recipients are separate persons—not only that the person undergoing harm is separate from anyone benefited—is relevant in deciding whether to perform an action that harms one person. By contrast, if we merely aggregate benefits over many people, then we ignore the distribution of the benefits over individual persons. (Notice that one person can be worse off than another through *intra*personal aggregation of harms, but aggregating over one life, even assuming constant personal identity, has problems of its own. For example, if one person will suffer a thousand headaches over the course of his life, but he will live seventy years and the headaches are interspersed evenly, he may be better off than someone who will have five hundred headaches over the course of a ten-year life, especially if they are bunched together.)

Arguably, the method of pairwise comparison is not adequate on its own. For sometimes it seems that a loss suffered by someone can be justified even though the benefit does not come to him but to others, each of whom would suffer less (if not aided) and benefit less (if aided) than he would. For example, suppose I refuse to save someone from death in order to save a million from paralysis. If aggregation in this case is permissible, it seems to diminish the significance of the separateness of persons in the way emphasized by pairwise comparison. Indeed, if I were to decide it was permissible to kill a person for the sake of saving the lives of a million people—a case in which each person would (if left unaided) suffer as great a loss as the one who is to be killed—this too would diminish the significance of the separateness of persons, at least as expressed by the requirement of pure pairwise comparison, since no one of the million would be any worse off (if not aided) than the one person would be if he died, nor would any one of the million receive a benefit (if aided) greater than the single person would receive if he were allowed to live.

There is, however, another way of taking account of the separateness of persons besides pure pairwise comparison. I call this "balancing of equals." Imagine cases where there is a conflict of interests and we must decide whether to *aid* a smaller or a larger group (of non-overlapping persons). A person on one side of a conflict is balanced out against another on the other side, and the side with the greater number is helped, at least when each stands to lose and gain as much. This is a form of substitution of equals; for in a conflict between persons A and B, we think, from an impartial point of view, that we accomplish as much if we save B as if we save A, and hence we accomplish even more if we save B plus C. We think

this even though A does not benefit if B is saved (because they are separate persons) and even though, from A's partial perspective, the outcome
in which she survives is better than the one in which B survives. The
balancing-of-equals approach can still respect the separateness of persons
by not weighing against A's loss of twenty years of life a combination of
B's loss of ten years and C's loss of ten years. That is, we can first engage
in pairwise comparison to check to see if a person will suffer the greater
loss and/or receive a greater benefit and only balance out those who
stand to lose or gain as much. The combination of pairwise comparison
and balancing allows us to justify saving a greater number rather than a
smaller number of people in a conflict situation. However, if we allow an
aggregation of losses suffered by several persons to outweigh another
individual's greater loss (for example, saving a million from paralysis
rather than one person from death), we still move beyond anything that
balancing entails.

In cases involving negative rights, balancing is ruled out more frequently, even when the greater good we would produce by transgressing
one person's negative right involves minimizing violations of comparable
rights in others (each of whom stands to lose as much). For example, we
may not kill one person to harvest his organs in order to save ten people
from death. What is being relied on here to reinforce the moral significance of the separateness of persons and rule out balancing, I believe, is
a claim on the part of a person to what would be taken from him (e.g., his
property or his liberty) that is much stronger than anyone else's claim to
it. By contrast, in cases where I must choose when to aid, each party may
have the same (or no) claim on my assistance.[11]

However, another suggestion that has been made to explain the cases
involving negative rights reminds us of yet another way in which the
separateness of persons has been thought to play a role in ethics. Some
have said that *my* transgressing a right in order to prevent others from
doing so produces the worse state of affairs from my perspective. The
emphasis in this account seems to shift from the significance of the separateness of the potential victim and the potential beneficiaries to the
significance of the separateness of a particular agent from other agents.
This suggests that if another agent were to transgress someone's negative
right for the sake of minimizing comparable rights violations, I would
have no reason to stop him. For example, suppose B will violate A's right
not to have his arm amputated in order to save many others from having
their arms amputated. Do I have a reason (even if not a duty) to put aside
my activities to stop the violation of A's right, rather than let it be the

---

[11] I am here omitting consideration of fine points that make it permissible to take something that someone has a claim to if we do it in one way (e.g., redirecting a threat to him)
but not if we do it in another way. For more on this, see my *Morality, Mortality*, vol. 2
(Oxford: Oxford University Press, 1996).

cause of the greater good? I think I do.[12] Also, if it were most important that *I* not be involved in violating a negative right, should I minimize the number of such acts that I commit? May I kill one person now to stop a threat I started yesterday that will soon kill five other people, making me the killer of five people? I think not. These cases suggest that it is a mistake to interpret the constraint on transgressing one person's right as expressing an agent's concern with his own agency.

So far, I have been characterizing some ways in which the separateness of persons is taken account of in certain moral theories. We can summarize these ways as follows: (1) not substituting one person for another, period; (2) not substituting one person for another unless there is an equal loss and/or gain to be sustained by each; (3) not substituting one person for another when the person has a claim to control what makes him separate; (4) an agent not substituting for other agents.

C. Substitutability and ways of mattering morally

Now let us consider creatures who have a good but are not rights-bearers, and also entities of value in their own right but not ones for whose sake we can act. Let us see whether there is any principle analogous to the separateness of persons that can be applied when dealing with such entities. Would it be permissible to destroy one non-rights-bearing animal in order to prevent the destruction of others? Arguably, yes. (Notice that the sacrificeability of one animal for others is consistent with the fact that it is the sort of being that has a life of its own and could have been benefited if we had not harmed it.) Does this further imply that we may be utilitarians and simple maximizers with respect to animals? No, because it may still be wrong to aggregate small losses to many animals against a big loss to one animal at least when the former would not be as badly off (if not helped) as the latter. It might also be wrong to sacrifice a higher animal (for example, one with a greater degree of intellectual and interactive capacities) to save a greater number of lower ones. (In these respects, Robert Nozick seems to have been wrong in suggesting deontology for people and utilitarianism for animals.)[13]

Would it be permissible to destroy one embryo to save others from being destroyed, at least when the latter will develop into people? I believe so. Would it be permissible to destroy one great artwork to prevent several other comparable artworks from being destroyed? I believe so. Would it be permissible to destroy one human embryo to allow many

---

[12] And this is not because I would otherwise be intending the act by another's hand, for I need not be intending it. For example, I may be a very busy person, and making some effort so that transgressions do not occur is an imposition I would like to avoid, yet I have a reason to make the effort.

[13] See Robert Nozick, *Anarchy, State, and Utopia* (New York: Basic Books, 1974), p. 40.

monkey embryos to develop? I believe so.[14] Would it be permissible to destroy one great art work for the sake of several less significant ones? Interestingly, this seems truly misguided.

This broad sacrificeability of one entity for the sake of others is in sharp contrast with the way it is permissible to treat a self-governing being. Yet it is also in contrast to the way we should treat some non-rights-bearing entities. For such sacrificeability is not true of entities whose value is purely symbolic, like flags, nor for holy entities. These things have no rights, and no good for whose sake we act, yet there are reasons not to destroy one for the sake of others that are analogous to reasons that apply to persons. For example, it may sometimes make no sense for it to be permissible to burn one flag to prevent many other flags from being burnt impermissibly. This is the case if it is their status as inviolable that we are concerned with in trying to save the many. For the *permissibility* of burning one to save others denies that very inviolability. If this is true of purely symbolic entities, but not of embryos, this suggests that the value of the embryo does *not* reside merely in its role as a symbol of human life. An embryo may serve merely as a symbol only when we are *not* interested in its future development. Hence, we may think that it makes sense to destroy one embryo for the sake of the *future development* of other embryos, but not for the sake of their survival as mere symbols of life in a freezer.

In Section II, I have considered different types of entities falling into increasingly narrow categories: those that count in their own right, those that have moral status, and those that can have claims against us. I have argued that the moral nonsubstitutability of the entities that can have claims against us is stronger than the nonsubstitutability of those that merely count in their own right or that merely have moral status. This is true even though those in the latter class can have separate points of view and interests of their own. In the next section, I attempt to apply these conclusions about nonsubstitutability to the issue of reproductive cloning.

III. Reproductive Cloning

"Your clone, Melford, has come of work age. You must leave now."

New Yorker cartoon, February 9, 2004

One sheep to another: "Sometimes I worry that I'm a wolf dressed as me."

New Yorker cartoon, February 2, 2004

---

[14] The argument for this is that even an embryo with the potential to be a person does not have the moral status of a person. Suppose for some reason it was good to produce monkeys but not necessary to produce another person, and the only way to produce monkeys was to sacrifice a human embryo. I think its lack of great moral importance makes the sacrifice of the embryo for a good purpose permissible.

There are many objections that people raise to reproductive cloning. My primary concern in this context is with the sense that it might be "a threat to one's personal identity" and to the nonsubstitutability of persons that I have discussed above. Let us deal with the substitutability issue first.[15]

As we have seen, nonsubstitutability in a strong sense—for example, not violating a strong negative right even to minimize the violation of comparable rights in others—pertains for the most part to the sorts of individuals to whom one can owe things: self-conscious, rational beings. Such nonsubstitutability seems connected to what we call the dignity of persons. Hence, some may think that cloning is incompatible with the dignity of persons because it would reduce nonsubstitutability. How could being a person who exists as a result of cloning deprive one of being entitled to such regard? Imagine you are under a massive delusion about the way in which you were actually produced. Everything about you remains as you are now, except that you are not the product, as you believed, of sexual reproduction, but of mono-parental cloning. Would you think that your rights had changed dramatically? I do not think you would, and I think you would be right not to. The question of the historical course of events that leads to the existence of a certain sort of being can, for the most part, be distinguished from the value of the entity that is produced and what gives it value.[16] And that is one of the most important things to remember in this area.[17]

Is a person, if he is genetically identical to someone else (as a result of cloning or otherwise), replaceable by that second person? Sometimes people want to say that a genetic clone is not going to have the same phenotype as you do, and thus is neither going to be you, nor be a replacement for you, on this account.[18] But we all know that, strictly speaking, the clone will not be you: "numerical nonidentity" dictates that there are two different beings; we do not need to point to difference in phenotype to know that a clone is not you. Indeed, I think that in arguing for nonsubstitutability, it is a mistake to focus on the fact that genotype alone

[15] Some material in this section is drawn from my essay "Cloning and Harm to Offspring," *New York University Journal of Legislation and Public Policy* 4, no. 1 (2000).

[16] But this is not always the case, since there are interesting philosophical cases in which origins do matter to the value of an entity. For example, that a set of marks on paper is an expression of the artist's view of nature, rather than produced by the random acts of a monkey, gives it value.

[17] I have criticized Ronald Dworkin for inordinately emphasizing origins in his account of value. See Frances M. Kamm, "Abortion and the Value of Life: A Discussion of Life's Dominion," *Columbia Law Review* 95 (1995): 160, 164–65, reviewing Ronald Dworkin, *Life's Dominion: An Argument about Abortion, Euthanasia, and Individual Freedom.*

[18] See Lee M. Silver, Comments at the *New York University Journal of Legislation and Public Policy* symposium "Legislating Morality: The Debate over Human Cloning," November 19, 1999, transcript on file with the *New York University Journal of Legislation and Public Policy.* One's genotype is one's genetic material. One's phenotype is one's characteristics due to both genotype and environmental factors.

does not lead to the same phenotype. The core point is that, even if there were a clone who was phenotypically identical to me—identical genotypically and phenotypically, but numerically nonidentical—that would not mean that I would be replaceable by it. *This is because the clone still would not be me.* It is tempting to say that it is because I would not be replaceable to myself (that is, from my own perspective). If this suggests that someone might not be willing to replace herself with another, that is not necessarily true.[19] The point is that I cannot replace myself with another and still continue being me. That is one crucial ethical point. The other crucial point is that I am still the type of creature who has a claim to what would be taken from me (life, job), and thus it should not be taken from me without my consent.

Suppose someone told me: "If we kill you, or fire you, we will also replace you with a being that is genetically and phenotypically identical to you, but, of course, numerically distinct." That would not in any significant way compensate *me* for my loss of life or job, given that I don't care about the clone. Now, this raises the question that philosophers often discuss: What is it that we ought to be concerned about in our survival? Is it just a type of gene, a phenotype, or the particular individual? It seems to many people that it is more the particular individual's survival than their type, either genetic or phenotypic, that is crucial. Now, suppose you were replaceable *to* everybody else; that is, suppose they do not care about you except for your genotype and your phenotype; they do not care about you as a particular person. This is not usually true, but suppose it were. It would still be the case that your right to life and to respect would be as strong as any other person's, given that you are the sort of creature who has a claim to his life and does not waive it. The crucial foundation for the idea of respect for the person or the right to life would not be changed by cloning, even if we allow for identity of phenotype.

In literature, the idea of one's double (as in Dostoyevsky's *The Double*)[20] is threatening, only in part because others take him to be entitled to what one would otherwise be entitled to. In Dostoyevsky's novel, the double is also threatening because the protagonist seems to lose his sense of himself as himself, actively confusing himself with the other. This is the problem of the sheep in the *New Yorker* cartoon who thinks he might be the other

---

[19] I owe this point to David Copp. He reminded me that a very altruistic person could be indifferent between his own survival and the survival of another. Also, someone who held an inaccurate metaphysics might not recognize the difference between himself and another.

[20] In this novel, Mr. G, a clerk, is rejected by all who formerly befriended him. It seems that either he has done something extremely objectionable to offend everyone, or he is not recognized by those whom he visits. As he wanders along the streets, trying to decide why he is being so badly treated, he encounters a man who looks very like himself and, in fact, calls himself by the same name and was born in the same village. Mr. G welcomes the new Mr. G into his life, sharing everything, including a position at his workplace. The newcomer begins to act outrageously, with the consequences being assigned to the first Mr. G. Life becomes unbearable for the first Mr. G, and eventually, he is tricked into entering a carriage bound for the insane asylum.

(the wolf dressed up to look like him). But we laugh at the joke and think the person who identifies with his double is literally insane, because there is no way for a being with a subjective point of view to correctly think such things. Hence, there is no way that a still rational being would identify his clone as himself.

In sum, it should be emphasized that an argument based on the fact that cloning will not result in the same phenotype, though well-intentioned and probably correct, is misplaced. Respect for persons entailing strong nonsubstitutability—even if all had the same phenotype and genotype— would be based on their each being self-conscious, being capable of responding to reasons, and having a claim to their individual lives greater than anyone else has.

Notice that I have so far been arguing against the view that cloning is inconsistent with the dignity of the person in the sense that this is inter- preted to meant that one could not be a person with such dignity if one had been cloned or if one had a clone in existence. But the view might be interpreted differently: Given that the clone will be a person with dignity, it is wrong to bring such a being into existence by cloning. But why should this be true? If cloning of persons were the natural form of repro- duction, would there be a prima facie moral obligation to develop sexual reproduction instead, out of concern for the dignity of persons? And if not, why is there something inherently wrong with introducing repro- ductive cloning? Would there be such a prima facie obligation if clones were phenotypically the same? Why is it an insult to one's dignity that others share the same phenotype?

I have tried to argue that the worth and strong nonsubstitutability of persons are not incompatible with reproductive cloning, either in the sense that cloning would rob persons of dignity or that it would insult the dignity that they have. I now want to consider the view that cloning is a threat to human identity and personal identification in a less than strict sense. My comments apply equally to the cases of human clones that already exist—genetically identical twins—except that I will sometimes imagine (for argument's sake) that twins have an identical phenotype as well as genotype.

There is a sense of "personal identity" that is commonly used by psy- chologists, doctors, and biologists. It is what I shall call a "holistic sense" of personal identity closely related to one's phenotype—the sense in which I am a philosopher, someone who is interested in art, or someone who makes jokes. All of this is part of my holistic identity, for someone would not be me in the holistic sense if she were not interested in philosophy or art or making jokes.

Consider a way of presenting the views of those who emphasize the importance of differences in the parts of the actual phenotype with which they say we identify ourselves holistically. Figure 1 represents four logical possibilities. (I do not mean to imply that all are physically possible.) In

	same holistic phenotype	different holistic phenotypes
same genotype	A	B
different genotypes	C	D

FIGURE 1. Logically possible genotype/phenotype relations.

condition A, we all have the same genotype and the same holistic phenotype. In condition B, we have the same genotype and different holistic phenotypes. In condition C, we have different genotypes and the same holistic phenotype. In condition D, we have different genotypes and different holistic phenotypes.

To those who think that what is worrisome about reproductive cloning is only identical holistic phenotypes, condition A (where, let us assume, there is cloning) is as worrisome as condition C (where there is no cloning), and conditions B and D are equally unworrisome per se. Suppose that (contrary to fact) the only way we could ensure holistic phenotypic nonidentity were by ensuring genetic identity. Then (if genetic identity did not occur naturally) cloning would be the preferred mode of reproduction, if all we were obliged to be concerned about was holistic identity differentiation. This view seems reinforced by entertaining the following thought experiment: Suppose that we have all been misled, and all our genetic makeups are already, in fact, naturally identical. If our phenotypic differences remain as they are, we would not worry about losing a holistic sense of identity differentiation.

This psychosocial, holistic notion of personal identity is not the philosopher's notion of personal identity, however. The philosopher's notion of personal identity concerns those properties that are essential to your nature, such that if we changed them, you would no longer exist in a strict sense.[21] It is a fact or a datum or a premise in most philosophical arguments that there are many things about you that could be very important facts about you (your holistic identity) and yet they could have been different and you would have continued to exist. For example, if you suddenly lost twenty points of your IQ, a holder of the holistic notion might say the person you had changed into was no longer you, but a philosopher could say that it was still you in a reduced state and that the decrease in your IQ helped explain why *you* were much worse off than *you* had been.

Some philosophers claim that if the same sperm and egg from which you arose had been placed in a different environment, or had been held

---

[21] See Harold W. Noonan, *Personal Identity* (London: Routledge, 1989), 2–3; and Sydney Shoemaker and Richard Swinburne, *Personal Identity* (Oxford: Blackwell, 1984), 4–5.

up in some laboratory and started dividing at a later point in time, it would still have resulted in you.[22] Just as most phenotypic properties are not essential properties, neither are many historical properties, like the date of your birth or the date of your death. These properties could change, and the new ones would still be true of *you*. Some genetic properties are similarly nonessential. Now, the question is: What are the essential properties? There is much debate over this, and I have no answers.

As I have already noted, many people who say that a clone will *not* be you point to the expected phenotypic difference, and they probably do this because they think that holistic phenotypic differentiation among people is very important, even though we would not literally fear we were someone else or fear that moral nonsubstitutability would disappear if there were no such differentiation. The fact that, in the philosopher's sense, it could have been *you* with a different holistic phenotype may make the response to the "threat of cloning" that emphasizes continuation of phenotypic differences seem weaker. For when I consider individuals who are holistically phenotypically different from me but genetically identical, I may think that any one of those individuals is an example of what I might have been like while (to be redundant) still being me. The idea is that, though we are holistically phenotypically different, I could have had your holistic phenotype, and thus it is not holistic phenotypes but something else that is crucial to who I am. (Of course, even if we have the same genotype and could have shared holistic phenotypes, I would not *be* the other person, since we are numerically distinct and *in fact* do not share the same holistic phenotype.)

In addition, consider that there is a tension between the importance of genetic connection with offspring, and the idea that holistic phenotype, and not genotype, determines who we really are. Suppose someone offers me a genetically unrelated child who is phenotypically very similar to me, including all the same interests and values that I have. Many people think that I still would not have satisfied a supposed intense desire for genetic connection. If genetic connection is so important, this suggests that people think their genes *are* very important to who they are. It is the latter thought that leads people to think that they should project their genes into the future. Thus, the idea that passing on his genes is so important to a person is at war with the idea that phenotypic difference is enough to distinguish individuals from one another (in a nonphilosophical sense) and that phenotypic similarity is enough to relate them to one another.[23]

---

[22] See Thomas Nagel, "Death," in Nagel, *Mortal Questions* (Cambridge: Cambridge University Press, 1979), 1, 8.

[23] I am aware that the underlying drive to have one's genes pass on may only give rise to a conscious *desire to reproduce,* not a conscious desire to pass on one's genes. One could have the first desire before one knows anything about genes. Once one is genetically literate, however, a new desire with passing on one's genes as its object may arise.

Perhaps considerations such as these—only partially grasped, not as a full-fledged philosophical theory of identity—may underlie some people's sense that it is undesirable to have beings who share their genotype, making condition B in Figure 1 worse than condition D. Here the presupposition is that it is a genotype, or at least part of it, that is essential to me. (Of course, it cannot be the only thing essential to me, since, by hypothesis, someone else has it too.) This leaves it open that phenotypic nondifferentiation would be too high a price to pay if it alone were compatible with genetic diversity, and thus condition A in Figure 1 is the worst outcome. Now, I do not believe that thinking along these lines would provide a decisive argument against cloning, because one's genetically identical natural twin now shares one's genotype as well, and do we think there is a strong reason to prevent natural identical twinning? But perhaps thinking along these lines may provide one with a reason to prefer a world in which there is no natural twinning and a reason not to seek such twins, even with phenotypic diversity.

Twins as we know them now are synchronic (that is, they come into being simultaneously). Clones might come into being diachronically (for example, a bit later than the original or after the original has ceased to exist). It might be thought that the very thing that makes one uncomfortable with even a phenotypically different clone existing synchronically with oneself could be desirable if the clone existed diachronically after one ceased to exist. For if we cannot be immortal, having a successor who is a clone could bring us as close as possible to immortality. (According to at least one philosophical theory of personal identity, a successor to you that had certain very tight causal relations to you, might actually be you.)[24]

This, however, seems to be the problem. Synchronic cloning is in one way less threatening because it seems clearer that an original and a clone are separate individuals when they both exist. When the original has passed away, however, the possibility that someone else will be identified as the original may seem greater. Suppose we think such identification of a closest successor with the original is a mistake (that is, we do not accept the metaphysical theory according to which such identification is correct). Then, if identification takes place, we shall be disturbed by the sense that acts and accomplishments that are someone else's may be added to the account of the original, making "his life" beyond his control. So long as I am a token of a type, I am definitely to be distinguished from other such

---

[24] See Robert Nozick, *Philosophical Explanations* (Cambridge, MA: Harvard University Press, 1981), 34–35. Having a successor is different from merely having offspring in ordinary reproduction. For example, the latter do not usually begin life just as the parent is leaving it. And offspring that fuse genetic material (and perhaps phenotypic properties) of emotionally bonded people may be the ideal in ordinary reproduction. Producing such a "chimera" of two people could even be preferred to two emotionally bonded people having a biological role in helping to produce the clones of each one.

tokens. If I cease to be a token of this type (because I cease to be), the fact that an instance of the type could supersede me becomes a cause of concern.

IV. WHEN IDENTITY MIGHT NOT MATTER MORALLY

A. The embryo of a future person

I have argued that a cloned person (just like a noncloned person) could not permissibly be harmed in order to minimize comparable harms to other persons, cloned or uncloned. Now I want to consider whether an embryo that *will in fact* develop into a person is also protected against less-than-lethal interventions that will negatively affect the future person and that are undertaken for the sake of benefiting other future persons by affecting other embryos from which they will develop.

Previously, I have argued against what I shall call the View:[25] We have as strong a duty not to do things to an embryo that will result in harm (or fail to prevent harm) to the person that the embryo will definitely develop into as we have not to harm (or fail to prevent harm to) that person when he is already in existence. Notice that the View is compatible with thinking that a pregnant woman is not obligated to do (or refrain from doing) certain things that a woman would have to do (or refrain from doing) for an offspring outside her body. This is because more of an imposition on her may be involved if she must do these things when the embryo is in her body than when it is outside, and the duty she has may not license such an imposition.

One premise in an argument (call it the Argument) for the View[26] that I have considered elsewhere is that, if we have duties to an embryo while it is still only an embryo, it is because of the person it will develop into. Those who make the Argument think that this premise implies the view that duties that exist while there is only an embryo should be as strong and of the same general type as duties that we have to the person once he has developed (at least if we are certain that the embryo will develop into a person and that what we do to it as an embryo will affect the person in the same way).

Recently, philosopher Elizabeth Harman has characterized the Argument as follows (speaking of early fetuses, whom she claims have no moral status but are capable of being harmed):

---

[25] See F. M. Kamm, *Creation and Abortion* (New York: Oxford University Press, 1992); Kamm, "Cloning and Harm to Offspring," *Legislation and Public Policy* 4 (2000–2001): 65–76; and Kamm, "Genes, Justice, and Obligations to Future People," *Social Philosophy and Policy* 19, no. 2 (2002): 360–88.

[26] Such an argument is made in Allen Buchanan, Dan W. Brock, Norman Daniels, and Daniel Wikler, *From Chance to Choice: Genetics and Justice* (New York: Cambridge University Press, 2000).

According to the existing account, we are prohibited from harming those early fetuses that will be carried to term not because of anything constitutive of the harming itself. It is not that these things, these early fetuses, are the kind of things we should not harm. It is merely that there is a bad further consequence of harming these fetuses: in the future, a baby is born who suffers from fetal alcohol syndrome or some other bad effect of the earlier harming. This bad account may fail to address the worry expressed by those who challenge the liberal view [on abortion]. The worry may not simply be that the liberal view is incompatible with prohibitions on harming early fetuses. Rather, it may be that the liberal view is incompatible with its being the case that some early fetuses are the kind of things [we are] prohibited from harming. The worry is that the liberal view cannot appeal to the nature and status of these early fetuses themselves in explaining why we are prohibited from harming them.[27]

In place of the Argument, Harman offers what she calls the Actual Future Principle: "An early fetus that will become a person has some moral status. An early fetus that will die while it is still an early fetus has no moral status."[28] (I assume Harman would apply the principle to embryos, too.) Notice that Harman's principle takes the view that the fetus does not merely give rise to a person. Harman thinks that it becomes a person in the sense that there is one human being from conception through personhood and the fetus that will become a person is that human being's earliest stage. Notice also that, as stated, the Actual Future Principle does not fully support the View. This is because it does not claim that the fetus's moral status is the same as the status of the person it will become and therefore that we have as strong a duty not to do things to an embryo that will result in harm to the person as we have not to harm the person when she is already in existence. Thus, Harman's principle may not strictly imply that the duty not to do things to the fetus that will harm (or not prevent harm to) the person it will become is as strong as the comparable duty to the person when she already exists. Nevertheless, it is not clear why Harman should not hold the View, for she also says: "The Actual Future Principle recognizes the moral status of early fetuses that will become persons; it is precisely these early fetuses in which *persons can be said to be already present.*"[29] If a person is already present, then the fetus's moral status should be the same as the status of the person.

A problem that arises for the Actual Future Principle that does not arise for the Argument is that the former implies (when combined with Harman's

---

[27] Elizabeth Harman, "Creation Ethics: The Moral Status of Early Fetuses and the Ethics of Abortion," *Philosophy and Public Affairs* 28, no. 4 (1999): 310-24, p. 311.

[28] Ibid.

[29] Ibid., 312 n. 3.

view that it is possible to harm early fetuses, and presumably embryos) that we may not do things to a fetus that harm it, even when the harm is short-lived and will not affect the person whom the fetus will definitely become. This is because we have a prima facie duty not to harm a person, even when the harm is short-lived and will not go on to affect the person in the future. I think (a) it is either not true that it is impermissible to cause a short-lived harm, or (b) if it is impermissible to cause such a short-lived harm (e.g., pain), this will be true even if the embryo/fetus will not develop into a person.

I shall put this issue aside, for I am interested to show that the View is wrong and that if the Actual Future Principle implies the View, it too is wrong. Hence, either the Actual Future Principle does not imply the View and we need to know why it does not, or, I will argue, the principle is wrong. With respect to the Argument, I claim only to show (as I have tried to do elsewhere) that while its first premise may be true, it does not imply the View. That is, we can agree that any duties we have to treat a fetus in a certain way exist only because of the person it will develop into, but this does not imply the View.

Here is an example which, I believe, shows that it is permissible to affect a future person by doing something to the fetus (or to the embryo) from which he develops, though it is not permissible to affect the person in the same way by doing something to him once he exists. Suppose a woman has given a fetus genes that will result in a person with an IQ of 160. She decides this is too smart, not for the good of the person who has the high IQ, but for the good of the family. As a result, she takes a drug during early pregnancy to reduce the future person's IQ to 140.[30] This is a case of causing a person to be worse off than he would otherwise have been (I shall assume). I believe this is permissible (for reasons to be given below). But it would not be permissible, I believe, for the woman to give her child, once it exists, a pill that reduces its IQ from 160 to 140 or alters its genes so that the child will have an IQ of 140 rather than 160 in the future. What is the difference between (1) affecting the person by affecting the fetus and (2) directly affecting the person himself? A fetus is not the sort of being that is entitled to keep a characteristic that it has, such as a genetic makeup that will generate a 160 IQ. This is because it is not the sort of being that can be the bearer of rights (to retain anything). It lacks moral status (as defined in Section II) and lacks additional properties that would make it a rights-bearer, in part, because it is not sentient or conscious. In addition, the person who will develop from the fetus will not fall below an acceptable level of intelligence if he has only a 140 IQ, so he (as a person) is not owed a 160 IQ by his parent. (An IQ of 140 is already far above the minimal standard that, it might be argued, is owed to the

---

[30] I first discussed this case in my book *Creation and Abortion* (Oxford: Oxford University Press, 1992).

people we create. I will here merely assume and not argue for this claim, that persons do owe their offspring certain things.)[31] These two facts are crucial to the permissibility of taking back from the fetus IQ points that the parent gave it. But since a child is already a person (I assume), it is entitled to keep a beneficial characteristic it has, even if doing so raises the child far beyond the standard it is owed. Hence, I believe it is impermissible to give the IQ-reducing pill to the child, even if doing so would not cause his IQ to fall below the minimum owed to one's child.[32] By contrast, suppose we owe a good chance of an IQ of at least 100 to people we create. In this case, doing something easily avoidable in early pregnancy to a fetus that results in a person who develops with an IQ below 100 may well be as impermissible as doing to the later child something that lowers its IQ to below 100.

Because the fetus is not yet a person (or does not yet have other properties that make it an entity that is entitled to keep what is given to it)—even though it will become a person—the act of taking away characteristics the fetus has (which will impact on the person that will be) is no different from not giving it those characteristics to begin with. And one would have a right not to give a future person that one created genes sufficient for a 160 IQ. Analogously, if a parent puts money into a bank account that will belong to someone when he exists as an adult, the fact that he will exist as an adult, by itself, does not imply that it is impermissible for the parent to take back the money before the person reaches the age at which he can claim his bank account. (This is true even if the parent has not earned her own money, but has inherited it from others as people inherit their genes.)

Suppose now that the fetus is not in the woman's body, dependent on her services in carrying it. Instead, it is growing in a mechanical gestation device. Yet imagine that the world is such that if the woman engages in an activity such as exercising (no matter where), this has the effect of altering the fetus so that the person who develops will have an IQ of 140 rather than 160. Would it be permissible for her to exercise? First, consider the variant in which she has given the fetus its intelligence genes. Here I think it is permissible for her to do what causes the drop in IQ, since she is taking back what she has given to an entity not yet entitled to retain this thing. However, it would be prima facie impermissible for her to engage in the same activity when it would affect a child of hers who is in possession of genetic material that will bring about the higher IQ, material he is entitled not to be deprived of. Now consider the variant in which it is the father who gave the fetus the intelligence genes. It is true that the fetus is not entitled to keep these genes, and on the basis of his donation, the father may remove them, but that does not mean that just anyone may

---

[31] For discussion of this issue, see my *Creation and Abortion*.
[32] I first presented this argument in *Creation and Abortion*.

take an action that would remove them (or alter their effects on the child's intelligence). Since the woman in this case has neither given the relevant genes nor is contributing any efforts necessary for the fruition of the genes, I think that she may not do those things that lead to a drop in IQ to 140. (Nor may any other entity, such as a government, without the father's permission, do things to lower the IQ to 140, other things being equal.)

What about the permissibility of a parent not rendering assistance to a fetus to prevent a natural change that will lead the person who develops from the fetus to have a 140 IQ rather than a 160 IQ? If the change would occur in the fetus before it is entitled to keep the traits, I believe that one need not make as great an effort to stop the reduction in IQ as one should make once one is the parent of the child who has the 160 IQ or the genetic traits that will lead to the 160 IQ. A parent's duty to help a child keep a beneficial trait that the child already has can be stronger than a parent's duty to see to it that her offspring comes to have such a trait by helping the embryo retain the genetic material.[33]

But now consider an in-between case.[34] Suppose the parent is not physically able to remove the genetic material at the fetus stage, and (as I have argued) not permitted to take an action that would remove IQ points from the child-person. May she give to the fetus a drug that will have a delayed reaction in childhood (like a slow bomb), eliminating the child's genetic material that would lead it eventually to have a 160 IQ rather than a 140 IQ? I do not believe this is permissible. I also do not believe that anything I have said implies that it is permissible. For it involves doing something at time t_1 that will remove something at t_2 when there is a person to whom that item belongs. (That is, the person will actually suffer a loss, rather than merely living with the effect of an earlier loss.)

Recall the View as I set it out at the beginning of this section: We have as strong a duty not to do things to an embryo that will result in harm (or fail to prevent harm) to the person that the embryo will definitely develop into as we have not to harm (or fail to prevent harm to) that person when

---

[33] Unlike the duty not to take away from (what is already) a person those things she is entitled to, the duty to provide aid does not rely so strongly on the presence of the person. For this reason, one may sense less of a difference in the fetus and child variants of cases when aiding is in question. Note that nothing I have said implies that it is better for someone acting in the interests of a future person to (1) cause a large loss to the future person by acting at his early fetus stage rather than (2) cause a small loss to that person through an action one takes when he exists. One argument for this is that if I know that I must or will do one or the other, it is ex ante in the future person's interest to waive his right against my doing (2) so that I do not do (1). A second argument is based on what I call the "principle of secondary permissibility." Very roughly, it implies that if I will permissibly cause someone a harm in one way, it may become permissible to cause a lesser harm in a way that would otherwise be impermissible. (For more on this principle, see my *Morality, Mortality*, vol. 2 [New York: Oxford University Press, 1996], and my essay "Failures of Just War Theory," *Ethics* 114, no. 4 [2004]: 650–92.) Hence, I think I should, in this case, do (2) rather than (1). I thank Richard Arneson for the question to which this is a response.

[34] I owe this case to Arthur Applbaum.

he is already in existence. Suppose that my arguments have shown that the View is incorrect. If the View is implied by the Actual Future Principle, then the latter is incorrect.

Now, imagine again that a mother has given a fetus genetic material that would give the person it will develop into a 160 IQ. Imagine further that if the mother takes from the fetus some genetic material, this makes the fetus develop into a person with a 140 IQ instead, and the mother can then transfer the material into two other fetuses, thereby raising their IQs from 130 to 140 each. What I have said above, I think, implies that doing this would be permissible. The mother would be morally free to equalize beneficial traits among future persons by affecting their embryos, even though she thereby makes some person worse off than he would otherwise be. However, I do not think it would be permissible for her to (safely) take from a child (already a person) some characteristic that will or does give him a 160 IQ, leaving him with a 140 IQ, so that she can transfer the material into two other children, raising their IQs from 130 to 140 each.

When modifying the genome of an embryo is contemplated, it is usually in a context where we can improve the life of the person who will develop from the embryo. I have raised the possibility that it might be permissible, for good reason, to alter an embryo in a way that will cause the person who develops to be worse off than he might otherwise be. It might be noted that in the real world there would be no need to take something from one embryo in order to place it in another embryo, as a means of improving the latter, as was true in my hypothetical case. And while making one person worse off without thereby improving others could increase equality between people, this sort of "leveling down" to achieve equality is often taken to be a counterexample to the value of achieving equality. However, taking something away from one embryo without transferring anything to others could still improve the lives of persons who will develop from the other embryos. For example, it might make it more likely that they will win their share of competitions with the other person. Then there could be an increase in their absolute well-being and the charge of "leveling down" would be defeated.

B. Future generations and the Non-Identity Problem

These results bear in an important way on our responsibilities to future generations. Take the imaginary case in which we know that certain particular people will definitely exist in a hundred years. Suppose we engage in activities today that will affect the environment in such a way that the air quality will not be as good in one hundred years, though it will still be above the level that we owe to future generations. Suppose, further, that there is no person in existence yet whose environment that future environment is. I believe we may engage in such activities. But if we were (somehow) transported one hundred years hence, it could well be impermissible to engage in the same activities that reduce to the same degree the air quality that the persons then living are already enjoying. In fact, it is not necessary that these people (or the children in my previous cases) actually already be in possession of the better environment (or the more advantageous trait, whether it is the higher IQ or the genetic trait that will lead to it). Given that they are already persons, if their *prospects* as persons are for acquiring such a superior environment (or advantageous trait), they should not be deprived of these prospects by an event that occurs once they are persons.[35] This means that we are permitted to act in ways that reduce the superior air quality (but not below an acceptable level) before future persons who will be affected by this exist. By contrast, we may not be permitted to have the same effect on the environment somewhat delayed, so that it occurs when the future persons already exist and impacts an environment they can claim as theirs. If we wish to do right by future generations, therefore, it will be very important to know what level of environmental quality they are owed and, surprisingly, when the alteration to the environment will occur relative to the existence of the persons affected by such an alteration. We cannot merely say that there is a duty not to make any future environment worse than it would otherwise be without our action.

Finally, let me consider the possible bearing of these issues on what is known as "the Non-Identity Problem." Derek Parfit famously argued that sometimes, at least, it seems not to matter morally whether we are affecting the same (identical) person for the worse or just making someone worse off than some separate (nonidentical) person would have been.[36] Moral principles that tell us not to make persons worse off than they would have been, or to make persons better off than they would have been, are called "person-affecting principles." The moral insignificance of nonidentity is a problem for those who think that all moral principles are person-affecting. Moral principles that tell us not to make there be people who are worse off than other people would have been (or to make persons who are better off than other persons would have been) are called "non-person-affecting principles." This is not because there are no effects on persons in the latter cases, but rather because no person is better off than *he* would otherwise have been, given that the better-off person is someone else. So, for example, suppose that if we behave in a certain way now, we will affect the environment so that future people who would otherwise have existed anyway are worse off than they might have been.

---

[35] It might be said that if we act now so as to worsen the environment in a delayed manner, the future persons could not ever be in possession of the prospects for a better environment. But what I have in mind are two different causal routes: one route leads to the prospects and the other would lead to their being undone; and the event of their being undone would occur during the lifetimes of the future persons.

[36] See Derek Parfit, *Reasons and Persons* (New York: Oxford University Press, 1985).

In this case, we affect people for the worse. Alternatively, suppose that if we behave in a certain way now, we will affect the world so that different people will exist in the future than would otherwise have existed, and they will live worse lives than those other people would have lived, due to changes our behavior also makes to the environment. In this case, we do not affect anyone so that he is worse off now than *he* would have been. Parfit claims that, morally speaking, it does not matter whether we affect existing persons for the worse or create worse-off persons.

Let us assume that the worse life in these examples is still a life worth living, and also that it is a life that is good enough to meet the standards that a responsible parent could be held to in creating new people. Then we cannot argue that people are entitled not to have the worse life because they are entitled not to be in certain states, whether by our making them worse off than they would have otherwise been or by our doing something that leads to the existence of worse-off people (than would have otherwise existed). That is, we cannot argue that person-affecting principles do not have special weight because people simply have a right not to be in the worse state. It is just the comparative worseness of one set of people that speaks against the act that produces them, just as it is the comparative worseness of the way in which a given person's life will go that speaks against acting in a way that makes him worse off.

How might what I have said against the View bear on the Non-Identity Problem? I have argued that sometimes *the way in which* we affect someone for the worse can make a moral difference, not just the fact *that* we affect him for the worse. If we affect him by doing something to him or to some trait or resource he is entitled to (only because he has it and it is or will be beneficial to him), this can have greater moral significance than if we affect him similarly by doing something to a trait or resource he is not yet entitled to because he does not yet exist as a being who can have entitlements. Standard cases in which we affect people for the worse are like the former. This leaves it open that *person-affecting* cases of the latter sort are not morally more significant than *non-person-affecting* cases, while cases of the former sort are more significant. Choosing to perform easily avoidable acts that lead to a given offspring having fewer resources may be no worse than choosing to perform easily avoidable acts that lead to creating a worse-off person rather than a different better-off person. Yet both sorts of acts may be less morally problematic than performing an act that will take from someone what he is entitled to keep (or not provide him with help he is entitled to get), resulting in his having fewer resources. If the person-affecting cases that are used to illustrate the Non-Identity Problem do not involve entitlement based on personal possession, then they do not compare the stronger form of person-affecting principles with non-person-affecting principles. This means that the argument for the moral equivalence of non-person-affecting and person-affecting actions is crucially incomplete.

V. Conclusion

In Section II of this essay, I argued that even those entities that, in their own right and for their own sake, give us reason not to destroy them (and to help them) are sometimes substitutable for the good of other entities. In so arguing, I considered the idea of being valuable as an end in virtue of intrinsic and extrinsic properties. I also concluded that entities that have claims to things and against others are especially nonsubstitutable. In Section III, I argued that reproductive cloning poses no threat to the nonsubstitutability of these entities (and in this sense, to the dignity of persons). I also considered the relation between cloning and (what I called) holistic identity, and between the latter and genetic identity. In Section IV, I tried to distinguish between (1) cases where identity over time and so-called person-affecting acts have greater moral significance than non-identity over time and non-person-affecting acts and (2) cases where they do not have greater moral significance. I tried to apply my results to cases involving embryos, future generations, and to the so-called Non-Identity Problem.

Philosophy and Public Policy, Kennedy School of Government;
Philosophy, Faculty of Arts and Sciences, Harvard University

THE IDENTITY OF IDENTITY: MORAL AND LEGAL ASPECTS OF TECHNOLOGICAL SELF-TRANSFORMATION

By Michael H. Shapiro

I. A Sketch of the Project

Changes in the world, arranged by us or not, sometimes drive us to reexamine the conceptual structures we use to describe and evaluate that world. In this essay, I review the ideas of personal identity, and certain related abstractions, that might be affected by technological developments in the life sciences. In particular, I consider whether the concept of identity might require revision under the impact of certain biotechnological developments—those that increasingly enable relatively precise modifications of the genetic development of traits and of their ultimate expression. I deal both with control of the traits of existing beings (including fetuses and developed embryos, whose germ lines, unlike those of early embryos and of gametes, can no longer be altered) and with germline interventions. I will, of course, try to explain what I mean by "conceptual reexaminations" that are "driven" by changes in the world—technological developments in particular.

If technology confuses us about identity, it will also, and necessarily, confuse us about the moral, legal, and political roles of merit and desert. And in turn, if merit and desert ascriptions are made more uncertain than they already are, then equality, fairness, and justice constraints also become, to that extent, more muddled. For many, keying the size of rewards to degree of merit (at least in some senses of "merit") does not violate standards of equality or fairness, and may indeed promote them. But if we cannot say who has true merit, or even who has won the race, our assignment of merit-based rewards cannot be fully justified.[1] Nor can we confidently say who should be admitted to any given educational institution, awarded a prize, appointed to a prestigious post, and so on. Confused attributions of identity may thus have far-reaching effects—serious enough to at least warrant rethinking the role and structure of that concept.

---

[1] For a discussion of trait change from an equality perspective, see Michael H. Shapiro, "Does Technological Enhancement of Human Traits Threaten Human Equality and Democracy?" *San Diego Law Review* 39, no. 3 (2002): 769–842.

Some aspects of this essay reflect legal frameworks of analysis.[2] There are two reasons for this. First, the ideas of "conceptual reconstruction" and "conceptual impacts" are partially filled out by considering several examples from the law, where conceptual strains are often particularly salient. Second, the conceptual histories of some basic abstractions, particularly value concepts, become embedded in law and thus in its argument structures—and these argument structures in turn illuminate the value issues at stake. The more fundamental the values, the likelier they are expressed or implied in basic legal documents such as the U.S. Constitution. Thus, toward the end of the essay, I launch the beginnings of a constitutional analysis of directed technological trait-changes that may impinge on personal identity. The effect that shaping of behavioral traits may have on perceptions of individual identity has already gained the attention of the U.S. Supreme Court. The Court has twice ruled that compelled administration of antipsychotic drugs that can sharply alter the behavior of a criminal defendant may, depending on the circumstances, violate a fundamental liberty interest in refusing such treatment.[3] In prosecutions where the defendant claims insanity, an important rationale for such constitutional rulings is that this defense is impaired by allowing her to appear "normal" during trial. (This is sometimes referred to as a problem of "synthetic sanity.")

II. Assumptions about the Nature, Scope, and Limitations of Prospective Technological Capabilities

This essay considers the possibility that what we think we know about personal identity should be reconsidered in light of technological capacities to (1) significantly alter traits of existing beings (persons, fetuses, some early embryos) through technological intervention without altering the germ line; or to (2) specify the traits of possible persons (loosely, those who do not exist but whose existence, in one form or another, is planned)[4] by reworking the genetic material in early embryos[5] or, possibly, in gametes.

---

[2] The idea of a "legal framework" is especially complex, but I have to rely on exposition and readers' schooled intuitions in clarifying it. For more extended remarks, see generally Michael H. Shapiro, "Lawyers, Judges, and Bioethics," *Southern California Interdisciplinary Law Journal* 5, no. 2 (1997): 113–92.

[3] *Riggins v. Nevada*, 504 U.S. 127 (1992) (ruling that on the record before the Court, the accused should not have been given antipsychotic medication over his objection to render him competent to stand trial); *Sell v. United States*, 539 U.S. 166 (2003) (ruling in another competence-to-stand-trial case that the conditions for forced medication had not been shown to be satisfied).

[4] David Heyd, *Genethics: Moral Issues in the Creation of People* (Berkeley and Los Angeles: University of California Press, 1992). I use the term "being" to include human adults, children, fetuses, and embryos.

[5] This has been done in some nonhuman embryos, e.g., mice whose genomes have been altered so that they grow larger than they otherwise would; and mice altered so as to delay senescence and thus slow the degradation of mouse aptitudes. For brief descriptions, see

These prospects represent a partial displacement of our *relative* inability to control the expression of a trait and its genetic underpinnings. Of course, training, practice, and effort may yield significant improvements in performance capacities,[6] but the process is gradual, time-consuming, and rigorous, and few believe (whatever they *say*) that such modalities of improvement enable us all to reach elite levels of accomplishment. We cannot all perform like Lance Armstrong, no matter how hard we try — at least when using the traditional mechanisms of self-improvement.[7] But the technologically enabled transition "from chance to choice" (as Buchanan, Brock, Daniels, and Wikler nicely put it)[8] may significantly affect how we view persons in relation to their constitutive traits.[9]

III. Trait Change and Identity

The *germ-line/non-germ-line* distinction is crucial in identity studies for several reasons. The most obvious is that altering the germ line does not involve the modification of an existing person's traits. Becoming more intelligent through ingesting certain substances is far afield from having been born with that higher intelligence after germ-line "enhancement." The distinction also bears, in complex ways, on one's personal sense of identity. A person whose traits were augmented in utero, or in infancy, or even in early childhood, may have no recollection of any transformative events, and is likely, though not certain, to take her traits as intrinsic and possibly — for better or worse — central to her identity.

Michael H. Shapiro, Roy G. Spece, Jr., Rebecca Dresser, and Ellen Wright Clayton, eds., *Bioethics and Law: Cases, Materials, and Problems*, 2d ed. (St. Paul, MN: Thomson/West, 2003), 270–97. See also The President's Council on Bioethics, *Beyond Therapy: Biotechnology and the Pursuit of Happiness* (Washington, DC: President's Council on Bioethics, October 2003); available online at http://www.bioethics.gov/reports/beyondtherapy/.

The President's Council notes the anticipation of the general topic of enhancement in René Descartes, *Discourse on the Method of Conducting One's Reason Well and Seeking Truth in the Sciences*, part VI, paragraph 2, quoting, among other things, the passage stating: "[I]f it is possible to find some means that generally renders men more wise and more capable than they have been up to now, I believe that we must seek for it in medicine. . . ."

[6] "Performance" as used here may refer to a variety of subjects — e.g., bare outcomes such as winning or losing, or completing a task in a given time; satisfying some evaluative standards for the manner in which a task is pursued; and achieving specified goals, however described (doing Nobel-quality work, actually winning the Nobel Prize, becoming a great scientist, etc.). It may thus have either descriptive or evaluative (including moral) meanings, or both, and may refer both to processes and outcomes.

[7] "Traditional" does not mean "devoid of technology" — itself an unclear term. "Scientifically" selected diets, for example, are not technological "fixes," but they are not entirely "natural" either.

[8] See generally Allen Buchanan, Dan W. Brock, Norman Daniels, and Daniel Wikler, *From Chance to Choice: Genetics and Justice* (New York: Cambridge University Press, 2000).

[9] I do not mean "constitutive" in a strictly reductive sense. The term is meant simply to note that there is a connection between our separate identities and our respective traits.

The distinction also suggests the idea of an alternative *counterfactual* ("default"; "natural"; "real") *identity*.[10] The idea applies to both germ-line and non-germ-line transformations, though it plays out differently in the two realms. In germ-line changes, we join, in a single course of procreative conduct, two physically and conceptually distinct aspects of the reproductive process: determining both the *existence* of a specific possible person or being (which we have always been able to do through ordinary sexual reproduction) and *the specification of the nature and measure of many of its traits* (which is a developing possibility).[11] The self-image of one who knows his genome has been deliberately modified in certain ways may include hazy notions of what he would have been like without the modifications, and might be coupled, however irrationally, with regret and anger.[12] If others know of his reproductive history, it may also affect how they view him, but it is hard to say in just what ways; much depends on what is transformed, and how the technologies for genetic modification are received by society and incorporated into some baseline of accepted practice.[13] In vitro fertilization, for example, though it still generates some controversy, has become conceptually well-integrated into the contemporary vision of human reproduction. The self-image of persons born of that process may differ somewhat from the norm, but is unlikely, on its own, to bear serious adversities.[14]

IV. Categories of Identity Problems

Our vocabulary for describing and evaluating trait changes may well expand with new techniques for technological transformations. We already

[10] This is meant to designate the set of traits that a person would have developed without germ-line intervention. They are, of course, often impossible to specify because of the complex interaction of the workings of genes and of environmental influences. See generally Heyd, *Genethics*, 170: "[W]e have to consider any genetic 'manipulation' against the background of the set of traits which the 'person' already possesses or that he or she will inevitably turn out to possess. This is the person-affecting principle in the context of identity formation." Counterfactual identity might also extend to identities that could have been but were not implemented by genomic change, as well as to the default or natural identity.

[11] See generally Joel Feinberg, "Wrongful Life and the Counterfactual Element in Harming," *Social Philosophy and Policy* 4, no. 1 (1986): 145–78, at 158.

[12] Anger may not always be irrational in such circumstances; parents and participating genetic engineers may have had plans that were defective or ill-informed in some ways, and may have been improperly executed. The "wrongful life" and "wrongful birth" cases are instructive here. See, e.g., *Turpin v. Sortini*, 643 P.2d 954 (Cal. 1982) ("rejecting" a wrongful-life claim and denying general damages, but—inconsistently—awarding special damages nevertheless); and Joel Feinberg, "Wrongful Life and the Counterfactual Element in Harming," 158.

[13] The idea of a baseline incorporated into an evaluation system from which changes are judged is important in many disparate fields—engineering, defining legal standards of care, everyday practical decision making, and so on. In some situations, it serves to "grandfather" or immunize certain practices from legal or other attack. In many fields, it serves as the content of a somewhat conservative presumption of rectitude for customary practices.

[14] See generally Shapiro et al., eds., *Bioethics and Law*, 625, 647.

have an abundance of "change" terms, however; their differences loosely mark variations in the kinds and dimensions of change they address and in the causal variables underlying the modifications. We speak of transformation, transfiguration, transmogrification, transmutation, transition, conversion, modification, amendment, and so on. Variables include the rate of change; the role of the trait in both basic species functioning and in the surrounding culture (e.g., the perceived moral importance or socioeconomic utility of the trait generally); the degree and breadth of trait change; the level of personal effort, technological input, and expense needed to effect a given change; the benefits and risks of both the process of change and its short- and long-term effects; the impact of the modification on personal identity, as perceived by others and as perceived by oneself; and the impact of the change on other traits—a "globalness of effect" notion involving the role of the cascading results of a given trait change.[15]

Among the various senses of "identity," our main interest is in personal identity ("The problem is that of what makes the identity of the single person at a time or through time"), rather than numerical identity or the causal theory of identity (and so on).[16]

V. Moral Risks of Expanded Choice: The Descent from Person to Object

A. Too many options?

The idea of responsibility for the effects of our decisions is not exactly new, but some of its aspects are highlighted when we encounter new arenas of choice. Here, the field of choice concerns important human "traits" that, without technological assists, are only marginally improvable or are adjustable only in incremental, relatively "unintrusive" ways.[17]

---

[15] I do not consider, except in passing, the identity problems associated with "beaming" mishaps (as when Commander Riker was duplicated by a malfunctioning transporter in an episode of *Star Trek: The Next Generation*), nor do I consider problems associated with "mosaic"-like persons resulting from transplanting hemispheres or other brain structures. See generally Derek Parfit, *Reasons and Persons* (Oxford: Clarendon Press, 1984); and Robert Nozick, *Philosophical Explanations* (Cambridge: Belknap Press of Harvard University Press, 1981).

[16] On the impressive variety of identity-related concepts, see Simon Blackburn, ed., *The Oxford Dictionary of Philosophy* (Oxford: Oxford University Press, 1996). Oxford Reference Online: http://www.oxfordreference.com/views/ENTRY.html?subview=Main&entry=t98.e1172 (accessed October 7, 2004). I do not consider any "unified field" theories to unite all versions of identity and of related concepts. For discussion of "the concept of identity as a life narrative," see generally Gaia Bernstein, "Accommodating Technological Innovation: Identity, Genetic Testing, and the Internet," *Vanderbilt Law Review* 57, no. 3 (2004): 965–1039, p. 973.

[17] I use the term "intrusive" to emphasize the more "discontinuous" aspects of technological change of traits. Despite its pejorative connotations, the term is meant to be descriptive and morally neutral for present purposes. See generally Shapiro et al., eds., *Bioethics and Law*, 389–96.

This—or any—expansion of choice may entail an expansion of the potential range of personal responsibility for one's conduct. One may face new opportunities for blame over matters gone awry, as well as the chance of credit for things going well in their new ways. The *ways* in which things go wrong may differ sharply from what we are accustomed to; and what we may be held responsible for (both causally and culpably) may be without clear moral or legal precedent. If a germ-line change to increase expected height does not pan out as planned or hoped—the procedure did not work well enough, it caused kidney damage, the offspring was unable or unwilling to trade on it commercially—the disappointed parents or athletic teams may search for someone at fault. Perhaps we will consider recognizing "wrongfully wrought identity" claims one might bring against trait engineers—or one's parents.[18] Of course, this increased risk of moral (and possibly legal) blame might be offset by the prospect of moral credit.

These are the considerations that underlie the idea of "too much choice"[19] and the accompanying idea of being "normatively worse off" *in certain ways*. There is a risk of censure for not acting in ways that formerly were closed off, whether for technological, legal, or moral reasons, but have now opened up with changed attitudes. An example from another bioethical region clarifies this. Suppose the head of a low-income family learns that sales of non-vital organs are no longer illegal.[20] Might she think that she is duty-bound to sell one to care for her family? To be sure, she may not be worse off *overall* with this new prospect: she has the option to save her family from living on the streets, an opportunity she did not have before. She may fear this opportunity, however, preferring to avoid a procedure that for her is a mutilation because there is no medical reason for removing the organ. This risk of blame (including self-blame) for bypassing the opportunity renders her normatively worse off in that respect. In rough parallel, one may find that the palette of traits one can choose for one's offspring—or oneself—presents the psychic burden of a sense of moral risk and a fear of regret. In particular, regret over a lost but once possible identity may also be one of the perils of enlarged choice.

[18] The analogy is to "wrongful life" claims brought on behalf of children whose lives, from their viewpoints, are dispreferred to nonexistence. (Parents or guardians would, of course, bring such actions.) "Wrongful birth" claims of various sorts are separate causes of action brought by parents on their own behalf, complaining of injury to *their* interests because of the birth of the impaired child.

[19] See Gerald Dworkin, "Is More Choice Better Than Less?" *Midwest Studies in Philosophy* 7 (1982): 47–62; and Michael H. Shapiro, "Illicit Reasons and Means for Reproduction: On Excessive Choice and Categorical and Technological Imperatives," *Hastings Law Journal* 47, no. 4 (1996): 1081–1221. See also Barry Schwartz, *The Paradox of Choice: Why More Is Less* (New York: ECCO, 2004).

[20] This is not far-fetched. See, e.g., Larry Rohter, "Tracking the Sale of a Kidney on a Path of Poverty and Hope," *New York Times*, May 23, 2004, available online at http://www.nytimes.com/2004/05/23/international/americas/23BRAZ.html?hp=&pagewanted=print&position ("'As of today, there is no law in Israel that forbids trafficking in human organs,' Meir Broder, a legal adviser to the Health Ministry, explained in an interview in Jerusalem. 'There is no criminal aspect at all.' ").

*B. The (possible) descent from person to object; the erosion
of noncontingent bonding*

The very idea of planned technological modification of traits entails an *intensified* focus on discrete traits, amplifying the attention we historically have paid to individual traits and their varying presentations, both in ourselves and in others. We do not, for the most part, view each other as indistinguishable or fungible, and we do not mate with or befriend trait- less wraiths. What, then, is the nature and significance of this enhanced attention to particular attributes?

Consider illustrations concerning control of the genetic processes under- lying reproduction. Our moral ideals generally call for *noncontingent* bond- ing to our children: we are to love and care for them *without question or reservation,* apart from any trait or traits they bear — whether they are male or female, physically and mentally sound or not, cute or repellent, colicky or peaceful. The ideal is regularly breached (some people abandon or abuse their children), but the ideal stands nonetheless and is widely (if not universally) respected. In procreation, then, we are to accept and cherish what we receive, as well as to make the best of it.

With the advent of population and pregnancy screening in the 1960s and 1970s, this situation changed sharply. For many unwanted conditions — Tay-Sachs disease, Down syndrome, sickle-cell anemia and other hemo- globinopathies, etc. — we can avoid the very existence of an afflicted child. Those who do not take advantage of such possibilities — including elective abortion — may be criticized by some as behaving immorally for burden- ing the community, themselves as parents, and possibly, if illogically, the afflicted offspring.[21] The affected persons and their conditions become more visible because the afflictions are preventable through nonreproduction, and, in many cases, this does not foreclose new attempts to have children.

There is, of course, far more to trait-control than screening out unwanted characteristics. As trait-modification technology develops, highly valued merit attributes — which are often strongly resource-attractive — may be subject to significant enhancement efforts, and ordinarily disfavored traits (e.g., a disposition toward impulsive violence) might be attenuated, or even deleted or replaced. The possibility of planning such maneuvers, of course, does not *create* our attention to traits and how they vary from person to person. But *the very perception of traits and trait differences* across persons (and cultures) suggests the likelihood that greater control over what some call the "genetic lottery" will, as suggested, sharpen our atten- tion to interpersonal differences. (Enlarging these differences might indeed be the very object of greater control.) In turn, this might well affect our valuations of the traits in question and of the persons who have them. It may even influence what we recognize or identify *as* a trait.

---

[21] The resulting child is not harmed unless its very existence constitutes a harm to it, from its viewpoint.

One possible historical example of re-valuations or recharacterizations of traits following technological developments is the expansion of concepts of disorder and treatment to match new capabilities, say, to alter mental states. In such cases, "treatment" precedes "disorder"[22]—that is, the definition of disorder expands to match the technological capacities for altering mental functions and behavior. Exuberance, in some forms, becomes "attention deficit disorder," and reactive sadness becomes "clinical depression," or so some might argue.[23]

Thus, if we do not always have to take what comes but can either screen out possible persons with unwanted traits, or adjust the nature and strength of the traits of a possible person who is to be born, our perceptions and valuations of persons may rest even more strongly than they do now on particular personal attributes and the extent to which these attributes fulfill our reproductive plans. A key moral concern is that failure of the plans inspiring the effort to change traits may spur devaluation[24] of the person born; our bonds to our offspring may become contingent on the success of our combined reproductive and transformative plans.

Technological adjustment of traits—and thus possibly of identities—thus compounds the risk of human reduction or objectification, and raises the likelihood that persons will be used as *mere* means. Hence the phrase "the descent from person to object." I note in advance, however, that I think these reductive risks have often been significantly exaggerated in the discussions of "assisted reproduction."

These risks are among the asserted perils of expanded choice, a notion introduced earlier. There are more such perils, however, including those involving personal moral and legal accountability and one's internal sense of culpability and regret. To the extent that trait changes are significant— perhaps enough to suggest identity shifts—we will be presumptively responsible for aspects of our own identities and those of our offspring.[25] This prospect of sharply expanded choice sets is rather bracing: it affects our notions of the nature and worth of autonomy, and seems to displace grand ideas of our historic subjection to Nature and Fate. Perhaps more choice is presumptively better, because of the direct (if incomplete and uncertain) link between the "size" of one's field of choice and one's autonomy. But presumptions can be overcome by considerations of risk,

---

[22] See generally Elmer A. Gardner, "Implications of Psychoactive Drug Therapy," *New England Journal of Medicine* 290, no. 14 (1974): 800–802.

[23] The nature and value of "attention deficit disorder" ascriptions has been controversial for decades. See, e.g., Lawrence H. Diller, "The Run on Ritalin: Attention Deficit Disorder and Stimulant Treatment in the 1990s," *Hastings Center Report* 26, no. 2 (1996): 12–18 (Westlaw: 1996 WL 10189234).

[24] This and allied terms (e.g., "reduction") are both complex and important. I do not present extended definitions, but try to clarify what I mean as I move along.

[25] This seems far more straightforward than the familiar moral position held by some that we are at least partially responsible for our individual characters, and thus for the expression of particular character traits.

or even uncertainty. As Lucy van Pelt might say: "Autonomy isn't everything, you know. It'll never bring you peace of mind."[26] We may come to
fear the reactions and regrets of our own children. Of course, a person
who exists because her embryo was selected over another that bore a
deleterious gene cannot coherently complain about the reproductive road
not taken.[27] But someone whose germ line was altered, or someone whose
nascent or existing traits are modified, may well complain that her parents, or trait-engineers, or she herself, took the wrong road.

Trait alteration is not *entirely* a new field of regret: bodybuilders may
complain of enhancing the wrong muscles or overenhancing the right
ones; patients may lament the results of plastic surgery; and so on. Serious and prolonged regret is not necessarily pathological, though it is a
kind of harm, and it is a standard risk of free choice. Moreover, it may be
instrumentally valuable in encouraging greater care in making choices.
The remarks of the late British philosopher Bernard Williams, though in
a quite different context, capture the issue well: "It seems to me a fundamental criticism of many ethical theories that their accounts of moral
conflict and its resolution do not do justice to the facts of regret and
related considerations: basically because they eliminate from the scene
the 'ought' that is not acted upon."[28]

This account of moral endangerment is of course consistent with saying
that, *overall*, we may be normatively better off in the new technological
regime; I am simply describing vectors in tension, not calculating the
resultant.

VI. The Concept of "Conceptual Impact": Can Concepts Get Broken? The Effects of Deconstructing and Reconstructing Basic Life Processes and Conditions

A. The normative nature of conceptual impacts and reconstructions

What is the "conceptual impact" of an idea? If we can speak of such an
impact, what impact does the known availability or prospect of technological modification of traits have on the concept of personal identity?[29]

---

[26] Lucy is a character in the late Charles Schulz's comic strip *Peanuts*. However, she was
talking about happiness, not autonomy: "Happiness isn't everything, you know. It'll never
bring you peace of mind!" Robert L. Short, *The Gospel According to Peanuts* (Louisville, KY:
Westminster John Knox Press, 1999), 112 (referring to the strip and quoting the remark).

[27] See Yury Verlinsky et al., "Preimplantation Diagnosis for Early-Onset Alzheimer Disease Caused by V717L Mutation," *Journal of the American Medical Association* 287, no. 8 (2002):
1018–21.

[28] Bernard Williams, "Ethical Consistency," in Geoffrey Sayre-McCord, ed., *Essays on
Moral Realism* (Ithaca, NY: Cornell University Press, 1988), 41, 49.

[29] Perhaps this is a question about "the identity of identity," assuming it makes sense to
refer to the "identity" of concepts.

An adequate response requires at least (i) an explanation of the meaning(s) of "conceptual impact"; and (ii) a description of the current "baseline" understanding of the idea of identity, or at least of the central contests concerning its meaning: without knowing this, one could not tell what features of identity, if any, were under "revisionist" pressure. Of course, it would also require (iii) an explanation of why it is important to take account of such impacts. In this section, I illustrate, without exactly defining, what a conceptual impact is.

Using terms such as "conceptual impact" and "conceptual change, reconstruction, revision, reinterpretation, modification, amendment, etc."[30] may seem a rather woolly way to describe how we understand and use given concepts across different settings. Concepts don't get battered in any straightforward sense. But they do get battered in some nonstraightforward senses, as I suggest through examples, some of which have applications to the idea of personal identity.

In other writings, I have suggested that some biological technologies are particularly hard to confront because their workings do not "fit" within the conceptual systems we rely on to describe and evaluate actions, events, and situations.[31] Sometimes this is because of a literal physical "deconstruction" followed by "reconstruction" or "reassembly" of *basic* life processes:[32] i.e., conception, gestation, and birth; the development of a person's traits; and the processes of dying. Beyond the clear physical fragmentation and reintegration of the elements of such processes, there are (in a metaphoric sense) conceptual "fragmentations," and, accompanying this, there may be observable rearrangements of familiar human relationships into less familiar and possibly unsettling forms. There are also physical "fragments" that uncharacteristically (and perhaps disturbingly) endure after being loosed from the body—say, cryopreserved embryos, stem cells, and various bodily parts or substances that have medical or other value. The upshot is that the abstractions and categories we hitherto used to frame and assess what we perceive through our senses seem to "run out," as it were: they are simply not up to the tasks of describing and evaluating what we see—or so it may seem. The question of conceptual reconstruction or respecification thus rests on moral and legal analysis of unfamiliar actions and situations.[33]

---

[30] These terms are far from interchangeable, and in an extended work would have to be differentiated.

[31] See generally Michael H. Shapiro, "Fragmenting and Reassembling the World: Of Flying Squirrels, Augmented Persons, and Other Monsters," *Ohio State Law Journal* 51, no. 2 (1990): 331–74.

[32] I am not trying to describe necessary and/or sufficient conditions for being a "basic" life process.

[33] Note Heyd's description of one aspect of his project, in *Genethics*, 69–70 ("in the same way as the issues of brain death and euthanasia, abortion and *in vitro* fertilization force on us a reconsideration of the metaphysical criteria of 'life,' so do the issues of genetic engineering and wrongful life urge us to reformulate the metaphysics of personal identity"). See

B. Examples of conceptual "failure and respecification" from the fields
of reproduction and the neurobiology of behavior[34]

So far, the clearest examples available for the ostensive definition of "conceptual impact" come from areas not directly concerned with identity, though identity issues may arise in some form.

1. Gestation and genetics. Think first of gestational surrogacy, where gametes from a man and a woman are united to form a fertilized ovum in vitro, which is then implanted in a second woman who is to gestate and give birth to the child, and then to deliver it to the genetic parents (or, perhaps, to other intended custodial parents, whoever they are). Assume that before the project is completed, the gestator threatens to withhold delivery unless she receives greater compensation. More profoundly, she claims the child as "her own" because she was the gestator—the birth mother—and that this outweighs the lack of a genetic link.

In such reproductive transactions, the gestational and genetic "components" of motherhood have been "split" or "unbundled"; the reproductive process, both physiologically and socially, has been fragmented and reassembled. There is no clear, dominating *conceptual* answer to the question, Who is the "true" or "natural" mother?—although some may believe that, given their particular evaluation of the physiological and social roles of gestation and genetics in identity formation, there is a clear answer.

Identifying the "natural mother" within the meaning of California's version of the Uniform Parentage Act was precisely the question in *Johnson v. Calvert*:[35] was it Anna Johnson, the surrogate gestator, or Mrs. Calvert, the genetic progenitor who planned to raise the child with her husband? The problem was a conceptual/normative one about the very concept of motherhood, and it is of considerable and immediate practical interest. It is the concept's *initial* technology-induced "inability" to perform its function in the situation at hand that draws our attention. The

---

also ibid., 163 ("The particular genethical problems of identity formation call for a new approach to personal identity in its dynamic change"). Later, however, Heyd obliquely suggests considerations cutting against reformulation. He explains why he discusses various fictitious examples in which identities are engineered: it is "both because [these examples] are theoretically significant and because they have the same structure as the much more common practical problems of standard identity" (ibid., 173).

[34] What follows is not a complete list of possible examples of conceptual reconstruction or replacement. If other examples were to be included, one of the first would be the idea of "brain death" (which seems to involve no change of meaning for "death") and "permanent unconsciousness" as death (which would entail a serious shift in meaning). See generally Michael H. Shapiro, "Law, Culpability, and the Neural Sciences," in Roger D. Masters and Michael T. McGuire, eds., *The Neurotransmitter Revolution: Serotonin, Social Behavior, and the Law* (Carbondale: Southern Illinois University Press, 1993).

[35] *Johnson v. Calvert*, 851 P.2d 776 (Cal. 1993), discussed below. In this case, the California Supreme Court awarded custody of a child to its genetic parents, rather than to the gestational surrogate, because the genetic parents were, *by the terms of the agreement*, intended to be the custodial parents. The court took that intent to be determinative of who was to be recognized as the child's "natural parents" under California's Uniform Parentage Act.

problem of understanding the structure of the concept of motherhood
arises rarely, but it surfaces dramatically when it "fails" as a decisive
instrument in a child custody dispute. As the German philosopher Martin
Heidegger put it, "When its [a tool's] unusability is thus discovered,
equipment becomes conspicuous."[36] Gestation and genetic parenthood
having been separated, "motherhood" falls between the cracks, and the
(possibly temporary) unserviceability of the conceptual equipment *as it
remains* is striking.

The problem reflected in the *Johnson* case is, in a plausible sense, a
question about the "conceptual identity" of parenthood generally and
motherhood in particular (is Mrs. Calvert or Ms. Johnson the *real* mother?),
and about whether "motherhood" has to be "reconstructed" or "revised."
I do not have a rigorous account of what "conceptual reconstruction"
means, but it seems unnecessary for present purposes. Perhaps "reconstruction" is in some cases too fancy a term: we may simply be "interpreting," or clarifying what is implicit, or applying a given concept to
new—but in this case very surprising—situations. In any case, when
concepts are pressed beyond their apparent limits, their innards are
exposed, revealing more of their strengths and weaknesses. This is an
important payoff, however we describe our conceptual explorations.

The California Supreme Court did not resolve the matter by comparative genetic and physiological analysis of the workings of genes and
gestation, or by inquiring into the possible exploitation of impoverished
women of color (Anna Johnson was African American),[37] or by raising
any other scientific or cultural questions. The court's interpretation of the
now conceptually challenged statutory concept of a "natural parent" relied
on a quite different reconstructive (reinterpretive?) method for specifying
the idea of legal parenthood. In dealing with the statute's newly apparent
conceptual "hole," the court looked to the primary aspects of the very
decision to initiate biological procreation in modern human cultures, and
saw that the intention to create an internally bonded and enduring nuclear

---

[36] Martin Heidegger, *Being and Time*, ed. and trans. John Macquarrie and Edward Robinson (New York: Harper, 1962), 102–3.

[37] The race of the parties is formally irrelevant under the court's rule of decision, and
questions of disproportionate burdens on minority groups are also irrelevant under federal
constitutional doctrine, unless there is independent evidence of purposeful discrimination,
or the disproportion is sufficiently extreme to warrant burdening the government with
establishing acceptable purposes. But gestational surrogacy, unlike "traditional surrogacy"
(where the gestating mother is also the ovum source), makes possible a reproductive practice in which women in minority groups—on the average, less wealthy than white persons—
would "rent their wombs" in disproportionate numbers. This might influence a legislature
to ban or heavily regulate the practice, although differential treatment of surrogacy agree-
ments based on the race of any of the parties would be constitutionally suspect. A court
might also craft a rule in which determining the intentions of the parties to a surrogacy
agreement is subject to rigorous examination in order to rule out "undue influence" or
"exploitation," particularly of women of color. This presupposes that in some situations,
members of minority groups are more vulnerable to the enticement or "coercive power" of
financial or other rewards. (I neither endorse nor reject such regimes.)

family seemed preeminent. This was an unpacking or a deeper specification of the idea of parenthood that reflected the social/cultural purposes of biological reproduction, *whatever its form,* in our society: the formation of a nuclear family in which genetic parents will raise their children. Briefly put, the decision to reproduce, in our culture, is (generally) a decision to become a *custodial* parent.

On that view, Mrs. Calvert, who was the genetic mother, was deemed to be the "natural mother" within the governing statutory meaning *in that case,* because that was how the transaction was set up: it was the Calverts' idea to create a family consisting of them and their genetic offspring, in close companionship.

If, on the other hand, the intention had been to assist the gestator in creating her own nuclear family, then, on the intention-is-determinative rationale, custody would have been awarded to her rather than to the genetic mother. This is not entirely unrealistic, especially if the gestator is a close relative or friend of the child's genetic sources.

The extent to which procreation is viewed as the intentional creation of a nuclear family as presently understood is a contingent social fact, though this view seems all but universal. To see this, compare human procreation as we know it with that in Plato's *Republic*,[38] where it is understood that genetic parents are generally not to be the custodial parents, and children are to be raised by members of a specified social class.

This illustration of conceptual reconstruction or respecification emphasizes both the descriptive and evaluative features of this process: we are not just redefining abstractions, but making moral decisions on how to deal with novel situations. This is a very tricky business, since we are reviewing and revising some of the very tools needed for moral analysis in the first place.

2. Human reproductive cloning. Human reproductive cloning produces a separate new person, as does traditional sexual reproduction. On that limited description, there is nothing new: the human population has increased by one. With sexual reproduction, however, we have conceptually (and morally and legally) clear ways to say who shall be the "default" custodial parents—that is, the parties automatically designated by law as custodial parents in the absence of evidence of a prior agreement on custody or judicial decree. The woman who brings a child to term is at least one of two default biological mothers. The sperm source is the biological father, period. But who would be the *clearly required* default biological parent(s) of the cloned offspring? Not the nuclear source, who is simply a previously born genetic twin. Not the woman who is the source of the enucleated ovum: she makes no genetic contribution (except

---

[38] Plato, *The Republic and Other Works,* ed. and trans. B. Jowett (Garden City, NY: Doubleday, 1960), book V, 151.

for mitochondria, carried in the cytoplasm).[39] Although many commentators would hold otherwise,[40] it is not the gestator either—who might be someone other than the source of the enucleated ovum: *as* gestator alone, she makes a biological, but not a genetic contribution. Nor is it the nuclear source's father and mother, despite the fact that they are the "genomic parents" of both the nuclear source and the cloned offspring; the source and the offspring are, in genetic terms, twins, whatever their age differences.[41] Asexual reproduction is thus, biologically and socially, something *quite* different from what we are used to, even against the backdrop of surrogacy, in vitro fertilization, and other social and technological mechanisms for assisting reproduction through sexual recombination. Sexual reproduction simply does not generate genomes identical to either of the parental genomes; we have, in general, only one-half the genome of each genetic parent. Moreover, there are no socially obvious default parents. Lacking biological and social markers for immediately assigning custodial parenthood, courts and legislatures are likely to turn to intentions, as in *Johnson v. Calvert*.

3. *Mood control*. An example closer to our topic of trait change and identity reflects the increasing ability to control mental processes and to understand their neurophysiological substrates. Compare the four responses to the following question: "Why are you so energized and enthused—so inappropriately cheerful—all the time?" (a) "That's just the way I am; it's an aspect of my character; it's *who* I am as well as the *way* I am (which are, of course, connected)." (b) "I have naturally high serotonin levels." (c) "I have naturally high serotonin levels, which largely accounts for that 'up' aspect of my personality—indeed, of my character— and helps makes me who I am." (d) "I have naturally low serotonin levels, so I take a selective serotonin reuptake inhibitor, and now my serotonin is *way* up; I will remain on the drug indefinitely. It's the *new me*. Or, better, it's the *real me* that was previously suppressed by my inadequate serotonin chemistry."

Are these descriptions and characterizations relevant to matters of personal identity? Are they relevant to assessment of character and actions? To the assignment of praise or blame? To freedom and responsibility

---

[39] We cannot say, however, that the genetic impact of the enucleated ovum is nil. For example, offspring might have serious mitochondria-related disorders. The case for assigning default parenthood to the source of the enucleated ovum seems thin, nevertheless. See generally Shapiro et al., eds., *Bioethics and Law*, 744–45.

[40] See generally Michael H. Shapiro, "How (Not) to Think about Surrogacy and Other Reproductive Innovations," *University of San Francisco Law Review* 28, no. 3 (1994): 647–80, 675–78 (discussing how to assess gestational effects on developing embryos and fetuses).

[41] The "offspring" of a nuclear source is not the "genetic child" of that source in the sexual recombination sense: in a sense, she is *too* closely related genetically; her genome and her source's genome are identical (subject to mitochondrial variation and transcription errors). Sexual recombination assigns only one-half of any parent's genome to the offspring. Thus, the notion of "genetic offspring" and, more generally, "offspring" itself would seem to require respecification when one discusses human reproductive cloning.

generally? Does the example indicate the need for any conceptual reconstructions, whether concerning identity or any cognate concepts?

As for personal identity, no revisions are occasioned by modest degrees of coherent, continuous change,[42] both from natural biological processes and from directed efforts at transformation. These variations over time are not only consistent with stability, they are *expected* within any social system that anticipates not only the usual transitions of maturation and aging, but of certain forms of personal growth and development. Those who *fail* to "evolve" in these ways over time may themselves be viewed as "unstable" because they depart from the paradigm of slow but steady change.

However, the situation is less clear with the prospect of serious and rapid trait-malleability. Whether or not this impels revisions in our conceptual frameworks, it will change our expectations; our perceptions of someone's identity may become more tentative, driving us to distinguish between "real" or "former" identity and "induced" identity. Of course, the salience of new facts that erode our assumptions does not always require revision or abandonment of ideas ("identity and personal responsibility as we knew them no longer make sense"), but it may stimulate new conceptual and normative structures that adjust how we see and order things ("perhaps we should take more seriously the idea of diminished capacity"). Clearly, it is hard to distinguish between (on the one hand) the various overlapping ideas of conceptual modification, and (on the other hand) perceptual changes that involve revaluing or reordering aspects of what we see or adding "new" aspects. In any case, *something* is likely to change how we assess ourselves and our places in a world where nothing is nailed down, including our identities.

4. Identity itself: imaginable worlds of "shape-shifting"; what are the limits on the work "identity" can do?[43] We do not generally think of discontinuous breaks in identity when maturity and aging take their usual courses; or when alertness is enhanced by caffeine; or even when steroids seem to generate visible results in appearance and performance. Still, even if we do not see breaks in identity, we might see "merit breaks" of sorts: Barry Bonds remains Barry Bonds, the baseball slugger, but those who believe he used steroids may downgrade the credit they assign to his otherwise impressive accomplishments (especially his setting the record for most home runs in a single season).[44]

---

[42] I refer to (in)coherence and (dis)continuity again below. I am not referring to immediate striking changes worked by, say, plastic surgery or surgical decoration. The emphasis is on personality and character traits, mental and behavioral dispositions, and skills.

[43] I use the term "shape-shifting" loosely to cover all significant changes in whatever we view as an attribute, physical or mental/behavioral. Some uses of the term are thus analogical—as in altering the contours of mental functioning rather than specific physical shapes as such. The term "shape-shifting" is familiar in studies of mythology.

[44] Barry Bonds plays for the San Francisco Giants, and is one of several candidates regularly mentioned for "greatest baseball player ever."

Nevertheless, it seems perfectly reasonable to posit far more radical changes—changes so salient within our customary[45] perceptual frameworks that the assumption of constancy-through-change is weakened: whatever remains constant is at so high a level of abstraction that it seems next to useless, even if we think that *something* must endure through these transmogrifications.[46] The idea of calling some figurative conceptual fragmentations "violent" may be overdone, but the metaphor at least emphasizes points worth noting about the nature of conceptual change. Indeed, despite the inaccuracy of saying that use of the current or near-term technologies may change one's identity, the ascription of identity change has some value as a hyperbolic comparison to true identity change because it calls attention to the seriousness of the trait changes.

To see this, simply recall H. L. A. Hart's "philosophical fantasy," as he put it, in which he asked readers to consider the fact that

> [t]he world in which we live, and we who live in it, may one day change in many different ways; and if this change were radical enough not only would certain statements of fact now true be false and vice versa, but whole ways of thinking and talking which constitute our present conceptual apparatus, through which we see the world and each other, would lapse. We have only to consider how the whole of our social, moral, and legal life, as we understand it now, depends on the contingent fact that though our bodies do change in shape, size, and other physical properties they do not do this drastically nor with such quicksilver rapidity and irregularity that we cannot identify each other as the same persistent individual over considerable spans of time. Though this is but a contingent fact which may one day be different, on it at present rest huge structures of our thought and principles of action and social life.[47]

Such "drastic" and "quicksilver" shifts in personal characteristics—which I take here to include changes in mental and behavioral dispositions as well as physical structure—would indeed seem to render "personal identity" irrelevant, unless perhaps we can identify *some* significant continuing invariant link across changes. But it is hard to believe we will soon, or ever, be faced with such a situation or its possibility—although

---

[45] To *some* extent, ideas of enduring/ruptured identity are functions of cultural variables.

[46] "The Hulk is guided by [David Banner's] personality, dealing with whatever distresses David. But unfortunately, David has no control over the creature's actions. Nor can he remember what he had done during his Hulkish states." "The Incredible Hulk," http://www.scifi.com/hulk/lowdown/ (accessed May 11, 2004).

[47] H. L. A. Hart, "Positivism and the Separation of Law and Morals," *Harvard Law Review* 71, no. 4 (1958): 593–629, 622. Hart introduced this "philosophical fantasy," as he called it, to "show what could intelligibly be meant by the claim that certain provisions in a legal system are 'necessary.'"

I say this from our present perspective. And from that perspective, the role of "identity" in a Hartian world may seem compromised simply because it is no longer necessary or useful, or is much enfeebled.

Even in situations less chaotic than Hart's world, however, we might still be reduced to viewing identity (if we think of it at all), as a placeholder for, say, interpersonal and legal coordination—a sort of template or fly-wheel to maintain some stability through change. If Fx means x *has the property F*, we might view x as some continuing, ill-defined subject of change across all changes in properties (whatever F is); x is a continuing "repository" of (possibly) transient individuality—possibly a set of "successive selves"—although this still sounds too identity-oriented. We might also see F as a placeholder for the shifting properties that complicate our identity attributions. This two-placeholder conceptual concoction is, however, a rather thin template for our ideas of personal identity.

One might question the novelty of any of these Hartian or other imagined shape-shifting developments, and so question the need for conceptual retooling; the idea that there is nothing new under the sun serves to remind us that few developments have no "antecedents" whatever; at some level of abstract description, nothing is without precedent (except, of course, The First Thing). This is, however, a trivial point about the nature of abstract description. In any case, the illustrations suggest that some technological maneuvers will simply be too different to be comfortably subsumed within customary categories and practices.

VII. IDENTITY AND LINKED BUT DISTINCT CONCEPTS

There are connections—hard to specify—between identity and other concepts critically important for description and evaluation. Personhood is a leading example. In a world of extreme trait-malleability, one would rightly wonder whether the concept of personhood itself can function in any coherent way. On the one hand, if the idea of personhood cannot function, there seems to be limited scope for the concept of personal identity. On the other hand, if there is limited scope for the idea of personal identity, it is hard to see how the concept of personhood can function. Each seems to presuppose the other.

To complicate matters still further, one might think that a defining characteristic of (at least human) personhood is the *capacity* to reflect on *whether* to change one's characteristics—and possibly one's identity—and to try to do so if desired. Here, perhaps, we have reached the limits of a concept's being bent but not broken. Identity and personhood seem too hard to use, and there are no concepts "more basic" that might assist us. "Autonomy" and, more particularly, "rational self-direction" may add insights, but they seem to presuppose personhood and identity, and we are again enmeshed in conceptual cycling; nothing stands as central and decisive, everything is mutually interactive or "entangled," and identity claims are indefinite. In H. L. A. Hart's world of continuing shifts in the properties of the (possibly) "continuing" entities around us, one might, as we saw, trace some faint and possibly arbitrary constancies, but it might (depending on the situation) be pointless. Mere physical shape shifters might retain identity, even after global reconstruction or partial merger with other entities. But in cases involving a sequence of huge shifts in mentational and behavioral characteristics, personal identity would be a shard, even if not wholly obliterated. Hart's image of continuously roiling properties represents a sort of limit: before reaching it, there may be a reason to retain the concept of personal identity. Beyond it, there might not be, although much depends on the exact nature of the setting.

Something now needs to be said about the baseline conceptual components of the idea of identity, particularly that of personal identity. The baseline is rich and complex, and its contents are contested, but the discussion to follow can only shadow the field. The literature is of course very extensive. After this overview of personal identity (in Section VIII), I will review (in Section IX, subsection C.2.c) some technological suppositions that return us to considering the conceptual reconstruction of identity's identity.

VIII. Tracking the Baseline of the Concept of Personal Identity: A Brief Accounting

A. Timestop[48]

The Oxford Dictionary of Philosophy refers to personal identity as "what makes the identity of the single person *at a time* or *through time.*"[49] This is an important contrast, so I divide things up accordingly. Suppose time stopped in our universe. By this I mean that nothing whatever is happening. It does not matter whether this is physically impossible. (Perhaps it is a state of maximum entropy.) It is just that no events occur and no processes proceed—including mental processes.

However, there are entities existing within our frozen universe, so ideas of identity would apply in some ways, although they are not among the principal ones relevant for analyzing personal identity. The issues might even be viewed as problems of other—though related—kinds. Thus, we might want to know whether what we see is one thing or several, and in what sense, and how properties differ from one entity to another. This raises familiar philosophical issues about individuation, number, predication, and the specification of sets and their respective memberships. We might want to know more particularly what an entity's distinguishing

---

[48] The term is taken from the science fiction novel by Philip José Farmer, *Timestop!* (London: Quartet, 1973), but the concept there differs from the one used here.

[49] Blackburn, ed., *The Oxford Dictionary of Philosophy* (italics added).

attributes are—an inquiry related to determining what that one thing is. Timestop or not, things might be characterized by necessary and/or sufficient conditions—"defining characteristics"—and these are identity-related notions.

When time is restarted (we plug the universe back in), there are two broad groups of questions. Timestart means that something is going on—events and processes. What answers would we now give to the questions asked earlier about what we see? We are likely to say that whatever we have identified as a single thing remains the same, at least for a while. What we see as important groupings may change. The chief thing about timestart for our purposes, however, is that not only do locations, positions, orientations, and so on, change, but so might anything we would refer to as a characteristic of anything.

B. Timestart; the deconstruction and reconstruction of life processes; the unit of identity

What exactly are the identity problems in timestart—particularly those involving personal identity? The task at this point is to identify identity problems that are likely to be pressing in the face of biotechnologies that divide and recombine life processes. As we saw, this unbundling and rebundling process can sorely test the basic abstractions we use to describe and judge actions, events, and situations. It can directly create "new" entities in the form of new processes (e.g., asexual reproduction), new things (extracorporeal enduring embryos), new life forms (organisms whose genomes contain artificially inserted DNA), and, indirectly, new relationships, new or reconstituted concepts and frameworks, and perhaps new social worlds. Whatever is "new" may be new because it has traits it did not have before, or has traits in greater or lesser strength than it did before (this may be hard to distinguish from having "new" traits), or has certain traits arising from a "genesis" involving genomic or early-life alteration.[50]

Some identity problems are ordinarily peripheral to the personal identity issues discussed here: numerical identity, individuation, and existence itself. Under more unusual circumstances—including technological alteration of traits—these facets of identity may become more important, as when we are faced with morphing entities that merge with each other, split into new forms, merge again, and so on. Our personal identity problems concern how to view a continuing entity whose characteristics have changed (and may be continuously changing), or an entity that has fragmented and recombined itself, possibly with other entities.

Although the "unit of identity" for present purposes is the human individual, we should understand that there are other plausible units. A

---

[50] Events that determine whether persons are to exist at all and what nature they will take are referred to as "genesis" events by Heyd, *Genethics*, 2, 4.

germ-line alteration, for example, changes not only a possible person, but the set of genomes of all her descendants, and, writ large, germ-line alterations may change species identity.

C. Some standard identity questions and illustrations

1. In general; examples for continuing reference; some assumptions. Explorers of the idea of personal identity sooner or later must ask about possible links and overlaps among the following:[51] one's characteristics observable by others; one's characteristics observable by oneself; the metaphysics/ontology of personal identity; one's subjective sense of self and of one's nature; the views of others about one's identity; one's place in various social systems; and the vectors of change in all of these factors.

In an era of substantial technological governance over traits, however, I suggest one more consideration: when we move along any of these standard identity variables, we should take extra note of counterfactual identity—that is, supposed outcomes of transformative options not taken, including the option *not* to transform. Choosing among these options can occur at any life stage: the gametic, embryonic, fetal, and neonatal stages, infancy, and early childhood through adulthood. Such "alternative" identities might seem to some to constitute "real" identity, and may also affect perceptions of one's identity, by oneself and by others. Alternative identities may thus bear on what we view as an actual identity.

In reviewing some of these aspects and issues of identity, we can use as an occasional reference point the situation in Poul Anderson's science fiction novel *Brain Wave*:[52] when the solar system finally emerged from the brain-dampening field that took Earth hundreds of thousands of years to pass through, everyone quite suddenly became *a lot* smarter. Each person's perception of the world changed sharply. With changes *that extensive* in attributes *that central*, one thinks about the (in)stability of identity. (Of course, this is still far afield from the Hartian vision of continuing shape-shifting and melding.) Each person could also view his earlier state as reflecting a now counterfactual identity, and could recognize the new state as embodying his real identity, hitherto suppressed. This opposition of "new me" and "old me no longer suppressed" may be a prominent conceptual issue with any sharp changes in major attributes.

A connected thought experiment (for future reference) involves somewhat different issues: deliberately induced memory loss targeted toward

---

[51] I do not mean these to be definitive or exhaustive. They are, however, among the most important.

[52] Poul Anderson, *Brain Wave* (New York: Ballantine Books, 1954). See also Daniel Keyes, *Flowers for Algernon* (New York: Harcourt Brace and World, 1966), involving a mentally impaired person who becomes exceptionally intelligent after brain surgery intended to enhance his abilities. The story was made into the film *Charly*, starring Cliff Robertson (ABC Pictures, 1968).

specific troubling memories,[53] or even toward broader forms of amnesia. For example, one's internal sense of continuity of identity may be more compromised with major erasures of memory than with suddenly improved intelligence.

It is now time to identify some important working assumptions in this essay: first, that a number of genes with "outsize" effects on intelligence and other major traits may be identified, and second, that it may be possible to work with them so as to significantly enhance the measures of those traits in the persons who will develop from an early embryo or from selected gametes.[54] In this situation, there is no existing individual personal baseline that is *presented* in more or less "finished" traits. This is quite different from the *Brain Wave* setting, or from a situation in which someone ingests a substance that sharply augments various intellectual functions. In the genetic control project envisioned here, we compare a constructed and actually developing intelligence (or other) profile with a different process that *would have* continued but for our intervention, but is now impossible to return to. Notwithstanding the theoretical difficulties of counterfactual analysis, the altered person and those observing and judging her will compare her as she is with the way she would have been had the genetic control (or fetal or infant alteration) project not been undertaken. This is, of course, not comparing her to some *other* once-possible person (i.e., a numerically different one), as one could do when, say, a "gifted" embryo is selected over a regular one for implantation. In our situation, a selfsame (numerically identical) person with particular traits is compared to herself with different traits—herself as she would have been: her "default" persona, interrupted by technology.

2. *Conceptual connections among identity, personhood, autonomy, and . . . ?* This investigation of inter-conceptual links was mentioned earlier. Ideas such as identity, personhood, and autonomy are conceptually joined in complex ways; perhaps they *are* each other in certain aspects. To say

---

[53] See generally Liz Else, "We Hold These Freedoms to Be Self-Evident," *New Scientist* 182, no. 2444 (April 2004), 46 (quoting Richard Glen Boire, cofounder of the Center for Cognitive Liberty and Ethics in California, referring to "memory management drugs" in the offing, some of which he states are "designed to help dim or to erase the memories that haunt people suffering post-traumatic stress disorder"). There are, of course, many different forms of amnesia. See generally Andrew M. Colman, ed., *A Dictionary of Psychology* (Oxford: Oxford University Press, 2001), s.v. "amnesia." Oxford Reference Online, http://www. oxfordreference.com/views/ENTRY.html?subview=Main&entry=t87.e364 (August 13, 2004).

[54] Broad skepticism about such technological possibilities is ill-advised if it is based simply on the complexity of human mental functioning and the fact that it takes a lot of genes and a lot of neurochemistry to generate mental functions of any sort, never mind the most complex. A single gene or set of genes may have immense influence on the development of memory and reasoning capacities. See generally Shapiro et al., eds., *Bioethics and Law*, part VIII. There are, after all, only a relatively few genes that separate us from chimpanzees. See Sharon Begley, "What Distinguishes Us from the Chimps? Actually, Not Much," *Wall Street Journal*, April 12, 2002, A13 (Westlaw: 2002 WL-WSJ 3391541). Of course, one can still doubt on other grounds that we will ever discover and master the techniques required for enhancement.

that one concept is an aspect of another concept, however, is not to say that there is really only one concept to identify; it is to link them logically. A distinctive feature of such mutually defining concepts is that they may refer to each other in an unending cycle. For example, whether a given trait change is thought to bear on identity may depend on the importance of the trait, but its importance may rest on ideas of personhood—say, on some attribute of cognitive understanding or perception. Are we dealing with separate concepts, extensionally equivalent concepts, or different ideas locked in conceptual ping pong?

D. A short list of questions concerning personal identity

The concepts designated by "identity" and its cognates are embedded in everything we do, but we rarely think about this (this includes philosophers and lawyers) because it is usually pointless to do so. For the most part, the presence of a concept (or anything else) is *noticed* only when the concept is in some sense challenged. Raising some pointed questions from a variety of contexts may help clarify some issues about the "identity" of the idea of personal identity, and, more generally, may reveal additional aspects of the conceptual impacts of technological control of traits.

1. What is the work done by the concept of identity in any given sphere—and specifically, what work does it do that is not done by other concepts, separately or in any combination?

2. What is the connection between one's identity and any given set of one's attributes or traits? To what extent is this dictated by species characteristics, and to what extent by cultural variables? Ted Williams is said by many to have been the greatest hitter in baseball history. Perhaps one could say that his exceptional ability to hit small, fast-moving objects with a stick was a defining characteristic of "what it means to be Ted Williams," as it might be put in everyday language. Perhaps this holds true from both his perspective and that of others.

3. Does the proper use of "identity" in formulas such as "X has undergone an identity change" require an all-or-nothing ascription such as "X has changed her identity; she is no longer the same person she was before, although her physical embodiment as the selfsame entity continues uninterrupted"? Or should the proper default usage be "X has undergone an identity change with respect to μ," rather than the more global ascription of flat-out identity change? If the ascription is not global, wouldn't it be misleading to refer to partial or limited-respect change of identity?

4. If it is technologically open to us to change personal attributes in ourselves and others, and to alter the default traits of possible persons via alteration of their genomes, what traits should we change, or allow to be changed? Are there standards, principles, and rules that serve as moral

channels, allowing us to distinguish among trait changes that are impermissible, permissible, desirable, or mandatory?

Note that leaving matters to the "genetic supermarket"[55] concerns only the specific question of *who decides* what traits are to be selected. It does not settle, whether for the individual within the market or for any other decision maker, *what to select*.

5. If choosing basic traits and/or their measures is possible, what responsibilities would the "designers" and "engineers" and the altered persons themselves bear for flawed outcomes and other adverse consequences? And what is a "flawed outcome" or "adverse consequence"?

6. Does the capacity to choose or alter traits entail the risk (or is it a benefit?) of human reduction, understood in part as the perception that a person, or persons generally, are "nothing but" (their capacities to bear children) (their intellectual abilities), and so on? And might such reductive perceptions be accompanied by the view that a person is an "object," subject to mere use by others?

7. What sorts of boundaries or limitations, if any, exist for this expanding field of choice? Is this a matter of moral concern? What reasons are there for using or avoiding authorizing/limiting concepts such as—

—*disorder models*[56] as limiting and authorizing tools for uses of technology. Are *social handicap models* too loose?

—*identity models* (or *identity-preservation models*) as limiting and authorizing tools for uses of technology—as in "No technological changes are permitted if they would compromise the endurance of personal identity."

—the idea of *nature* (and its links to identity and disorder).

---

[55] Robert Nozick, *Anarchy, State, and Utopia* (New York: Basic Books, 1974), 315 n. *. See generally Jonathan Glover, *What Sort of People Should There Be?* (New York: Penguin Books, 1984).

[56] For present purposes, a model is an abstract guide for pursuing certain tasks, such as description and evaluation, and justification or limitation of various kinds of action. A disorder model, for example, might authorize certain interventions into someone's physiological processes upon diagnosis of certain disorders (say, growth hormone for pituitary disorders), and might authorize withholding interventions when not justified by confirmation of disorder (no growth hormone for short but non-disordered persons). A social handicap model would use a criterion for intervention based on excessive difficulty in pursuing standard human activities (e.g., operating a motor vehicle). Under such a model, extremely short (but not necessarily disordered) persons might qualify for growth hormone. Tall persons who simply want to be taller would probably not qualify under either model; being not quite tall enough for the National Basketball Association would probably not evidence either a disorder or a social handicap. An enhancement model would be extremely broad-based—authorizing interventions to augment traits, but not to diminish them. (The unenhanced or less-enhanced might, depending on the circumstances, also invoke a social handicap model.) An identity model might be incorporated within an enhancement model to limit enhancements to those that do not threaten the integrity of personal identity. The concurrent applicability of all these models in given cases might reinforce or diminish arguments for intervention. What the moral and legal foundations for these models might be is not discussed here.

—the *continuity and coherence* of change (integrity?).
—the preservation of traditional notions of *merit and blame*.
—*coordinating matters of ownership*, entitlement, and the like.

These are conceptual standards meant to tell us when we may, must, shouldn't, and mustn't exercise a power in order to avoid its getting out of control. But why would limits on trait change be necessary? What does "out of control" mean anyway? The most obvious background idea here is using disorder models—to the exclusion of enhancement models—to implement ideas of human nature as normative, to be restored when impaired but not otherwise tampered with;[57] to control medical costs (insurers are reluctant to fund cosmetic measures, for example, unless related to the amelioration of defects or injuries); to conform to religious injunctions concerning healing; and so on.

8. What is the moral significance, if any, of the lost possibility of an alternative or default identity that would have come into existence, or would have continued to exist or develop, had the technological intervention not occurred? If the felt notion of a default, "would have been" identity bears any moral significance, does it derive from anything other than psychological burdens? Is the default identity in any sense a person's "true identity" whose integrity was breached?

9. Are there special—or *any*—problems of identity associated with *cloning?*

10. The problem of "Who merits merit?" Would enhancements of merit attributes such as intelligence and physical strength be self-reinforcing because they step up the basis for still more expansion of powers to attract wealth and other rewards? Would facing such questions, bearing on central aspects of equality, fairness, and other basic values, be so troubling that we should not enter this region of technological resources at all?[58]

11. Do affirmations or denials of change in identity embed moral as well as empirical/conceptual claims? For example, would a significant shift in someone's moral attitudes be a better case for ascribing identity change than a significant shift in intelligence, unaccompanied by such attitude changes?[59] Do changes in physical appearance and capacities count for less than changes in mental functioning? In what sense? Is there a moral hierarchy of identity-relevant changes? This may in theory eventually be reflected in legal problems—such as who is to inherit from an estate when two persons have exchanged brain hemispheres.

[57] See Shapiro, "Fragmenting and Reassembling the World," 343.

[58] See generally Michael H. Shapiro, "Who Merits Merit? Problems in Distributive Justice and Utility Posed by the New Biology," *Southern California Law Review* 48, no. 2 (1974): 318–70; and Michael H. Shapiro, "The Technology of Perfection: Performance Enhancement and the Control of Attributes," *Southern California Law Review* 65, no. 1 (1991): 11–113.

[59] Such changes are hard to view as discrete changes, allowing for a ceteris paribus assumption; they will all have cascading, polycentric effects.

IX. The "Identity Effects" of Technological Alteration
of Human Traits

A. Suppression and highlighting of traits

Personal identity has a complex and uncertain connection with a person's traits. At its simplest, it is a functional link of sorts—as in "*x* is a (partial) function of *y*." But when and why should we be concerned with the connection between trait change and identity—with determining when the nature and degree of trait change bears on personal identity?

Finding an answer to this question (if there is one) will require attention to an obvious but sometimes overlooked fact: sometimes we stress interpersonal differences and sometimes we suppress or at least ignore or downplay them. Indeed, in many contexts whether we suppress or highlight such differences may be viewed as required by basic values. Differences in characteristics among persons often rightly dominate decision making in forming personal relationships, or in accomplishing major social, political, and economic tasks; this is such a global point that extended discussion is unnecessary. In other contexts, however, interpersonal differences may not only make no difference, but relying on them would be thought morally and legally unacceptable, on now-standard accounts of equality, fairness, and justice. In distributing rights to vote, for example, we are interested in only the simple, intuitive notion of whether we are dealing with the qualified voter Jane Smith or some imposter—an "identity" issue in a very simple sense—and her personal attributes are largely irrelevant for any purpose beyond serving as identity markers.[60] With voting, then, we suppress most interpersonal trait differences, many of which are relevant in other contexts.[61]

B. What does "trait change" mean?

Here I draw briefly on an earlier work discussing the idea of trait change in persons.[62] The general points are these:

"Trait" is close to primitive. It is thus hard to respond clearly to the questions, "What is a trait? How do we recognize something *as* a trait?" For our purposes, a trait is best understood as an aspect or feature of someone,[63] and it can refer to things that are ontologically quite different:

---

[60] Of course there may be (dis)qualifications required by law—a minimum age, no felony convictions, residence, etc.

[61] Such political equality is not an objectionable move toward interpersonal fungibility, but the point is unimportant for present purposes.

[62] Shapiro, "The Technology of Perfection," 45–46.

[63] It is "[a] particular feature of mind or character; a distinguishing quality; a characteristic. . . ." *Oxford English Dictionary*, 2d ed. (Oxford: Oxford University Press, 2004); http://dictionary.oed.com/cgi/entry/00255902?query_type=word&queryword=trait&edition=2e&first=1&max_to_show=10&sort_type=alpha&result_place=1&search_id=UQxP-mYET7B-599&hilite=00255902 (accessed August 1, 2004). This is ambiguous because (among other things) it does not specify the subject of the quality, which could be an individual, a set, or

appearance, characteristics of muscle tissue, particular configurations of neurons, properties of electrochemical processes, great physical strength, the ability to draw usefully on that strength, memory, analytical abilities in one field or another, mentational and behavioral dispositions of variously described sorts, and so on.[64] This is a wide-ranging assortment, and some readers may want to displace several entries by "reducing" them to others (e.g., mentalist notions reduced to materialist constructs). I have already noted the "cultural relativity" of some trait designations.

We are, of course, talking about traits in contexts where sharp technological alteration of our physiological structures and processes—and hence of our behavioral and mental dispositions—is increasingly possible. We thus need to understand clearly that, whatever we think a trait is, there is no assurance that any technology at any time will precisely target "it" for desired modification. For one thing, the conceptual uncertainty may prevent us from designating a "trait" that could be fixed as a target. For another, the physics and chemistry of life do not necessarily "track" our designations of traits. Even if we had a clear idea of the trait we wished to address, there may be no way to control and alter it because it may rest on physiological conditions too complex and diffuse—possibly not even subject to clear specification—to be manageable.

As for changes in these traits, they can occur in various ways, under various circumstances, whether "by chance or choice." For now, I simply say that, for various reasons, we generally applaud alterations authorized by disorder, trauma, defect, and handicap models; they are likely to be viewed as curing or repairing rather than as "trait changes." Our views of technological alterations outside these models of justification are less favorable—for example, use of stimulants for entertainment purposes; perhaps using memory-enhancing substances to increase current abilities not impaired by disorder; or creating capacities that did not exist before, either in a given person (e.g., the ability to run one hundred meters in less than ten seconds, which a few persons have) or in humans generally (running that distance in five seconds).

C. Identifying identity-relevant trait changes

1. The traits that seem to matter most to most people.[65] The traits that matter most include merit attributes and/or resource attractors.[66] (The

---

any entity. Also, I use the term "trait" to apply even to qualities that do not distinguish an entity as an individual rather than as a member of a set.

[64] I use "trait," "attribute," and "characteristic" interchangeably here.

[65] This discussion has parallels to that of "centrality" of traits, as discussed in Amélie Oksenberg Rorty and David Wong, "Aspects of Identity and Agency," in Owen Flanagan and Amélie Oksenberg Rorty, eds., *Identity, Character, and Morality* (Cambridge, MA: MIT Press, 1990), 19–21.

[66] The resources attracted are not restricted to pure economic resources—e.g., they might include mates, friends, and business associates. Of course, for certain purposes, economic values can be estimated and placed on such resources.

two sets overlap.) Such characteristics help explain the survival and adaptive successes of humanity, and the achievements of particular persons or groups in particular social settings. These characteristics may be viewed by some as aspects of human nature, however defined. (No doubt some believe that aspects of these very traits—intelligence, foresight, ambition, aggressiveness, industry, sociability—will help bring about humanity's fall.) There are, of course, cultural variations in the recognition of traits as traits and in how they are valued and measured. Detail is not required here; I simply note that we generally admire various mental and physical aptitudes and abilities, physical attractiveness and stature, and, in a more explicitly evaluative domain, mentational and behavioral dispositions that display sound character and virtue.

2. *Characterizing the nature of the change: Coherence and continuity, now and in the future; intrusiveness; disorder and handicap; nature; impact on merit and blame ascriptions.*

a. *Coherence and continuity of trait changes; merit, desert, and distribution.* To some extent, "coherence" and "continuity" in individual lives and in personal interactions are needed if we want some degree of stability and predictability, and indeed they are required for many common social and political goals of human society. In turn, such stability depends on the relative constancy of the respective identities of individual persons. To close the loop, "incoherent" and "discontinuous" trait changes might be thought to compromise identity, and thus the stability of individual life paths and social interactions.

We invoke ideas of coherence in many contexts: judging scientific hypotheses, formulating theories of meaning, interpreting texts, evaluating developments in decisional law, and, more broadly, in assessing social relationships, societal goals, and personal life-plans. Like identity itself, coherence is an explicit or implicit constant or consideration across everything we think and do.

Analysts who rely on ideas of coherence often state that it is not a matter of simple consistency—as in requiring that a set of propositions not lead to both x and not-x. There is no reason to try to settle this. I observe only that it is at least arguable that whenever a conceptual system is said to be incoherent, that system—conceived of as a set of formulas or propositions—must at some point, however complex the path, lead to an inconsistency. However, demonstrating the inconsistency may be difficult or contested: a showing of contradiction presupposes interpretation, to put it loosely, and if there is no agreement on the meaning of the propositions whose consistency *inter se* is challenged, there is no closure on the issue of coherence. This is likely to be so with attributions of "incoherent" or even "discontinuous" trait changes: what seems to be a sharp change in behavior may be coherent, even smooth, in light of considerations that are not readily apparent. Coherence may be indeterminate because it rests in part on matters of perception and valuation, which in many cases must precede any search for formal inconsistency.

Ideas of (in)coherence may be important in distinguishing trait changes that are identity-relevant from those that are not. If any trait changes are indeed identity-relevant, they probably involve merit and resource-attractive attributes. In turn, this is relevant because, for better or worse, the ideas of merit and desert are broadly used to distribute the rewards of life generally. This holds to some extent in market systems: one's ability to compete for goods and services in such systems is often viewed as a (very) rough proxy for underlying merit.[67] Incoherent and discontinuous changes in traits may compromise one's merit claims by compromising one's identity—as when a technologically enhanced runner wins a race he otherwise would have lost badly. Of course, depending on circumstances, we may prefer to say that the runner's identity is intact but that his performance lacks the proper merit credentials because of serious trait changes that rendered the contest unfair or pointless. The two locutions easily blend into each other.

b. Merit attributes and resource attractors in distributional systems. Goods and services can be distributed through many different mechanisms. I note simply that outcomes of market transactions may be taken as rough proxies for merit of certain sorts, although the bare ability to command and bid resources for goods and services within a market can stand alone as a functioning (if not entirely sound) distributional criterion and does not *require* reference to "merit" at all.[68] Some commodities—for example, access to educational institutions—are more explicitly (though not exclusively) merit-based, often resting on measurements of aptitudes and skills acquired through prior training.

Of course, markets and explicitly merit-based systems are not the only ways to distribute commodities. Some are distributed by, say, kinship relationships, conquest, theft, or competition within something akin to

[67] I do not probe the concept of merit here. See generally George Sher, *Desert* (Princeton, NJ: Princeton University Press, 1989).

[68] The idea of merit is particularly tricky in some commercial contexts. However, I cannot fully investigate the extent to which any particular distribution system—market, kinship, centralized administration—reflects or departs from merit. Much depends on what "merit" is thought to include. Some find it odd that attractive thin females can earn substantial sums modeling clothes, but their particular traits are culturally defined merit attributes. Perhaps the ability to find prime numbers or return tennis serves reflects greater merit, but within each domain, differences in income may at least loosely correlate with skills and talent, even given the substantial effects of "luck," "chance," or sheer persistence (the capacity for which may itself reflect a merit attribute). To be sure, simply having money in itself has no necessary connection to merit. Nevertheless, if someone outbids a competitor at an honest auction, it would be considered unfair to deny her the commodity she seeks, in part because of the reasonable expectations and reliance generated by the market institution she entered. Her legal action, if any, would be "meritorious" in that restricted sense. She *merits* the commodity *within the "game" as defined*. One could go on to say, in addition, that in a market system, possessing resource-attractive traits is a form of merit *within the market culture*. "Merit," it seems, is quite protean.

localized states of nature. However, at least in much of contemporary civilization, Western or Eastern, there is a rough correlation between characteristics viewed as morally praiseworthy merit attributes and those that can be described more neutrally as resource-attractors: intelligence and abilities of certain sorts; virtues such as reliability and loyalty; diligence and the capacity to exert effort. In this respect, markets are far more merit-related than, say, kinship systems.[69]

These merit attributes and resource-attractors are historic targets for improvement and upgrading in traditional ways—e.g., "practice," as the historic directions to Carnegie Hall go. They will certainly be prime targets for technological enhancement. Increases in the strength of one's resource-attractive traits may bring ever-increasing and ever-accelerating enlargements in one's economic, political, and personal powers. Increments in the very resource-attractors that brought in earlier resources continuingly expand one's "merit base" and thus one's bidding powers to command resources of all kinds in an accelerating positive feedback cycle. The distributional issues for merit-enhancing traits thus take on an importance lacking in other commodities that do not, *by their very consumption*, significantly raise the power of the distributee to make future merit claims for "merit-enhancing" (or any) resources—the very resource-attractors that allowed accumulation to begin in the first place.[70]

Elsewhere, I refer to this as the problem of "Who merits merit?"[71] The phrase should be taken (at least tentatively) as metaphoric because of moral doubts that technological enhancements can indeed count as enhancements of *merit*,[72] rather than of the pure power to attract resources. This distributional situation bears the possibility of irreversible entrenchment and enlargement of social, economic, and political inequalities because of the increasing "distance" in abilities and other merit qualities between those who receive enhancement resources and those who do not. Them that hath will get more, and the rest will lose what little they do hath, as was said, more literately, in the Bible.[73]

c. The ways of change in attributes; personal betterment. There may be limited exceptions, but most contemporary civilizations seem, in varying ways and degrees, to have absorbed the idea of progress, both for groups

---

[69] To be sure, kinship relations—by "bloodlines," marriage, etc.—might be seen as constituting merit within some normative/conceptual systems. ("Blood is everything.")

[70] There are clear analogues to this that do not involve technological elite-creating resources. Consumption of educational resources, for example, elevates one's starting claims for still more education services, and so on. Similarly, accumulating money increases one's "commercial merit" for securing still more money.

[71] See note 58.

[72] The merit ascription can apply both to the process of enhancement (including its pre-planning) and its outcome.

[73] "For unto every one that hath shall be given, and he shall have abundance: But from him that hath not shall be taken away even that which he hath." Matthew 25:29. The phrase "Matthew Effect" was coined by Robert K. Merton, "The Matthew Effect in Science," *Science* 159, no. 3810 (1968): 56–63.

and for individuals: progress, in some sense, has become part of the canon of desirable, possibly morally mandatory human goals.

But personal progress has generally (if not exclusively) been understood to require effort, and perhaps luck. Advancement is expected to be incremental and gradual, and to require struggle, even for the natively endowed elite, at least when they are at the outer limits of their abilities.[74] Of course, the capacity to expend strong effort is itself a merit attribute, and, in theory, can also be strengthened.

Consider next the possibility of (partially) bypassing effort and using technological routes to higher attribute measures and skill levels. Popular commentary aside, there is an enormous difference between what present technologies of performance enhancement can do and what some people think they can do (or may do in the future). The public discussion of the use of various forms of steroids is an obvious example. Some people seem to think that ingesting them enhances strength or endurance with little or no effort, and the athlete becomes something that he or she "really" isn't. For that audience—especially the young and presumably more impressionable—the use of steroids may reinforce objectionable visions of free rides and bigger bangs for the buck. It seems far more accurate to say that ingesting steroids *may* have effects on physical (and possibly mentational) attributes *at the margin*, which *may* improve performance *in small, if telling, increments*. Small increments in performance may of course mark the difference between winning and losing, and require ever greater inputs of effort, with or without steroids. Although the time needed for any given degree of enhancement may be reduced compared with traditional efforts, one still doesn't just swell up with muscular bulk all at once.[75] One has to keep working out and expending effort—beyond what is required to swallow pills or prepare for an injection—and the returns are diminishing. Indeed, one of the enhancing effects of steroids is said to be to increase the physical capacity to keep expending physical effort, and this is part of the effectiveness of steroids in improving performance. In this somewhat paradoxical sense, steroid use may at once enhance the value of true effort in one way and devalue it in another.

Inflated beliefs or not, few think that anyone's identity is seriously compromised by using steroids. If Marsha wins Wimbledon and is found

[74] The degree of "struggle" required to master a given task is roughly inverse to one's baseline abilities. There is some tension between the relative merit-status of native endowments and of effort. Some people have difficulty in deciding whether it is the less-talented but determined competitor who is more praiseworthy, or, instead, the more-talented, less resolute party. Of course, the analysis is even more complex because the capacity to mount efforts is also a function of native endowment.

[75] But cf. David Cohen, "Cheating Is Easier Than You Think: Steroids Boost Performance in Just Three Weeks," *New Scientist*, no. 2460 (August 2004): 6–7; available online at http://www.newscientist.com/ (stating that "[e]ven a low dose of testosterone can give athletes a big performance boost—and in a fraction of the time thought necessary, a study initiated by *New Scientist* has found").

to have taken steroids, we don't say: "It wasn't Marsha who won, it was someone else, someone she turned into, like Billy Batson saying 'Shazam' and turning into Captain Marvel." We say instead: "Marsha—our Marsha— seems to have won, but she really didn't *win*, not because someone else won (she-who-had-been-Marsha-but-isn't-anymore), but because she *cheated*."[76]

If we assume that steroid use had been "decriminalized" and proved harmless,[77] that the substances were available to all who wanted them, and that users gained identical increments in performance ability (however defined), we might now be more willing to say that Marsha had won, this time without cheating. Our view of the nature of the contest may have shifted to include a *technological baseline* for what constitutes acceptable enhancement, as with the "Mentats" in Frank Herbert's novel *Dune*—a group of very talented and significantly enhanced "wizards" retained by competing feudal Houses about ten thousand years in the future. On these quite strained assumptions—used here to help clarify some issues—the bell-shaped performance curve will simply have been shifted to the right, preserving the relative positions of the competitors.[78]

Next, given the technological and nontechnological (or less technological) routes to similar results,[79] we need to ask when and why the moral qualities of these end-states—that is, performance abilities and outcomes— might be path-dependent.

   d. *Betterment and path dependence—the paradox of perfectionism;*[80] *the relevance, if any, of what preceded bottom-line betterment.* This is how the "paradox" is structured: Consider the personal characteristics a society values the most at a given time—for example, intellectual abilities of certain sorts, physical strength and aptitude, and diligence in pursuing goals requiring strong efforts. These are the prime traits for improvement via traditional "upgrading" methods: study, training, and practice. Yet they seem to be the most untouchable with respect to technological

---

[76] The concept of cheating bears analytical difficulties that I leave undiscussed.

[77] Steroid use clearly bears serious risks. See Shapiro et al., eds., *Bioethics and Law*, 1438–43. I do not address the possibility of unfair coercive incentives for athletes to take risks they would prefer not to take. I note only that the existence of "traditional" risks inherent in the game and in training does not suggest that just any new incremental risks required to maintain competitiveness must also be acceptable.

[78] Of course, comparing records over time would be difficult if the baseline keeps changing.

[79] "Result," "end-state," and "outcome" are ambiguous, but the ambiguities are of little consequence for present purposes. They may be important in more detailed studies of performance enhancement and identity.

[80] I am using "perfectionism" loosely. The term has several varying (though linked) meanings. See generally Will Kymlicka, *Liberalism, Community, and Culture* (Oxford: Clarendon Press; New York: Oxford University Press, 1989), 33 ("A perfectionist theory includes a particular view, or range of views, about what dispositions and attributes define human perfection, and it views the development of these as our essential interest"). For a critical analysis of perfectionist theories, see Tom Regan, *The Case for Animal Rights* (Berkeley: University of California Press, 1983), 233–35. See also Ronald R. Garet, "Self-Transformability," *Southern California Law Review* 65, no. 1 (1991): 121–203.

alteration—a kind of tampering with the inviolable. Why inviolable? Perhaps because these traits are ordained by Nature or by God, or because the uncertain effects of rearranging basic life processes render it intrinsically (and at least instrumentally) immoral, or because of some vague precautionary principle that privileges nature and tradition as the presumptively safest routes. I have to leave this line of inquiry open, however.

The traits that we most want to develop, then, are also the traits that are to be the most insulated from artificial, unnatural, externally generated, and thus (possibly) identity-threatening augmentation. On this view, such augmentation would not be praiseworthy, would not result in enhanced merit, and might be affirmatively wrong. It may increase the resource-attractiveness of one's merit traits, but such an increase in resource-attractiveness does not, standing alone, really increase one's true moral merit; it only increases one's moral entitlements given compliance with the rules of the distribution system in place. (And perhaps whatever reward or credit is due must be shared with parents and bioengineers.) There is nothing intrinsically praiseworthy about *merely* enhancing such traits; the outcome is praiseworthy only if it is the terminus of the right paths. Improving ourselves in morally unsuitable ways thus does not perfect us; even worse, it seems to lessen us. In this sense, more is less. Or so one could argue.

The supposed paradox, then, is that (a) the merit traits most favored for enhancement are those for which technological means—the most efficient road to enhancement—are the most suspect; but (b) if they are indeed the most favored, they are probably the most resource-attractive and thus the most socially/economically useful; and (c) if so, we should want to enhance the measures of these most-valued traits in the most efficient way we can, so everyone can be better off through greater productivity, innovation, and economic advancement. There is thus a tension between maximizing (true) merit and maximizing socioeconomic utility, and in some cases, doing the latter defeats the former. The claim that *technologized* enhancement of merit attributes does *not* enhance or reflect merit constitutes one "arm" of the paradox, the other arm being our continuing interest in both merit and utility maximization.[81] The paradox, such as it is, would wither if we gave up on merit or gave up on wealth maximization, or, possibly, if we reconstructed the concept of merit to comprehend technologized increments in the strength of merit attributes.

We can now say, tentatively, that technological augmentation at least suggests breaches of the integrity of personal identity—without altogether obliterating it—and leaves us confused when it is time to assign credit or blame and bestow awards or penalties. The process of

---

[81] These are not fully disjointed. A given utility function may include preferences concerning the moral values associated with true merit.

technologized trait development may present results that seem incoherent or discontinuous with customary modes of self-improvement.[82]

Moreover, to the extent that assignments of merit become dubious or even vacuous when we face technological enhancement, equality criteria in judging distributional schemes are also confused. On some theories of equality, the accumulation of greater rewards to the more meritorious not only does not violate equality standards, it is required by them. If we cannot tell who *really* won without cheating, how would we assign the reward? Who would be admitted to what educational institutions or awarded what positions? Should we just drop consideration of the person's prior trait profile and start dealing with the new one, *however* it was developed? Or, on the contrary, should we ignore the new configuration of traits and use the previous (now a counterfactual) one as the distributional guide? After all, we are, under current conditions, still dealing with the same person: despite the possible developmental incoherences and gaps between the before-and-after profiles, there remains a clear line of continuance that preserves overall identity.

e. Disorder control[83] *and personal transformation: Operating in the shadow of identity.* One of the moral claims embedded in a disorder model is that various nontrivial interventions[84] into body and mind are justified only if they are meant to cure or mitigate the effects of disorder (disease, illness, trauma, defect, injury). This justification is not available when intervention occurs for other reasons: entertainment and recreation; the closely related goal of escape from reality; enhancement of traits and performance; happiness; and so on. The illustrative distinction between use of a memory-enhancing drug by a dementia patient and one used by a student preparing for exams is relatively familiar—although we might loosely say that both the dementia patient and the student have been "enhanced" if the intervention is effective.

Many think it obvious that use of enhancement modalities "outside" a disorder model is wrong. It may be wrong, but this is not obvious. Consider the claim that "it wasn't really Jack doing the memory work—it was the medicine." Medicine for disorder restores you to yourself by releasing your real self from captivity. Medicine for enhancement, however, takes you away from yourself and establishes a new, artificial plane of being and performance—or so it might be put. The moral monopoly of the

---

[82] See, e.g., Nozick, *Philosophical Explanations*, 65–66 ("For us to understand why identity matters, we must understand why the closest continuer, when it exists, gets special caring. . . . '. . . [W]hy do I especially care about my future self if it is simply (merely?) my current self's closest continuer?'").

[83] For an exploration of the nature and limits of disorder and other models, see Norman Daniels, *Just Health Care* (Cambridge and New York: Cambridge University Press, 1985).

[84] "Intervention" is something of a weasel word. Talk therapy, for example, is a kind of intervention into one's dispositions, as are sound waves impinging on one's eardrum. In this essay, however, the term refers primarily to intrusive physical interventions directly into the body.

disorder model is thus reinforced by these comparative accounts of causal attribution: in the one account, the self maintains its integrity while being restored by treatment—a process that is absorbed into an intact identity; in the other account, the self is transmuted into a new one by a process that remains "external" to the original self, however well integrated into the new.

Perhaps, then, there are realms of trait change in which there is a pathology that is identifiable, relatively discrete, and substantially removable without serious side-effects. In those cases, the removal of the pathology does not result in anything like global identity change. No one will say, "This isn't Sally"; they'll say, "This is Sally, flourishing, the new Sally who has the same identity as the old Sally but is better equipped for life because both her depression and her obsessive-compulsive disorder (OCD) have been controlled." For such cases, it seems off the mark to apply psychiatrist Peter Kramer's phrase "better than well"[85] (from his book *Listening to Prozac*) to Sally's case: she is better than she was because two disorders, depression and OCD, were dealt with—one that presents in cycles (depression), and another that is almost always present (OCD). It is the amelioration or subtraction of the latter that may inspire "Behold the new, improved Sally," as opposed to "Our old Sally is back."

As for the role of identity: In Sally's case, perhaps the idea of identity, while instructive in many ways, does no significant obvious work. Still, our account seems to take place "in the shadow" of identity as an abstract descriptive and evaluative criterion:[86] "go no further than this, or we might be in moral trouble."

3. *Identity, person-perception, reduction, and objectification. Is cognitive psychology relevant? Trait alteration and identity change as risking reduction.*

a. *The idea of person-perception in cognitive science, and its connection to human reduction or devaluation; the bearing of objectification on identity.* In part, we perceive persons as persons—and as particular persons—by recognizing (perhaps not fully consciously) particular traits from the chaos of our sensorium. The nature of this process is contested both by scientists and by philosophers. But in whatever way it is accomplished, we see that this person is huge, that that one is rotund, and that the one over there is playing the piano. In many cases, we resist—for good reason—focusing on any given characteristic; we try to see the person as (very roughly speaking) an "entirety" (a gestalt perception of sorts), though with obvious emphases here and there. It is also clear that, at the same time, we

---

[85] Peter D. Kramer, *Listening to Prozac* (New York: Viking, 1993), xv (stating that although patients occasionally are "remarkably restored," Prozac made many patients "better than well").

[86] This roughly parallels the jurisprudential phrase "bargaining in the shadow of the law." In the context of such bargaining, the point is that private parties may reach accommodation among themselves in ways that would not be generated by formal adjudication—but the threat or possibility of formal adjudication affects the bargaining process and specific outcomes.

often view persons *as* one thing or another, in varying respects. For example, here is Donovan the quarterback (or, sometimes, Donovan the black quarterback), and yonder is Martha the pianist. Most of the time, these are not viewed as reductive descriptions, and the people described would rarely protest them; the descriptions affirm their value as persons of strong talent and accomplishment.

Persons may not want to be described *solely* in these ways, however. They may fear that some forms of person-perception might be vehicles for reduction of a person's overall value to the value of a specific trait or group of traits (however "value" is understood in context). Donovan would surely insist that he has a life beyond quarterbacking, and Martha is not simply a pianist—and neither of them wishes to be viewed as a commodity.

Thus, we have another paradox (or irony), this time in person-perception: What seems to be one and the same perceptual process is intrinsically both part of an affirmative valuation of a person because of her favorable traits, say, Y and Z, and *also* part of her reduction to a merely useful entity because she bears those very traits, Y and Z.[87] Perhaps valuing and devaluing persons—and differentiating persons from each other beyond noting their separateness—are all the same thing, looked at from different value perspectives and goals. Operationally, if not conceptually, the processes of human reduction, human elevation, and interpersonal differentiation may in many respects be indistinguishable.

"Reduction," in this context, of course does not refer to claims that, say, all talk about mental entities is "reducible" to talk about physical entities and processes, or that, ontologically, one sort of thing (say, mental stuff) is really nothing but another sort of thing (material stuff). It is about human reduction—a psychological, perceptual, and evaluative matter. Full human reduction is the process or the product of viewing persons as having little or no intrinsic moral value; their worth, at least to persons other than themselves, is instrumental only. This instrumental value lies exclusively in a discrete trait or set of traits. I suppose the most obvious and total form of human reduction is slavery in its various forms, although one could argue whether the reduction was "complete" in any given setting.

In other forms of human reduction, however, persons are at least sometimes reduced to specific traits, in the eyes of particular persons or groups. To a customer, a prostitute might be "nothing but" her sexual attractiveness, sexual prowess, and her willingness to make them available commercially. To the owner of a professional sports team, perhaps the team members are viewed simply as mechanisms for assuring profit through the exploitation of their athletic traits.[88]

---

[87] See generally Robert A. Stewart et al., *Person Perception and Stereotyping* (Farnborough, England: Saxon House, 1979), 14–15.

[88] Cf. Sharon E. Rush, "Touchdowns, Toddlers, and Taboos: On Paying College Athletes and Surrogate Contract Mothers," *Arizona Law Review* 31, no. 3 (1989): 549–614, 573–74.

The connection between this relational concept of human reduction and the often used term "objectification" is obvious.[89] Indeed, the connection may be one of identity (depending on context and usage), or at least extensional equivalence. To say that prostitutes are (fully) objectified is to say that they are reduced to objects with little or no intrinsic value in the eyes of *some* persons or groups; they bear primarily only the instrumental value identified with their sexual traits. It is also to say that prostitutes are used as mere means—by certain parties.[90]

If persons with certain traits—dwarfism, for example—become valued for purposes of, say, space travel in cramped quarters, then "breeding" them and impressing them into such service would be a paradigm of reduction of persons to nothing but (i.e., to being fully identified with) the value of a particular trait. Many refer to such reproductive "manufacturing" processes as "genetic diminishment," but of course, relative to the tasks involved, the users of these persons—and perhaps the persons themselves—may view their traits as enhancements, not diminishments, at least when they are compared with others who wish to travel in space. It nevertheless seems clear that reduction and objectification are bound up with the notion of mere use, in the sense of the second formulation of Kant's categorical imperative, which enjoins us to treat persons as ends in themselves, and never as mere means.[91] I do not try to specify the exact conceptual connections among reduction, objectification, and mere use.

How do reduction, objectification, and mere use bear on personal identity, if at all? They would seem to affect identity as perceived by others and by oneself, and in some extreme situations the reduced/objectified/merely-used party may operate functionally *as* an object, from all viewpoints, including his own. To display the link to the idea of identity more specifically: Saying that "X has been reduced in value to her capacity to serve as a procreative vessel (e.g., a surrogate mother)" is saying, still more loosely, that she is "identified with" her reproductive capacities and her willingness to rent them out.

b. Planned identity change and the risk of reduction. The very idea of directed trait change requires us to *focus* on the trait(s) in question: whatever drives this focus—self-improvement, enhancing the value of our slaves, ruling the world—is a matter of *planning*. If, for example, we have a reproductive plan at a fairly specific level of generality (compare "We want to have a child" with "We want to have a girl" with "We want to have a child with a genome identical to Meryl Streep's"), we are neces-

---

[89] "Commodification" is mainly the commercial form of objectification.

[90] These are hyperbolic descriptions; prostitutes, professional athletes, artists, etc., are not usually viewed as devoid of all intrinsic value, although this may vary across settings.

[91] "Act in such a way that you always treat humanity, whether in your own person or in the person of any other, never simply as a means but always at the same time as an end." Thomas E. Hill, Jr., *Dignity and Practical Reason in Kant's Moral Theory* (Ithaca, NY: Cornell University Press, 1992), 38–39.

sarily *centering our attention* on a subset of attributes (variously described) to the exclusion (at least temporarily) of others.

If technological intervention into personal attributes were serious or striking enough to raise identity questions, then the risk of reduction would probably be elevated, although not necessarily at a maximum. This is *not* part of an argument on my part against human enhancement; I think the risk of reduction/objectification/mere use is greatly overblown. It is not zero, however, and it seems likely that there will be instances in which directed trait change effects a reduction of one's *perceived* identity, and an elevation of one's perceived objecthood, both defined by the deliberately selected and altered traits.

I note one more perspective on trait change and its connection to reduction, objectification, and mere use of persons. Compare technological alteration of traits with the modifications of machines. If we are doing *the same sort of thing* to persons as we do to machines (compare adjusting the toaster from "toast" to "bagel" with switching Donovan the quarterback from "pass" to "run"), perhaps we are objectifying persons by assimilating—reducing—them to things.[92] (This is not necessarily a matter of conscious awareness.)

When one makes comparisons, however, one is identifying differences as well as similarities. Upgrading a computer by installing more memory may bear an analogy to human memory improvement, but it bears fairly strong disanalogies also.[93] It will not do simply to say that memory improvement for the non-demented, or muscle-bulking for athletes, is just like souping up your car's engine.

c. The cascading (perhaps chaotic) effects of directed trait change.[94] A trait change—particularly a sharp one—cannot be adequately analyzed without considering the relationships between that trait and others, and the complex network of effects deriving from the alteration. A significant change in appearance, for example (whether through plastic surgery, accident, disease, or aging), will have multiple, interacting, polycentric, and cycling effects that may be impossible to predict. And even the most effective and nonintrusive "magic bullet" treatments cannot just "subtract" or "delete" a disorder. When a patient's clinical depression departs, many things may change in complex ways. Moreover, with both enhancement and treatment, risks of error—however "error" is defined—are enormous. This is part of the reason why critics of enhancement technology

---

[92] On the breakdown of the "discontinuities" between the realms of persons, animals, things, and machines, see Bruce Mazlish, *The Fourth Discontinuity: The Co-evolution of Humans and Machines* (New Haven, CT: Yale University Press, 1993).

[93] For more on objectification, see generally Michael H. Shapiro, "I Want a Girl (Boy) Just Like the Girl (Boy) That Married Dear Old Dad (Mom): Cloning Lives," *Southern California Interdisciplinary Law Journal* 9, no. 1 (2000): 1–294, 120–21 (and see part VI generally).

[94] Aspects of this "impact analysis" are discussed in Rorty and Wong, "Aspects of Identity and Agency," 19–21.

tend to invoke "neophobic" preferences or "precautionary principles."[95] The uses of technology to alter traits may over time alter the valuations of those very traits that drove the intervention in the first place. A community's normative system may be revalued and reordered because of the learning effects of enhancement and treatment practices. Thus, the very ability to drastically alter traits may itself generate hierarchical changes in how we rate those and other traits.

d. A note on cloning and identity.[96] There are plenty of serious issues about whether we should engage in human cloning. Philosophical analysis of the idea of personal identity, however, is of no special importance within that discussion. The cloned offspring's traits are not altered from some previous form: the cloning process does not transform her any more than coming into existence transforms anyone. She is not an appendage of the nuclear source, does not share a consciousness with her, received no physical material from her beyond the molecules containing genomic instructions, and is not a "continuation" of her. She is genomically a delayed identical twin of the nuclear source. Nor has the cloned offspring appropriated or been forced to accept the source's identity as an individuated person. To deny this would entail an extreme form of genetic reductionism that few hold to: a person is not just her genome. There are, however, pragmatic issues about identity formation and person-perception in cloned offspring. Anyone who knows the story of James Mill's highly focused and rigorous training of his son, John Stuart Mill,[97] can understand the general issue, even though John Stuart wasn't a clone. To go to the trouble of creating a person from another's genome suggests issues about overintrusive nurturing and compromises of the offspring's autonomy by severely narrowing her options.[98] But cloning raises no striking

---

[95] Although I do not deal with "the precautionary principle," or risk aversion/preference, or neophobia (fear of new things), these ideas require attention to the sharply varying kinds of moral risk attending the development of technologies for altering human traits. See generally Frank B. Cross, "Paradoxical Perils of the Precautionary Principle," *Washington and Lee Law Review* 53, no. 3 (1996): 851–925; and Cass R. Sunstein, *Risk and Reason: Safety, Law, and the Environment* (New York: Cambridge University Press, 2002), 102–5, 182–183.

[96] For a more extensive treatment of cloning issues, see generally Shapiro, "I Want a Girl." I use the terms "clone" and "offspring" to refer to the person generated from the use of a somatic nucleus.

[97] See, e.g., Bruce Mazlish, *James and John Stuart Mill: Father and Son in the Nineteenth Century* (New York: Basic Books, 1975), 169–72 (discussing the idea that John Stuart "seems never to have been a child, or to have had a childhood").

[98] There are more general issues of "genetic planning" that I cannot go into here. Some reproductive transactions that have already occurred foreshadow, to a limited extent, problems of nurture that one can expect from cloning. For example, some children were conceived for the specific purpose of providing bone marrow for transplantation into a sibling. See Shapiro et al., eds., *Bioethics and Law*, 1276–80. I have no clear examples replicating the Millian childrearing example, but Richard Williams, father of tennis stars Venus and Serena, has been described as having decided, "before they were conceived," that "his daughters were going to be tennis champions." See "Hardball Is the Only Game She Knows," *The London Times (Sunday)*, July 9, 2000, p. 19; http://www.timesonline.co.uk/. Perhaps this isn't much different from having children to carry on the family business or tradition.

issues in the fragmentation of identity such as those posed by exchange of brain hemispheres or Star Trekian transporter accidents that duplicate a person. Nor is it straightforwardly about induced trait change, although it is certainly concerned with trait selection. The idea that cloning (in fact, not fiction) replicates "identity" or "consciousness" and thus provides a form of "immortality" deriving from "rebirth" is silly.

Still, cloning "magnifies" certain aspects of regular sexual reproduction, creating some puzzles for some senses of "identity." Striking physical resemblance to the nuclear source is all but guaranteed. *Genetically,* a clone and her nuclear source are time-separated twins.[99] The clone's sense of separate identity and independence may very well be questioned by both the clone and others—possibly more so than with twins—for several reasons. The nuclear source may be significantly older, and highly influential by her presence, instruction, or example; similarly, the source might be dead, her life serving as an influential template; and, most important, the specific planning and investment of resources, hopes, and expectations are likely to be powerful forces. Moreover, if critics of cloning keep telling the clone that she is a mere genetic rerun, the child might indeed be adversely affected. This would be the critics' fault—a self-fulfillment of the prophecy that cloning will ultimately be harmful to the clone. As psychologist Kenneth Gergen put it: "If the social environment continues to define a given individual in a specified manner, we may reasonably anticipate that, without contravening information, the individual will come to accept the publicly provided definition as his own."[100] As I noted in an earlier work, Pogo might have said of cloning's critics, "We have met the enemy and he is Us."

Given both the technological risks of producing gravely impaired persons and the risks of intrusive nurturing, some may believe that the prospect of harm to the clone renders the cloning enterprise immoral. But whether a clone is harmed turns on whether her life is, from her viewpoint,[101] dispreferred to nonexistence because of injuries or a warped upbringing. From society's (not the clone's) perspective, there is something to be said for disapproving reproductive practices that yield many miserable persons. Many observers will worry over the fate of the cloned offspring, even when they understand that the clones' lives, from their

[99] This is fully correct when a woman is cloned, using her own ovum. In other cases, there will be genetic differences because mitochondria remain in the cytoplasm of the enucleated ovum. If cloning did not involve use of ova, including mitochondria, the genetic identity would hold across the board, errors aside.

[100] Kenneth Gergen, "The Social Construction of Self-Knowledge," in Daniel Kolak and Raymond Martin, eds., *Self and Identity: Contemporary Philosophical Issues* (New York: Macmillan, 1991), 372, 375.

[101] However, there are objective "reasonableness" constraints on the impact of one's subjective evaluation of the worth of one's life vis-à-vis nonexistence. For example, a suicidal cloned offspring who believes her life not to be worth living would not, because of that view alone, be living a life so terrible that nonexistence would be objectively preferable from her viewpoint.

respective viewpoints, are generally still preferable to nonexistence. Net social utility may thus decline. Existence as clones was, of course, *the clones'* only option for existence, but it was not the world's only option for reproduction.

Although the risks to the clones are not best seen as affecting identity, the ills suffered may be serious nonetheless. Philosopher Joel Feinberg's notion of a child's right to an open future is a good talking point for assessing such harms.[102] Once again, we face a practical paradox. We worry about "intrusive" tracking of children's interests, even as we note that they cannot be left to run amok. Channeling a child's interests and activities is both a threat to, and an essential feature of, promoting autonomy. This holds for clones at least as much as for others. The presence of a genetic plan for cloning or trait revision raises the antecedent risks of overdoing the tracking of a child toward a parentally favored path.

If Mozart were cloned, however, one would expect the child to be at least introduced to music, and not left solely with the options of learning golf or studying philosophy. Indeed, trying to match a child's interests to her revealed or projected aptitudes is something that parents presumptively *ought* to do: such link-ups between interests and abilities promote the individual's opportunities, and thus, *pro tanto*, her autonomy, her chances for "success," and her prospects for personal satisfaction in life.

D. A closer look at identity's work

1. In general; enhancement and its impact on awards, ownership, causal attribution, and identity; ascriptions of identity as moral claims. If the concept of identity is a tool, what are the tasks, moral and legal, for which it is—or is thought to be—a tool? What descriptive and moral freight do our present notions of identity bear?

In a rough sense, the term "identity" seems to carry with it the gravitas of Nature, Fate, and God.[103] Perhaps this translates into a morally useful maxim: If the technological use proposed (e.g., memory transfer from one person to another) would make us wonder who any of the persons involved have become—as when the transformation seems incoherent or discontinuous with a given person's "baseline" trait collection—then we are leaving the realm in which human alteration projects are presumptively

---

[102] Joel Feinberg, "The Child's Right to an Open Future," in *Freedom and Fulfillment: Philosophical Essays* (Princeton, NJ: Princeton University Press, 1992), 76.

[103] Recall also the idea of our creation *imago Dei*: if we are made in God's "image," can we change it? Does enhancement conflict with this image—or *vindicate* it, on the theory that if an aspect of God is life-creation, it is also rightly viewed as an aspect of humanity? But creativity with respect to what? See generally Garet, "Self-Transformability," 127 (arguing that "we are most human when we transform aspects of our self that are usually taken for granted or regarded as given"). See also ibid., 159–62 (discussing the "imago Dei argument for human nature as self-creation or self-transformability"). And see Heyd, *Genethics*, 2–7 (discussing image-of-God arguments).

permissible. Henceforth, such efforts would be presumptively wrong (or possibly morally indeterminate).

But just what are the underpinnings of this maxim? There is a link between what-is-natural-to-our-species (possibly including a self-improvement vector) and the idea of identity; it was not "unnatural" for us to come to the ideas of progress and perfection. Of course, determining why nature is a morally preferred standard of thought and action is yet another unbounded project. For our purposes, let us rest on this consideration: Nature may, in many cases, be the default or presumptive guide to what courses of action will "work" with reasonable efficiency, given our goals, and will produce a net benefit, all risks considered. This, however, is simply a loose "precautionary maxim," not a deep moral principle.[104] It is riddled with obvious holes (for example, what is the standard for judging "goals" and the effects of the means used?), but it will do temporarily.

Consider next the possibility of identity-challenging transfigurations. A working assumption bears restating: We presuppose continuity of personal identity through the inevitable changes of aging and experience, through the effects of traditional self-improvement, and through medical maneuvers accepted as treatments of disorders or repairs of defects or injuries.

But there are treatments and treatments: "I know Tommy had to have a new arm—but did they have to give him Koufax's?"[105] This remark by Pete Rose was occasioned by the apparent improvement in Tommy John's pitching after parts from his healthy arm were grafted onto his damaged one—but no one was really moved to say that Tommy John wasn't pitching. Did he nevertheless "cheat" by using his "repaired" bionic arm because the repair went beyond restoring the status quo ante (even if not by design)? There is an even greater hint of identity-challenge from a different source: "[T]he Swedish skiers [in the Swedish Ski Games of March 1985] found themselves wondering who—and what—they had been skiing against [after they had discovered that some of their competitors had resorted to blood doping]."[106]

Earlier, I described the view that technological "improvement" might not enhance one's merit (although the project might be morally creditworthy for other reasons).[107] Still, might it not be an act of courage to take

---

[104] See generally Albert R. Jonsen and Stephen Toulmin, *The Abuse of Casuistry: A History of Moral Reasoning* (Berkeley: University of California Press, 1988).

[105] Pete Rose, quoted in Jim Murray, "They Rebuilt Her Knees, She Rebuilt Her Game," *Los Angeles Times*, March 5, 1991, C1 (the title refers to Martina Navratilova).

[106] John M. Hoberman, "Sport and the Technological Image of Man," in William Morgan and Klaus Meier, eds., *Philosophic Inquiry in Sport* (Champaign, IL: Human Kinetics Publishers, 1988), 319, 322.

[107] Enhancements designed to enable air traffic controllers to handle ever-greater loads might be one example.

the risks of ingesting new substances to improve one's performance?[108] Pumping iron, special diets, and other forms of training are not risk-free. Lives have been lost and careers ruined on the practice field. It is said that Robert Schumann's career as a performer (rather than as a composer) was destroyed when the contraption he devised to aid his piano practicing (the digital version of pumping iron?) injured him. Perhaps it is praiseworthy to effectively intermix native capacities and technological self-alteration to produce superior performance (the Mentats from *Dune* again). We could evaluate the skill with which this is done, whether in the context of sports or games, or in other spheres of human activity. The degree of improvement might also suggest highly meritorious antecedent traits.

Finally, can ascriptions of identity be understood, at least in some cases, as moral claims? Think of these competing assertions: "The person (or creature) formed from the joining of brain structures from Marshall Artz and Tai Kwando is [more Marshall than Tai]; [more Tai than Marshall]; [both in equal parts]; [none of the above—we have a new person with certain memories and dispositions linked to the two earlier persons (have they ceased to exist?) and that's all we can say]."

Selecting the best of these claims is not a purely descriptive issue—but then, what sort of claim is it? What turns on it, and what does it turn on? If Artz was scheduled to inherit something from a recently deceased parent, a formal distribution *must* say whether the resulting creature is to take the inheritance because he *is* Artz, or is "the closest continuer" of Artz (or is this the same thing, exactly, as "being Artz"?). This is a question about the best description within a given social distributive system, and "best" clearly has morally evaluative components.

2. Hierarchies and gradients of traits.[109] When transformations—technological or otherwise—occur, how are they to be dealt with by the persons transformed and by others, within the framework of the reigning normative system? How are they characteristically dealt with now? (We do, from time to time, catch people having epiphanies.) The answers to these questions rest partly on the nature of the transformed trait—its "centrality" or importance for given purposes—but in whose view and on what standards? The views of the transformee, of the persons she interacts with, and of others who observe or know of her may all differ *inter se*.

Much depends on the relative importance of the trait for normal species functioning and for various culture-relative tasks and expectations; the

---

[108] It may also take courage to cheat or break the law. However, I am not suggesting that all acts of courage are morally praiseworthy.

[109] Again, see the discussion of centrality of traits in Oksenberg and Wong, "Aspects of Identity and Agency," 19–21. See also Nozick, *Philosophical Explanations,* 105 ("When people disagree about some of the problem cases of personal identity, for example, transfer of self from one body to another, this may stem from their different views of which dimensions, with what relative weights, constitute the metric of closeness. What is the correct measure of persons, then, and upon what does its being the correct one depend?"). See also Heyd, *Genethics,* 163–64.

nature, degree, and scope of trait change; the suddenness of change; its continuity or coherence with the trait as it was, and with coexisting traits; its cascading, and perhaps chaotic, personal and interpersonal effects; and so on.[110] A sharp increase in the already ample quantitative/spatial-relations aptitudes of a reclusive theoretical physicist is likely to be viewed by all (herself included) as coherent and only somewhat discontinuous. The installation of a new trait of physical aggressiveness, however—the sort of trait one might wish to enhance in some soldiers and professional athletes—would seem not to cohere well with her other traits, unless situational variables explain it. (Perhaps she had to move to the place formerly known as "Yugoslavia" and needed the trait for self-defense.)

Finally, I offer one more illustrative question about how to sort and rank traits and trait changes by assessing their impacts on personal identity: How are we to view "gender transformation" procedures? Defining what this means is difficult: the idea of genomic changes in existing persons seems far-fetched, and not everyone views the results of the surgical/hormonal procedures involved as gender changes. Still, for those who view gender largely as a matter of social/legal "construction" or perception, the continuation of certain unchanging genetic or other physical variables does not block acceptance of gender transformation. In any case, gender transformations as now understood obviously involve trait changes of various sorts, and the personal identity issues that arise are obvious: gender seems universally of central importance to identity as resting on self-perception and perception by others. For those whose interior vision compels them to view themselves as "a woman in a man's body" or the reverse, gender transformation might be viewed as an "enhancement"—or perhaps as "relief of a handicap," or even "amelioration of a gender-dysmorphic disorder." Whether the physical interventions should be seen as generating a "biological" sex change or a "perceived-sex" change or any other sort of change is a hard conceptual problem that I do not address. Whatever form the intervention takes in particular cases, however, it may not be clear whether we should say, or deny, that a person is still whoever he was even after his gender has in some sense been transformed.[111] I leave this topic by suggesting (as a subject for discussion on another occasion) comparisons among various forms gender transformation, intellect enhancement (recall *Brain Wave*), and targeted amnesia.

---

[110] Glover puts one aspect of this nicely, in *What Sort of People Should There Be?* 109–10: "In asking these questions [about identity], [people] are using the word 'identity' in a way philosophers usually do not. [This doesn't seem to be so with personal identity.] They are not asking where they stop and where the rest of the world begins, or which of several people they are. Rather, they are thinking about what they are like: about the characteristics that make them distinctive, the things that make friendship with them different from friendship with someone else."

[111] See generally Garet, "Self-Transformability," 123 (discussing "human nature as self-transformability," which he explores "by considering the experiences, choices, and identities of transsexuals").

3. "Identity models" and "disorder models": Can they properly authorize and limit technological alteration of traits? Can they operate concurrently? At a high level of generality, the abstract logic of an identity-preservation model is identical to that of disorder and enhancement models: to establish authorizations and limitations on what we may, must, shouldn't, and mustn't do in modifying our traits.

Here is a very simplified account of what might be intended as a disorder model,[112] our current chief guide for nontrivial manipulations of body and mind: "Serious or intrusive technological intervention into bodily (including brain) processes and structures, including reproduction, is justified only if it is intended to, and reasonably likely to, ameliorate, cure, or prevent the occurrence of a disorder, whether by addressing the causes, including genetic causes, or the adverse effects of the disorder." (Cosmetic alteration of appearance generally belongs in an enhancement model, discussed below.)[113]

A disorder model is thus a set of rules, principles, and standards for sorting the conditions we observe (and infer) into disorders, diseases, injuries, defects, etc.; for making specific diagnoses; and for authorizing and limiting certain forms of action (treatment, dealing with persons in certain ways when they are "ill"—i.e., installing the "sick role"—and so on). The key conceptual ingredients of such a model are highly contested in various situations. There is, for example, the view that specific disorders are often "constructed" in response to available technological fixes—or, more pointedly, that disorders are simply invented so that certain medical/surgical procedures can be used.[114] These possibilities are of some importance when considering radical expansions in the powers of technological intervention: it might be a short trip from invented disorders to the (partial) abandonment of disorder justifications altogether. The "serious or intrusive technological intervention"[115] qualification within the disorder model is

---

[112] One might say that there is just one overarching disorder model of which all others are submodels based on contextual variations. "Disorder," as used here, is meant to embrace notions of disease, sickness, illness, affliction, ailment, infirmity, injury, trauma, and—possibly—defect, disability, and handicap. Perhaps not all of the notions are rightly listed within a disorder model; they are clearly not synonymous. But I avoid efforts at a "unified field" concept that is more precise than "something is distinctively wrong here that merits correction."

[113] There are, of course, cosmetic alterations occasioned by traumatic injuries or by disease—rebuilding faces, dealing with scar tissue, etc. On cosmetic alteration in the dramatic arts and its bearing on identity, see Thomas Morawetz, *Making Faces, Playing God: Identity and the Art of Transformational Makeup* (Austin: University of Texas Press, 2001).

[114] This is often said about the use of Ritalin (methylphenidate) and other stimulant drugs for the family of conditions thought to involve an attention deficit. See generally Gina Kolata, "Boom in Ritalin Sales Raises Ethical Issues," *New York Times*, May 15, 1996, C8; Gardner, "Implications of Psychoactive Drug Therapy." This position may be overstated, but the issue is theoretically and practically important.

[115] The idea of "intrusiveness" has been used in various technological contexts, one of the more prominent being the field of behavior control through use of "biological" or "organic" therapies. More specifically, it is used as an authorizing and limiting tool in the process of

meant, in part, to exclude certain measures designed for entertainment or minor transient augmentation—for example, the use of caffeine, nicotine, alcohol, and possibly hot sauce. These are part of the currently accepted "baseline" for self-transformation and for that reason are probably not even viewed as trait changes: within our present framework, they are insignificant. Still, the very existence of this baseline as a rough border suggests limits we have already placed on the authority of disorder models.

What is "intrusive" is not a matter of pure empirical and conceptual analysis: it is heavily influenced by custom and other situational variables, and it is in many cases, at bottom, a moral characterization. Compulsory education throughout the years of one's childhood and adolescence has massive effects on one's development, but is not generally compared in "intrusiveness" to brain surgery used to reduce maladaptive behavior.

Handicap models are structurally isomorphic to disorder models but have quite different contents. For example, in the absence of pituitary or other disorders that impede normal growth, some physicians will not prescribe human growth hormone: its use is not authorized—and is implicitly banned—within a disorder model because it is pure augmentation.[116] However, one could craft a notion of severe social handicap—partly based on cultural/environmental contingencies, including government assistance opportunities—resulting from extremely short stature.[117] This may apply to a variety of traits that are so far from the mean or median as to qualify as "outliers." Depending on the circumstances, extremely tall persons may be handicapped in some ways. But an expansive handicap rationale blends smoothly into departure from a "something is distinctively wrong" model to a much looser enhancement justification.

As an action-evaluation tool, an identity model implements the claim that "doing X (to) (for) (on) person W is justified for enhancement (or other) purposes only if it does not risk changing his identity (or his identity with respect to trait μ)."[118] Of course, it is possible that we will come to endorse a quite different identity model pointing in the opposite direction: a model that views achieving identity-change as a reason *for*

---

justifying (or not) the use of certain treatments. For a more extended account of intrusiveness, see generally Shapiro et al., eds., *Bioethics and Law*, 389–96. The concept seems useful in considering what might trigger use of an identity model, as well as a disorder model.

[116] Some physicians may believe that such lack of authorization entails that no treatment risks are justifiable. In the absence of risks, they might endorse the treatment. Their operating disorder model rests heavily on the risks of intervention.

[117] "Handicap" models may straddle both disorder and enhancement. Thus, short stature resulting from disorder and "normal variation" short stature may be equally "handicapping." See generally David B. Allen and Norman C. Fost, "Growth Hormone Therapy for Short Stature: Panacea or Pandora's Box?" *Journal of Pediatrics* 117, no. 1 (1990): 16–21, 18–20.

[118] "Identity with respect to μ" is an awkward formulation that I do not discuss, except to say that it reflects the tension between recognizing *really* big changes in someone, on the one hand, and the fact that such changes may be consistent with remaining the same someone, on the other.

certain interventions—and for running their attendant risks—rather than *against* them.[119]

All of these justificatory models require their own justifications. Attempting to provide them often involves use of a family of morally freighted categories for determining the proper occasions and limits for modifying ourselves, temporarily or permanently. There may be overlapping appeals to what is natural; to what is internally rather than externally generated; and to what is authentically "of or from" the person—an aspect of causal attribution distinguishing "self"-agency from outside determinants. Some of these concepts are taken as bases for pejorative (if hyperbolic) ascriptions ("It wasn't you, it was the steroids that won") or for excusing conditions ("It wasn't you, it was the [booze] [depression] talking"—or even "It wasn't you, it was your medicine that committed the murder").[120] Sudden or "punctuated" self-modification (rather than gradually induced changes) may be taken as a sign of unnatural and thus presumptively improper amplification. The effects of intellect-enhancing pills may be taken as not attributable to one's internal, natural self, and "credit" for one's work would rightly go (at least partly) to the chemicals ingested.[121] Or so it might be argued.

Legal issues of "synthetic sanity," mentioned earlier (at the end of Section I), roughly illustrate some of these problems in moral ascriptions relevant to questions of personal identity. As we saw, it is possible that an insanity defense in a criminal trial would be weakened if the accused is medicated in order to render her competent to be tried: if her symptoms indeed remit with treatment, she will not seem to be crazy. Instructing juries to disregard her "induced sanity" at trial in judging her insanity *when the act was committed*—and thus her culpability—is unlikely to be an adequate corrective.[122] In the civil domain, courts on occasion have refused

---

[119] I leave out constraints concerning the role of risk of injury or other adverse effects. Whether running such risks is justified within an enhancement model depends in part on how the prospects of enhancement are valued.

[120] The idea that selective serotonin reuptake inhibitors (SSRIs) have (paradoxically?) been responsible for suicides and murders has been suggested, but the current weight of medical opinion is against this view. As to murder, see Wade C. Myers and Monica A. Vondruska, "Murder, Minors, Selective Serotonin Reuptake Inhibitors, and the Involuntary Intoxication Defense," *Journal of the American Academy of Psychiatry and Law* 26, no. 3 (1998): 487–96. On suicide, see Simon Wessely and Robert Kerwin, "Suicide Risk and the SSRIs," *Journal of the American Medical Association* 292, no. 3 (2004): 379–81.

[121] See generally John McGinnis, "Attention Deficit Disaster," *Wall Street Journal*, September 18, 1997, A14 (Westlaw: 1997 WL-WSJ 14166812) (". . . if Tim is behaving, his parents and teachers believe his Ritalin's working; if he's not behaving, the ADD is at work. Either way, the medication for the 'disorder' is responsible; Tim's just along for the ride. [¶] That's a corrosive lesson for a little boy to learn. . . . ADD kids are learning an early lesson in the mores of 1990s America: Don't take responsibility for your own conduct; instead, declare that you're in the grip of uncontrollable impulses, seek professional help, and start making excuses"). I am not endorsing such arguments, but they reflect serious moral and legal issues.

[122] See *Riggins v. Nevada*, 504 U.S. 127 (1992), and *Sell v. United States*, 539 U.S. 166 (2003), described in note 3 above. See generally Shapiro et al., eds., *Bioethics and Law*, 368–70 (discussing synthetic sanity).

to release persons confined in mental health facilities even upon complete remission of their symptoms, if the improvement was externally induced by treatment—an artifact—and was not generated by the self.[123]

In many ways, then, these jurisprudential problems are identity (or identity-connected) arguments: to recognize a person as having a particular identity is to establish a template for determining what *she*, as opposed to someone or something else, has done or avoided. The insanity defense itself, for example, is implicitly bound up with notions of identity as one's "true self"—a true self that is overwhelmed by an "external," "non-self-related," identity-alien sickness. Identity, moral agency, and causal attribution are thus logically linked, at least in this respect.[124]

There thus seem to be important intersections among identity, disorder, and enhancement models, beyond their obvious links as rough gauges for judging interventions into body and mind. In many situations, the models reinforce each other; indeed, perhaps they are connected elements of a larger model, or are aspects of each other. For example, some interventions not justified by disorder because they "go beyond" the applicable therapeutic logic (Tommy John's new pitching arm?) may also fail within an identity-preservation model because the induced changes are too discontinuous and radical.[125] Another illustration is the treatment of persons incompetent to make therapeutic decisions because of disorder, injury, or defect: they are often viewed as "not themselves" and treated medically over their objections, possibly as part of a duty to their "real (or future, or even possible) selves." Moreover, given the usual features of mental disorder, the very idea of cure or palliation embeds notions of restoring the person to what he was before—to his preexisting but currently impeded identity—rather than of creating an artifactual new identity.

Identity and disorder models are generally (though not inevitably) arrayed against enhancement models, which purport to justify serious intrusions at least when they are exercises of the subjects' or their parents' (or proxies') autonomous choices, or because of the expected gains from modification. Suppose, for example, a substance that provides one with eidetic perceptual powers for an extended period carries serious risks— say, subsequent memory impairments, blood-pressure spikes, and purulent acne. The reasons for declining this trait-change might not rest exclusively, if at all, on memory enhancement as an outcome; the main

---

[123] In *State of Louisiana v. Boulmay*, 498 So.2d 213 (La.App. 1986), the appellate court reversed a trial court's judgment denying an inmate's release from a state forensic facility; the trial court had found the inmate "only 'chemically sane'."

[124] Some issues involved in "multiple personality syndrome" overlap identity problems. See generally Elyn R. Saks, with Stephen H. Behnke, *Jekyll on Trial: Multiple Personality Disorder and Criminal Law* (New York: New York University Press, 1997).

[125] See generally Joshua Rosenkranz, "Custom Kids and the Moral Duty to Genetically Engineer Our Children," *High Technology Law Journal* 2, no. 1 (1987): 3–53, 26 ("The seldom-acknowledged focus of the noninterventionists' argument must be on whether the changes suffice to turn one person into another *different* person").

reason might be to avoid the risks in accord with a maxim telling us not to ingest dangerous substances unless there is a disorder-based reason for it. In contrast, an enhancement model might specify that a significant improvement in an important trait might be a strong reason to run the posited risks. And embedded in these considerations is the possibility that the acquisition of the powers of eidetic imagery might have transformative effects on one's capacities, behavior, and self-image. For some, this may either weigh against the intervention (an identity-preservation model) or pull for it (an identity-seeking model).

Identity, disorder, and enhancement models may thus enjoy an uneasy coexistence in which they may reinforce or limit (or have no effect on) each other. Each model helps call attention to the strengths and vulnerabilities of the others. Disorder and identity models may form pragmatic standards for limiting what might be unchecked distributional pressures generated by enhancement models—or autonomy models ungoverned by notions of disorder, identity, or enhancement. They may also be simultaneously invoked or challenged when particular interventions are in question (e.g., "gender transformation"). Here, issues of treatment of disorder, remediation of handicap, gender identity and its bearing on personal identity, and enhancement (should gender transformation be withheld from persons not suffering from a "transsexual disorder"?) are all immediately present. Of course, all of the models are embedded in complex regions of general moral and political philosophy from which we can raise still deeper issues: on what moral theory should disorder or identity-preservation ever limit autonomous self-change?

Finally, for some observers, disorder and identity models, insofar as they limit enhancement models, are valuable primarily to vindicate principles derived from the moral force of nature. Although nature's moral standing does not rest exclusively on religious premises, it holds a rather higher station within many theological systems than it does in secular thought. To be sure, some views of nature, secular or religious, may support enhancement models, but this does not seem to reflect currently dominant views.

4. *What is the relevance of alternative identities not chosen? In particular, what is the relevance of the fact that one's parents rejected one's default natural identity, or any alternative identities?* What is the significance of counterfactual or, more particularly, default natural identity? First, knowing of it may affect a person's self-image, both with respect to identity and with respect to his sense of autonomy, individuality, and uniqueness. Second, knowing of it may affect the views of others who know of the now nonexistent but once possible identity.[126] Third, knowledge of a natural default identity and of what particular attributes were affected may contribute to human reduction by calling attention to the specific traits involved, to the *reasons* for the change, and to the rejection or discarding of the identity that would otherwise develop.

[126] These first two considerations interact.

To illustrate some of these risks, consider this remark from the President's Council on Bioethics, referring "to the question of what it might mean for a child to live with a chosen genotype: he may feel grateful to his parents for having gone to such trouble to spare him the burden of various genetic defects; but he might also have to deal with the sense that he is not just a gift born of his parents' love but also, in some degree, a product of their will."[127]

On the surface, at least, the problem described does not seem to raise issues of personal identity. It suggests risks of overly aggressive parenting in fulfillment of the plans of the reproductive enterprise, and risks to the child's sense of autonomous individuality—his belief that he is someone whose preferences are authentically his, rather than his parents'. It may also inspire fears that his parents' bonds to him were and are contingent on their reproductive/enhancement plan's favorable outcome.

But shifting the genome of an early embryo or a gamete from what its basic developmental fate might otherwise be may indeed bear on perceived identity, at least from the viewpoint of the parents and other external observers. What would be the point of intervening if not to generate benefits from it—for the child, for the parents, and possibly beyond? And how would one promote these goals without careful implementation that may heavily affect the child's development and ultimate "identity"? Planning drives realization.

It remains, however, that such programs are unlikely to generate lives not worth living from the viewpoint of the offspring, despite the emotional impact of learning of one's not-fully-natural origins and of one's abandoned default identity, and despite the risks of excessive constraints being imposed on the offspring's lifestyle and life path.

E. Is conceptual reconstruction necessary? The inevitability of indeterminacy[128]

If identity did not do any useful work (at least in particular contexts), there would not be much point in "reconstructing" it (in those contexts).

---

[127] The President's Council on Bioethics, *Beyond Therapy: Biotechnology and the Pursuit of Happiness* (Washington, DC: President's Council on Bioethics, October 2003); http://www.bioethics.gov/reports/beyondtherapy/.

[128] I do not try to define "reconstruction." Carnap's idea of rational reconstruction may have some purchase here. See generally Rudolf Carnap, *Logical Foundations of Probability* (Chicago: University of Chicago Press, 1962), 576–77. For our purposes, the term refers to the difficulties of applying certain concepts under radically changed circumstances, and to the decision maker's responsive handling of the concepts. *Johnson v. Calvert* illustrates the process. I can only note without elaboration that reconstruction or respecification may occur with respect to varying aspects and levels of generality of a concept. Thus, the "double helix" theory of DNA newly specified both its molecular structure and its function in reproduction. But cf. Heyd, *Genethics*, 12, arguing that "genesis problems" are "unique, not in being new, or in requiring novel adaptation of ethical principles, but in the fact that they resist any kind of ethical treatment." One might view this as a hyperbolic way (*any* kind of ethical treatment is resisted?) of describing the sort of conceptual fragmentation or disintegration discussed in this essay. However, I don't think it applies to any of the main concepts used as examples in this essay, including identity.

Indeed, even for those who reject disorder-model limits on trait change, identity-preservation may be looked to as a desirable limitation on such transformations; on that view, the idea of identity-preservation should be reinforced as an ideal, largely as it is. This stance is fortified by the possibility that attaining the power to create and shape traits in relatively precise ways will affect how we deal with human attributes generally, and thus how we deal with human reproduction. This will inevitably highlight the properties of identity and the possible need, at least in some eyes, to hold fast to it as a constraint on human modification.

In any case, reconstructing the idea of identity does not seem required where truly drastic "shape-shifting" alterations are *not* involved. The extent to which the concept is revised or respecified depends, as I said, on the need to vet the underpinnings of basic concepts in order to reach moral and legal conclusions in strikingly new situations. Think back to *Johnson v. Calvert*, the gestational surrogacy case. There, the concepts of genetics and gestation were not reinterpreted, never mind reconstructed, although many observers were moved to think harder about matters of "nature and nurture" generally. The situational pressure on "mother-hood," however, did seem to require a reconstruction or respecification of sorts—one that required investigating the very purposes of speaking of motherhood, and more generally, of parenthood, within our cultural systems of family formation.

Similarly, the pressure of enhancement possibilities requires probing the very purposes of ascribing identity in various contexts—which in turn requires exploring another layer of concepts concerning the foundations of praise and blame, merit and desert, and the distribution of rewards generally. But this investigation may send us looping back to identity. Does a particular accomplishment reflect true merit if it derives from the technologically enhanced traits of the actor? That depends on what we mean by "merit," and what we mean by it has crucial links to matters of attribution, a notion that presupposes an understanding of identity: to *whom or what* are we to impute an action, an insight, a discovery, a writing, and so on? There is nothing new in this general question. Techno-logical enhancement simply pushes us into familiar issues of freedom, determinism, culpability, merit, and desert. In any case, until we approach the Hartian chaos of continuous reshaping, we do not need a new foun-dational specification of the idea of identity as such. At this point, the analogy to the reconstruction of "motherhood" weakens.

Still, we have in store for us an array of technological interventions that seem somewhat discontinuous and incoherent—changes that are out of line with customary expectations of the progress of particular persons within their existing trait profiles. This is likely to fix our attention to the status of traits and those who bear and change them. Even when a revised baseline of expectations of sharp changes is integrated into our social norms, this new situation, by hypothesis, includes widespread planning and intensified immersion into assaying human attributes.

What, then, of the more extreme worlds, such as that in the Hartian philosophical fantasy? Does the idea of identity simply "run out"? What can it do for us? Recall the Artz/Kwando brain hemisphere exchange. This does create a situation akin to that in *Johnson v. Calvert*'s motherhood muddle: literal sunderings and recombinations of physiological features and processes. If the result of the Artz/Kwando hemisphere exchange does not clearly reflect the "dominance" of "Artzness" or "Kwandoness," then perhaps there is no metaphysically defined closest continuer for either one of them. "The real Artz/Kwando" then seems to have no referent. Situational variables, however, may require stipulated assignment of identities, old or new, as a matter of basic social ordering. Artz may be the sole heir of his wealthy parents, as we saw. But there is no "essence of identity" that would cogently lead to identifying one transplantee or the other as Artz, and this is rather unlike the situation with motherhood in *Johnson v. Calvert*: there, loosely speaking, the "essence" of motherhood in most modern societies rests on the intended familial association with one's offspring.[129]

Identity does not seem to be a totally empty concept in any of these situations, however, and there may be some analogy to the reconstruction of "motherhood." In an age of technologized "mega-enhancement," the idea of sequential continuity of a succession of entities (whether they are thought to bear the same identity or not) could serve as a primary standard for inter-entity relations. One could see this standard, on the one hand, as a reconstruction of identity that rests on its ultimate practical rationale of stability: maintenance of relationships of *some* sort among entities of *some* sort. These are matters essential to any society's viability. On the other hand, one could view the standard as a "replacement" for identity, but I will not try to distinguish between reconstruction and replacement.

Finally, in considering technological pressures for conceptual modification, what is the relevance of increased knowledge of the neural substrates of thought, behavior, and physical structure? Does this enhanced knowledge mean we "know ourselves" better, or know better "who we are"? Does it mandate a reconsideration of our individual identities, or of "humanity's identity" as a species? Consider a familiar sort of philosophical problem (with many echoes in law): Does the concept of (say) gold—our notion of what gold is, what its "identity" is—change when we learn its molecular structure and how that molecular structure bears on the more directly observable properties of gold? In parallel, suppose we discover important neurophysiological processes that are said to "explain" or account for a variety of hot-button—if ill-defined—traits, such as intellectual assets or deficiencies of certain sorts, sexual orientation, violent dispositions, and some forms of mental disorder or of psychopathy. Do we now "know" or "see" Dick and Jane differently if we discover a specific physical causal foundation that accounts, at least in significant

---

[129] With adoption, intended association is also key.

part, for their already known sexual orientations or other mental or behavioral dispositions? Why *would* we view them differently? Did we really think their dispositions and behaviors were uncaused? If we didn't think that, why would getting the causal details matter for any purpose other than more precisely controlling mental functioning and behavior—or is it *that* very prospect of the determinate, algorithmically governed person that fixes our attention?

So far, despite calls for the renovation of the idea of identity occasioned by assorted technological changes, a radical restructuring of the *concept* of identity does not seem "compelled" by any given set of developments that erode its presuppositions, except perhaps in the most extreme and remote cases. In those cases, needs for reasonable certainty in dealings among separate entities (whoever and whatever they are) may require criteria for identifying continuing "repositories" of legal and social attributes. And if we no longer even have notions of identifiable continuing entities that could constitute such repositories, the world would be so different that life would no longer be as we know it, and even basic communication would be difficult or impossible to pursue.

Still, it remains that some forms of new knowledge and capability, by their vividness, call attention to the rough foundations of both everyday and technical concepts. As philosopher Antony Flew observes, "although familiar differences [as between external compulsion and self-direction] cannot be abolished by discoveries, such discoveries may sometimes demand some revision in accepted ideas about the significance of those differences." [130] An instructive example is that a person who comes to see his problem as a disorder linked to (or even constituted by) anomalous functioning of the brain may be inclined to say—against all pulls toward reduction—that something is wrong with his brain, rather than that something is wrong with him.[131]

X. Legal Issues in Identity Formation

At the very least, the law concerns disputes and conflicts among persons, groups, officials, and other entities; that is the *stuff* that occasions the

[130] Antony Flew, *Crime or Disease?* (New York: Barnes & Noble, 1973), 106. The claim that revision is "demanded" may be overdone, but the general point is sound. In speaking of ordinary, nontechnical views of moral and legal accountability, Flew says: "In so far as these distinctions are rooted in familiar differences, and in so far as the words and expressions used to mark these undoubted differences carry no theoretical load, then they cannot be impugned by any discovery whatsoever, whether scientific or theological" (ibid., 105). But in our contexts, the qualification "rooted in familiar differences" does not always apply, at least in full strength. See also Norman Daniels, "The Genome Project, Individual Differences, and Just Health Care," in Timothy F. Murphy and Mark A. Lappé, eds., *Justice and the Human Genome Project* (Berkeley: University of California Press, 1994), 110, 124–25, where Daniels indicates that knowledge gained through the human genome project "might make the distinction between disease (including genetic disease) and the normal distribution of capabilities seem more arbitrary."

[131] Joseph Dumit, *Picturing Personhood: Brain Scans and Biomedical Identity* (Princeton, NJ: Princeton University Press, 2004), 161.

need for such authoritative systems.[132] To put it a bit (but only a bit) more precisely, the initial task of law (at least as it is known in many parts of the world) is to address disputes by adjudicating or otherwise resolving them, and by initiating measures—rules and their constituents—to avoid future disputes. The latter goal is promoted by systems of "coordination" (e.g., as reflected in traffic rules) and by the fact that legal systems and their constituent institutions are meant to reinforce preferred societal values.

The contours of interpersonal disputes track the conflicting perspectives and viewpoints of the adversaries, ranging from the most elementary—"As I see it, this is my space"—to the extremely complex: "Did Presidents Truman, Kennedy, Johnson, Reagan, Clinton, $Bush_1$, and $Bush_2$ commit impeachable offenses in not seeking congressional declarations of war for their military actions?" The law-personnel involved in disputes are required to identify these perspectives, and the more adept among them try to "get inside" the perspectives so as to see them from the internal viewpoint of the participants on all sides. Highlighting the perspectives is a necessary precursor to bringing them within the surrounding legal institutions so that some form of legal closure is attained.[133] "Doing law" within a modern legal framework, however, is not simply about attaining closure *simpliciter,* but about illuminating the conflicting issues and clashing frameworks within a relevant body of rules, standards, and principles, and setting up at least rough templates for future guidance.

Why bother with this elementary (though contestable) account? If technology enables the sort of disaggregations and reformations of life processes discussed here, then every element that is "cut and pasted" and every severed and reattached aspect of a process may be reflected in someone's or some entity's "perspective" or set of interests that can be argued for by others. We can thus speak of the perspectives of a gestator, a non-gestating genetic mother, a cryopreserved embryo, a stem cell, reproductive engineers, a community, and so on. The splitting and re-lumping may raise new disputes involving the distinctive new perspectives of the disputants, and, even more fundamentally, disputes about

---

[132] This is meant to cover both civil disputes and crimes, and disputes between government entities or personnel and any other entities, including persons and other government entities. If a basic legal system already exists, it is likely—but not certain—that a criminal case would be styled as one between "the community" and the accused, as well as between criminal and victim. The formulation in the text is also meant to include both actual and possible disputes and conflicts. Of course, this loose description presupposes the existence of some legal or law-like system that identifies entities as "officials" and other entities as proper subjects of dispute.

[133] On the perspective-vetting missions of lawyers, judges, and legal systems, see generally Shapiro, "Lawyers, Judges, and Bioethics." I leave terms such as "perspective" and "framework" undefined, and note only that they do not entail that the entity working within them has any conscious awareness of this, or is even conscious. Thus, embryos have perspectives connected to their interests in continued existence and development. As for "interest," it too is left undefined. For those who do not assign value to "potential" or projected developmental lines, embryos have neither interests nor perspectives.

who or what should be recognized *as* a disputant reflecting some sort of interest. And the disputants may be involved in relationships largely unheard of before; the link between a genetic father and a genetic surrogate—the true genetic mother of his child, to whom he is neither married nor personally affiliated—is an obvious example.

The identification and clarification of perspectives, old and new, is open to anyone, but it is one of the essential tasks of modern legal systems. Perhaps lawyers, judges, and lawmakers have no special moral expertise or access to it—assuming that there is even such a thing as moral expertise. But they do have expertise in laying the groundwork for moral analysis by identifying and searching the interiors of rival frameworks to help determine what might be morally and legally material, and for placing what they find into a legal matrix to aid resolution.[134] Thus, though it may seem counterintuitive to some, legal analysis is a fruitful way to begin sorting things out, however uncomfortable it might be for the participants.

I now apply these considerations to some examples of actions and situations relevant to our studies of identity and then conclude this essay. With and without technology, we try to control disease, the reproductive process, the genetic profile of succeeding generations, our physical appearance and stature, our sensorium, and our behavior; and we try to cure, improve, enhance, and entertain ourselves. There are, of course, moral limits to what we can do to (or for) ourselves and others, and much of what we do is subject to external regulation, most prominently by government. Laws may impinge, deliberately or incidentally, on matters over which we might wish to exercise full control—including choices affecting our health, our characteristics, and various aspects of what we (and others) see as our identities. On the one hand, if we, as individuals, wish to do these things, we may place on government the burden of explaining why, despite our wishes, we should be stopped or regulated in some or all of these pursuits. On the other hand, if we, as "society" or "government," wish instead to prevent, say, identity-threatening technological interventions, individuals may be required to show why they should be free to act. Deciding who rightly bears the moral and legal burdens of justification may turn on deep issues within political and moral philosophy—and it may determine the outcome of the debate.

Why is any given human behavior regulated in any given way? Why is the use of alcohol permitted (with certain limitations) and the use of marijuana prohibited (with certain contested exceptions)? Why must our medicines and medical devices be vetted by the Food and Drug Administration before we gain access to them? (And why aren't surgical procedures similarly vetted?) Why are so many medicines barred from use

---

[134] There is a familiar circular (or cycling) paradox here. What is legally material is determined by the existing legal rule structure, but that legal structure presupposes having already identified the legally material considerations.

without physician authorization? Why are nonmedical uses of steroids prohibited by law and by nongovernment organizations such as the International Olympic Committee? What business is it of the government to interfere with such ingestive/digestive preferences? On the other hand, why should we recognize personal rights to drastically alter our individual God-given, or at least Natural, attributes?

It is particularly characteristic of the West that when government impinges on what we, as individuals, view as intensely personal matters that should be largely *up to us,* we invoke ideas of autonomy, privacy, choices concerning our bodily and mentational integrity and structure, and arbitrary government interference with these interests. Just how this political-moral-legal framework came to characterize many sectors of many societies I cannot investigate here.[135] I can, however, outline certain aspects of the American constitutional framework that may be critical when matters of technological alteration of human traits come up. Applying constitutional templates to government restrictions—and enablements—can thus be a powerful heuristic tool to aid analysis.

In the United States, what we view as the most important individual interests sooner or later appear as important players within constitutional adjudication. So also do the most important countervailing societal interests.[136] The U.S. Constitution is (among other things) an authoritative legal text announcing the dominion of certain very basic values. The text's references to liberty, equal protection of the law, due process, freedom of speech, press, and religion, the security of our persons and homes, and so on, are not morally neutral: as a repository of core values, *the Constitution takes and reflects moral positions.* (This fact about the Constitution is neutral with respect to issues about the separation or joinder of legal interpretation and moral analysis; the soundness of legal positivism is not an issue.) What those exact moral positions might be, and how we identify and apply them, are defining issues in legal, political, and moral philosophy.

Within this constitutional universe, there may be disputes between and among governments, persons, and entities of various sorts—including disputes about technological modification of traits. These disputes have been and will continue to be reflected in legal and constitutional adjudication.[137] As technology develops, there will be calls for recognizing strong rights in self-creation and transformation, and, on the other side,

---

[135] There is a sizable literature criticizing supposedly excessive reliance on conceptions of rights and entitlements. For some references in a bioethical context, see generally Shapiro et al., eds., *Bioethics and Law,* 14–17, 134.

[136] To be sure, the described "societal interests" may include a "collective" interest in promoting individual interests, and individual interests may prosper more in a regime where communitarian interests of various sorts are touted.

[137] Recall the earlier references to "synthetic sanity," as where defendants in criminal prosecutions are forcibly medicated to render them competent to stand trial, and references to controlling behavior generally while in custody. There are also cases involving "street drugs" that peripherally illustrate this. See, e.g., *People v. Werber,* 97 Cal.Rptr. 150, 156 (Cal.App. 1971), where the court mentioned defendant's claim that marijuana produced "a new awareness of various unfamiliar and abstract concepts."

for promoting social interests said to require prohibition or regulation of these personal-transformation projects—say, the avoidance of human reduction, or of the uncertain outcome of altering our present conceptions of identity. This is at least one of the major constitutional "balancing" frameworks in which the radical transfiguration of personal attributes will be litigated.

The Constitution does not *clearly* specify argument structures well-suited for addressing issues of physical, mental, and procreational autonomy generally, or interests in enhancement and self-realization in particular.[138] But the very nature of an abstraction is to comprehend and relate many things without specifying any of them. Law (and other domains) cannot do without abstractions, and a bare reference to a text's lack of "specificity" cannot settle interpretive questions without more. The interpretive issues[139] here are at bottom matters of disagreement about the best ways to work within rule-governed systems of certain sorts under certain conditions. Having made this pronouncement, I subject it to no analysis. I use it simply to set up what are likely to be interpretive maneuvers in constitutional adjudication of claims of right to (or against) serious modification of one's attributes.

The U.S. Constitution does not "say" anything about a right to procreate, but such a right seems to be recognized by the Supreme Court as "implicit" in or implied by the textual references to liberty (and, in some eyes, privileges and immunities of national citizenship). The Court first announced this right in response to a suit by an incarcerated thief who objected to being sterilized, a procedure apparently inspired by a desire to further negative eugenics goals—that is, reducing the number of genetically "unfit" persons in coming generations by discouraging or preventing their birth (or survival).[140]

The operational effect of designating something as a fundamental right or a fundamental liberty interest is, at the outset, to burden the government with justifying what it did, rather than to require the individual to demonstrate the worth of his claim.[141] The government must present a strong ("compelling," or at least "important") reason for interfering with

---

[138] Not all will concur with this use of "clearly." "Liberty" comprehends "liberty to X," and, absent restrictions on what "X" refers to, it would seem to comprehend self-realization, the consumption of chocolate, and other instantiations of the pursuit of happiness. Clearly, this issue must be left aside.

[139] I do not discuss possible disagreements on what are interpretive disputes and what are arguably disputes of other sorts. For an argument that what passes for interpretation is in fact "metadoctrine" that "implements" the Constitution, see Mitchell N. Berman, "Constitutional Decision Rules," *Virginia Law Review* 90, no. 1 (2004): 1–168.

[140] *Skinner v. Oklahoma,* 316 U.S. 535 (1942). "Genetic unfitness" presupposes that the supposed adverse characteristics in question have a significant genetic component. Obviously, "unfit," standing alone, is too vague to be serviceable. See generally Shapiro et al., eds., *Bioethics and Law,* 807–17.

[141] Whether the proper terminology is "fundamental right" or "fundamental liberty interest" remains unclear. As is often so in constitutional law, official conceptual designations and their operational legal consequences are in flux.

personal choice, and must interfere in the manner least intrusive on the right claimed, assuming the less intrusive means are as effective in fulfilling the government's goals as the mechanism under attack.[142] Of course, this use of the "strict scrutiny" standard of review for government action presupposes that the rights claimant has adequately shown that whatever he wants protected is indeed within the scope of a strongly protected right; if that opening burden is not met, no heavy burden of justification falls on the government. The claimant's required threshold burden may be hard to meet, both conceptually and empirically, as when one questions whether cloning is "procreation" within the meaning of the constitutionally protected concept. With interacting changes in technology and culture, this problem of constitutional characterization comes up frequently.[143]

Outside the realm of fundamental rights,[144] however, the presumption is that the government acted within its powers, and one must show that the government's actions were "irrational," which is usually impossible on the current *constitutional* meaning of "irrational."[145] These burdens of justification are generally embedded in "standards of review."[146]

---

[142] This "equally effective" constraint is part of the canonical formulation of "strict constitutional scrutiny." However, a close inspection of the cases might indicate that on some occasions less intrusive alternatives have been required even when they are likely to be less effective. See generally Roy G. Spece, Jr., "The Most Effective or Least Restrictive Alternative as the Only Intermediate and Only Means-Focused Review in Due Process and Equal Protection," *Villanova Law Review* 33, no. 1 (1988): 111–74.

[143] The point is illustrated further in Michael H. Shapiro, "Constitutional Adjudication and Standards of Review under Pressure from Biological Technologies," *Health Matrix: Journal of Law and Medicine* (Case Western Reserve) 11, no. 2 (2001): 351–486, 389–92.

[144] I am confining my remarks to matters of fundamental rights within what constitutional lawyers call "substantive due process"—a realm contained within the Fifth and Fourteenth Amendments' injunctions against depriving persons of life, liberty, or property without due process. I do not address fundamental rights that might be tied to the equal protection clause or to other clauses in the Constitution. I also do not discuss standards of review in equal protection, which in many ways parallel standards of review in substantive due process, except to note that strict scrutiny is triggered in equal protection adjudication where suspect classifications (e.g., race) are in use; and intermediate scrutiny arises with semi-suspect classifications (e.g., gender). Strict scrutiny also is required in equal protection contexts where government classifies persons, groups, legal entities, actions, viewpoints—virtually anything that marks out people or proxies for particular classes of people—in ways that burden fundamental rights or interests.

[145] There are several key cases that do not fit this analytic scheme, particularly in equal protection jurisprudence, where "rational basis" analysis may be more than minimal. See generally Erwin Chemerinsky, *Constitutional Law: Principles and Policies*, 2d ed. (New York: Aspen Law and Business, 2002), 753–59.

[146] Standards of review are (according to this writer) text-derived "meta-rules" directing courts (and others) to assign weights to competing interests and thus to establish burdens of justification on the parties. Standards of review are not optional items in constitutional law. I argue that they are mandated by any constitutional interpretation recognizing that some constitutional interests—of individuals, governments, or other entities—outweigh others. This hierarchy necessitates greater or lesser burdens of justification on government action that impinges on these interests—i.e., varying standards of review. Because these standards generally receive names—"strict scrutiny," "intermediate scrutiny," "minimal scrutiny"—they give the appearance of being step-functions rather than continuous ones. For more extensive analysis, see Shapiro, "Constitutional Adjudication and Standards of Review under Pressure from Biological Technologies."

It is, of course, perennially unclear what fundamental rights are. Some individual interests are so designated (at least in part) because they are actually mentioned in the Constitution—speech, the free exercise of religion, the security of person and home against unlawful intrusions, and so on. In turn, other fundamental rights are derived from the specifically mentioned rights—as associational rights are derived from free speech rights.[147] Still others are thought to be derivable from the protections of "liberty" standing alone, and perhaps from certain other constitutional concepts (as "association" is derived from speech protections). One cannot be deprived of liberty without due process of law, but, by the rules of inference of ordinary language, one *can* indeed be deprived of it *with* due process. How these rights are derived from the unspecific idea of liberty, and what constitutes due process, are crucial matters, but I leave them for another forum.

Procreational autonomy's current constitutional status is somewhat unclear, but most commentators would agree that government cannot require licenses for reproduction *tout simple* or install any serious blockades to it. It does not matter whether procreation would be a good thing in a given case, or whether a given couple would be behaving immorally in seeking to reproduce under seriously adverse conditions (as where they are homeless and destitute). The exercise of a basic constitutional right does not require as a precondition that the claimant provide a rational reason for doing so.[148]

We do not know exactly what "procreation" comprehends, however.[149] Suppose government gets the idea that in vitro fertilization is objectionable. (Someone convinces a legislature that this reproductive aid "commodifies" children.) Suppose a man wants to hire a woman to bear a child

---

[147] In some of these cases, one might object that what is derived is not "another" fundamental right, but a necessary aspect of the expressly mentioned right. Some might claim this for (at least) political speech and association.

[148] This claim requires some qualification. In free speech jurisprudence, for example, some reasons for exercising a right—say, to cause a riot—are logically linked to government interests (say, in protection of persons and property) that may successfully qualify the right, or take it outside the realm of First Amendment protection altogether. Where the soundness of reasons might be constitutionally material—say, a woman seeking a post-viability abortion because of a threat to her life or health rather than because of a late decision not to be a parent after all—the right itself functionally falls short of fundamentality. There is either no fundamental right or liberty interest in post-viability abortion, or, if there is, the government's interest in assuring live birth is presumptively (perhaps *per se*) compelling. The first formulation seems less confusing. Other formulations that more specifically circumscribe a right are of course possible—e.g., one could assert a presumptive right of noninterference with use of accepted medical and nonmedical measures to protect one's life. How to select the best of the alternative ways of framing individual and social interests in either moral or legal contexts is a very large enterprise. See generally Michael H. Shapiro, "Choosing Conceptual Systems in Constitutional Law, and Some Other Locations" (unpublished manuscript, 2003/2004, on file with the author).

[149] "Procreation" and "reproduction" are used synonymously in most contexts. "Reproduction" seems somewhat broader, and may carry, for some, the pejorative connotation of "duplication" or "Xeroxing" of persons, not just genomes. Of course, reproductive cloning does not replicate anyone.

who is to be transferred to him shortly after its birth; or that government wants to prohibit prenatal or preconception screening for defects; or that a couple wishes to infuse a gene known to code for substantial quantities of growth hormone into the early embryo of their child-to-be; or that someone wants to clone herself. And so on. It will not do, in these cases, to say simply that procreation is procreation—if we get a new person, it's procreation, however it is arranged. There are substantial arguments holding that at least some of the fundamental rights protected by the Constitution are defined and limited by their commonly perceived paradigmatic forms. Of course, the contents of paradigms may be contested, and their decisive roles may be rejected.

Move now to enhancement maneuvers directed at already existing persons.[150] It seems pretty clear that government would violate the Constitution's liberty clauses if it told us we could not study for more than ten hours a day, or pump iron for any length of time, or run marathons, etc. Such radical egalitarian (or anti-elitist) measures are unlikely to be upheld, but it is not certain how our rights to be free of such intrusions on our preferences for self-improvement would be couched. Certainly, most litigants would speak not just of liberty, but of "privacy" (a particularly muddled term), intimate personal choice, physical and mentational integrity and autonomy, personal security,[151] self-realization, a First Amendment right to learn (for the study restriction), and a right to control the informational and emotional contents of one's mind (a right to be euphoric? to space out? to remember more—or less—through memory enhancement or erasure?). (These rights claims overlap considerably.)

How could such basic questions about rights characterization remain unclear after all this time? For several reasons. For one thing, government has not yet been quite stupid enough to (say) require people to get permission before pumping iron, etc.[152]

Could the government restrict the intake of caffeine? On what grounds? On the grounds that artificial enhancement of alertness is intrinsically wrong? Or that the price in frayed nerves and lost tempers is too high?

---

[150] Again, this category would, in a finely calibrated analysis, be broken into age or memory-capacity segments, and possibly extended to fetuses or embryos in which global genome changes are no longer possible.

[151] There is a recognized liberty interest in personal security, which is closely related to the most intuitive meaning of "liberty" in the Fifth and Fourteenth Amendments: freedom from physical confinement, as by imprisonment, shackles, etc. This right of personal security underlies the decision in *Youngberg v. Romeo*, 457 U.S. 307 (1982), which recognized a mentally retarded inmate's right to "habilitation" treatment to reduce his physical aggressiveness, which resulted in his own injuries when other inmates defended themselves against his attacks. The standard of review, however, was strongly deferential to professional judgment concerning what treatment programs to use—if any.

[152] But government can heavily regulate the iron pumping business in ways that might seriously impair access by restricting the supply of entrepreneurs in the field, thus elevating prices. Even more intrusively, government might require prescreening of would-be iron pumpers, and limit degrees of effort based on some appraisal of risks and benefits. One could compare this—perhaps not too closely—to regulating hours of work and safety conditions at the workplace.

What is to stop the government from doing so? Irrational justifications do not necessarily make for unconstitutional justifications—unless there is a very important right at stake. What *is* that right? This line of argument has never worked for access to, say, marijuana, and government can generally tax the hell out of liquor sales without violating the Constitution.

Caffeine consumption might be insulated from prohibition by the existence of a long-standing tradition of noninterference with its use; such histories and customs of noninterference are sometimes relied upon to establish the existence of a fundamental right of noninterference with some enterprises—for example, refusing medical care, getting married, and so on.[153] "Liberty," after all, must apply to *something,* and, as things stand now, no Supreme Court justice has insisted that it comprehends *only* the specific interests mentioned in the Bill of Rights. The fact that we have traditionally and all but universally avoided certain forms of governmental interference seems a reasonable clue to what we mean by "liberty," both in general and as it appears in the Constitution. Perhaps, then, we have a fundamental liberty interest, per tradition, in access to caffeine. (But suppose we find out something really nasty about caffeine. Could this trump tradition? Could government ban tobacco consumption?) If this seems curiously specific or trivial,[154] bear in mind that the Supreme Court has announced a liberty interest in refusing antipsychotic drugs, but did not say anything about other medical psychotropics—for example, antidepressants and antianxiety drugs.[155] In this case, being somewhat oddly particular betokens the absence of a general theory, or an unwillingness to try to construct one when not clearly necessary. There is much to be said both for and against this judicial reticence, but not here.

Could the government prevent the use of intellect-enhancing drugs for persons not suffering from some pathology of the mind—dementia, brain trauma, etc.? What exactly would we invoke as the constitutionally unmentioned fundamental right or interest? Would it be a right to control the contents of our minds and our mental processes generally without restraint? (All *constitutional* arguments for government noninterference with access to nonmedical mind-altering drugs have failed.)[156] Or would we seek

---

[153] *Cruzan v. Director, Missouri Department of Health,* 497 U.S. 261 (1990) (acknowledging a liberty interest in refusing lifesaving and other medical treatment but declining to award relief because the permanently unconscious patient's preferences were unknown); *Turner v. Safley,* 482 U.S. 78 (1987) (among other things, striking down marriage restriction in prisons). The absence of such tradition does not, in practice, always foreclose such rights, as is illustrated by *Roe v. Wade,* 410 U.S. 113 (1973). The exact role of finding a protective tradition in establishing the existence of a strongly protected right is an actively debated issue in constitutional analysis. The problem is greatly compounded by the difficulties in settling on an acceptable description of the supposed tradition. See generally Laurence H. Tribe and Michael C. Dorf, "Levels of Generality in the Definition of Rights," *University of Chicago Law Review* 57, no. 4 (1990): 1057–1108; and Chemerinsky, *Constitutional Law,* 764–66.

[154] Recall the level-of-abstraction problem in describing "tradition." Perhaps we should be talking about our access to non-food substances generally, or to ingestion of anything.

[155] *Washington v. Harper,* 494 U.S. 210 (1990).

[156] Peyote use has a special history of scattered legislative and administrative protection because of its religious use by some Native Americans. See generally *Employment Div., Dept.*

recognition of a right to control mental functioning for the more specific purpose of improving ourselves? Could the government properly seek to block serious enhancement techniques that bear on core aspects of our identities? What social/governmental interests would this serve? What rights do we have to resist government interference with how we control our personal attributes and our identities? Is our constitutional liberty to mold or remake ourselves constrained by a disorder model, to the exclusion of enhancement?

Even when important rights are recognized, they are subject to qualification by countervailing societal interests, as framed by government. Assuming we have a presumptive right to technologically modify ourselves, at least for self-improvement, what compelling or important interests of the state suggest that the presumption is overcome? Does the government have compelling interests in avoiding the risk of medical injuries, in preventing the social chaos of runaway identity change, in avoiding the descent from person to object, in preserving existing normative systems against the observed "lesson" that we can get something for nothing—or at least for very little?

It is not even entirely clear how we would characterize our rights in easier cases—say, rights to use medically indicated intellect-enhancing substances. Assuming the constitutional soundness of traditional levels of federal and state regulation of the efficacy and safety of medicines, biologics, devices, etc., how would we formulate a claim that we should have a right against government interference with treating true disorders by way of medically indicated intellect enhancement? On the one hand, no broad right of noninterference with medical selection of therapy has been recognized.[157] On the other hand, we have yet to face a situation in which government has prohibited, across the board, the use of the only confirmed cure for a grave disorder.[158] Perhaps in such cases we would speak of a right to the continued integrity of our personhood—including our existing aggregations of attributes—when gravely threatened by disease. The government would defend its prohibition by turning to this very ideal, asserting the power to preserve the integrity of personhood on behalf of the person when he threatens it by seeking treatment via dangerous or inadequately tested measures. The government might also fear uncontrolled expansion of the use of treatments from medical to non-

---

of Human Resources v. Smith, 494 U.S. 872 (1990) (ruling that the peyote restrictions in question did not impair the free exercise of religion protected by the First Amendment).

[157] Cf. United States v. Rutherford, 442 U.S. 544 (1979), where the Supreme Court left the right-of-privacy issue aside, offering no encouragement for its use in securing access to experimental therapy (in that case, the drug Laetrile for cancer). States are free to recognize broader constitutional rights under their own constitutions and statutes. This has been explicitly held by California courts applying the California constitution. See, e.g., Warfield v. Peninsula Golf & Country Club, 896 P.2d 776 (Cal. 1995).

[158] This excludes rationing and triage situations, as well as general pricing mechanisms. The move to permit medical use of marijuana in treating various disorders has been strongly resisted by the federal government. Cf. United States v. Oakland Cannabis Buyers' Cooperative, 532 U.S. 483 (2001) (no medical necessity exception to federal marijuana prohibitions).

medical needs, or it might simply believe that the risk-benefit profile is unacceptable. Moreover, there is no recognized "fundamental right to health"; nor is there a fundamental right to "noninterference in personal health care decisions" (beyond the right to refuse treatment); nor, more generally, is there a global right to maintain one's physical and mental integrity through treatment of one's choosing to blunt the ravages of disorder or injury. We might indeed invoke the well-accepted right to personal security and enlarge it to embrace the integrity of body and mind—but here, the government can seize on this formulation and assert that such integrity is precisely what it is trying to protect, through paternalistic interference if called for. The claim of right would then have to be understood as a matter of dominion over mental and physical integrity, including the option to install a new scheme of integrity that we prefer to the existing one—or simply to give up the notion of integrity because of its double edge.

In general, it is conceptually impossible to form a complete, coherent theory of constitutional interpretation to guide the formulation of fundamental rights (and even to tell us if these rights are "found," "recognized," or "created"); we will thus never have a full account of what sorts of personal interests are presumptively protected.[159]

Some cases are, to be sure, clearer than others. The right to procreate was not extensively discussed by Justice William O. Douglas in *Skinner v. Oklahoma* (1942), in which the Supreme Court struck down a statute authorizing involuntary sterilization of some felons,[160] but it could have been explained, in part at least, by the fact that there is no American tradition of broad government invasion of private choice concerning whether to reproduce.[161] This and other histories of nonintervention into personal choice are often invoked as interpretive criteria for "liberty" in the Fourteenth and Fifth Amendments, and for other constitutional concepts.[162]

---

[159] This "conceptual impossibility" does not foreclose the (unlikely) prospect of complete consensus on certain matters, from interpretive theories to particular interpretations. Everyone might agree, for example, on the proper interpretation of "equality" and on the application of the particular equality conception in all cases that arise. The basic abstraction itself remains partially indeterminate.

[160] *Skinner v. Oklahoma*, 316 U.S. 535 (1942). The Oklahoma penal law permitted involuntary sterilization of persons convicted of three or more felonies involving moral turpitude, but via a scheme that made genetically senseless distinctions, such as that between larceny and embezzlement. The majority opinion recited its reliance on the equal protection clause rather than the liberty clause of the Fourteenth Amendment, but the equality argument would have collapsed without the assertion of a strong liberty to reproduce.

[161] The history of forced sterilization cuts the other way, but its very condemnation and substantial termination suggest the strength of the overarching tradition of noninterference with procreative decisions. Still, there is a significant body of cases on preventing reproduction by incompetent persons. See, e.g., *Conservatorship of Valerie N. v. Valerie N.*, 707 P.2d 760 (Cal. 1985). Also, there are peripheral rules that bear on reproductive choice—e.g., administrative requirements for marriage may slow matters down for some would-be reproducers, and requirements for post-birth screening of infants may intimidate some persons.

[162] It is likely that there has always been a degree of private and largely hidden conduct in which individuals and health care providers pressure patients to accept unwanted treatment. Courts also have often deferred to professional ascriptions of incompetence to make

Indeed, the right to refuse certain forms of lifesaving care was articulated, in more or less this fashion, by Chief Justice William H. Rehnquist, who simply cited the long common-law tradition asserting that a competent person's refusal of treatment cannot rightly be overridden, even if nontreatment would likely be fatal. Invoking tradition, history, and custom are intuitively plausible interpretive maneuvers, though they have severe limitations, especially when traditions are fractured and multivocal.[163]

As for the most famous unstated fundamental right, abortion, all I can make out of the constitutional argument structure of the watershed case, *Roe v. Wade*,[164] is that the Court's majority acted on a belief that the Court was a delegatee of We-the-people's assumed authority to announce new moral insights and to say that they are embedded within the Constitution. Whatever it was doing, it was not relying on a long-standing American tradition of noninterference with deliberate termination of pregnancies, because there wasn't one.[165] What a more constitutionally satisfactory opinion reaching the same outcome might look like is a subject of continuing scholarly and political debate.

Finally, I want to stress a particular analytic/interpretive point. Much of fundamental rights analysis involves matching a rights claim with a paradigm case of what is concededly protected. (Such comparison is an inevitable feature of much abstract thought.) Our procreative urges, by custom, are almost entirely up to us. Suppose that government sought to prohibit or more heavily regulate artificial insemination by donor. A woman seeking access to artificial insemination services would press the *identity* of the *biological* sexual recombination process in *standard* reproduction—a married couple having sex—with that in artificial insemination, arguing that the social/relational variations are unimportant (e.g., an extrafamilial genetic source and the lack of sexual intercourse). One could argue more pointedly that the variations are simply not material within the paradigm— they are not dictated by the "standard" case, even if the standard case was the most common. (This is a classic display of a dispute over specifying the proper level of abstraction for any paradigm or exemplar.) In any event, government insistence on preserving the values distinctively linked to the standard case of nuclear family formation would likely be rejected as either incoherent or too weak to override individual procreational preferences.

---

therapeutic decisions, leaving the way open for imposed treatment. The actual behavioral "tradition" is thus fractured, and there may be a gulf between legally expressed ideals and common practice. This is an important problem in constitutional interpretation, to the extent that history, custom, and tradition are invoked for text-interpretation purposes.

[163] See generally Tribe and Dorf, "Levels of Generality in the Definition of Rights."

[164] *Roe v. Wade*, 410 U.S. 113 (1973).

[165] Justice Harry Blackmun purported to describe the history of abortion and its regulation over the last two-plus millennia, including the American experience. Although there were somewhat less restrictive regimes early on in the U.S., nothing resembling a clear tradition of noninterference was ever apparent, and Justice Blackmun did not claim otherwise.

The comparison to the paradigm is much murkier for cloning because consensus on the core elements of the procreative paradigm itself breaks down.[166] Some deny that cloning is human "reproduction" at all, insisting that the human reproductive paradigm is much more than simply generating a new person.[167] (Eve wasn't "procreated"; she was built out of Adam, and whatever "process" it was, it didn't stem from human sources. The unnamed creature created by Dr. Frankenstein was not procreated either, despite its human provenance.) There is of course no sexual recombination in asexual reproduction. Still more, asexual reproduction is far different from reproduction by sexual recombination because we know far more about what sort of physical entity we will get. If we cloned Queen Elizabeth II, we would know almost exactly what the offspring would look like at various stages of her life, although whether she too would develop odd millinery preferences would be unknown in advance.

Working through these difficult stages of constitutional argument structures will unearth most of the constitutional, moral, political, and policy issues that commentators both within and outside the law professions would agree are central. Constitutional argumentation as a heuristic drives colloquies such as the following: "We're not reproducing; we're duplicating people to enslave them or for other impermissible purposes." (This is an essential question at the very threshold of argumentation, determining whether there is a constitutional interest of significance that demands recognition.) • "No, there's no 'duplication' in any coherent sense; and the prospect of clone slaves is too remote and speculative to worry about; in any case, slavery is already unconstitutional, forbidden to individuals as well as governments by the Thirteenth Amendment." (This responds to the threshold attack, and anticipates a later argument stage in which government offers its justifications, if required, for its interference.) • "What about the risks to the child?" • "What risks? The technological bugs have been worked out [we assume *arguendo*] so that the 'error rate' is not much greater than that accompanying 'regular' reproduction." • "We mean the sense of burden in knowing that your life has already been lived by the prior owner of the genome." • "No one's life has already been lived; genomes don't have independent lives as persons." • "Let me put it otherwise. If we found Beethoven's nuclear material and cloned him, the offspring's autonomy would be nil; he would be improperly pressured into being a composer of classical music." • "He apparently will have some serious genetic endowments of musical talent. What's wrong with a little gentle channeling of preferences toward abilities, to promote greater opportunities and satisfaction?" • "Suppose he decided to be a rock star instead." • "His choice." • "Conditioning would deprive him of true choice. The risk of mere use and reduction is just too great. And who needs to clone

---

[166] See the discussion of the constitutionality of regulating cloning in Shapiro, "I Want a Girl," 238–92.

[167] Nor would a change in personal (not numerical) identity constitute procreation.

anyway? What is it *for*?" •"Why does it have to be 'needed'? Who needs
to reproduce *at all*? We don't need a reason to procreate." •"It isn't
procreation." •"It is too." And we have a new go around. The post-
threshold exchange tests justifications for government interference and
also re-explains aspects of the threshold right.

With trait change not involving germ-line alteration, much of the constitutional analysis is similar, but it bears its own uncertainties. The Supreme
Court has already said that there are rights to refuse treatment, including
treatment with antipsychotic drugs, and presumably other forms of medicine for the mind. One would also expect recognition of a right to refuse
enforced enhancement, outside disorder models altogether. The Court
ruled long ago that government cannot constrain the education of children by prohibiting the learning of foreign languages, or prohibiting
attendance at private parochial schools.[168] Major portions of how we
construct ourselves nontechnologically seem clearly to be part of this
general liberty, though often crystallized in more specific terms as First
Amendment speech and religion rights, and rights against imposed medical treatment.[169]

With germ-line alteration, the comparison to a paradigm is also difficult
because such alteration does not exist in any but primitive form. Invoca-
tions of magic and requests for miraculous intervention aside, we have
never tried to alter human traits via the germ line. The nearest "tradition"
is the practice within recent decades of prenatal and preconception screening, but this screens persons out without specifying characteristics of
persons left in. For obvious reasons, our pre-1960s historical practice of
procreational freedom lies in protecting the bare decision to procreate, not
in specifying the "contents" of reproduction via screening or germ-line
modification of specific characteristics. The former is likely to be considered a now-traditional aspect of reproductive choice. It is reasonable to
wonder whether the latter—the affirmative intrusion into the genome—
will become a common practice and be viewed as an aspect of reproductive choice, and what rank it would be accorded, when compared to
screening. And, again, it is hard to say what the government's overwhelming interests might be here. Maintaining species identity? Reducing the
risk of human reduction? Maintaining our normative systems—invoking,
perhaps, a neophobic or precautionary principle? Political philosophers

---

[168] *Pierce v. Society of Sisters*, 268 U.S. 510 (1925) (invoking an expansive idea of liberty and
invalidating a requirement that children attend public rather than private schools); *Meyer v.
Nebraska*, 262 U.S. 390 (1923) (also offering a similarly extensive view of liberty, and invalidating a law prohibiting the teaching of foreign languages to young children).

[169] The (limited) First Amendment aspect bears mention. First, the customarily invoked
rationales of a strong free speech principle include considerations of opportunities to learn,
to train, and, more generally, to better oneself through communicating and receiving communications. Second, there is a conceptual connection between mental functioning and
speech, so that impingements on the former—perhaps even lost opportunities for mental
functioning—may have a First Amendment component. See Shapiro et al., eds., *Bioethics and
Law*, 468–69.

have been known to say that communities have rights to preserve themselves *as* themselves, within limits.[170] Is this a constitutional principle—or does it prove too much? Doesn't the U.S. Constitution exist—in *part*—to preserve personal choice against communitarian demands? It does, but it also exists to maintain an enduring political entity framed within an identifiable, if fuzzy, liberal tradition. Are any of these asserted interests strong enough to overcome our personal interests in self-modification through technology?

Legal dispute resolution cannot settle the moral issues about rights to self-transformation and rights to adjust or revise or replace one's identity in any respect. Such resolutions achieve a limited, though possibly significant, form of closure. But the moral and political issues will emerge because the task of the law—as we now know it in many parts of the world—is to resolve the dispute in accordance with legal rules that require the search for, articulation of, and defense of all the contending perspectives.

XI. CONCLUSION

Continuous, extreme "makeovers" of individual persons will "conceptually require," if anything, losing the idea of identity rather than reconstructing it. Short of never-ending shape-shifting and melding of formerly separate persons, however, the idea of personal identity remains intact and serviceable. The emerging practices that create this failed conceptual challenge nevertheless involve, by hypothesis, close attention to the ordering of traits in a hierarchy of importance, and to their particular values in particular persons, before and after their respective makeovers. Technological enhancement clearly has its dark side, but that is not its only aspect.

Law, University of Southern California

---

[170] See generally Will Kymlicka, *Contemporary Political Philosophy: An Introduction,* 2d ed. (Oxford: Oxford University Press, 2002), 246 (on "[d]uties to protect the cultural structure").

INDEX